STAGGERING FORWARD

BY THE SAME AUTHOR

Why India Is Not a Great Power (Yet)

Strategic Sell-out: Indian–US Nuclear Deal (co-author)

India's Nuclear Policy

Nuclear Weapons and Indian Security: The Realist Foundations of Strategy (Second Edition)

Future Imperilled: India's Security in the 1990s and Beyond (editor and main contributor)

STAGGERING FORWARD

NARENDRA MODI AND INDIA'S GLOBAL AMBITION

BHARAT KARNAD

PENGUIN
VIKING
An imprint of Penguin Random House

VIKING

USA | Canada | UK | Ireland | Australia
New Zealand | India | South Africa | China

Viking is part of the Penguin Random House group of companies whose addresses can be found at global.penguinrandomhouse.com

Published by Penguin Random House India Pvt. Ltd
7th Floor, Infinity Tower C, DLF Cyber City,
Gurgaon 122 002, Haryana, India

Penguin
Random House
India

First published in Viking by Penguin Random House India 2018

Copyright © Bharat Karnad 2018

All rights reserved

10 9 8 7 6 5 4 3 2 1

The views and opinions expressed in this book are the author's own and the facts are as reported by him which have been verified to the extent possible, and the publishers are not in any way liable for the same.

ISBN 9780670089697

Typeset in Adobe Garamond Pro by Manipal Digital Systems, Manipal
Printed at Replika Press Pvt. Ltd, India

This book is sold subject to the condition that it shall not, by way of trade or otherwise, be lent, resold, hired out, or otherwise circulated without the publisher's prior consent in any form of binding or cover other than that in which it is published and without a similar condition including this condition being imposed on the subsequent purchaser.

www.penguin.co.in

For
Ranju and Raj Ketkar, Ravi and Savita Karnad, Nima and Kayo Noble
and
Nikhil Singhal, a lover of books

'Scepticism is a virtue in history as well as in philosophy'

Napoleon Bonaparte

Contents

Introduction		xi
1.	'Alpha Male' Leaders and 'Country First' Power Politics	1
2.	Impact of Modi's Persona on Government	37
3.	Creeper-vine Foreign Policy	78
4.	Adversarial Geopolitics: BRIS and Mod Quad	154
5.	Affirmative Inaction	221
6.	Perennial Security Muddle	270
Conclusion		379
Notes		399

Introduction

INFLECTION POINTS IN national and international affairs are routinely heralded, and each decade is perceived as more dangerous than the previous one. Invariably, there's a person, a country, an event or a series of incidents or an emerging situation that is identified as the trigger for things going askew. The second decade of the new millennium has been marked, in this respect, by the rise of political strongmen in major countries across the globe—Vladimir Putin in Russia, Xi Jinping in China, Recep Tayyip Erdogan in Turkey, Shinzo Abe in Japan, Donald J. Trump in the United States and Narendra Modi in India. These are highly motivated leaders who by the force of their personalities and ambitions and sometimes quirky policy agendas have changed the international relations dynamic. Their similarity means they are each alive to what drives the others, and this makes for wariness all round, as well as, perhaps, a strained sort of regional and international peace. But it is peace all the same.

In the two vital democracies, India and the US, moreover, there are the walrus-moustachioed individuals coming into their own as influence-wielders. If Mohan Bhagwat, the head of the powerful right-wing social service organization Rashtriya Swayamsevak Sangh (RSS), represents Hindu triumphalism and is the acknowledged éminence grise of the ruling Bharatiya Janata Party (BJP) government headed by Narendra Modi, John Bolton, no friend of India, the new US national security advisor (NSA) who replaced the steady General H.R. McMaster, will likely put teeth into President Trump's truculent 'America First' policy and increase the dilemma for Delhi.[1] Inclined to wage wars of denuclearization and regime change against Iran and North Korea, Bolton will encourage Trump's worst tendencies and set the world up for a hair-raising ride to the nuclear abyss, because it is unlikely Putin and Xi will sit idly by and see Washington take out these states that are potentially levers to stall America's regional designs.[2] India will have to negotiate this international milieu, already rendered unpredictable and difficult by Trump's 'rash' foreign policy 'instincts', and face the hazards of US policy fuelled by his pet peeves.[3] That Modi has developed a rapport with Trump augurs well. But it also means that the White House will expect New Delhi to fall in with its policies without demurring and contribute to furthering US objectives, which expectation if belied can lead to Trump turning on India. Meanwhile, at home, Bhagwat and the RSS have hurrahed Modi along as he seeks recognition for India as the 'jagat guru' (world guru) and pushes the Indian state towards a palpably Hindu identity, heightening tensions in society along caste and religious lines and affecting the Indian polity—a problem Modi has publicly avoided addressing.[4]

Global power politics is a serious game requiring countries that matter to think and act big. Given its many attributes, India belongs in this group but has not been in the running for want of an inspiring leader with a clear national vision, the ability to get things done and the will to put India on the path to accelerated economic growth and prosperity and to great power. But the pursuit of great power requires a lean and effective apparatus of state that is able to efficiently implement policies and deliver on programmes in double-quick time and enable the ease of doing business. It also needs talent for conceiving and implementing agile realpolitik-minded foreign and military policies and obtaining an appropriate mix of war-fighting and credible strategic deterrent capabilities for the purpose, along with the knack for using hard power effectively as a tool of diplomacy.[5]

Narendra Damodardas Modi was elected with a thumping majority in 2014 in part because the people believed he would make the country progress on all these fronts. But he was sidetracked; his government got mired in the Hindu fringe politics of cow worship, beef-eating, 'love jihad' and the Ayodhya Ram Temple instead, and failed to initiate any kind of system transformation. Contrary to expectations, Modi also retained the rickety administrative structure—centred on generalist civil servants working in silos, immersed in the minutiae of cross-cutting laws, rules, regulations and procedures—that has hindered the nation's progress. It is no wonder that so little was achieved during Modi's first term, moving the stalwart diplomat K.S. Bajpai to lament the fact that 'the country [seems] unaware of the deficiencies of mechanisms it has devised to serve its needs'.[6]

What is particularly surprising considering his big talk is how, in the external realm, Modi has stayed with the small stakes game anchored in short policy horizons that the previous governments had locked the country into. Continuing to lean overmuch on the United States, and keying on Pakistan and Pakistan-sponsored terrorism in Jammu and Kashmir rather than on the primary threat from China, is the sort of foreign policy a lesser state would follow for marginal gains. As a result, India has belied hopes, piled on disappointments, messed up on economic and strategic opportunities and underperformed in every sphere of national and international activity.[7] The world, therefore, while not having given up on India just yet, has moved on from the 'India story' which, along with the 'China story', was all the rage on either side of the new millennium.[8] While China has advanced by leaps under the strategically driven Xi and an enabling system, with its economy generating wealth at a rate that sees it racing to replace the US at the top of the heap, India has meandered, its global impact far less than the sum of its small successes.

This trend was expected to slow down, if not actually reverse, with Modi's advent. His qualities as a self-made man, a showman and a strongman all rolled into one inspired confidence that he would get things done. India, it was widely believed, would be taken by the scruff of its neck as it were and frog-marched into economic plenty and the great power club. Too long victimized by a tardy nanny state spawned by pseudo-socialist ideology and politics and a diffident foreign policy, the Indian people desperately desired change. With his clean reputation, proven track record as chief minister of Gujarat and his formidable leadership qualities on display, Modi seemed the right fit for the prime minister's job, and just the man to turn the country around after the decade-long rule by the meek and mumbling Manmohan Singh.

In the Modi era, there is drive and bustle all right—corruption is at a lower ebb, at least in the higher reaches of government (counterpointed, however, by stories of 'crony Gujarati capitalists'), some structural changes have been engineered in the economic sphere, new ideas to improve the lot of the people are being tried out and the focus on technology to provide development solutions is a departure from the norm. The government seems more responsive and the mechanisms to deliver public services and benefits to the masses have improved. Coupled with the high hopes he held out for a new India, this part is what initially created the sizzle. But in the context of his many slogans heralding a new dawn for the country—'Minimum government, maximum governance', 'Government has no business to be in business'—the radical makeover of the apparatus of state and economy along with a system redesign and overhaul, which Modi had hinted at, never came to pass. This is the reason for the fizzle.

Where the situation has changed for the worse is on the domestic scene. Social peace has a tincture of violence against Muslims and Dalits in it, with Hindu extremist groups interpreting the fact of Modi and the BJP in power as licence to create mayhem, fray the social fabric and exacerbate societal fault lines. Modi has tried to douse communal passions, but only half-heartedly, because the ruling party benefits electorally from religious polarization of the heterogeneous Indian society that is immune to other means of political mobilization. This is so because the majority Hindu community is divided into too many sects and diverse traditions to form a coherent political whole.[9]

On the foreign and military policy fronts, there have been no surprises. The initial surge of international curiosity in Modi's leadership and his foreign policy orientation was stoked by a flurry of foreign trips and summits in his first years in office. But his personalized diplomacy, complete with the unselfconscious hugging and embracing of sometimes startled, usually awkward Western leaders in frequent foreign tours, produced no signal departure from the policies of previous governments, nor any stellar results. The exception was the Arabian peninsula where Sunni Saudi Arabia and the Gulf emirates and sheikhdoms have been receptive to Modi's overtures because they hope to distance India, to the extent possible, from Shia Iran, safely invest in its growth and clean up their own image as purveyors of the corrosive Wahhabist brand of extremist Islam that spawned the Islamic State terrorist group in Iraq and the Levant by associating with a heterogeneous and democratic country. India's armed services remain hobbled, as before, by short-term objectives, shortsighted policies and ad hoc procurement of military hardware from abroad at the expense of indigenous defence industrial efforts that have made India an object lesson to aspiring states on what not to do with respect to national security.

What is evident is the paradox of Modi's liberal internationalist foreign policy and the growingly illiberal Indian state. He stayed with the Paris Climate Accord, for instance, even as President Trump withdrew the US from it, and shoehorned India into a leadership role in the International Solar Alliance.[10] At the same time, by not publicly discouraging excesses by Hindu outlier outfits, he nudged the fairly tolerant social order that has evolved over the millennia to accommodate an extraordinarily complex Indian society into a Hinduist straitjacket in line with the thinking of the RSS, which Modi was once an office holder in. The tension between the liberal push and the illiberal pull, between impulse and instinct, is as much a result of Modi's psychological make-up as his politics. It has affected his policies and India's relations with countries far and near without really changing their course and direction. Understanding this aspect makes him more transparent.

Modi's humble background and the time he spent in the RSS has led to the prime minister's views and values resonating with those of this 'social service' organization. It has imbued in him discipline and conservative notions of order and influenced his attitude and approach to government and governance. Under Modi's watch, hitherto secondary issues such as the ban on cow slaughter have turned into a national preoccupation, and beef-eating has become a spurious test of national identity and the reason for the social and cultural differentiation of the Muslims in the country, who are ethnically indistinguishable from the majority community. Moreover, RSS ideas of a stable society premised on an established hierarchy predispose Modi to act and react in external situations and crises in ways deferential to the powerful, which may explain, for instance, his inclination to accommodate the superior US and China while berating a plainly inferior Pakistan. In Modi's thought universe, the internal affects the external and vice versa. How such factors possibly shape his thinking on national security and foreign and military choices will be explored in this study.

A strong personality, strong views and a strong hand on the policy rudder mean that for the first time since the heydays of Jawaharlal Nehru and Indira Gandhi the Indian government is wholly pivoted on one person: Narendra Modi. All policymaking emanates from him and is overseen by the Prime Minister's Office (PMO) staffed by handpicked functionaries, most of whom served him in Gujarat and so are attuned to his manner of command and control and his preferences and predilections. It is curious, in this respect, that Modi's emergence in Delhi parallels the rise of nationalist-minded strongmen in other parts of the world and in different political systems. They share many traits, such as enormous self-confidence and self-centredness—everything that happens in their countries is about them. Having minimized the opposition within their own parties and in their respective polities, they appear intent on consolidating their power and fashioning their country's polities to reflect their own views and values. Thus, Modi's 'new India' and Erdogan's 'new Turkey', for example, are not dissimilar in that the concepts have gone beyond slogans to become 'projects' and subsume the leaders' long stay in office.[11]

All these strongmen, moreover, prize winning in domestic political battles at any cost but are careful when competing with other strongmen.[12] But because there can be no certainty of victory in the international sphere, they have weighted the odds in their favour by picking on weak targets to burnish their image and assure a higher probability of success. Thus, Putin exerted himself against Ukraine by annexing Crimea, Xi flexed his muscles against the littoral states on the South China Sea, Erdogan moved forcefully against the Kurds, and Trump bombed Syria and now picks on Iran and North Korea. Similarly, Modi is concentrating on the smaller, weaker Pakistan while giving the more dangerous and challenging China a free pass. Modi has disappointed because he has failed to articulate a national vision, fully unshackle the economy and incentivize the private sector to lead it. His Make in India programme to make the country self-sufficient in arms is stillborn. His unambitious foreign and military policies, by being restricted to small steps and reinforcing India's supposed reputation as a 'responsible state', have missed out on the huge strategic benefits of being assertive and disruptive. This has diverted India, it will be argued, from stepping legitimately into the great power game.

This book is in the main a critique of Modi's foreign and national security policies—an audit, if you will, principally of his government's performance in these spheres. If readers find the analysis suffused with disappointment, they will not be wrong. Based on his public pronouncements in the run-up to the 2014 general elections and such snippets of his philosophy as could be gleaned from them, I was among the first in the commentariat, assuming there is such a thing, to laud Modi as an unusually forthright and desirable candidate for prime minister. It was impressive, I thought, that he exhorted Indians to 'think big, dream big', and his ideological tilt convinced me, as I wrote in September 2011, that he would 'fill the need that Rajaji writing in *Swarajya*, in August 1957, voiced for "a strong and articulate Right" stressing small government and good governance'.[13] (Rajaji or C. Rajagopalachari, the first Indian governor general, was the tallest leader to oppose Nehru's socialism on ideological grounds. He left the Congress in 1959 to found the right-of-centre Swatantra Party.[14])

Then there was the 'India First' concept that Modi popularized in his election campaign. This phrase was first used, conceived and fleshed out, incidentally, by this author in 2002 and in my books and writings (including op-eds in newspapers) since.[15] 'India First' has now become a tag line every TV channel and website freely uses. It was prompted by what I saw happening as adviser, defence expenditure, to the Tenth Finance Commission chaired by former defence minister, the late K.C. Pant, in the Congress government of P.V. Narasimha Rao in the early to mid-1990s, and several years later experienced as member of the (first) National Security Advisory Board (NSAB) formed by the BJP government of Atal Bihari Vajpayee, and outside of it when I interacted closely with a few cabinet ministers, in particular Jaswant Singh, even as a series of foreign and national security policy disasters unfolded.

Among these were the ill-thought-out initiatives to please Washington that prevented the Indian nuclear deterrent from achieving full-scale thermonuclear weapons capability with the announcement of the 'voluntary test moratorium' in May 1998 and the programme for the development of ballistic missiles from achieving intercontinental range, and the Next Steps in Strategic Partnership initiative with the United States that followed, eventuating in 2008 in the civilian nuclear cooperation deal predicated on the non-resumption of nuclear testing by India. There was also the December 1999 hijack of the Indian Airlines flight to Kandahar, which could have been stopped from leaving the Amritsar airport but wasn't, leading to the shameful exchange of passengers and aircraft for the release of the Pakistani terrorist, Azhar Mahmood. This was succeeded some time later by the Vajpayee government ordering the useless general mobilization for war instead of instantaneous retaliatory strikes on the major Pakistani Army's Inter-Services Intelligence (ISI) targets and/or special forces actions to decapitate the Hizbul Mujahideen and Lashkar-e-Taiba (LeT) leadership for the attack on Parliament in December 2001.

I was struck then, as I am now, by how inept the Government of India seems to be other than in consistently misreading the strategic geography and threats, avoiding significant action, making the wrong choices and shying away from securing decisive military wherewithal, which in the present day are tested and proven thermonuclear weapons of medium to high yields atop tested intercontinental ballistic missiles (ICBMs) and long-range cruise missiles. And in addition, hankering to join the United Nations Security Council (UNSC) as a permanent member without veto power and going along with technology denial regimes that victimized India, such as the Nuclear Suppliers Group (NSG), Missile Technology Control Regime (MTCR) and the Wassenaar Arrangement, and then not on our own terms. The other ways India shot itself in the foot was by cueing to lesser dangers, emphasizing the wrong security issues and switching from relying on the ex-Soviet Union/Russia as main military supplier to leaning on the US when history suggests that for a would-be great power like India it is folly to depend on any foreign country for arms and any big power for deliverance. In this respect the US has had a particularly bad record of hurting Indian interests. Just as dispiriting to see was the spectacle of a supposedly 'nationalist' BJP dispensation, this time under Modi, compounding the existing problem of arms imports with the fundamentally flawed Make in India programme—

Modi's flagship policy to promote manufacturing, spread technological innovation and generate employment—that has had no economic impact and made not the slightest dent in arms imports. This is so because of the confusion about its concept and its stuttering implementation, the unwillingness to take hard measures and to integrate the resources and capacities of the public sector and the private sector to form a core cost-efficient national defence industry, and the absence of political will to promote self-sufficiency if necessary by compelling the armed services to induct successful indigenous weapons systems (Tejas light combat aircraft [LCA] and Arjun main battle tank [MBT]) in large numbers to achieve economies of scale and fire up a nascent industry. Without these correctives, all Make in India may end up doing is that instead of Russian military hardware being assembled in defence public sector units (DPSUs) with transfer of screw-driver-level technology, obsolete Western armaments (F-16 combat aircraft, M-777 howitzer) would now be screw-drivered together under licence in the private sector.

Equally galling was the discovery that Modi did not have a grand idea or design for the country other than recovering for India its 'civilizational power', which in terms of advancing the country's interests means little, and that he did not mean what his campaign slogans said about 'No red tape but red carpet' for investors and entrepreneurs, and 'Government has no business to be in government', because he actually believes in the bureaucratized Indian state and those manning it to deliver the goods that they have failed to do in the last seventy-odd years. Further, his surrounding himself with pedestrian intellectual talent from among the ranks of retired and serving civil servants means his foreign and military policies have lacked freshness and strategic imagination. Complicating the situation is the fact that his big power–focused foreign policy has neglected neighbouring states, and estranged traditionally friendly countries and regions of special importance to the country. Thus, almost all of South Asia is alienated as is Russia. With regard to the states in the middle-abroad, such as Iran and the Central Asian republics (CARs) and, in the east, the countries crucial to ring-fencing China—Vietnam and Japan in particular—India has talked the talk better than it has walked it. Modi's India comes across as an inconstant friend to states that are kindly disposed towards it, while its petty-minded policies towards smaller and weaker states in the vicinity has helped China strengthen its presence in precisely the strategic space that is legitimately India's to dominate. It is hardly to be wondered then that in the eighth decade of its existence as an independent nation, India is emerging as something of an anachronism: a hefty economic power (per macro indices) that politically, diplomatically and militarily is pulling itself down to the second rank and is widely perceived as 'all mouth and no trousers'.

The infirmities in Modi's foreign and military policies are stark and tragically constitute the new normal. Having earned the trust of the people and received their mandate for massive system reform, rather than junking the whole caboodle of foreign and military policy and the administrative system propping it up, and starting afresh with new thinking and new ways of conducting the government's business, Modi chose to trust the same cautious and muddling bureaucrats to conjure up very different results. If not fundamental changes of the kind that allowed China to force its way into the global reckoning, were the people wrong to expect disruptive policies to shake things up a bit?[16] Yes, because 'change', Modi sombrely noted in his second year in office, 'does not happen all of a sudden'.[17] And his alpha male chest-thumping nationalism that voters were enthused by in 2014 has, other than with Pakistan, nowhere been in evidence. Candidate Modi roared like a tiger; as prime minister he has been a purring kitten when dealing with the big cats.

The chapter-wise delineation is as follows. Chapter 1 fleshes out the emerging international context of the alpha male political strongmen that have come to the fore the world over, and how their 'country first' bent of mind has affected regional and international relations and the global order, and how Modi has contributed to this milieu. Chapter 2 examines Prime Minister Modi's political personality and temperament from a psychological angle and traces how his early-life factors and socialization in the RSS may have made him more of an establishmentarian than a revolutionary, how this may have influenced his thinking and outlook and impacted his government's attitude, policies and manner of functioning and his outlook on international relations. This includes his respect for hierarchy, which has translated into being over-respectful of powerful states like the US and China and less tolerance towards weaker states. The same factors can explain why many of the most explosive socioeconomic problems he confronted when entering government, such as the millions of unskilled youth chasing after too few jobs and the perennially woeful agricultural sector, have worsened.

Chapter 3 explores the reasons for the continuation by Modi of India's creeper-vine foreign policy that winds itself around some great power patron or the other in order for the country to rise. It deconstructs his surprisingly obsequious stance vis-à-vis the US and the West as the central pillar of his foreign policy and approach to the world, ignoring a long history of Washington deliberately and with forethought hindering and obstructing India strategically and undermining its national security interests. In keeping with this approach, Modi frowns on even the slightest unsettling of the existing global and regional orders, even though as a revisionist power seeking to change the rank ordering of nations, India's interests are better served by dismantling the status quo and building new regional and international systems. In support of policy and posture bending towards America is a new policy ecosystem in Delhi that is in place, headed by the Indian chapters of reputed Washington think tanks. These also feature senior civilian and uniformed officers and bureaucrats seeking immigrant status (Green Cards) and other considerations for progeny and family members at all levels of the government and the military, happy to finesse and push a US-friendly policy line. This new phenomenon will be scrutinized.

In Chapter 4, two new geopolitical groupings—BRIS (Brazil, Russia, India, South Africa, i.e., BRICS minus China) and Mod Quad (India, Japan, Australia, the South East Asian nations, i.e., the Quadrilateral minus the US)—are mooted as means to escape the thrall of the proto-hegemons, the United States and China, and the reasons why this makes geopolitical, economic and military sense analysed. This slant to gain India political–military traction will be contrasted with Modi's preference to ride US coat-tails and seek accommodation with China.

Chapter 5 will delve into the failure of the Indian government, with the Ministry of External Affairs (MEA) in the van, to work in a coordinated fashion for timely delivery on promises and development projects announced by the prime minister during his foreign trips and when hosting foreign leaders in Delhi. We will see how tardy implementation and affirmative inaction has sapped goodwill and hurt India's credibility and standing in the neighbourhood, in Central Asia and in Africa, and why in trying to please the US Delhi has eroded India's clout in Moscow, strained relations with Iran, lost India its special place in Myanmar, and generally harmed the country's freedom of strategic action. There's also a short case study about the deal for the ShinMaywa US-2 amphibious aircraft hanging fire even though it is critical to building a strong relationship with Japan and a comprehensive Indian aerospace industry with global supply chain links. What it highlights is Modi's reticence to get a lazy and rules-bound bureaucracy to deliver the outcomes he desires, and to bring in accountability and a high rewards, harsh punishment regime to motivate civil servants. A common thread running through chapters 3, 4 and 5 is how the BJP government's fixation with Pakistan continues to skew India's external orientation while China benefits from Delhi's fearfulness and pusillanimity.

Chapter 6 scrutinizes some perennial but assorted national security problems, other than deconstructing in some detail Modi's confused and confusing Make in India programme. In this context are analysed the Tejas LCA programme, the prospective acquisition of a single-engine fighter plane, and the Indian Navy's Project 75i conventional submarine project, which would be best off with buying just the design and select technologies the country is deficient from a foreign vendor for a fraction of the $10.4 billion already allotted this project, rather than signing another spendthrift deal, like the one with France for the Scorpene diesel submarine, that won't fetch the country the critical technologies it really needs. In the strategic sphere, revisions in the nuclear doctrine and posture will be suggested with an eye to blunting China's comprehensive military edge with a nuclear first use strategy. And there will be brief analyses of, among other military issues, the costs of the army's preoccupation with counter-insurgency operations, the air force's future air order-of-battle (ORBAT) and the navy's emphasis on aircraft carriers. The concluding chapter will summarize the main themes and conclude that Modi's performance in government has not matched the prime minister's outsized poster persona and promises.

There are three conspicuous policy voids, which are also the running themes in this book, that Modi, like the other prime ministers after Nehru, has failed to fill, confirming, in the process, India's potential status as a little more than a 'great power lite'.[18] These have to do with the absence of a clear national vision, plan and timetable for its attainment, the absence of armaments self-sufficiency based on indigenous design-to-delivery capability by a profit-minded, private sector–led comprehensively capable defence industry, and of geopolitically bold and imaginative policies stressing India's neglected hard power as a diplomatic tool. There is an imperative need for policies to be disruptive and assertive in equal measure, aimed at elbowing India into the forefront of nations and increasing its global strategic profile and autonomous stature.

The policy ills that are elucidated at the heart of this book are something most Indians who voted Modi to power in 2014 had hoped he would remedy. But that has not happened. His long-term political ambition to cement a Hindu-majority support base has led to the ruling party's discreet support for Hindu extremist groups to polarize domestic politics along communal lines. The BJP government has failed on the socioeconomic front, including to generate employment, expand skilling programmes and incentivize the manufacturing sector into leading the charge on sustained double-digit GDP growth. It would have spread prosperity and a sense of well-being in the country and realized Modi's promise of 'sabka saath, sabka vikas' (with everybody, and for everybody's progress). His mix of personalized diplomacy, showmanship and bonhomie with foreign leaders, while an asset, has failed to achieve much, attempt anything new or embark the country on anything really big. It has been mostly more of the same, except the attitude towards Pakistan has become shriller, making India lose out on the greater strategic benefits that would accrue from pacifying the neighbourhood. It has only helped China consolidate its foothold in the subcontinent.

Little wonder then that the country appears to be stuck in neutral gear, if not actually sliding back. In a situation where India's formidable resources cry out to be used more holistically, expansively, strategically and productively, the Modi government has been found wanting. In nautical terms, India seems like a large stricken ship that started on its journey with much fanfare but soon developed engine trouble, and is bobbing aimlessly mid-sea with the captain and crew having no clue about how to fix the problem while the restless passengers on board await the next big wave to beach it somewhere. That somewhere, however, may be a place the country would not like to find itself in.

[1]

'Alpha Male' Leaders and 'Country First' Power Politics

'Maybe the ... human alpha male is a combination of disgruntled male wish fulfilment and borderline-pseudoscientific justification for resorting to bullying, intimidation and generally all-round unpleasant behaviour by men hoping to impose their will on a world they find too complex and unnerving so revert to their baser instincts to get what they want, despite knowing deep down they don't deserve it and shouldn't have it'—Dean Burnett, neuroscientist[1]

WHAT IS COMMON to Narendra Modi in India, Xi Jinping in China, Donald J. Trump in the US, Vladimir Putin in Russia, Recep Tayyip Erdogan in Turkey, Shinzo Abe in Japan, Marine Le Pen in France and Geert Wilders in the Netherlands? Besides relatively trivial things like the penchant of some of them (Modi and Trump in particular) to use social media for direct communications with the people, they are all 'alpha male' personalities who run their governments autocratically. Most of them are often brash and impetuous in their actions, have strong, if not always well-informed, views on everything and are used to conceiving the policy line and issuing orders, not confabulating with advisers. Quick to engage their egos to even ill-considered positions, they stick by them. They are mostly 'top-of-the-heap' loners surrounded by acolytes and functionaries ready to do their bidding, and focused on pushing their own agendas and besting their internal and external adversaries. These are powerful *jefes maximo* who have come to the fore after shaking up their respective polities. Other than Le Pen and Wilders, who lost their respective elections but unsettled the internal politics of both France and the Netherlands nevertheless, they have taken charge. Delhi, Beijing, Washington, Moscow, Ankara and Tokyo are awhirl, marching to a new drumbeat. When there is such a collection of flinty and strong-willed leaders striding the world stage, fireworks are always an incident away from happening.

It is significant that in this group of countries, five boast of strong militaries (US, Russia, China, India and Japan), three are civilizational states (India, China and Turkey), three are hegemonic powers (Russia, China and the US), three are genuine great economic powers (US, China and Japan), and all of them barring India are self-sufficient in arms and are generators of high technology. But they are all also nations seemingly dissatisfied with their lot. A strange phenomenon is thus abroad of countries that happen to be the biggest beneficiaries of the existing global order and verily its pillars are, in different ways, dissatisfied and bent on undermining it. They are behaving like bloody-minded revisionist states desirous of changing some crucial aspect or another of the international system, whose actions taken singly weaken the system and together can bring it down.

China figures in all these different subgroups, tilting towards upending the global balance in the different realms of state power and influence—cultural, economic, diplomatic and military. Therefore, it poses the central threat to the existing system. In the new age, China is emerging—as the US did at the Bretton Woods Conference after the Second World War—as the principal node of comprehensive power and the state that other countries take their bearings from. Except, the passing of the dominant state baton this time around is unlikely to be as peaceful as the US assumption of overlordship from the then fading power, Great Britain, in the early 1900s. This 'transfer of power', so to say, was unusually smooth because the successor Pax Americana, backed by the globe-girdling US Navy in its essentials, resonated with the trade-driven and liberal Pax Britannica enforced by the Royal Navy in the previous hundred-odd years.[2]

The new power shift will be more contentious because there is no consonance in the values and strategic aims among the US, the new contender China, and Russia which is determined to remain strategically relevant. While gaining from the prevailing economic and trading regimes, China, far from reflecting the essential Anglo-Saxon values of the current global order, favours imposing its own international schema: the *tianxia* system of Confucian origin. This ancient Sino-centric concept, given new gloss by Xi, envisions 'harmony and cooperation without hegemony' and is regarded by some Chinese as 'the best blueprint for world politics in the future'.[3] But this latter construct is unfamiliar to the international community and has little legitimacy, notwithstanding Beijing's rhetorical use of variations of the theme of 'harmony under heaven' central to tianxia.[4] Xi's programme for the 'rejuvenation of the nation' is, however, the practical template that Asia and the rest of the world need to be mindful of. The time it will take Beijing to 'rejuvenate the nation' and establish a harmonious order advantageous to itself is the time afforded India and the other countries to derail China's hegemonic designs.

The fact is, if world politics prior to the meltdown of the Soviet Union in the early 1990s orientated to the superpower US–Soviet rivalry, hereafter it is likely to be animated by opposition to an overbearing China. In the context of a receding America and the natural rebalancing of global power against a coming hegemon, the problem for Xi and his Chinese Communist Party cohort is that Messrs Modi, Trump, Putin, the European Union (EU) (as unitary actor) and Abe, in their separate and joint, planned and unplanned and sometimes faltering ways, will ensure that Xi's plans for realizing his 'new China dream' do not fructify. That said, all these leaders are realists, grounded and no pushovers when it comes to marshalling the formidable strengths and resources of their countries. Thus, just as Xi feels free to pursue his objectives in the larger geopolitical game that is under way, the others feel motivated to restrict Beijing's ambitions because they know that China can achieve its goals only at the expense of their countries. Interesting tests of will are hence in the offing. There is already evidence of this: India and China over the disputed border and in the Indian Ocean region; the US and China over trade, the south China Sea and a nuclearized North Korea; the US and Russia over Crimea and Ukraine; and these two and China over Iran.

Tests of will between nations are ultimately manifested in wars, of course, but also in testy, often literally physical, interactions between leaders, especially if they happen to be the strongman type. This is no trivial matter, but Modi, Xi, Trump, Putin and Abe are solidly built men who endow their public personas with physicality. It is often slyly used by them as a means of intimidation and is glimpsed in their personalized diplomacy. The most impressive thing about the Indian prime minister's first meeting in Washington on 26 June 2017 with the US President, for instance, was Modi imposing himself physically on Trump, who is a head taller. Despite being warned about the Indian prime minister being a habitual hugger, Trump, a self-confessed germophobe, was unable to do anything other than acquiesce tamely to Modi's full-frontal bear hugs—once in public view in the White House garden and twice in other meetings.[5] Modi had famously bragged during the 2014 general elections about his 56 inch chest, as if chest size mattered in running the affairs of state, but it was a standard the Indian people quickly cottoned to as a measure of his ability to deliver on promises. Perhaps appreciating that Modi was on to something, especially as the Indian leader's public hug reverberated more with the worldwide public than his handshake, Trump, following Modi's visit, firmed up a longer, stronger and more lingering handshake with his foreign counterparts (which he successfully tried out on the much younger, slightly disdainful French President Emmanuel Macron in Paris on 13 July 2017).[6]

But predating Modi and Trump in the beefcake sweepstakes was Putin, a martial arts expert and former Russian counter-intelligence agent for sixteen years (1975–91) in the KGB (Komitet Gosudarstvennoy Bezopasnosti) Second Chief Directorate. Photographs of a bare-chested and muscular Putin on horseback wearing khaki cargo pants, posing with a hunting rifle and, most recently, angling, convey the impression to his own people and to audiences abroad of a man and a country that are not to be trifled with. In contrast, Shinzo Abe appeared at the closing ceremony of the Rio Olympics in 2016 representing Tokyo, host of the next edition of the Games, dressed up and seemingly uncomfortable as Super Mario, the video game plumber. He made up for this faux pas by kicking off the Autumn Festival at the Yasukuni Shrine war memorial with a ritual offering in the face of shrill outcries by China against the revival of Japanese militarism.[7]

Xi is a 'princeling', the son of Xi Zhongxun, one of Mao Zedong's chieftains and founder of the North-west Revolutionary Base Area that offered refuge at a critical time to the People's Liberation Army (PLA), which was reeling from attacks by Generalissimo Chiang Kai-shek's Kuomintang army. Xi *pere* was later the commissar of the military campaign to subdue the Uyghur warlords of Xinjiang. Xi Junior seemed to be aware that he is privileged and destined for bigger things. With his anti-corruption drive he has done two things: rid himself of rivals within the party and addressed the disillusionment of the Chinese people fed up with the greed and corruption of the senior party cadres.[8] He has also effected a 'rapid centralization of power' and sanitized the social media space so that there is place only for 'gushing praise' of his leadership.

With the second best-funded military in the world, President Xi has reorganized the PLA structure to tighten his control. He has taken to reviewing parades in uniform and is referred to in some official media as the 'Supreme Commander of the people's army'.[9] He has gone about augmenting his personal power and strengthening his grip on the Chinese state and the military so methodically that an Australian Broadcasting Corporation commentator likened him to 'Vladimir Putin on steroids'.[10] But whether it is a hug (Modi), a vigorous handshake (Trump) or a Baikal rifle hung casually over the shoulder (Putin), it is a gesture designed to get under an adversary's skin. Meanwhile, pictures of Xi being a stern supremo reviewing troops reflect his forceful nature and resolve. These are no bad things to telegraph to the world.

Even with so much physicality on show, the North Atlantic Treaty Organization (NATO) Summit in May 2017 was extraordinary for the display of Trump's boorishness, when he physically shoved aside Dusko Marković, the prime minister of Montenegro, to get to the front for a group photograph, an incident captured on TV. French President Macron was going to have none of this, so when he met his American counterpart for the first time, the seventy-year-old Trump and the thirty-nine-year-old Macron clasped each other's hands in a hard, knuckle-whitening grip from which the older man pulled out. The Frenchman later confided to the French press that this was no 'innocent' gesture but was meant to convey to the American leader that unlike Marković he was no pushover. 'Donald Trump, the Turkish president [Erdogan] or the Russian president [Putin],' Macron explained, 'see relationships in terms of power. That doesn't bother me. I don't believe in diplomacy by public abuse, but in my bilateral dialogues I won't let anything pass [or] make small concessions, even symbolic ones.' It was a warning to strongman leaders everywhere that should any of them get physical in a way that was not nice, they'd get a taste of the same medicine in return.[11]

But Modi's friendly hug at the July 2017 G20 Summit in Hamburg elicited something else altogether with Macron reciprocating warmly (in contrast to his predecessor Francois Hollande's manifest discomfort with Modi's embrace). This spectacle of international meetings as physical contests between leaders—obvious alpha male behaviour—is not entirely alien to the political sensibility in the subcontinent. Recall that just after India's nuclear tests in May 1998, the then BJP chief minister of Delhi Madan Lal Khurana, in a fit of braggadocio, had challenged Pakistan to step into the *akhada* (wrestling pit)!

Alpha Maleness and the 'Country First' Foreign Policy

Other than their manly attributes, what is the thinking of these leaders, what do they believe in and what are the ideas that drive their outlook, approach and policies? In these respects and others, how does Modi stack up when compared to Trump, Putin, Xi, Abe and Erdogan? And what do these strongmen portend for the world?

For one thing, they all seem to share a certain antipathy to militant Islam. Sebastian Gorka, a former denizen of the Soviet bloc and a Hungarian who ended up in the US as a propagandist for Trump, hinted at what's in store soon after the latter came to power. 'Our foreign policy,' he said on a television show, 'has been a disaster. We've neglected and abandoned our allies. We've emboldened our enemies. The message I have—it's a very simple one . . . The era of the pyjama boy is over . . . and the alpha males are back.'[12] Gorka, deputy assistant and apparently principal adviser to the US President on matters relating to terrorism and the Islamic world, supposedly shaped Trump's call during the presidential campaign for a Cold War–type of confrontation to 'take on the ideology of radical Islam'. This included policy kinks like banning Muslim immigration from terrorist-infested societies in West

Asia and weeding out American Muslims who 'believe that sharia law should supplant American law'. In a profile of the influential deputy assistant, the *Washington Post* wrote: 'Trump's foreign policy, Gorka says, will be a macho foreign policy, when tough guys will once again rule the world and wimp[s] are left on the sidelines.'[13] Early in his days at the White House, Trump was prevailed upon to reverse the previous US stance and invite one of Gorka's favourite West Asian leaders, President Abdel Fattah el-Sisi, battling the Muslim Brotherhood in Egypt, to visit Washington, which the latter did on 3 April 2017.

The incoming Trump administration's display of machismo in rhetoric and policy was all too much for three 'alpha ladies' experienced in top-level affairs of state and diplomacy: Madeleine Albright, US President Bill Clinton's secretary of state in the 1990s, Wendy Sherman, undersecretary of state during the Barack Obama presidency, and Michele Flournoy, who would have been the first woman US defense secretary had a Hillary Clinton presidency come to pass. What they said as regards Trump's policy and posturing could apply equally to the other alpha male leaders. 'One of the lessons for the alpha males,' observed Flournoy tartly, 'is to actually start with the facts.' Sherman pitched in, saying, 'Tough talk is quite easy. Bullying is quite easy. Getting something done in the world is quite complicated.' Albright, on her part, voiced the hope that 'we are not in the world of the alpha males, because they have made an awful lot of mistakes'. Worse, 'they prod each other', she said, 'into more alphaness' and, she implied, into making more mistakes and getting their countries into bigger messes.[14]

The alpha maleness of these leaders has not, by itself, spawned the Country First principle separately espoused by them. That has come mostly from the widespread disaffection with the ideology of geoeconomics and interdependence that had heretofore held sway, and its inhering conceit that national boundaries don't matter, concerns of sovereignty are irrelevant and the free flow of capital and labour across borders is as natural as the openness of the global marketplace that supposedly works for the benefit of all. Curiously, the Country First phrase was expressly coined in 1858 by the German historian Heinrich von Treitschke with the motto: 'The Fatherland before everything else'.

This was at a time of tremendous middle-class angst with the unrealized ideals of the revolutions of 1848 in many European countries, particularly Denmark, the Netherlands and the Austro-Hungarian Empire.[15] There has been a similar churn on a much larger scale since the mid-1990s.

The evidence suggests that high labour and manufacturing costs in advanced societies have led to the relocation of jobs and factories abroad, leaving large sections of the working class that had moved to the middle class without employment. This propelled right-wing populism and politics of discontent. It led, for instance, to Brexit—the British decision via a referendum to leave the EU—the election of Trump in the US and the nearly successful electoral campaigns by Marine Le Pen in France and Geert Wilders in the Netherlands. Fuelling the social discontent was also the unhindered demand-driven movement of skilled and unskilled labour across borders. The resultant influx of foreign workers has led to a watering down of host country cultures and the forced homogenization of societal values and norms. It has flattened national identities, erased territorial distinctions, disturbed local economies, destabilized social orders and run smack into nativist reaction and resistance. People do want to continue receiving the benefits they are accustomed to, the national borders to be protected and national identities to be preserved. This leads to the demand that governments exercise the sovereign imperative to advance their particular economic, political and national security interests rather than some vague universal or corporate good in the guise of free trade. From this has sprung the India First, America First and Japan First kind of thinking.

But India, a latecomer to globalized economics and a laggard in the international marketplace, is discovering that plugging into the global supply chains and getting mega-transnational corporations to invest in the country on the basis of its presumed comparative labour cost advantage is not easy. The march that China and the smaller, more politically and economically agile states of South East Asia have stolen on India is not something these top racers are going to give up without a fight, and then only if the tortoise can match up with the hares in all the areas the latter excel in.

India cannot, unfortunately, follow the China model of a centralized command economy run on capitalist lines, which is replicated by a host of 'small dragon economies' in Asia. The path it has to follow is the more onerous one of becoming economically efficient. But to make headway will require catching up in areas like ease of doing business. It will also need to make arrangements for a smooth and corruption-free interface with the host government and society, easily accessible pool of skilled and relatively cheap manpower, simple rules, effective laws, fair regulatory mechanisms, strong protection for intellectual property rights, efficient infrastructure, ready availability of land, and other basics such as water and electricity and a conducive investment and labour milieu. This is the evolutionary approach Modi, like his immediate predecessors, has adopted. Evolutionary progress, alas, is slow, and the country's inability to muster up these attributes fast enough means it cannot rise economically and race with the best. This exacerbates India's internal contradictions, resulting in growing economic unrest and social turmoil and the consequent falling of its political and diplomatic stock.

In this regard, the US and the EU countries have more leeway, because however much they slip in the economic indices, they will remain at the top because they are already at the post-industrial stage of development. China got its way by being disruptive in all spheres—especially in foreign and military policy—something Delhi has shown little talent and no appetite for. If neither happens, India is damned perpetually to remain in the 'between and betwixt' stage—never completely out of the global reckoning but not quite making it either. This is to say that Modi's India First ideology has different wellsprings compared to the Country First policy of Trump, Putin, Xi, Abe or Erdogan, and will play out differently in terms of outcomes depending on how these leaders and their nations translate such thinking into policies. But it helps to have an alpha male leader at the top because it injects credibility into the effort he is putting in and can get the people behind him to create a bigger ripple effect at home and abroad.

To contextualize Modi's India First thinking, it will help to see what some of the other Country First pronouncements are about, and how they compare and contrast with the Indian version. Let's start with some of the outlier leaders who didn't make it but represent a large slice of public opinion in their countries.

The party manifesto for Marine Le Pen's National Front Party (NFP) in the 2017 presidential campaign was 'France First' in all but name, featuring 144 points. Some unrealistic promises apart—such as redrafting the Constitution—this list promised 'national preference' for French citizens in hiring and in dispensing housing benefits, the return of the franc as the national currency, closing of borders, opting out of the European free travel zone, seeking exemption for France from the EU's fundamental tenets, asserting the 'right to close the national borders permanently, prioritizing French workers over others, and rescinding all free trade agreements [FTAs] unilaterally'. Also in the NFP election manifesto was withdrawal from NATO's integrated command system, and cutting the migrant flow into the country by 90 per cent. Lesser objectives included a ban on the hijab for Muslim women residing in France.[16] Whether this was merely Le Pen's 'vision' and hence not implementable or a policy 'roadmap' is not as germane to this analysis as the fact that most such provisions were populist, directed at formalizing the discrimination faced by Muslims in France, closing off the immigration channel for Arab Muslims mostly from the former French colonies in the Maghreb region (Algeria, Morocco and Libya) and otherwise de-Islamizing the immigrant communities in the country. She capitalized on the anti-Muslim and anti-Arab sentiment among the people at large and justified such thrust of policy as recovering for France its essential nature as a Christian country. But because her Catholic faith always rested lightly on her, she used it mainly to mask her populist schemes relating to jobs and immigration.[17] It is not unimportant that Le Pen's more strident take on national security, say, had spillover effects on the new regime—the head of the French armed forces General Pierre de Villiers, for example, resigned over President Macron's proposed cuts in the defence budget.[18]

To France's north-west, the colourful Geert Wilders and his Party for Freedom enlivened the Dutch parliamentary elections in March 2017 that he lost. His demand to stop Muslim immigration into the Netherlands and for a 'Drexit' (Dutch exit from the EU) gained a wide following. The support for Wilders, a 'former punk rocker' with Indonesian roots on his maternal side, wrote Ian Buruma in the *Sunday New York Times*, reflected the yearning in Dutch society for 'the old certainties of a more traditional and ethnically homogeneous society'.[19]

Whether Le Pen and Wilders would have decisively turned France and the Netherlands inward, Trump's America First set of policies has turned the US isolationist with a vengeance. His administration is committed, says a document released by the White House, to 'a foreign policy focused on American interests and American national security' in pursuing which, the paper states, 'we will embrace diplomacy. The world must know... that we are always happy when old enemies become friends and when old friends become allies.'[20] This suggests that Trump will try and improve relations with Putin's Russia despite the US policy establishment's hesitation on this count, and should any friendly country, such as India, choose to come to America, Trump will demand, as he did of NATO partners, that they contribute their fair share and pay up for such security as provided them by the US military.[21]

Elsewhere, the US has already pulled out of the Trans-Pacific Partnership (TPP), and Trump has warned that unless 'American workers get a fair deal' the US will also withdraw from the North American Free Trade Agreement (NAFTA), 'crackdown' on nations violating trade accords and fight 'for fair but tough trade deals [to] bring jobs back to America's shores, increase wages, and support US manufacturing'.[22] On this issue, Trump has fired the first shots in what could become a full-fledged trade war. He imposed a 10 to 25 per cent tax on imported steel and aluminium. While Canada, Mexico, the EU and Japan were subsequently exempted from these taxes, the same was not true for India, which retaliated with duties on US goods.[23] And China retaliated against the $50 billion worth of tariffs on Chinese technology companies by cutting down on imports of American agricultural commodities, like soya.[24] Defence-wise, the US president says he will 'not allow other nations to surpass' the US military capability, and to prove the point he signed a $1.3 trillion budget.[25] Trump is committed to achieving 'energy independence' by tapping 'the estimated $50 trillion' in shale oil and gas reserves within the country and by 'reviving America's coal industry'—the reason for his yanking the US out of the Paris Climate Accord.[26]

Trump's views representing 'ethno-nationalist, nativist, ideas' promising 'far-right populism' and his dismissive attitude to traditional alliances, security cooperation, multilateral institutions, an open trading system and democratic solidarity has raised alarms about the end of the liberal international order that the US created and led after the Second World War.[27] This order is weakening because of the rising disaffection with it owing to the economic dislocations in the countries of the First World, until now its prime beneficiaries. They have suffered as corporations in search of bigger margins of profit close down factories, divert investments and throw people out of work. It is to this section of the US population that Trump's (and Le Pen's) 'mercantilist, or zero-sum, understanding of trade' and his view of it 'as a game of winners and losers, not an exchange that generates mutual gains' appeals.[28]

Trump has followed up his excoriation of FTAs and alliances with policies and executive action to upend them. It fits in with the 'leave us alone' backwoods Protestant belief of the American evangelical right that majorly supported Trump and ensured his success in the presidential elections. But it doesn't quite explain how 'a thrice married, biblically illiterate sexual predator hijacked the religious right'. Writing in the *New Republic*, Sarah Posner explains that this was because Trump mixed ethno-religious solidarity, attitudinal belligerence and embedded racism in white evangelical circles, especially in the American south, and alt-right revisionist politics to advantageous effect, highlighting the fact that the postmodern societies of the West are just as vulnerable to religious appeals as any country in the developing world.[29] Does it really matter that in one case religious prejudices are used to milk votes and in the other to rouse people for jihad? Both instances reflect the limited reach of international liberal norms and values.

Shinzo Abe freely admits that his view was derived from Trump's America First slogan but with differences. 'I am the prime minister of Japan, so I am for Japan First,' he said at a May 2017 event in Tokyo hosted by the *Wall Street Journal*. He, however, noted that his concept conceives of a 'Japan that walks the path of global peace and prosperity'. Abe particularly supports the TPP that Trump has ditched. 'My conviction that the Asia-Pacific region, which is a centre of world growth, needs the TPP,' he said, 'remains unchanged.' Importantly, he referred to the May 2017 G7 Summit in Taormina, Italy, as dilating on 'the route the world should take going forward, and strengthen the ties among leaders who share universal values'.[30]

With Trump attending, the summit swerved around differences on climate, immigration and free trade, but deferred to his pet policy themes, including ambiguity about just how to tackle Russia. This was reflected in the communique issued at the end of the meet. Interestingly, while calling out Russia on its 'illegal annexation of the Crimean peninsula' and demanding that Moscow implement its commitments under the Minsk Agreements (respecting the sovereignty of Ukraine, among other things), it nowhere mentioned China by name or its aggressive behaviour in the East Sea around the disputed Senkaku/Diaoyu Islands. Nor did Beijing's virtual takeover of most of the South China Sea merit a mention in it other than as a hope voiced about respecting UNCLOS (United Nations Convention on the Law of the Sea). And, despite being the chief beneficiary of free trade, China, with its state-subsidized and protected market, was not hauled up by the G7 for its protectionist policies.[31] Treating China with kid gloves is apparently the new norm because it is just too big and powerful to upset.

Thus, at Taormina, Japan's seconding of the G7 line on Russia and Crimea didn't fetch it condemnation of Beijing on the Senkaku issue. Abe has time and again been given the brush-off by Washington, first during Obama's presidency and now by Trump and the West European countries when he sought their support on this dispute. If Japan, a treaty ally, cannot get the US to back it, India's chances of getting Washington to line up on its side against China are remote, whatever the quality of an Indian prime minister's personal rapport with the US President of the day. Looked at from the perspective of India's territorial dispute with China, it means that Delhi cannot rely on the US and G7 for any assistance, no matter how egregious China's provocations and even aggression, because they would fear being at the receiving end of Beijing's big economic stick.

If the US hesitates to take on China, what role will Japan play in blunting China's economic edge in Asia and its military assertiveness? Its uncertain response to Beijing's use of its geopolitically expansive Belt and Road Initiative (BRI) as a means of extending Chinese military reach and clout is telling. After initially shrugging off the BRI, Abe in June

2017 lauded its 'potential to connect East and West as well as diverse regions found in between'.[32] On the other divisive subject, the TPP, Abe considers it of 'awesome' strategic value despite Trump's rejection of it. Yoichi Funabashi, chairman of the Rebuild Japan Initiative Foundation, the influential Tokyo think tank, voiced his fears in the run-up to the US presidential elections about the Republican Party candidate's view that 'US–Japan relations were one-sided, with America shouldering too many burdens', and concluded that 'Japan would have to step up . . . or be left to its own devices'. Funabashi speculated that if not the TPP, Washington 'will realize soon enough that, for both economic and strategic reasons, America must participate in multilateral trade agreements in the Asia-Pacific region . . . [or] be left out [and] in effect [cede] the area to China and its economic expansionism.'[33]

Consistent with this view, Funabashi had earlier supported Japan joining the China-led Asian Infrastructure Investment Bank (AIIB), which is in direct competition with the Asian Development Bank (ADB) principally funded by Japan. He argued, 'By distributing financial assistance to states in the Asia-Pacific, the bank [and hence China] will inevitably help shape the region's future economic architecture, as well as, implicitly, its security relations [and therefore] Japan has a major strategic interest in participating [in it].' Apparently, Funabashi had in mind Japan's involvement in the AIIB to pre-empt the emergence, collaterally, of an overtly China-centred security arrangement. Prime Minister Abe, however, was cautious, stating that his government was keeping a 'careful' eye on the AIIB's lending operations and, as part of his Japan First slant, expressed his willingness to join the bank pending the resolution of certain issues relating to its governance. Some Chinese analysts have criticized Abe's Japan First principle as contradicting his interest in the TPP and AIIB.[34] But the thrust of the Japanese policy is clear: It is for a strong economic counterpoise to China in Asia. In security matters, because Tokyo would prefer not to be left alone to deal with China, it will continue to rely on the US military's prowess for as long as it is available, and also on partnering potentially strong countries such as India.

For a country where religion was ostracized by the Soviet state for some seventy years, the Russian Orthodox Church has not merely revived but become a significant factor in that country's domestic politics. In the religious vacuum created by the fragmentation of the Soviet Union, American religious organizations (Jehovah's Witness, evangelicals, et al.) rushed in imperilling the indigenous Church's latent influence. The 1997 law forbidding the practice of faiths 'foreign' to the country helped it to spring back. The speculation is that Vladimir Putin, who for a short while in the 1980s spent time away from counter-intelligence and in KGB Fifth Directorate monitoring religious groups, built personal relationships with patriarchs of the Church. As head of the United Russia Party government, he restored to the Church its vast estates, wealth and status in Russian society. Together, Putin and the Church have moved to 'sacralize the Russian national identity', a valuable asset in shaping and legitimating an authoritarian order in the country. Externally, the Church has portrayed Putin-led Russia's conflict with the US and its ongoing differences with western Europe as spiritual and civilizational in nature. A 2015 poll revealed that 60 per cent of Russians believe the US is a threat, and half as many (31 per cent) think the US would invade Russia.[35] This is the kind of public paranoia that has fanned support for Putin's aggressive style in foreign affairs while strengthening his authority.

Putin's Russia, which allegedly helped Trump get elected with some well-executed cyber operations against his opponent Hillary Clinton's campaign staff, has traction with the Trump White House.[36] Whether Trump chooses to stay on the sidelines or not, Moscow is resolved to reclaim for Russia its old Soviet sphere of influence in eastern Europe and in Central Asia, and to once again be a meaningful player in the world. This goal is being realized, due in no small part to Washington's hesitation on a pushback on Russia's periphery. Trump's insistence that the European states contribute their fair share for collective security has divided NATO and diluted the threat to Russia from the West to an extent, some analysts fear, of emboldening Putin to next do a Crimea in Belarus.[37] In West Asia, in contrast to what Hillary Clinton would have done in Syria with the imposition of a 'no fly zone', say, Trump withdrew US backing to the Syrian rebels, making life easier for the Bashar al-Assad regime surviving on a Russian life-support drip.[38] Elsewhere, the US is putting the squeeze on Pakistan to rein in the leadership of the terrorist Haqqani Network residing in Quetta and shoring up the Kabul dispensation of President Ashraf Ghani propped up by Russia and India.[39] In light of the infirm US military commitment, even its longtime allies are making separate arrangements. Abe, for one, has thought it prudent to arrive at a compromise with Putin on the Kurile Islands. During Putin's state visit to Japan in December 2016 a 'special system' was proposed for the joint development of these islands occupied by Stalin four days after the Second World War formally ended with the Japanese surrender in May 1945. Abe hopes it will be the first step in recovering for Japan this four-island chain. Putin, on the other hand, expects by such means to weaken Tokyo's support for the US military base in Japan.[40] It is a mutually beneficial Russo-Japanese move that could end up benefiting China most of all.

In the league of strongmen simultaneously helming numerous countries, Erdogan in Turkey has the most relevance for Modi in India, perhaps because of the cultural affinities. The ruling AKP (Adalet ve Kalkinma Partisi or Justice and Development Party) has traditionally been a centre-right umbrella party inclusive of Islamists, political conservatives and votaries of the free market economy. The 16 April 2017 referendum and the follow-up 2019 elections are expected to usher in a presidential form of government with a weak Parliament and fortify Erdogan's hold on the country. This development is complemented by Turkey's growing Islamization with Ankara rising as a champion of Islamic causes, including Palestine and, much to Delhi's discomfiture, Kashmir.[41] Turkey, moreover, has abjured the earlier cordial relations with Israel by turning anti-Zionist, even anti-Semitic.[42] And the ruling AKP has over the last several years gravitated towards becoming an Erdogan 'personality cult' with the projection of the leader by his political appointees as an infallible, larger than life, figure of Islamic rectitude and assertiveness, even endowing him with a mythical backstory.

Because the dynastic principle matters, Turkish Prime Minister Binali Yildirim in autumn 2016 traced Erdogan's ancestry to an Ottoman-era sultan. Another ruling AKP official on Facebook described him as 'the Caliph of the Presidency'. Secondly, Erdogan's stature is sought to be raised by lowering that of Mustafa Kemal Ataturk, who founded the modern, secular Turkish state on the ruins of the Ottoman Empire after the First World War. Ataturk is portrayed as a westernized person and foreigner to boot who was not in sync with Islamic traditions and customs. An AKP youth leader has made much of the fact, for example, of Ataturk hailing from Thessaloniki, the once Ottoman city in Greece on the Aegean Sea, adding that he 'doesn't [even] look Turkish'.[43] Combining Islam with nationalism has garnered Erdogan popular support, a base he means to use for transforming Turkish society. Thus, school curriculums have been changed to emphasize the Islamic way of life, with a view to producing a more 'pious generation' of Turks.[44]

But what about Erdogan's New Turkey (Yeni Turkiye) programme? In AKP's telling, the country's history is divided between the Kemalist period that saw the entrenchment of a centralized, authoritarian and autarchic Turkish state run by an oligarchy composed of the military, bureaucracy and judiciary, and the more 'democratic' system that Erdogan is said to have obtained by structurally rejigging it, particularly by loosening the clasp of the Turkish armed forces, the mainstay of the ancien régime, by such tactics as the forced en masse resignations in 2011 of the top military brass. Successive AKP victories in elections, moreover, have led to a 'regression into the old ways' and the emergence of an authoritarian Erdogan under the cover of greater 'democratization'.[45]

Modi's India First Orientation and 'New India'

Narendra Modi has never really articulated his India First policy in extenso but spoken about it in dribs and drabs and broad-brush terms. In a town hall setting in New Delhi in August 2016, he elaborated on this concept as the 'central point [of Indian foreign policy]. It is about protecting India's strategic interest [and] ensur[ing] that India marches forward in achieving economic prosperity by leaps and bounds and reach[ing] the position which it is destined to reach.' But unlike Trump's, Le Pen's and Wilders's notions and more in line with Abe's outlook, Modi's engagement with the world is in the geoeconomics-motivated interdependence mould. Rejecting the interstate politics of an earlier era when the US, the Soviet and the non-aligned blocs held sway, he averred that 'the time of grouping has come to an end. Every country is linked to some other country [and] walking together has become the norm.' It is in this milieu of cooperative internationalism that Modi claimed 'India is making its place with new energy and prestige' and, en passant, cautioned against labelling Indian foreign policy as aggressive, progressive or even proactive.[46]

It may be instructive to gauge Modi's India First ideas with the concept as it was first mooted in 2002 by me, and to see the extent of deviation and the reasons for it. The context at the time was the Atal Bihari Vajpayee government's foreign and military policies that seemed to me to be keeling over to please the US government and, in the process, emasculating India's national interests and security. Thus, the 'voluntary moratorium' on nuclear testing was announced in the wake of the Shakti series of tests in May 1998 despite the government being aware of the failure of the thermonuclear weapon that was tested. Further, the nuclear deterrent was disaggregated with the nuclear warheads/weapons de-mated from their vectors (missiles and aircraft) to enhance crisis stability, something that Washington favoured, with the Indian strategic strike capability capped at the ballistic missiles of intermediate range because it was apprehended an Indian ICBM capability might excite US paranoia. Moreover, a 'general mobilization for war' was inappropriately ordered in response to the Pakistan-sponsored 13 December 2001 terrorist attack on Parliament, rather than instantaneous retaliatory aerial strikes on terrorist facilities and installations within Pakistan and Pakistan-Occupied Kashmir (POK). Forgoing the last option, predictably, drew praise from Washington, which was fully prepared for and would have condoned Indian retaliation, but was taken aback by the forbearance shown by Delhi and lauded the Vajpayee government for its responsible behaviour. Similar forbearance was shown after the November 2008 attack on Mumbai from the sea.

The reasons for such sensitivity to US concerns post-1998 was firstly the unwarranted fear of America taking 'the non-proliferation stick to India' and, more positively, the lure of advanced technology. These two streams merged, culminating in the 8 July 2005 agreement signed by Prime Minister Manmohan Singh and President George W. Bush that promised India entry into the international nuclear mainstream. With this would come 'the rights and privileges' of a nuclear weapons state, the civilian nuclear cooperation deal in 2008 and collaterally collaborative projects to develop sophisticated military hardware and support for India's candidature for a permanent seat in the UN Security Council. As I had pointed out at the time, this was tantamount to India seeking 'great power' as 'entitlement', and achieving it on the cheap and at the sufferance of a big power patron instead of securing it the old-fashioned way: by earning it with 'blood and iron' as Bismarck had done with 19th century Germany and Mao with China in the 20th century. Practising restraint and self-abnegation, I had said, only 'earns derision, not respect'. Further, because national vision, self-respect, self-belief and the necessary comprehensive national effort are the 'building blocks of great power', that the 'single-minded' pursuit of 'narrowly-defined national interests at the expense of every other principle, ideology and value' is what, I argued, defines 'the India first, always, and at all cost mindset and attitude'. Such 'India First' thinking, I had suggested, needed to be imbibed by every official and agency in the Indian government, especially the MEA, Ministry of Defence (MoD) and the Department of Defence Production, all military men, defence scientists and engineers, and the entire defence industry for India to have a chance at becoming, within a relatively short period of time, a country of consequence.[47]

In the end stage of his first term as prime minister, Modi, the sole fount of all policy ideas in the BJP government, has done nothing very meaningful in meeting the India First metrics. In early May 2017, he defined his foreign policy priorities to an assembly of the country's ambassadors as follows: increasing India's economic profile in the newer, untapped markets of the world, enhancing its security in a difficult neighbourhood and building it into a leading power and net security provider.[48] These are unexceptionable goals, not the stuff to vault India into the heaving scrum of international power politics. The impression of Modi's small-time objectives is backed by the fact that there is no mention anywhere in his many pronouncements of the inherent strengths and resources of the nation and how he means to harness them. More troublingly, there's no hint, much less a detailed articulation, of a national vision, of the preferred global order and rising India's place in it, the time-frame in which he expects the country to achieve it and with what effect on the Asian region and the world and, most significantly, utilizing what plan and strategy. Indeed, there has been nothing from Modi by way of a national vision, game plan or strategy. Nor has there been a public mustering of the iron resolve and political will necessary to signal to the people his intentions, just a series of mostly alliterative slogans and, in practice, staying with the foreign and military policies charted by his predecessors, Vajpayee and Manmohan Singh. It doesn't come close to fleshing out a genuinely 'new India', much less an India First attitude and policies.

Consider in this respect what Modi sees as constituting a 'new India': A more efficient apparatus of state (better coordination between government agencies, distribution of LED bulbs, etc.), speeded up governmental processes (less time to get passports, income tax refunds), streamlined delivery of social benefits (farmer insurance, free gas connections, rural electrification, bank accounts for the poor), more effective implementation of infrastructure programmes (rail projects, increased electricity generation), and accelerated creation of jobs (extending shop hours).[49] The impression one has of these markers is that of a list of ingredients and tools a car designer may crave without an inkling of what he is supposed to create. The result could be a Rolls-Royce or a Tata Nano. If all Modi's vision for the country is a bagful of relatively small achievements, meagre economic accomplishments and unspecified but timid objectives in the external realm dressed up in acronyms (such as SAGAR—Security and Growth for All in the Region), his 'new India' is much like the old India he inherited. It's the 'same old, same old' with Modi's ministrations, producing only marginal changes because he is relying on the existing rickety government system and the old way of doing things to deliver new, different and dazzling outcomes. So, India continues to lag way behind the South East Asian states to go no farther out than that and, where China is concerned, remains overmatched.

Compared and contrasted with the agendas of the other strongmen, Modi's vision and schemes appear meagre, mostly of local import, and not designed for anything other than minimal international impact. If he has been restrained and convivial in his dealings with foreign countries, his government at home, like Trump's in the US, Xi's in China, Putin's in Russia and Erdogan's in Turkey, has been only about himself. Having first ruthlessly eliminated the residual resistance to his primacy within the ruling BJP with some deft political manoeuvring, Modi has, with the help of his confidant Amit Shah (installed by him as party chief), reduced the opposition to bumfuzzled irrelevance, sharing the fate of the Kemalists at the hands of Erdogan in Turkey, of the Communist Party and the Liberal Democratic Party by Putin in Russia, and the shrinking of the support base of the Democratic Party and Constitutional Democratic Party by Abe in Japan.

But it is hard not to attribute this outcome to Modi's political skills and rhetoric, his keen social sense, insights into caste arithmetic in various regions and the gripes and grievances of the common man.[50] Combined with his killer instinct, it has assured Modi and his party a longish stint in power. A domineering presence in national life has resulted in the Indian system and policy establishment—the deep state—adjusting to Modi's likes and dislikes, becoming attentive to his every tick and ready to do his bidding. It has reinforced the prime minister's autocratic style of functioning, rooting the top-down decision-making model that's presently in vogue—very different from the more collegial model of the previous regimes that fitted the personalities of Manmohan Singh and Vajpayee. It mirrors developments in the US, China, Russia and Turkey, and a good part of the developing world, and in the states formerly comprising the Soviet bloc. It represents what John Lloyd, founder of the Reuters Institute for the Study of Journalism at Oxford University has called 'semi-authoritarian nationalism'.[51] Whatever their differing ideologies, autocratic regimes find other governments of the same ilk easier to do business with.[52]

Commonalities

What is most striking is just how determined this lot of alpha male leaders appears to be to pull down iconic leaders in their own countries from their pedestals, and to belittle the work of their predecessors in order to pump up their own importance and legitimize their policies. In Turkey, Erdogan's backers have tried to diminish the seminal role of Kemal Ataturk in conceiving and imposing by the force of his will a secular state, with all the trappings of modernity, on a society that only a few years earlier was the hotbed of the Ottoman caliphate, and whose abrupt ending roused the Muslim masses as far away as India to the 'khilafat' cause.[53] The equally remarkable achievement in post-Independence India was of Jawaharlal Nehru's to install a liberal state and democratic order when he could as easily have succumbed to the temptations of outright dictatorship, considering there was a pliant colonial apparatus of state at hand to implement his orders as it previously had done the British viceroy's. He is today derided by the ruling BJP and the RSS for seeding dynastic politics.[54] In the US, Trump, likewise, loses no opportunity to belittle his immediate predecessor Obama or Hillary Clinton, whom he defeated in the 2016 presidential elections. His obsessive, almost pathological, hatred for them is an aberration that helps to define him politically.[55]

Naturally, all of them are self-centred chest-thumpers and self-promoters to a fault who do not like to be upstaged by anyone, are concerned about the impression they make, whether addressing large crowds at home, jaw-jawing in summits abroad or exchanging ideas in small groups. They are also adept in communicating directly with the people through public speeches or social media.[56] Perceptions matter more to them than policies; they dream big for the country without necessarily acting big.

Trump's aim is recessive: to prune America's role in the world. Erdogan's desire to make Turkey the Islamic pivot in international politics is grand but the path to realizing it is dangerous. Modi's strategic ambition for India is muddled, mostly a continuation of past policies garbed in new rhetoric.[57] Because he has not detailed his national vision or offered anything substantively new and novel, Modi has the latitude to adjust the vision so that it is in line with whatever he can claim up to any moment in time to be his achievements. This is clever tactical thinking, because had he elaborated in more exact geostrategic and economic language, for example, what he actually had in mind to do, by when and using what means, his success or the lack thereof would become measurable. This way his failures cannot be easily fixed as his vision is a shifting goal. Putin's and Xi's objectives are more definite. The former means to ensure that a reinvigorated Russia once again becomes the arbiter of Europe's fate and central to the international scene a la the Cold War era.[58] Meanwhile, China is bent on shaking off the reserve of Deng Xiaoping's China weighed down by the Great Helmsman's '24-character strategy': 'Observe calmly; secure our position; cope with affairs calmly; hide our capacities and bide our time; be good at maintaining a low profile; and never claim leadership.'[59] Xi believes that while Dengist China was a country on the make, his China has arrived, and is at a point where it is able, by force if necessary, to pacify its periphery, regain its pre-eminence in the Asia-Pacific and plan realistically on becoming the dominant power by 2049: the hundredth anniversary of the founding of the communist regime.[60]

Of the six major alpha male leaders considered here, three are impulsive: Trump, Erdogan and Modi. Xi and Putin are system-trained apparatchiks focused on achieving what they set out to accomplish with careful preparation and long-term plans. And Abe teeters between abrasively taking on adversaries such as China and North Korea and hesitation owing to the uncertain political and military backing by Washington. Trump is the least predictable, acting on his hunches, which means policies that can change by the hour or the minute as his fancy strikes him, prompted by the next incident, Twitter response or television comment. It makes for potentially mercurial policies that keep international relations permanently on the boil. Trump can afford such recklessness because of the very large margin of error afforded the US President by America's wealth, trading heft and military prowess, making him virtually mistake-proof. Hence, Trump's lies and misstatements that would have cost the leaders of lesser states dear are passed off with a shrug. Erdogan's impulsiveness lies in his ambition, inserting Turkey, for instance, as mediator in long-standing disputes in the extended region, including Kashmir, as armed interventionist against the Syrian Kurds to ensure they don't link up with the Turkish Kurdish community to promote 'Independent Kurdistan', and as a perfervid supporter of Palestinian terror organizations such as Hamas and of Islamist groups such as the Muslim Brotherhood, which puts Ankara at odds with Israel and the regional Arab regimes fighting them, like the el-Sisi government in Egypt.[61]

Modi is impetuous with his decisions-as-announcements. Whether or not these are designed to surprise and cause consternation all round, the fact is they have done just that. His impromptu decision when visiting Paris in April 2015 to acquire thirty-six Rafale combat aircraft from French firm Dassault Aviation caught the host President, Francois Hollande, off guard as much as it did the Indian foreign secretary accompanying him. While France and the Indian Air Force (IAF) were elated, the numbers didn't add up and the deal made no economic sense. It was too small a buy of an inordinately expensive weapons platform to be justified in terms of augmenting the fighting strength of the country's air arm and too costly to dismiss as a mistake.

The medium multi-role combat aircraft (MMRCA) sweepstakes won by Rafale was for 126 aircraft with transfer of technology (TOT) with the 2012 price tag of $12.4 billion.[62] The Modi announcement means India will pay only marginally less: ₹63,000 crore or $9.88 billion (at the 9 August 2017 rate of ₹63.77 to the US dollar) without TOT and lifetime spares and servicing support for less than a third as many aircraft bought off the shelf with minimal first and second line sets of spares and the barest minimum stock of weapons such as the Meteor air-to-air missile. The then defence minister Manohar Parrikar made it plain that this was a one-off purchase to meet the 'urgent requirement' and not the proverbial wedge as the IAF had hoped it would be to ease 200 more of this make of fighter plane into its fleet.[63] The demonetization initiated on 8 November 2016 was another such move sprung on the nation which unhinged the country to a far greater extent. It was an action the governor of the Reserve Bank of India (RBI) had no prior notice of, and was taken despite expert advice against it, including from the Vivekananda International Foundation (VIF), the think tank that supplied Modi with his NSA, Ajit Doval, and other staffers in the PMO.[64] Supposed to unearth black money and end corruption, which it did to some extent, this measure also slowed down the economy, hurting cash transactions, which account for 87 per cent of commerce at all levels.[65]

The other attributes apart, what the six alpha male leaders have significantly in common is their use of cultural differentiation to deepen ethnic, religious and racial divides within their own societies with a view to winning elections, solidifying their political position at home, strengthening their support base and even extending the 'us versus them' thinking to the external realm to conceive of vexatious issues in terms of civilizational clashes.

In Poland, Trump called on the West to 'summon the courage and the will to defend our civilization' and at a NATO meet urged the alliance members to 'never forget who we are' and to hold on to 'the bonds of history, culture and memory'. This reflected the popular sentiment against the waves of immigrants entering Europe to escape the turmoil in the Islamic world. It meshed with the view he has often espoused of the US being under siege by illegal immigrants from Mexico and Central America, by Indians misusing the H1B visa to chivvy Americans out of high-paying jobs, and by China and other countries with a favourable balance of trade exploiting unfair labour practices and non-tariff barriers to hurt US exports and to run the American manufacturing sector into the ground. 'In the Trump era,' writes Carlos Lozada, 'moralism, cynicism and hypocrisy coexist [but] not peacefully', threatening 'the ideology of multiculturalism' at the core of modern, socially complex, culturally heterogeneous, countries,[66] such as the US and, even more, India.

Other than a few lapses, such as his repeated mention during the 2014 general election campaign of the 'pink economy', referring to the nearly $4 billion bovine meat exports industry, which, owing to the cultural aversion of Hindus, is dominated by and employs millions of Muslims, Modi has been nowhere as divisive in his polemic as Trump.[67] The marked Hindutva undertow, if not in his personal politics, then in that of the Hindu fringe and the RSS the BJP is associated with, is problematical, however. Comprising some 14 per cent of the Indian population of almost 1.3 billion, Indian Muslims constitute in theory a large enough electoral mass for the BJP to be mindful of it. But with the polarizing of society, the ruling party finds it can do without Muslim support and, therefore, that it need not be overly sensitive to minority sentiments. But Modi has cleverly used a 'Muslim issue' such as 'triple talaq' to create a gender rift in the Muslim community.[68] This together with social welfare schemes such as the Ujjwala programme that has fairly and equitably distributed free cooking gas canisters among the poor has created goodwill for Modi and the BJP among Muslim women, thus splitting to a degree the Muslim vote in elections.

On the negative side, the very processes of consolidating the Hindu vote requires the BJP to overlook where it can, and pooh-pooh where it must, the excesses of the so-called 'gau rakshaks': the Hindu lumpen element who as protectors of cows extort money and occasionally have lynched and physically abused Muslim men.[69] Because most such incidents are happening in the cow-belt states of Uttar Pradesh, Madhya Pradesh and Bihar, and also peninsular provinces like Karnataka and Maharashtra either ruled by the BJP or where it is the main opposition party, Modi can, if he wishes, instantly put a stop to such targeted violence with stern actions and instructions to state chief ministers and police agencies to go after the miscreants. He has instead been lightly censorious and even then days after the incidents, encouraging bad behaviour by unemployed Hindu youth sympathetic to the BJP-qua-Hindutva cause. The larger leitmotif is, however, civilizational, with the RSS claiming that Indian Muslims being converts, their religion of extra-territorial origin notwithstanding, they are culturally and civilizationally Hindu. And should this fact be accepted by Muslims and they refrain from doing what good Hindus supposedly don't do, such as eat beef, oppose singing 'vande mataram' and do yoga, there'd be no communal tensions and the communal divide would, well, disappear.[70] This belief is of the same genus as Trump's contention that Western countries accept only those immigrants 'who share our values and love our people'.

Xi, heading a country that is population-wise 92 per cent Han, would, on paper, appear to have no reason to worry about a minority problem. Except among minorities, the Tibetans in Tibet and the Muslim Uyghurs of Xinjiang inhabiting the vast tracts of land that make up much of the landmass of China are seriously disaffected and agitating for freedom for a long time. They are dealt with by Xi in the manner Chinese rulers have historically done, a solution endorsed by Sun Yat-sen, the founding president of the Chinese Republic in 1911. This involves physically rubbing out the minorities with a programme of Han-ization or forcible assimilation. In his famous 'San Min Chu I' lectures of the 1920s, Sun Yat-sen justified violence against minorities, telescoping in the bargain the issues of territory, ethnic diversity, state building and cultural homogenization, saying, 'In simple terms the race or nationality has developed through natural forces, while the State has developed through force of arms.'[71] Curiously, it is a justification that converges in part with the RSS view of Hindus and Indian Muslims being of the same racial and ethnic stock and nationality. Whence in the Indian context it follows that the need for forced or even voluntary Hinduization or, to use Hindutva jargon, 'ghar wapsi' (homecoming), is obviated at least in theory, making for a society at peace with itself.

Clash of Civilizations or Country First Ideologies?

With so many strongmen on the international stage, the possibility of interpersonal friction is high. But what factor will decide whether they will clash: because they are at odds with each other over differing civilizational values and norms, or because their national interests and their respective Country First policies collide? It is evident that, barring Trump—a fairly unique political phenomenon—the rest, Modi, Xi, Putin, Abe and Erdogan, are creatures of the extant political systems. Naturally, to get to the top, they have had to be a bit cleverer, more ambitious, more hard-nosed, and better managers and manipulators of domestic political forces than their rivals.

Trump, because he was elected President without the Republican Party's help, owes nothing to precedents set by the previous Republican Party, leave alone the Democratic Party presidents of the United States. As a true outsider, he has no track record as an elected official, never having been previously elected to any office, and feels completely free to follow his whims and fancies and, is therefore, the most unpredictable of the lot. Because he heads a country that is very wealthy and militarily the most powerful, the vocabulary-challenged Trump is also the most dangerous, as his inexperience with international diplomacy and use of force can lead to a crisis where none exists or escalating them. Such as the one he needlessly precipitated in early August 2017 by warning North Korea of 'fire and fury'—a synonym for nuclear weapons use, presumably, if it again threatened the US. It prompted the practised provocateur in President Kim Jong-un in Pyongyang to do just that, calling Trump names and his bluff by issuing a threat of nuclear destruction of Guam, the US island territory in the mid-Pacific and major American military base. It left Washington red-faced and Trump's aides scrambling for face-saving excuses.[72]

But Trump lays great store by his personal relations. His attitude to foreign countries seems to be dictated by how comfortable he feels with their leaders. Thus, he was at ease with Putin when they met on 7 July 2017 in Hamburg, telling the Russian President 'it's an honour to be with you'.[73] Whether or not it was a decision by Trump to please Putin, the next thing that occurred was Washington stopping covert aid to the Syrian rebels, thereby lessening the pressure on the Bashar al-Assad government that is dependent on Russia.[74]

Modi, in contrast to Trump, is more deliberate when consorting with other leaders. He went to Washington, for instance, with the intention of winning over the US President. Modi succeeded with his warm gestures, such as his hug. Of greater import given the US President's closeness to his family was Modi's personal invitation to the first daughter and reportedly Trump's favourite child, Ivanka Trump, to lead the US delegation to the Global Entrepreneurship Summit held in Hyderabad from 18 to 20 November 2017.[75] The former Delhi correspondent of *The Economist* Adam Roberts summed up the similarities between Modi and Trump well. Both of them, he writes:

> . . . are nationalist, fond of performing before large rallies of adoring fans as well as on social media; both came to office with a history of showing hostility toward Muslims and foreigners; and both whipped up support among voters who liked talk, however simplistic, of making their respective country 'great' and favouring a 'strongman' in the highest office.[76]

Warmth in personal relations is all very well, but it hasn't overridden the America First bias in Trump's policies. As early as January 2016, presidential candidate Trump placed India in an adversarial matrix, juxtaposing America's economic slide against an ascendant China and India. 'We've gone from a tremendous power that is respected all over the world,' he said in a TV interview on CNN, 'to somewhat [sic] of a laughing stock and all of a sudden, people are talking about China and India and other places.'[77]

And, for all the friendliness with the Indian prime minister, it was Trump who asked for the removal of restraints on American exports to India while Modi, aware of the US President's strong feelings on the H1B visa issue, considered it politic to not even raise it in his White House discussion.[78] So, the new visa policy restricting the flow into the US of low-cost skilled information technology labour from Bengaluru and Hyderabad has been tightened. Modi had even less success with the more reserved Putin, his hug not being returned by the Russian leader. In the Trumpian vein, however, Putin was able at the November 2017 BRICS Summit in Goa to supposedly secure Modi's commitment to jointly produce the fifth-generation fighter aircraft (PAK FA or FGFA) programme. As a supplicant, Modi's India First policy is necessarily flexible, with far less leeway than that enjoyed by the Country First policies of Trump, Putin or Xi. But he is on more even ground with Abe as the Japanese prime minister is eager for a larger, more active, Indian military role in the Asian security context. He is also in a similar situation with Erdogan because little was left to be transacted once the Turkish President, who is majorly into hyphenating India and Pakistan with regard to membership, in the NSG, for instance, inserted himself, unbidden, as mediator in the Kashmir dispute. The Indo-Turkish trade of less than $7 billion, moreover, is not big enough to matter.

In the context of the prophecy by Samuel Huntington of civilizational clashes in the future, what will the big power scene look like? The great fault line in global society today is the division between the Islamic and non-Islamic worlds exacerbated by Islamist terrorism. While there is 'secular' terrorism, if you will, of liberation wars and separatist/secessionist movements, it is the diehard Islamist variety represented by the Al-Qaeda organization that in the years since its founding by Osama bin Laden in 1988 has spawned many offshoots. The most barbaric and ruthless among these is the Islamic State group in Iraq and parts of Syria that before its decimation caused huge concern. The fact that most of the major countries, including the US, Russia, China and even India have for reasons of realpolitik often materially helped and assisted terrorist organizations has complicated international relations. There's no country that is, in this respect, clean. Even so, Al-Qaeda and Islamic State propagating worldwide the harsh fundamentalist values of Wahhabi desert Islam, financed by the so-called Arab 'Islamic charities' in Saudi Arabia and the wealthy Gulf states, are the *locus genesis* of extremist Islam and terrorism but are not held to account owing to the cross-cutting big power stakes in their petroleum sector.

The oil-rich Arab states are suppliers of energy to the world. Energy security is important to the developed world, especially the US but also Britain and France, all of whom have oil companies drilling for, processing and selling Arab oil. Therefore, they are keen to protect their economic stakes and keep the often medievalist but pliable Bedouin tribal regimes in place. Thus, the central paradox: The US is at once the chief protector and target of rabid Islamism. Except the Saudi–Gulf funding of the Al-Qaeda, IS and Wahhabi missionaries the world over fuels Islamic terrorism, targeting not just the 'kaffir' US and the West, but also countries such as India, Thailand, and the Philippines with significant Muslim populations and Muslim-majority provinces. If Al-Qaeda sympathizers ramming passenger aircraft into the World Trade Center towers in New York in September 2001 was shocking, the routine beheadings carried out by Islamic State with grisly videos of these events uploaded to the Internet supposedly to attract adherents are mind-numbing. The lure of Islamic extremism is such it has infected Muslim societies in Central Asia, Malaysia and Indonesia, and Muslim separatist movements in non-Muslim states, such as in Jammu and Kashmir in India, Mindanao in the Philippines and southern Thailand. So the US is engaged in Afghanistan and Iraq fighting Islamic State and the Taliban and in protecting the ruling Sauds and the Gulf emirs and sheikhs who coddle the Wahhabi sect and fund its activities.

The effects of radical Islam have been felt in Europe, particularly by countries that are open and democratic, and tolerate the ebb and flow of people across their borders, such as France, the UK, Germany and Belgium. In India, the growing presence in Assam and West Bengal of Bangladeshi Muslims and, more recently, of Rohingya Muslims from Myanmar is, however, roiling the social milieu.[79] The US and the West have always been magnets for political refugees disgorged by the wars in Iraq, the Levant and Afghanistan involving US forces. The Algerians and Moroccans have had problems fitting into French society; same is the case of subcontinental-origin Muslims in Britain. Their presence is resented because these migrants/refugees come loaded with traditional Islamic values and cultural traits that do not mesh with the secular ethos and norms of Western countries, prevent easy assimilation and constitute an ill-fitting cog. It has steeled the Western governments into pre-emptively reducing the immigrant inflow to avoid social disorder and instability and, in Trump's case, to restrict the intake by the US of even those Muslims legally seeking to relocate to America in order to please his domestic white-majority Christian base.

In India, which has a Muslim population that will by 2050 be the largest of any country in the world, the consequences of Islamic radicalization could be devastating.[80] Muslim extremism in Pakistan and Bangladesh and the activity in Kashmir of jihadi terrorist groups patronized by Islamabad are spurring parallel Hindu extremist outlier outfits in India, which are encouraged by the apparent laxity of the Modi regime in dealing with them, and thus widening the Hindu–Muslim rift in society. In the Philippines, relations have soured between the Christians and Muslims of Mindanao, and in southern Thailand between Buddhists and Muslims. Islam and Muslims have thus emerged the world over as the bugbear of most countries and regional and global powers. In Huntingtonian terms, the potential for large-scale clashes between militant Islam on the one hand and all the other major religions—Hinduism, Christianity, Buddhism, etc.—on the other, is real. Further, with terrorism being the asymmetric means of choice of the weaker Muslim states to deploy against stronger states, it is easy to see why it is the preferred mode of the minority to make a splash, and also why anything Islamic is universally in bad odour.

Arrayed against Islam is China, where any organized religion or religious activity is anathema and considered a threat to state security. The oppression of Tibetans and the cultural genocide in Tibet is long-standing.[81] So is the treatment of the majority Muslims in Xinjiang, where the hostility to Islam is such Beijing has decreed that children cannot be given Muslim names and males under fifty years of age cannot sport beards.[82] The support for the Turkistan Islamic Movement among the majority Uyghur Muslims of Xinjiang, which is turning violent with the returning Uyghur veterans of Islamic State, Iraq and Afghan wars taking to insurrectionary violence, is one reason why. But China is caught between trying to stealthily help Pakistan, a very useful client state, maintain terrorist pressure on India to keep its Asian rival distracted and ensuring there's no Islamist terrorist blowback in Xinjiang.[83]

The antipathy of the communist Chinese state to all non-conforming sections of society has produced harsh results. Members of the gentle Falun Gong sect, for example, are imprisoned and used for grisly practices such as organ harvesting.[84] The reason why there is virtually no outcry in the liberal West or anywhere else against such institutionalized atrocities is that China is powerful enough to get away with its excesses as no country wants to court its displeasure. Even so, the communist rulers have failed to rid China of religion, with a recent poll showing 85 per cent of the people owning up to religious beliefs.[85] Support for Pakistan-based terrorist gangs notwithstanding, its anti-Uyghur attitude bands China together with countries hostile to terrorism and extremist Islamic ideology.

The differing national and vested interests mean that countries will join to fight extremist Islam and jihadi terrorism if and when it suits them and will individually prosecute military actions to wipe out this menace within their own bailiwicks without fear of international moral sanction. This is why India has drawn so little international criticism for its tough methods to subdue the militancy in Jammu and Kashmir of the Hizbul Mujahideen with mostly Srinagar Valley recruits, and the Pakistan-based LeT and Jaish-e-Mohammad (JeM). It has occasioned consternation and even frustration in the Pakistan policy establishment, which banks on the international hullabaloo against Indian humanitarian outrages to further its case for plebiscite. But the time for a referendum is long gone as Pakistan did not meet the pre-condition of vacating its police and military presence from the part of Jammu and Kashmir it occupied as mandated by UN Security Council Resolution Number 47. Seventy years later, it is unrealistic to expect the situation in that erstwhile princely state can be returned to that old start point.

More than combating violent Islam, the issue potentially provoking a civilizational collision is elsewhere. China is the revisionist power seeking to impose, if it can, its tianxia system on the rest of the world. It will fail to do so even in proximal regions—seaward in the South China Sea and landward in Central Asia. This is because the tianxia scheme, premised on the central role of China as the superior power and adjudicator, does not have wide acceptability. Unlike the fairly flexible Anglo-American system of free trade that has been around for the better part of 200 years and was bolted into place by the British Navy and its extensively located coaling stations on the major littorals of the world that defined the reach of Pax Britannica in its heyday, and since the First World War by the bigger and even more powerful American Navy and military generally, tianxia has many shortfalls. Firstly, China does not have the military muscle to foist it on the world as a replacement system; and secondly, it lacks both the architectural elasticity required of a globe-spanning trading order and multilateral forums such as the World Trade Organization (WTO) to accord it legitimacy. Moreover, China being the chief beneficiary of the current global economic order subtracts from Xi's commitment to tianxia.

Then again, unlike in past epochs, great powers do not today enjoy absolute freedom of action. The four largest multitrillion-dollar economies—the US, China, the EU and India and even Russia, because its enormous military clout cannot be ignored—may at most be able to establish, and then tenuously, a certain kind of order in their immediate vicinities (a Pax Americana in its hemisphere, tianxia around China, an Indian Monroe Doctrine in the Indian Ocean basin, the East European-cum-Central Asian circle around Russia, and the EU in western Europe) while the political, economic and military spaces in the overlapping areas and in West Asia, Africa and Latin America are contested. The world may actually evolve into four or five sometimes clashing, sometimes cooperating congeries of states around these main powers. Influence in the Muslim world, however, will also be up for grabs. Strung out as it is between Sunni Turkey and Shia Iran, with Saudi Arabia, minus the components of comprehensive power drifting to the sidelines, the five global power groups will, in different ways, jockey for stakes in the numerous Islamic countries and otherwise prevent a solid Islamic bloc from emerging.[86]

To round out the argument, what are the more enduring effects of the alpha male leaders at the steering wheels? Predictably, many of them have a number of traits in common. On the domestic scene, they tend to be social polarizers, indulging in the politics of majoritarian grievance. Modi has split Indian society between the Hindu majority and the Muslim minority. The Hindu middle class and intelligentsia may not be enamoured of the methods used by the RSS and the Hindu outlier sections but poll evidence shows that they vote for the BJP.[87] Trump, likewise, is solicitous of his white American working-class Christian supporters, willing to stoke their anger and prejudices at the expense of societal peace.[88] Erdogan won by the barest majority (51.2 per cent) the referendum on installing a presidential form of government that centralized power, leaving the secular half of the Turkish society believing in 'liberal Islam' worried.[89] Xi and Putin are the two rulers without any domestic opposition to speak of, with the former having negotiated his way around the various centres of power within the party and the PLA and ascending formally, after the historic Nineteenth Communist Party Congress, to Mao-like status in China.[90]

However, it is in the cleaving of societies that one glimpses the disbenefits of having alpha male leaders at the helm. Dividing societies to win elections has brought to the fore the anti-modernist thrust of the traditional, socially conservative-minded citizenry that finds it hard to cope in a time of rapid change driven by technologies advancing at warp speed. Modi is a traditional Hindu at heart, harking back surprisingly often to the values of an India of myth and lore. More on this in the next chapter. Into his eighth decade, Trump appears to be an American of the 1950s when the country was mostly white, immigration was highly regulated, the Church was strong and the minorities, particularly African-Americans, were consciously marginalized. Erdogan talks of Turkey's resurgence in terms of the country's past glories.[91] Xi has made no bones about wanting to reclaim the vast imperium and sphere of influence that China boasted of at its civilizational apogee during the Tang Dynasty around 422 BC.[92]

With the attributes of these strongmen on view, the evidence of their interpersonal relations and interactions over the past few years suggest that they are mutually respectful and get along well, perhaps because they understand and empathize with each other, as all have successfully run the arduous obstacle course to gain power. Trump has made no concessions to any country, but has been extremely respectful of Putin; even thanking him for saving his government money by expelling over 750 American diplomats in retaliation for Washington's shutting down certain Russian government properties in the US.[93] Modi hasn't reacted harshly to Trump's H1B visa measures, gets along with Xi but without a scintilla of warmth in their personal relations, has been proper with Erdogan, and treats Putin with respect, which the Russian leader has reciprocated. While averse to Modi's trademark hugs when they first met, Putin has since been more engaging. In a television interview with Megyn Kelly at the 2017 St Petersburg International Economic Forum at which Modi was invited to be the chief guest, when asked what he thought of Putin and Trump as leaders, Modi's ambiguous reply, 'Who am I to judge such leaders!', drew from the Russian President the remark 'That's ancient philosophy!' and, more self-deprecatingly, that 'persons [like himself, by implication not versed in "ancient philosophy"] say what comes to our head'.[94]

Inherent in the mutual regard they have for each other is the wariness and prudence against pushing other strong-willed counterparts around, lest it entail unpleasant surprises. It is why Trump, for instance, has put off starting a trade war with China. Assuming that like Manmohan Singh, Modi would buckle under threats and calibrated military pressure tactics, the Chinese President discovered that the Indian prime minister simply wouldn't back down from a possible military confrontation in the India–Bhutan–China trijunction area around Doklam in the summer of 2017. By physically preventing PLA construction crews from bulldozing a road in this disputed region, the Indian Army halted the creeping annexation by China of Bhutanese territory that would have brought the PLA nearer to the Siliguri corridor—the long, thin strategically important strip of land connecting West Bengal to Assam and the north-eastern states—and rendered the Indian states both to the east and west of the corridor vulnerable.[95]

The more lasting benefit to international affairs from having a number of important countries led by alpha males is that the nations may test each other's resolve and political will all the time and probe for weaknesses, and regional tensions and international crises may ensue. But, ultimately, the alpha male leaders are attentive to a fellow alpha male's reputation and will not provoke beyond a point when the situation could spin out of their control. History suggests that wars usually occur when there's a strong state led by a strong leader surrounded by weak states.[96] The contrafactual conclusion, however, is that there's unlikely to be major wars in the 21st century with alpha male leaders in charge of major countries, even when each is trying maximally to advance his nation's interests and to undercut that of others. Not a bad outcome from the perspective of international peace.

This prognosis meshes with Modi showing himself to be a pussycat abroad, traipsing around in the company of big cats, taking care to see he gives no offence to them, while uncoiling his ruthlessness only against a weak and enervated Pakistan, on the one hand, and his domestic political opponents on the other. One wishes, however, that Modi had shown at least as much ferocity and ruthlessness with respect to China and in furthering India's national interests and strategic security.

[2]

Impact of Modi's Persona on Government

'Groups take on the personality of the leader'—Sigmund Freud

FOR DECONSTRUCTING NARENDRA MODI, independent India's fifteenth prime minister, it is necessary to have an insight into the man: what motivates him, why he thinks and acts the way he does, and what factors shape not just his worldview but, at the core, his persona—the driver of his policies and, indeed, his government. Modi is an intriguing subject for an in-depth study. That is a challenging task and will not be attempted here. Rather, such information as is available about a very private public person will be parsed, and his politics as well as his mindset and their possible connection to the manner and method he employs to run the government and rule the country analysed.

Modi broke out on to the national scene when the BJP Parliamentary Board in September 2013 declared him the party's prime ministerial candidate for the general elections the following year despite opposition by stalwarts, including L.K. Advani, Murli Manohar Joshi and Sushma Swaraj, a rival who lost out in the race.[1] He had by then become known for his business-friendly reputation and the splashy annual Vibrant Gujarat soirees that drew national and international interest, but most of all for his non-role in curbing the anti-Muslim riots in the wake of the deaths of scores of Hindu pilgrims travelling by the Sabarmati Express at the Godhra railway station in February 2002. His slogan 'nayi soch, nayi umeed' (new thinking, new hope) hinted at change from the ten years of Prime Minister Manmohan Singh's Congress party rule, scarred by financial scams and scandals, and led to the BJP winning a majority in Parliament in 2014 and Modi assuming the top job. The pitting of a chaiwala (tea seller) against the wearisome dynasts of the Congress party and political heirs elsewhere, including in the BJP, was a winning election theme. Modi's rags-to-political-riches story inspired millions, making them believe that they too could transcend their social limitations, overcome poverty and make good. His electric oratory apart, Modi's communications outreach using social media and high-technology contrivances like holographic imagery, moreover, entranced voters in the countryside, etching him in their mind as a modernizer.[2] At the same time, his sly attempts at communally polarizing society for electoral benefit—for instance, by repeatedly referring to the 'pink' economy, the bovine meat export industry traditionally dominated by Muslims, and the Congress's 'appeasement politics'—stoked the pent-up majoritarian sense of grievance and anger, motivated the RSS and the Hindu extremists to bring out the Hindu vote and signalled a less tolerant social order.[3]

The popular discontent with the Congress party and its corruption-ridden decade-long government, combined with the socially potent ideology of change and the symbolism of a backward-caste person as the agent of it, were factors that afforded Modi near-absolute sanction to radically restructure the system of governance and take an axe to the deadwood that is the administrative apparatus of the Indian state. He had led the people to believe that this was his priority given another of his oft-repeated slogans: 'maximum governance, minimum government'. Other than Jawaharlal Nehru in the first years of the republic, no prime minister had entered office riding such a wave of public anticipation and vested with so comprehensive a popular mandate to take on the establishment and entrenched interests, roll out drastic reforms, and do whatever was necessary to fast-forward the country into the 21st century and prosperity. Modi was in a position to realize a revolution and overhaul the government to make it a lean and efficient instrument to implement effective policies. He squandered that opportunity by relying on the very same hidebound bureaucracy that has been the main barrier to progress all along. He fiddled with some administrative procedures but has left much of the decrepit, dysfunctional and corrupt machinery of state he inherited intact. This notwithstanding nearly seven decades of evidence showing that a government run on colonial-era conventions, regulations, norms and 'rules of business' is inherently incapable of good governance in the digital age and verily an unbearable burden.

Radical transformation of the government is what the people expected of Modi, and this he has failed to deliver. The disillusionment with him has spread and grown with time, which is sought to be countered by the prime minister making more promises.[4] Modi's surprising cautiousness, his inability to produce results to match his tall talk, to undertake system change on a grand scale and to take political risks are weaknesses that (like his many strengths) may be traced to his family background—the small-town milieu he grew up in, the early influences of the RSS that shaped his thinking about the world and his attitude to it, his outlook on life and, in politics, his ambition and administrative style. What will be plumbed in this chapter is how his background and the play of forces that socialized him may have effected Modi, made him the sort of political leader and prime minister that he is and, more significantly, why under his watch Indian society has become more illiberal and what the ramifications are for the country's external policies and for national security.

The Psychological What, How and Why of Modi

So far, Mahatma Gandhi is the only Indian leader considered psychologically intriguing enough to merit detailed psychoanalytical scrutiny.[5] Considering the many interesting characters that have filled India's political stage, the wonder is there have not been more such studies. Even at the level of popular media, political personalities have rarely been examined through the psychological filter. An attempt was made in 2009, curiously by a pink paper, the Sunday edition of the *Economic Times*. But such judgements as were made about the political leaders it examined on the basis, among other things, of questionnaires filled out by them, were uniformly positive. After all, no Indian newspaper or media house would wish to anger politicians by printing psychologically tinged adverse comments about them. 'Mapping the leadership style of Indian leaders' was an exercise done jointly, the *Economic Times* informed its readers, with 'the ODA consultancy' using 'the Enneagram tool' touted as 'a globally accepted personality profiling method' sourced to 'the teachings of esoteric guru George Gurdjieff' and his pupil Oscar Ichazo.

This report describes the Congress party president Sonia Gandhi as 'highly loyal and responsible' but also suspicious, sceptical and with a 'sharp and incisive mind' and as someone 'guided by her head . . . [which made] her a natural leader'; Manmohan Singh as objective, dispassionate and calm 'under extreme pressure' and as 'a blend of a strategist, integrator and a visionary'; the veteran BJP leader L.K. Advani as 'self-confident and straightforward'; the Bahujan Samaj Party supremo Mayawati as a control freak and something of a political dominatrix; Akhilesh Yadav as 'warm and friendly'; the Congress party leader Sachin Pilot as 'prim and proper'; DMK Rajya Sabha member Kanimozhi as 'deeply creative and intuitive'; the former minister of state for external affairs and Congress party member of Parliament Shashi Tharoor as adaptive and 'a go-getter'; the young BJP leader Manvendra Singh from Barmer as 'self-aware, sensitive, and painfully intuitive'; and Rahul Gandhi, president of the Congress party and, by the newspaper's reckoning, 'future prime ministerial material' and the only leader in this survey to not fill the required questionnaire, as 'exuding confidence' and having 'an aristocratic aura of a successful, confident and inspired individual' about him. His personality, the newspaper went on to add, comprises 'equal doses of sophistication, flamboyance, ambition and energy'.

This survey did not ignore the then Gujarat chief minister, Narendra Modi, but it was less effusive about him. Modi, the report observes, displays 'tremendous drive, ambition', shows self-belief, takes care in 'being presentable and appropriate', always puts his 'best foot forward', and presents himself 'in a way that highlights [his] energy and confidence'. He is praised for 'his excellent organizational capability . . . and focus', and for being 'highly adaptable' in 'different social settings'. Modi, the report adds as an afterthought, always wants 'to exemplify the values of whatever group [he] is in' and tries 'different approaches to problems until [he] find[s] a formula that seems the most effective'.[6]

Whatever the techniques of the Enneagram method, the above thumbnail sketches seem commonplace appraisals based on publicly available information that almost anybody who reads newspapers would have come up with. Modi's pronouncements, his behaviour in public fora and private settings, biographical writings and media reportage and coverage about him will be analysed here but through the filter of the psychological aspects of political leadership, with a view to developing deeper insights into the Narendra Modi persona and phenomenon.

James David Barber, a political scientist at Duke University, created a stir in the early 1970s with his book on 'presidential character'. Based on his research he categorized US presidents into one of four phenotypes that he had conceived: active-positive, passive-positive, active-negative and passive-negative. According to Barber, those falling into the active-positive bracket (Franklin Roosevelt, John F. Kennedy, Jimmy Carter) are distinguished by their optimism, readiness to act, and appreciation of the high post they hold; the passive-positives (Ronald Reagan, William Taft, Warren Harding) suffer from low self-esteem compensated by attempts to please everybody and are shallowly optimistic; the active-negative persons (Richard Nixon, Woodrow Wilson, Herbert Hoover) are aggressive, carry out their tasks joylessly, are rigid in their thoughts and in functioning, and view power as means of self-realization; and the passive-negatives (Dwight D. Eisenhower, Calvin Coolidge) try to avoid power but have a strong sense of duty, low self-esteem made up by public service, and aversion to political give-and-take.[7] Transposed to the Indian scene, these Barber phenotypes can be easily matched with Indian prime ministers. Nehru, Indira Gandhi and Rajiv Gandhi fit the active-positive mould; Lal Bahadur Shastri, Vajpayee and P.V. Narasimha Rao are passive-positives; Morarji Desai, Charan Singh and V.P. Singh fit the active-negative category; and Manmohan Singh falls in the passive-negative slot. Gulzari Lal Nanda, Chandrashekhar, I.K. Gujral and H.D. Deve Gowda were prime ministers for too short a time to matter.

Barber's phenotypes are helpful; less an accurate read on political leaders than a tool to identify them by their distinctive traits. In reality, politicians often exhibit qualities spanning two or more of the categories. Thus, Modi seems a mix of the active-positive and active-negative types, at once an ambitious go-getter with a clear goal and aggressive nature, and seeking power to reinforce the positive view he has of himself. This may be seen in his unprecedented rise in state and national politics and his record of achievements, which is unlike that of any other Indian politician. He rocketed from a social service organization to party functionary to chief minister of a state to prime minister in a relatively short period of time without the fuel political dynasties provide, which, for example, instantly elevated Rajiv Gandhi from an Indian Airlines pilot one day to the prime minister of the country the next. Modi's success is due in no small measure to his keen political sense, of course, but also to his relentless motor, and thespian and rhetorical skills to beguile the masses that were honed in debating sessions and dramatics in school.[8] Modi's sharp organizational talent, capacity for hard work, and the diligence with which he performed his assigned tasks at each level is what impressed his seniors and talent-spotters in the RSS and the BJP.[9]

But it is his instincts and acumen to do the right thing politically, and especially his 'administrative facilitator' skills, that fast-tracked him to the higher levels in the RSS and BJP hierarchy.[10] Inside of seven years, he graduated from menial work in the local RSS office to the covert task of resisting the Indira Gandhi–era Emergency—pamphleteering, arranging the distribution of anti-Emergency literature, setting up safe houses for resistors, adopting disguises (activity that instilled in him deep dislike of the Congress)—to appointment in 1978 as the Sangh organizer for the Surat–Vadodara region. A year later, he was transferred to the Delhi office of the RSS, returning some five years later to Gujarat on attachment to the BJP. As poll manager, he ensured that the party handily won the 1985 Ahmedabad municipal elections.[11] With L.K. Advani, former deputy prime minister in the first BJP government at the centre, taking over as party president, Modi was shifted to the party's national election committee. He successfully organized Advani's 1990 Rath Yatra and, a couple of years later, the new party president Murli Manohar Joshi's Ekta Yatra, creating in the process powerful mentors and racking up valuable IOUs up and down the party chain.[12]

His rise thereafter was swifter still. Modi's habit of mastering organizational details, working the levers of power and achieving results confirmed his reputation as a go-getter in the RSS and later the BJP, resulting in his being tasked with progressively bigger jobs.[13] Persuaded by Advani to manage the poll campaign in the 1995 state elections, Modi's electoral strategy won Gujarat for the BJP, which success was repeated in the 2000 elections. In 2001, when failing health necessitated the removal of Chief Minister Keshubhai Patel, the BJP prime minister Vajpayee and Advani offered Modi the deputy chief minister's job which, as the story goes, he declined, saying he was 'going to be fully responsible for Gujarat or not at all', whereupon he was installed in Patel's place as chief minister.[14] Modi by then had taken care to eliminate his main rival in the party, Shankersinh Vaghela, forcing him out of the BJP, eventuating in the latter's defection to the Congress.[15] It showed a politician with ruthless instincts, strategizing ability and foresight, and a knack for engineering situations that advanced his personal aims and ambition, illustrating the fact that a mix of talent, keen political antennae, drive, luck and systemic factors usually spells success in politics.

The blot on his escutcheon—his government's inability to contain the anti-Muslim violence—apart, his tenure as chief minister in Gandhinagar was notable for building up 'Brand Modi' and the 'Gujarat model of governance', which helped vault him into 7 Race Course Road.[16] It was characterized by the minimization of corruption at all levels of government, delivery of reasonably efficient public services (inclusive of water and electricity), enhancement of agriculture through innovative means such as drip irrigation, particularly in the semi-arid Kutch and Kathiawar regions, wider downstream distribution of the dammed Narmada river water, and the rooting of an industry and business-friendly milieu that induced large Indian companies to set up manufacturing hubs and foreign financial institutions to invest in the state. It was a model for development that did not pander to the Muslim minority as the previous Congress party governments drawing support from the KHAM (Kshatriya, Harijan, Adivasi, Muslim) vote base had done. It strengthened the party in the state and pleased the RSS.[17]

Clearly, what is notable is not just that he craved the next higher job, but his calculation of what would fetch him that post and how he negotiated the political waters and juggled his actions and public pronouncements to keep moving upward. By the time the BJP anointed him its candidate for prime minister on 13 September 2013, it seemed like a mere formality, considering Modi had ticked the right boxes along the way and had wide-ranging support within the success-hungry party that he had served as its organizing general secretary for many years when he networked and cultivated party cadres and familiarized himself with the minutiae of party politics and organization.[18] These are factors that overrode the concern of many BJP veterans such as Advani, who had greased his climb but now regarded him as the wrong choice for the top job.[19] Modi's opponents within the party argued that his Hindutva calling card made him a divisive figure who would lose BJP votes.[20] Obviously, the BJP seniors had misread both the balance of power within the party and the mood of the country. They also misapprehended his supposed commitment to Hindutva and issues such as anti-Muslim riots, cow slaughter and Ram Temple, which to Modi were only the means to enthuse, mobilize and motivate the voters, not a binding election plank.[21] By his own admission, Modi is an easygoing Hindu, not unlike most Indians, and has repeatedly said that he is 'spiritual', not 'religious'.[22] However, the cultivation of votes of the majority community using emotive issues has had unintended consequences such as 'cow vigilantism' which both Modi and the RSS chief Mohan Bhagwat had not expected.[23]

The late James MacGregor Burns, a Harvard University political scientist, in his 1978 tract had defined 'Leadership' as 'power governed by principle, directed toward raising people to their highest levels of personal motive and social morality'. It is different from 'power', he argued, in that 'Power manipulates people as they are; leadership as they could be. Power manages; leadership mobilizes. Power impacts, leadership engages. Power tends to corrupt, leadership to create.' He elaborated further, saying leadership is the ability 'to engage followers, not merely to activate them, to commingle needs and aspirations and goals in common enterprise, and in the process to make better citizens of both leaders and followers'. Burns then distilled these aspects of leadership and the quest for power into two separate streams: 'transformational leadership' and 'transactional leadership'. Transformational leaders, Burns contends, are agents of change who help their followers to better themselves. However, 'Truly great and creative leaders do something more,' he wrote. 'They arouse people's hopes and aspirations and expectations, convert social needs into political demands, and rise to higher levels of leadership as they respond to those demands.' Transactional leaders, on the other hand, often resort to 'a short-term approach' using 'negotiations and compromise', because achieving goals matters more to them.

By the Burns standard, Modi has simultaneously aggrandized power and acted the inspiring leader, motivating the masses and encouraging them to see him as the vehicle for their aspirations. With his government's programmes for direct delivery of social welfare subsidies, making the people technology-conversant, drawing them into the formal, cashless economy, stressing personal hygiene and civic cleanliness (Swachh Bharat) and bettering the condition of women in society (by supplying cooking gas cylinders, opposing 'triple talaq'), he is a leader seeking to transform a maddeningly traditional society rooted in medievalist norms (treating women as chattels, carrying out honour killings). But he has also shown himself as a transactional leader, compromising on his campaign promises in terms of retaining the decrepit apparatus of state to implement his grand promises and, in the foreign policy realm, undercutting his India First rhetoric by tilting towards short-term solutions hurtful to national interest (as will be shown in later chapters). Central to Burns's theme is the leader's ethical tendencies. 'Divorced from ethics,' he wrote, 'leadership is reduced to management and politics to mere technique.'[24] Modi's political management style and techniques may be questioned but his success with them is undeniable.

However, Modi's ethics have occasioned concern. His attitude, for instance, to acts of violence against minorities seems tinged with political calculation. Whether it was the lynching of Muslims on the beef ban/cow slaughter issue in Uttar Pradesh and Maharashtra, or the widespread rioting by devotees of Gurmeet Ram Rahim Singh, a 'god-man' and founder of the Dera Sacha Sauda sect propagating a mish-mash of religious beliefs and bizarre rituals, protesting his conviction for the rape of two women, Modi's reaction has followed a pattern. He has censured the wrongdoers and warned people not to take the law into their own hands.[25] But—and this is what has aroused suspicion—the interval between the murderous acts of the cow vigilantes and the Dera Sacha Sauda mobs and the prime minister wagging his finger at them was long enough to allow the anti-Muslim impulses of Hindu miscreants to run their course, the punitive-minded feelings of the majority community to be satiated and for the extremist Hindu outfits to feel reassured. Acting thus meant Modi was able to do the politically correct thing, albeit belatedly, without alienating the Hindu fringe or the party's support base.

In the Ram Rahim case, which led to a serious breakdown of law and order in parts of Haryana, moreover, the prime minister did not pull up the Haryana chief minister Manohar Lal Khattar for failing to impose Section 144 of the Indian Penal Code in Haryana and the rest of the state, prohibiting the assembly of persons in public areas. Had he criticized Khattar, like himself a former RSS pracharak, Modi would have impugned his own choice of Khattar as state chief minister and estranged the RSS and the legions of Dera supporters who, instructed by the god-man, had dutifully voted for the BJP in the 2015 state elections. It resulted in the Haryana police treating the Dera rioters with kid gloves long after they had run amok.[26] This is the transactional Modi, damned by some for his 'moral paralysis'.[27] And slammed by others for his standoffish attitude to the targeting of Muslims by letting majoritarian bias play out and for sparking a recrudescence of communalized politics in the country of the kind that begot—and this reading seems unduly alarmist—Partition and Pakistan in 1947.[28] The fanaticism of the Dera followers in Haryana and Punjab, however, pointed to a still larger issue: the failure of the state to meet basic needs. 'The Dera offered free education to its members [the bulk of them lower-caste Sikhs] and their children and free food for the hungry. It kept the faithful off drugs, and provided employment in its enterprises, offering not only a livelihood, but also a sense of meaning and purpose,' explained Shashi Tharoor, the erudite Congress party member of Parliament. '[W]here government and civil society failed, an apparent charlatan succeeded.'[29] It is these fundamental deficiencies of the Indian state that Modi promised to correct, but well into his term, the system, by and large, remains as it was, principally because of the methods he has adopted.

The question about whether Modi is more transactional than he is transformational is valid also because the former implies a small-time, short-term political orientation. The emphasis of the BJP government seems to be to rack up just enough visible changes to satisfy the electorate in the next general elections.[30] If genuine transformation is not what the prime minister is into, what are the lesser aims? At one level, transformation can be seen as a process involving a series of transactions the leader has with the system and its constituent elements. Necessarily, this involves minimum disruption, which approach is something Modi is inclined towards anyway, especially in the foreign policy and defence fields, as the next two chapters will make clear. As Burns points out, the transformational type of leader, while more desirable, may be 'initially impelled by the quest for individual recognition, [but] ultimately advances collective purpose by being attuned to the wants and wishes of his or her followers'. In this respect, he mentions Mao Zedong and Mahatma Gandhi.

Given how well and easily he connects with people in the cities as well as in the countryside, and how enthusiastically they respond to him personally and his initiatives, it is hard not to make the case that while there may be a low politics angle to some of Modi's moves (such as deploying the Central Bureau of Investigation to unearth corruption in deals involving political opponents, as charged by some), he is generally in sync with the people's thinking. He strives to better their lives and, by his lights, brighten the prospects for the country: the reason why voters continue to trust him to deliver the goods.[31] Burns further distinguishes between 'leaders'—persons whose motives resonate with those of the people—and 'power wielders'—motivated mainly by the potential for personal gain.[32] This distinction is particularly relevant in the Indian scene because politics has become so much a means for self-enrichment that the advent of the likes of Modi sans family and the usual hangers-on, a leader without any stain of corruption and insisting on probity in public life, has pretty much rearranged the political game. It has led to the popular belief that clean government is possible when upright leaders such as Modi are at the steering wheel rather than the usual power-hungry politicians.[33]

Political psychology is still an iffy science. Even with all the necessary data and information, there's no way to predict with certainty just how a person elected to public office will turn out once he gets power. Too many imponderables—situational, personal and milieu-related—remain unmapped and outside the public realm to make definitive judgements. This hasn't, however, deterred psychologists and political scientists from conceiving certain broad categories to fit politicians into. Having earlier placed Modi as part active-positive and part active-negative phenotype, a mix of the transformational as well as transactional leader, and as a leader rather than a run-of-the-mill 'power wielder', let's see what more can be divined about his persona.

American psychiatrist David Rosen lists six types: narcissist, obsessive-compulsive, Machiavellian, authoritarian, paranoid and totalitarian. All politicians are some combination of these types. According to Rosen, narcissists are charismatic, 'attention-seeking... extremely convincing liars and are the ultimate users [of people]— demanding loyalty from others they seldom give in return, and don't always make the best decisions but . . . [they] generally make the best leaders.'[34] Modi seems naturally to slip into this category. A person who wears an expensive coat with his name weaved in gold thread into the pinstripes, as the prime minister did during his one-on-one meeting with the more modestly clad US President Barack Obama during the latter's trip to Delhi as chief guest at the 2015 Republic Day celebrations, is, arguably, not someone who values humility. But there's a story to Modi's sartorial fastidiousness related to an early life of deprivation. The short-sleeved 'Modi kurta' that has become a fashion statement was originally 'designed' by him by simply lopping off the sleeves at the elbow of a kurta he possessed to make it easier to wear, wash and carry in his bag during his wide-ranging travels all over the country in early adult life.[35]

The prime minister no doubt believes in the adage of clothes making a man, and has done so from his childhood days when straitened family circumstances limited him to a single set of clothes, despite which he took care at all times to wear clean, look clean.[36] It is an attribute manifested in his quick-change artistry in later life—the frequent change of stylishly cut clothes at home as well as during his frequent trips abroad.[37] Narcissists attract a loyal following, but loyalty in politics may sometimes be a liability. As a loner and doer, Modi has marched to his own drumbeat, with his eye always on the political main chance.[38] He has gathered followers by the millions but also won the admiration of his seniors for his work ethic.

So, it is remarkable how many senior leaders in the BJP, whom he assisted and who helped Modi on his way up, resent the callous treatment they feel they have received at his hands. A stalwart BJP leader refers to Modi as 'overambitious' but 'a hollow man, a very insecure person'.[39] It has spurred them to challenge the prime minister in party conclaves and criticize him for his political failures, such as when the party suffered a resounding defeat in the November 2015 Bihar state elections. Considering how important Advani and Murli Manohar Joshi were in promoting his political career by installing him as general secretary and later as Gujarat chief minister, their disillusionment with Modi is striking. In reviewing the party's failure in the Bihar elections at a meeting of the BJP Parliamentary Board, these two elders, joined by Yashwant Sinha, external affairs minister in Vajpayee's cabinet, charged Modi and his confidant, party chief Amit Shah, with 'emasculating' the party and for 'shrugging off responsibility' for its misfortune in a crucial cow-belt state'.[40]

However, psychologists consider narcissism a personality disorder, which the Mayo Clinic, a highly regarded research hospital in the US, perceives as a 'mental [condition] in which people have an inflated sense of their own importance, a deep need for admiration and a lack of empathy for others'. But many caution that there's a very thin line separating a certifiable narcissist from someone with, as American neurosurgeon Bobby Azarian put it, 'a healthy amount of confidence and a burning desire to achieve great goals'. With Trump firmly in mind, Azarian said, 'Beneath the surface layer of overwhelming arrogance lies a delicate self-esteem that is easily injured' and presciently wondered if 'World War III' will follow if Trump, 'a loose cannon', confronted the 'notoriously Anti-American dictators' such as Kim Jong-un who won't 'kiss his ass' as [Trump] expects everyone to.[41] A delicate self-esteem may be Modi's problem as well considering how he doesn't brook criticism nor tolerate dissent. Obsessive-compulsives are identified by Rosen as 'hardworking, conscientious, and ethical personalities driven by a need for accuracy . . . [whose] professional capabilities outshine their personalities . . . [whose] deliberative decision-making and love of complexity makes them extraordinarily good at policymaking, but terrible at leading—particularly in crises when quick decisions have to be made with limited and often ambiguous information', and who avoid actions that rock the boat.[42] Modi is hardworking, has an abstemious lifestyle bereft of frivolous pastimes and is demanding as a boss. These are attributes he apparently cultivated in his youth under the guidance of the local RSS head, Laxmanrao Inamdar—'Vakil Sahab'—a father figure and early RSS mentor.

Unbidden, Modi would go off after school to help his father in his tea stall at the Vadnagar railway station, and then repair to the local RSS shakha, to which he was drawn when still in his adolescence to help out with petty tasks. It showed his appetite for toil. And Modi's conscientiousness was apparent when, as a youngster he suggested to his teachers to their great annoyance ways of improving their teaching methods and showed his mother better ways of doing chores at home. 'Narendra's enthusiasm for changing and improving things, his need to align the world to the way he saw things,' writes a biographer, 'gives additional weight to the idea that [he felt constricted and] wanted more than Vadnagar could offer.'[43]

So, Modi's ambition was not a late development. His desire to escape small-town constraints, to see the wider world and make something of himself in it, was a corollary. The person crucial to shaping the young Modi's mind and his future was Inamdar, who advised the individualistic lad on the importance of being part of a 'system' to accomplish big things, and eased his passage upwards through the RSS system.[44] The respect for whatever system he found himself in at any given time was drilled into Modi then, as also the desire to work within it and to make it work. Inamdar may have broadened Modi's horizons but there's a Gujarati cultural factor to his outward-thrusting impulses. It led to the young, penniless Modi taking off for distant places—Kolkata and the Himalayas—for two years when he was barely seventeen years of age. It may have endowed him, as it has other enterprising Gujaratis, one of his biographers notes, with the 'adaptive culture nous' essential to adjusting quickly to new environs and to engaging with all sorts of people.[45] It is seen in Modi's self-confidence, especially its physical dimension, which too was hardwired into his persona at an early age.[46]

This is manifested in the way the prime minister physically forces himself on foreign leaders with his unselfconscious hugging—a gesture at once intimate and friendly that breaks down the walls of formality and reserve, establishes instant rapport and publicly signals his comfort level with them. It doesn't matter whether it is the cerebral Obama or the visceral Trump, the self-composed Putin or the phlegmatic Xi—they have all thus been seemingly put at ease. Modi's embraces are in a sense a diplomatic innovation, considering most international leaders are entirely unused to such ready and easy physical intimacy in the conduct of international relations. If the famously 'touch-me-not' President Trump tolerated it, there must be something to it as the medium for traditionally stiff-necked diplomacy to become more informal, if not always more productive.

It is, perhaps, the secret behind the warm personal relations Modi has forged with his foreign counterparts despite serious differences on issues between governments. How vehemently, after all, can one disagree or be disagreeable with someone you have been in a tight squeeze with? It is no bad tactic to ensure an irreducible minimum degree of goodwill and fellow feeling in the fraught world of interstate affairs. But, in the context of the earlier mention of narcissism by the neurosurgeon Azarian, an uncomfortable question arises: Was Modi's bear hug and overfriendliness on display in the Rose Garden at the White House during his June 2017 visit interpreted by US President Trump as the Indian leader 'kissing ass'? Is that why Trump got along well with Modi? Then again, as many commentators have observed, strongmen do relate better to each other in the international arena.[47]

Machiavellians, Rosen suggests, are 'master manipulators [who] focus on the game more than the outcomes... cool and calculating [they] are not... burdened by the ethical qualms... Winning is everything [to them], the rest is negotiable.'[48] All successful politicians are Machiavellians to a lesser or greater degree. Manipulating people without being overly burdened by ethical concerns are, in a sense, the requirements of the job, these being routine attributes of the trade to ensure survival and success. Certainly what is plain from the twists and turns in Modi's personal life and political career is that there is a Machiavelli, or Chanakya if you will, in him. The steadiness of intent, the single-minded focus on realizing goals and the manner in which he has negotiated the shoals and currents of Indian politics is an indication of a 'political man' at work. There's more to this than is perceptible. Should Modi succeed in replicating on a national scale the success of his economic policies in Gujarat, for example, he will end up doing more for India's democracy in terms of strengthening it than most of his predecessors.[49] So his success matters. That he did it all his own way in Gandhinagar and is trying to repeat it in Delhi is something to be marvelled at. Except Modi has not quite garnered the success on the national stage as prime minister that he did as Gujarat chief minister.

Modi's chief ministerial tenure was distinguished by centralized decision-making and the absence of corruption and patronage. His ministers were not permitted to pad their accounts or appoint their supporters to government posts—the innumerable chairmanships of official commissions, state-owned companies and the like—or to appoint their lackeys to lesser sinecures in the state government. Further, the RSS did not get any special consideration any more than any other social service organization.[50] As in Gujarat so on the national stage, he has not cavilled—and this is Chanakya/Machiavelli stuff—from cold-bloodedly using socially combustible 'anti-Muslim' issues such as cow slaughter, Ram Temple or 'triple talaq' as political stratagems to cleave society and consolidate Hindu votes. As far as Modi is concerned this is '*dhanda*—business, political business, his business, even though, as his biographers attest, he personally feels no ill-will for Muslims, having grown up in interior Gujarat with many Muslims as friends. He is not conspicuously pro-Hindu or anti-anything, but he is against unduly placating any particular section of society, especially minorities, and, hence, against the attendant politics that he charges the Congress and other parties of practising.

In an interview to the *New York Times*, he had this exchange: When asked what he had done for Muslims, Modi replied, 'Nothing.' 'So you admit it?' the reporter said. Modi then suggested the reporter ask him what he had 'done for Hindus'. 'What have you done for Hindus?' the reporter demanded obediently. 'Nothing,' Modi said. 'Everything I have done has been for Gujaratis.'[51] On the national stage, he can likewise claim that his policies have not benefited any specific section of the Indian society, but all Indians. He elaborated his 'no appeasement' view thus: 'If one of your hands is perfect but the other weak then you cannot be considered healthy. There can be no discrimination. But this does not mean that there is any advantage in appeasement. The path of appeasement is damaging the nation and it has become a part of the politics of vote banks. I want to . . . put an end to the politics of vote banks.'[52]

In practice, this non-appeasement stance of Modi's translated, in the wake of the Godhra riots, for instance, into relief, food and protection for the riot victims at large, but these were not advertised as exclusively serving Muslims.[53] Even so, the equal treatment under Modi's rule pleased a large section of the minority community. Twenty-three per cent of the Muslim vote went to the BJP in the 2012 state elections that returned Modi to power.[54] In any case, the ruling party's caste arithmetic added to the Modi government's welfarism, anti-corruption measures and heavy-duty nationalism, which pretty much made the Muslim vote redundant for the BJP.[55]

His perceptions of the world are coloured by his conviction about the basically secular nature of Hindu culture and Indian society. 'Our society has believed in *vasudhaiva kutumbakam* [the whole world is one family] from the time when there was no religion in the world,' Modi maintains. 'This is also the case with Hindutva—take the agenda of any country, any government in the world—the political and economic agenda and compare with [what] our society has believed in from the Vedic periods. Forget the literal meaning—in essence it means the well-being of all without any distinctions of sect, or of one geographical area. Now this is the philosophy some people term as Hindutva [Swami Vivekananda and philosopher and former President Dr S. Radhakrishnan, among them]. And, this is my understanding also.'[56]

Modi understands that this more expansive view of India's uniqueness in the world does not dovetail with the BJP's championing of domestic issues such as the building of the Ram Temple in Ayodhya and the abrogation of Article 370 according special status to Jammu and Kashmir within the Indian Union, which ends up riling the Muslim community and exacerbating communal discord. He labels the Ram Temple type of issues 'core issues' that, he suggests, may be implemented only when his party secures a two-thirds majority in Parliament. The implication is that because such a majority—enough to amend the Constitution—may be hard to come by, these emotionally charged promises, while electorally profitable, are in no way practicable and, hence, there's no point in harping on them. It is a position that provides the BJP with plausible reasons for ignoring these issues when in government. 'What can you achieve by taking up any [such] agenda?' asks Modi, rhetorically.[57]

Winning is everything in politics and so it is for Modi as well—the reason, perhaps, why he thinks that there is no political premium in being an ideologue of any kind. 'People often confuse ideology with programmes. The programme is not ideology, and ideology is not programme,' he said, and added, 'Programmes are made at particular moments depending on the situation prevailing at that time.' So does that mean he has no ideology whatsoever? It turns out that if he has one, it is of the secular variety. 'Our ideology,' Modi averred, 'is simple—India First. Rest are all projects, programmes.'[58]

It may, therefore, be inferred that 'projects' and 'programmes' are merely the means to win votes and to consolidate the party's rule at the centre and in the states. Alas, Modi's India First is not a fully fleshed out ideology or corpus of thought but only a sketchy policy guideline and as such a fairly innocuous, diffuse, flexible and patriotic-sounding all-purpose catchphrase that can mean a lot of things to lots of people, can cover a lot of ground or, alternatively, mean nothing at all. But the concept can subsume any policy, project or programme. Whether or not his domestic and economic policies have adhered to the India First principle, most of his foreign and military policies, as the subsequent chapters will show, reveal only a passing acquaintance with the hard India First principle requiring the government to pursue the national interest in terms of extracting the maximum possible economic, military and strategic benefit, and to deploy disruptive policies to reshape the regional and international order inimical to India and Indian interests. The experience so far of Modi's India First policies, however, suggests that it is nothing like the Country First philosophy of Trump, Erdogan, Putin, Abe or Xi.

The Authoritarians, according to Rosen, are 'quintessentially hierarchical, sycophantic towards superiors, competitive toward peers, and domineering toward subordinates. They value toughness, believe might makes right and have contempt for mercy. They also tend to be conservative, sexually prudish, rule-oriented and prejudiced—

projecting their own flaws and insecurities on to low status groups.' The next category, the Paranoids, are 'Secretive and suspicious', believe in conspiracies, 'harbor doubts about the loyalty of even close confidants', and hold grudges. The paranoia, Rosen says, is 'compensation for deep feelings of inferiority, often mixed with anger and resentment.' And, finally, there is the Totalitarian type; they 'demand absolute obedience from underlings, believe in their own infallibility and wield power through a combination of awe, terror and the gullibility of their supporters', foster 'the cult of personality' and reject 'facts that contradict goals and fanaticism'.[59] Modi's public life has not revealed any signs of paranoia in him, though some like the sociologist Ashis Nandy contend he is a 'fascist' and has 'clear paranoid and obsessive' traits.[60] Fascist is a strong word, but there is no doubt about the authoritarian streaks in his personality.

Modi's stern, no-nonsense bearing, disciplined deportment, strict views on what is acceptable and unacceptable, his differential pattern of behaviour—solicitous and eager to please where his superiors (RSS leaders and party stalwarts he dealt with on his way up) are concerned but autocratic, brusque, dismissive and often mocking when dealing with inferiors, namely, other politicians and civil servants—reveal authoritarian, even totalitarian, tendencies. As do the calculatedly serious mien he adopts to create an aura of unapproachability, his self-assurance bordering on arrogance, the 'I, me, myself' attitude that comes from a regime he has imposed on the government revolving around his personality and his inclination to spring decisions that are not thought through and end up costing the nation plenty (such as demonetization and the Rafale deal).

The factors that impel such behaviour and have shaped the political Modi, his mindset and worldview can, in the main, be sourced to his socialization in the RSS, to his indoctrination and immersion in the Sangh's ethos and worldview. Modi readily acknowledges the RSS's impact and influence on him. 'Whatever I am,' Modi confessed, 'is because of the basic foundation of the Sangh. Hard work, the idea that the nation is more important than the party—I got the ability to think this way due to [this] association. There are many such traits that I picked up from my early days and they stand me in good stead now.'

This includes the administrative skills central to running the government which, Modi claims, he 'learnt from the Sangh', especially 'how to use manpower resources to the hilt, to the optimum levels'.[61] The RSS's role as something of a management school honing Modi's organizational talent is important from the point of view of his rapid advancement in the Sangh, and in the BJP to which he was deputed. Its more personal and intimate value to Modi lies in the Sangh being his family and home, affording him a sense of 'belonging' and comradeship. His experiences in and of the Sangh provided him the model, once in power, to order the reality around him in a similar manner.

Modi values the RSS also for 'inculcating [in him] a sense of responsibility' and 'how to work within [any organization]'. This is a clue to Modi's conservativism and his ability to work within whatever system he finds himself in, in other words, towards status quo and evolutionary change. And as the prime minister, he is mindful of the usefulness of the RSS cadres to push his agenda at the grassroots level and, along with social media, to promote trust in him and propagate his image as a clean, careful and diligent leader working hard to do good for the people.[62] It has emboldened the RSS, as quid pro quo, to push its own agenda of spreading 'traditional values' in society, advising women, in particular, about the benefits of vegetarianism and the perils of 'foreign culture'.[63]

'Conservatives tend to be higher in a personality trait called orderliness and lower in openness,' writes a researcher in psychology from the University of Toronto, almost as if he were describing Modi. 'This means that they're more concerned about a sense of order and tradition, expressing a deep psychological motive to preserve the current social structure.'[64] It explains why Modi as prime minister is so into preserving the extant system of government, into making it work and against dismantling it or even radically changing it, let alone transforming it. As he rose in the RSS and saw how seniority was respected in the organization, and the higher-ups in the hierarchy given deference with their views considered the last word on the subject, Modi too expected that as he ascended his view would be deferred to by all. As chief minister in Gujarat and now prime minister, he has arranged the already hierarchical decision-making and administrative structure into the still steeper top-down system that he was familiar with from his time in the RSS, where only the top person gives orders and everybody else buckles down to implementing them in earnest. Except, first in Gandhinagar and then in Delhi, Modi went a step further and set himself up as an overarching authority figure, and not only in government. Gordhan Zadafia, a former minister in the Gujarat government, said of Modi that he 'thinks of himself as above the organization whether it is Parivar or the BJP—he has a very autocratic style of functioning'.[65]

Modi apparently sees the position of head of government as similar to that of the *sarsanghchalak* atop the RSS, but with far greater responsibility—a sort of very superior sarsanghchalak. Modi has accordingly fashioned the PMO as the locus of all authority and power in the government, and as a tool to ensure that what he says or wants gets done even as he has retained the creaky colonial-era administration with all its constraints because that's the system he was given to work with. This, however, flies in the face of his own reading of why good governance is not possible with such a system. 'In governance, the major problem in our system,' says Modi, 'is . . . compartmental thinking and in water-tight compartments, psychologically and physically. I wanted to change this environment.' But compartmentalized or silo-based decision-making cannot be removed by anything other than major organizational reforms, which he is unwilling to undertake.

In other words, while he is not for radical administrative reforms, he will tinker around at the edges with the existing system by, for instance, telling bureaucrats heading ministries in the government to adopt the mindset of chief executives and present him with their plans.[66] Except, chief executives of companies don't have to negotiate the byzantine maze of cross-cutting rules, regulations, bureaucratic norms, protocols and procedures that is the Government of India. It is a strategy for governance that may have worked in Gandhinagar but cannot be scaled up to Delhi. The PMO has always been the handmaiden of strong-willed prime ministers. Nehru was too much the liberal democrat to misuse it. Indira Gandhi had no such qualms and, in her second full term as prime minister (1971–77), imposed the Emergency, upended the Constitution, suspended habeas corpus and the rule of law, and ran the country like her private fief. It is only the second time in the history of the republic that as strong a PMO has emerged in Modi's time with the Union cabinet reduced to a formality. The present setup has achieved several things, though. It has done away with the pretence of the prime minister as primus inter pares—the first among equals. Modi is the boss, what he says goes. His cabinet colleagues know it, his party knows it, the opposition knows it, every functionary in the central government and in the states knows it and now so do the people of India. Ministers are not expected to have programmes of their own but to take orders from Modi and realize them along the lines he decrees. The PMO keeps track and checks up on whether and how well the prime minister's advice is followed and his wishes carried out. Ministers who disappoint are shunted off to lesser jobs.[67]

Some of those ministers who meet Modi's expectations, such as Nitin Gadkari, are rewarded with more politically valuable work. The instituting of a rewards and punishment system has made the ministers more active and accountable and streamlined the processes of making decisions, ridding it of some of the inefficiencies and delays due to inter-ministry squabbles and bureaucratic foot-dragging endemic to governments in the past. Secondly, there is no question of a laid-back prime minister allowing bureaucratic flunkies to steal the show. This happened during Vajpayee's time when the former diplomat Brajesh Mishra as NSA and principal private secretary (PPS) to the prime minister made no bones about the fact that he was the de facto chief executive. The division of labour then was Vajpayee dealing with the political aspects of government—managing the disorderly National Democratic Alliance coalition partners and opposition politicians—and Mishra manipulating the bureaucratic levers to execute policies, often of his own devising.[68] Or, the situation that obtained during the Manmohan Singh regime when the NSA M.K. Narayanan with direct access to his political patron Sonia Gandhi, president of the Congress, wielded his clout to undermine the MEA's negotiations with the US on the civilian nuclear cooperation deal that the prime minister desired.[69]

In the Modi dispensation, in contrast, neither the NSA, Ajit K. Doval, formerly from the Indian Police Service, nor the PPS, Nripendra

Misra, a retiree from the Indian Administrative Service (IAS), presumes to be in any way in charge or entertains the faintest notion of being the fount of policy ideas. As Doval reportedly told a former senior functionary in the Manmohan Singh government who called on him: 'The boss knows his mind. I am here to implement what he tells me to.' Doval was also clear that this ruled out his offering Modi policy choices for the prime minister to select from.[70] Thus, in the Modi universe, those working for him know their place in the pecking order, where they stand with him, and what he expects of them—so does the rest of the whole bureaucratic caboodle of secretaries in the line ministries, and the foreign secretary in the MEA. They all take their cues from Modi and, on matters important to the prime minister, report directly to him, often bypassing their own ministers. There are numerous forums—some old, some new—to facilitate such interaction between the prime minister and his ministers, between Modi and the secretaries in the ministries, agency heads, etc., where procedural barriers are ignored and bureaucratic turf issues resolved, all by prime ministerial fiat. The upside of this arrangement is that the responsibility is clear and unambiguous. Modi can corner the credit for such success as his domestic, economic, external and national security policies and the central government's development and social welfare schemes, programmes and projects achieve. But he can pass on blame for things going wrong to the bureaucrats for shortfalls in implementation.

At the apex level in the party and government and with the experience of the RSS model in mind, it is natural that Modi treats no one as his equal in the domestic realm. But he finds foreign leaders he meets with or visits worthy of respect. Even here, his conduct differs with the foreign leader in question. If the foreign leader is from the West, especially the US or western Europe, Modi tends to be deferential; in the case of Putin and Abe he is personable; and with Xi, Modi's attitude has evolved from seeking to please to being proper even as India's policy has gone from wanting peaceful resolution, standing its ground in Doklam to cagily countering China in the Indian Ocean region. And where the heads of government from the developing world are concerned, he is stiff, distant and officious. There are two norm-related factors at work here.

The esteem shown by Modi to Western, usually white, leaders—Obama was the exception—stands out in contrast to how he carries himself with Third World leaders, especially from Africa, whom he meets but not with his trademark hugs. This may have something to do with that old but resilient Hindu affliction of social differentiation by skin colour, varna, that the RSS has not disavowed and Modi may be unconsciously manifesting. In the Hindu social universe, the lighter-skinned people are at the top and the darker-skinned people at the bottom. Necessarily, in this social schemata, the persons at the top have power and exercise it. The colour consciousness in Indian society is something to marvel at—it manifests everywhere in India, from 'whitening creams' to the demand for fair-skinned brides to the awful discrimination faced by African students in Indian universities. The ramifications of this, albeit indirect, varna-effected diplomacy are serious, for instance, with regard to Indian policies vis-à-vis African countries, where diplomatic posts are vacant because few in the Indian Foreign Service (IFS) want to serve there.

The other factor that shapes such behaviour is simply power. Modi's demeanour with foreign leaders may be a function of the power of the countries they represent. Being effusive and physically friendly with Trump, Putin, Abe or Macron, Modi perhaps calculates, will gain him and India more than a similar treatment of, say, the South African President Jacob Zuma. In other words, Modi's physical intimacy with foreign leaders, other than the varna considerations, may be less genuine gestures of friendship or friendliness than a reflection of what he assesses as the power quotient of the country the person he embraces belongs to.

This last may be no great revelation, however, considering successful politicians everywhere are good at gauging the relative power and standing of those they interact with and trimming their behaviour accordingly. Modi has always been adept at sizing up people and shifting power situations and exploiting them to his advantage. Consider the quite extraordinary episode pertaining to the 2002 Gujarat riots: the low point of Modi's career. The context was the ongoing riots with Gujarati Muslims at the receiving end of violence which the state government seemed unable to control. Modi was in Delhi to consult with the central leadership. Prime Minister Vajpayee on that occasion famously urged Modi to perform his 'raj dharma' and act in a non-discriminatory manner to restore law and order. This much is well known and critics time and again bring it up to highlight the supposed flaws in Modi's character and his failings as chief minister. What is left out of such accounts is more revealing.

After their official discussion, presumably on how best to curb the rioters and the sort of help the central government may be able to render, Vajpayee and Modi met jointly with the press. It was the occasion when the prime minister made his 'raj dharma' comment. What was not as well reported was that immediately after Vajpayee's statement Modi cut in and, without ceremony, declared that he in fact had acted 'exactly' as the prime minister had counselled. Faced with this public challenge, Vajpayee back-pedalled. 'I believe,' said the prime minister lamely, '[that Modi] is performing his raj dharma properly.'[71] It was a stunning finish to a much advertised public hanging that ended up with the hangman having the noose round his neck! It showed Modi's steely political instincts and reading of the balance of power in the state and within the BJP and the inclination of the RSS. It is a reflection of what the British journalist Lance Price in another context identified as Modi's 'indomitable will' to succeed, and his 'determination ... never to recognize the possibility of failure'.[72] It has helped him resist pressures from the RSS for a more ideological government and, by his own account, even to try and change that organization's views on certain issues.

Thus, to stave off hunger and meet the basic needs of the drought-affected people in 1985–86 the RSS first decided to collect funds from Hindu communities and well-wishers abroad but instead ended up following an alternative solution proffered by Modi. 'Why do we appeal to foreign nations? What's the need for this?' asked Modi. 'We are a nation, we have human power. Our whole relief work must be on the basis of our human energy, our nation, our manpower, and for that we could have a different strategy' for mobilizing food and other resources from within the country itself.[73]

An individual's will and instincts are fine, but in the Modi-centred government what is of critical importance is whether there is a system to generate imaginative, high-quality ideas that are in sync with these instincts, and to process them into policy choices for the prime minister to mull over, so that they can be fleshed out in the PMO and elsewhere and transmitted to the ministries. Insofar as can be discerned, there's no such system. Nor, being a 'loner', does he have a circle of intellectually inclined friends and acquaintances, formally or informally batting policy ideas with him, as Indira Gandhi did with her 'kitchen cabinet'.[74] So, as in Nehru's time, the capillaries of the government—the PMO and the various ministries, departments and agencies of the Government of India are open to oxygenation only and exclusively by Modi. They pick up on his every utterance as potential content or direction for policy. In the event, it matters a great deal how and where the prime minister gets his ideas from.

The widely travelled Nehru—a liberal politician, an acclaimed author and a classical historian of international repute with many brilliant books to his credit, and a man who hobnobbed with the best and the brightest everywhere, including Bertrand Russell and Albert Einstein—still relied for policy ideas on a bevy of outsiders, albeit ennobled and highly placed Britons. Chief among them were Lord Kaldor for socialist economics, Lord Blackett, the 1948 Physics Nobel laureate, for structuring the armed forces, Field Marshal Claude Auchinleck, commander-in-chief, India, for a possible nuclear military, and Lieutenant General Sir Francis Tuker, the last Englishman to command India's Eastern Army, for geostrategics. One may fault Nehru for banking on advice from the colonial metropole, as it were, but it showed that even though intellectually fecund, he felt he needed help.[75] Where Modi is concerned, he apparently doesn't have to look far for ideas. By his own admission he does not need outside help.

Thinking policy and creating policy options are generally considered a job for experts. Modi has no such outside talent bank advising him and feeding him ideas, only serving and retired civil servants and policemen and such around him. But like diplomats, who may have learned a thing or two about international relations during their careers, their powers of conceptualization of policy options are constrained by long exposure to the official line. It is a hindrance when it comes to formalizing imaginative policy choices for the prime minister. The newly constituted

NITI Aayog, which replaced the Planning Commission, is thought of as the BJP government's think tank. Except, its members are frustrated because (as a later chapter will show) their recommendations are rarely paid heed to. Then again, Modi wants everyone manning his PMO and other parts of the government not so much to think up bright new policy ideas for him but simply to carry out his instructions and generate data. But a large volume of information does not, by itself, make for quality analysis or produce insights. In any case, all such considerations seem to be irrelevant. Modi values his memory and his recall ability, which he believes assist him in keeping on top of the bureaucracy and in following up to see that his guidelines in diverse policy fields are properly followed, and this is the 'Modi operandi'.[76] He is also, by his own account, enthused by innovative thoughts and the possibility of improving things. 'Innovation, new ideas, that [is] basically my temperament,' he confessed elsewhere.[77]

Modi frankly believes he is his own best think tank. He disclosed how his policy ideas are spawned. 'It is probably a god-gifted ability,' he explained. 'Even I would be surprised at times about how I got a particular idea. It just came to my mind.'[78] It was thus that the idea came to him of placing solar panels on agricultural canals to prevent the evaporation of water and to produce power for the grid, and to separate the electricity distribution system between domestic and agricultural use to make available power for homes 24/7 and adequate supply to farmers during nights and off-peak hours to work their water pumps. As practical solutions go, these are inspired but of a localized nature. But what about policies that require more than the momentary bright idea? Here the process gets a bit murky and mysterious. Persons who worked with Modi in Gujarat were uniformly of the view, as Nilanjan Mukhopadhyay, who published the then chief minister's biography in 2013, notes 'that Modi did not like to listen to any viewpoint besides his own'. It is a trait Modi himself confirms, saying that while he listens to, and learns from, experts and studies [the issues at hand], 'I am,' he admitted, 'never influenced by anyone, or any place. There is no need—I get inspired, not influenced.'[79]

It's nice that he thus occasionally finds inspiration from outside of himself. But, surely, somewhere at the bottom of the pile of this (non)intellectual activity are books and serious treatises that he reads to firm up his notions about the various aspects of the complex reality he confronts and the kind of policies he needs to engineer to have a 'big' effect. The evidence that he reads anything at all is spotty. Only one of his numerous biographers vouches for his reading habit, asserting that Modi is a 'ferocious reader'.[80] This is a curious thing to say about Modi. Does it mean he devours books by the truckload, or that he reads at a fast pace, or that he is both a fast and diligent reader, taking notes and filing away nuggets of information, ideas and insights as his reading provides him for future use. It is not clear. Those who have researched his life discovered that Modi is not into books much and makes do at most with short articles.[81] A senior BJP leader backs this perception, saying Modi 'trusts nobody, consults no one, allows no one any real access, reads no books, but every morning gets a folio of opinion-page pieces culled from newspapers by [P.K.] Mishra'.[82] (Additional PPS to the prime minister and a self-effacing former IAS officer who speaks fluent Gujarati, Mishra is regarded as the only PMO official close to Modi.[83]) The picture of Modi that emerges is that of a lonely workaholic, with no interests outside of his job; his solitary nature, in particular, being exemplified by the infrequent days off he used to take in the past to commune with nature, to be all by himself in distant, uninhabited, places.[84]

However, Modi seems to have more in common with Trump than any previous Indian prime minister had with a US President: alpha-maleness and regimes they run centred on themselves. There is something else they share. The sociologist Shiv Visvanathan has lamented the fact that in the age of mobile telephony, television and proliferating social media, information has premium, not knowledge.[85] Small attention spans and complicated problems shrunk to simple, often simplistic solutions coexist in this high-impact universe, which both Modi and Trump seem to inhabit and which the latter even joked about.[86] If, as is known, Modi favours short policy presentations in bullet points on a single page, colourful computer graphics and whole programmes encapsulated in no more than five slides and pie-charts, and gets ideas about what next to do and in what policy realm on the basis of no systematic method but by way of something somehow popping up in his consciousness, one can see why he bonds well with

Trump, who can't be bothered with reading policy briefs but trusts himself to wing it.[87]

Instincts matter even more to Modi. Lacking serious formal education, he has made the most, by his own account, of his 'god-given' intellectual gifts to gauge, study and understand the world around him.[88] From this it may be deduced that he is a keen observer of human nature, quick on the uptake and a fast and motivated learner, soaking up snippets of information, insights and factoids from where he can find them and from his experiences peregrinating in India and abroad. These are then stored in his memory bank. All this material apparently simmers and stews in his head before congealing into slogans and policy parameters. Former prime ministers Nehru and Narasimha Rao, for example, patronized talented people because they were secure enough in their own intellects and abilities.[89] Modi is known neither to seek the advice of domain specialists or even his cabinet colleagues, nor does he consult senior officials in government before approving policies. In the foreign policy area, therefore, the MEA is 'sidelined'.[90] A senior IFS officer backing this view said a bit acerbically, 'How many people do you need to make policy? Two? Three? And that's done by the prime minister.' And so what work remains for the MEA to do is that of 'glorified peons'.[91]

Then again, as a self-confessed loner—'I actually enjoy loneliness,' Modi has said—the prime minister communes a lot with himself. He did so as late as 1995–96, using his annual ritual of getting away for a 'meet myself programme' to 'completely unknown places', such as the Gir forest, there, in his own words, to do nothing but 'just think'.[92] As prime minister he may not have the time for walkabouts in the wilderness, but it is safe to assume that by habit he thinks of policy issues that concern him and works things out in his own mind and within his understanding of the subject. Unencumbered by official duties in his early years in the RSS, he attended seminars, lectures, etc. to bone up on subjects of interest to him. He has no time for such activity any more.[93] Nor do experts find a place in his advisorate. Having made up his mind and alighted on a policy track, he doesn't like anybody criticizing or opposing it.

His sometime home-minister-turned-political-foe in Gujarat, Gordhan Zadafia, recalls how as RSS pracharak Modi 'never liked anyone to disagree [with him] but only [to] listen to his commands. [And how] even then he always tried to remove his opponents.' But this may have been the result of his socialization in the RSS and his imbibing its workplace norms in which disagreement with a senior is not countenanced.[94] If he didn't brook ideas that differed with his own when he was not in government, it is unlikely he has become more tolerant of dissonant views as he graduated from chief minister to prime minister. The RSS further embedded in him, in his own words, 'a sense of responsibility, [and the desire to study] an organization's setup and how to work within it'.[95] This explains why Modi is ultimately an arch establishmentarian and a statist—not one to reform or make over the extant bureaucratic system in the country but satisfied with making do with what he has. What's new is that he trusts the system to perform by motivating its functionaries. Talking before a Silicon Valley crowd in September 2015, he said that 'India is not a scooter whose direction you can see changing easily [but rather a] forty-compartment train [which] takes time. India is a huge country.'[96]

But this metaphor of India as a train unfortunately suggests why the country with Modi as engine driver will chug along in the same old way on the same old track and turning in a new direction only very slowly and then perhaps with the same old results. Modi has given no hint here or anywhere else of the need to rip up the vintage rail tracks and to lay them in an entirely new direction and, to stick with this metaphor, to introduce new rolling stock and locomotive technology. Thus, about his slogan 'minimum government, maximum governance' that promised a thorough overhaul of the system, a prospect that had so enthused voters, he only meant, Modi told Adam Roberts, the correspondent for *The Economist*, the cutting of some red tape and a more efficient administration. In the same vein, he confessed his antipathy to privatization and reluctance to sell off loss-making PSUs because he feared having to tangle with labour unions. And he talked of being 'pro-business', while promoting 'crony capitalists', when what he needed to do for the sake of the country was to be 'pro-market', fuel competitiveness, sell off moribund PSUs and, by these means, enhance productivity in the economy—two very different sets of policies with very different outcomes. Consequently, notes Roberts tartly, 'Where

India needed liberalization and removal of the dead hand of bureaucrats, to help unleash economic growth, Modi . . . delivered . . . the great cash withdrawal' and 'Modi's plan for 600,000 villages to have high-speed Internet by 2017 was in trouble from the start . . . because it relied on slow-moving bureaucrats'. Modi, moreover, confessed he didn't know what 'big bang' reforms were but argued that the changes he had effected had made India 'the most open economy in the world' for foreign investors. It was Trump's kind of untruth readily uttered, considering that the International Chamber of Commerce in 2017 ranked India 64th of 75 countries, behind Egypt, Tunisia, the Philippines and Indonesia, among others.[97]

That still leaves the mystery intact about the ideational wellsprings of Modi's policies. Modi reads no books or serious stuff like that. He occasionally meets with experts and media people but it seems less to initiate an exchange than to convey his views and indicate the issues he is preoccupied with at the moment.[98] This is a channel for one-way communication to suit Modi who, it is claimed, is not 'open-minded', with such sessions being in the nature of the RSS-style *charcha*s that the prime minister seems well versed in as a means of legitimating his own thinking.[99] Such outside experts as have been recruited are mostly economists, an indication perhaps that in the economic policy area he is less sure of his knowledge and instincts. Though even here one can detect his childhood experiences as motivating many of his government's populist programmes.

For instance, the successful Ujjwala programme to distribute free LPG gas cylinders to poor households surely harks back to Modi remembering his mother slaving over a smoky earthen stove fired by cow dung fuel in the small windowless house in Vadgaon where the Modi family of eight lived.[100] In other economic policy spheres, however, Modi's decisions cannot be traced to any particular source. A senior staffer in the Modi government's favourite think tank, the VIF, complains that their policy papers when not ignored have their recommendations so twisted as to undercut their effectiveness. A VIF paper on demonetization sent to the PMO, for example, expressly advised against the printing of any high-denomination currency to replace the ₹1000 note. But the introduction of the ₹2000 note has ended up, the VIF staffer fumed, giving a fillip to the black market economy—doubling the value for the same weight of paper and facilitating underhand transactions, which the VIF authors had warned the prime minister about.[101]

Even so, everyone is aware that Modi has 'strong' personal views and a reputation fostered during his career of being rebellious and a leader willing to brave the odds.[102] Very little of this supposed risk-taking proclivity of the prime minister is evident, however, in the external realm. (More on this in the next two chapters.) Modi is a self-contained leader in that he works inside his own bubble and is so certain about his views and what he wants to do with them, it is natural for him to abhor too great a diversity of views within his setup. It has resulted in the higher reaches of the ruling party, the PMO, the cabinet and the government being peopled by 'yes-men'.[103] Psychologists call this 'the doppelganger effect' of political leaders tending to surround themselves with people who think and act like them.[104]

Modi has been particular in populating even advisory agencies such as NITI Aayog with people who he is certain will affirm and support the policies he has pursued.[105] Further, to minimize friction, he has embarked on economic populism that is in line with the thinking of the RSS, which believes in socialism of sorts and the central role of the government in removing poverty and economic disparities. It clashes with Modi's free-market nostrums of enlarging the economic pie so that there's more to go around for more people, but this is the price he is willing to pay. 'Always there was resistance [to the laissez-faire philosophy], always there were questions,' Modi told one of his biographers. 'But if I am convinced, I will prove the results. Then results will make them convinced.'[106] But he failed to push through the kind of reforms that would have obtained a 'bigger pie' and achieved the RSS aim of diminishing poverty faster, perhaps because he was apprehensive about Sangh outfits such as the Swadeshi Jagran Manch opposing them.[107]

Its flipside is the Hindu fringe's belief in the 'crony spiritualism' of the BJP regime that has convinced the mostly lumpen-populated outlier groups that they have the licence violently to enforce restrictive norms and behaviour in the culturally pluralistic Indian society.[108] There's a still more regressive side to the over-the-top glorification of Hinduism and everything Hindu that tends towards absurdity. Prime Minister Modi has repeatedly indulged in it. A stunned audience of doctors and medical researchers at the All India Institute of Medical Sciences in October 2014 were told by him that ancient India was advanced in many branches of science including genetics and plastic surgery and as proof offered the elephant-headed Hindu god, Ganesha. 'We worship Lord Ganesha,' he said. 'There must have been some plastic surgeon at that time who got an elephant's head on the body of a human being and began the practice of plastic surgery.' He then mentioned the great Kaurava warrior Karna who is described in the Mahabharata as being born outside his mother's womb. This episode was adduced by Modi as evidence of prehistoric India's competence in genetics. Such forays by Modi into India's mythical scientific achievements are not new. As Gujarat chief minister he wrote a foreword to a book that claimed that ancient India featured radar-equipped aeroplanes and stem cell research.[109]

The fusing of mythology with science has time and again got scientists' goat. The 2009 Nobel Prize winner, the University of Cambridge biochemist, Venkataraman Ramakrishnan, for example, dismissed the 103rd Indian Science Congress in 2016 as a 'circus' and vowed never to attend another one after hearing Lord Shiva being extolled as a great environmentalist, and having the audience's senses assaulted by the ceaseless blowing of a conch shell by someone who claimed its curative powers.[110] But what does this say about Modi that he actually believes such nonsense is science?[111] It has exposed him to ridicule. More such incidents and what international credibility he has mustered will begin to erode to his detriment and the country's. He may end up as exotica, like Prime Minister Morarji Desai who is remembered, if at all, in the West for drinking his own liquid waste as part of 'auto-urine therapy'.

If ideology is irrelevant and his personal conviction does not impinge on his approach, and such views as he holds have no real depth and deliberation behind them, but nevertheless provide direction to policy, how he comes by his views in the first place is a matter of public concern. How he gathers information and operates with it has already been dilated upon. An alternative explanation is that the strong social media cell in the PMO comes up with attractive alliterative slogans for the PM to popularize through his public speeches and mass outreach programmes, such as the 'Mann Ki Baat' (Saying what's on my mind) radio programme. These slogans, while taking on a life of their own, appear most times to be the new raiment for policies of previous governments. This charge has some credence considering how the bureaucrats—the bellwether of the system—have adjusted to Modi. They have rejigged their language and their standard operating procedures to stress the appropriate Modi slogan and rhetoric but otherwise have carried on much as before with the template of existing social welfare policies from Manmohan Singh's time.[112]

The minister for electronics and information technology, Ravi Shankar Prasad, misrepresented this process by saying it is 'new wine in old bottles', as he himself confirmed. The Modi regime, he wrote, fixed the 'various flaws' in the prevailing policies, reduced the leakages with the direct delivery mode and 'has been better in terms of designing new schemes and improving previous schemes [which] is what governance is about'.[113] A third possibility—and this applies in particular to the government's foreign and defence policies that will be scrutinized in the rest of the book—is that other than being persuaded by the virtues of continuity, Modi gets his ideas from a relatively new source—the novel policy ecosystem in Delhi helmed by the local chapters of reputed American think tanks (Aspen Group, Brookings Institution and Carnegie Endowment for International Peace) funded by Indian corporates. American experts parachute into Delhi from their home base to canvas for this or that Indian policy line. In fact, they often pitch it directly to the prime minister to whom they have ready access, and which advice, while designed to dovetail with US policies, do not serve India's national interests.[114] More on these American think tanks in the next chapter.

Further, his belief in pseudo-science apart, Modi by his own reckoning is a practical man of the world—a doer, not an ideologue; he is a spiritual, not religious, person and has no strong prejudices except two and these are reflected, in one case, in his politics and, in the other case, in his foreign policy.[115] His intense dislike of the Congress, spawned from a young age, got calcified during Indira Gandhi's Emergency into 'hatred' for dynastic politics and animated his subsequent roles in the 1973 'navnirman' movement to oust the Congress from power in Gujarat and to resist the Emergency in 1975–76.[116] On the national stage, it transmogrified during the 2014 general elections into his iconic 'Congress-mukt Bharat' (Congress-free India) politics that has met with success.[117] The BJP now rules in twenty-one of the twenty-nine states in the Indian Union. 'The threat to democracy is bureaucratic and dynastic; it comes from red tape and nepotism,' maintains Modi, neatly conflating systemic ills with Congress rule.[118] But having identified the system's besetting problems he has been unwilling to do anything meaningful to rid India of the millstone round its neck: its lumbering bureaucracy.

The only thing to match his anti-Congressism is his visceral hostility to Pakistan, the other prejudice, which was fired in the 1965 war, surfacing as ultra-patriotism.[119] This hostility was apparently reinforced when he joined the RSS, which is known for its anti-Muslim sentiments. His childhood friendship with Muslim kids in the locality notwithstanding, Modi could not have remained unaffected by the communally polarized society in his home state with antecedents in the razing of the Somnath temple by the Afghan looter Mahmud of Ghazni and in the pre-Independence era by the separate electorates introduced by the 1909 Morley–Minto Reforms. Post-Partition, the religious separation became trickier to mesh with secular politics, resulting in the popular anti-Muslim feelings taking on an anti-Pakistan hue and looping back into state-level politics.[120]

However, the traditional intermeshing of the economic interests of the Hindu and Muslim communities remains firm and has led to a two-faced Gujarati mentality wherein social cohabitation is frowned upon but economic collaboration is considered a fact of life.[121] In Modi's case this jumble of anti-Muslim-qua-anti-Pakistan attitudes stewed in the RSS's Hindutva pot has resulted in his government's plainly schizophrenic policy vis-à-vis Pakistan. It is highlighted by Modi's spontaneous reaching out to his receptive Pakistani counterpart Nawaz Sharif with the invitation to attend his inauguration in May 2014 and by his dropping in, virtually unannounced, on the Pakistan prime minister in his hometown of Jati Umra on the latter's birthday in December 2015.

These gestures generated much warmth in relations but the ceaseless international demonization of Pakistan coupled with the threat of 'surgical strikes' that may be popular with the public has kicked bilateral ties to the basement. It has, in the process, messed up India's great power ambitions by alienating the immediate neighbourhood and, worse, hurt the country's strategic and military ability optimally to meet the challenge posed by China.[122]

Crucial to the success of the BJP government is the combination of Modi's impressive personality, his talent for communicating with the people, the schemes for direct transfer of subsidies to the people and the fairly clean, corruption-free, government he has presided over. However, a growingly illiberal Indian state coupled to the shenanigans of cow worshippers has disaffected Muslims, other minorities and the growing middle classes in the country, and motivated the opposition parties to unify and pushback the BJP in Karnataka and in the cowbelt with electoral victories in 2018. It hasn't helped the Modi government that the Indian economy isn't doing too well, exacerbating problems of poverty, wealth disparity, farmer discontent, youth unemployment, inadequate skilling programmes and rising discontent all round. It is clear the BJP government's failures on the economic and social fronts have shrunk Modi's political capital. Political capital, psychologists researching leadership claim, is an aggregate of three sets of resources: skills, relations and reputation. Skills can be 'hard'—transactional expertise in cutting political deals, transmitting his views to the people and tackling the power centres and vested interests—or they can be 'soft': providing a compelling vision or inspiration to the people. Here the leadership style assumes importance. One style of leadership is repressive, the other more successful style is associated with bargaining and accommodation.[123]

In Modi's case, he switched from the latter style used during his years when he was learning the political ropes and rising in the RSS and BJP hierarchies to the former, when having attained a high position, he tended to use fear in his method of governance, as many even in his own party allege.[124] 'Relations' refers to a politician's ability to gather and grow a following among the masses and the personal connection he is able to establish with them. Hard work may help a politician climb the greasy pole but it is his ability to sway voters that keeps him at the top. 'Reputation' is a factor that is a politician's biggest vulnerability. And the source of his credibility, whence the need to carefully nurse and protect it; Modi has kept it unsullied, eliminating the usual source of corruption—family, by having no truck with his mother, wife or brothers, all of whom continue to lead their normal, small-town, lower-middle class lives. Modi obviously scores high on all these counts.

People believe in Modi and hence believe in his message, so much so an entire political party, the non-dynastic BJP, is wrapped up around him, almost reducing it to a personality cult.[125] As the Congress was during Indira Gandhi's prime ministership when a sycophantic functionary declared: 'Indira is India, and India is Indira.'[126] Modi has become for the BJP what the dynast Rahul Gandhi is to the Congress—the person who is both masthead and mascot. The prime minister's chief lieutenant, Amit Shah, the ruling party president, inadvertently admitted as much. 'After [Swami] Vivekananda, [Modi] has become the torch-bearer of the nation's pride globally,' said Shah and praised the prime minister for ending 'policy paralysis' and 'the era of communal, dynastic and appeasement politics' and, without a hint of irony, 'individual-centric' politics.[127]

There are other attributes of Modi's persona and thinking that have implications for his foreign policy. His belief in hierarchy and hierarchical order translates, as already indicated, into Modi's almost reflexive subservience to top rank-ordered countries. He is thus instinctively placatory towards the US and respectful of China and Russia. Naturally, he embraced the '100-year' relationship with India that Trump talked around and the then US Secretary of State Rex W. Tillerson offered India during his maiden visit to Delhi in October 2017.[128] The US tilt in Modi's policy has, however, a personal angle to it. As an RSS pracharak he backpacked through the US, travelling frugally through twenty-nine American states in the 1990s, and in 1994 was part of an official tour of that country hosted by the US State Department under its Young Leaders programme. That was when he developed an abiding fascination for America. It did not lessen despite the humiliation he suffered in subsequent years owing to the revocation of his tourist visa in 2002 and the denial of a visa three years later while he was chief minister of

Gujarat on the grounds of human rights violations (of Muslims in the 2002 riots).

Normally attired in spiffy native ensembles—closed-collar coats and short-sleeved kurtas—the American influence shows, as one of his biographers noted, in his 'wearing stylish Texan hats along with jeans and T[shirts]' publicly, like in the Rann of Kutch Festival.[129] It was a tremendous investment that Washington made in Modi then that is only beginning to pay off now. A US diplomat's assessment of Modi in the early years of the millennium was, 'He is insular, distrustful person who rules with a small group of advisers . . . He reigns more by fear and intimidation than by inclusiveness and consensus, and is rude and condescending and often derogatory to even high-level party officials. He hoards power, and often leaves his ministers in the cold when making decisions that affect their portfolios.' Another diplomatic cable referred to his 'abrasive' style that leaves him isolated and inspires no loyalty. By 2009, however, sensing change in the air, the US diplomatic view of Modi began changing. He was now seen as a 'star campaigner' and 'the best brand manager India has seen' and as 'exemplify[ing] the entwining of two major themes in modern India—communalism and economic development'.[130]

His beguilement by the US has even overcome Modi's deep prejudice against non-vegetarianism. 'Meat-eating people,' he asserted, 'have a different temperament.'[131] So, are American and Western leaders, and in fact, most leaders in the rest of the world, including Abe and Jinping, all meat-eaters to a man (or woman), outside the pale? Apparently not. His culinary bias apparently shows up only with respect to Muslims in India. Such downside aspects of Modi's persona reflected, for instance, in his government's anti-cow slaughter policy and targeting of the leather processing industry populated by Muslims, echo the disapproval of the Hindu majority with 'secular' parties who pander to the minorities. According to Fareed Zakaria, the Indian-origin CNN commentator, this has 'made India more democratic' but also 'less liberal'.[132]

That a leader matters and entities take on the personality of the man or woman heading it are by now truisms. The Indian cricket team playing under the in-your-face competitive captain Virat Kohli reflects his attacking attitude and will to win. The prime minister's belligerence in the external world likewise is mirrored by the Indian people. Modi's toughness against Pakistan, with Islamabad threatened at every turn by 'surgical strikes,' is mirrored in the people, various regional outfits and the public opinion becoming rancorous about anything Pakistani, including agitations (such as by the Mumbai-based Shiv Sena) against visas for Pakistani actors and musicians shooting for Bollywood films, and playing cricket and hockey matches with that country, even though such sports encounters attract houseful crowds and Pakistani actors, vocalists and musicians have a large fan following in India. Underlying Modi's anti-Pakistan stance may be the Hindutva politics and the notion of 'akhand Bharat' or 'undivided India' and the perception of Pakistan as an abomination, which also fetches electoral benefits.

The relentless demonization of Pakistan, ostensibly on the terrorism issue, when even India seems to be paying back in the same coin with support for the Balochistan freedom fighters and pressuring the Indian Muslim community on trivial social matters such as beef-eating, 'love jihad', etc, have predictably resulted in the country becoming noticeably less tolerant, less liberal, more anti-Pakistan and more anti-minority since the advent of the Modi regime. Meanwhile, the Indian Muslim has all but disappeared from the domestic political reckoning with even the Congress becoming aware of the pitfalls of too close an association with Muslim causes.[133] While the BJP capitalizes on majoritarian prejudice, which gets reflected in polls showing the popular perception of Pakistan and its border dispute with India as the chief threat, Modi's China policy has emphasized peaceful resolution of the undelineated border with Tibet as a means of mitigating the far more strategically difficult situation Beijing has created for India in the north and the north-east by deliberately and with great foresight befriending the adjoining states that India has offended with its big-brotherly attitude. So, Pakistan, posing only a linear threat, could have been dealt with by a similar China policy—of composite talks on Kashmir and other outstanding disputes at one level, and normal trade and economic relations with potential for cross-investments and free cultural exchanges at the other level.

Except, an FTA is on the anvil with China, which would lead to an economic swamping of the India market by cheap Chinese goods.

This when economically co-opting Pakistan and the other neighbouring states into the Indian economy and plugging them into the vast Indian market would, for instance, yield rich politico-economic and strategic dividend without any attendant dangers. Alas, there's venom in Modi's thinking about Pakistan, in part also because in his deeply ingrained notions of hierarchy and order, a lowly Pakistan, an inferior, ought to be submissive but is instead insolent and has to be put in its place. China, contrarily, has by dint of its own effort, become a superior nation and needs to be handled, per Modi's policy, with care, caution and empathy, notwithstanding the fact that it is both an imminent and immanent military threat and security challenge. So, as regards Pakistan, Modi's conciliatory approach to China has made the Indian people sanguine, lulling them into believing that it poses less of a danger than Pakistan.[134]

As a one-man government, Modi is credited with being able to 'walk the talk'.[135] What's less certain is whether his 'talk'—his vision and plans for the country, especially in the external and national security domains—were ever really expansive and ambitious enough, or simply cobbled together to provide him a platform to burnish his personal image and leadership credentials. What's also in doubt is the manner of his 'walking' or realizing his policies. Bereft of an overarching and practicable strategic vision—something he has never bothered to articulate—such actions as his government has taken were never as ruthless and single-minded as they needed to engage in a drag-out fight with China.

Asked by an Israeli TV journalist about his vision, Modi reduced it to yet another slogan, 'Reform, Perform and Transform', coupled to a set of government programmes to tackle the country's problems of illiteracy and homelessness.[136] Even without a grand vision, the implementation of Modi's foreign and military policies, most of them with continuity as their defining principle, has been tepid at best. Assuming his secret design to make India a standout nation is sought to be achieved by concentrating all the power and authority of the government in himself, it has worked against Modi's effectively executing it. He is like a juggler with too many balls in the air, unable to keep his eye on any particular policy ball. Given Modi's larger-than-life image and personality that no other Indian politician can match, the results of his exertions are a dispassionate metric to judge his policies by. Unfortunately for him, the outcomes of his policies seem only slightly better than when that 'shrinking lily' of a prime minister, Manmohan Singh, with very little political power, ran the show.

[3]

Creeper-vine Foreign Policy

'*Most vines travel vertically if they have a means of support, such as a pole, a fence or a wall*'—homeguides.sfgate.com

CATHERINE THE GREAT of Russia was in two minds about converting the 1766 Commercial Treaty she had signed with Britain into a military alliance. Britain was the victor in the Seven Years War that saw its rivals Spain reduced and France defeated. The empress finally decided against it on the advice of Countess Yekaterina Vorontsova-Dashkova, whom she appointed much later as the head of what became the prestigious Russian Academy of Sciences. The intellectually gifted countess convinced the empress that Russia was too big and potentially a great power itself to ally with another great power, and that doing so when European power was hanging in the balance would end up demeaning Russia's standing and endangering its security.[1]

One wishes the Indian prime minister Narendra Modi had an adviser with Dashkova's intellect and insight to guide him on foreign policy. Then he would not be misreading the emerging distribution of global power and mistaking the expedient policy he is pursuing for something that serves the country's enduring national interests. International politics is racked to an unusual degree by doubt, uncertainty and the fluidity of power, much as it was in Catherine's time. It was a Dashkovan kind of thinking that persuaded the classical historian in Jawaharlal Nehru to do the statesman-like thing and alight on non-alignment as the most compelling posture for a down-in-the-dumps India to gain from the competing attentions of the two Cold War protagonists—the United States and the Soviet Union—while preserving its freedom of action and choice. A Polish economist from that time, Michal Kalecki, an admirer of India's non-alignment policy, likened it to 'a clever calf sucking milk from two cows'.[2] Nehru instinctively understood that to be too intimate with any big power is to sign away the hope of playing any independent role.

Since the mid-1990s, however, this basic precept of India's foreign policy has been progressively undermined—first by the Vajpayee government coining the phrase 'strategic autonomy' as cover for its policy of getting close to Washington while retaining the room for manoeuvre that the hoary concept of 'non-alignment' inherently possessed, and the later governments of Manmohan Singh and now Narendra Modi carrying on in the same vein.[3] In pursuing this policy, Delhi paid the price demanded by Washington—accepting the US conditions of capping India's strategic capabilities short of the hydrogen bomb and the ICBM, eventuating in the Manmohan Singh government taking the next step of losing the country its nuclear sovereignty (no nuclear testing on the threat of abrogation of the India–US civilian nuclear cooperation deal). The discarding of even the pretence of strategic autonomy as organizing principle has reached a point in Modi's tenure where Delhi seems more convinced than ever before that leaning more and more on the US will be worthwhile and fetch India untold economic, diplomatic and security dividend.

This despite US President Trump making no bones about the fact that he is interested in India only to the extent that it continues to buy US-made military hardware, partners American security ventures in the Indian Ocean region, provides military assistance in the form of land, naval and air bases for US forces in the extended region (as per the 29 August 2016 Logistics Exchange Agreement) and helps his country retain jobs, increase employment and ensure the health and commercial prospects of American industry. He intends all this to solidify his presidency and his personal reputation as a great 'deal-maker', all under the rubric of countering China. James J. Carafano, a member of Trump's transition team, confirmed this at an interactive session at the Confederation of Indian Industry, saying that where India is concerned the US President is majorly into pushing defence and energy exports, and in cooperation with India and Japan, to leveraging private sector investment to counter the Chinese BRI. Contradicting the US government stress on military hardware sales is Carafano's take on what he thinks is Trump's 'conceptualization' of Asia. It is 'broader', he says, than George W. Bush's 'muscular' engagement policy and Obama's selective 'disengagement' combined with a 'pivot to Asia'. Trump, according to Carafano, is intent not on containing China but on 'minimizing its destabilizing tendencies'. Because 'India is at the heart and centre' of this geostrategic policy, the Trump White House, he says, means to identify what the Indian government wants from Washington in terms of advanced military technologies, for instance, and to see how that can be delivered. This includes drafting enabling laws and, at the executive level, fine-tuning rules and regulations to facilitate it, rather than trying to fit India's demands within existing laws and regulatory schemes.[4]

The troubling part of Carafano's view of Trump's policy is its aim: 'the minimizing' of China's 'destabilizing tendencies' in Asia. Because destabilization will obviously and naturally be judged from the US perspective, there will be more disagreement than consensus and India, as the lesser power, will end up litigating with the US government on issues important to it. This is not an encouraging template for cooperation and only emphasizes the dangers of trusting Washington to do the right thing by India. In any case, Modi has apparently not focused on this aspect of Trump's policy at all. He seems rather to have bought into the notion that a US-educated Australian analyst articulated soon after the prime minister's first flurry of foreign trips to the ASEAN and G20 summits, Japan, the US and Australia in 2014, and which is diligently parroted by the bulk of Indian commentators ever since. Heralding with considerable foresight the 'end of [India's] strategic autonomy', David Brewster argued that this concept while a 'nice sounding' principle is a 'mistake', 'an excuse to avoid building connections' with the US and its allies, and that 'just as economic interdependence actually enhances a nation's economic power, strategic connectedness [with the US] enhances [India's] military power' and holding on to strategic autonomy distracts

India from its 'focus on outcomes'. He concluded with the questionable statement that 'India's sovereignty will come to be measured by its actual ability to exert national power and influence . . . by its ability to engage' with the US and the West.

In practical terms, however, such a view suggests that the West will judge India's sovereignty by the extent to which it is willing to dilute it by becoming part of the US alliance system in Asia and the world.[5] At the very least, this sort of thinking is to tread dangerously into Orwell's 'newspeak' territory where war is peace and subservience freedom. Further, such motivated and ahistorical analysis wrongly couples the benefits from fostering economic ties with the US with security gains from strategically linking up with it, when economic and national security policy are separate policy spheres. A country can have serious disputes with another country and simultaneously have mutually fruitful economic ties. To wit, Sino-Indian relations and China's managing in the last forty-odd years to forge the strongest possible economic, commercial and trade links with America and yet emerge as not only its virtual economic equal but also as a strategic-military rival and peer-competitor. Of course, the difference is that India is not China, and in Delhi there has been no Deng Xiaoping, only a succession of small-visioned political leaders devoid of strategic sense who were majorly into prosecuting what former prime minister Manmohan Singh called 'short-term maximizing' policies to please Washington. This basically involves doing the US's bidding rather than exploiting the chinks in American policy as Deng's China did to gain fairly free access to the US market and build itself into a multitrillion-dollar economy and far from conceding even an iota of its strategic space or liberty, in fact, expanding it.

For Modi to stay with the economic–security interdependence line in foreign policy without modifying it to suit India's unique geostrategic circumstances is for the country to once again miss out, this time on a substantial de-globalization trend owing to technological advances that are changing the nature of industrial production and military capabilities and making great power patronage passé. Globalization occurred due to four factors: 'extensivity, the extensiveness of interdependence; intensivity, the rise in the number of networked and interdependent relationships; velocity, the speed with which these networks transmit the effects of interdependence; and impact, the degree to which the interdependencies extend into cultures, states or networked societies'.[6] While once significant, globalization is giving way gradually to de-globalization, which is occurring owing to two not unrelated trends in technology, one economic–industrial, the other military. Automated manufacture—artificial intelligence, robotics and 3D printing (also called additive manufacturing)—that today constitutes 10 per cent of all manufacturing will by 2025 increase to 25 per cent. It is making global production chains and economic intermeshing both increasingly obsolete and unnecessary, undermining the basic logic of geoeconomics and leading increasingly to the localization of production, services and agriculture.[7] De-globalization is already beginning to affect India because of the dilution of the extensivity and intensivity factors as the American market overseen by Trump begins to detach itself economically from the outside world, including Indian manufactures, outsourced back office operations and other engineering and financial services.

The other trend is of weaponry becoming small, smart, lethal and cheap and, therefore, available in large numbers to even the poorest and weakest nations, which are now able to impose potentially high costs and deter even the biggest powers from interfering in their affairs.[8] This rids smaller countries of their security fears and motivation to seek big power protection, dating in the process such concepts as 'collective security' and 'extended deterrence'. Thus, the Philippines, for instance, would see nothing positive coming out of invoking the 1953 security treaty with the US as long as it was adequately armed with large numbers of, say, supersonic BrahMos cruise missiles to thwart any future attempts by the Chinese Navy to wrest away more of the Philippine islands falling within the former's Nine Dash Line claim in the South China Sea.[9] The trend towards smaller, cheaper and smarter weapons, because it will mean more easily affordable security, will free poorer and weaker states from being easily intimidated by stronger ones. Big power bullying manifested in the modern version of the old-style 'gunboat diplomacy' may for all intents and purposes become a thing of the past.[10]

The global political landscape that will likely obtain will revert to a 'fragmented' international system of ultra-sovereign states, with each country responsible for its own security with the desire for economic well-being permitting FTAs, bilateral accords and industrial partnerships. This to say that international trade will increase but have less collateral or spillover effect into the security realm.[11] These convergent trends, writes T.X. Hammes, a former US Marines colonel and one of Washington's well-regarded 'ideas man', will result in Americans being 'no longer . . . willing to underwrite international security with their tax dollars [and] may demand a return to a limited strategic concept of defending the hemisphere and assuring access to the global commons'.[12] It will reinforce the urge for security self-sufficiency in the Asian states and their need to arm themselves appropriately. A more isolationist and recessive US under Trump anticipates this de-globalized future. This may persuade its allies and friends to turn inward as well.

Since Independence, India has been a free-rider on security offered as international public good by the US (except during the 1971 war when the Treaty of Friendship and Cooperation signed with the Soviet Union allowed Indira Gandhi to cleave Pakistan unmolested by the US).[13] That period is ending just as the Indian government with Modi at the wheel is getting serious about globalization and economic interdependence and trying to dovetail the country into the global economy. 'Globalization and global economy is on a growth trajectory—no one can stop that,' Modi asserted, somewhat mistakenly. 'The market will remain global [and] we will have to develop accordingly.'[14] This makes him a believer in a situation that is gradually ceasing to exist. Coming in at the tail end of the globalization phenomenon and generally misreading international reality has costs, especially if this also includes leaning on the US as crutch—as seems to be the case. This is recognized by the MEA as a problem.

'After decades of American internationalism,' said former foreign secretary Subrahmanyam Jaishankar at the 2017 Raisina Dialogue, 'we are finally face to face with its nationalism. Now it is true that Russia and Europe too became less internationalist in their outlook. Emerging powers, including regional ones, have shown little inclinations in that direction. India actually is an exception. So, is nationalism the new normal and can India make a difference—by being different?'[15] This would suggest that Modi's foreign policy is prepared to swim against the international current of nationalism with the big fish—the US, Russia and China—in the van. It is a tack that does not hold out much hope, considering Delhi mismanaged the country's affairs in terms of setting India on the course to great power when the milieu was helpful. With the conditions turning less conducive, its chances of getting things right are negligible, unless Modi is happy to see India as a second-rate power in thrall to the US, Russia, China or some other passing big power.

There is a certain poignancy to Jaishankar's question, however, because, post-Nehru, India has been the perennial latecomer and laggard in almost every sector because its government, elected rulers, policy establishment and military have proved especially inept in trend-spotting. Always late and damagingly low and slow on the learning curve, progress has inevitably been fitful in every field. So the Modi government is embarking on economic interlinks with the US and the world just when the era of geoeconomics is ending. Worse, geopolitics-wise, it is shifting from 'strategic autonomy' and relying mainly on Russia for critical assistance in the strategic military field to wrapping itself around the US for security, technology and political support. It is doing so at a time when America, unwilling any longer to exhaust its resources—already stretched by unending wars in distant locales—is, under Trump, calling it a day. Moreover, the axiom attending on Washington's unwillingness to any longer permit free-riding by its friends means that India will have to continue paying the price demanded by Trump for such security and security-related measures that Delhi hopes to avail of, just as US NATO allies and Japan and South Korea are asked to do.

What will naturally follow is pressure on India to follow up the Logistics Support Agreement (LSA)—a relabelled LEMOA (Logistics Exchange Memorandum of Agreement)—with signing the other 'foundational accords'. These include the Communications Interoperability and Security Memorandum of Agreement (CISMOA) that has been notionally changed to adjust to India's sensitivity and is called COMCASA (Communications Compatibility and Security Agreement), and the Basic Exchange and Cooperation Agreement for Geospatial Cooperation (BECA) that Washington has been pushing since the George W. Bush administration. Except, neither the LSA nor the COMCASA are really necessary. The former formalized an arrangement that has existed since the 1991 US Operation Desert Storm mounted against Iraqi ingress into Kuwait, during which American transport aircraft and ships transiting from the east to the war theatre were routinely refuelled and replenished in Mumbai on a barter basis to avoid negotiating the complex accounting systems in each other's country and the handling of cash. COMCASA, sought by Washington ostensibly to promote interoperability, will override objections by the Indian military which fears that it will enable seamless penetration horizontally and vertically of the official Indian communications grid, including the most sensitive strategic communications network. It will also be a red line for Russia because such penetration will compromise many of its advanced military assets in India's employ, such as the Akula-II-class nuclear-powered attack submarine leased to the Indian Navy.

In fact, the US makes no bones about the fact that COMCASA will allow original US communications equipment on board US-sourced platforms such as the C-17/C-130 transport aircraft and the P-8i maritime surveillance aircraft to enable both forward and backward integration of the Indian security communications network with the US's global communications grid. In other words, it will mean that nothing in the Indian government and military will remain secret but it is being justified by Washington on the laughable basis that it will ensure the security of VIPs in India![16] The US pressure has apparently worked and the Modi government has been softened up enough to consider signing COMCASA.[17] Because the Indian leaders' fear of security lapses is being played on by the US, it implies Modi's lack of confidence in Indian intelligence agencies and the armed services to protect him and his colleagues and, in the larger context, the country.

The LSA, on its part, has ended up re-hyphenating India with Pakistan, as Islamabad has a similar accord but more extensive experience of dealing with the US and in extracting reimbursements from Washington for sustaining and servicing American forces in Afghanistan. This has required Islamabad to jump through procedural hoops and for the Pakistani Army to face US congressional scrutiny. By signing the LSA, Modi has exposed India and the Indian military to this kind of public humiliation in another country. Apologists for the accords claim they will extend the operational reach of the Indian Navy and Air Force. But why should the Indian government opt for such a short-term salve when the long-term solution of developing distant bases (Duqm on the Oman coast, the Agalegas in Mauritius, northern Mozambique, Assumption Island in the Seychelles, the Farkhor base in Ainee, Tajikistan, Trincomalee in Sri Lanka, Sabang in Indonesia, et al.) is readily available?

This is happening, moreover, at a time when Russia is recovering its Cold War elan and China is stepping up to fill the power vacuum created by the receding US. Trump, Putin and Xi are apprehended as constituting 'the axis of disorder' with Trump opposing free trade and alliances, Putin finding the current order directly threatening his regime and therefore seeking to undercut it and Xi in a hurry for China to displace the US from its pre-eminence in Asia.[18] This is not an occasion for Delhi to careen into trouble by sidling up to Washington, but rather to pause and consider whether the country is on the right track. A dominant China in Asia is not in India's interest. But neither is jumping into a strategic bedfellowship with US the answer for the looming dangers. Any kind of crypto-alliance with America will impose shackles on Indian foreign and military policy (regarding relations with Iran, Russia, and other countries the US may fall out with)—ask Asian states that have felt the lash of the US's coercive alliance diplomacy.[19] The loss of policy freedom, latitude and choices, estrangement from old and tested friends such as Russia, distancing from natural partners like Iran and the consequent shrinking of India to the status of a Pakistan— as just another junior partner of America—is the outcome that the Modi government has apparently not considered in any depth or seriousness.

It is a situation compounded by the rapid advances in technology that are shoving India's dated industrial-age military into obsolescence and rendering it unemployable as a diplomatic tool—assuming the Modi government ever means to use it, which, on the basis of India's inaction to move against the Abdulla Yameen regime in the Maldives, Delhi has clearly signalled it is not willing to. Adding to the country's woes is the Modi regime's befuddled implementation of its Make in India programme that is set to squander national wealth on importing antiquated US weaponry: F-16 and F-18 combat aircraft and screwdriver technologies in the guise of 'technology transfer' at the expense of indigenous defence industrial capabilities. (More on this in Chapter 6.) It reflects the knack the Indian government has developed over the years for always doing the wrong thing, taking the wrong policy turn at the wrong time and being on the wrong side of history.

Steering Problems

Narasimha Rao steered 'a deft course', as his foreign secretary Krishnan Srinivasan put it, 'between nationalist aspirations in the security field and the need to keep the USA in friendship and positive play', when the essential wisdom of the Nehruvian modus operandi was retained but barely.[20] The new concept of 'strategic autonomy' floated by the BJP government of Vajpayee proved expedient, conforming to the party's rightist orientation and justifying the nineteen sessions of the Jaswant Singh–Strobe Talbott 'strategic dialogue' that culminated in the Next Steps in Strategic Partnership (NSSP).[21] The NSSP was achieved at a substantive strategic cost to India—Delhi agreed in general terms to curtail the natural advancement of the country's strategic arsenal towards high-yield and tailored thermonuclear armaments and to cap Indian missiles at the intermediate (5500 km) range.[22] It was a concession made precisely to keep the US 'in play' at a time when the comfortable certainties of the Cold War had been replaced by the insecurity-breeding uncertainties of an international system trying to find its feet in a new century.

It is not for nothing that President George W. Bush's Secretary of State Condoleezza Rice revealingly described the NSSP as 'a turning point and the camel's nose under the [Indian] tent'.[23] Her reference may have been to improving the India–US relationship, but it aptly defines its uses to slowly solidify and gradually extend a strategic partnership on American terms which with the progress on the foundational accords front is exactly what's happened since then. This turn in policy became a fullish slide into the American camp with Prime Minister Manmohan Singh agreeing to the 2008 civilian nuclear cooperation deal. Delhi had hoped this deal would immeasurably elevate bilateral relations—it has not. The US has by these means succeeded, however, in bottling India's nuclear testing option and preventing it from becoming a credible thermonuclear weapons state with long-range strike capability and an independent power. Delhi's sticking to its 'voluntary moratorium' on testing has resulted in the freezing of its nuclear weapons at the 20 kiloton fission technology level (as the fusion device tested in the S-1 test on 11 May 1998 was a dud with only partial combustion of the Lithium-6 fusion fuel).[24]

India's institutional habit of respecting the letter and, even more, the spirit, of agreements it signs with foreign countries is something that no great power or would-be great power ever does. Indeed, bilateral and international agreements are respected by big powers only to the extent it suits their national interest. Thus, the US, the pillar of the 1968 Non-Proliferation Treaty, conveniently ignored it and was purposely blind to Beijing's missile-arming Pakistan in the late 1970s because it needed Pakistan as the CIA base to stage Afghan Mujahideen actions against the Soviet military in Afghanistan. And China pays lip service to UNCLOS but flouts its provisions in the South China Sea. What the Indian government seems not to appreciate is that international agreements are to be followed only if it serves its purposes and should not be seen as a constraint on any policy or action in support of its sovereign national interest. The trouble is that Indian leaders are seduced by Western praise for India's 'responsible state' behaviour and show of restraint when these same traits are not exhibited by the powers themselves. It is a policy liability that has convinced Washington that it can thus prevail on Delhi to not do anything it doesn't want India to do.

There's already evidence of this with Delhi not using potential trigger events—North Korea's repeated testing of nuclear and thermonuclear weapons at its Punggye-ri test site and its test-firing of intermediate range and genuinely intercontinental range Hwasong ballistic missiles at a rapid clip, Pakistan's nuclear build-up and China's modernization of its nuclear weapons inventory. Any other country possessing a half-baked deterrent such as India does would have seen these incidents as precursor to these strategically lethal technologies being transferred to Pakistan as part of the rogue nuclear triad dynamic (China, North Korea and Pakistan), and justified an immediate resumption of testing to put in place a certifiable thermonuclear arsenal and to green light the development and production on a war footing of multi-warheaded ICBMs with multiple independently targetable re-entry vehicle (MIRV) technology. MIRV designs, incidentally, have been on the shelf of the Defence Research and Development Organisation's (DRDO) Advanced Systems Laboratory in Hyderabad since the early 2000s.[25] That Delhi has done none of these things is particularly galling considering that high yield-to-weight hydrogen weapons atop ICBMs are gaining currency as the new arbiters of global power, a lesson driven home by an impoverished North Korea with the mojo, brandishing thermonuclear-warheaded long-range missiles to make strategic deterrence more 'adversarial' and keeping Trump's America at bay.[26]

Moreover, with the certainty of what Pyongyang perfects with Chinese technical and material help today being in Islamabad's hands tomorrow, the Pakistani strategic arsenal too will inevitably progress fast towards thermonuclearization even as the Indian government twiddles its thumbs with its 'do-nothing nuclear policy'.[27] India, armed with just the puny 20 kiloton fission device—its only reliable, tested, and proven weapon—will be the 'odd' country out in the triangular India-China-Pakistan deterrence game. An unscrupulous China, having previously armed Pakistan with nuclear missiles, will use the North Korean channel to upgrade the Pakistani deterrent to the fusion level against India, which acts unmindful of the danger heading its way.

Delhi's commitment to the US to not do things like resume nuclear testing, which it should have done before signing the deal not to do them, when juxtaposed against Kim Jong-un's acquiring hydrogen weapons and ICBMs, cocking a snook at Washington, shrugging off the intense US-led international pressure and buying his regime an insurance policy against assault on its sovereignty by any power shows up Modi in bad light. It has exposed India to a far greater strategic risk—the pincer of a thermonuclear-armed China and Pakistan—just to please and pacify Washington. The fact is that starting with the reticence of the Vajpayee and Manmohan Singh governments and now the Modi regime in procuring proven thermonuclear weapons with new underground test explosions and ICBMs, India has assumed the status of a 'lesser nuclear state', a category, incidentally, that Indira Gandhi had rejected for the country when she initiated projects indigenously to produce strategic armaments of the type possessed by the superpowers, namely nuclear-powered submarines firing ballistic missiles and long-range Agni missiles.[28]

Further nuclear testing is the key and absolutely essential, but the Indian government has not seen the light. The Indian public as also the lead Indian negotiators of the nuclear deal—Foreign Secretary Shyam Saran and Joint Secretary (Americas) S. Jaishankar—had been forewarned about the shape of things to come by a small, active and technically competent set of opponents at home, whose uncompromising campaign mostly in the print media to nix the nuclear deal almost succeeded (but for certain Indian politicians in touch with Washington and the shenanigans in Parliament before the vote on this deal on 8 July 2008).[29]

There was also ample warning about the US's hard-nosed non-proliferation intent and thrust prior to negotiations on this deal. President George W. Bush's NSA, Stephen Hadley, told Strobe Talbott, President Bill Clinton's deputy secretary of state, ere he got down to negotiating the NSSP in the early 2000s, 'We're not going to unravel the [1968] NPT [Non-Proliferation Treaty] for the Indians. We're not going to let whatever is permitted in [commercial space launch and nuclear commerce] bleed over into their military missile or nuclear weapons program. We'll have firewalls to prevent that.' Another high-ranking US official told Talbott that 'when we get [to an agreement, it] won't be Nirvana for the Indians'.[30] Talbott, it may be recalled, was the person who had extracted from Jaswant Singh in their 'strategic dialogue' the undertaking that India would voluntarily stop short of securing thermonuclear armaments and very long-range missiles. According to an old India hand, former US ambassador Teresita Schaffer, the success of these negotiations centred on the fact that 'India had made a unilateral promise not to test [again to get the deal going which] it was quite unwilling to turn into an agreement . . . [and that the Indian negotiator Jaishankar] walked right up to the edge of that . . . but they didn't step over the line.'

So the agreement text bridged this gap between the US seeking termination of testing and India walking around it, as per Schaffer, with 'a very long passage—3–6 pages, single-spaced, very fine print, heavily lawyerized language . . . to spell out everything that would have to happen if either party felt it was obliged to cutoff cooperation . . . It talks about different types of consultation, what has to happen when, and how long it's to take when. But what it does preserve for the US is the option to respond.'[31] More than Washington abrogating the deal, what the Indian government feared was the US nuclear forces targeting an India armed with thermonuclear-warheaded ICBMs, which likelihood was communicated to the Indian government. It is the standard operating procedure of the US Strategic Command to bring within its threat ambit any country, including non-allied friendly states such as India, with armaments and delivery systems to reach continental US targets.[32] Why this normal precautionary measure should so unsettle Delhi is hard to understand except as the Indian government's trademark quality of taking no risks whatsoever, however remote. The pity is that Indian leaders have rarely shown the patience to wait out not just adversaries but friendly states bent on goring their ox at India's expense.

North Korea's pugnacity was on exhibition at the time a nuclear deal was sort of jelling in Delhi and Washington, with the 2006 Six Party talks to de-nuclearize the Korean Peninsula on the table. There was every prospect that Pyongyang would test again and develop long-range missiles as Kim Jong-un had warned it would do. Why wasn't the MEA more on the ball and why didn't it advise Prime Minister Manmohan Singh that a nuclear deal was not time-critical? With China's nuclear proliferation connections with Pakistan in mind and North Korea's impending nuclear test that year providing a legitimate reason for India to resume testing and firming up its thermonuclear weapons profile, India could have stalled the US pressure for compromise until after India had completed a series of new open-ended nuclear tests to remove doubts about its fusion weaponry. The US was in no position to react punitively as it had done in knee-jerk fashion after the 1998 tests considering that by then China was lighting up the US threat radar and the first signs of the George W. Bush administration perceiving India as a desirable partner in Asia were apparent.[33]

If, as foreign secretary and later NSA Shivshankar Menon makes clear, Delhi had by then accepted and internalized the Chinese negotiating tactic of treating time as a diplomatic asset and not forcing a final border solution with China, why was the same metric not applied to the nuclear deal? Given that by almost any reckoning the situation in Asia was turning to India's advantage; if it had in the interregnum seized the North Korean explosive nuclear test as reason for its own resumed testing, it would have placed India in a better position to secure a nuclear bargain with America to subserve Indian interests.[34] Mind that the 2002 National Security Strategy drafted by Philip Zelikow, the very influential counsellor in the Colin Powell–run US State Department, had noted that

> differences remain including India's nuclear and missile programs . . . But while in the past these concerns may have dominated our thinking about India, today we start with a view of India as a growing power with which we have common strategic interests. Through a growing partnership with India we can best address any differences and shape a dynamic future.[35]

Ignoring the emerging advantageous milieu for India, Delhi rushed pell-mell into a nuclear deal that for all intents and purposes surrendered the country's freedom to develop high-yield fusion weapons and ICBMs. It also compromised India militarily and politically, with the Manmohan Singh regime even preparing the ground for it by legislating the 2005 Weapons of Mass Destruction Act to control the export of dual-use technologies to comply with US law.[36]

The two foreign secretaries during Manmohan Singh's tenure, Shyam Saran and Shivshankar Menon, with the latter swearing by 'strategic autonomy' in a strange twist to the concept, ended up mocking the very notion of India as power balancer in the 21st century between the US and China, US and Russia, and Russia and China by rejecting the 'balance of power' system itself as so '19th century'.[37] This seems to be the MEA outlook at large. Natwar Singh, also a former diplomat and external affairs minister in Manmohan Singh's first term, wondered out loud often enough times, including when there were US officials around that, with the Cold War ended, 'who[m] India is to be non-aligned against'.[38] The inference to be drawn is that with no superpowers to contend with, the balance of power system was obsolete and India's balancing role had lost its salience and, hence, that siding openly with the US will be without cost and have benefits. It is a line that establishment- and America-friendly media commentators in the Indian media keep embellishing. As an example, one of them wrote, 'Half-baked ideas about strategic autonomy and preserving the legacy of non-alignment . . . constrained India's ability to build a genuine partnership with the US.'[39] Except, that was so 21st century. Since then, Russia is back in a big way, China is on a roll and America's old Asian ally Japan is contemplating nuclear weapons for its security because Trump is proving more reluctant than Obama to take on China.

The fact is the international reality of sovereign states-qua-balance of power system is not only a constant but with the technology trends discussed earlier it is being reaffirmed. This is the nature of the evolving beast and in its essentials it is no different from the situation that existed when the Chinese Empire was at its zenith in the Tang Dynasty some 200 years before Alexander the Great invaded north-western India, during the reign of Charlemagne, when Britain worked its 'Continental Strategy' and Catherine the Great managed a budding Russian Empire, when Otto von Bismarck waged wars to establish Germany's supremacy in Europe, in the nearly fifty years of the Cold War, and in any of the historical epochs in-between. So flawed a take on the international system, in which balancing of power is a constant, reflects poorly on the quality of 'professional advice' available to successive Indian prime ministers.

In this respect, a recent study deconstructing the IFS and its functioning is pertinent. Talking about the quality of the IFS, it reports a foreign secretary lamenting that 'Now, we might be wonderful and very efficient, but we are not that efficient or that good. I mean it really is a problem.' As regards the quality of advice given the prime minister, it depends on the intellectual quality of the entry-level officers; if they are of inferior quality so will be the advice offered by them as they rise to important positions within the MEA. According to this book, this quality, steadily declining since the mid-1970s, had reached so low a point by 2008 that the last vacancy in the IFS was filled by a person 709th in the merit list. By 2014 over half the 483-strong IFS-A cadre comprised people who entered via quotas and the reserved category.[40] (The IFS-B cadre comprises the clerical staff at headquarters and in Indian outposts abroad.) That the policy of denigrating the balancing of regional and international power is the template for Modi is, therefore, a matter of continuing concern because it confirms the prime minister's personal US-leaning proclivities. The difference between the present and the previous Indian government is that Modi is less politically constrained than was Manmohan Singh (who had to threaten to resign before the Congress chief Sonia Gandhi permitted the nuclear deal with the US to go through) and seems determined on following a path that could end up taking an India used to leaning on some power or the other beyond 'strategic partnership' with America into client status, whether he so intends it or not. Ironically, it is happening just when India is acquiring, however unevenly, the economic and technological resources to ascend on its own.

In an international system that involves sovereign states competing for power and slivers of advantage, the natural tendency in case any one country becomes too powerful and throws its weight about is for the other nations to automatically band together and balance its power and prevent its excesses. If China is that power everybody fears, countries around it are naturally going to gang up to stop it. So that's a ready solution for neutralizing the would-be Asian hegemon, in which situation no special advantages accrue to India from siding prominently with America—an unreliable, extra-territorial power that can withdraw to its fortress behind the moats of the Pacific and Atlantic oceans whenever it chooses to do so or, in the case of Trump, on his whim, and especially if it stands to lose much in a live-fire confrontation with China. It is an option not available to Asian states that have to deal with the putative hegemon on their land and maritime borders the best they can with the resources they are able singly or jointly to muster.

Moreover, as the heftiest nation on the Chinese periphery with a long-standing territorial dispute to boot, smaller Asian countries in the Indo-Pacific region, including Japan and Australia, are mindful of how Delhi deals with China. Thus, the developments in the seventy-day Doklam confrontation at the Bhutan–India–China trijunction in the late summer of 2017 were closely watched by the states in South East Asia and farther east. That India stood its ground in that face-off with Xi's 'new China' helped strengthen the view that India has some steel in its spine after all, and that that it is a credible potential security provider in the region, a role Delhi has curiously hesitated to fill.[41] On the other hand, the US, safely separated from Asia by the expanse of the Pacific Ocean and whose enormous cross-investments with China are such as to inhibit Washington's moves, is far more reluctant to rile Beijing on any 'Asian' issue. This renders America suspect as a reliable security partner for Asian littoral and offshore states in their bigger mission to somehow frustrate the realization by Xi of his geopolitical tianxia design of Asian states peacefully acquiescing in a 'harmonious' order presided over by China.[42]

In the circumstances, China's smaller neighbours have to delicately balance their individual economic ties with China, which makes them susceptible to pressure, and their associating with the US as security guarantor, which China frowns upon. In this context, Trump's habit of sweet-talking Beijing is not reassuring.[43] Washington's disinclination to clash with China economically and militarily is not an anomalous development that will go away with the ending of the Trump presidency but, given the enormous economic stakes the US and China have in each other, it is, to use Xi's favourite phrase, the 'new normal' that India, Asian states and the rest of the world have to contend with. There is also the matter of the Chinese reaction. Asian countries pivoting to India in a loose coalition is unlikely to spark the same sense of foreboding in Beijing as would their leaning towards an activist America. This is because India is less wealthy and military-wise less capable, and even a grouping of Asian nations around it would, ipso facto, be less threatening to China. But to draw together such a coalition, unfortunately, is not the primary aim of Modi's policy, closing in with the US is. The downside of this last is the gradual separation from an old and trusted friend, Russia, which will disturb the international power equipoise and have bad geostrategic consequences for India. Moreover, the strategic wisdom of getting intimate with America as core policy given its downside is perplexing, as is the downplaying by Modi of India's role as balancer in Asia and the world. This issue warrants a deeper examination.

The Dashkovan logic of India's potential and ability to rise on its own, if so visioned, willed and properly guided by its political leaders to do so, is obviously lost on Modi and his advisers, as it escaped the two previous prime ministers. The kernel of the hard policy turn to America in recent years lies in Modi's personal admiration for that country. His beguilement with America, other than his travel in the 1990s on $500 Delta Airlines tickets that allowed foreigners unlimited flights, was as a rising member of the RSS–BJP complex. He availed of hospitality provided him by the Sangh sympathizers among the Indian diaspora in the US—whence his great regard for US-based NRIs. These visits were followed by US government–sponsored trips to cultivate promising foreign politicians, and in 1999 under the aegis of the Fulbright American Studies Institute a trip during which he partook of a month-long 'young diplomat' course and the Congress of World Religions in America. These visits were supplemented thereafter by more frequent travels to that country, often with party elders to raise funds.[44]

The modernity, material plenty, intellectual wealth, technological advancement and civic order in that country must have dazzled Modi with his impoverished *mofussil* background. It perhaps did four things: instil in him an abiding love and respect for America and all things American, mould his thinking of technology and free market as possible engines of change, shape his brand of aspirational politics, which won him state elections for over a decade in Gujarat and the 2014 national elections, and awaken in him an appreciation of NRIs as a socioeconomic–cultural bridge between India and the countries they resided in and who could be mobilized as a political–diplomatic tool for India.[45] It meshes, for instance, with the priority his regime has accorded the retention and enlargement of the H1B/L1 visa quota by the US government as a means of winning the vote of the aspiring Indian middle class at home even if, unfortunately, it results in a still bigger Indian 'brain drain'. Liberal values such as religious diversity and freedom of expression and of the press—also supposedly American attributes—did not, however, leave as big an impress on Modi, resulting in his 'good friend Barack' lecturing him, in light of the murders of Muslims on the cow issue, on the virtues of religious tolerance and the need to be nice to Indian Muslims.[46]

Modi is a self-taught, self-made man and is cocky about the views he holds, confident of the conclusions he has reached, presumably, after cogitating mostly with himself and on the basis that he has seen the world, knows how it works and is confirmed by whatever selective material is put up by his staff in the PMO for his perusal. He is also convinced that he needs no 'experts' to tutor him on foreign policy or anything else for that matter. Nor is he afraid to make his personal likes and dislikes (such as his pro-US, anti-Pakistan bias) and his assessment of his own ability to strike deals with difficult foreign leaders (Xi and Trump, for instance) the basis of his foreign policy. On the evidence of much of his first term, Modi appears, from many angles to be what American psychoanalyst Michael Maccoby calls a 'true narcissist'. Such a person, he argues, (1) 'doesn't listen to anyone else when he believes in doing something', (2) 'has a precise vision of how things should be', (3) has 'the charisma and drive to convince others to buy into [his] vision or embrace a common purpose' and (4) 'communicate[s] a sense of meaning that inspires others to follow [him]'.[47]

Further, because leadership to him has always meant demanding obedience and imposing his will and views on others, he does not countenance anyone in his retinue (and that includes his cabinet colleagues, his appointees in government and civil servants) contradicting him or disagreeing with him. Even less does he like views that clash with his own or to share the spotlight with anyone. The result is that no one around him in the PMO and elsewhere in government dares to come up with better ideas, assuming they have it in them to do so. Thus, what he says goes.[48] Little wonder that in this BJP regime he is the sole source of policy ideas, with his office acting more or less like a post office passing on the prime minister's views for the line ministries and agencies to flesh out.

Some appointees in NITI Aayog like Amitabh Kant and Bibek Debroy are permitted to mouth off only because they are distanced from quotidian matters of policy implementation and can be safely ignored, their periodic public ejaculations conveying the impression of the Modi dispensation being more open to new ideas for the myriad problems rocking the country than it really is. Many of these persons happen to 'have the gift of the gab', which as a corporate insider said counts for much with the prime minister who prides himself on being a facile and forceful speaker.[49] The fact is Modi is a one-man show, with the lesser lights dressing up his ideas as policy nostrums.[50] The pattern seemingly involves Modi voicing ideas, many of them of American provenance, which are then popularized, propagated in the media and legitimated, in no particular order, by Ram Madhav, the BJP general secretary and RSS-anointed 'expert' adviser to the prime minister on foreign affairs, the NSA Ajit Doval and the foreign secretary of the day, and others down the food chain.

Take, for example, the concept of India as 'leading power'—the organizing principle of Modi's foreign policy. Not long after assuming his post, Modi proposed that the MEA 'help India position itself in a leading role, rather than [as] just a balancing force, globally'. Why the prime minister believed that a leading role was separate from a balancing role is not clear. In any case, the locus genesis of this concept appears to be the US Secretary of State Hillary Clinton's speech in Chennai on 20 July 2011. She spoke then about 'This not [being the] time when any of us can afford to look inward at the expense of looking outward. This is a time to seize the opportunities of the 21st century and it is a time to lead'.[51]

Obama's ambassador to India, Richard Verma, made it plainer that 'India as leading power that can uphold international norms and support what Defense Secretary [Ashton] Carter called . . . a principled security network in Asia' was the 'US vision for India'.[52] Hillary Clinton reiterated President Obama's description of India–US relations as 'one of the defining partnerships of the 21st century' and sketched India's leadership role in the Indo-Pacific (she called it Asia-Pacific because that was the term in fashion then). Besides 'India's growing role in South and Central Asia', she talked about 'India straddling the waters from the Indian to the Pacific Ocean [and] is, with us, a steward of these waterways. We are both deeply invested in shaping the future of the region that they connect.'

She added that 'there are big questions for us to consider. Will this region adopt basic rules of the road or rules of the sea to mobilize strategic and economic cooperation and manage disagreements? Will it build the regional architecture of institutions and arrangements to enforce international norms on security, trade, rule of law, human rights and accountable governance?' After suggesting, sotto voce, that it was China that violated 'rules of the road or rules of the sea' and that India and the US and other rule-abiding countries in the region had to make common cause against it, Clinton pirouetted around to proposing that

India, China and the US 'coordinate our efforts' to 'address, manage, or solve some of the most pressing issues'.[53] Among other things the US secretary of state spelled out was America's primacy in India's strategic calculus. Significantly, it is virtually a snapshot of what Modi has tried to do but, judging by the outcomes, with limited success. This is because of the basic confusion at the heart of his 'leading power' concept.

In the prime minister's estimation, a 'leading power' is higher up on the ladder than a mere 'balancing force', though it seems not to have occurred to him, as history shows, that powers that lead or are 'leading' also invariably balance power among other states in the neighbourhood, the extended region, the continent they are in, and in the world, and that leading and balancing, far from being mutually exclusive tasks of ambitious states, are complementary aims. Did any of the designated 'advisers' around Modi point this out to him? Apparently not, but it did not really matter because the joint statement issued after the prime minister's first visit to the US in 2014 to meet with President Obama declared that Modi 'emphasized the priority India accords to its partnership with the United States, a principal partner in the realization of India's rise as a responsible, influential world power'.[54]

This enunciation of the 'principal partner' role merely cemented America's prominence in India's policy universe that Hillary Clinton had hoped for three years previously. India having officially designated the US as 'principal partner', there was no question about the BJP government wanting to also try and be a balancer in the international balance-of-power system. With this as the central plank of Indian policy, the phrases describing what India aspires to be—'leading power', 'responsible, influential power', 'important power in . . . a great power continent'—lose their relevance because India's ambitions and policy horizons are clipped to whatever conforms to Washington's thinking.[55]

Ram Madhav, for instance, pulled together the various themes to state that the US's role was as 'a principal partner in the realization of India's rise as a responsible, influential power'.[56] So America is supposedly the lever helping push up India, an already 'responsible' state, also become an 'influential power' and, in terms of the quality of such help, the US stands head and shoulders above other friendly powers that are merely 'strategic partners' (Russia, Japan, etc.) and who count but not for as much. It follows that the US is the preferred country for any cooperative or collaborative activity, and for trade and technology programmes and projects. But Modi's thinking on great power and foreign policy is often at odds with his pro-American instincts, thereby scrambling his conceptualization. Soon after becoming prime minister in May 2014, for instance, he said:

> Thus far we have been a balancing power, always seeking other's favours. How long can we continue to do that? Why don't we grow into a global power? It is clear in my mind we are more than just a balancing power, but a global player. We speak on equal terms with all, whether it is the US or China. Today we approach the world with greater self-assurance. We have shown the confidence to engage all major powers simultaneously and effectively.[57]

In this view a global power is apparently autarchic in that it doesn't need anybody and therefore doesn't have to seek favours from the 'major powers'. This thrust of Modi's is undercut by his policy of getting close to the US, courting American foreign direct investment (FDI), buying more US-sourced armaments, trying to get bigger access for Indian goods to the US market and, most conspicuously, by his deciding to upgrade the security relationship by signing the LSA, with COMCASA possibly to follow. The LSA permits Washington to treat Indian naval bases, army infrastructure and air force stations, in effect, as locations for its worldwide military presence and profile. It is a concession that exceeds anything the Soviet Union, for instance, enjoyed vide the 1971 Treaty of Friendship and Cooperation. The fact that the text of this agreement has not been made public, says a former foreign secretary, causes suspicion that some onerous provisions such as carving out of the Indian naval and air base areas for exclusive if contingent use by US military units have been agreed to, something denied by the Modi government. Such provisions, he says, were resisted by the Manmohan Singh dispensation.[58] What it signals is Delhi's willingness to be co-opted into the American security architecture.

It is hard in the event for the prime minister to argue that this is an 'equal' relationship and India is dealing on 'equal terms' with the US.

Reduced to its essence, India is no more equal than any NATO member state is to the US. More tellingly, it may not be wrong to conclude that Modi is reflexively pro-American in a way no previous Indian prime minister has been, and combined with Trump's America First orientation may incline Delhi to bend to the US's will. Does relying on the US so fully serve would-be great power India's interests? And what has America's record been vis-à-vis India?

Turning Indian Traits against India

Modi's accommodation of the US and the West and seeking their approbation (like Manmohan Singh before him) is a historical affliction that former diplomat and insightful chronicler of the Indian middle class, Pavan Varma, contends owes much to the colonized mindsets of our elected rulers Nehru on down. It has bred a sense of racial, cultural and intellectual inferiority, which last is manifested, he writes—and this is particularly germane to Modi's rule—'in the tendency to seek solace in an idealized past whose achievements, imagined or otherwise, could reduce the erosion of self-worth . . . in excessive sensitivity to any criticism or praise emanating from the West . . . [and in] vast initiatives which dulled the pursuit of excellence and creativity'.[59] This observation contextualizes the analysis of Modi's policy that follows.

It may be instructive at this point to look at how Washington has diplomatically played Delhi over the years by turning peculiarly Indian policy conceits and characteristics against India. And secondly, how an ecosystem has come up within the country in the new century that encourages not just a US-leaning Indian stance but reinforces Delhi's policy sways conforming to American interests. What is referred to here is a trellis embedded in the Indian milieu to support a US-leaning foreign policy and posture that, creeper-vine-like, wrap themselves around it to rise. Among the conceits Indian leaders beginning with Nehru have entertained is that unlike other countries, India is a preternaturally moral and pacifistic state. Nehru was canny enough to understand, however, that morality is a double-edged sword but nevertheless exploited *moralpolitik*—the use of morality as an instrument of realpolitik—to sidestep ideological pitfalls and equip India surreptitiously in the founding decades of the republic with indigenously developed strategic capabilities the West would have frowned upon had they been definite about what he was up to.

Thus, the nuclear weapons capability masterminded by the nuclear visionary Homi J. Bhabha was acquired, as was combat aircraft design and development capability by hiring Kurt Tank, a leading designer of Nazi Luftwaffe fighter-bombers, to produce the first supersonic combat jet aircraft, HF-24, outside of the US and Europe at Hindustan Aeronautics Limited (HAL), Bangalore. Similarly, a defence–industrial complex was seeded, right under the nose of a censorious West that would have looked askance at a Third World country surviving on food aid seeking the wherewithal for becoming a nuclear and conventional military power.[60] As Nehru told former foreign secretary M.K. Rasgotra, then a young MEA staffer, in October 1960, 'What I am trying to do is lay the foundations in all areas of [India's] present and future needs ... My priorities could be wrong, but priorities can be reviewed from time to time and changed if necessary.'[61] Except Nehru was intellectually and diplomatic practice–wise agile enough to calibrate his morality-tinged rhetoric with actual policy to mask his real intentions and programmatic thrust, and particularly to protect his 'Janus-faced' nuclear programme from Western scrutiny and shut down pressure.

Nehru's successors, however, lacking his great power vision, will and statesmanly skills, frittered away the head start the country had gained, reducing India by the late 1970s into its present state—armed with a nuclear arsenal in petrified animation and the status of the biggest arms importer in the world and an abject technology dependency. This happened, in part, because successive prime ministers paid more heed to his disarmament rhetoric and speechifying about the bomb as moral horror, for instance, than his albeit understated thrust for dual-use nuclear expertise and wherewithal, about which he freely hinted but which nobody in the Indian policy establishment apparently paid attention to.[62] It was this Nehruvian rhetoric Washington successfully turned back on Delhi to dampen the enthusiasm for nuclear weaponization during the Lal Bahadur Shastri and early Indira Gandhi years. After India's first test in 1974, American public opinion leaders recalled Nehruvian idealism to virtually coerce Indira Gandhi into abandoning rapid progress towards full weaponization.[63]

A glimpse of the rhetorical counter to the Nehruvian disarmament bombast that ended up influencing Delhi and hurting India's strategic interests is seen in the revealing take by President John F. Kennedy's assistant for national security, McGeorge Bundy, on a nuclear-weapon-armed India—a status the Kennedy administration resolutely prevented the country from achieving in the years prior to 1964 when India reached the nuclear weapons threshold. 'The bomb for India remains,' Bundy stated, 'a doubtful prize in that something about this apocalyptically destructive standard of greatness is not truly Indian.'[64] Working on the narcissism characteristic of the Indian government and leaders, Bundy in this way conceived an atypical standard of greatness just for India that at once massaged the Indian ego and prodded the Indian elite to act to limit the country's hard power, which theme can still be heard in certain non-proliferation quarters at home and abroad. It is a moral stance Nehru had originally adopted for realpolitik reasons returning to bite the country.

The other singularly Indian conceit that has harmed the national interest is that India is a 'responsible' state that trusts mostly in its soft power to have international impact. This is centrally a part of Modi's rhetoric and an attribute that meshes with the other qualities that define his government's approach which, in great power terms, is unambitious, cautious, passive, reactive, defensive and, military-wise, minimalist.[65] Delhi keeps ballyhooing India's being a 'responsible' country as a tremendous national virtue. Predictably, aware of the Indian leaders' susceptibility to flattery, Washington has firmed up such thinking by heaping praise to ensure Delhi stays 'responsible', meaning doesn't stray from the laid-down line and suddenly do something disruptive that may hurt US interests. Thus, Obama's Defense Secretary, Ashton Carter, praised India's 'responsible' behaviour because, he said, it hasn't peddled or transferred its indigenously developed nuclear civilian and military technologies to anyone.

However, not being part of any technology control or denial regimes, the Indian government was not bound by any agreement and could have easily sold heavy-water-moderated reactors and associated technologies its nuclear energy programme specializes in to energy-starved nations in the developing world. With the 'first mover' advantage, moreover, it would have created and consolidated a worldwide commercial market for its nuclear goods and, in the bargain, have had a whole bunch of countries strategically beholden to it. These sales could have been under International Atomic Energy Agency safeguards or not, depending on what India could get out of the buyer state by way of, say, military basing rights, access to natural resources and their markets on concessionary terms, etc.

The US and the West would not have appreciated such an Indian policy because, besides skewing their strategic calculi, India would thus have stolen a march over them in economic and energy terms and robbed their own nuclear industries of potential custom and export revenue. Further, with China in mind, a separate, special category of potential politico-strategic partners—Vietnam, the Philippines, Mongolia, Indonesia—could have been cultivated with the transfer of Indian nuclear or heavy conventional explosive-tipped short-range and medium-range missiles, BrahMos supersonic cruise missiles and similar armaments to stifle Chinese adventurism, and as legitimate payback in kind for Beijing's transferring nuclear missile technologies to Pakistan. All these options have been formally surrendered by the Modi government without getting anything in return.

Following India's entry into the MTCR in 2016, the invitation to become a member of the Wassenaar Arrangement was accepted in December 2017, with membership in the Australia Group to follow as a lead-up, China permitting, to its entry into the NSG. This last won't happen without Pakistan being accorded the same nuclear treatment. Risibly though, the MEA trumpeted India's putting these shackles on itself as a 'slap' to China for its opposition to India's entry into the NSG, when the joke was on India because it binds the country to the MTCR and now the Wassenaar strictures on trade and commerce in strategic technologies, goods and materials.[66]

Further, the contention that India's admission will motivate Japan to invest in nuclear power plants in the country and enter into joint ventures with Indian entities overlooks the unwillingness on the part of Japanese technology purveyors to part with technology lest it create an industrial competitor.[67] These developments highlight Delhi's long-standing but politically incomprehensible eagerness to join clubs that selectively restrict the diffusion of technology, and illustrates the all-consuming naivety of the MEA and Indian government about power politics and how the world functions. Instead of undercutting and undermining these schemes that for long have victimized India, Modi's regime is turning into their champion and booster. In effect, such moves have proved Modi's commitment to the cause of non-proliferation of nuclear and missile technologies without first firming up India's security architecture and technological profile in the world, and its market share for relevant nuclear and missile technologies, goods and materials, as the US, Russia, China, the UK and France have done. Delhi has thus willingly sacrificed the leverage it had in terms of its potential for seriously discommoding and disrupting the self-serving activities of these big power–dominated technology cartels.

Beijing kept away from these self-limiting groups and deigned to join them only after it had masterfully set up the 'rogue nuclear triad' with itself at the centre, assisting Pakistan and North Korea to become proud owners of nuclear weapons of mass destruction and delivery systems. It is this habit of the Indian government to casually circumscribe India's policy freedom and foreclose its options that has hobbled India strategically over the years, gladdened Washington's heart and reassured Beijing that India is its own worst enemy. The BJP regime (like the predecessor governments) sought these memberships mainly to win the approval of the US and the West and for Modi, perhaps, to bolster his personal cachet in Western capitals. Voluntarily ceding policy ground, not leveraging India's capabilities, resources and indigenous technologies to secure advantage, and not getting something equally substantive in exchange for giving away so much seems to be an appalling way for the Indian government to conduct business. It is so far distanced from the realpolitik strategies pursued by every other major country that it merits a separate category of politicking—timidpolitik, which is not all that new, considering timidity is an Indian characteristic that foreign powers have historically used to subjugate India.[68]

The theme of a responsible India that is peace-minded and dedicated to helping out other peoples caught in crisis situations and natural disasters, and relying on its cultural presence in Asia and other soft power to make a mark is a standard Modi spiel.[69] This desire of the prime minister to project a non-threatening, boy-scout image of India sits well with the 'vishwa guru' vision he has articulated for the country. It is an abstract national ambition which, because it eschews hard power, covers up for an Indian policy of militarily fixating on a small-time Pakistan while outsourcing strategic security vis-à-vis China to the US via bilateral agreements with Washington and the strategic quadrilateral in the Indo-Pacific of the US, Japan, Australia and India.

Modi's depiction of India as harbinger of peace, for example, is on the trivial basis of the country providing a large number of troops for UN peacekeeping missions.[70] By this standard, Bangladesh and Nepal too could claim similar status, when the fact is South Asian militaries eagerly seek such UN billets simply because it enables at least a small portion of their armed forces to earn tax-free, dollar-designated salaries. It is to completely misread the basis of power and influence within the UN, what to speak of the world at large. In the UN, power is proportional to the country's contribution for its upkeep. India provides for just 0.737 per cent of the UN budget compared to China's 7.92 per cent and the US's 22 per cent, and its influence in the world body is, therefore, proportionately little.[71] This, of course, is not a true reflection of India's international influence, of course, but it does suggest limits to its supposed clout.

Modi, however, has an alternative vision as well, and it is to contend with China for the leadership of Asia. This is a sound and reasonable vision but not supported, any more than his notion of India as 'vishwa guru' is, by an adamantine will and realpolitik policy drive of the kind that helped China achieve its goals. Realpolitik was succinctly described by President Obama's adviser Rahm Emanuel as being 'cold-blooded about the self-interests of your nation'. The classical definition of 'realpolitik' by the mid-19th century German politician Ludwig von Rochau, who coined the word, concerns not the 'realization of ideals but the attainment of concrete ends ... Ultimately [this concept] is an enemy of all kinds of self-delusion.'[72] This definition does not obviously mesh with Modi's thinking. Rather, Modi thinks he has conceived of an effortless way for the country to attain global prominence.

First, based on his reading of international power politics, he believes that the US is in decline, China is shaky, and hence that India has a chance to become leader by default if it plays its cards well.[73]

This doesn't explain why, in the event, Modi's policy is pivoting to the US. Secondly, take his formula for India to gain power, which he calls 'panchamrit'—a mix of five elements—'samman' (dignity and honour), 'samvaad' (greater engagement and dialogue), 'samriddhi' (shared prosperity), 'suraksha' (regional and international security) and 'sanskriti evam sabhyata' (cultural and civilizational linkages).[74] One can see why this seems attractive—it alludes to great power coming easily to India's hand as long as it keeps out of confrontations and trouble with more powerful countries, with 'suraksha' also implying that security is not just a sovereign and singular concern of the country but a public good that can be obtained collectively or in concert with the other powers. This is where, presumably, the US comes into the picture.

In fact, the 'vishwa guru' idea drawing on India's cultural resources and its ability civilizationally to connect with states in the near- and middle-abroad (via Buddhism to Afghanistan, Mongolia, South East Asia, China, the Korean Peninsula and Japan; via Hinduism to South East Asia and the island states in the Indian Ocean, via Sufi Islam to Iran and Central Asia) naturally distances India from the strong-arm aspects of international relations. It is a prescription for maintaining the status quo and quite different in nature than the traditional Kautilyan statecraft emphasizing the aggressive use of *sama* (conciliation), *dana* (economic aid or other assistance), *bheda* (sowing dissension in the enemy ranks) and *danda* (punitive action or war) to further the national interest. Striving powers follow Kautilyan advice, but countries that have made it, that have already arrived as global powers—and Modi counts India among them—do not need to exert themselves in the same way, do not need to indulge in crude intimidation tactics, and can get by with making minimal adjustments here, widening its circle of friends there, waxing pacific and exercising its soft power. For the rare contingencies when national security may be at risk and military prowess is necessary, he thinks he has India covered by having the US military as backstop.

For Modi to believe that India has already made it and need only putter around is to commit the cardinal mistake that Bismarck warned against, in German historian Friedrich Meinecke's words, of not making the 'sharp distinction between a policy of national interest and one of national prestige'.[75] Modi aims to garner prestige for India (and, incidentally, for himself) by highlighting India as a peaceful, non-threatening, non-provocative nation. In his perorations on India's Act East and Act West policies, for instance, there is nary a mention of India's military power and capability. This seems to be an attempt to leapfrog over the excessively difficult stage of first making the country a consequential power that the world has to reckon with. Whether the prime minister likes it or not, hard power is the only basis for achieving great power and even the 'vishwa guru' status he hankers for.

Emperor Ashoka, the last of the great rulers of the Chanakyan age, for example, instinctively understood this and it was only after he had bloodily pacified the subcontinent and eliminated all conceivable threats to his realm—the last being the kingdom of Kalinga which he made an example of by remorselessly killing every man, woman and child in it—that he fell in with the Buddha's teachings and propagated peace and non-violence. When all enemies and threats are eliminated, non-violence becomes a feasible proposition.

For modern India, which is still taking baby steps in great power politics, Modi would be better off having the Ashoka-on-the-make as model and obtain for the country strategically meaningful and discriminate hard power than carry on as if the coercive power of the state doesn't matter and act as Ashoka of the Buddhist persuasion. The hard power that matters is not the kind of armed services capability the nation presently has but a strategically consequential force no friend or foe, however geographically distant, can ignore. The irony is it can be acquired for the same level of resources currently expended in maintaining a mostly short-legged, limited capability and an industrial-age Indian conventional military that is good for nothing strategic. (More on this in Chapter 6.) Instead, Modi thinks he can take a shortcut by clinging to the US and hoping that will do the trick.

Variations on Modi's thinking have been around since P.V. Narasimha Rao's time. Rao changed the direction of Indian foreign policy by veering gradually away from Russia for two reasons. As the sole superpower standing after the Cold War, he hoped and expected that Washington would put out for a democratic India as it had done for Deng Xiaoping's communist China and pave the way for its comparable rise as a manufacturing and economic power. It was a policy slant seconded by Vajpayee who, as per Washington's wishes, disavowed nuclear testing and long-range missiles, and got himself the NSSP. Manmohan Singh followed up by cementing the nuclear deal, even if these understandings have left India stranded with a non-credible strategic arsenal. Modi, on his part, is more fully orientating Indian policy in Washington's direction.[76] The US government, meanwhile, has been diligent in observing India's weaknesses and, over the last seven decades, has exploited them, subtly and not so subtly. A prime weakness is a set of Indian conceits that have been turned into foreign policy gold by the US. Among them that India is a naturally pacifist nation uninterested in acquiring power. To the US Secretary of State Condoleezza Rice's offer to make India 'a great power', Foreign Minister Natwar Singh airily replied: 'We are not in the game of becoming a great power. Our job is to eradicate poverty.'[77] Prime Minister Manmohan Singh put it a little differently: 'Foreign policies are not just empty struggles on a chessboard . . . Ultimately, foreign policy is the outcome of economic policy.'[78] Combine such political thinking with Indian diplomats' abhorrence for nationalism and their love of 'practical pragmatism', and foreign governments find Indian interlocuters perfect pliable dupes.

Furthermore, Washington has repeatedly capitalized on India's timidpolitik soaked in 'over cautiousness' that the former nuclear energy czar, the late Raja Ramanna, dubbed an 'Indian cultural trait'. It has bred in Delhi its risk-averse mentality justified by the all-purpose rationale of the country being a 'responsible state'.[79] It has disabled India, preventing it from acting and reacting strongly in support of its national interest while hoping that adversaries will not take advantage and, if they do, friendly powers will pick up the slack. Hence, rather than do something decisive for a change, successive Indian governments have looked in the new century to Washington to deal with the terrorist threat from Pakistan. Thus, settled policies are prevented from reaching their natural end point and well-planned strategies from being implemented either to pre-empt threats or to punish adversaries for their egregious actions. Examples of each will clue one to the Indian government's follies.

Indira Gandhi was deterred in 1974 from open-ended testing and nuclear weaponization, among other reasons, because of 'external pressure'.[80] Except, the US was in no position to forestall Gandhi going down that route.[81] It was the same fear and unwillingness to take risks that militated against her deciding on new tests after she returned to power in 1979 when Ramanna pushed for them, saying the Americans would 'crack our heads'.[82] Indira was just as weak-kneed when it came to making hard decisions of the preventive kind, cancelling virtually at the last hour two planned pre-emptive strikes on the Pakistani nuclear complex at Kahuta in the early 1980s, the first one jointly with the Israel Air Force, with the Israeli F-16s conducting the strike and the F-15s providing protective escort, and India pitching in with infrastructure and other support, to take out the uranium centrifuges and Pakistan's bomb-making capacity because she apprehended an adverse reaction by Washington, and the second time when Rajiv Gandhi in 1984 cancelled an IAF operation designed to take out these targets on its own.[83]

In 1998, before ordering the limited nuclear tests, Vajpayee asked the finance ministry to assess the likely effects of economic and other sanctions. Because the ministry bureaucrats were aware that the prime minister was determined on the explosions and did not want to fall afoul of him, they produced a report saying the consequences would be manageable. Had the civil servants sensed a weaker resolve on the part of the leadership, they would likely have played safe and advised against the tests. Indeed, the Vajpayee government stopped further tests that would have obtained certifiable high-yield thermonuclear weapons and instead announced a 'voluntary [testing] moratorium' because the same finance ministry officials then turned around and counselled that India would be able to inflict 'serious costs' on any sanctions-imposing countries only after the hard currency reserves were built up to the $100 billion mark and India became a trillion-dollar economy.[84]

Twenty years later, India is a trillion-plus-dollar economy and has a foreign exchange hoard of nearly half a trillion dollars but there's no sign of any guts on Delhi's part to resume nuclear testing. And finally, how to make sense of the Manmohan Singh regime not reacting at all to the 26/11 Pakistan-sponsored terrorist attack on Mumbai in 2008? It was a virtual replay of the inaction of the BJP government of Vajpayee to the December 2001 terrorist attack on Parliament. The NSA at the time of the 2008 incident, Shivshankar Menon, confesses to have 'pressed at the time for immediate visible retaliation of some sort' which, he writes, 'would have been emotionally satisfying and gone some way toward erasing the shame of the incompetence that India's police and security agencies displayed'. But on 'sober reflection and in hindsight' he writes that the decision to do nothing was correct, reasoning that a retaliatory strike would have (1) 'obscured' official Pakistani involvement in the attack, (2) 'united Pakistan behind the Pakistan Army' weakening, in the process, the Pakistan People's Party government of Asif Zardari, (3) 'limited practical utility' and no lasting effect, (4) dimmed the prospect of bringing the perpetrators of this terrorist action to justice, and (5) started a war that . . . [would have] imposed 'heavy costs and set back the progress of the Indian economy'.[85] The reason none of this is convincing is because it is a permanent justification to neither act pre-emptively nor react strongly no matter what the provocation.

The real reason may be, as Rice indicated in her memoir, that Manmohan Singh 'was determined to avoid war'.[86] In the Indian system, what the prime minister wants is what the country gets, and what the prime minister desires is often gut-level stuff, not the outcome of deliberation and coordinated fast-think involving, among other agencies, the military. Predictably, India's restraint was fulsomely lauded by the US government, which knew more than it let on about the Mumbai strike action at the planning stage but did not warn the Indian authorities lest its cooperation with Pakistan's ISI in Afghanistan be affected.[87] This is not an isolated incident. So, how good a friend to India does that make the United States and how committed is it to wiping out terrorism?

The Indian government's ingrained tendency to not upset the applecarts of big powers is firmed up by high-up US officials patting Delhi on the back for its restraint and stoking its 'responsible state' conceit. Thus, Obama's Defense Secretary, Ashton Carter, referred to India as a 'responsible nuclear state' and, knowing it would please the Modi government, added that Pakistan was an 'unstable nuclear weapon state'.[88] Trump's first secretary of state, Tillerson, upped the ante flattery-wise by saying India was a 'more responsible' nuclear weapon state than China.[89] In another words, India is not only hog-tied by informal understandings (on the non-development of ICBMs) and agreements (like the nuclear deal) that are not binding (on nuclear testing), but by flattery and other blandishments and also by unwarranted fears. What accrue are self-imposed restrictions that dovetail with self-advertisement as a moral, idealistic, pacifist, responsible, passive-defensive and reactive power. That this sort of thing purveyed by myopic, strategically challenged leaders never becomes cause for public ire is, to say the least, strange.

There is a long history of the US, in particular, using praise and flattery as diplomatic tools to meet its ends and to subtly reinforce Delhi's fear of consequences. In the lead-up to the 1971 Bangladesh war when the inflow of millions of refugees from East Pakistan was forcing the Indira government to consider drastic action, US Undersecretary of State John Irwin urged the Indian ambassador in Washington that as a 'responsible power' India must exercise restraint. The US assistant secretary of state, Joseph Sisco, helpfully informed the Indian embassy that President Nixon and his NSA Henry Kissinger both expected India to absorb millions of Bengalis from East Pakistan because of its history 'of taking into its fold' waves of foreign migrants.[90] Simultaneously, Nixon was ordering the USS *Enterprise* carrier task group into the Bay of Bengal just in case India acted against East Pakistan.

The fact is, the US has issued military threats, imposed hurtful economic sanctions after the 1974 and 1998 nuclear tests, forewarned Pakistan of India's pre-emptive actions (such as the planned aerial strikes on Kahuta), openly urged China to attack India and open a 'second front'— as Kissinger did during the 1971 Bangladesh war to get Pakistan off the hook—disclosed the secret letter Vajpayee had written to President Bill Clinton explaining that a thermonuclear weapons–armed and aggressive China was the reason for India carrying out the Shakti series of nuclear tests, and hurt the indigenous Tejas LCA project by simply expropriating massive amounts of design and test data related to this warplane by the US government at the Wright-Patterson air force base in the US where the Tejas model was undergoing wind tunnel and other tests on the announcement of economic sanctions in the wake of the 1998 nuclear tests. And the US has worked overtime to undermine Indian strategic programmes and to gang up with the other four NPT-recognized nuclear weapon states, including China, to relentlessly force India into signing the Comprehensive Test Ban Treaty at the UN Commission on Disarmament.

The US has been equally flagrant in treating contractual obligations as scraps of paper. Washington abruptly terminated the enriched uranium fuel supply for American light water reactors in Tarapur after the 1974 Indian nuclear test, forcing that power plant to run at reduced capacity to stretch out the stockpiled fuel, resulting in diminished electricity in the grid and enormous opportunity costs and economic losses for India. And in recent years, despite the friendly overtures by Delhi, the US government did not think twice before pressing Israel against using the Elta 2052 computer for DRDO's indigenous active electronically scanned array (AESA) radar being developed for the LCA, forcing India to initially settle for the lesser Elta 2032 computer. The 2052 unit was approved for use only when the US became aware that DRDO's AESA prototype was reaching the same performance threshold.

If India, a declared 'strategic partner' of the US, is treated this way, how is it different from Washington's treatment of India in all the years when India was not close to it? The fact is that the US, because it can, does whatever its government of the day feels it has to do to safeguard and advance American interests. India, on the other hand, as Foreign Secretary Jaishankar said with respect to the nuclear deal, is used to 'making do', in other words eating whatever is plonked on the policy plate by the big powers, however meagre the fare, because it does not have the will, Oliver Twist-like, to ask for more, or to throw away the plate and, like China, start its own kitchen.[91]

US-tilting Policy Ecosystem

There are several building blocks to the policy ecosystem supportive of India's tilt to the US that's in place in Delhi. The first is the America-friendly section of the political class in which can be subsumed the leadership of all the political parties, except the odd communist party ideologues. Originally constituted by the right wing of the Congress around stalwarts such as S.K. Patil and Morarji Desai who wore their antipathy to Nehru's socialist economics on their sleeves, they looked to the US for solutions and welcomed generous US (PL 480) food aid and development programmes.[92] Today the government and society seem to look to America for everything, including national security solutions. Public opinion-shapers, the intelligentsia and the media and the burgeoning information technology sector annually earning for the country export revenues of over $10 billion and whose interests converge with that of the large, youthful and growing Indian middle class enthusiastic about Hollywood, American cultural icons, consider US education and H1B/L1 visas as the gateway to the good life in the US. The middle class, being more politically conscious and organized, forms a powerful voter base which no party can afford to alienate. It is a constituency with a stake in good relations with the US and the West because that's where middle-class youth aspire to go for higher education, settle down and make good.

From the practical foreign policy point of view, however, it is the senior members of the IFS, IAS and armed forces who have always provided both the float and the ballast for the US-friendly outlook and approach of the government. Exposed to the US since 1947, Indian diplomats were the first bridgehead (after the waves of Sikh immigrants to the west coast of North America in the 1920s). By the early 1960s it became fairly routine for Indian diplomats to have their progeny settle down in the US. The former IFS officer and the Congress's agent provocateur, Mani Shankar Aiyar, who joined the service in 1963, discovered to his surprise that in his batch 'not a single officer's child is in India'.[93] Since then the senior officers of the other Indian civil services too have cadged resident US visas for their children. By Aiyar's estimate, 98 per cent of all officers joint secretary and above in the Government of India and in the MEA are thus compromised. 'And don't forget,' he added, for good measure, 'the guys in the military and in other areas.'[94]

It is a figure that tallies, according to a former home secretary with an exceptionally clean reputation, with the information he says the home ministry collects.[95] Senior officers in crucial ministries are 'softened up', according to an Indian intelligence source, by various means, the most effective being 'scholarships' offered their children to elite universities and offer of resident visas (Green Cards).[96] It is also by now routine for retired Indian diplomats and military officers to be appointed as visiting faculty at universities and colleges in the US, with a former Indian naval chief even taking up a lecturer's post at the US Naval War College, Newport, Rhode Island, immediately after pulling a diplomatic posting despite being warned about the 'cooling off' period by the MEA. It is reasonable that these beneficiaries were afforded American largesse because they helped push the American agenda during their careers in the Indian government and military.

Moreover, there are some forty-odd programmes which facilitate visits for the training of Indian officials in the US. The US State Department and the Pentagon together are invested, for example, in the showpiece International Military Education and Training Programme (IMETP), which annually permits scores of mid-career Indian armed services officers to spend time at US military training institutions. According to a 2017 joint document of the State Department and the Department of Defense, the IMETP 'favourably impacts India's military leadership, doctrinal developments, and perceptions of the United States' and more significantly 'provides access and leverage for US diplomatic, military and regional objectives'. It notes by way of success of the programme that 'In recent years, there have been two occasions in which all three service chiefs were IMETP graduates.'[97]

The budgetary allocation request for India in the IMETP for fiscal 2017 was $1.3 million of the $3 million for all countries of South and Central Asia, constituting 4.1 per cent of the total worldwide IMETP spend of $31.4 million.[98] Considering the high returns it fetches Washington, this relatively minuscule amount of money is apparently well spent. The consequence of the top echelons of the MEA, the rest of the Indian bureaucracy, intelligence services and the military wanting to be in Washington's good books is that US-friendly policies fairly sail through official channels in Delhi. Much of this is known to entities in the Government of India but with intimate relations with the US as the main plank of the previous two governments and now the Modi foreign policy, there is no one publicly to sound the tocsin considering just about everybody of any consequence in the Indian government is feeding at the American trough.

The Indian military officers trained in the US return with uniquely American capital-intensive notions of war-fighting that are not relevant to the financial circumstances of the country, but increasingly form an influential cadre within the government and the military, as US official documents testify. This is particularly evident in the navy where alumni of the US Naval War College, for example, are in the forefront of advocating aircraft carriers and support arms (naval aviation) as priority. As regards this powerful civilian–military lobby within the government and the armed services, Rahul Bedi, a correspondent for *Jane's Defence Weekly*, wrote this: 'So blatant, widespread and generous is Washington's largesse' to the sons and daughters of Indian officials of all kinds that 'It is worth asking to what extent Indian policy on a range of issues of interest to America [is] "hostage" to the children of a growing number of Delhi's powerful decision-makers'. He continued, 'The scholarship recipients' list is embarrassingly revelatory. It is also not unknown for senior Indian intelligence, security and military officials travelling to Washington to negotiate sensitive bilateral issues and agreements to ask their obliging hosts, who by now have a measure of their Delhi counterparts, for favours like immigrant visas or Green Cards, H1B visas, extension of student visas and even jobs for family members in the US. Needless to say, negotiations the following morning become significantly compromised by the promises of the night before.'[99]

Asked about the effect on Indian policy of the Indian government and military staffers seeking consideration from US authorities, former foreign secretary Shyam Saran candidly admitted, 'It is there at the back of our mind.'[100] Another foreign secretary had a more nuanced view on this issue. While conceding that most senior Indian diplomats and government officials have an American connection, they have, he said, 'internalized' the distrust of the US and used it as an intellectual sieve to filter, by institutional habit, all US-related policies. Thus, Washington is often disappointed, he claimed, when it expects 'anticipatory compliance' with its wishes. This distrust, he said, is separate from the appreciation of the US as a free society, and its democratic values are the reason for that country's attractiveness to children, family, etc. He, however, cautioned that military officers who haven't had exposure to foreign policymaking and dealing with foreigners are more easily impressed by the weapons and war-making technologies equipping the US military.[101] A former naval chief says that of the ninety top-level officers in the Indian Navy, thirty were tagged in his time by Indian intelligence agencies as 'suspect' in terms of passing sensitive information to their US Navy counterparts, with a former naval chief, in fact, considered a 'conduit' for such information leakage.[102] Despite the hair-splitting about which sections of the Indian government are prone to leaks or are friendly to the US, the fact is that there is an infrastructure in place within the Indian government supportive of an America-friendly stance, and pushing for Indian actions, measures and policies to fortify it.

The extensive 'influence operations' carried out by the US State Department and the Department of Defense—observed a report for the director, net assessment in the Office of the US Defense Secretary first submitted in 2002 and updated six years later—are meant to translate into procurement decisions by Delhi for American military hardware and to culminate in 'basing [facilities] and access for US power projection'. In the ten years since that report, Indian armed services have purchased in excess of $15 billion of C-130J and C-17 transport aircraft, P-8I maritime surveillance aircraft, Harpoon anti-ship missiles and M-777 lightweight howitzers. With the LSA, Washington has all but realized its India-based power projection options, which a July 2017 'Joint Report to the [US] Congress' has tried to sanitize in line with Indian government pronouncements by stating that it only seeks 'to simplify logistics exchanges' between the US and Indian militaries.[103]

Still another important part of the ecosystem or the trellis for the creeper-vine Indian policy to wind itself around is the Indian presence in US academia which complements a new phenomenon—the Delhi chapters of Washington think tanks established with Indian corporate monies. Old Indian money as well as newly rich IT billionaires alike have in the last two decades endowed numerous multimillion-dollar 'chairs' in prestigious universities in America (Narayana Murthy at Harvard, Nandan Nilekani at Yale, Ratan Tata at Cornell, etc.) and in Washington think tanks (Ratan Tata at the Carnegie Endowment for International Peace) and funded whole buildings (Mukesh Ambani at Wharton, Ratan Tata at the Harvard Business School). These are enormous resources that could have financed the founding of half a dozen world-class academic and research institutions in India. That's not, however, the priority of these Indian benefactors who'd prefer to pad their reputations in America with their largesse.

Complementing this show of Indian money power in US academe is the founding of Indian branches of reputed Washington-based think tanks—the Brookings Institution, Carnegie Endowment for International Peace, Aspen Institute India and its offshoot, the Ananta Aspen Centre, all active in Delhi, and the New York–based Asia Society working out of Mumbai. The Delhi chapter of the Brookings Institution, for example, opened in 2013, promising to disseminate 'recommendations for Indian policymakers'. Three years later its Washington twin, Carnegie, set up shop, hoping to develop, its website says, 'fresh policy ideas and [to] direct[ly] [engage] and collaborat[e] with decision makers in [Indian] government, business, and civil society'. It is reasonable to surmise that the policy advice proffered and the 'fresh policy ideas' that are promised by these two organizations will, at a minimum, be in tune with US geopolitical security and economic interests. At the inauguration ceremony of Carnegie India on 6 April 2016, Sunil Mittal, the owner of Airtel and chairman of the board of trustees, for example, removed any doubts on this score. 'We have put out our flag here,' he declared, without a trace of irony, and pleaded with the numerous Indian moneybags in the audience to show more 'generosity in moving *our* agenda forward' (italics mine)—meaning, presumably, the Carnegie–US government agenda in India.[104]

The generosity of wealthy Indians, newly minted IT billionaires, Indian industrialists and business houses funding such organizations no doubt mirrors the yearning of their American counterparts in the US to 'amplify' their influence in the host society and government, especially if the regime in Delhi is perceived as keen to improve relations with Washington. Indian funders of the American think tank presence, moreover, thus complement their reach into the Indian government with like access to the movers and shakers in US policymaking circles.[105] These American outposts in Delhi conduct 'Indo-US strategic dialogues', hold policy meets, arrange seminars and conferences and afford eminent American visitors and senior Indian officials a forum to air official positions and to engage Indian policy audiences. The Ananta Aspen Centre, according to its website, additionally focuses 'on [Indian] leadership development and open dialogue on important issues facing Indian society, to help foster its transformation'.[106] This is the US think tank's contribution and the flipside of the US State Department–sponsored programmes to bring carefully selected young and impressionable political leaders for visits to the US: the channel that first acquainted Modi with America.

These think tanks have many things in common, among them the fact that they fish in the same small pool of serving and retired Indian government and military officials and a growing but still size-wise small community of younger-generation foreign and military policy scholars and analysts who slip into the influence network stream, participate in seminars and conferences hosted by their principals in the US and, advertently or otherwise, get sucked into furthering American policy aims in India. The Indian chapters of these organizations get their message across to the Indian public via institutional tie-ups with Indian newspapers and media outlets, who think that a Carnegie or Brookings label is a mark of quality that lends them prestige and enhances their content.[107]

A glimpse into how this information–influence network functions was disclosed by foreign secretary Jaishankar. He revealed how when he was negotiating the nuclear deal he regularly discussed issues relating to the ongoing talks on the nuclear deal with his father, the late K. Subrahmanyam, ex-IAS officer and for many years the Indian government's go-to person for advice on strategic matters. He spoke about how as ambassador in Beijing he regularly talked with his father about the 'challenges of two countries like India and China rising in near time frames in near proximity' and, in an aside, how Subrahmanyam took time to relate 'the inside story of how the 1965 war almost went wrong for India' to Jaishankar's son Dhruva, who, as it happens, is on the staff of Carnegie India, run by Jaishankar's close friend, C. Raja Mohan.[108] Assuming that as with his father, the then foreign secretary, adhering to family dinner table norm, conversed on Indian foreign policymaking with his son, giving the latter an insider's account of how this or that policy choice was made or is progressing within the Modi government, it is not far-fetched to conclude that such information would have quickly wended its way via Carnegie Washington to the US State Department and the Pentagon and that Jaishankar and Raja Mohan would have had a mutual back-scratching arrangement.

To add to the punch of these American think tanks in Delhi is the trend of retired foreign secretaries and NSAs ending up on their faculties, thereby strengthening the semi-institutional ties between the MEA, India's National Security Council and the US government, which link-up Jaishankar initiated, no doubt with the prime minister's blessings, and the Foreign Office makes no attempt to hide.[109] It points to another part of the US influence-peddling complex, peer-group comprising

Indian university students who branched off into government and think tanks and over their careers ended up as mutually supportive entities. This has helped Modi's US-leaning foreign policy gain traction in the Delhi think tank and media circuits.[110] Yet another influence stream is the growing tribe of NRI academics in the US, who strive manfully to be noticed by US policy circles by pitching policy choices for India that are in sync with Washington's thinking and which tack, incidentally, firms up their residency status and tenure track appointments in American universities.

So, they dutifully flog, for instance, the South Asia as nuclear 'flash point' thesis beloved of Washington, push for India to minimize its strategic deterrent in line with US non-proliferation rhetoric, argue for India buying American military hardware, argue for India as subsidiary partner of the US to contain China, call for Indian laws to protect American intellectual property rights and generally propagate the line US think tanks do in Washington and their branches do in Delhi. Indian media persons are lured into propagating the US-friendly line with offers of short stints in US research and training institutions and 'lecture tours' because, as Rahul Bedi writes, their patron, the US government, 'does not believe in free lunches and admits as much'.[111]

The Indian bureaucrats and military men who are exposed to America are the Trojan Horse within the government. As far as is known, there has been no official examination of the consequences for the national interest and prospects of an independent Indian foreign policy owing to the personal payoffs in kind to Indian civilian and uniformed officers by the US, and the role of the India-based Washington think tanks in legitimating a pronounced listing of Indian policy towards the US, nor about the role of the Indian corporate sector in rendering Indian policy subservient to American interests through direct and indirect means via these think tanks. It is not that other countries are not active in trying to shape the Indian government's attitude and policies by similar means—the UK with its British Council, Russia with its Indo-Russian Cultural Centres, France with its Alliance Francaise. Rather, it is to point out that no other country possesses the sort of allure and resources or can offer the kind of inducements that Indians in government, military, universities and media find irresistible. This makes the United States unique in that it is a dangerous friendly state because of this ready 'Fifth Column' available to it within the Indian government and society.

The corrective lies with the Indian government. It needs to institutionalize the prohibition against anyone on the public payroll consorting with foreign officials in any way at any time for any reason other than the prescribed one, and in the prescribed manner. Special units of the intelligence services need to be established with the mandate to track and monitor all official and 'unofficial' interactions, and then see if children of senior Indian government, intelligence and military officers are beneficiaries of 'scholarships' to famous American universities by checking up on the basis of such largesse and to impose serious deterrent punishment—long jail sentences and career-ending penalties for guilty or culpable officers—and real-time monitoring of the activity of susceptible officials and potential targets. All major countries without exception police and punish wrongdoing of this sort.

The Criminal and Enforcement Divisions in the US Department of Justice, for example, mount comprehensive surveillance of US government officers dealing with foreign states to make sure American public servants are on the level and do not do things at the behest of foreign capitals and get remunerated for it in any way. Wiretaps are maintained, as also regular but covert checking of bank accounts, property purchases and any unusual events like expensive holidays, etc.[112] In India, in contrast, there's virtually no surveillance of this kind, with R&AW officers, including in its counter-intelligence wing, being found to have been 'turned' while in service and now residing in comfortable retirement in the US.[113] Something has to be done to arrest this trend of Indian government employees being easy pickings for foreign governments and to be mindful of the working of the various foreign state–friendly, policy-influencing think tanks and similar influence-peddling organizations that are active in Delhi and elsewhere in the country.

A central figure in legitimating the role of Americans and US think tanks in the shaping of Indian foreign and military policies is the affable, Mumbai-origin, Ashley J. Tellis, who occupies the Tata Chair at Carnegie Washington. A crafty insider and heavyweight policy wonk who finessed the nuclear deal through official Indian corridors in its early stages when he was posted in Delhi in the mid-2000s as adviser to the US ambassador Robert Blackwill and was reportedly shortlisted by Trump for the ambassadorial appointment in Delhi, Tellis is not a run-of-the-mill NRI academic or think-tanker. His utility to the US government, given his reach and influence in Indian government, is immense. In the last stretch when negotiations for the nuclear deal hit a bump, Tellis, by then back in Washington was, for instance, deployed by the US State Department as the offline channel to try and convince the Indian negotiators to accept a new demand that was sprung on them in February 2006. The US chief negotiator insisted that in the scheme to 'island' the weapons section of the Indian nuclear programme in Trombay—which concept the Indian negotiators (led by Jaishankar) had by then unwisely accepted—that Indian scientific and engineering personnel in the Department of Atomic Energy too be divided into the military and civilian streams, and threatened that without this provision the US Senate would reject the deal. Tellis tried hard to impress on the Indians that non-acceptance of this provision would be a 'deal breaker'. Thankfully, the Indian team were not persuaded and the US backed off.[114]

There's a lesson here that the Indian government and the MEA are loath to learn, which is that if Delhi is hard-headed and no-nonsense and sticks to its position and wears the other side down by a strategem of stonewalling, the US has little choice other than to accept, because in Asia, with China in the mix, America cannot do without India. The trouble is the Indian negotiators have to be so instructed not to budge from a high tough line by the prime minister, without which the MEA officials with an eye on personal gain can end up giving away the store in negotiations. But to revert to Tellis, apart from being a critical cog in Washington's South Asia policy machine, he enjoys unprecedented access to Modi, being reportedly the only 'foreigner' to get an appointment with the prime minister at short notice. He uses such privileged access to push US objectives in the guise of serving India's interests, like selling Delhi on the virtues of the F-16s and F-18s, which Trump is keen that India buy. While admitting that the F-16, designed in 1969, is old in the tooth, he jauntily argued, for example, that agility-wise it can still match the supposed front runner in the IAF's 'single engine' aircraft race, the Swedish Gripen combat aircraft. But buying the Swedish product, he slyly warns, would expose India to licensing problems owing to 50 per cent of the technologies in it being US-sourced. Tellis also makes the case that buying the F-16 will make India 'a critical node in supporting the 3,200 F-16s still in service in 25 countries' and give a fillip to Modi's Make in India programme.[115] He thus makes the unsellable attractive.

With a talent for clearly and eloquently enunciating complex issues in simple, easily understandable language, he is a hit in Indian policy circles because it provides bureaucrats and military officers 'talking points' they can advance in their ministries and armed services. Tellis is convincing because he does their thinking for them, providing them with the rationale and articulating India's role in grand terms in the US geopolitical design for Asia in a way that makes it acceptable, while liberally casting doubts about India's capabilities and easing in snide comments about India's inability to handle China, terrorism, etc. on its own. In a recent paper he contended, for example, that India's best bet is to ally with the US and Japan because it will 'never be capable of holding its own against . . . China or defining the international system to its advantage in the face of possible opposition' and that even Modi's more modest goal of making India 'a leading power' will require it to lean on the US.[116] It is a self-serving thesis, of course, for the obvious reason that the Indian government has failed so far to do anything to make the country capable of 'holding its own' when it so easily could have.

Should India tighten up its act, align its efforts to the correct threat—which is China, not Pakistan—roll out a realpolitik-driven policy, discriminately build up its strategic capabilities and practice proactive diplomacy with intensive use of its military as both a coercive instrument (to ensure a friendly regime in the Maldives, say) and diplomatic tool (by offering security cooperation with the Indian Ocean littoral and South East Asian states, for example) it can change the policy course for the better (as will be discussed later). Most troublingly though, Delhi refuses to retaliate in kind to China's kicks in the shin and elbows to the face by exercising its hard power countermeasures and make life difficult for Beijing. This ends up bolstering Tellis's case about the country's incapacity. Further, the wrong set of policies and strategic orientation that have obtained as a result are interpreted by

Tellis as India's shortfalls which, in turn, helps him to highlight India's weaknesses, reinforce Delhi's diffidence and air his belief that the US is indispensable to India's security and, in fact, is doing India a favour by providing it. It is India, he asserts, that 'seeks a resolute American presence in the region to hedge against possible Chinese excesses'.[117]

Tellis is also the most visible part of the NRI iceberg which can capsize India's national interests. NRIs are a big thing for the BJP government whom Modi personally courts as India's best and brightest. The presence of NRIs in the American media, in higher corporate circles, in industry and in colleges and universities and especially in the US government and the American Foreign Service is viewed as a winning situation for India. This is a wrong perception. Just because they look Indian doesn't mean these NRIs and, growingly, US-born Americans with parents who are NRIs, are Indians in any real sense, or that they will unfailingly help in advancing India's interests. In fact, the basic requirement for NRIs to succeed in any sphere of economic, political and cultural activity in America is that they are mainstream and propound and relentlessly push American policy themes and US policy interests. Thus, there is no harder supporter of US interests in the media than Fareed Zakaria, the CNN commentator who fancies himself as a future US secretary of state and is therefore careful never to transgress the bounds of US mainstream views.[118] Less talented people than Tellis and Zakaria beaver away in universities, think tanks and increasingly in the US civil services, in the hope of becoming players in the Washington power game—they are in no way minders of India's interests.

While the supportive milieu and ambience in Delhi and elsewhere in India have obviously helped, what is crucial to Washington's extracting enduring value from Modi is the personal warmth he feels for Trump (on display during his late June 2017 visit to the US) and, as stated, his personal regard and admiration for America. Trump prides himself on being a 'deal-maker', Modi too trusts his business instincts. 'Being a Gujarati is in my blood . . . commerce is in my blood,' Modi has said. 'I understand these matters.'[119] In short, he seems ready to give some to get some. How well has this worked so far with Trump who believes in all take and no give? There's the complicating factor of the physicality of these two leaders in the 'strongman' mould. If Modi boasts about his 56 inch chest as reflecting his muscular politics and approach to international affairs, Trump's 'broad-shouldered leadership' is praised as proof of his foreign policy acumen.[120] When these two men sit down to negotiate, or instruct their teams on the negotiating parameters, there may be less willingness to compromise on either side because ceding ground and making concessions would be seen by either party as succumbing to an opponent, as bending to superior will, which is unpalatable to them.

In the context of several Modi–Trump meetings and interactions, let us briefly analyse the issues of importance to the Indian leader and whether the US government has given him satisfaction on any of them, and what it portends for bilateral relations. Modi started out with a self-inflicted disadvantage by adopting Delhi's ingrained policy habit, tin cup in hand, of begging for more H1B visas for the new-age Indian coolie, for advanced technology and for a more punitive US policy against Pakistan. The Indian prime minister perhaps expected that having established a personal rapport with Trump, massaged his ego, and pleased him by according the visit by his favourite child Ivanka Trump the trappings of a state visit, the US President would make concessions on these three issues dear to him. The evidence suggests the Trump White House hasn't budged at all.

Since the economic reforms and the surfacing of the Indian information technology industry as a high revenue earner for the country and as the site for back office operations for the postmodern economies of the US and western Europe and the growing intake by them of Indian doctors, engineers and financial managers, the entire Indian socioeconomic system underwent a sea change starting in the late 1990s. With the aspirational middle class in the forefront, the US became for large sections of Indian society the glittering city on the hill where ambitious youth would go to seek fame and fortune and, at the very least, a higher standard of living. This was done on the basis of professional degrees earned by them at the All India Institute of Medical Sciences, Indian Institutes of Technology and the Indian Institutes of Management, institutions subsidized by the Indian taxpayer that Nehru had founded in the hope, ironically, of producing the skilled manpower to run the India of tomorrow. Modi, with a different perspective, sees such outward rush of professionals to the West as a good thing because it sets up India as a bountiful supplier of skilled and employable youth which the ageing societies of the West lack. 'The world has money and industries but no youth to run them,' said Modi when laying the foundation stone of the Indian Institute of Information Technology in Guwahati. 'After 2030, India can globally supply manpower for running the industries. That day is not far off.'[121]

Once settled abroad, these Indians comprise the country's high-end diaspora that is the source of the ruling party's funds. The aspirational Indian middle class as a vote bloc for the BJP is keen on keeping the H1B/L1 visa route open and hurrahs along the Indian government's policies accommodative of America. Whence, the Modi regime's disproportionate expenditure of diplomatic capital on enlarging the intake by the US of qualified Indian professionals. Whether it is the prime minister himself or External Affairs Minister Sushma Swaraj or Finance Minister Arun Jaitley, the H1B/L1 visa is uppermost in their minds when meeting with their opposite numbers. Similar representations in the past had made no difference to Obama's policy of 'in-sourcing' to limit the Indian techie inflow, nor have they moderated Trump's 'Buy American, hire American' position even a bit. 'Right now, widespread abuse in our immigration system is allowing American workers of all backgrounds to be replaced by workers brought in from other countries to fill the same job for sometimes less pay,' Trump said at the signing of the order that made it more difficult for American companies to hire Indians. 'This will stop. American workers have long called for reforms to end these visa abuses. And today, their calls are being answered for the first time. That includes taking the first steps to set in motion a long-overdue reform of H1B visas.'

The H1B/L1 visa facilitates intra-company transfers of techies by Indian IT companies from their home base to worksites in the US while paying them Indian salaries. It is the differential in remuneration and the ease of moving the skilled workers as needed from point to work point that makes for flexibility in operations and higher profit margins for Indian companies. Even before Trump assumed office, two bills were introduced in the US legislature to raise the minimum annual wage of H1B visa holders from $60,000 to $100,000 in order to compel Indian IT companies to hire locally.[122] Then, on the very day (18 October 2017) that Secretary of State Tillerson was selling his US-led security scheme for the Indo-Pacific region and outlining a prominent role for India in it and Sushma Swaraj was urging Washington to do nothing to hurt Indian economic interests, the Trump White House inserted very sharp teeth in Obama's policy, issuing a directive making it difficult for Indian software engineers already in the US to extend their stay on H1B/L1 visas.[123] Also in the offing are changes to US immigration laws, such as the one disallowing 'chain migration', i.e., legal immigrants from bringing immediate family members to America, which will demotivate Indian professionals from going there.[124] In the wake of the 1 November 2017 terrorist attack in New York by an Uzbek immigrant, the US president again iterated his intention to replace the 'visa lottery system' with a 'merit-based' immigration policy.[125] And in mid-December 2017, Trump twinned the lottery and chain migration issues and promised 'to end both of them'.[126]

With the aim of shoehorning Delhi's H1B concerns into the growingly restrictive US outsourcing policy, Finance Minister Jaitley tried piggybacking on Trump's views by characterizing Indian H1B visa seekers as 'high-value professionals' who 'contribute immensely to the US economy'.[127] From the perspective of its interest, the US would rather that small numbers of highly qualified Indian engineers and doctors migrate to America than a horde of taxi drivers, cooks and pizza delivery boys. How encouraging Washington to thus decant top Indian talent will serve India's national interest is not clear. In any case, despite every possible evidence that neither the Obama government nor the Trump administration has bought the Modi–Jaitley argument, Delhi persists. It is not certain what more Trump can do to slam the H1B immigration door shut in India's face that would convince Modi that the US will not budge.

A series of measures after the initial moves to close off the H1B/L1 route have included the imposition of a 21 per cent tax on offshoring, which as Rentala Chandrashekhar, president of NASSCOM (National Association of Software and Services Companies), said specifically targets the Indian IT–business process management (BPM) industry.[128] This sector is huge—a workforce of 3.7 million, over 15,000 small and large firms and 600 offshore development centres of 78 countries, contributing some 9.3 per cent of India's GDP and constituting 38 per cent of its total services exports estimated in 2017 at $117 billion (IT services: $65 billion; BPM: $26 billion; engineering and R&D: $25 billion).[129] With proper up-skilling in new areas such as artificial intelligence and machine learning, robotic process automation, advanced analytics, virtual and augmented reality, chatbots and digitally assisted voice search, the industry estimates an increase in its global market reach and a rise in its earnings to $50 billion by 2020 and $55 billion five years later, with exports growing at a yearly 10 per cent rate.[130]

But here's the rub. What Obama began with his 'in-sourcing' policy that sought to create and keep as many of these high-value jobs as possible within the US and to generate employment in this sector, Trump has propelled with vigour.[131] 85,000 H1B visas are annually issued by the US government with 20,000 of these reserved for foreign students in US universities. The bulk of the H1B quota is monopolized by Indians. The MEA's protestations that this is not an immigration but a 'trade and services' issue has not cut ice with Washington.[132] In fact, the Trump administration seems determined to not just end the H1B visa channel for legal immigration that the Google chief Sundar Pichai and the Microsoft head Satya Nadella, for example, availed of to become US citizens, but to close off the loopholes as well. Thus, Trump's initial decision to shut down this route led quickly to not extending this visa for workers already in America, which will compel as many as 7,50,000 Indian techies to return home.[133]

The US Immigration Service then decreed an end to the H4 visa that permitted spouses of H1B visa holders to hold jobs.[134] This injunction coupled with the earlier mentioned decision to restrict the chain migration of immediate relatives of immigrants by testing for English language proficiency and ensuring they are financially solvent would lower the incentive for Indian techies and their ilk from trying to become latter-day economic refugees to America. While temporary relief is possible, the fact is that it is Damocles's sword hanging over the Indian government that Washington can threaten to bring down at any time and that can be used to get Delhi to do things that the US wants done.[135]

Trump's unreceptive attitude in the face of strong lobbying by US business circles to keep the H1B visa system open and repeated pleadings by Modi and his cabinet colleagues about it being the lifeline of the burgeoning Indian technology industry—one of the few bright spots in a generally ho-hum Indian economy—is proof that Washington is prepared to throw the US's strategic partners and their interests under the bus to protect its own interests.[136] It is coercing Indian IT companies into doing what Trump wants: invest in the US, create jobs for Americans and sell to the world.[137] This leaves Modi and the Indian government in sackcloth and ashes.

Delhi should retaliate by playing hardball but of this there's not the faintest sign, what with the US-supportive policy ecosystem working overtime to convince the Indian government to stay on course and, in effect, play second fiddle to America. The larger point Trump's inflexibility should drive home to Delhi is the fact that while the revenue gains to the US from so taxing and disadvantaging the Indian IT sector is small, the impact on India is disproportionately large and could hurt Modi's political prospects. If Modi, the supreme political animal, fails to reverse this trend and is content with India making adjustments as per Washington's whims, then Trump will be quick to see this as a weakness to cash in on and ratchet up the hard-line and the pressure on other issues to push Modi into making more concessions. This is a foreign policy defeat for Modi.

Terrorism: Problem Strategique

Let's now consider the issue of terrorism. It has two angles. There is the Pakistan angle, which Delhi is fixated on, and then there is the Afghanistan aspect, in which India plays a part. Like his predecessors but with a lot more spite and verve, Modi has invested a lot of his and the country's political–diplomatic energy in getting Washington to target Pakistan as a terrorist scourge. This is being done, it would appear, less with a view to dealing with terrorism per se or with seeking political cover for independent Indian actions against terrorist leaders—Hafiz Saeed of LeT, Azhar Masood of JeM and the criminal ganglord Dawood Ibrahim—than to financially hurt Pakistan and, if possible, to turn the

US against it. The US parallel of this exercise is Washington's campaign to replace Russia in India's policy universe and as main military hardware supplier, and to minimize Moscow's salience to Delhi. Just as Russia is thus unlikely to be easily marginalized in Delhi's policy universe, Pakistan will not be abandoned by the US.

To believe that Washington can be persuaded to leave Pakistan to the tender mercies of China is to entirely misread the extant geopolitics and Washington's South Asia policy, and is belied by what transpired in Washington. In response to India's entreaties, Tillerson in late October 2017 undertook to get tough with Pakistan on terrorism, coming out with a vacuous statement—the sort of thing that sends Delhi into raptures. Just then, the Pakistan foreign minister Khwaja Asif, possibly with the sly intent of showing up American perfidy, disclosed that the name of Hafiz Saeed, on whom some years back Washington had announced a $10 million bounty, was missing from the list of international terrorists released by the US government.[138] Washington reacted by warning that if Pakistan failed to act against twenty terrorist groups active in Afghanistan and enjoying a safe haven in Pakistan and listed in a paper handed over by Tillerson to Islamabad during his day-long stopover, the US would act against them on its own.[139] Some ten days later, the US Congress with Trump's Republican Party in majority in both Houses amended a provision in the National Defense Authorization Act 2018 requiring the US defense secretary to certify that Pakistan had taken steps to 'significantly disrupt' the activities of both LeT and the Haqqani Network, but removed the mention of LeT from the draft bill.[140]

It proved once again that the US government is interested in resolving the terrorist problems that matter to US security, not tackle the asymmetric terrorist threat Pakistan wields against India. After all, the terrorists the US wants removed from the scene are not the same jihadis India seeks to neutralize. The twain does not meet, whence this legislative measure. Washington will, however, continue to make noises about terrorists in Pakistan to placate Delhi, as US Vice President Mike Pence did on a secret visit in December 2017 to the US forces in Afghanistan.[141]

In practice though, the US sympathizes with Pakistan because it is aware that for Islamabad to move whole hog against the Afghan

Taliban residing in that country would be to blow up the tenuous peace Islamabad has sewn together with the Quetta *shura*, and to harbour real domestic violence and disorder with the strong Pakhtun enclaves, especially in the economic hub—the Karachi metropolitan region—and that this would destabilize the country and be inimical to US regional interests. And secondly, the US cannot afford to alienate Pakistan because it continues to be a 'front-line' state geographically in a way India can never be. Other than facilitating a direct US role in Afghanistan by providing US forces a relatively safe and secure military staging area for its 'tsunami of air power' against the Afghan Taliban, Pakistan offers a great vantage point to monitor Iran and check Chinese influence in Pakistan (building up via the China–Pakistan Economic Corridor [CPEC]), China's 'new silk route' through Central Asia, and such inroads as Russia is making in Pakistan and the rest of southern Asia.[142]

Islamabad, in turn, realizes that closeness to China and Russia balances US influence in the country and helps it resist excessive American demands to 'do more' in Afghanistan.[143] This means that India will have to take care of the danger posed by Pakistan-based terrorist gangs by itself, and that the US government will do nothing other than mouth displeasure and issue empty threats. Trump announced the fact of his withholding $225 million in aid to Pakistan as an anti-terrorism measure to please India, except it was only a slap on the wrist for providing sanctuaries to the Afghan Taliban and in no way targeted the Pakistan-based terrorist mujahideen active in Kashmir. But it did help a gullible Delhi to crow that the punitive American action validated its position.[144]

In any case, this suspension of funds is temporary and monies will begin flowing to Islamabad, having only minorly inconvenienced Pakistan in the process.[145] Chalk up another success for Trump and a loss for Modi. Washington's generally cavalier attitude and treatment of Pakistan, a partner of historic standing, is more recently mirrored in the US's cold-shouldering the Kurds, whose Peshmerga forces were the fighting element that defeated Islamic State in Syria and who, until the referendum for independence ordered by their leader Masoud Barzani in September 2017, were Washington's favourites. This has alerted many Israelis to wonder if their country won't similarly be abandoned by the

US to serve its larger regional interests.[146] In the event, can India ever expect to be a more prized ally of the US than Israel or Pakistan and, therefore, can it afford to rely on it in a crisis against China?

High-tech Desires Hitting a Dead End

Then there is the Indian government's unusual yearning for US high-technology without factoring in the political and economic costs involved, particularly in the context of availability of alternative sources of equally advanced technology. It hands over the initiative and negotiating advantage to Washington, signalling that Delhi is prepared to pay any price for whatever America is prepared to sell. The Indian government's eagerness is doubly mystifying, considering that the highest levels of technology are formally fenced off by Washington and the technology that is available to India can be acquired via competitive bids from elsewhere. So successive governments in Delhi have made major strategic concessions to America, resulting in Indian commitment to limit the range of its weapons and the quality and yield of its nuclear weapons vide the MTCR and NSSP nuclear deal. Worse, it has aligned its rules, regulations and procedures for the export of indigenous nuclear and dual-use technologies with the US laws as a precondition for membership into the various technology denial regimes (MTCR, Wassenaar Arrangement, NSG, etc.).

Thus, it has foresworn the option of developing its own global market unhindered by constraints for its nuclear goods, including pressurized power reactors, and the use of transfer of sensitive technologies as strategic leverage as China has done by arming Pakistan and North Korea with nuclear missiles. It has not, and will not, fetch Delhi anything in terms of real frontier technology that it craves, except prohibitively expensive buys of such things as the untested and unproven Westinghouse AP 1000 light water reactor and the electromagnetic aircraft launch system (EMALS) for aircraft carriers. If a deal for the Westinghouse transpires, it will make India a guinea pig for potentially hazardous power plant technology that the US Nuclear Regulatory Commission has not certified for safety reasons.[147]

Moreover, in order to lubricate such deals, the Manmohan Singh and Modi regimes took the executive arrangement route to render infructuous an Act of Parliament, making foreign reactor technology providers liable for the full amount of damage and destruction, and signed the International Atomic Energy Commission's Convention on Supplementary Compensation limiting payouts by the original equipment manufacturers to $300 million. In effect, Modi's efforts to seek a looser system of total technology transfer have been no more successful than Manmohan Singh's. The official US rhetoric on this score has been uplifting but delivery on the Defense Technology Trade Initiative and the other Indo-US institutional mechanisms is negligible. This is because the US does not trust India with its technology.

US Secretary of State Tillerson revealed this in the interactive session following his October 2017 speech at the Center for Strategic and International Studies in Washington on the eve of his first trip to Delhi. Questioned by the host, John J. Hamre, a former deputy secretary of defence, about why despite being designated as 'major defence partner' India is not able to access cutting-edge military technology, Tillerson replied with unusual honesty:

> I think everyone appreciates, the US has the finest fighting military forces on the planet, first because of the quality of the men and women in uniform—all volunteer force, but they are also equipped with the greatest technologies and weapons systems that are unmatched by anyone else in the world. So that's an enormous advantage to our military strength, so we don't provide that [cutting-edge technology] lightly, and that's why we have such rigorous review mechanisms when we get into technology transfer.

He thereby indicated that its formal designation as 'major defence partner' notwithstanding, India (a) does not pass the 'rigorous review' test and, therefore, will not be trusted with cutting-edge US military hardware and technology, and (b) has to reconcile to the fact that Washington has to protect 'America's competitive advantage in this area'. Perhaps, realizing that he had gone too far with his candour, the then US secretary of state tried to pull back and ended up contradicting himself.

'Our most important allies and partners have access' to the armaments and technologies the US armed forces utilize and India, he said, 'has been elevated to that level'. He then climbed down again to identify the approved level of military technology the Indian armed services can realistically access: the Guardian maritime drone, 'aircraft carrier technologies', 'the future vertical lift program', and the old warhorses trundled out of retirement from the Boeing and Lockheed Martin stables, the 'F-18 and F-16 fighter aircraft' respectively.

Except, the Guardian drone sold to India is unarmed, good only for surveillance, and not in service with any of the US armed forces because better technology is available to them; the 'carrier technologies' refer to the extraordinarily expensive EMALS which with a $3 billion price tag on the newest nuclear-powered carrier in the American Navy, USS *Gerald Ford*, is being sold to India as non-lethal technology (with a marked-up price of $2 billion to $3 billion), but mainly because this sale would reduce the unit cost to the US Navy and help the San Diego-based General Atomics company producing it amortize its huge R&D investment in this system. The 'future vertical lift program' could mean anything from helping build the Osprey tilt rotor plane that was supposed to enhance mobility for the US Marines but has grave engineering and flight control problems (in the transitioning phase from vertical lift to horizontal movement) and which the Indian military have evinced interest in as a Special Operations platform without seriously considering its drawbacks, to the licensed manufacture of some fairly harmless utility helicopters; and the F-16 and F-18—fifty-year-old aircraft for sale along with the production rights but minus the 'know why', meaning no source codes, no operational algorithms, etc.[148]

That Tillerson referred to these items 'as potential game changers for our commercial and defence cooperation', the salesman's hyperbole apart, suggests not only the level of threat that Washington perceives that India faces from China, but a collateral US motivation for a restrictive policy, namely, of helping the American defence industry commercially to wring the last penny of profit from the sale of obsolete weapons platforms and overpriced hardware that its own military is phasing out or finds too expensive. The overarching US industrial interest evident in its not transferring 'know why' technology is to prevent

India from gaining comprehensive capacity to design and develop its own fighter planes and aerial combat technologies and systems and become independent of US suppliers and a competitor in the lucrative arms export business.[149] The upside of this Tillerson speech is that, for the first time, Delhi has been publicly alerted to the exact qualitative ceiling of American military technology India is cleared to buy. It takes all the guesswork and uncertainty out of the military's plans and the Indian government's policy calculations, and should disabuse Modi, the MEA and elements in the America-supportive policy ecosystem active in Delhi of their belief that access to higher levels of technology is a matter of the prime minister working his personal charm on Trump and of stiff negotiation. Despite hints in the clearest possible language, it is doubtful the Indian government and military as a rule quite appreciate the nature of the systemic constraints on the free flow of American high-technology to India. While recent US administrations removed some procedural hurdles to facilitate the sale of certain military-use, non-lethal goods (like transport and maritime surveillance aircraft), they have never been as upfront about their unwillingness to sell advanced technologies until Tillerson came along. Ring up yet another distinct success for Trump and the US and a defeat for Modi and India.

The most significant disagreement is on the economic and trade front. At the end of the stalemated Eleventh Ministerial Conference of the WTO in Buenos Aires on 14 December 2017, India, as a developing country, found its interests resonating more with those of China than the US—both in terms of the embodied principle of multilateralism in trade agreements that America refused to reaffirm and of the specific developed north versus the developing south issues where disagreement led to the breakdown of talks. Trump is for jettisoning all multilateral accords such as the WTO and the Doha Round, and favouring bilateral trade agreements in the hope that he will be able to obtain for the US a string of better trade deals and cumulatively a bigger slice of the global trade.

India and the US disagree fundamentally on other issues as well, such as intellectual property rights on which the US wants stricter Indian laws and supervision and on the flow of labour that Delhi wants liberalized but Washington is putting a stop to. Further, the US along with the developed economies are progressively using the WTO forum to advance their interests, such as e-commerce, investment facilitation, medium- and small-scale industries, etc., subjects on which there's no political consensus within India and where the domestic infrastructure is weak as compared to the US and Europe. Then there are specific provisions that Delhi has zealously protected, most recently at the conference in Argentina, such as the 'peace clause' relating to its food security programme. It permits a minimum support price for agricultural commodities and the stockpiling of foodgrain, which the US strongly opposes as it does other similar issues, like subsidies on fisheries, etc. So divergent are the interests of India and the US and so keen is Washington to upend the WTO and the Doha Development Agenda that India took the unusual step of all but publicly calling out America.

'Unfortunately, the strong position of one member against agricultural reform based on current WTO mandates and rules led to a deadlock without any outcome on agriculture or even a programme for the next two years,' said a statement issued by the Indian delegation in Buenos Aires. It also reiterated its 'stand on fundamental principles of the WTO', other than multilateralism, 'rules-based consensual decision-making, an independent and credible dispute resolution and appellate process, the centrality of development [underlying] the DDA, and special and differential treatment for developing countries'.[150] This has riled Washington because it believes that as a burgeoning economy India should no longer enjoy the benefits due a developing state—which is the basic policy premise of Trump's economic and commerce-related policies with respect to this country.

On the means and methodologies of international trade, the interests of India and the US are in collision, something that even an unduly America-friendly Indian leader such as Modi will not risk averting. On this issue, consider it a wash, with neither India nor the US backing down or gaining much at the expense of the other. India may, however, gain from Trump's antipathy to multilateral trade accords, in particular from the US pulling out of the TPP. Consistent with these moves, he next all but blew up the G7 grouping of advanced economic powers at the June 2018 summit in Toronto over their reluctance to get Russia back into the G7 fold and reform into G8, and to agree to an absolute free trade regime. 'We are,' he said, 'like the piggy bank that everybody's robbing and that ends.'

Not content with riding roughshod over old allies, he gratuitously lashed out at India, a new friend that Washington desperately wants in its corner. 'This isn't just about G7, I mean, we have India, where some of the tariffs are 100 per cent. And,' Trump added to make a point, 'we charge nothing. We can't do that . . . And it's going to stop. Or we will stop trading with them.'[151] Sure, the US president was reacting to the Indian government seeking a retaliation claim from the WTO for the recovery of $31 million due to the US levy on Indian aluminium exports and of $130 million on steel exports. But he was missing out on the larger picture of a generally beneficial free trade system in place, just as he ignored the bigger aim of having strategically friendly India with his threat to penalize all Indian exports to add to his other actions that have hurt India economically. In the event, can Modi act as if nothing is amiss and America is a friend?

In the absence of even a single Indian policy advantage or gain, the principle of mutual benefit, which is the basis of stable relations between sovereign nations, seems not to be applied by the Indian government to dispassionately assess its one-sided relationship with the US. The US's relentless pursuit of its own national interests and about not caring a hoot about India's concerns, of Washington's attitude of taking more and more from India while conceding less and less to it, is leading to bilateral ties fast becoming iniquitous, with one side mostly getting what it wants and the other side getting nothing. But this unilateralist thrust of US policy conforms to the way the US in recent times has conducted its alliance politics—'give us what we want or face the music'—leaving its NATO and Asian allies and partners frustrated and fuming. India finds itself in a similar situation because Indian governments mid-1990s onwards have believed that getting close to the US has value. So far this value has not shown up. For India to thus disadvantage itself makes no sense and would appear to be a self-defeating policy and strategy, but it is precisely the tack Delhi has so far taken.

Consider some of the policy leverages India has surrendered over the last decade to the US. The freedom to resume testing to obtain a proven, tested and credible thermonuclear arsenal, courtesy the 2008 nuclear deal, has been given up as also the option to transfer indigenous nuclear and strategic missile and other sensitive technologies to China's adversaries in South East Asia as payback for Beijing's missile-arming Pakistan, which is now foreclosed by India's signing on with technology denial regimes—MTCR, Wassenaar Arrangement and, prospectively, the NSG. And agreeing to the LSA and prospectively the other 'foundational accords' such as COMCASA and BECA has stampeded India into the American camp, proportionately separating it from Russia—the only ready source of advanced military hardware and of assistance in strategic technology areas.

And what are India's gains from wilfully giving away so much, what has India gained in return? Repeated acclaim from Washington and pats on Manmohan Singh's and Modi's backs for their leadership qualities, praise for India always acting as a 'responsible' state and a prized 'strategic partner' and promises and still more promises of 'high technology'. To date this has consisted of offers to collaborate in developing things like 'battery packs' and to sell prohibitively expensive carrier aircraft launch technology the US cannot afford and so wants to rope in India in order to rein in its own carrier costs and the museum-ready F-16s and F-18s.

Other than hindering India's natural growth as a thermonuclear weapons power, there is also the dubious aspect of the civilian nuclear cooperation deal—the rescue of the bankrupt Westinghouse Company by buying six of its AP1000 power reactors, whose commercial prospects in America have dimmed with the US Federal Energy Regulatory Commission's refusal in January 2018 to publicly subsidize nuclear power to make it viable.[152] Worse is this reactor's history—not a single power project anywhere in the world featuring it has come in without massive time and cost overruns. The six units that Westinghouse expects to sell to India will have a price tag upwards of $70 billion to $90 billion (based on reasonable cost escalation of the French 1000 MW Areva power project in Olkiluoto, Finland, originally priced at $3.8 billion, which will end up costing $12.5 billion and is expected to go on grid a decade late, in 2019).[153] The US cannot be blamed for striking such bargains when Delhi seems bent on giving things away.

Are such giveaways by India part of a proactive negotiating strategy to purchase American friendship and goodwill to equalize Delhi's perceived disparity in resources? If this is the case, how does Modi propose to cope with the differential in the level and quality of foreign policy resources, the divergence of interests and threat perceptions in the strategic partnership with America and, simultaneously, to hold off China, hold on to Russia's friendship and still retain for India its independent power status and standing? Trying to please the US at any price is bad policy. Flattering allusions to India's importance to America mixed with a steely advancement of its own interests while, at the same time, scuttling India's national interest is by now the US's stock-in-trade. It is an approach mirrored, for example, in the National Security Strategy (NSS) document released by the White House in early December 2017.

In it the Trump dispensation delineated the 'Indo-Pacific' region, a concept the US President has popularized, as stretching 'from the west coast of India to the western shores of the United States'. But as regards China, the NSS says that it is 'using economic inducements and penalties, influence operations and implied military threats to persuade [Asian] states to heed its political and security agenda', 'the militarizing of the South China Sea' and rapidly modernizing its military, which actions, the document states, 'risks diminishing the sovereignty of many states in the Indo-Pacific'.

Elsewhere, though, the NSS is a mite more combative, talking of China 'challenging American power, influence, and interests, attempting to erode American security and prosperity', and which competition it says will 'require the United States to rethink the policies of the past two decades—policies based on the assumption that engagement with rivals and their inclusion in international institutions and global commerce would turn them into benign actors and trustworthy partners. For the most part, this premise turned out to be false'.[154] But this conclusion has been rubbished in the US policy community as 'a mixture of truisms, appropriate exhortations, dubious analysis and bad history' and, in practice, as being incapable of delivering on its promise which would require the ousting of China 'from international institutions and its role in global trade [and to] be marginalized . . . neither [of which] objective will be achieved, in whole or in part'.[155]

Given the Chinese economic investments in the US, including more than one trillion dollars in US Treasury bonds, Trump may at most risk a limited trade skirmish—correcting the existing balance of payments problem by taxing certain imports from China, such as steel, by factoring in the hidden state subsidies on Chinese products, cutting off sale of telecommunications paraphernalia because of security fears and preventing Chinese purchases of high-technology companies, etc., but not hugely inconveniencing it.[156] The two countries have a good thing going—China sells cheap consumer goods to America that Americans lap up, the dollars that China earns buy US Treasury paper which, in turn, means cheap credit is recycled back to the Americans to buy more Chinese goods in an endless virtual cycle.

The merest hint by Beijing in January 2018 about slowing down its purchase of these bonds had the value of the US dollar plunging, the stock market diving and Wall Street all aflutter.[157] The last time such action was contemplated was in 2011 by President Hu Jintao. There was talk then in US financial circles about 'Plan B' of the Obama administration urging its own citizens and friendly foreign states to buy the bonds that China might unload in the market.[158] In this situation, India—which already holds part of its portfolio in US bonds—will be one of the first countries America will approach to invest in its debt: a leverage India has never exploited, perhaps because the volume of India's buys are not big enough to matter. Such action by China may be damaging but is a far cry from threatening anything military, an aspect highlighted by the fact that the NSS nowhere labels China as troublemaker, disruptor or even prime security threat.

It is this American angle Delhi habitually pays less attention to even though it is supposedly the shared perception of danger from China that brings India and the US together. Delhi just seems happy with the attention it is getting in US military, especially the US Navy, circles. This document, for example, welcomes 'India's emergence as a leading global power', seeks 'to increase quadrilateral cooperation with Japan, Australia and India' and declares that America 'will expand . . . defense and security cooperation with India' which it confirms is 'a major defense partner', adding that it will 'support India's growing relationships throughout the region'. It will be tragic if the Modi regime understands such references to mean the US sides with India, considering how consistently Washington has opposed potential Indian actions—resumption of nuclear testing, acquisition of ICBM capability, the covert transfer of strategically meaningful nuclear/

strategic armaments to Vietnam and other states on China's borders to deter Beijing and to complicate China's security calculus—moves that a gutsy Indian government (an oxymoron?) can easily justify as actions to counter China and to legitimately impose like costs on it. If Delhi prosecuted such actions, it would pump up India as a nodal power and a credible rival to China in Asia while puncturing China's expansive role, ambition and pretensions.

So how does Trump propose to handle China? His NSS significantly says little other than engaging with China and Russia in 'competitive diplomacy' and makes fairly innocuous references about China aspiring 'to project power worldwide' while conceding that the US seeks 'to continue to cooperate with China'.[159] As regards the Pakistan bone thrown for the Modi regime to gnaw on, the NSS says that the US 'will press Pakistan to intensify its counterterrorism efforts' but— and very plainly—only against the Taliban operating against the US forces in Afghanistan, not the LeT and JeM that are bothering India in Jammu and Kashmir.[160] The NSS, geared exclusively to enhancing American interests, confirms that India will have no respite on issues ranging from military security to trade to technology to H1B visas. It, in effect, highlights the US's historical record as an unreliable friend and partner. It is for good reason that even a US-friendly diplomat such as Shivshankar Menon was careful to write that Indian and US interests were 'contiguous', not convergent.[161] Contiguous is a word, it may be noted, that suggests spatial differentiation and is open to interpretation; the word convergent is not.

The differences notwithstanding, Washington will continue to use its networks to push its agenda in Delhi, to penetrate the Indian government and military, and to pass the responsibility for erasing the trust deficit in relations on to India by requiring that Delhi keep making periodic multibillion-dollar purchases of mostly non-lethal military hardware, and using high-technology as bait for selling obsolete weapons platforms. It is interesting, in the event, to speculate about how any Indian government will negotiate with a Trumpian Washington or even a Washington without Trump when there's virtually no substantive meeting ground on any outstanding issues.[162] India is endowed with several big leverages which can be used but which no Indian prime minister including Modi has so far deigned to do. These are its (1) size and geostrategic location centred on the Indian Ocean; without a friendly India willing to offer bases (now facilitated by the LSA), the US military will be stretched hard to be effective in the expanse at the eastern end of the Indo-Pacific region, (2) a professional, if unimaginative, Indian military competent in basic territorial defence but which, if properly equipped with three offensive mountain corps, can hold up the Chinese PLA at the Himalayas line, worry the Chinese occupation troops in Tibet and distract Beijing from wielding its land power to overawe the rest of Asia, and (3), most importantly, the access to its vast and growing market populated by the 300-million-plus consumerist-minded middle class, the largest outside China. It is market access that economically is something that is to die for and, if strictly regulated, can seriously hurt the prospects of global companies, especially American firms, and can be used as the 'currency of exchange' to secure whatever India wants and needs from the US or any other country, not excluding China.

Further, Delhi could legislate that all foreign countries and companies wanting to sell in India will compulsorily have to make their products wholly within the country—design-to-delivery, a recipe for speedily setting India up as a global manufacturing hub. Secondly, it can decree, like China, that any company seeking to sell technological goods in India will have to part with the product and manufacturing technology to its Indian partner to grow the technology base in the country. These legal requirements will address the frightening unemployment problem and in the bargain give Modi's Make in India programme traction (which decision will, of course, have to be accompanied with the easing of labour laws, land acquisition rules and tax regimes, which the Modi regime has only fitfully undertaken). Alas, the Indian government, including during Modi's tenure, has acted as if entirely unaware of these leverages, particularly economic and trade leverages, which India has never used to virtually extort or extract anything it wants from any country. Indeed, Trump's 'scorched earth' trade policy provides a perfect rationale for Delhi to effectively use access to the Indian market as leverage to get the terms it wants from Washington on the pain of other countries complying and getting a march over American firms. It is the sort of policy that requires a bravura political will that no Indian leader has to date been able to summon.

Of course, this is not to be unmindful of the assets in the US armoury. In the main it is the plenitude of every kind of resource that Henry Kissinger, former secretary of state and adviser to US presidents explained, makes it unnecessary for the US to have any strategic vision at all, because US foreign policy becomes just a series of external problems to be solved by mobilizing and deploying the appropriate resources to the required level.[163] The US's financial muscle may be gauged by the fact that America's wars (in Iraq and Afghanistan) just in the two decades of this century have already cost the US exchequer some $5 trillion, or almost a third of the current GDP of $17 trillion, with no end to the Afghan war and similar expenditure in sight.[164]

Where India is concerned, Washington does not have to exert itself much at all because, as discussed, it can simply hand out Green Cards, H1B visas and 'scholarships' and jobs in US companies to progeny of the nomenklatura in Delhi. It is a nice, clean and easy solution to resolve any of its India-related problems. Thus, even inflexibly strong positions taken by Modi on bilateral issues can suffer because Indian officials susceptible to allurements can implement strong policies weakly. The formal US strategy, however, is one of playing to the Indian establishment's frailties, or as the former US ambassador who had numerous postings in South Asia, Teresita Schaffer said, of 'playing to India's uniqueness'. 'Uniqueness' here is seemingly a code-phrase for Delhi's concern for preserving India's 'image' even at the cost of its sovereignty. Washington has learned that Indian negotiators can be persuaded to concede anything just so long as the 'image words' they desire find mention in the agreement under negotiation to, presumably, provide them with political cover, and because ultimately the Indian government has been shown to wilt under sustained pressure.[165]

Modi is further handicapped by Trump's foreign policy modus operandi, which he adopts with most countries except, for obvious reasons, China and Russia. His use of bluff and bluster or sweet words with a hint of strong-arm tactics as the situation demands is a way of conducting business that he perfected as a real estate mogul. With Trump overturning seventy years of NATO convention and ordering traditional European allies either directly to pay up or reimburse the US for the upkeep of American military forces on their territories and, at the other end of Eurasia, publicly prompting Japan to do a rethink on nuclear weapons and to take care of its military security against China by itself, what are the chances he will not push Delhi to follow up the LSA with permission to base US military units in India and to compel the Indian government to share the costs? Recall, in this last respect, that Washington refused to allow the US armed services in the 1990s war in the Balkans to serve under Indian Army Lieutenant General Satish Nambiar of the Indian army, who was the first commander and head of mission of the UN Protection Force in the then united Yugoslavia.

The larger, more delicate point to make is something else. Modi may be convinced that his Gujarati small trader's commercial instincts will stand him in good stead when tackling Trump, but he will discover soon enough, if he hasn't already, that he is overmatched because the billionaire US President brings his rich-brat-who-always-has-his-way steamroller mentality to the table. He can, quite literally, trump the Indian prime minister at every turn by combining the enormous resources of the US with his patent whimsicality that can turn the situation from friendly to adversarial in a trice. This is not the stuff most democratic heads of government can handle with aplomb—the reason why West European regimes find themselves all at sea in conducting bilateral and G7 relations with the US. Is Modi better placed? He may call upon the brazenness of a commercial-minded Gujarati in response, but this will fetch him little. Trump approaches allies and partners as a superior with a sense of entitlement and privilege; what he says, he thinks, should go. Would this be acceptable to the Indian prime minister? The fact that Trump played along with Modi in their first meeting in the White House in the summer of 2017 should not lead the prime minister to believe that hugging the US President will translate into anything other than US policies being thrust down his throat, which is what subsequent developments (on the H1B visa, technology transfer, trade, etc.) have proved.

By way of illustrating the point about the double-edged deals that will be short-term panaceas for India and benefit mostly the US in the long term, consider the following: What will Modi do, for example, if

Trump, say, offers to carve out a two- or three-year window for Indians and Indian IT companies on H1B visas in exchange for the Indian prime minister buying the obsolete F-16 and/or F-18 combat aircraft and/or finalizing the sale of the Westinghouse AP 1000 reactors? The defence, telecommunications and power ministries, the Department of Atomic Energy whose ministerial head is concurrently the prime minister, and the entire Indian IT industry will be vociferous in support of such exchange. And, what if the US President conceives a special purpose vehicle to allow Indian exports of manufactures to the US on a preferential basis, last afforded Dengist China (which, in reality, will undermine Trump's own policy of favouring US jobs, industry and exports and, therefore, is highly unlikely) in return for full military basing privileges for the US Navy and the US Air Force in India? Such a gambit will have the finance and other economic ministries and some of the armed services counselling Modi to accept it. This is to say that politically and economically attractive inducements can result in trade-offs that can subsequently be rationalized in a host of ways and sold to the Indian public under the aegis of a friendly media. It can quickly become a means for a transactional-minded Washington to manipulate a transaction-minded Modi, and for the former to pull even more value from the bargain than the latter was originally inclined to give up.

The meta-problem for India is this: With Indian governments for a long time now tending to undervalue India's inherent strengths, strategic options and capabilities and overvalue the US's (or any other big power's) potential contribution and role in making India a prosperous/great/major power or, in the phrase used by the NSS, 'leading global power'—the kind of 'image words' that makes the Indian government and media go weak in the knee—India's creeper-vine policy of clinging to the US to rise may have a bad ending. A creeper vine, after all, has to cling to a pole or a trellis, and can fall down in a heap should this support be removed, in which case, the threat of such removal itself becomes a pressure point and provides the US incomparable political leverage. It is a danger Modi did not contemplate before staying with the policy tilt Vajpayee initiated and which Manmohan Singh consolidated. American influence spreaders in Indian society, seeing the direction in which Modi is headed, are cheering him on, urging him to compromise India's national interest and bring it in line with US economic interests because, as one of them put it, that's 'the key to an enduring and productive bilateral partnership', which he avers, could fetch India a reprieve on the H1B visa count, as if the H1B visa is the pivot for India's strategic interests.[166]

What Modi desperately needs to do is pause, think and realize that his India First goals, while less easy to achieve, are strategically far-sighted, and also in the present circumstances, realizable. If Obama and Trump, Putin and Xi, Erdogan and Shinzo Abe, Angela Merkel and Emmanuel Macron, are all guided only by narrowly defined notions of national interest, meaning that which mostly benefits only their own countries, why have Indian prime ministers not been so motivated as well? It is time for Modi to not take too seriously the rhetoric of friendship by big powers that have shown their inconstancy in the past, and to be moved only by hard calculations of national interest.

Here, it may be appropriate to recall an episode related by the former foreign secretary Rasgotra. At the height of the build-up to the Bangladesh war, US Undersecretary of State John Irwin counselled, what else, 'restraint' to the Indian ambassador in Washington, L.S. Jha. When Rasgotra, then on the embassy staff sitting in the meeting, reacted by suggesting that the Nixon administration could end the refugee flow that was creating the crisis for India by restraining the Pakistani martial law government of General Yahya Khan, Irwin blew up. 'We are doing what is in our national interest and we shall continue to act in our national interest,' an enraged Irwin asserted. 'We do not need advice about what we should or should not do.'[167] Ideally, this Irwinian riposte may be no bad thing for the Indian government to repeat when next Delhi is asked by Washington to restrain itself and act responsibly. Modi can, however, exploit Trump's doctrine of 'principled realism' to legitimize India's economic and national security interests independent of America.

Delhi's Blind Spots: America and China

It is India's hesitancy to impose costs on China that has permitted Washington to insert itself into the power game in the Indo-Pacific and convince Delhi about the necessity of having the US on its side. As a result, both Washington and Beijing have been given a free pass by Delhi. It is important to note here that the Indian government has followed the late K. Subrahmanyam's observation that 'With the Americans you purchase not just weapons but a security relationship . . . [and] build it into [your] calculations'. Fine, but in lieu of really advanced military hardware that Washington won't give to India for love or money, the IAF may get stuck with obsolete late-1960s vintage F-16 and the navy with the F-18 combat aircraft, which the Pentagon, the concerned US companies and American think tanks with Tellis in the lead have lobbied for at both the Washington and Delhi ends, and which option Jaishankar and the MEA supported likely because they saw Modi tending that way.[168] More generally, Jaishankar defined India's foreign policy aphoristically at the Carnegie India inauguration as 'leverage[ing] the dominant, collaborat[ing] with the convergent, and manag[ing] the competition'.[169] It can be inferred from this statement that China is the target and that the US is crucial for India succeeding in all these three streams of policy.

Let's briefly analyse here only the first stream and see why it is wrong-headed and hollow. 'Leveraging the dominant' implies that Washington has to be courted by India and that Delhi needs to put out for the US. The geostrategic reality, however, is contrary to Modi's, Tellis's and Jaishankar's construct. The US's continuing desire to retain its influence and remain relevant in Asia at a time when it is in a growingly tenuous financial condition, sports a weakened political resolve, and in terms of its thinning military wherewithal and strength of deployable forces is in no position to match either China's purse or its comprehensive capability and that is the reason why Washington needs India far more than the other way around.[170] It is the upper hand that Delhi doesn't seem to realize it has, and this doesn't even take into account the potential ruthless use of access to the Indian market of American trade and commerce that can be wielded to demand really big things—complete transfer of advanced technology, including source codes, for designing and producing combat aircraft jet engines, for example, which would be evidence of US good faith—or else tell the US to take a hike. Delhi doesn't do this, preferring to act like the supplicant it is used to being.

This Modi–Tellis–Jaishankar formulation, moreover, does not begin to address the basic trust deficit existing between India and the US, which is wide, deep and difficult to paper over with nice words in the face of self-centred US policies. Washington has historically sought and continues to undermine India's strategic weapons capability and its attempts to become self-sufficient in conventional armaments; it seeks to balance Indian power and influence in the subcontinent by arming and aiding a puny Pakistan to the extent of being complicit in its nuclearization by China and, in the present, by trying to constrain India's ties with friendly countries in the extended neighbourhood, including Iran and Russia, all the while making pleasant noises about India as 'security provider' in the Indian Ocean region.[171]

What no US government official or think-tanker has ever been able to explain is why, if India is the central pillar of an Indo-Pacific security edifice (because Japan for all its economic and military muscle is, comparatively speaking, piddling in size, and Australia has the size but lacks the population), Washington is so vehemently against Delhi resuming thermonuclear testing to obtain credible thermonuclear weapons and, at a stroke, to achieve at least notional strategic parity with China and psychologically to blunt Beijing's hegemonic ambition? This is so, former US ambassador Richard Verma hinted, because such were not the terms Delhi negotiated, which it could have done in the 2008 civil nuclear cooperation deal with the US had the Indian government and negotiators acted as if aware of India's larger geostrategic location and the leverage it afforded Delhi and refused to be railroaded into an agreement that did not comprehensively serve India's interests.[172]

Of course, the Indian diplomats who negotiated this accord with Jaishankar as joint secretary (Americas) in the lead, as per their socialization in the IFS, came pickled in the vinegar of antipathy to 'primordial nationalism', spiced with the dislike of hard power (epitomized by nuclear weapons) and in the oil of 'practical pragmatism'—which mix, presumably, lubricated their acceptance of US terms.[173] This agreement bars India from conducting nuclear tests on pain of termination of the deal and reimposition of the technology-denying NSG strictures— which apparently is so intolerable to the Indian government, it apparently can see nothing beyond them and even though other technologies are extraneous to the country's needs.[174]

Not that non-proliferation is all that big an American concern. If it were it wouldn't have been complicit in China's arming Pakistan with nuclear missiles, something President Jimmy Carter's NSA Zbigniew Brzezinski explained thus: 'Our security policy cannot be dictated by our non-proliferation policy', a statement that was welcomed by Chairman Deng Xiaoping in Beijing.[175] That India got suckered into the 2008 nuclear deal is because MEA negotiators swallowed hook, line and sinker the line about the US's supposedly sacrosanct non-proliferation goals, when what they should have had their eyes on was the objective of securing a credible thermonuclear deterrent and left it to Washington to back out or adjust. In any case, the larger US game plan is transparent, but not to the Indian policy establishment, and that is to string India along as potential collaborator, an aim that a compromised and pliant Indian officialdom keeps nudging forward.

There is a pattern here. Consistent with its goal of securing a string of dependencies in Asia, Washington has been just as ruthless in tamping down policies and popular sentiment for the Bomb by Japan, South Korea and Taiwan, because armed with nuclear weapons these countries will be less malleable.[176] In the context of Indo-US relations over the last fifty years—and ample proof of bad faith, distrust, retroactive changing of treaties (Tarapur fuel), deliberate hurting of India's security interests and unwillingness to part with any meaningful technology—it is extraordinary but par for the course for Tellis to claim that the US has shown 'strategic generosity towards India'.[177] It leads one to wonder whether India wouldn't be better off with strategic meanness on America's part—assuming it can afford it in 21st century geopolitics, which is not exactly going the US's way.

In any case, the US may be in no position to challenge China and Russia militarily because, according to defence secretary James Mattis, it is just 'emerging from a period of strategic atrophy'—a situation that realistically will take several decades to mend, assuming the US Congress votes the necessary funds and defence expenditures are prioritized as per Mattis's recommendations.[178] It may become a long-term debility given the dysfunctional Trump administration and the political headwinds it is running into. In this milieu, the fact of an enfeebled US military, drained by the war in Iraq and weakened by an unending conflict in Afghanistan, will only buttress Washington's shortage of political will to take on Beijing. It is not a state of affairs to inspire confidence in its traditional Asian allies. For India, it only accentuates the US's unreliability as strategic partner.

Be that as it may, the India–US relationship, in any case, is unidirectional in that influence flows only one way—from Washington to Delhi—and is often used by Modi to seek US government validation of his views, which is promptly made available. Consider Modi's concept of 'India as leading, not balancing, power' again. Tellis was first off the blocks to argue that Modi's 'leading power' notion is proximal to the 'great power' idea, and that India can, in fact, realize this ambition, by doing three things: (1) 'Complete the structural reforms necessary to create efficient product and factor markets' requiring the government 'to redirect its activities toward producing better public goods, while establishing an institutional framework that stimulates private creativity and increases rationalization across Indian society', (2) 'Create an effective state to leverage India's capacity to build its national power' by vastly improving 'its presence in society as well as better extractive and regulatory capacities—all of which require a more autonomous state—India cannot accumulate material capabilities to rapidly become a great power', and (3) 'Foster a strong relationship with the United States' as it 'is an important host for India's skilled labor; remains a critical source of capital, technology, and expertise; and constitutes the fulcrum of strategic support for India's global ambitions'.

If India maintains robust ties with the United States, even as it strengthens relations with key US allies in Asia and beyond, it will continue to gain indispensable benefits'.[179] The first two are stock recommendations that Indian economic and social commentators regularly make. The last is the geostrategically loaded one and has been proffered in the past two decades by US presidents George W. Bush and Barack Obama as a means of gently nudging India more fully into the American camp. What with a revived Russia under Putin giving the US and western Europe the jitters, and China's emergence as an all-round rival putting America's place in Asia in jeopardy, this is now imperative for the US.

The Americans, however, stress that linking up with the US and its allies in the Indo-Pacific will help India enlarge its role in the wider landward and maritime Asia and help it gain global recognition as a major player. Global recognition? For what, for being a cog in the

American machine? They emphasize that this is a 'natural' path for India to pursue because of the shared democratic systems and values. What is not mentioned is the cost to India in terms of its reputation and image as a self-respecting and independent-minded country of its thus skittering over to the US side, rather than retaining the distance with the US as also with China and Russia (which will assuage all the parties) while preserving policy space and latitude for itself to side with any or none of them as dictated by the circumstances. Contingently partnering the US, Russia or China and other powers to advance its specific and distinct interests and generally being free to put together short-, medium- or long-term security and economic coalitions or, simply, issue-based working arrangements from among other countries in Asia and the world to keep the major powers—especially the proto-hegemons, the US and China—on their toes, is the power game India should be in.

It is this aspect that was implicit in Modi's first articulation after the 2014 elections of the country's foreign policy when he talked of being on 'equal terms' with the major powers. It showed an understanding of India's inherent strengths and his intention to convert them into diplomatic clout. It, moreover, fitted in nicely with the history of several millennia of alliance politics, starting with Thucydides's account of the Peloponnesian Wars (431–404 BC) which shows that a potentially powerful country can be marginalized, transformed into a strategic appendage, taken for granted and its interests sidestepped if it joins up with a still more powerful state and gets absorbed in its alliance system.[180] It is a sharp lesson that history offers that a seemingly America-besotted Modi and Indian foreign policy establishment has lost sight of.

Another lesson that history time and again teaches is the primacy of hard power in a country's rise married to expansive vision and unwavering will. This is evidenced in the Phoenix-like rise of Putin's Russia from the ashes of the Cold War defeat and the dismantling of the Soviet Union, and of the economic basket-case North Korea, armed, owing to China, with thermonuclear-warheaded ICBMs, thumbing its nose at Washington, reducing the US, already reeling under the impulsive, almost infantile, presidency of Donald Trump, into sputtering ineffectualness. Yet, in India the case is frequently made about the need to first become an economic power conjoined to the exercise of its enormous soft power before it can become a strategically consequential state. Indeed, Delhi's priorities have traditionally been economy first, soft power second, and military power and power projection last. The country has suffered grievously for it. India has been consigned to the fringes of great power, left vulnerable to the machinations of the extant big powers, all of whom by nature proactively protect and advance their national interests at the expense of all other countries. Going by what's emanating from the government, Modi, the PMO, MEA and MoD are equally oblivious to the emerging international distribution of power and the decreasing importance of economic interdependence and globalization. They seem to be unconscious of the trending military technology, wherewithal, strategy and tactics that are evolving towards strengthening the sovereignty of individual states.

The fact that Modi, despite great initial promise, is at a sorry pass at the end of his first term where he finds associating with the US essential, may be blamed at least partly for his not knowing any better, and on the existing dysfunctional government system monopolized by a generalist bureaucracy, whose senior ranks are occupied by officers with personal and familial stakes in good Indo-US ties. The way the apparatus of state is structured, the colonial-age 'rules of business' followed and the discretionary power of civil servants exercised without any trace of accountability, it makes misgovernance, hesitant half-measures, inefficiency, corruption and costly delays in government decisions and policy implementation a byword for, in Lance Pritchett's memorable phrase, a 'flailing state'.[181]

Yet, Prime Minister Modi insists on seeing the existing bureaucratic system as the instrument to effect change, which only makes for a still bigger problem. Despite being saddled with a manifestly ineffective administrative structure, he blithely claims, as he did at the Asia-Pacific Economic Summit in Manila in November 2017, that everything is well and India is 'transforming' itself. When a malfunctioning government system is not recognized for the problem that it is, far-reaching solutions, it stands to reason, are not attempted. Thus, even though Modi has repeatedly claimed that the business milieu has eased and his policies have spurred economic activity, what is apparent is that economic progress is slow and unsteady, FDI is largely missing, the Indian private manufacturing and services sectors are in the doldrums, doing business in India is still an ordeal, the profligate public sector, particularly in defence production, survives on government favours, contracts and subsidies, the unemployment problem is going from bad to alarming and Modi's reputation as a doer and one for lighting a fire under the economy has taken a hit at home and abroad.[182]

Moreover, with a foreign policy in which India is the dependent variable and the US the independent variable, solid achievements are missing. Quick-fixes will not work but a start could and should be made on two policy fronts as antidote to the country's America-centric policies of the first two decades of the 21st century, which have failed to do other than push the country deeper into a hole. India should regain centrality in the Indian foreign policy by cutting out the would-be proto-hegemonic powers from the two groupings with the utmost strategic importance and the greatest potential to the country. Delhi should hereon strive to put together a BRIS group, that is BRICS without China, and a Modified Quadrilateral or Mod Quad. These constructs need not replace BRICS and the Quadrilateral but flourish independent of them. This is discussed in the next two chapters.

[4]

Adversarial Geopolitics: BRIS and Mod Quad

'Geopolitics is all about leverage'—Thomas Friedman

INDIA HAS FOR a long time now stopped being thought of as a large country that matters, for the reason that it seems unable to stand by itself, for itself and do things on its own in its interests. The fact of Indian foreign policy tilting America-wards so far in the 21st century is supposed to help Delhi and Washington demarcate the Sinic-sphere in Asia and, in time, shrink it. Had the Indian government (headed successively by Atal Bihari Vajpayee, Manmohan Singh and now Narendra Modi) instead been driven by hard realpolitik coupled with what the pioneering theoretician of geopolitics Halford Mackinder called 'The map reading habit of mind', India, with its size and location alone, would have emerged as a decisive player on the world scene, the ultimate balancer of international power and central to shaping the future of Asia and, by extension, the world. Because successive governments have not done this, India seems only another self-absorbed Asian state that can't see beyond its nose and grabs at any available great power's coat-tails to save itself. India's foreign policy in the new century, strangely enough, is not dictated by its geography, belying Napoleon's view that 'If you know a country's geography, you can understand and predict its foreign policy'.

The confusion and not a little bit of incoherence in Indian foreign policy appears to be because in its fundamentals, the driver of policy,

Prime Minister Modi, is not clear about the difference between its two distinct and separate organizing principles, namely, 'non-alignment' and 'strategic autonomy', conflating the datedness of the former with the supposed disutility of the latter and throwing out the baby of strategic autonomy with the bathwater of non-alignment. True, Vajpayee's regime conceived of 'strategic autonomy' to mask its cultivating the US (which resulted in the NSSP). The subsequent decade-long Congress party government of Manmohan Singh and its successor BJP dispensation under Modi not merely stuck to this course but embellished it, subscribing, as a staffer at the VIF founded by NSA Ajit Doval has called it, 'alliance diplomacy' with the United States.[1] The question is, how does this affect India's foreign policy stance?

The basic difference between non-alignment and strategic autonomy that Modi and his cohort seem ignorant of, and which the MEA has not grasped, has scrambled policy aims and objectives and distorted the perception of the means to achieve them. The policy of non-alignment that Jawaharlal Nehru practised and formalized in 1961 when the Big Four of the movement—Nehru, President Josip Broz Tito of Yugoslavia, President Gamal Abdel of Egypt and President Sukarno of Indonesia—met in the northern Adriatic Sea port of Brioni (or Brijuni in present-day Croatia) was based on a sensible reading of the then 'correlation of forces'. Each of them led countries that singly were too feeble to influence world events or even matters concerning their own immediate regions, but together they comprised a spatially dispersed and vocally powerful presence drawing on support from the uncommitted nations of Asia, Africa and South America. They were able to wield disproportionate diplomatic clout in the initial years of the Cold War when what side the non-aligned tipped the scales on mattered to the two superpowers of the day: the USA and the Union of Soviet Socialist Republics (USSR).

Genuine 'strategic autonomy' (not Vajpayee or Manmohan Singh's kind), on the other hand, is a concept that more neatly fits India and the geopolitical terrain in the new century. Economically prospering after partial reforms, beginning to accumulate power and, with the proper use of resources, being in a condition to spread its wings within the region and beyond, a strategically autonomous India, on its own, can disrupt, stimulate and guide the direction in which power will shift in Asia and the world. This hasn't happened because autonomy is being frittered away on the altar of pleasing the United States. A non-aligned India, by comparison, was mainly an international nuisance in the larger global power politics.

Modi, however, has avoided risk, and taken the line of least resistance. Guided by his admiration for America, he has sought safety by clambering on to the US bandwagon that is conveniently at hand, and which he expects will help India get to where it wants to go. But, unwilling or unable to conceive a national vision, Modi finds his India in the position of Lewis Carroll's Alice, discovering in Wonderland that if you don't know where you are going any path will get you there. The pity is that the enormous capability and leverage India has acquired for the first time in the modern era is thus being wasted. A medley of flawed policies has followed as Modi, like his immediate predecessors in office, has reached for the crutch of the US's big power protection and patronage because he foresees a limp in the future: India's inability to handle a bellicose China. This reflects the fact that Indian prime ministers of late have been devoid of strategic imagination and habituated to safe, Pavlovian reflexes to external stimuli-qua-threats.

The country's characteristically overcautious, predictable and legalistic style of diplomacy—an Anglo-Saxon legacy of the Raj—moreover, is lauded by the US and its European allies because it is high on predictability, they are familiar with it and it serves their purposes. The Western praise strengthens Delhi's instincts of always acting as a 'responsible state', seemingly the central policy tenet of its approach to international affairs in the Manmohan Singh and Modi years. In practice, it means that it is better for India not to gain by being venturesome than to fail by taking risk.

In fact, the US Secretary of State Rex W. Tillerson, on the eve of his first trip to Delhi in October 2017, praised India for just this peculiarity, praising it for, unlike China, 'rising . . . responsibly' without 'undermining the international, rules-based order' which, incidentally, is of US and Western construction.[2] What the Chinese understand well but the Indian establishment apparently does not comprehend is the fact that a country only behaves 'responsibly' to uphold an order that is beneficial to one's own country and there's a stake to protect. If the existing order is not configured to advantage India then it behooves Delhi to try in every manner and form to undermine it, disturb the ongoing power plays and make it clear with its deeds that it will take down the system unless its interests are recognized and the 'rules of the road' rectified to accord it a founder status in a new 'Power-4' grouping in line with the new balance of power—of India, the US, Russia and China at the apex of the international system. The United Kingdom and France, relatively small European states that have been riding on their historic role as colonial and imperial powers too long, no longer merit a place at the top and the Indian government should make this clear in its dealings with them and ease them off the high table.

Alas, this is not how the BJP government views the world or seeks to enhance India's standing. In fact, Foreign Secretary Jaishankar was clear about this when he juxtaposed, without actually saying so, at the 2018 Raisina Dialogue, India's rise against China's 'disruptive rise', echoing what the US Pacific Command chief admiral Harry Harris said about China being 'the disruptive force in the Indo-Pacific region'. In the existing disruptive ambience, Jaishankar also included 'the posture of the US, the challenge of terrorism, and the . . . implications of non-market economics' and ended up strangely thanking China for 'open[ing] up the international order, which allowed India to make its presence felt'.[3]

In other words, Indian foreign policy seems premised on being beholden not just to the US but to China as well. It is a policy of avoiding risks and slipstreaming into prominence on the strength and initiative of countries that do take risks. This may be good tactics, but it is certainly not good strategy because a country can take a free ride on another country's wings only so much before finding itself stranded in a place that is far from its destination. Surely, Modi is not planning to ride at the same time two differently aligned horses—US and China—cantering in a direction that serves their separate interests or joint purpose but not India's. The limitations of a policy relying on friends and adversaries to afford India opportunities to make good are self-evident. Moreover, there's the little thing about 'trust deficit', which Admiral Harris dumped on China, saying, 'The trust deficit that exists in the region should be addressed by China.'[4] But as discussed previously, India has as big if not a bigger trust deficit with America.

The inability to differentiate between tactics and strategy is an old failing of the Indian government. Modi's defining trait appears to be to mistake vaporous feel-good statements for strategy. Trust or the lack of it with the US or with China does not really matter because Indian policy is based on the contingent reading of the unfolding situation by the prime minister. Consequently, the country's foreign policy seems strung out between institutional myopia and the prime minister's trustful, high-flying rhetoric, ensuring that India when not falling between these two stools advances only by default. For example, Modi cherishes India as a civilizational power, which in harsh power politics terms translates into a lot of hot air because there's no aspect of it readily translatable into power politics. He talked when in China about his civilizational approach fuelling 'the image of India as a responsible rising power that seeks to lead through the strength of its ageless wisdom that had once radiated across most of the civilized world'.[5]

This must have come as a relief to Zhongnanhai—the seat of the government in Beijing (like the North and South Blocks in Delhi)—which has relied on the Indian government to continue to act 'responsibly' so that Chinese ends can be furthered without facing the danger of tit-for-tat actions and punitive measures by an aggrieved India. Such as, for a start, arming the states on China's periphery with nuclear missiles as payback for Beijing's dastardly proliferation of nuclear weapon and missile technologies to Pakistan, assisting the Tibetan and Uyghur freedom movements, and putting relations with Taiwan on a higher plane, walking back Delhi's acceptance of Tibet or even the Tibetan Autonomous Region as part of China owing to Beijing's position on Kashmir, etc. It highlights the Indian government's aversion to proactive, offensive, pre-emptive policies for fear of upsetting friends and foes, the regional and international orders, power balances and the prevailing great power setup.

Given the America-friendly policy ecosystem (elaborated in the last chapter) that has been allowed to take root in Delhi, playing footsie with the US, which is leery of an assertive India, is tantamount to providing Washington a means of ensuring that India does not emerge as an independent player. US policy is, in some ways, congruent with China's of exercising its well-thought-out strategy to hamper India's rise and shrink India's reach, clout and influence. What has transpired as a result of the Modi government's desire to play along with the US and China is its policies have been shaped accordingly. The rationale provided by the MEA is that India needs to be seen as more flexible and to be less a global 'naysayer'.[6] But are taking action in its national interest, countering the policies of extraterritorial powers seeking to expand their influence at the expense of India in extended South Asia, and simply saying no to injurious big power initiatives tantamount to being obstructionist? And if so, what's wrong with that? Did the US in the Pacific rim and China in South East Asia not make clear that these areas are their backyards where they will tolerate no outside presence, interference or role, and do they not act to ensure that these redlines are respected?

But seemingly Modi is not keen on keeping this region as India's semi-exclusive domain at the cost of bad blood with, say, Beijing, and in any case is not prepared to get into a bidding game with China for the loyalty of the regimes in southern Asia and in the Indian Ocean region which, given the resources available to Beijing, is a losing proposition anyway. But India's proximity permits Delhi to exercise other sorts of leverage, like coercive military and economic force, which India has not used despite being offered every provocation. So, willy-nilly, Modi is complicit in India's strategic shrinkage. Consider the evidence with respect to India's new, more forbearing policy in the immediate neighbourhood that has permitted China to root its presence in the region, specifically the Maldives.

Politics in the Maldives has always been a zero sum game. In the latest version, the winner in the last general elections, Abdulla Yameen, forced the losing former president Mohammad Nasheed into exile, and hauled the long-time former president and cousin Abdulla Gayoom up for treason. Gayoom's rule was restored in 1986 with the intervention by the Indian Army's airborne brigade (Operation Cactus) and the coup d'etatists—a bunch of Sri Lankan Tamil adventurers, having failed to establish an *eelam* in their country, failed again in taking over the government in the Maldives, an archipelagic country strung out north to south over nearly 1200 coral islands grouped in some 26 atolls over some 2000 km of the Indian Ocean south-west of the Indian

Lakshadweep island chain. The last time there was a hint of use of Indian force was in 2013–14 when the Indian Navy pre-empted Yameen's initial moves to gift an atoll just 19 km from the southern-most island in the Lakshadweep chain to China for it to establish a radar station there. A Chinese radar installation in that strategic location would have enabled the Chinese Navy to carry out sweeps of the entire arc seaward and landward to monitor the traffic of Indian naval vessels in and out of its west coast bases, and otherwise to mount 24/7 real-time surveillance.

The appearance of two Indian warships dispatched by Vice Admiral Shekhar Sinha, then head of the Western Naval Command, was enough for Yameen to return to his senses and call off that deal. As per the established modus operandi, this entire episode was treated as a local issue with the nearest operational naval command having the jurisdiction to act on the basis of its own intelligence, with Delhi merely kept in the loop.[7] So what has changed? The reluctance of the Modi government to upend the defiant Yameen regime. It goes against the grain of the prime minister's own pronouncements when the Maldivian President last visited Delhi in April 2016.

'India understands its role as a net security provider in the Indian Ocean and is ready to protect its strategic interests in this region,' Modi had declared. He also added, 'The prompt implementation of a concrete action plan in the defence sector will strengthen our security cooperation.'[8] This cooperation involved, besides training and equipment for the Maldivian military and police forces and investment in several developments projects, the posting of Indian naval personnel on a rotational basis to man powerful radar stations and other facilities on various Maldivian locations. Post-2016, however, the always unsettled domestic politics of this island state took a turn for the worse with Yameen's cabinet colleagues deserting the ruling coalition and making common cause with the Nasheed and Gayoom factions of the opposition, a situation compounded by the Maldivian Supreme Court ruling against Yameen for election irregularities.

Always fearful of India's intervention, Yameen had never made any bones about cultivating China as a counter, but his leasing an atoll to China gifted Messrs Nasheed and Gayoom the issue they believed would prompt Delhi to oust Yameen.[9] Beijing, asked by Yameen, was quick to caution India to let the Maldives be.[10] Instead of preserving the Maldives as exclusive Indian turf and acting boldly to keep China out of the country's oceanic vicinity by ordering the navy into action as was standard practice, he consulted with Washington, which counselled—ah, yes—restraint.[11] It emboldened Yameen, who, perceiving an infirm will, asked Beijing for an expeditious show of military muscle whence a Chinese naval flotilla pulling anti-piracy duty in the western Indian Ocean duly turned up in the Maldivian waters.[12]

It must have been the size of the Chinese naval force of eleven ships—several missile destroyers, a frigate, a 30,000 tonne amphibious transport dock and three fleet tankers—that spooked Delhi or at least set off MEA officials on their usual appeasement options. Led by Mandarin-speaking China 'experts' in the Foreign Office, headed by Foreign Secretary Vijay Gokhale, who when not easily frightened are ever so mindful of Chinese sensitivities to do India's national security interests much good, and invariably counselled caution. The next thing that happened was the quite extraordinary development of the BJP government, that has consistently attacked Nehru and Congress governments of the past for their pusillanimity in tackling China, conceding what was until now an exclusive Indian 'sphere of influence' to Beijing.

'The days when India believed that South Asia was its primary sphere of influence and that it could prevent other powers such as China from expanding its own clout are long gone,' said a senior government official to the press. It is the clearest proof available that Modi and his national security team in the PMO are devoid of basic strategic sense and understanding of geography. As far as is known, there were no quick studies or even assessment based on intelligence reports about whether the Chinese naval flotilla off the Maldives could sustain its presence in those waters for any length of time, let alone conduct offensive operations so far from home base in defence of the Yameen regime, and whether the Indian Western Fleet couldn't have been rapidly deployed to impose at least a minimum blockade of the Maldives and show India's resolve to stop China by force if necessary. The fact is that the Chinese naval flotilla, already near the end of its patrolling time, lacked the resources to do much had India deployed its proximal naval assets in force. It would have compelled the Chinese warships to either risk starting hostilities by running the blockade that they couldn't possibly have done or peeling off and heading home, reaffirming in the process this area as India's bailiwick.

These were the ideal circumstances to show up Xi's China as a paper dragon, increase the confidence of the littoral states in the South China Sea about India's capability, win grudging acknowledgement even from the sceptics about India's steadfastness in crisis and reinforce Modi's claims for India as 'security provider'. It would have sobered up Yameen, K.P. Oli in Nepal and every other regime in South Asia, including Pakistan, signalled that Delhi is not to be trifled with, and sent a message to Beijing that the Indian Ocean is not the South China Sea and that it can't patrol the Indian Ocean with the insouciance it shows against the small and weak states east of Malacca. Most importantly, it would have conveyed to Beijing that China's military presence in the Indian Ocean would always be at India's sufferance. It is a position that India can physically maintain, albeit with some effort, but China cannot forcefully contest because of the sheer distances and its tenuous logistics support line that cannot be ramped up in a hurry, if at all. Such action, moreover, would have burnished Modi's strongman image at the expense of Xi's.

That opportunity was lost with the same senior official explaining the Modi government's wish to escape militarily clashing with China thus: 'India cannot claim sole proprietorship of the region. We can't stop what the Chinese are doing, whether in the Maldives or in Nepal, but we can tell them about our sensitivities, our lines of legitimacy. If they cross it, the violation of this strategic trust will be upon Beijing.'[13] What does 'lines of legitimacy' and 'the violation of strategic trust' mean? In any case, if the Modi government didn't have the resolve to enforce India's sphere of influence in the Maldives, what are the chances of its being able to insist on its 'lines of legitimacy' elsewhere in India's near abroad ? In the event, does this phrase not signify Delhi's lacking the stomach for a fight with China even for India's own backyard? The record makes it plain that for Beijing 'strategic trust' means little and won't stop it from getting what it wants. It also raises the question: What would Beijing have to do get India to react forcefully? Let's say the Chinese begin constructing a naval or air base on a Maldivian atoll, and submarine pens at Hambantota port, which Colombo has leased for ninety-nine years to a Chinese company; that would be violating 'strategic trust' wouldn't it? What will Delhi do other than protest weakly and have the Indian Foreign Office repeat the same shopworn phrases about not being able to prevent these areas from being used strategically against India? Expectedly, Malé was quick to rub in the salt, equating the political turmoil in the Maldives to the unrest in Kashmir and pretty much sealing India's reduced status in South Asia and the Indian Ocean region.[14]

Obviously, the Modi dispensation has thought of a solution for just such situations: It is to minimize India's risk of dealing singly with China by spreading it among several powers. Thus, other than the LSA allowing US armed forces to stage out of India, Delhi signed a similar agreement for 'reciprocal logistics support' with France when President Macron was in Delhi in early March 2018, which Modi rather fulsomely described as 'as a golden step in the history of our close defence cooperation'.[15] So Indian ships can put into harbour and replenish stores in the naval base on Reunion Island in the French Indian Ocean territory and the Heron naval base in Djibouti in the Horn of Africa. French ships, more frequently, can be hosted along India's long coastline, and together Indian, US and French naval units can scare off the Chinese Navy. But the policy of dissipating the risk this way in a collective security enterprise minimizes India's singular stake in the Indian Ocean region, and that's the point China will have taken to heart from this Maldives episode, besides being reassured by India's unwillingness to fight for its interests.

Other than the Maldives, Modi also followed the Chinese dictates on the Dalai Lama by preventing public events organized by the Tibetan community to mark the sixtieth year of his exile from being staged in Delhi and instructing Indian politicians and officials to not attend them.[16] After Doklam, Delhi seems intent on a 'reset' of bilateral relations with China at any cost and, hence, generally on Chinese terms.[17] With such an understanding, India, said the reassured Chinese foreign minister Wang Yi, the Chinese dragon and the Indian elephant can indeed dance together.[18] The message that India does not have what it takes to fight for its interests was telegraphed to all. In quick succession, Iran offered the Chabahar port to Pakistan and China, former Sri Lanka president Mahinda Rajapaksa, who is likely to vault back into power in the 2019 elections, talked confidently about Pakistan and China as 'valued friends' and about Delhi looking 'at things differently now', and the political opposition in Seychelles quickly mobilized against India's taking over Assumption Island for military purposes.[19]

The locus genesis of this recessive Indian policy, if one were to reach back into history, was in the aftermath of the disastrous 1962 war with China when India began seeing the West, and America in particular, as saviour. This policy undergirding was cemented in the institutional mind and attitude of the Indian government even as Indira Gandhi erected the superstructure of Indo-Soviet ties on top of it. This latter carapace was dislodged by Narasimha Rao's active courting of the US while retaining India's links with Moscow. These last are being weakened by the Modi regime doing the inexcusable: parlaying disinterest in Russia's strategic imperatives and taking Moscow for granted. If carried too far, India will have a huge price to pay. At the national security end, an equally debilitating political directive was issued to the armed services post 1962 enjoining them to 'not lose an inch of territory'. It still stands and is the principal reason for the Indian military's overly defensive stance and its uselessness as an instrument of an activist diplomacy. When the bulk of the armed forces are arrayed for a passive defence, they cannot quickly be mobilized for agile expeditionary missions in strength on a regular basis in tune with a nimble and expansive policy. But when, as has been the case for a very long time and in the present, there is no sprightliness in policy, what is the need for a quicksilver military? Such are the predicates of India's solipsistic foreign and defence policies that Modi has left undisturbed. (More on this later and in the next chapter.) For a country that has all the makings and most of the endowments of great power, these self-inflicted liabilities are hard to overcome.

In contrast, China, believing centrally in the beneficial effects of disruption at every turn and, unlike India, absolutely trusting no other country—something enjoined in the ancient statecrafts of Chanakya and Sun Tzu—has forced itself into the great power ranks in the same timeframe as India has barely inched into middle-power status.[20] When an otherwise lowly Kim Jong-un–led North Korea, by moving rapidly from fission devices of questionable provenance and short-range Scud missiles to testing and fielding proven high-yield thermonuclear weapons and ICBMs and, significantly, offensive cyber warfare capabilities—all with

China's covert material and other assistance in the face of sanctions and unremitting global pressure orchestrated by Washington—stole a march over India, it should have given Delhi pause, but didn't.[21] Simply put, who is feared and hence respected more, forget China—North Korea or India?[22] In this context, will Washington worry about saving itself from a salvo of North Korean Hwasong missiles or hold Delhi's hands in its next crisis with China? Israel, with an all-azimuth security outlook, is troubled that what is 'paraded in Pyongyang ends up in Tehran'.[23] Not so the Modi regime, which, like the previous Indian governments, seems unrattled by the inevitability of China-sourced hydrogen bomb design, material and technology ending up, as per Beijing's plans, in Islamabad's nuclear arms inventory via North Korea (to afford Beijing plausible deniability).[24] This is bad news, especially because Delhi complicates the country's security problems by tackling the proliferatee—Pakistan—with gusto rather than vengefully countering the proliferator, China, and ends up darkening what little prospect there is for a rapprochement with Pakistan while letting Beijing push India around. One would have thought that based on seven decades of experience, the Indian government would by now have learned some basic foreign policy truths, namely that it doesn't help punitively to deal with the cat's paw and coddle the cat. Or, to put it another way, take on the lesser foe, Pakistan, because that's an easier task, than challenge a comprehensively superior China, which it fears doing.

How best to handle China is a policy concern the Indian government has long been bedevilled by, and consistently gets wrong. Jawaharlal Nehru's policy of unrequited empathy for China in the 1950s when he conceived of an India–China duopoly in Asia and expended scarce political capital in garnering legitimacy for the Mao Zedong dispensation and canvassing for a permanent seat in the UN Security Council for China—a seat that was first offered Delhi by both the US and the USSR—boomeranged on India. It all but terminated India's chances of ever making it to the UN Security Council and confirmed Chinese perceptions of this country as weak-minded and, therefore, to be made light of.[25] The chances are that Modi's policy, filled with goodwill, laced with sentiment and laden with hopes of bagging infrastructure investments in billions of dollars from Xi, will not fare much better.[26]

In his speech at the elite Tsinghua University in Beijing during his state visit to China in April 2016, for example, the Indian prime minister spoke of 'the centuries old story of our relations [being that of] of spiritualism, learning, art and trade [and of] respect for each other's civilization and shared prosperity'. He followed this up with more such patent nonsense: 'Neither [India nor China] can be contained or become part of anyone's plans,' he said. 'So our partnership . . . should not be determined by the concerns of others, but [by] the interests of our two countries.'[27] This sentiment was echoed by Chinese Foreign Minister Wang Yi who stated that 'If China and India are united, one plus one will not equal two but eleven.'[28] If this were actually true, how to explain China's successfully containing India by arming Pakistan with both conventional and nuclear weapons, supporting Islamabad in right or wrong and, in light of the sheer disparity in economic and military power between India and China, Delhi's all but committing to a security architecture for the Indo-Pacific on Washington's terms, which may not serve India's interests?

Scepticism is merited in any case about whether this is the correct foreign policy course to follow considering there is a long history of US unreliability as security partner—of pressuring the Indian government on the Kashmir dispute, balancing power in the subcontinent by weighing in on the side of Pakistan to the extent of acquiescing in the clandestine Chinese arming of Pakistan with nuclear weapons and missiles, and of undermining India's nuclear and strategic military interests and defence–industrial capabilities. In fact, many of these inherent traits of the US's India policy are seen in the clear, wide-ranging and fairly candid espousal of it by Trump's first secretary of state, Rex Tillerson. It removes all doubt about what it is that Washington means to do and where India stands vis-à-vis the United States. Referring to India and the US as the 'two bookends of stability, on either side of the globe', Tillerson, in effect, offered Delhi an informal '100 year' alliance to 'uphold' in the 'Indo-Pacific region the rule of law, freedom of navigation, universal values, and free trade'. Acknowledging that 'The world's center of gravity is shifting to the heart of the Indo-Pacific', and that the Indian Ocean 'is the focal point of the world's energy and trade routes' involving 40 per cent of 'the world's oil supply', he pointedly mentioned that China, unlike India, has risen 'less responsibly'. He meant it did not obey 'the rules-based order' installed by Western countries, chiefly the US, and hence has single-mindedly pursued its national interest unconstrained by Western notions of propriety, but which freedom Delhi long ago signed away because it was more keen to some cheap acclaim from the West by playing by the rules of the international power politics game it had no role in writing.

So, China thumbed its nose and sought to upend the existing system and subvert, as Tillerson put it, 'the sovereignty of neighboring countries, and disadvantage the US and our friends'. North Korea is embarked on the same course as is, in its own way, Pakistan. In this situation, the US and India, he concluded in nautical terms, 'must serve as the eastern and western beacons', '[a]s the port and starboard lights between which the region can reach its greatest and best potential'. The '100 year' time-frame apart, Tillerson's speech on 18 October 2017 had the stock ideas fleshing out the 'Asia pivot' that were last voiced by Obama's secretary of state, Hillary Clinton. 'One of the most important tasks of American statecraft over the next decade,' she wrote in a 2011 article in *Foreign Policy*, will be 'to lock in a substantially increased investment—diplomatic, economic, strategic and otherwise—in the Asia-Pacific region'. A 'strategic turn' to Asia, she argued, will 'secure and sustain America's global leadership', and is a development she compared to the Marshall Plan to reconstruct western Europe and the founding of NATO after the Second World War. In this scenario she called India 'the linchpin' for 'a more economically integrated and politically stable South and Central Asia'. But Clinton's article had few details in part because of the problem she alluded to, namely, of operationalizing the concept of connecting the Indian and Pacific oceans. This is the same issue the Trump administration's design faces along with the problem Hillary Clinton specifically mentioned of a 'more broadly distributed military presence across the region'.[29]

'Principled Realism': No Bad Guideline for India

'Principled realism' predates the Trump administration's NSS document, having been first articulated in Riyadh in May 2017 when the US president visited Saudi Arabia. In an address, he declared that 'principled realism [is] rooted in... common sense' and that 'Our friends will never question our support and our enemies will never doubt our determination. Our partnerships will advance security through stability, not through radical disruption. We will make decisions based on real world outcomes, not inflexible ideology. We will be guided by the lessons of experience, not the confines of rigid thinking. And wherever possible we will seek gradual reforms, not sudden intervention. We must seek partners, not perfection. And to make allies of all who share our goals.'[30] The NSS has all these elements but appears to be the US State Department's bureaucratic product that says the right things, touches the right cords, hits the right cadences and sits right by the diplomats, but in reality has little do with Trump's off-the-cuff policies which, as the evidence shows, is what matters.[31] It is for this reason that this jumbled and confusing doctrine has been panned in the US as 'belligerent narcissism', as being long on realism and short on principle, and of being devoid of both realism and principle.[32] Still another analyst wondered if the phrase was not coined by his minders to pre-empt Trump being called unprincipled and unrealistic.[33]

Joseph Joffe of the Hoover Institute at Stanford University encapsulates the Trump Doctrine in the NSS as 'Reassert yourself big-time, but mind the risk and look for a deal with your rivals'.[34] How are India or any of America's Asian allies and partners to feel reassured by this, particularly because whatever deal-making with China that takes place will be at their cost? It would be reasonable to conclude that Trump expects that in a crunch the Asian states, left to their own devices, will somehow fend off China with minimal US participation. While the high-noon for a condominium of America and China— or 'Chimerica' as the Harvard historian Niall Ferguson labelled it in the 21st century—came and went, possibly because, as social anthropologist Ian Morris wrote, 'In economics as in strategy, every action has a culminating point beyond which Clausewitz observed, "the scale turns and the reaction follows"', there's good reason for Washington's hesitation in taking the China bull by the horns.[35] 'Democratic globocops pay higher costs still,' Morris explained, 'and when the intended victim is also the globocop's banker—as China is for the United States—beating him becomes a truly terrible idea.'[36]

This to say that despite all the passing drama and concocted war plans and force structures, heightened tensions and crises and frequent exchange of hot words, the US and China are unlikely ever to engage in actual hostilities because both have too much to lose. This is not going to affect their very sharp rivalry and competition because each will be intent on having its say and in showing up the other at every juncture. If an actual conflict between them is, therefore, less probable, their willingness to go out on a limb to protect the interests of third parties—their respective camp followers—is also much less likely. It is very good reason, therefore, for India to plan and configure its foreign policy and security strategy on the basis that it will have to work on a concert of nations that have the most at stake in keeping China tethered and quiet, can rifle up the resources and are prepared to pay the price if push comes to shove because in India's case no US cavalry is going to ride to the rescue of Indians.

In the event, what the Trump doctrine actually means, if it means anything at all, is of no real relevance to India. But his phrase 'principled realism' does provide the Indian government—if only it has the strategic wit to use it this way—the rhetorical shell under which to grow policies maximizing India's distinct interests and foreign policy manoeuvring space and for Modi to justify his India First policies. A dexterous Indian strategy is called for with the aim principally to maintain a power scheme in the Indo-Pacific and the world at large to tilt against China, solely motivated by the logic of hard realpolitik and backed by activist Indian military diplomacy. This overbalancing for caution is a form of balancing power and can be managed with either the Palmerston–Disraeli approach that Britain used in the 19th century, as Kissinger writes, of waiting for the power equilibrium 'to be threatened directly before engaging . . . almost always on the weaker side', or by Bismarck's method of 'seeking to prevent challenges from arising by establishing close relations with as many parties as possible, by building overlapping alliance systems, and by using the resulting influence to moderate the claims of contenders'. The US and China, it turns out, follow the Bismarckian mode.[37] Modi seems to be, in some sense, on the Bismarckian track given that he has left no region unvisited and no political leader unhugged, nor neglected the alphabet soup of multinational groups ranging from BRICS, SCO, RIC (Russia, India, China), ASEAN, to G20, East Asia Economic Summits in the economic sphere, and in South Asia BIMSTEC (Bay of Bengal Initiative for Multi-Sectoral Technical and Economic Cooperation), SAARC (South Asian Association for Regional Cooperation) and SAFTA (South African Free Trade Agreement). But, insofar as can be made out, there seem to be no strategic aims driving his travels to realize a grand strategy to keep both America and Russia in play, and combine the resources of Asian states fearful of Beijing's intentions to collar China. If there is such a plan and grand strategy, it is Modi's well-kept secret.

Modi may not be entirely bereft of foreign policy ideas. It may even be that what Lord Palmerston supposedly said about Napoleon that 'ideas proliferated in his head like rabbits in a hutch' applies to Modi. The trouble where the French emperor was concerned, says Kissinger, was that 'these ideas did not relate to any over-riding concept'.[38] Unfortunately, in Modi's case as well, there's no discernible 'over-riding concept' knitting his ideas into a comprehensive national vision and strategy that do not stray into vaporous abstractions. As a result, Indian foreign policy appears a mish-mash of concepts laced with helter-skelter foreign visits and attendant activity—denoting the absence of a single, overarching, strategic game plan, which is a debilitating flaw. More serious still is Modi's near emphasis on the country's soft power as a means of reaching out to, and making it, in the world. He and the MEA seem unaware that soft power, as Joseph S. Nye Jr, the originator of this concept, has written, because 'it is not controllable, it cannot be directed with precision—and, indeed, sometimes, it cannot be directed at all'.[39] At best then, it is an unpredictable foreign policy instrument that will not always produce the desired results, and is an unreliable diplomatic instrument in a fundamental way that hard power of the state is not. Whence the US President Teddy Roosevelt's annoyance with what he called 'high-sounding principles backed by neither the power nor the will to implement them', a charge that can be safely directed at Modi's foreign policy.[40]

If Modi's time as prime minister is not to be written off as a lot of hot air and fluff, he will have to insert some steel into his foreign policy—less against Pakistan, his government's favourite whipping boy, than

China—and to instil in the MEA and Indian diplomats an appreciation for the hard power of the state and the willingness to call on it to advance the national interest. Diplomacy, howsoever adroit, cannot, as Eliot A. Cohen, George W. Bush's counsellor in the US State Department, has argued, substitute for 'real power' represented by military force.[41] Were Modi to recognize the potential utility of the Indian military, he can see to it that the MEA amalgamates it into a new approach that the thinking behind it is fully ingested by the Foreign Office and the people manning it, and that it becomes the Indian diplomats' second nature.

Alas, in this respect, Modi's first term has been a waste. All is not lost, however. An opening, fortuitously, is still available to Delhi to recoup its position, and it has to do with the widely held view in US policy enclaves that one of the few external successes the US has enjoyed since the early years of the 21st century is with its South Asia policy. President Trump, writes Robert Kaufman, 'has revived President George W. Bush's prescient initiative to facilitate a decent democratic India's rise as a counterweight to China and radical Islam both also existentially threatening Indian democracy'.[42] The idea, however, should be for the prime minister to ignore the fawning reference ('decent democratic India') but ride that sentiment. China and radical Islam are all but universal threats that are here to stay. China is a particularly useful adversary to have, considering there's no Asian state that does not fear it, and almost any Indian move, independent of a shaky US, directed at chipping away at Chinese power and strategically and economically discomfiting it will be welcomed in Asia and, because it helps American interests, lauded by Washington. Such assertive Indian behaviour will also subtly delimit US institutional tendencies to hurt India (through forums such as the US Human Rights Commission and the US Commission on International Religious Freedom), proportionately increase its policy freedom and leverage with Washington and decrease the need for India to accommodate the US.

But what is the Indian establishment's thinking on how best to take on China? Three representative views about sum up the Delhi establishment's view of India's China policy. Former foreign secretary Shyam Saran believes that with Xi 'benchmarking' China with the US and emphasizing a possible G2 condominium to oversee the affairs of the world, the strategic and global dimensions of Sino-Indian relations have been weakened and have declined in importance. Beijing now not only feels no urgency to resolve the outstanding border dispute with India but to be more militarily active on the Line of Actual Control (LAC). He recommends that Delhi heed Kautilya's advice 'to act with prudence, not provoking a conflict with a stronger power while building one's own strength'.[43] This has a status-quoist recommendation and defines Modi's policy.

Former NSA and foreign secretary, Shivshankar Menon, apprehends that if India joins the US and upgrades its nuclear missile quality with terminal accuracy and MIRV technology and develops its anti-satellite capability 'it will feed China's fear of encirclement' and accelerate its own capacity development. That is the sort of development that will unsettle 'strategic stability' which, because it is the preferred condition, could be more effectively furthered by strengthening 'the processes and institutions to manage [the] changing security dynamics' that are presently 'underdeveloped' given that China, India, Vietnam, South Korea, Indonesia 'are rising and rapidly accumulating power'.[44] It is a multilateral solution to contain China beloved of Indian diplomats that does not address the basic problem India faces of unequal security where China is concerned, one exacerbated by Delhi's reluctance to do anything that Beijing will look askance at or will clash with Chinese interests, such as asymmetrical methods of transferring armaments with strategic impact to states on the Chinese periphery, co-opting Pakistan, wrenching the other neighbouring countries from China's grasp by facilitating their assimilation into a greater Indian and South Asian marketplace, etc.

Ajit Doval, Modi's NSA, unable to write and conceptualize as well as Messrs Menon and Saran, is just as risk-averse in his thinking. China, Doval states, 'is converting its economic power into strategic and military power at a very, very fast rate, faster than we had anticipated' to reach a stage where its 'comprehensive strategic power' is three times that of India. 'We have to accept this reality as it is,' he adds.[45] In other words, that India can do nothing except presumably try and modulate Beijing's posture and policy but otherwise grin and bear it! All these three approaches reek of defeatism at the core of India's China policy. In any case, this 'don't poke the beast in the eye' stance is only a tactic, not a policy or strategy. Not surprising then that China is almost contemptuous of the supposed heavyweight, India, and refuses to take its pretensions or professions seriously as a military, economic or any kind of power. This is in contrast, say, to how respectfully it treats the bantamweight Vietnam that displays fighting spirit, having bloodied China's nose in the 1979 war Beijing initiated, and fearlessly strengthening its island outposts in the teeth of China's opposition.[46]

The fact is that Indian foreign policy needs to be that of an unsatisfied, discontented and pugnacious power that will do whatever it takes to raise its credibility as a rival to China in Asia and the country's regional and international leverage and stock. But this is not how Modi thinks. India's external relations have been keyed, as minister Sushma Swaraj disclosed in the Rajya Sabha debate on foreign policy in August 2017, on winning 'prestige' for the country.[47] Without the inclination to use coercive power to push national interest and the will to put an Indian fist to China's face, Modi's foreign trips, his talk of India's civilizational influence and the reach-outs to the local diaspora all count for zilch in power politics.

The metric to judge India's success is how much it diminishes China, hamstrings its power and curtails its flexing of the Chinese military. It will mean Delhi pushing back and reversing China's geopolitical successes in India's near- and middle-abroad, which are stacking up owing to the Indian government's inattention and lack of desire to be proactive in the extended regions around India and to pre-emptively nip any Chinese foray in the extended region in the bud, and to resort to the deft marshalling of the military resources backed by economic and other inducements. When regimes in small island nations, such as the Maldives, and landward, such as Nepal, cosy up to China without fear of swift and telling retribution, it shows just how little India is feared and respected or is counted in its own South Asian neighbourhood.

In the event, it is not to be wondered at that Beijing has grown its footprint in all of southern Asia at India's expense. Delhi has been too much the passive onlooker—quiet and obliging, happy to play a minor role assigned it by Beijing as potential 'loser' in the Chinese strategic game of Wei Qi that is underway, which Indian foreign policymakers know nothing about, nor have shown interest or competence in playing.

The aim in Wei Qi, translated as 'encirclement game' (or 'Go'), is to occupy more and more squares on the board, dominate the geographic expanse, crowd out adversaries and restrict their freedom of physical movement and policy manoeuvre and, while doing this, to also balance 'the need to expand with the need to build protected clusters'.

'Go features multiple battles over a wide front rather than a single decisive encounter,' writes Keith Johnson, summarizing the views of David Lai, who as professor at the US Army War College has tried to familiarize American strategists with this game and its ramifications for tackling China. 'It emphasizes long-term planning over quick tactical advantage.'[48] It is the geopolitical Wei Qi setting that India needs to turn inside out. Selective exclusion of rivals and proto-hegemonic powers—the US and China—from coalitions it features in is central to this geopolitical great game. This is the strategic underpinning for the BRIS (Brazil, Russia, India, South Africa) and for the Mod Quad (India, Japan, Australia, South East Asian states). The TPP formalized in February 2016, for instance, was notable for precisely such exclusion—keeping China out of this free trade pact which Trump torpedoed by withdrawing America from it and jeopardizing, in the process, 'the possibility for a trade pact in the Pacific to exist free of Chinese influence'.[49]

BRIS (Brazil, Russia, India, South Africa)

Crucial to wresting the geopolitical advantage from China is the rearrangement of the geostrategic board such as to slant the Indian Ocean and its littoral and, importantly, Eurasian politics, against China. The vital elements in this latter scheme is to configure a BRICS without China—i.e, BRIS (Brazil, Russia, India, South Africa), and to cut out the US from the original Quadrilateral concept to form a modified version, or Mod Quad, of India, Japan, Australia and a group of South East Asian states—anchored by Myanmar and Vietnam at the land end and Indonesia and the Philippines at the sea end, with Singapore, Thailand, Indonesia, Brunei and Malaysia in the middle, and to weaponize both these groups by making cooperative security as much the shared objective as free trade and economic interlinks. Laos and Cambodia—China's spear-carriers in ASEAN—are kept out of this reckoning tactically because until they begin pulling away from China, which as we'll see is sought to be engineered by India, the security aspects necessitate their exclusion. Why try and constitute power configurations minus these two big competing powers? Because given their comprehensive power and capabilities, any organization in which China and/or the US figure naturally tilts to serve their interests and concerns to the detriment of the other countries in these combines, with the latter ending up being subsumed in the putative hegemons' respective security and economic or trade schemes.

But why is America clubbed with China? Because it is a 'fading power' which, Richard Haass, a former head of policy planning in the US State Department, contends, has not so much given into its isolationist impulse under Trump as 'abdicated' its international responsibility.[50] For India, as discussed, the US is a liability if it is relied upon overmuch to provide security, and a boon if, as a result of America's gradual withdrawal from Asia, India is forced to give up on its habit of freeriding on security afforded by the great powers of the day and is compelled to secure itself by its own means.[51]

To highlight the tendency of the US and China to monopolize the organizations they are part of, let's first consider BRICS and, because this group has an essentially economic raison d'etre, the BRICS trading patterns. According to the latest figures available, in 2015 the intra-BRICS imports as percentage of the group's global imports was 6 per cent for China versus 6.8 per cent for India, 10.2 per cent for Russia, 13.9 per cent for South Africa and 22.5 per cent for Brazil; in other words, imports-wise China had the smallest stake. However, in terms of intra-BRICS exports it was predominant with 56.3 per cent (compared to 17.7 per cent for Brazil, 15.5 per cent for Russia, 7.5 per cent for India and 4.5 per cent for South Africa).[52] More generally, China is the number one source of imports for Russia (19.3 per cent), South Africa (18.3 per cent), Brazil (17.9 per cent) and India (15.8 per cent). No other BRIS member makes it as a top ten import partner for any of them. Among BRIS states, moreover, Brazil is the top exporter to China, being the ninth largest, Russia is tenth and India is eleventh.[53]

If the export and import numbers of each BRIS state are seen as a percentage of global trade, they are even more skewed in favour of

China.[54] All of these statistics are topped by the huge BRIS states' trade imbalances with China. In 2015–16, India's trade deficit was a whopping $52.7 billion.[55] Brazil and South Africa too have balance of payments deficits. Only Russia, because of its exports of oil and gas, minerals and military hardware and technology, is in a relatively good place vis-à-vis China but finds itself unable to cope with the scale of resources Beijing can bring to bear to gain its strategic ends. The conclusion is not hard to reach that because China so outpaces every other group member as a trading partner Beijing has the upper hand. It uses this to both preserve its top economic status within BRICS and, owing to the uniquely Chinese concept of state capitalism with its complex skein of hidden tariffs and subsidies to its manufacturing sector, prevents other member states in the group from competing with it. It makes ample sense, therefore, for BRIS states to get together on their own and develop a preferential trading regime to build up their individual and collective trade-driven economic power than to continue having China in their midst and help it to become richer and more powerful at their expense.

It helps that forming such a group is eminently doable. A recent audit of BRICS states, for instance, shows a high degree of compliance on commitments (on e-commerce, development of the African Union, cooperation on terrorism, cooperation on corruption, economic global value chains, automatic exchange of information on taxes, information and communications technology).[56] It suggests that if the constituent states decided to found BRIS, it could get going by bolting together the necessary supportive economic vehicles and diplomatic instruments. Such as the 'payment versus payment (PVP) system' Moscow has devised with Beijing that permits mutual trade contracts to be settled in local currencies minimizing, in the bargain, their risks and improving their foreign exchange transactions. PVP now constitutes a quarter of all Sino-Russian trade.[57] It is the sort of arrangement that will seal the institutional commitment of the member states to the BRIS grouping and insulate them against the vagaries of the US dollar-driven international trade and the threat of economic sanctions. The potential economic punch of the BRIS bloc is indicated in the table on page 177, listing the GDP in nominal terms and related statistics of BRIS states, and of the US and China in 2017, with projections for 2022.

The combined total GDP of BRIS in 2017 is $6.6 trillion, about half that of China, and a third that of the US. By 2022, the BRIS GDP figure goes up to $8.78 trillion—just short of half that of the US and a third that of China, with the Chinese economy going past the American economy to be number one. China's becoming the dominant economic power in the world by then means that the BRIS states don't have much time to solidify themselves into an economic-trading bloc. The economies of India, Brazil, Russia and South Africa as it is are ranked sixth, eighth, eleventh and thirty-fifth and by 2022 would be the fourth, eighth, eleventh and thirty-ninth largest and richest in the world. What BRIS perhaps lacks in economic heft as compared to China and the US it can make up by controlling China's economic fate, owing to its geostrategic virtues: the immense, resource-rich frontages on three oceans—Atlantic, Arctic and Indian—and on the Eurasian landmass, that BRIS members front on. This is no mean leverage for the BRIS states individually or jointly to wield against China, or even America.

GDP of BRIS States (nominal) ($ trillion)

	2017	Share of world GDP (%)	Rank	2022 (projected)	Rank
US	19.4	24.9	1	19.4	2
China	11.8	15	2	23.8	2
India	2.5	3.15	6	3.9	4
Brazil	2.14	2.75	8	2.7	8
Russia	1.6	2	11	1.8	11
South Africa	0.318	0.4	35	0.38	39

Source: *Statistics Times*, 23 April 2017, http://statisticstimes.com/economy/countries-by-projected-gdp.php

With only limited openings—and that too contested—on the East Sea and South China Sea, China finds itself in a deeply unhappy position for a premier trading but energy-deficient nation. Its trade and West Asia–sourced energy traffic has long distances to negotiate—just the distance from Hainan Island to the approaches to Malacca, for instance, is some 3500 km—and it is vulnerable to being bottled up at the eastern ends of the Malacca, Lumbok and Sunda Straits by India, motivated South East Asian nations, and Japan and Australia as part of the Mod Quad, which can intervene in this theatre with powerful forces. At the same time, China has to focus on the East Sea where really provoked Japanese maritime defence forces can wreak havoc.

BRIS security arrangements, moreover, will not attract the kind of attention that BRICS, because of China, would, if it established itself even as an informal security collective. Due to territorial disputes with India, Russian anxieties of a Chinese 'demographic creep' into Siberia, and trade deficits it has with almost all the BRIS states, China couldn't possibly be on a common security platform with them anyway. However, rough economic parity between the BRIS states will mean more equitable security cooperation between them—a natural corollary of their shared interests and outlook to prevent hegemonism everywhere. This aspect of BRIS will particularly appeal to Russia, whose relations with the US and NATO have deteriorated with military build-ups, tit-for-tat reductions in embassy personnel, American sanctions on Russian arms exports companies and energy industry, and with both sides beefing up their conventional military profiles in Europe and developing new strategic armaments.

A defiant Russia is also seeking protection for itself against US sanctions by, among other measures, exploring trading partnerships with Japan and South Korea in East Asia, Turkey, Saudi Arabia and Egypt in West Asia, and 'the Moscow-led Eurasian Economic Union' to 'expand ties' with China and Iran. Beefing up Indo-Russian relations will segue into these developments. But Modi appears reluctant to acknowledge Russia's importance to India even as he publicly shows favours to the US, evident, for example, in his address at the 2018 Shangri-La Dialogue in Singapore. There, his measly mention of the Sochi summit with Putin as expressing 'the need for a strong multi-polar world' contrasted sharply with the effusive reference to 'India's global strategic partnership' with America that, he said, 'has overcome the hesitations of history and continues to deepen across the extraordinary breadth of our relationship'.[58]

While the dip in Indo-Russian relations is troubling from the point of view of realizing an effective BRIS and an independent role for India in the world, there's no way its potential can be ignored. For instance, with regard to a prospective greater defence–industrial cooperation among the four member states which could produce an enormous defence-industrial combine of Russia, India, Brazil (RIB) to match anything in the West. RIB would enjoy worldwide reach and have available to it the political, diplomatic, economic and military clout of the four countries and their marketing reach and power. Properly configured, BRIS could thus become an active force for peace and order in the world as at once the global balancer between hegemonic-minded China and the US, and as a military and economic counterweight to either or both of them. It will naturally raise the regional and international standing and status of the BRIS countries and, should the UNSC ever be expanded in light of the new reality and distribution of power, enhance the claims for a permanent seat of India from Asia, Brazil from Latin America, and the Republic of South Africa from Africa.

The BRIS concept is supported by India's cautionary experience of the Shanghai Cooperation Organization (SCO) and Russia's moves to constrain China generally. Kept out of the SCO by China, which has dominated it, India formally joined it at the 2017 Astana Summit only because Russia wanted India in to balance China. Beijing permitted this move but dragged in Pakistan as quid pro quo. Given this history, it is not surprising that in Astana and in the subsequent meeting of foreign ministers, Beijing controlled the proceedings and the agenda. Further, with Pakistan in the mix, India failed to make headway in getting this organization to even acknowledge terrorism as an issue.[59] Meanwhile, Beijing continues to use the SCO conferences to progress its BRI, also called the New Silk Road, by getting its members—Russia and the CARs—repeatedly to endorse it, which endorsement China has used to expand and enhance the BRI zone of activity and to improve its own economic prospects with preferential bilateral trade and other schemes with the CARs.

Except, the SCO, riven with ethnic tensions between Kyrgyzstan and Uzbekistan, water conflicts between Tajikistan and Uzbekistan, and as a stage for a showdown between the heads of Kyrgyzstan and Kazakhstan, is not a very effective grouping. But India's membership in this organization could be a lightning rod for Washington's pressure.

Trump may at any time complain that a democratic India should be no part of a 'dictators' club' comprising five states rated 'unfree' and two 'partially free' by Freedom House. But, significant from the point of view of constructing BRIS, the SCO showcases President Putin's discomfort at being relegated to the status of sidekick to Chinese President Xi.[60] It is a neat reversal of the 'junior partner and apprentice complex' that Mao's China suffered at the hands of first Stalin and later Nikita Khrushchev's Soviet Union in the 1950s. It has spawned, avers the analyst Timofei Bodarchev of St Petersburg University and programme director at the influential Valdai Club, a disjunction between the Russian and Chinese policy elites and an 'ambiguity of intentions [which] is the biggest obstacle to cooperation between states and the main reason for mutual mistrust'.[61] Moreover, given the clash of US and Chinese interests that makes a 'conflict between them unavoidable' and in which Moscow prefers to remain 'neutral . . . rather than choosing between two rival giants' there's no chance, he writes, of 'a formal union' of any kind between Russia and China that some Chinese commentators have mooted.[62] In this regard, there's another aspect of Sino-Russian relations of even greater interest: Russia's oil and gas deals with China, inclusive of infrastructure, such as the 3000 km long 'Power of Siberia' gas pipeline.[63]

No fool, Putin sees the supply of Russian natural resources as a powerful means of moderating China's behaviour and checking its territorial spread northwards into a scantily populated Siberia that offers it lebensraum (territorial space to grow in), and of Beijing's influence westwards via BRI. With 30 million tonnes of oil gushing annually through the two Siberian pipelines, Russia has replaced Saudi Arabia as the main source of energy to China.[64] And as such Moscow now has a hand on the throat of the Chinese economy with a grip that can be tightened or loosened at will. In trying to escape what is called its 'Malacca dilemma' of having to rely on the Gulf oil traffic that can be easily interdicted at the three Straits chokepoints in South East Asia by India, Beijing may find itself in a soup because of the land-borne energy route. Moscow has not quailed, for instance, from turning off the oil and gas spigot to the central and eastern European states of the European Union as punishment for their adverse reaction to Russian moves in the Ukraine.[65] And it was the threat of cutting off the oil and gas supply in 2014 that deterred Germany,

Europe's strongest economy, from sanctioning Russia at America's behest over Moscow's annexation of Crimea.[66] In other words, Russia is sitting pretty, able to use energy to manipulate the politico-economic levers to wield some control in Europe and its impressive military to drive a wedge between the US and its NATO allies in the west. In the east, Moscow is well placed to influence Chinese moves in Central Asia, to establish parity in its relations with China, and otherwise to emerge as an independent and substantial global player, regaining to a great extent the standing of the Soviet Union in the Cold War. Russia has also positioned itself as a critical balancer of Chinese power in landward Eurasia and of US influence in South Asia. This last policy is sought to be augmented by Putin courting India and Modi personally. In this context and with no ideological glue to keep Russia and China bonded, convincing Moscow about BRIS may not be difficult. It will make this group at once more viable and credible, its economic and military power affording BRIS the ballast it needs to make it a going concern. Indeed, the common twin goals of containing China and limiting America's free-wheeling attitude would justify a comprehensively missioned BRIS. Russia certainly wouldn't be averse to it because of the geopolitical gains.

It was as part of Putin's policy of cultivating the Indian prime minister that Modi was invited as the chief guest at the 2016 St Petersburg International Economic Forum. The most startling imagery from that meet was Modi's walk in a city park hand-in-hand with Putin.[67] The Russian President, not one for touchy-feely stuff, nevertheless indulged in such physical intimacy to please Modi, or because they genuinely get along well. It says a lot about Putin's eagerness to foster personal intimacy with the Indian leader because he believed it served the larger strategic purpose he has in mind, other than China, of keeping India from keeling over to the US side. But what may also be deduced from this event is Putin's readiness for a BRIS group as a bulwark against both China and the US or NATO establishing a bigger footprint in Eurasia and oceanward. The foundation and cement for such a concert of nations is mutual trust, which is precisely what Modi talked about when extolling Indo-Russian relations, in contrast, to his never mentioning the word trust with regard to the US in any of his statements. 'Our relationship is not about give and take, buy and sell,' said Modi in a

2 June 2017 interview to Russian TV outlet RT News, comparing India's relationship with Russia and America. 'It is about trust.'[68] This trust has been built up over the decades by Moscow making available some of its most advanced military technology at 'friendship prices' and equipping the Indian military with over 70 per cent of its hardware needs.

Not only is India allowed access to its advanced weapons platforms, such as the lease of the Akula-II nuclear-powered attack submarine (SSN) and offer of technology transfer of the fifth-generation fighter aircraft (FGFA) technology but also in terms of technical expertise and assistance for the country's highly sensitive indigenous strategic armaments projects, including the Arihant-class SSBNs (nuclear-powered ballistic missile submarines), the long-range Agni missiles and even nuclear weapons (in terms of Indian scientists being able to use the inertial confinement fusion chamber in Troitsk, near Moscow, to refine Indian thermonuclear weapon designs). This relationship has dipped a bit owing to the ongoing problems with spares supply, which has soured many in the Indian military to the Russian connection.

'The spirit of "Hindi-Russi bhai-bhai" vanished along with the dissolution of the USSR, when the friendly Soviet [agencies dealing with arms sales] were replaced by predatory conglomerates such as Rosoboronexport, RAC-MiG, United Aircraft and United Shipbuilding Corporations and their ilk; all controlled by corrupt oligarchs linked to Putin. While quality control had plummeted alarmingly, and Russian product support (never very strong) had become—and remains—virtually non-existent,' writes a former naval chief in a long and detailed personal communication to the author. 'After my retirement, I have learned that the Russians have only grown in arrogance when dealing with the [Indian] navy and shrug off all accountability. The "grapevine" regularly speaks of premature engine and airframe failures [of Su-30MKI combat aircraft and MiG-29K carrier aircraft] and it is a mercy that the IAF and Indian Navy have not had many fatalities. Proof of all this can be found in the report that CAG tables in Parliament annually. The thinly disguised "Fighter-A", "Tank-B" and "Submarine-C" are all Russian origin weapons whose average availability hovers around 40 per cent to 45 per cent. Are we, then, ready for war?'

He also notes that 'despite having manufactured/assembled over 850 MiG-21s and a couple of thousand R-11 and R-13 engines the Russians did not transfer an iota of technology to HAL'. In this context, he refers to programmes on the anvil that he considers of dubious value. 'The FGFA project, touted as an Indo-Russian "joint development" is one of the biggest fiddles ever. Half a dozen prototypes—designed and built for the Russian Air Force—are already flying in Irkutsk. However, India has shelled out a neat $300 million (out of $4 billion) without being allowed to make any design contribution or technological participation. It is in this context that we must view [the possibility of] Russian assistance in designing and developing a powerful nuclear reactor for the two indigenous aircraft carriers with great skepticism.'

He then cites an example of what he calls 'Russian blackmail/intransigence'. The work on the first Indian-made aircraft carrier (IAC-1) at the Kochi shipyard begun in 2016 was 'held up for months due to the languid manner in which the [Russians] provided consultancy and documents for the "aviation support complex" of the ship as per a consultancy contract signed in the mid-2000s'. The reason for such unprofessional Russian actions, he suggests, is because Moscow 'would like this project to fail so that they can build our next carrier in Severdovinsk'. And he then raises a seriously worrisome question with regard to the premier strategic system leased from Russia—INS *Chakra* (the Akula-class submarine)—with the lease contract for a second such boat under negotiation. 'Where's the guarantee,' he asks, 'that software bugs will not be activated the moment a missile or torpedo is fired from it in anger, disabling the warheads?'[69]

There is much to contest in what this highly regarded former naval chief says. Some are quibbles; the 'predatory' nature of Rosoboronexport, et al. is a function of commercial agencies whose prospects rise and fall based on the foreign sales they rack up. Their mission shared with Western arms companies is to lock India into a perennial arms import cycle, not contribute to indigenous projects to help India become independent of them and the wares they sell. The complaints relating to unpredictable Russian spares supply and inconsistent product support are, however, genuine. The move by the Indian government to insist that Russian companies make the spare parts for their weapons systems in India may address this problem.[70] The surprise is that this remedy was not attempted earlier for which the service and the MoD may be to blame. Manufacturing spares in India to alleviate the problem of shortages was always Delhi's call. The fact that the Indian MoD made it so late in the day cannot be blamed on Russia. As regards his observation on the FGFA project, he fails to mention that India's existing limited combat aircraft design capability, focused on the Tejas LCA, was never large or proven enough to contribute substantially to designing the FGFA and, indeed, such ill-thought-out changes in the aircraft's architecture as the IAF had originally suggested were seen in retrospect to be wrongheaded and reversed by the Air Headquarters itself.

For example, a two-seat configuration was proposed without realizing that this would undermine its stealth characteristics. Further, his suspicions about the Russian offers for collaboration on the FGFA and to design nuclear reactors for the Indian carriers beg the questions: Is any other country willing to collaborate with India on the Sukhoi T-50 FGFA type of warplane that is the equal of the US F-22 Raptor? No. And is any other country willing to help India design and construct a nuclear plant for its aircraft carriers? Again, no. The US point-blank refused any such assistance when it was requested as part of the deal for EMALS and France and the UK are incapable of building a powerful enough reactor for a carrier operating in Indian conditions.[71]

And as to the fear about 'bugs' in the Akula boat, they cannot be ruled out. But, equally, shouldn't the Indian military equally fear 'bugs' in all US, UK and France-sourced hardware, and continue vehemently to oppose signing the 'foundational' COMCASA that Washington is pressuring Delhi to sign that will permit US intelligence agencies to penetrate India's most sensitive communications networks, including the Strategic Forces Command. This, a former service chief says, is not happening.[72] Such issues underline the perils of India's status as an abject arms dependency, as also the fact that, absent a strong-willed government taking the risk of closing off the arms import channel for good to achieve the higher aim of self-sufficiency, the country cannot do without Russia as strategic partner.

The Indo-Russian model of technology cooperation is in contrast to the ties with the US where it is all transaction and very little trust and meagre progress, with the 2012 Indo-US Defense Technology and Trade Initiative going nowhere. What Washington is eager to sell India is the 'know how' involving licensed production and screwdriver technology for F-16 and F-18 fighter aircraft, while refusing to transfer the 'know why', including source codes and operational algorithms for these aircraft even though these relate to 1970s vintage combat planes because, as pointed out earlier in this chapter, Washington does not trust India enough to part with even its obsolete technology. It is not a record as partner that Delhi can be enthused about.[73] The contrast with Russia's more open and forthcoming attitude to transferring high-value hardware and to render technical assistance for indigenous strategic projects was hard for even Modi to ignore. 'Russia will remain India's major defence and strategic partner,' the prime minister said at the 17th India–Russia annual summit on 15 October 2016. 'The enduring partnership between them is an anchor of peace and stability in a changing World Order.'[74]

Other than the SCO, Putin has tried to firm up the Russia–India–China (RIC) trilateral in the hope that Moscow and Delhi will together be able to curdle China's ambition and capability. This 'eternal triangle' is, after all, a concept originally floated by Nehru in the 1950s when it seemed natural for the three 'socialist giants' to help each other progress and to secure their interests. Prime Minister Yevgeny Primakov revived the idea in the 1990s after the demise of the Soviet Union in order to retain for Russia a semblance of its past importance. It didn't work out in the earlier two periods because of China's economic, political and strategic interests colliding with those of India and Russia.[75] Its prospects are not much improved today principally because China has grown so big and powerful that it dwarfs India and Russia, neither of whom is about to tolerate Beijing's big brother tendencies. So this geopolitical contrivance won't take off.

Some Russian analysts, however, see a different end. They believe that with an ambitious India swinging more and more towards America because the latter has more to offer by way of commercial technology, trade and commerce, and for security towards the US-conceived Quadrilateral, and Russia, for reasons of economics and to balance American power in Asia will mosey over to the Chinese side. It has the oil, gas, minerals and military technology to sell Beijing and China has the money to pay for them, which will keep Russia financially afloat, and with India and Russia thus on diverging paths, they will end up splitting.[76] Whether or not this is the motivation for the two parties, there has indeed been a bit of a cooling off. Moscow is upset that the Modi government, unappreciative of Russian help and assistance and in developing strategic systems and historic closeness, is being niggardly in negotiating deals with the Russian arms industry—that country's technology showcase—even as it doles out rich contracts to American corporations for non-lethal goods, such as transport aircraft (C-17 and C-130J planes) and to the French aviation major Dassault (for the Rafale multi-role combat aircraft) with the intent of 'diversifying' India's sources of armament supply.

Putin is especially upset that on the big-ticket items—the collaboration with India on the FGFA project, the production of the Project 75i diesel submarine for which the Russians offered a more advanced version of its Amur-class boat and the offtake of large numbers of upgraded 'super Sukhois' to replace the 272-strong IAF fleet of older Su-30MKIs—there has been a lot of to-ing and fro-ing but no deals, which Putin had banked on to ameliorate Russia's dependence on China and to keep his revenue-earning defence industry from hurting.[77] Moscow is in an overdrive to modernize and augment its military for what it believes is a revival of its armed competition with the US, and selling India advanced weapons systems is one way of generating funds for Russia without compromising the technology, and to strengthen Indian capacity to handle China.[78]

But there's Russian unease with India getting too friendly with the US. A Russian foreign policy insider confirmed a certain negativity entering into the bloodstream of bilateral relations. The Kremlin sees India as an essential piece in China's containment and to keep the US unsteady in Asia. But his attempts to pally up with the Indian prime minister notwithstanding, Putin does not 'trust Modi' and neither do the Russian diplomatic corps or the Russian military, he said. The Russian read on Modi's seeking a concert with the US is, the Russian said, that he is 'a bit naive', has a 'narrower' view of the world and cannot envision 'India's role in global terms'. He was definite about what he called Moscow's 'redline' that he hoped Delhi would not cross, namely the failure to hew to India's long-standing policy of 'strategic autonomy'.

The Russian military's more immediate worry, he said, is about front-line Russian weapons systems, such as the Akula-II SSN, being compromised by the American penetration of the Indian armed services.[79] Getting too intimate with Washington, he apprehends, would trigger a major geopolitical realignment. It may precipitate an intimidating Russia–China–Pakistan bloc and the sort of strategic high-technology arms sales and transfers by Moscow to Pakistan of the kind that saw India add muscle to its military in the three decades from the 1960s to the 1990s.[80]

Already a Pakistani regional adviser to the World Bank, Haroon Sharif has conceived of just such a bloc with Iran, Afghanistan and Central Asia added to it.[81] Should it come to pass, this grouping would create difficulties for India's Iran, Afghanistan and Central Asia policies, and for the Indian trade plying the overland route from Chabahar or via the Caspian Sea to Russia's Northern Distribution Network connecting to Baltic seaports and Europe as an alternative to the sea route via Suez. Worse, the Russian arming of Pakistan, possibly subsidized by China, with the latest Russian military and strategic-use equipment could put India in a vice between two closing ends on the landward side, which pressure a seaward-strong America will not be able to relieve. It will have punch because such Russian actions will be laced with bitterness, a sense of betrayal and with punitive intent to impose high costs on an ungrateful India. This aspect is pertinent to Putin's management of Russian foreign policy. As a former spy, he has the eye for detail and, as a hands-on manager, keeps himself in the know of the nuts and bolts of what India buys or doesn't, and why or why not.[82]

It was Narasimha Rao who saw the unravelling of the Soviet Union and warned the MEA not to exploit the situation nor show ingratitude. 'Never forget what the Indo-Soviet relationship was like and how much we have gained from it,' he cautioned Indian diplomats. 'We should never be ungrateful. You don't forget friends when they are less powerful or less influential, or anything like that. You have to stand by them.'[83] It explains why his regime authorized a grant of ₹6000 crore to keep the Sukhoi plant producing the Su-30 combat aircraft in Irkutsk afloat, and why Moscow returned the favour by offering the best weapons and missile designers and engineers from the Russian defence industry to work in India, which offer the prime minister foolishly refused.[84] The Russian 'redline', moreover, will definitely be crossed if the Indian government acts on the US ambassador Kenneth Juster's suggestions. After commending India for becoming part of the technology denial regimes—MTCR, Wassenaar Arrangement, and soon possibly the Australia Group and the NSG, Juster urged the Indian government on 11 January 2018 in a speech at Carnegie India to 'put a strategic lens on our economic relationship', sign an FTA, and seize 'the strategic opportunity, through trade and investment, to become an alternative hub for US business' now that American companies are facing 'increasing difficulties [in] conducting business in the largest market in the region—China'. The bait is juicy but the hook on which the US hopes to impale India sharp.

More significantly, just two years after the signing of the LSA, he asked the Modi regime to get a move on, 'expand officer exchanges' at the training facilities in the two countries and 'at some point, post reciprocal military liaison officers at our respective combatant commands'.[85] The Modi government has responded by tasking the Indian defence attache in the embassy in Bahrain, where the US Fifth Fleet is based, to also function as the liaison between the Indian and the US navies. And it has also agreed to post an Indian military officer at the Pentagon's Defense Innovation Unit Experimental (DIUx) to gain first-hand experience of how the US military identifies and prioritizes technology for development and invests in private sector companies.[86]

This Juster theme, incidentally, was repeated in a piece the US ambassador co-wrote with the Carnegie India head that called for the 'building' of 'a durable relationship in the 21st century'. It underlined just how the American influence networks detailed earlier work in tandem with the US embassy and government to realize US goals. In quick order the inevitable followed: Washington asked Delhi to choose between 'us or Russia' and, while the trigger was India's move to buy the Russian S-400 air defence system, it indicated how the US government would frame issues of Russian arms supplies in the future. It was a short step from such stark Manichean thinking to Washington exercising coercive means to achieve its strategic objective of terminating India's defence ties with Russia. Washington threatened to bring India within the punitive ambit of the Countering America's Adversaries Through Sanctions Act (CAATSA) enacted by the US Congress in early 2018 if Delhi signed up for the S-400. With Washington not above using the CAATSA threat to get India to sign the other two pending accords, COMCASA and BECA, supposedly to improve 'interoperability'.[87]

In this regard, it is interesting to consider the parallel case of the US and Egypt. The Egyptian armed forces, like their Indian counterpart, are majorly equipped with Russian weapons, the country's President, General Abdel Fattah el-Sisi, who cracked down on extremist groups such as the Muslim Brotherhood in his country, was fawned over and feted by Trump in Washington, just as Modi was. But el-Sisi decided not to anger Putin's Russia by succumbing to Washington's blandishments. Egypt, like Pakistan, gets an annual billion-dollar subvention from the US but has suffered from a flapping US policy that cuts off military aid to Cairo one moment on the basis of el-Sisi's human rights record and restores it the next by Trump overruling his own State Department, a process that the Israeli ambassador in Cairo called 'botched'.[88] The US foreign policy for long years now has been confused and unpredictable—undermining friendly states (Obama supported the Mohammad Morsi regime that el-Sisi overthrew), taking allies and partners for granted and surprising them with widely varying decisions.

Five months after his meeting with Trump at the White House, the Egyptian leader decided he had had enough of the unpredictable shifts in American policy and, on a visit to Moscow, finalized an accord allowing Russian military aircraft use of Egyptian bases and air space. Russia has been on an arms-selling spree to states considered American partners or inching towards the US: $3.5 billion worth of armaments to Egypt apart, arms valued at $2 billion to Turkey, a NATO member, and $3 billion to Saudi Arabia. It has permitted Moscow to be more militarily active in West Asia and to fill the political space vacated by the US because Trump, into his second year in the White House, failed to appoint ambassadors to various capitals in the region and to fill key posts in the US State Department. Consequently, many Gulf and Arab states find Russia more attractive and reassuring than the US's quicksilver approach.[89]

The bigger game was geopolitical one-upmanship. In the aftermath of the 1973 Yom Kippur War, Washington succeeded in wrenching Egypt away from the Soviet Union. Putin has repaid the compliment by now distancing Cairo from the US. And Russia is helping North Korea evade UN sanctions while China reduced its support for Pyongyang.[90] In South Asia, the US is trying to bag India, traditionally close to Russia, as its partner of choice in South Asia. In light of America's track record in the wider region, however, how wise is it for Modi to somersault into Washington's lap and make an enemy of Russia, rather than continuing with India's very effective and productive policy of 'strategic autonomy' that's in thick with both? This policy enables India to pick and choose from whatever Russia and the US have to offer, play one off against the other, cut competitive-priced deals without committing to either of them, but with an eye chiefly to securing the economic and military wherewithal and capabilities to strategically hamper, hinder and harass China in every possible way—a proto-adversary also of the US and Russia. This choice of policy, of remaining strictly 'strategically autonomous', is a no-brainer, but the way it is struggling to get traction, Modi's government has made it out to be rocket science. A BRIS coalition in this context would be a perfectly good solution to further such objectives especially when twinned with the Mod Quad without the US.

To ponder the US's credibility as strategic partner, let's mull over the state of the American military in Asia. In the Indo-Pacific region, the US Indo-Pacific Command controls the US 8th Army in Japan, the Pacific Army in Hawaii, the US Army in Alaska, which can reportedly get its units to any Asian trouble spot inside of eighteen hours, and I Corps out of the American West Coast. These are the US fighting forces on call for contingencies in Asia.[91] Three carrier strike groups with reserve forces constitute the US 7th Fleet based in Yokosuka, Japan, policing the eastern Pacific, and the US 5th, 7th and 11th Air Forces, based respectively in Yokota, Japan, Osan, South Korea and Elmendorf, Alaska, maintain aerial watch. They are not only the lead US elements in the region, but tasked in a crisis with coordinating with the militaries of allies—Japan, Australia, South Korea and the Philippines.[92] This force disposition may look good on paper but owing to the 'sequestration' of defence funding during the Obama years there are doubts about whether the US military in Europe and in East Asia can adequately 'counter' what a US Congressional Research Service report of June 2017 calls 'hybrid warfare and gray-zone tactics' involving intense cyber warfare onslaughts by Russia in Europe or China's 'salami-slicing tactics in the East and South China Seas'. It calls into question whether the deployed US forces in these theatres even have 'appropriate and sufficient' capabilities for 'high-end warfare' considering the continuing 'constraints on defense funding' and uncertainty about making 'tradeoffs' between 'balancing capabilities for high end warfare' and 'other [US Department of Defense] priorities'.[93]

According to an American legislator and former one-star general, Don Bacon, the US Air Force cannot even conduct electronic warfare against radio and radar in Afghanistan and Iraq or carry out 'standoff jamming' to pave the way for attack aircraft against Russia and China, what to speak of more complex warfare.[94] For option-less allies and partners, relying on a thus handicapped US armed presence entails a lot of grumbling, showing of defiance, falling in line with American policy and taking chances.[95] An additional point for Delhi to ponder: of the ten nuclear-powered aircraft carriers of the eleven available at any given time, the US Navy is struggling to farm out these assets between four live theatres: NATO or the Atlantic, Mediterranean, Indian Ocean and the Far East.

Indeed, during a brief period, late 2016 to early 2017, there was no US carrier deployed anywhere.[96] If the Trump administration stays with President Obama's decision of pivoting to Asia and deploying 60 per cent of the US Naval Fleet to the Indo-Pacific or six of the ten carriers, it will mean falling into the 'ends–means gap'. 'Decisionmakers need to concede that the pivot to the Indo-Pacific is a massive undertaking, tantamount to remapping the US global strategy,' wrote Toshi Yoshihara of the US Naval War College, anticipating the extant difficulties. 'The US may not be able to achieve its ambitious aims alone. Setting more realistic expectations about what can be done with like-minded regional powers to complete the rebalance should be part of the policy narrative.'[97]

It hints at the enormous leverage India has with the US, which the Modi government has not utilized. The Indian Navy is the only force in Asia, other than the Chinese Navy, with aircraft carriers but with much longer experience of deploying these in fleet operations. Trump's $886 billion defence budget for 2018–19 is expected to fund the more serious capability deficits but it will take a decade and more for the effects to show in terms of better-equipped battle-ready forces.[98]

There's, moreover, the experience of a long-time ally and partner of the US nearer home that the Indian government should heed. Notwithstanding its record as a front-line state staging the U-2 high-altitude spy aircraft out of the Peshawar base for surveillance of the Russian nuclear testing site in Semipalatinsk in the 1950s and 1960s, facilitating first the CIA-managed mujahideen guerilla war against the Soviet occupation troops in Afghanistan in the 1980s and, post 9/11, the conduct of US military operations against the Mullah Omar government in Kabul and, currently, against the Afghan Taliban—'the sturdy child of terror' (to use Winston Churchill's phrase for deterrence as a by-product of nuclear-armed US and USSR) of the original US-assisted mujahideen—Pakistan was targeted by the Trump administration in January 2018 with suspension of both US military aid and reimbursement funds for support of US coalition forces active in Afghanistan. His excuse was that Islamabad was not doing enough to bring the Afghan Taliban leaders enjoying safe haven in Pakistan to book.[99] The American attitude of asking friendly states to do more and still more may have at last led to the Pakistani worm half-turning. There was the predictable response by Pakistan Foreign Minister Khwaja Asif predictably charged the US with buying into India's lies.[100] The more thoughtful reactions, however, were more damning.

The head of the Pakistani Army's Inter-Services Public Relations, Major General Asif Ghafoor, revealed on a television news show in early January 2018 that while his country had received 'between $15-20 billion in coalition funds for our military expenditure . . . the national exchequer incurred $123 billion in losses' and reminded Washington that Pakistan does not need the US. 'We are a nuclear power; we do not need security guarantees from anyone.'[101] Because, he might have added, Pakistan now has a financially powerful China to fall back on.[102] Referring to the 'insatiable demands' of the US, Lieutenant General (retd) Talat Masood of the Pakistani Army wondered if his country was being punished for 'improving its relations with Russia . . . deepening its strategic relations with Saudi Arabia, moving closer to Turkey and reinforcing ties with Iran'—moves not liked by Washington. He also asked whether America's punitive mindset reflects the US President's 'contempt and ingrained prejudice towards Muslims', and 'Being a super power, [whether] the US considers [it] its right to impose policies without any regard to Pakistan's interests.'[103]

General Masood's concerns are pertinent to Modi's policy of long term and extensive strategic interlinking with the US. Setting aside the parallel moves Delhi has made vis-à-vis Russia, Iran, Turkey and Saudi Arabia to also 'broaden its options', and the prime minister's apparent dislike of, if not hostility towards, Muslims that mirrors Trump's antipathy, because it spells out the perils India may face down the road. Pakistan is, by Masood's account, 'a middle ranking power'—realistically, a category India fits into as well. Notwithstanding its $2.5 trillion economy, India, a typical Third World state not that far removed from Pakistan, looks, in the memorable words of the development economists Amartya Sen and Jean Dreze, 'more and more like islands of California in a sea of sub-Saharan Africa'.[104] In terms of lack of governance, an aggrandizing political class, an inefficient and corrupt bureaucracy and prevailing religious strife and social disorder, there's little to distinguish India from Pakistan.

Moreover, as the analysis has so far indicated, India is getting to be no less pliable a partner of America than Pakistan, considering that in recent times it has bent to Washington's will just as much as Pakistan has. The Indian government will also do well to bear in mind the Pakistani General Ghafoor's warning about how the US has not reimbursed the quantifiable costs to Pakistan for support of US coalition force operations in Afghanistan. It is an issue that could come to the fore were Delhi to rush into provisioning US forces in the region now that the Modi regime has agreed to the stationing of US military personnel on Indian territory vide the LSA. Then there's a sociocultural issue that could explode the bilateral ties. However liberal the environment in big cities, off-duty American military personnel will socialize and, as happened in Saigon and the larger towns of South Vietnam, and in nearby countries, such as Thailand during the Vietnam War, a whole economy will spring up to service the 'Yankees' with women, alcohol and drugs. The RSS will likely lead the campaign against the consequent breakdown of local norms and social values with Indian women fraternizing with American soldiers.

Serious law and order problems could be engendered especially if the agreement also puts US military miscreants outside the pale of Indian law. This is a pattern evidenced in all the countries (including NATO states) where America has had military presence that could be replicated here. Delhi would do well to give such aspects careful thought before taking the plunge.

The Mod Quad

The quadrilateral of India, US, Japan and Australia is an obvious enough geopolitical construct for the Indo-Pacific as an arrangement to try and bring a vaulting China to heel. The growing economic interweaving of the Asian littoral and offshore economies, including India's, constitutes the economically prosperous and militarily competent Asian rimland that the American geostrategist of the 1950s Nicholas Spyman envisioned as sufficient to contain a heartland power, communist China. But China, courtesy its investments, manufacturing supply chain links and its innovative 'debtbook diplomacy' with billions of dollars in loans that cannot be paid back, has obtained for Beijing a vast captive marketplace and a string of debtor countries willing to do Beijing's bidding on its extended periphery.[105]

Stretching from the eastern littoral of Africa, Djibouti, to Iran, Pakistan and India, through Central Asia, the Indian Ocean island states, South East Asian nations and across the Pacific to the US, China is the main source of cheap consumer goods and infrastructure credit. The US is, in this sense, as much in thrall to China as Laos or Cambodia are, for reasons already dilated on—China's access to the US market in return for Beijing's purchase of American government bonds translatable into credit on easy terms in the US and the propping up of the 'American lifestyle'. These deep and extensive mutually reinforcing cross-stakes mean that while more of Asia will be in thrall to and willing to accommodate Beijing, America will not go to war with China as that would be fatal to both.

Power politics will, however, occasion conflicts of interests that the two countries will manage via their proxies. It is in this last respect that the US seemingly excels. 'America,' a Russian foreign policy expert said, echoing sentiments from the Cold War when the then superpowers powers accused each other of being 'master of war by proxies.'[106] It is essentially as a proxy then that India figures in the US's larger security design for Asia. The US and China's tussle over Pakistan is, likewise, to gain a proxy. But Japan, which once jumped every time Washington asked it to, has grown more confident even as the US has become less sure. It prompted the Japanese premier Shinzo Abe in 2007 to talk of the 'confluence of the two seas' in order to corral India into a scheme that he outlined as 'the security diamond'—the quadrilateral by another name—to stiffen up an anti-China front. It encapsulates the effort by non-Sinic Asia to ring-fence China and ensure it doesn't become a security problem.

At the core of this reach-out by Tokyo to Delhi was Japan's recognition that it had to become more capable and therefore more independent, security-wise. In 2011, with the dispute over the Senkaku/Diaoyu Islands on the boil and Beijing propounding its 'nine-dash line' claims in the South China Sea in earnest, Tokyo affected a sea change in its military orientation. It reformed its military organization and fighting structure, and shifted its security focus from Russia and the Kurile Islands in the north to China. On the basis of a political directive, a chief of defence staff (CDS) system was set up along with seven theatres of command with allocation of the necessary resources to enable such organizational changes all inside of a year (compare this to twenty years of talk and promises regarding a CDS in India with little forward movement).[107]

The changing power dynamic with a thermonuclear-armed North Korea supported by an unscrupulous China juxtaposed against Washington's policy that moved from issuing threats to near paralysis at the thought of Kim Jong-un initiating a nuclear attack must have convinced Tokyo that the change in its attitude to rely on itself for security and to reorient its military accordingly was both necessary and correct. The reason for the US hesitation is understandable. America cannot take precipitate action against the Pyongyang regime, because it would risk certain nuclear destruction of almost anything Pyongyang wants to target in Japan and South Korea, Guam and even the Hawaiian Islands and, according to the mid-October 2017 statement by the then US Central Intelligence Agency chief and secretary of state, Mike Pompeo, any American city that Kim Jong-un wanted to take out. What the US can do, as Pompeo hinted, is eliminate Kim Jong-un—the words used were 'separate him from his regime'—and, as a last resort, use 'military force if necessary', which he said Trump was prepared to do.[108] Such American threats, if actualized, will likely bring China and Russia into the fray even though, in the wake of the Trump–Jong-un 'ice breaking' meeting in Singapore on 12 June 2018, such US intervention seems improbable.

When the US, in the aftermath of the North Korean thermonuclear test of 280 kiloton yield on 3 September 2017 flew a strike sortie headed by two US Air Force B-1B long-range bombers over South Korea as a warning to Jong-un, Russia, as it had done in the past, reacted by sending a brace of Tu-95MS nuclear bombers to the Korean peninsula as well to caution Washington against rash action.[109] If Beijing decides to stay out, the fact of Moscow entering the lists on the side of Pyongyang for reasons of realpolitik permanently takes the option of armed coercion off the American table. In that sense, it is a return to the Cold War–type scenario—when one protagonist enters the scene, the other inevitably follows but on the other side, and an impasse follows. With the situation tense, Washington marshalled a bit of psychology. As an antidote to both Beijing and Pyongyang, Trump resurrected the bogeyman from the Second World War days of a militarized 'warrior nation'—Japan.[110] But a nuclear-weaponized Japan, because it is feared by a China psychologically scarred by the wartime Japanese atrocities (such as the 'Nanjing massacre'), will also scramble Sino-US relations which may be no bad thing from India's perspective.

It is this possibility that likely persuaded Trump once in Tokyo to take another tack. He talked of the Japanese shooting North Korean nuclear missiles 'out of the sky' with 'massive amounts of military equipment' purchased from the US which, he reminded his domestic audience, means 'a lot of jobs for us and a lot of safety for Japan'.[111] It is the sort of simplistic, off-the-cuff kind of statement trademarked by Trump—connecting job creation at home with the certainty of US-sourced systems neutralizing the enemy threat, a solution he recommended to South Korea as well some days later, despite Seoul demanding the re-stationing of US tactical nuclear forces on its territory.[112] The reluctance to tangle with Pyongyang laced with the desire to sell US armaments seems to be the all-purpose Trumpian panacea for the security problems of Asian states. It is the same solution that Tillerson incidentally offered India, except the military goods on sale are either cost-prohibitive EMALS or junk (F-16/F-18 combat aircraft).

Australia, geographically more distanced than Japan from China, simultaneously senses greater foreign policy space for itself, but in its 2017 Foreign Policy White Paper seems concerned about the US's gradual pullback from the Indo-Pacific region and the likely dilution of its military presence, and apprehensive about China and its rocketing ambition, economic power and military capability. 'Power is likely to shift more quickly in the region, and it will be difficult for Australia to achieve the levels of security and stability we seek,' it said. 'A number of factors suggest we will face an increasingly complex and contested Indo-Pacific.'

'Australia is particularly concerned by the unprecedented pace and scale of China's activities,' the white paper added. 'Australia opposes the use of disputed features and artificial structures in the South China Sea for military purposes. Elsewhere in the region, Australia is concerned about the potential for the use of force or coercion in the East China Sea and Taiwan Strait.'[113] There's more than a hint of queasiness about the future of the continent-sized island nation, with the conservative party government of Malcolm Turnbull aware that the economic boom Australia has enjoyed in the last twenty-five years was the result mainly of huge Chinese investments in infrastructure and extractive industry and of massive exports to China of Australian coal and minerals.

'This is the first time in our history,' said Turnbull very pointedly about China, 'that our dominant trading partner is not also a dominant security partner.'[114] Australia's 2016 Defence White Paper defined its wider strategy as obtaining 'a secure nearer region, encompassing maritime South East Asia and the South Pacific' by helping to build 'effectiveness of regional operations to address shared security challenges' and, with these and other aims in mind, to maintain 'a regionally superior ADF [Australian Defence Forces]' with the highest priority accorded to submarines to sanitize the approaches. India is described in the document as 'a rising major power' and 'key security partner' with whom Australia has 'shared strategic interests'.

In a similar vein, Japan is regarded as a 'major power in North Asia with advanced military forces and an increasingly active approach to regional security' and with 'common strategic interests in secure and free-flowing trade routes, a stable Indo-Pacific region and a rules-based global order'. And as regards the disputes in the South China Sea, the Defence Paper talks of the 'combination of competing territorial claims and growth in military capability' as having 'the potential to destabilize the region and threaten Australia's interests' without mentioning the ersatz islands mid-South China Sea that the Foreign Policy Paper, in fact, casts a wary eye on. It refers with anxiety to China's 2013 unilateral declaration of an Air Defense Identification Zone (ADIZ) over the disputed seas, suggesting that Canberra's perceptions of the threat posed by China had hardened inside of a year. In this respect, however, the reference to the periodic trilateral military exercise—'the northern Jackeroo', involving the US, Chinese and Australian navies—raises an eyebrow.[115] What's the point of such confidence-building exercises with China? This is a question to also ask the Indian government which has approved joint military exercises with the Chinese PLA.

Australia's commitment to any security arrangement without America is doubtful, even in the face of doubts of many Asian countries about the US and China being too into each other to actually fight each other. This supposedly is the 'paradox of power'—mutual vulnerability leading to Sino-American strategic restraint.[116] The need is all the more, therefore, for the Asian littoral and offshore states to come together as the Mod Quad to have up and running a system of organic security— of regional states collectively responsible for their own security. It is precisely such thinking that undergirds Japan's moves to join India in establishing a sea route through the Indian Ocean to Africa's eastern littoral and the Gulf in competition with China's so-called 'maritime silk road' (or BRI). It will superimpose on Modi's Project Mausam that is seeking to revive the historical maritime trade ties to Indonesia at one end and Africa and the Gulf at the other, which has stalled for want of adequate funding.[117]

Japan, however, may be stepping in to rescue this scheme. Its policy liberated from its post–Second World War constraints by the activist prime minister Shinzo Abe, Tokyo has agreed to finance such undertakings and to collaborate in building shipping trade and related infrastructure in Africa, fund the development of the Chabahar port in Iran and the transportation grid connecting the Gulf coast to Afghanistan and Central Asia that India has undertaken to build, which will link up with the existing Russian network to Europe.[118] What is more noteworthy still is Tokyo's interest in working out a defence and security arrangement with India that is 'non-American and non-European'.[119] How this proposal will fare in light of India's wanting to clamber on to the American security bandwagon is something for Delhi and Tokyo to work out. (More on why this new Japanese policy initiative has not taken off in the next chapter.) On the other hand, the extent of Australia's involvement in Mod Quad will depend ultimately on how that dilemma of whether this nation is a European outlier or an 'Asian' entity is settled by Canberra.[120]

Underneath all such ideas is the tremendous discomfort of Asian states and the countries of the proposed Mod Quad, including India, with the unreliability of the US and how undependable it is. Instead of exploring more such credible arrangements for Asian security by littoral and offshore states, and its own experience to the contrary, the Modi government has chosen to believe that the US is the answer. As a result, Delhi is acting as America's apologist calming regional nerves by suggesting that the US presence is credible and durable.

After asserting that 'These are still early days [and it] is important not to jump to conclusions', Foreign Secretary Jaishankar, who demitted office January 2018-end, did just that in a Delhi conclave. 'The United States is, generally speaking, reframing its terms of engagement with the world. In some arenas, there may be a redefinition of its objectives. In others, we may be looking at a redrawing of its posture,' he said in Singapore in July 2017. 'At the same time, let us be clear what is not happening: the US is not withdrawing from the world. On the contrary, it is seeking to get what it hopes to be a better deal from the rest of the world . . . The continued presence of the United States in the Asia-Pacific is an important factor in the calculations of all nations.' He ascribed this reading of the situation to 'a nuanced understanding of the unfolding situation'.[121] There may be less nuance than uncertainty and befuddlement in his remarks than Jaishankar let on, considering that Trump proved an enigma to even the trio of his top minders—US Defense Secretary General James Mattis, the former secretary of state Rex Tillerson and the former NSA General H.R. McMaster, the last two of whom called Trump a 'moron', and a 'dope' and 'idiot', and ended up getting kicked out.[122]

The Mod Quad, like BRIS, represents what the Russian geopolitical expert Timofei Bordachev calls a 'macro-region' which, he sees as reflecting 'emerging and constantly growing interdependences . . . [and as] larger than conventional regions, but . . . still relatively localized on a global scale'.[123] Meaning that BRIS and Mod Quad have only localized military effect, their individual security efforts concentrated on threats primarily in their own immediate regions. This, it may be argued, is as much a function of their truncated national visions—and here Russia is the exception—as the paucity of financial resources, where Japan and Australia are the exceptions. Many of these states—India, Japan, Australia, Brazil and South Africa and the ASEAN members—have been allies or partners of America, or security freeriders on the US military presence in their vicinities. India, exceptionally, rode the US and Soviet/Russian security horses in turn—the US in the 1950s and 1960s, the Soviet Union from the 1970s to the 1990s, and the US again in the new century.

But there's only so much freeriding that's possible before growing ambition renders big power security cover iffy, sparking fresh thinking and leading the bigger and more capable countries to seek out other security solutions. To varying degrees these two factors make macro-organizations such as BRIS and Mod Quad more feasible now than ever in the past. A third factor is the proliferation of nuclear weapons and the revolution in military technology with the development of new mobile and miniaturized armaments or tweaked older systems with range that enable smaller, weaker countries to deter and dissuade great powers. A single test of a thermonuclear-warheaded ICBM, for example, was enough for Kim Jong-un to make Trump eat his words about raining 'fire and fury' on North Korea and bring him to the negotiating table.

Unfortunately, a hard-nosed and aggressive strategy has never been thought up, planned and implemented by the Indian government because that is not its forte. The MEA and the MoD are habituated to perceiving and keeping India as a bystander upholding the status quo even when it hurts India's national interest and prevents it from attaining great power. The Delhi policy establishment, moreover, is inclined to play safe and sees any departure from the status quo as 'disruptive' and necessarily bad which, if pursued, they fear, would rankle the United States and China—the two main beneficiaries of the current global order, which it is convinced, it cannot afford to do. The Indian government does not want to risk disruption of any sort despite Trump setting the pace and precedent for disruptive policies and practices by overturning seventy years of American foreign policy.[124] Novel strategies, policies and plans seem beyond the ken of the Indian PMO, MEA or MoD, however. This is so mainly because Indian prime ministers in the 21st century have quailed from going off the beaten path. To them the US and China have been the big constants with whom they feel it is best to get along with.

In an earlier chapter I had analysed why, owing to his imbibing, childhood onwards, the norms and values of the RSS, which is disciplined and hierarchically structured, Modi is almost reflexively deferential to the US and China and their heads of government, Trump and Xi, acknowledging them and their countries as his and India's superiors in the rank ordering of nations and leaders. This attitude is reflected in his foreign policy based on giving minimum offence to these two countries, as also in his respectful and placatory behaviour where Trump and Xi are concerned. This fits in nicely with Trump's and the US's idea of their exalted place under the sun, and it conforms to the Confucian notion of order 'under the heaven'. It has led Xi and China to act on the belief, as Henry Kissinger says, that 'foreign policy is a hierarchical set of relationships'. It explains why, for instance, there was never any foreign ministry but only the Ministry of Rituals at the Chinese court of yore, which graded nations by their tributary status, and why that Chinese mindset still prevails.[125]

But what is the economic potential of the Mod Quad? The table on the following page reveals the economic promise.

Mod Quad GDP (nominal) (in $ trillion)

	2017	Rank	Share of world GDP (%)	2022 (projected)	Rank
India	2.5	6	3.15	4	4
Japan	4.8	3	6.2	5.4	3
Australia	1.4	13	1.74	1.7	13
ASEAN	$2.06	9	2.6	3.64	9
Indonesia	1.02	15	12.3	1.6	14
Thailand	0.433	26	0.55	0.519	29
Philippines	0.330	34	0.42	0.489	26
Malaysia	0.310	36	0.4	0.380	39
Singapore	0.292	41	0.37	0.341	43
Vietnam	0.216	47	0.28	0.314	47

Source: Statistics Times, 23 April 2017, http://statisticstimes.com/economy/countries-by-projected-gdp.php

It is important to note that the collective GDP of the South East Asian group almost equalled that of India in 2017 and surpassed Australia's. ASEAN trade is, unsurprisingly, unbalanced with China, with the latter also having trade surpluses with most of the Mod Quad states. According to the latest available figures, ASEAN imports from China were worth $21.5 billion; its exports $13.4 billion, for a trade deficit of $8.1 billion.[126] This compares with China's trade surplus of some $52 billion with India, $41 billion with Japan, but a deficit with Australia of some $2 billion.[127] In comparison, India–ASEAN trade was some $72 billion in 2017–18, an increase of 10 per cent over 2015–16, but still only a sixth of the two-way ASEAN trade (of $452.3 billion) with China. But ASEAN enjoyed a trade surplus of $10.9 billion with India in 2015–16 which decreased marginally the following fiscal year (to $9.1 billion).[128]

More telling, though, is the huge differential in ASEAN's trade links with India as compared with China. China constituted 15.2 per cent of all ASEAN trade in 2015 (the last year for which figures are available), India barely 2.4 per cent, a drop of 0.3 per cent from the previous year. Obviously, this trade as a basis for security cooperation needs to be strengthened, but it is how much Delhi puts out in the security field that will decide how India is viewed by this group, not whether the trade goes up or down. This was evidenced in the two themes the ASEAN leaders pounded on during their 25 January 2018 summit with Modi in Delhi: The need for the Indian government to bring closure by year end to the ongoing negotiations for the Regional Comprehensive Economic Partnership (RCEP) that the Singapore Prime Minister Lee Hsien Loong called 'a historic opportunity to create the world's largest trading bloc' and for it to up its military game so as to offer a credible counterweight to China that the ASEAN states seriously desire, which Modi's taking digs at China's expansionism did not address.[129]

On RCEP, Delhi is on the horns of a dilemma. Were an accord to be finalized, China, as an RCEP member, would end up benefitting most, consolidating its trading advantages vis-à-vis India and other states. Modi's talk of 'balanced trade' flagged precisely that Indian worry.[130] The other issue about India shoring up maritime security east of Malacca as public good is more germane to ASEAN concerns. Modi's promise at the summit to make freedom of navigation a 'key focus area' of Indian military activity in that part of the world and his promise to ensure respect for the 1982 UNCLOS was well received. Except India did not follow up by dispatching naval flotillas on freedom of navigation patrols (FoNPs) in the South China Sea, which gesture would have cemented India's credentials as security provider.[131]

China's heavy-handed tactics in the South China Sea compels ASEAN to court big powers and involve them in their security as hedge. While the US is still the go-to country to get protection, Trump's antics are a disheartening reminder that ASEAN's well-being continues to hang on Chinese goodwill. Were India to take its role as a trustworthy security partner seriously it will afford the South East Asian countries the diplomatic space to push back against Beijing. In this context, delivering on its military commitments and a higher level of military presence will more than make up for India's understandable hesitation on the RCEP/trade front.

The military pressure on the South East Asian nations and Japan and India is daily felt with the 'islands' that China has created mid-channel in the South China Sea that bristle with radar, long-range artillery and missiles and combat aircraft. Security cooperation is thus an imperative, its success measured in terms of whether or not and to what extent the pressure on ASEAN states is lessened. But such thinking has still a rough passage to negotiate because in the economic sphere the trade-offs are more complex as each country has a different payoff matrix with regard to China. For instance, the Modi government's tolerance of India's gross trade imbalance with China may be due to the fact that it seeks to enlarge Chinese investment and economic presence to a point where the threat of the loss of access to the revenue-generating Indian market can become an effective political leverage. Or, it may be that Delhi expects Beijing to right the balance on its own by investing $20 billion in infrastructure that Xi had promised during his 2014 visit, less than a quarter of which amount has so far materialized.[132] While access to the Indian market is an excellent device to keep Beijing interested, Modi should appreciate that Beijing's investment decisions are based on strategic considerations and not influenced an iota by the Modi–Xi summit optics and similar extraneous factors.

Other countries of the MoD Quad will have their own reasons for not disturbing the existing economic pattern. Nevertheless, the shared concern for national security and sovereignty means that the nested military capabilities of this group of countries are easier to weave together into a collective effort. India, for instance, has ongoing naval cooperation with most of these states and Japan, and by now it is normal for Indian naval ships sailing east to exercise with the US, Russian and Japanese navies in the Sea of Okhotsk, the East Sea and well past Guam and into the western Pacific Ocean, respectively, and to also practise joint manoeuvres with the Vietnamese and Singapore navies and to anchor in Manila Bay. Indeed, along with Vietnam's offer of Nha Trang on its central coast as a site for India's naval base and electronic intelligence station, Singapore has revived the original 1965 offer by its first prime minister, Lee Kwan Yew, for the Indian Navy to use its Changi base as a logistics hub, enabling Indian warships to carry out sustained FoNPs in the contested waters of the South China Sea.

The Indian Navy began regularly to patrol the western approaches to Malacca since June 2017. Singapore, 2177 km from the Indian base at Port Blair in the Andaman Sea, will substantially extend India's sea legs, keep more ships on station, permitting it more comprehensively to police these waters through which pass 80 per cent of China's oil and 11 per cent of its gas imports from the Gulf.[133] The basing and supply chain schemata with Vietnam and Singapore allows India to pre-position its military and naval stores in the region, particularly helpful when a surge presence is required in crisis. It could be the prototype agreement that India can propose to other states to militarily cement the Mod Quad.

The Indian Navy, as the medium of defence links, has been establishing its credentials in this sub-region, jointly keeping watch, for example, with the Indonesian Navy with the biannual coordinated patrols (CORPAT) since 2002. The cooperation will grow with India building the port infrastructure in Sabang on the western tip of Sumatra with 40 metre depth sufficient to let Indian submarines slip into pens, in the plan generally to strengthen, as the Indonesian president Joko Widodo hinted, the Andaman–Sumatra maritime security grid to keep China in check.[134] Navy-to-navy interaction with the Mod Quad countries has been at the level of regular naval staff engagements, participation in each other's fleet reviews, and in the annual Indian Navy–initiated Indian Ocean Naval Symposium (IONS), which has emerged as the principal forum for naval chiefs of the region to get to know each other, familiarize themselves with the others' standard operating procedures, discuss strategic and operational topics, and promote all-aspect maritime cooperation. It is an embryonic security organization that many participating countries put much store by.[135] IONS is in embryo a formal organization for coordinating the maritime and wider military operations of the Mod Quad.

In the larger context, were it not for the doubts and scepticism about the country's resources and capabilities entertained by many in the Indian government, and were Indian leaders and officials not susceptible to American advice and material inducements, India would have long ago ventured to seriously discomfit China. A mere listing of the options that Delhi has so far foresworn (and which have been mentioned earlier) will hint at their potency and the effect they will have of bridling China: Transferring nuclear missiles or, at a minimum, conventional high-explosive-armed BrahMos supersonic cruise missiles to Vietnam, Indonesia, the Philippines and other South East nations; formalizing relations with Taiwan; and activating the Tibet and Uyghur 'cards'. If expeditiously implemented, it can create no end of trouble for Beijing as payback, given that China cannot up the ante as it has already shot its bolt, done its worst, and because there are more states on China's periphery fearful of China's expansionist and aggressive tendencies than there are neighbouring countries that want to stick it to India.

Moreover, Beijing has a good economic thing going—India has tolerated an entirely skewed and unbalanced trade, providing Chinese manufacturers with access to a vast consumer market in India, the second largest in the world, a foothold it would not like to lose. This may have been one of the reasons for President Xi to back out of a fight on the Doklam plateau in July 2017 (the other possible reason may have been the apprehension that Modi would use this incident at the Twelfth East Asia Summit and the Fifteenth ASEAN–India Summit in November 2017 to stoke alarms about China and ruin the meeting for Xi). The fact is that Xi's China is a wealthy state desirous of increasing its global market share and wealth and will, therefore, be more averse to starting an affray with a militarily less powerful India than it was in the past when Mao launched the PLA in the 1962 Himalayan war 'to teach a serious lesson' to 'Indian reactionaries'.[136] So, a relatively poorer India with less to lose can be more risk-acceptant and prosecute more assertive policies with good amount of confidence that Beijing, because it has more to lose, will not chance an escalatory spiral.

This will require the jettisoning of a principal tenet of Indian policy since Nehru's time of needing to prove India's friendship and fraternal feelings for China with deeds in exchange for nothing but banalities and hot air from Beijing. It parallels India's buying more and more expensive US military hardware and capital equipment, such as nuclear reactors, to engender US trust in India when, given its record, it is the US that needs to reassure Delhi about its strategic intentions by, for instance, nudging the Indian government to resume nuclear testing so that India can attain notional parity with China with a proven thermonuclear arsenal. India's policy of helping China gain acceptance on the international community in the 1950s must have occasioned mirth for the hard-headed Mao and Zhou Enlai, unapologetic practitioners of realpolitik, which the Indian philosopher and second president of the republic, Sarvepalli Radhakrishnan, described in bovine terms as 'It is good when I steal your cow, and bad when you steal my cow'.[137] Never mind that such a stance assists China and violates Machiavelli's basic dictum that 'the prince who contributes toward the advancement of another ruins his own'.[138]

But, learning no lessons, Indian prime ministers have carried on in the Nehruvian vein regardless. During his 2003 visit to Beijing, Vajpayee for the first time recognized the Tibetan Autonomous Region as 'a part of the territory of the People's Republic of China' in return for Beijing's agreeing to recognize Sikkim as part of India, which recognition China incidentally refused to have mentioned in the joint statement. Two years later, Manmohan Singh decided in his talks with Chinese Premier Wen Jiabao to go a step further. He agreed to drop the qualifier 'autonomous region' and accepted 'Tibet' as part of China. This, according to Shyam Saran, foreign secretary at the time, was 'a more nuanced' position for India to take keeping in mind China's sensitivities.[139] The Modi government, while showing some steel in Doklam and in strongly opposing the BRI, nevertheless has been just as reluctant to pay Beijing back in its own coin, by beefing up the Mod Quad's collective military capability and in consolidating India's presence with a full-fledged naval and air base at Nha Trang with line of sight on the Sanya naval base on Hainan Island, home to China's powerful South Sea Fleet and the still nascent Indian Ocean Fleet.

It has, moreover, been tardy in not publicly challenging the Xi regime's take on regional developments. For instance, the Chinese Foreign Office never misses the chance to castigate India for its terrorism charges against Pakistan.[140] Other than usually being mealy-mouthed, the MEA says little in response. Next, Beijing excoriated Hanoi for inviting Indian investment in the offshore oil and gas extraction industry, claiming this was an 'infringement of its legitimate rights' to which the Indian government reacted not at all.[141] The right thing would have been for the Foreign Office spokesman to vociferously remind China that it has occupied Indian territory—5180 square km of the Shaksgam Valley ceded to Beijing by General Ayub Khan as per the 1963 Sino-Pakistan agreement, which land transfer Premier Zhou Enlai had promised not to formalize pending a final India–Pakistan settlement of the Kashmir dispute, a commitment China broke long ago.[142] And it can object to China's creation of islands in the South China Sea in defiance of the claims of the ASEAN states and the international law, warn Beijing against enlarging its presence in Sri Lanka and in the Maldives, publicly criticize it for constructing a military base in Gwadar while accelerating the build-up of Indian military bases at Nha Trang, in the north and south Agalega Islands of Mauritius, in Assumption Island in the Seychelles, in Maldives by leasing from Malé the Gan base that was once used as a Royal Air Force mid-ocean refuelling post in the Indian Ocean, and on the northern Mozambique coast, and generally task the Indian Navy to harry Chinese naval units operating in the Indian Ocean.

The case for an extensive chain of Indian military bases in the Indian Ocean and the oceanic littoral to tighten the pre-emptive Indian control of 'India's ocean' has long been obvious to strategists as also the non-strategic-minded Delhi's aversion to them.[143] The Modi government has been slow in appreciating their utility. While it has succeeded in getting the consent of host nations, such as Mauritius and Seychelles, it has not put this programme on a war-footing as needs to be done to match the pace of China's maritime and expeditionary capability build-up. Indeed, it is only in the Modi government's last (2018–19) budget that outlays were earmarked for the infrastructure development for these bases, such as ₹300 crore for constructing a jetty to berth warships and an airfield to host combat aircraft in the Seychelles, ₹350 crore tasked for the Agalega Islands, ₹150 crore for upgrading the Kankesanthurai port on the Jaffna peninsula in Sri Lanka, ₹125 crore for the Maldives, besides $500 million as continuing support for extending the facilities at the Chabahar port in Iran.[144]

The fact is that India's languorous, generally noodle-spined diplomacy on display vis-à-vis the Maldives that shies away from coercive measures mirrors India's diffidence and defensiveness and desire to seek big-power cover for its actions and undermines India's stature in the region and the world. It encourages Chinese expropriations of land and maritime territory and offshore natural resources openly or by stealth even in India's near-seas. BRIS and Mod Quad constitute a regional entente in Asia to hold off China independent of the US, particularly important now and in the future owing to the real possibility of Washington choosing to step back from any confrontation with China. But these groupings will mean nothing if India exhibits no political will to push back when China pushes in the first place.

The need is to exploit China's maritime security situation, which in reality is quite flimsy. Freedom of navigation in the East Sea and the South China Sea has been the bedrock of Chinese prosperity since the 1980s. Should it be hampered by a concert of regional nations and extraterritorial powers, whose interests have been adversely impacted by China's outlandishly expansive claims in these areas by the creation of synthetic islands mid-channel in the South China Sea, loud threats and aggressive naval postures and by its imposition of the ADIZ, Chinese economic progress could be seriously impaired and impeded. No small reason for the dragon to stop breathing fire. But Chinese leaders will be deterred from doing anything untoward only if they see the proposed Mod Quad states getting their act together and agreeing on structures of coordinated dissuasive military action.

As it is, China is facing the might of the modern Japanese Navy to its east and, north and north-eastwards, confronts the strong Russian Pacific Fleet out of Vladivostok. In the south-east, there's the powerful Australian sea-denial element that can scupper Chinese trade in the surrounding waters. And, in the Indian Ocean, the Chinese Navy cannot sustain a large enough deployment of warships and submarines for it to make a statement of power. China's real maritime predicament is that it is surrounded by adversaries and quasi-adversaries, which cannot easily be overcome by simply building a larger, flashier, more visible surface fleet.[145] Even a Chinese Navy with 500 capital ships may be inadequate to manage the oceanic space prowled by five other formidable navies—Indian, Russian, Japanese, Australian and the extraterritorial US. BRIS and Mod Quad with their extended oceanic and littoral presence can hamper Chinese access to the natural resources and the markets of Africa and Latin America. It is not a situation a prospective base in Gwadar and Djibouti can diffuse. Sure, Gwadar will help a part of its requirement of Gulf oil and gas meant for the mainland to be transported via the CPEC. But it cannot prevent the bulk of its energy flow via the sea routes from being potentially knocked off in a conflict it intiates in South East Asia.

The Chinese Navy's use of Gwadar, moreover, will be hindered for some of the same reasons that the Pakistan Navy has never been much of a factor in India–Pakistan 'wars'—there are only so many warships that China can deploy and maintain off the Pakistani coast and in the Indian Ocean. Besides its aircraft carriers, peninsular India can cover much of the trade-bearing Indian Ocean sea lines of communications (SLOCs) by land-based air. There will be more reasons for China to act timorously once Chabahar in Iran is operationalized as an Indian naval outpost, just 70 km up the coast from Gwadar, because then it is not only outflanked in the west by the Indian Navy but will find itself in a naval pincer, assisted by such Mod Quad and US naval and air assets as are readily available and deployable in this sub-region. In other words, China will never be in a position to command and control the SLOCs in the Indian Ocean, and even less the confluence of the Atlantic and Indian Oceans or the Indo-Pacific. This reality will put China's wealth-producing seaborne trade at the mercy of BRIS and Mod Quad militaries, making it hostage to its good behaviour in the South China Sea and the East Sea and on the disputed land borders. With positive inducements for good behaviour, China can be expected to become more sedate and manageable, helping BRIS and Mod Quad to consolidate themselves.

Assuming the 100-year partnership with India proposed by Tillerson can survive Trump's foreign policy by Twitter, what are its prospects? There's agreement about the original quadrilateral of India, Japan, Australia and the United States as the cutting edge of the Indo-US strategic partnership. The prospects of this group, however, rests on the thin reed of US will. But its derivative proposed here, the Mod Quad, is inherently more flexible and will endure because it is organic to the region, meaning it will involve regional countries in their own security. The original quadrilateral took form during the December 2004 tsunami that hit Indonesia when Indian, Japanese, Australian and American navies raced to the west Sumatra coast to render humanitarian aid and found it necessary to coordinate their separate assistance efforts in order not to get in each other's way. It led to the US government of President George W. Bush appreciating India's naval capabilities and concluding that contingent maritime cooperation witnessed in the South China Sea had the potential for possibly coalescing into a useful collective security arrangement.

It was Japanese Prime Minister Abe who was most enthused by the Quad as a means of maintaining peace, order and stability and as counter to China in Asia and began pushing for it in 2005, leading two years later to his conceptualization of this quadrilateral in an address to the Indian Parliament. In the meantime, the then foreign secretary Shyam Saran met with the long-serving Australian prime minister, John Howard, who too evinced interest in this concept. A year later, however, Washington's gaze had shifted to negotiating a stop to Russia's nuclear assistance to Iran and getting Moscow to participate in the Six Party Talks to denuclearize North Korea and to calm Chinese apprehensions about the Quadrilateral as a budding security arrangement.

According to Saran, Washington sought India's help in dousing Abe's enthusiasm for it by pointing out, for instance, that if not placated China would veto India's entry into the NSG, and provided the Manmohan Singh regime a reason to softly stonewall Tokyo's hard-sell—another instance of the US working against its Asian partners' interests and also the Indian government's stupidity in furthering the American security goal of reassuring China. But what subsequently upset Delhi was Howard's successor in Canberra, the Mandarin-speaking Kevin Rudd. His intemperate rejection of the proposed quadrilateral and cosying up to China created such bad blood that even after Rudd demitted office in 2010 India blocked Australia's joining the Malabar annual naval exercises and other security-related initiatives and discussions.[146]

China, always on the lookout for margins of advantage, praised India for keeping Australia out, even though it was Canberra that had prevented such a Quad from taking shape which had served Beijing's purpose.[147] The first formal discussion involving the quadrilateral states took place in Manila in 2011 and the second more meaningful meeting again in the Philippines capital, in November 2017. By then the so-far-shunned Australia was allowed back in by Delhi, its entry eased with Indian warships first exercising with Australian Navy vessels in 2015 and two years later in the second AUSINDEX (Australia–India Exercise). It is expected to lead to regular participation by the Australian Navy in the Malabar exercises.[148] Delhi, however, continues to entertain doubts about Canberra's commitment.

What will be crucial is the priority the US accords India's security in particular and Asian security in general. Given that the Quadrilateral is supposed to militarily hog-tie China, thwart Beijing's designs in the South China Sea and rein in its troublesome proxy in north-east Asia, North Korea, US attitude to these two 'flash points' and towards its treaty allies, Japan, South Korea and the Philippines, will indicate whether Washington can be counted on to support India in its struggle with China. Predictably, America's record on this score is not encouraging.

The Quadrilateral, when it was first mooted, jelled with the 'Asia pivot' of the Obama presidency. The pivot policy was spawned by the awareness of a China that, not satisfied with merely being an economic behemoth and the engine of global economy, was becoming a formidable military power and intent on physically carving out an exclusive sphere of influence for itself. China's Nine Dash Line claim over most of the South China Sea as its exclusive economic zone (EEZ) is based on 'historical fiction' and was so rejected in July 2016 by the International Court of Arbitration at the Hague, which further decided that Beijing had no jurisdiction whatsoever on the natural resources in this maritime sphere.

By the time the judgement was given, though, Beijing had already fabricated a chain of island bases with miles of cement poured on rocky protuberances and coral outcroppings in the contested area that it had forcefully annexed in the Paracel Island and the Spratly Island chains claimed variously by Vietnam, the Philippines, Indonesia, Brunei, Malaysia and Taiwan.[149] Beijing's strategic cleverness lies in the fact that most of these synthetic islands are bunched in the near centre of the Nine Dash Line curving short of and around the coasts of Vietnam, south-central Kalimantan (Indonesia), Sarawak and Sabah (Malaysia), Brunei and the Philippine islands.

These island facilities, equipped by Beijing with radar, artillery, surface-to-air missile batteries and naval and air assets protected by reinforced hangars for combat aircraft, has divided the South China Sea into two deliberately engineered 'narrow' seas for maritime traffic to play on either side of this newly constructed central verge. It enables Beijing to more effectively police the two channels, mount offensive surveillance over the entire sea and, should the situation hot up, launch strike and dissuasive sorties by fighter-bomber aircraft embarked from Fiery Cross, and the Mischief and Subi reefs, to compel in-area and out-of-area navies bent on challenging Chinese control to conduct inherently trickier and more risky operations.[150] What complicates freedom of navigation operations even more is that the Hague Tribunal, because it considered these 'land reclamations' faits accompli, in its verdict endowed each of them with the 12 mile territorial sea designations.

With instantly available military forces and the removal of many logistical constraints, 'first contact operations' in its vicinity have become easier for the Chinese Navy to prosecute, affording Beijing an unrivalled capacity to influence politics and developments in the countries on the littoral and offshore.[151] China is also in a position to dictate terms to its maritime neighbours, bend conflict or dispute resolution to its advantage, influence trading nations with its control over the now-bifurcated oceanic highway in the South China Sea and, with the threat of applying the tourniquet to one or both of the newly created narrower sea channels, prescribe what is permissible by way of maritime conduct and interaction and command a good part of the global trade passing through them. So what was the supposedly pre-eminent global power, the United States, doing all this while? It did nothing during the time the island bases were constructed and in the wake of the Hague verdict the Obama administration chose not to vocally side with the beleaguered nations in this region, or to challenge the Chinese construction of the ersatz islands in the South China Sea. It was sometime after the verdict that it deployed its ships on FoNPs, and then these patrols skirted around the 12 mile territorial sea around each of these 'land reclamations' so as to not offend China, which had by then also imposed an ADIZ in the extended area.

With the Trump takeover, Defense Secretary James Mattis declared that America 'will continue to fly, sail, and operate' freely in the South China Sea. The US warships will assert, he said, 'their right to free passage in the manner law allows, and demonstrate resolve through operational presence in the South China Sea and beyond'. In practice, Trump (like President Obama) has avoided conflict by only safely 'stalking' these islands.[152] Such caution resulted in Obama's time in his NSA Susan Rice even 'gagging' aggressive US military commanders saying it was done to preserve 'maximum political maneuvering space' in talks with Beijing.

Admiral John Richardson, the US chief of naval operations in 2016, defined this policy succinctly: 'Cooperation would be great, competition is fine. Conflict is the thing that we really want to avoid.'[153] An American policy that strains to eliminate even the slightest chance of friction with the Chinese is worrisome for the majority of Asian states habituated from the Cold War era to view the US military presence as the guarantor of their security. The loss of America's will to protect its friends has happened in tandem with its depleting purse and was reflected in candidate Trump's urging Tokyo to acquire nuclear weapons for self-preservation because the US, he said, could no longer afford to provide security to them.[154] As President, Trump changed his tune somewhat. He now peddles US-made armaments in Asian capitals to tackle regional threats and is not any more reassuring. Further, his earlier mocking of the North Korean president Kim Jong-un as 'Rocket-man' had an unintended effect. Far from rescuing the US's plummeting reputation, it heightened Asian fears about Trump's mental stability.[155]

Trump's fourteen-day jaunt through Asia in November 2017 actually worsened matters. Other than acting as a 'travelling salesman' for American defence companies, plugging the virtues of US-produced weapons at every stop as a means of tackling the threats from China and North Korea, and reminding the American people that such sales helped boost America economically, he failed to inspire Tokyo, Seoul, Hanoi and Manila that he visited. Further, his decision to withdraw from the TPP in late January 2017 led to the eleven remaining members hammering out a 'framework agreement' at the Asia-Pacific Economic Summit in Hanoi, reflecting their intent to launch the TPP any way in the face of 'protectionist winds' in the US. The Japanese economy minister heading this initiative, Toshimitsu Motegi, hoped 'that bringing [this] agreement into force as quickly as possible' may induce the US to return to it. This gambit failed. Trump did not amend his decision to be no part of the TPP encompassing 40 per cent of the global economy and conceived in 2013 as the largest free trade area in the world and, en bloc, as prime economic competitor to China.[156]

Actually, Trump exacerbated the Asia–US economic divide because of his strident call for 'fair and reciprocal trade' at the summit and his warning that America would not tolerate 'chronic trade abuses', among these, 'product dumping, subsidized goods, currency manipulation, and predatory industrial policies'.[157] Curiously, these are the very vices candidate Trump had accused China of and which he had vowed to take Xi to task for.[158] But once in Beijing, he was all prudence—sweet talk and conciliation, and signing deals with China worth $253 billon involving American technology and finance majors, including Honeywell, General Electric and Goldman Sachs. This was proof, if any was needed, that he will do anything as long as it leads to perceived gains for the US and/or enhancement of Trump's image.

In order to make it seem that the June 2018 summit with Kim Jong-un was a great diplomatic success, without consulting Seoul and opposed by his own Pentagon, Trump weakened the security treaty with South Korea by suspending joint military training exercises and 'war games' in exchange for reiterating the vague promise of working towards 'de-nuclearization' that the North Korean leader had already made to his South Korean counterpart, Moon-jae-in, vide the 27 April 2018 Panmunjom Declaration.[159] If the US can behave so shabbily with a treaty ally, what awaits India as strategic partner is a lot worse, and Delhi already has an inkling of it.

These standoffs in south-east and north-east Asia occasioned two very different types of reactions. They persuaded the more technologically and economically advanced among America's allies—Japan and South Korea in particular—to seriously contemplate getting nuclear weapons of their own as Trump had originally advised them to do.[160] Less well-endowed countries around the South China Sea, on the other hand, are watching to see what happens and, given the right circumstances, could follow the lead given by the irascible President Rodrigo Duterte of the Philippines who cut a separate peace deal with China—a precedent Beijing hopes other disputant nations will follow.[161] This is important because it was Manila that had dragged China to the arbitration tribunal and having won its case settled on an entente, permitting Beijing to make an end-run around the Hague ruling.[162] China lost no time after the 11 July 2016 verdict to conduct a live fire drill and impose an ADIZ to test the US response.[163] Significantly, it was a gauntlet Washington refused to run. America's disinclination to forcefully contest strategic spaces in Asia is something China will exploit to the fullest to both show up the US as an undependable ally and to intimidate Asian states into becoming more amenable.

It may convince those countries around the South China Sea with more pride and fighting spirit, such as Singapore, Indonesia, Vietnam and the Philippines, to enhance security cooperation with India, a big power in the vicinity and also one which has a territorial dispute with China, than rely on the tender mercies of the US with a more fungible stake in their security, and with a record lately of not standing by its friends.[164] The question is, is India motivated enough to be a strong and reliable partner to these Asian states?

BRIS and Mod Quad in a Nutshell

The US is a 'fading power', China is racing to replace it at the top, and Russia has the military wherewithal to stop either of them cold but lacks the economic heft to make it on its own. Great power politics are thus in a state of flux now more than at any time in the recent past. The goal for India, in this context, should be to cobble together coalitions to deny China the upper hand on its periphery, in the Indian Ocean region and in Asia at large, while rendering the role of the US less central to the security of Asian states. The natural tendency of the US and China as proto-hegemons is to dominate whatever groups they are part of, leading lesser powers to sacrifice their own interests and concerns. Hence, it is imperative that the 'middle powers' cobble together strong economic–security arrangements organic to their regions, relying principally on their own individual and joint capabilities and prowess.

New arrangements can be derived from the two existing economic groupings India is part of—BRICS and the Quadrilateral—except that China and the US have to be separated, freezing China out of the BRICS configuration and cutting America out of the Quadrilateral and making its contribution secondary to the Mod Quad's collective security activity aimed at hamstringing China. Greater intra-BRIS and intra–Mod Quad parity will mean a higher level of trust, a more equitable and democratic style of functioning, and greater policy latitude and freedom of action and strategic autonomy for member states. It will result in better-coordinated BRIS and Mod Quad actions with their formidable collective economic, trade and military capabilities restraining China, while making the US redundant to Asian security. As the country common to both BRIS and Mod Quad, India will be pivotal to the success of both and will gain for Delhi maximum leverage with both China and the US. Indian governments in the 21st century have, however, been timid, eager to reinforce the country's status as a 'responsible state' that is rising without disturbing the international order.

For BRIS and Mod Quad, China is a useful adversary, considering that most countries fear it, and almost any move directed at chipping away at Chinese power and advantage, and strategically discomfiting it, bolsters everyone's sense of well-being. It will require the 'weaponizing' of these coalitions by making cooperative security as much a shared objective as free trade and economic cooperation. What BRIS lacks in economic heft relative to China, it can make up by controlling the Asian behemoth's economic fate. The BRIS states control the oceanic frontages crucial to the Chinese economy. This is no mean advantage individually and jointly for BRIS states to wield against China. With only limited openings—and that too contested—on the East Sea and South China Sea, China finds that its trade traffic has to negotiate adversary-controlled waters. At the other end, Trump's imposition of tariffs on steel imports to punish China victimizes India as also Brazil and other South American countries, while US sanctions on Russian companies hurt Russia economically and, owing to the punitive aspects of the CAATSA, endanger India's long-standing friendship and military supply relationship with Russia.

It has already led to a backlash of Latin American states looking to Asia for trade partners—an opportunity the Narendra Modi government cannot afford to pass up to form a trading scheme to spur economic growth in the country and help it find new markets for its traditional exports and light manufactures south of the Rio Grande river, and to counter Washington's moves, for which purpose BRIS will come in handy. With BRIS opposed to hegemonism everywhere, it can balance China and the US and become a force for peace and order in the world and a military and economic counterweight to either of them and boost the UNSC candidature of India, Brazil and South Africa.

The Mod Quad of India, Japan, Australia and the South East Asian nations, on the other hand, is an obvious geopolitical construct, interweaving the economic and security interests of the littoral and offshore states on the Asian rimland to contain the heartland power, China. The Mod Quad is a trillion-dollar club with Japan, India, ASEAN and Australia boasting of a collective 2017 GDP of $10.8 trillion, each of whom fears China. So what will elicit a positive response to the Mod Quad concept are two things: a plainly overmatched US armed forces, and Washington's reluctance to militarily tangle with China in maritime territorial disputes involving Asian states. The US withdrawal from the TPP only confirmed the worst Asian fears about an America happy to throw its partners under the bus. Geographically more distanced from China, in its 2017 Foreign Policy White Paper Australia has voiced concern about an ambitious China and about the gradual military withdrawal of the US from the Indo-Pacific region, which last may convince Canberra to think of the Mod Quad as an alternative security buffer. More recently, ties with China have gone into 'deep freeze' owing to the harsh Australian criticism of Chinese infrastructure projects in the Pacific island states and measures to curtail Chinese espionage activity and interference in domestic politics with financial contributions to Australian parties by Chinese entities.[165]

China's military pressure on India, South East Asia and Japan has to be countered. Except, each country has a different payoff matrix with China to preserve. Even so, the shared concern for national security and sovereignty means that the combined military capabilities of the Mod Quad can mesh into an informal collective effort. India, for instance, has ongoing naval cooperation with most of these states and Japan. It has also proposed agreements on naval and air force basing arrangements with other South East Asian states, other than Vietnam, with the Philippines and Indonesia. These agreements are of the kind

Delhi signed with Singapore to assert the freedom of navigation rights in the South China Sea. With Subic Bay and the Clark air force base in the Philippines coming into the reckoning as stations for Indian naval and air units to periodically rotate out of, the Chinese Navy will find itself in difficulty with too many adversary navies in too many active sub-theatres to contend with. This is precisely the sort of operational dilemmas BRIS and Mod Quad need to create for Beijing.

In the Sino-Indian context, India has been shoved into a strategic corner. It is time Delhi retaliated with cold-blooded calculation. The solution of arming every state in China's maritime with strategic impact weapons will be enthusiastically received. The fact is that even with a modernized military, China is unable to command the SLOCs in any of the relevant Asian seas. It cannot control the extended littoral or risk the situation getting out of hand in the South China Sea. And the wealth-producing Chinese seaborne trade is at the mercy of adversary states on either side of Malacca and the 'narrow seas' created by the Chinese cement-on-coral islands in the South China Sea and in the sea lanes in the Indian Ocean. This will serve as a guarantee of China's good behaviour. With BRIS shoring up the land and Indian Ocean fronts, China will be rendered manageable for Mod Quad, making any US role as security provider unnecessary and in excess of need. This is organic security, with regional states as the main stakeholders, at its best. It makes even more economic sense with the ongoing Sino-US trade war that India can exploit for its own ends.[166] Delhi can induce US manufacturing companies active in China to relocate to India. But this presumes a quicksilver Indian government system which is entirely absent and so yet another opportunity to make good will go abegging.

The whole point about the disruptive aspects of the new and novel geopolitics that BRIS and Mod Quad represent is that it increases India's negotiating leverage with the US and China and widens its foreign and military policy choices.[167] It is the danger of losing the freedom of action on the one hand and the perils of partnering America on the other that is motivating Erdogan to push away from the US and NATO and have Turkey fall in with Russia and even Iran—two of Washington's biggest bugbears.[168] More tellingly, German Chancellor Angela Merkel urged Europeans 'to take our fates into our own hands', a sentiment that led to the EU establishing its own expeditionary forces independent of NATO 'to help reinforce', an official statement said, its 'strategic autonomy to act alone when necessary, and with partners whenever possible'. That Europe is discovering 'strategic autonomy' at a time when Modi is moving away from it underscores this inadequate grasp of the emerging world order and the need for India to configure coalitions to balance the US and China.

In this respect, Delhi needs to recall just how far the US will go to advance its interests even if it sets the rest of the world on fire. It concerted with the Sauds in Riyadh to use Wahhabism in Pakistan and Afghanistan to create the jihadi cadres to battle the Russian military in Afghanistan in the early 1980s and then departed the scene, leaving the two South Asian countries in the grip of Islamic extremism.[169] That's the kind of tragic denouement usually visiting America's clients who side with it, because client states cannot negotiate themselves out of trouble, leave alone get what they believe they deserve. As the boxing impresario Don King averred, 'You don't get what you deserve, you get what you negotiate.'[170] With no chips on India's side of the table of the kind that BRIS and Mod Quad would afford, and with depleted leverage owing to the downgrading of Russia by Delhi, India will soon discover, that the US will further its own interests without reducing China's in any way and drive India's national interest into the ground, which surely is not the bargain Modi has been looking for.

[5]

Affirmative Inaction

'There are risks and costs to action. But they are far less than the long-range risks of comfortable inaction'—John F. Kennedy

THE MOST STRIKING aspect of Modi's foreign policy are the seventy-odd foreign trips he has racked up in his first four years as prime minister. These underline the fact, writes A.R. Kohli, a ruling BJP member, that 'India's voice today matters on the world stage'.[1] A growing Indian economy based on a massive market of 1.2 billion people is, by itself, enough to register on the global consciousness. Undoubtedly, some strategic purpose has been served by these visits, but its impact has been lessened by the unease in international quarters about the domestic political situation teetering on the edge of turmoil, and Modi's meandering foreign policy.

Modi has notched up some notable successes, including the military-basing agreements at the two ends of the Indian Ocean—with Oman for the Indian Navy's use of the Duqm port, with France to use its Heron base in Djibouti, with Singapore for pre-positioning naval stores, and with Indonesia to build up the Sumatran port of Sabang as a naval base to enable sustained Indian naval patrols and presence in the eastern Indian Ocean and the South China Sea. Predictably, the MEA is crowing about Duqm's uses to shadow the Chinese forces out of Gwadar, but not about its utility, along with the Chabahar port in Iran, strategically to limit the Chinese military ex-Djibouti, which Beijing views as its base anchoring its Indian Ocean forces and serving for the

Chinese Navy the same purpose as Aden once did the Royal Navy. Duqm on the Trucial coast along with Chabahar is a double-barrelled flanking move to bring the prospective Chinese naval base in Gwadar within range, and Duqm and the French Heron base in Djibouti as staging points for Indian naval and air sorties to engage Chinese forces out of their newly constructed base also in Djibouti. Chabahar and Duqm, once plugged into the existing surveillance grid involving Indian military units in northern Mozambique, Seychelles, Mauritius, Maldives and Trincomalee in Sri Lanka, will make for a fairly strong Indian naval presence in the western and southern Indian Ocean. However, the lack of urgency to follow up the Duqm–Heron–Singapore–Sabang type of diplomatic successes to gain geostrategic advantage with actual military deployment, and to speed up basing preparations in the Agalega Islands in Mauritius and Assumption Island in the Seychelles—all of which will make possible for the first time expeditionary missions by the Indian military—is discouraging.

It reflects Modi's disinclination openly to pursue hard power–oriented diplomacy. Why this is so is not immediately discernible other than his belief that India's soft power counts for more in relations with countries in its extended abroad that have historically had close trade and cultural ties with the subcontinent and, in fact, exemplifies India's standing as a civilizational power, as 'vishwa guru'. In the event, the fact that a 'soft power matrix' was drawn up by the BJP government reportedly to gauge the success of its outreach policy is along anticipated lines. In this context, the MEA's cultural diplomacy arm, the Indian Council for Cultural Relations (ICCR) is to be accorded prominence and encouraged to establish Indian cultural centres in the Gulf and other proximal regions.[2]

This is fine, except there is as great a need to sell India's hard power and design policies for its use, something that Modi has avoided doing. On his visits to the kingdoms, sheikhdoms and emirates in the Gulf, he has mostly stressed Indian Islam and, by indirection, the large Indian Muslim population—second largest in the world after Indonesia. His success in facilitating Indian investment in oilfields, getting the Gulf regimes to allow the construction of Indian temples, and getting the Indian embassies in the region to look after the welfare and interests of the predominantly Muslim expatriate Indian community responsible for nearly $69 billion in remittances would have had a domestic multiplier effect and fetched the BJP rich dividend in terms of an enlarged Muslim voter support had the Modi regime not been viewed as condoning the excesses of the Hindu fringe. In the event, Modi's policy has spawned the suspicion that the 'ghettoizing' of Muslims in the country complements his foreign policy aimed primarily at crowding Pakistan out of the Gulf.[3] Together with Delhi's concerting with the US on Pakistan's role in fanning terrorism, it suggests that the BJP government's Neighbourhood First policy has been unwisely yoked, not to obtaining a peaceful South Asia premised on normalization of relations with Pakistan, but to the limited objective of scoring political points against Pakistan owing to its 'jihadi culture' as a failed and dangerous state.

To get a perspective, Modi's foreign policy has to be compared and contrasted with Nehru's achievements in the 1950s with minuscule resources but ample strategic wit and imagination. Nehru's rhetoric—other than on nuclear disarmament—was all Third World (anti-imperialism, anti-colonialism, anti-racism), whence the US Ambassador Loy Henderson's snarky 1951 note to the Secretary of State Dean Acheson that 'Nehru is constitutionally unhappy when he [is] not leading some cause of downtrodden peoples . . . against real or imagined oppression'.[4] But Indian foreign policy in practice was more focused, intent on extracting whatever benefits it could from the superpower politics of the Cold War. In the second decade of the 21st century, the business end of Indian policy is still tuned to the big powers even as Modi's invocation of India's age-old links to, and his government's intent to reconnect with, the island nations of the Indian Ocean, and countries in South East Asia, Central Asia, the Gulf states and on the East African littoral, has remained mostly talk.[5] The irony is that while the country lacked the resources in Nehru's time to stamp its presence in the *tiers monde*, what development aid and assistance his government did muster had impact. Programmes, such as the one that sent Indian schoolteachers to East African countries, for example, are recalled with gratitude to this day by its beneficiaries (including diplomats posted to Delhi). They generated goodwill and strengthened India's claims of leadership of the Third World. Sixty years on, what is missing, on the one hand, is the political will and, on the other hand, the institutional capacity of the MEA and the Indian government, in general, to deliver on the prime minister's promises to friendly states.

Modi has made commitments during his official travels to these parts and in regional and international fora, such as the India–Africa summit in Delhi, but little has materialized on the ground. The list of such projects is long and it makes no sense to detail the promises Modi has made in various countries or retail the failures of non-implementation, because they don't matter much considering they have remained largely unrealized. This is so because the tools and intragovernmental structures that are necessary for coordinated follow-up action is, when not absent, grossly inadequate, and the manpower assigned such work small. It has eroded the credibility and respect India once enjoyed, weakened its influence and enabled a resourceful China to quickly make friends and influence countries with offers of credit, trade and infrastructure investment, and to replace India in their affections.

This is especially noticeable in the subcontinent itself. With India unable to match or up the ante in material terms, Delhi has to offer something more and different, such as FTAs to recover the country's near-abroad from China's clutches. This the recent Indian governments, including Modi's, haven't been able to do. As a result, a number of adjoining states—Nepal, the Maldives, Myanmar—are all but lost to China, which, coupled with the unresolved problems with Pakistan, make for a doleful prospect for the country's neighbourhood policy.[6] A largely unpacified neighbourhood means that India's grand plan to rise peaceably to great power status, or even be recognized as a 'civilizational power', does not stand a chance because the country is likely to be tripped up at its doorstep by the ill will of adjoining states which the 'China–Pakistan Axis' seeks to stoke.[7]

Good Relations with Pakistan: the Crux

India's besetting foreign policy fault, which is also the country's greatest military weakness, post-Nehru, is that bereft of a significant and formally articulated national vision, it wallows in the shallows, its once grand design as the geographically centred pivotal power in the swath of land and sea from the Maghreb to the Far East, going by the weight of the armed forces deployed on the western and north-eastern fronts, shrivelled to perceiving Pakistan as principal adversary, a small, weak country with a tenth its GDP![8] It is all the more disturbing because this threat perception got rooted after the 1971 war to liberate Bangladesh when the last vestiges of Pakistan as even a remote threat disappeared. Yet, the consolidation of the Indian Army's armoured and mechanized post–1971 war might when there was no credible threat to wield it against is a bit curious. Its purpose is particularly opaque once Pakistani nuclear weapons hove into view, when large-scale mobile warfare with tanks became extinct, the nonsense about the 'Cold Start' doctrine notwithstanding.

Cold Start plans assume that the three Indian strike corps will be able to disaggregate and form into eight integrated battle groups (IBGs) while racing into war, which is almost impossible to achieve, and then they will not be able to go very far or very deep inside Pakistan beyond what the stores of POL (petroleum, oil, lubricants) integral to the formations, permit them to. In the event, Cold Start is good only as a justification for the army to keep its armoured strike corps and the current force structure that are long past their sell-by date.[9] The oldest of these 'Strike Corps', XXI Corps, was formed in 1942 for duty in present-day Iran as part of the Allied forces in the Persian theatre, I Corps was founded even as the 1965 conflict with Pakistan was underway, and II Corps was raised by Lieutenant General T.N. Raina a little before the onset of the war for Bangladesh. In other words, the bulk of the country's strike formations and the supposed main force to use against Pakistan on the Punjab plains and the Rajasthan desert were operational long after these could be put to any real test. Unless the idea is to carve up what remains of Pakistan in the west, which in the nuclearized milieu is infeasible.

Further, it is one thing, in a military context, to to and fro on a disputed border—gain some territory here, lose some there—on the LoC in Kashmir and on the LAC with China. It is quite another thing altogether to engage in a map-changing exercise or, short of a nuclear exchange initiated by Pakistan, to try and rub that nation off the face of the earth, which doesn't make geostrategic sense even if it was tolerated by the international system, which it won't be, even with the reasonable cause of ridding the world of a hotbed of Islamic terrorism. There's, however, the 'Sialkot grab' kind of option this analyst has detailed elsewhere that the current Indian armoured and mechanized forces can productively prosecute to achieve the political aim while pre-empting the Pakistani nuclear first use. In this scenario, the aim is to militarily invest a border city, such as Sialkot, in strength and to press forward with armour and mechanized units forcing back the civilian population and the Pakistani formations into the city and the Pakistani hinterland with the Indian armour and mounted infantry advancing in lockstep with the retreating Pakistani people and military units. This will prevent tactical nuclear first use by Pakistan for fear of vaporizing its own people and armed forces. And when the ceasefire is called, to use the captured city as a card to negotiate a final LoC-as-formal-border solution, the sort of victor's bargain Indira Gandhi could have legitimately imposed on Pakistan in 1971 but didn't.

Pakistan will be less deterred, however, from using tactical nuclear weapons in the open terrain of the Cholistan desert and the approaches to Rahim Yar Khan—the traditional ingress route for Indian armour.[10] The 'Sialkot grab' type of operation, moreover, does not require the kind of fighting mass that three strike corps can bring to bear, which are capital-intensive and way in excess of need. They can be safely pruned to a single composite corps plus several independent armoured brigades for any realistic Pakistan contingency, with the resources thus freed being sensibly diverted to raising three corps capable of offensive mountain and high-altitude desert warfare, enabling the army to take the fight to the Chinese PLA on the Tibetan plateau.

With the crippling blows to Islamic State (or Daesh) in Iraq and Syria, rabid Islamic terrorism is migrating eastward with reports suggesting that Islamic State elements are ensconced in Afghanistan. This is a troubling development, in which context it is foolhardy to in any way undermine Pakistan which, whether anybody likes it or not, acts as a cordon sanitaire against Islamic State, a buffer against extremist ideology and influences seeping east from Arab lands through Pakistan, aided and abetted for realpolitik reasons by the US and China.[11] So far, neither the Indian strike corps nor threats of 'surgical strikes' has dissuaded the Pakistani

Army from assisting terrorist outfits to target Indian Army units, camps and cantonment areas in Jammu and Kashmir, an activity made possible by the apparent inability of the Indian forces in the field to get even the basics of 'perimeter security' right, reflecting, perhaps, the lax work ethos permeating the army as it has done the rest of the government, and the home ministry–controlled police and paramilitary forces.[12]

Then again, as the 'front-line state' late 1970s onwards, Pakistan experienced the influx of millions of Afghan Pashtun into Pakistan. The spread of jihadi sentiments and the ready availability of Kalashnikovs changed the socio-religious and political dynamic in that country where state-sponsored terrorist units such as LeT and JeM, mixed with the Afghan Taliban, the home-grown Tehrik-i-Taliban Pakistan (TTP), and other jihadi groups in simpatico with Islamic State, have produced a combustible social compound that has taxed the Pakistani state to breaking point. Pakistan, in a sense, finds itself in an unending fight with itself, its internal cohesion rent by ethnic and sectarian violence, misgovernance and a febrile mode of politicking that only worsens the situation. Pakistan does not need India to tear it apart; it is doing a good job by itself.

In the larger context though, an isolated Pakistan, pressured by the US, hounded by India and on the brink of insolvency, has nowhere to turn except China. With the CPEC and associated infrastructural build-up, China has not only won access for its western provinces to a warm water port for year-round trade and commerce, a naval base in Gwadar for its Indian Ocean fleet—the so-called secret Fourth Fleet—and, with the yuan becoming legal tender in that area of Balochistan, there is every possibility of Pakistan becoming, as many in that country apprehend, a Chinese colony. It doesn't make a whit of a difference to the Pakistani Army that the CPEC will, in stages, erode that country's financial sovereignty, or that it will render Pakistan a pariah to the West. They'll suffer this because of their attitude fostered by a long-running animus against India—that readily countenances Pakistan's cutting off its own nose to spite India's face.[13] This is reflected most starkly in the prevailing belief in that country that tactical nuclear weapons are Pakistan's deliverance with no reflection whatsoever about the consequences to it of first use. The stance of 'first use'—assuming it is not just a ruse de guerre to deter India from overwhelming it by conventional military means—is powerful rhetoric that could be blinding the Pakistani security enclaves to the certainty of Indian retaliation that, in case of intemperate escalation will, given Pakistan's narrow spatial geography, mean its certain end as a social organism at the cost, of course, of quite considerable damage to India.[14]

Except Pakistan's pathological obsession with India is mirrored in the Modi government's fixation with Pakistan. To suggest this is exactly to define the end state of the artificial Hindu India–Muslim Pakistan enmity fuelled by the religious fringe in both countries. It can be easily squelched by Modi's coming down hard on the lumpen element, furthering the communal divide on frivolous issues that distracts from his twin mission of restoring India's civilizational stature with the 'live and let live' principle that has characterized Indian culture and society for millennia, and of raising the country's economic stock. It would rob the Pakistani outlier groups of much of their motivation and make it more difficult for the Pakistani Army's ISI to recruit Indian Muslims for its 'sleeper cells'.[15]

But as stated earlier, Prime Minister Modi is too much the political animal not to espy the benefits from polarizing the electorate. Sure, Pakistan-sponsored terrorist groups active in the Srinagar Valley are a nettlesome problem. But it is better tackled by the hammer and kid glove treatment of the local population, including harsh military–police actions to root out the secessionist/separatist elements, complemented by aggressive policing of the LoC. Waging *kutayuddha* (covert war) while carrying on placidly with normal bilateral relations, including dialoguing to resolve the Kashmir dispute, would be something Chanakya would have recommended. It is another matter that the General Headquarters' ([GHQ], the Pakistani Army's headquarters in Rawalpindi) covert war management system is sharper than Delhi's.[16] By making so much hoo-ha about 'surgical strikes' and boasting publicly about the Indian hand in Balochistan and, historically, in the emergence of Bangladesh, Modi has fanned the fear of 'Hindu India' that Islamic extremists in neighbouring countries nurse into full-blooded paranoia, strengthening, in Pakistan's case, the hand of the Pakistani Army and its institutional opposition to a Kashmir compromise–rapprochement with India.[17]

As a calculating and worldly wise politician and a man of the world, the above reading of the situation should not be difficult for Prime

Minister Modi to understand. He started out in office as if understanding where India and Pakistan stood with each other and what India needed to do to break the vicious cycle of mutual enmity and bad blood when he invited Prime Minister Nawaz Sharif along with the heads of government of other South Asian states to his inauguration in May 2014. Hope was still alive when he 'dropped' in on Sharif at the latter's Raiwind estate outside of Lahore in December of the following year on his flight back home from Kabul, surprising the Pakistanis and impressing them with his humility and uniquely subcontinental gestures, like touching Sharif's mother's feet, which warmed the cockles of many a Pakistani heart. This was ambush diplomacy at its best, at once disarming a putative foe with a low cost, high value move and holding out the prospect of a new beginning and a better tomorrow for both countries.[18]

Developments thereafter rapidly returned to 'normal'—the same old terrorist incidents, cross-LoC small arms and artillery duels, trading of charges and harrumphing by the beribboned generals on both sides, except in 2017 a retaliatory attack by the Indian Special Forces led to the insertion of a novel phrase into the bilateral ties: 'surgical strikes'. The Indian government used it to denote a ramped-up military response to Pakistani provocation, which the ruling BJP insists on portraying as reflecting an India that is willing to hit back. Whether it meets the requirements of Modi's 2014 election campaign rhetoric that his response to Pakistani provocation would be 'a bomb', not 'chicken biryani' is less clear.[19] The short-term payoffs from such theatrical belligerence apart, there may be some other factors at play here.

But to set the picture straight, consider the contrasting views and approaches of Modi with respect to Pakistan and China that he aired at the 2018 Raisina Dialogue, which a newspaper aptly described as proposing the 'terms' for resuming dialogue with Pakistan and wooing China for trade. 'Pakistan must walk away from terror if it wants to walk towards dialogue with India,' the prime minister said. 'It also has to be Pakistan's journey to make. India cannot walk the path of peace alone.' Admitting that relations with China had hit a low (due to the Doklam crisis), he talked about globalization as opening up the 'vast area of commercial and business opportunities'. 'It is not unnatural for two large neighbouring powers to have some differences,' Modi said soothingly, but 'for peace and progress in the region, both our countries need to show sensitivity and respect for each other's core concerns and interests'.[20]

The Indian government, by this reckoning, is prepared to overlook China's driving the CPEC through territory claimed by India—POK—along with its constant armed provocations along the LAC, its blatant aggression against Bhutan (an Indian protectorate in all but name), its cultural genocide in occupied Tibet, its support for assorted rebellions in north-eastern India, its predatory economic policies that have ballooned India's trade deficit vis-à-vis China to $53 billion, its support for Pakistani-funded terrorists and terrorist outfits, its veto of India's membership to a permanent seat in the UNSC and of the NSG; but Modi cannot bring himself to talk to Pakistan—similar to India in every social, cultural and even political aspect—because of the ongoing kerfuffle over Kashmir (and the terrorism that it has spawned)? There are obviously personal and visceral factors at work for the prime minister as regards Pakistan that are missing where China is concerned, despite its being India's main security and geopolitical challenge.

In other words, Modi's China policy of sponging up pain that Beijing inflicts by various means is bearable and the Indian government is prepared to carry on with a bilateral relationship at multiple levels despite getting hammered on every one of them, but is unwilling to countenance other than a single-pronged, unidimensional, policy of making terrorism the metric for normalcy with Pakistan when, all said and done, the police forces and the military have been able successfully to contain terrorism in Kashmir and put the lid on the insurgencies in the north-east. This is a policy twist that's worth plumbing.

The psyches of political leaders develop along different lines (as we have seen in the first two chapters). This matters because their likes and dislikes, which have jelled early in life for reasons as diverse as events that had a scarring effect, personal slights and socialization in milieus where social biases and ways of thinking are imbibed, end up shaping the policies of countries. Two wars impacted Modi. He recalled to a biographer that the 1962 war with China was the first time that he had patriotic feelings and how he plied Indian soldiers in trains rushing to the warfront with tea and biscuits at the Vadnagar railway station. The humiliation India suffered in that conflict apparently played on Modi's mind in terms of the lack of strong leadership which the country desperately needed. In that context, Nehru paled in Modi's estimation in comparison to Vallabhbhai Patel—the Gujarati leader, chief organizer of the Congress party and a rival of Nehru's for the prime minister's post. But Modi's patriotism, by his own account, took off during the 1965 war with Pakistan when it comingled with the indoctrination of the RSS that he had by then been exposed to.[21] He became ultra-patriotic, the heightened patriotism making him, a biographer noted, voluble about the need to destroy all Pakistanis.[22] While the China war served to emphasize the need for a strong national leadership for Modi, the 1965 war apparently had the effect of solidifying Pakistan as India's chief adversary. Conveniently, tensions in relations with Pakistan were easy to conflate with the Hindu–Muslim tensions in the country and the subcontinent at large, which was mirrored in the Gujarati society he grew up in where communal frictions are endemic.

The conflict with Pakistan had a more lasting effect, perhaps, also because he was older and the anti-Muslim prejudices inherent in the Sangh's Hindutva ideology congealed in his mind in a manner his antipathy to China didn't when he was younger. It may have firmed up a tilt of attitude which says that Indian and Chinese culture and ethos are ultimately flexible and, whatever the differences, India and China can do business with each other but that, for reasons of the rigid, exclusionist Islamic religion and ideology, normal and reasonable transactions with Pakistan are more difficult to obtain. Whence as pointed out in earlier chapters, his unwillingness as Gujarat chief minister and prime minister to treat Muslims as a minority requiring special consideration. And once he became chief minister and conversant with international affairs, Modi may have noticed the similarities between the Indian concepts of 'unity in diversity' and 'cooperative pluralism' or 'multi-polar world order' with the traditional Chinese principle of 'divergence in harmony'. This apparent resonance in Indian and Chinese values and ways of dealing with the world has, perhaps, led to the Modi regime's anomalous behaviour.

The BJP government will happily face off with China in Doklam, react to frequent military incidents triggered by the Chinese PLA along the LAC, say nothing about the PLA build-up in Tibet, suffer China's safe-havening of India's north-eastern rebels, tolerate its damming and diverting the Brahmaputra river in Tibet that could gradually lay waste the downstream estuarine economies of Assam and Bangladesh, which, according to international law, is casus belli (cause for war), smile through the procedural barriers erected by Beijing to mar India's progress in international forums, bear the China trade deficit burden, and still engage in interminable border talks and in normal cultural and other exchanges. But where Pakistan is concerned, he demands that as precondition for resuming 'composite' talks, Islamabad first swear off terrorism when, by his own public disclosure, Indian agencies have had a hand in the troubles in Balochistan. This doesn't make sense except in terms of the long-ingrained Indian (and South Asian) historical and cultural (caste-induced?) habit of bowing to the powerful and bullying the weak.

The irony is that in the manner in which he began his innings as prime minister, Modi gave every indication of a reset of India–Pakistan relations. Implicit in this was an acceptance that Islamabad has to be allowed the space to work out the troubling dynamic between its army and the political class which is at the root of how much and how strongly the Pakistani state supports the malcontents in Indian Kashmir, and expends scarce resources as an ultimately futile asymmetric warfare against India. That this is a way to keep the Indian Army occupied and distracted to contemplate for conventional war is fine but it is a costly option. It is this aspect that led General Pervez Musharraf to offer the 2007 compromise on Kashmir which would have formalized the LoC as international border, and afforded Pakistan the fig-leaf of the joint commission to 'oversee' along with India the affairs of the erstwhile princely state of Kashmir. Had that agreement been approved by Manmohan Singh, India could in the present day have exercised a veto over the CPEC passing through Gilgit and Baltistan.

Even so, that compromise still offers the outlines for a mutually acceptable solution for what's not really all that intractable a problem. The grand aim of a geopolitical design to restore to the subcontinent its strategic unitariness depends on Delhi's display of 'strategic generosity'. This may entail impressing the Pakistani Army by unilaterally restructuring the Indian land forces with a diluted armoured component as discussed earlier and pulling back nuclear missiles from the border with Pakistan. Simultaneously, the Pakistani trading and agricultural communities and industry can likewise be enticed with free and open access to the Indian market, allowing Pakistan-sourced and produced goods of any kind, including light manufactures, entry to the vast Indian market. If the Indian economy is big enough, rich enough, to bear the costs of unbalanced trade with China, it can surely absorb the infinitely smaller costs of even one-way free trade not just with Pakistan but with all other South Asian states. The substantive strategic benefits to India will outweigh any economic imposition. As it is, the informal Indian exports to Pakistan of some $13 billion to $14 billion via the 'switch trade'—goods ostensibly bound for Dubai offloaded from ships off Karachi or smuggled across the Thar desert—dwarfs the formal Indo-Pakistan trade of $3 billion. Good India–Pakistan relations boil down to, the former Pakistani commerce secretary Zafar Mahmood said, 'dominant' India showing 'large-heartedness' and being 'more accommodating toward its neighbors', wrote Zafar Mahmood, former Pakistan commerce secretary. 'Granting trade concessions to its smaller neighbors would not hurt it economically. It would not only earn goodwill and respect for India in the region, but would also contribute to the economic integration of South Asia.' This is more possible now, he concludes, with the previously reluctant private sector in Pakistan becoming growingly receptive to economic intercourse with India.[23]

Once the Pakistani Army sees that the restructured Indian forces are there to stay and do not constitute a danger it will be less averse to the peaceful resolution of Kashmir and other territorial disputes (Sir Creek, Wullar Barrage, where there's substantial agreement) to opening up economically to India. This will lead to increased trade flows and commercial and industrial linkages whose benefits to the Pakistani people and economy will surpass whatever good the Chinese-funded CPEC may do. The gigantic Chinese debt overhang owing to the CPEC, moreover, may convince Islamabad to rethink that country's over-reliance on China. India has for too long acted as an economic equal of the smaller, weaker neighbouring states that need to be dealt with on a strictly reciprocal basis, when a less petty, more open approach would mesh these countries into one of the largest markets anywhere. Instead, because Delhi drips condescension and disdain India finds itself disliked and distrusted by most of the smaller neighbouring countries. It has provided China the opening to insinuate itself into the subcontinent's affairs. India has further harmed its relative position with China by aligning its policies with the human rights concerns of the US and lost traditional friends such as Myanmar. And yet Modi hopes and expects that India can become a great power, a 'civilizational' and cultural node, on the backs of seriously disaffected states in the abutting regions.

The Modi government may not acknowledge this, but crafting good relations with Pakistan is the fundamental building block of a truly peaceful and economically integrated extended sub-region, one that is plugged into the Indian economy which, thus enlarged, can become the driver of economic prosperity and the kernel around which a loose collective security arrangement can over time grow to protect it. It won't happen at all if Pakistan's security fears are not squarely addressed and ameliorated by India. Even if Delhi takes all the friendly economic measures, peace initiatives will only get the Pakistani Army's support if the compromise Kashmir solution becomes reality.

The nub of the problem, which the GHQ has publicly voiced, is the structure of the Indian land forces with the capacity for deep penetration operations. That such an objective is unattainable is not the point. What is is the fact that such massive Indian armoured and mechanized formations, however meagre a threat they actually pose, do require Pakistan to invest disproportionately in a like blocking force. This may be fine by the Pakistani generals but robs social welfare and development sectors in Pakistan of monies they desperately need to not plunge headlong into social dislocation and bankruptcy. Such a Pakistani state at sixes and sevens with itself is even more perilous for India because of the ease with which the trends of social, sectarian and ethnic identity and fragmentation and attendant divisive ideologies can ooze across the border. The issues of Khalistan and Indian groups (like the Students' Islamic Movement of India) boasting cross-border influences is a reminder of how things can go very wrong when Delhi combines low politics in the border provinces with bad relations with Pakistan.

So, unless India undertakes a major restructuring of its armed services to emphasize the China threat, there will be no relief to the peoples of South Asia from their current predicament. Moreover, with terrorism as the prime Pakistani threat, a vast armoured force is hardly the necessary antidote for India. It is, in fact, a stupendous misuse of the taxpayer's money, which defence resources that can be better spent in constituting a capability as previously argued, for operations across the LAC. Three such offensive-tasked formations will mean that the Tibet-based PLA group armies cannot count on the Indian Army being forced to fight defensively and downhill and will have to factor into their consideration Indian attacking units debouching on to the plateau in the rear of their aggressor units. It entirely changes the conflict calculus and the PLA's logistics plans and will automatically lighten the Chinese pressure on the LAC. The army alignment towards China as primary threat has, in fact, been voiced repeatedly by the army chief General Bipin Rawat.[24] But there's still not the gumption in the army headquarters to undertake the reallocation of resources from the strike corps usable only in the flat open terrain of the Great Thar Desert, the Punjab plains on either side of the border being rendered difficult for armoured and mechanized armies by the network of criss-crossing agricultural canals and anti-tank ditches-cum-bunds.

With the Indian military bogey removed, Pakistani generals will be hard-pressed to justify their posture of unrelieved enmity towards India. Islamabad has always banked on two factors. The US strategy of defeating the Taliban in Afghanistan means no early end to America's small footprint or large footprint war. It guarantees Pakistan's indispensability as front-line state to Washington and at the same time maintains its importance. Pakistan will equally remain crucial to China in its plans to establish itself in southern Asia and the Indian Ocean.[25] These imperatives of the two big powers are often ignored by Delhi with Modi hoping that the terrorism issue will help his government draw the US away from Pakistan. That won't happen. In the drama attending on the minor military hostilities on the LoC, what is often disregarded in India is the professionalism of the Pakistani armed forces.

This is reflected in their very practical riffs on the kinds of wars they can in fact fight and survive, and about the limits of their nuclear first use posture. Even the nuclear situation so beloved of Western think tanks as a 'flash point' can be easily denatured were India to affect a more relaxed nuclear deployment by unilaterally removing its nuclear-tipped short-range and medium-range ballistic missiles from the border with Pakistan because the presence of such missiles shortens the nuclear fuse without any compensatory benefits. India's divesting the forward areas of Agni missiles would be in the full knowledge that the longer-range Agni missiles fired from hinterland areas can cover all of Pakistan.[26] These are the sorts of meta-strategic actions Delhi needs to take if it is to emerge as a credible power on the world scene which, alas, it doesn't do and which acts of omission by the government will guarantee India will not become a great power.

In this respect, Pakistani Army chiefs have been ahead of their Indian counterparts. Generals Ashfaq Parvez Kayani and Qamar Javed Bajwa publicly stated that terrorists within Pakistan are a bigger threat than India.[27] These remarks reflect the uneasiness within the army with the old shibboleths, the old threats, the old mode of thinking and the usual way of doing things. In this context, General Bajwa's well-publicized interest, soon after he assumed office, in having his officers read a book dealing with how the Indian Army adjusted to the democratic Indian polity and became apolitical was a cue for the Indian Army to suggest to the Modi regime parlays with their Pakistani counterparts.[28]

In an evolving situation where the potential for easing relations is signalled quite openly by the Pakistani Army, and where a sustained period of artillery shelling by Indian forces across the LoC begat not artillery salvos in return but a call from the Pakistani side for a meeting of the directors general of military operations for a pow-wow as a confidence-building measure.[29] In such a situation, for the Indian military to parrot the BJP government about the 'Pakistan threat' is to belittle itself and waste the chance for a smart restructuring of its own forces and for pushing the government towards ending the discord with Pakistan so that it can more effectively focus on China. But how to get around Modi, who seems to have become a victim of his own anti-Pakistan rhetoric?

In the coming fight with China, the centrality of getting Pakistan into a neutral corner cannot be overstressed. No matter what India does, an unfriendly Pakistan will always be India's weak flank for an enemy to exploit. It also complicates India's policy to the Islamic world—Modi's apparently successful diplomatic forays in the Gulf region and Palestine. After all, there will always be the pull in the policies of these Muslim states stretching west to North Africa and as far east as Indonesia, towards Pakistan, a country founded on the basis of Islam, Islamic identity and Islamic nationalism, and which has proved a loyal foot soldier for Arab and pan-Islamic causes. They all have to pussyfoot around this politico-religious minefield. Also, more obviously because Pakistan is the barrier to the natural flow of Indian trade to Afghanistan and the countries on the Central Asian steppes via the Khyber and Bolan passes. And, most damagingly from the point of view of Indian national interest, it permits China to insert itself into the politics of the subcontinent, and the power games in the extended region.

Consider China's geopolitical position if Pakistan were taken out of the equation. There would be no CPEC, no possibility to supply its western provinces from the Gwadar port, no potential naval presence on the Baloch coast and no Pakistan to manipulate to contain India. Many in the Pakistani intelligentsia suspect that the CPEC and BRI generally is an exploitative ruse to put Pakistan in economic thrall to Beijing.[30] In the same vein, a nuclear-armed and militarily secure Pakistan, rid of the incubus of terrorism and at peace with India, plugged into the latter's economy and market, like the rest of South Asia, will be prosperous and able to connect with the proposed east-west Ganga–Mekong grid to South East Asia and points farther east, and become rich with, among other things, the royalty paid by India for the Turkmen gas flowing through the north-south TAPI (Turkmenistan, Afghanistan, Pakistan, India) pipeline, and for the road-borne trade on the Karachi–Peshawar Highway to Afghanistan and points north.[31] TAPI would be complemented by the east-west Iran, Pakistan, India (IPI) oil/gas pipeline to mesh the economies of these networked countries, except IPI has run into foul weather for the same reasons TAPI has faltered: mutual Indo-Pakistan relations.[32]

Delhi's success in rendering Pakistan a friend despite a difficult history will impress and reassure other Asian states about India's bonafides and good faith, and its determination to take on China will, in turn, inspire confidence about India's leadership and its willingness to be the backstop for their security against a China grown too powerful too fast and being too aggressive to boot to be trusted not to do wrong by them. It is one thing to talk of India's age-old civilizational links with fellow Asian states, quite another for them to have living proof of India's comportment and the ease with which it generates goodwill and spreads a sense of well-being while at the same time displaying steel where it matters. These are no bad virtues for India to cultivate in a time of raging uncertainty and unpredictability precipitated worldwide by impulsive Trump and unreliable America and rampaging China.

Except, Modi is considered by many Pakistanis to be the archetypal Hindu extremist.[33] But it is precisely the reason why he is well positioned politically to make a breakthrough in relations with Pakistan if he chooses to do so (and, per chance, share a Nobel Peace Prize in the process?). After all, it was the arch anti-communist US President Richard Nixon who broke through the bamboo curtain to establish path-breaking relations with Mao's China in 1972. But will Modi do it? Highly unlikely because, unlike Nixon who had a realistic view of the world and its possibilities, Modi seems too dogmatic, too set in his views to seek a basic change in Indian foreign policy that he believes is not required. This is affirmative inaction at its starkest.

The case for drawing Pakistan into a less cantankerous relationship by offering it substantial incentives goes up against the argument that this approach is premised more on 'hope' than on 'realism'.[34] On the other hand, if the Indian government were to put Pakistan behind us, as it were, and to militarily concentrate on China, it would gain credence with the Pakistani Army. After all, it would rather see China deal with three Indian offensive mountain corps than that it face these ready-to-rumble land forces on their border. A former NSA opines that the leadership echelons in the army appreciate the problem but no Indian Army chief of the day will risk calling for the necessary force restructuring because then he would be tagged as 'not being a good team player'.[35] A good team player in this context is a chief who preserves powerful combat arms, not reduces them.

Intensifying Engagement with Afghanistan

However India's relations with Pakistan pan out, they are inextricably linked, for historical reasons, to India's ties with Afghanistan. In the present day, Pakistan sees its interests as served by having a Taliban government once again running the country. It was during the Mullah Omar government (1996–2001) when Afghanistan was internationally isolated that Pakistan's stock shot up in Kabul. It fronted for the Taliban regime and was its window to the world and the medium through which it conducted its severely limited diplomatic and economic relations. Moreover, being militarily weak, Mullah Omar's Kabul permitted the GHQ to once again think of the Afghan territory in terms of 'strategic depth' for the Pakistani Army to retreat to in case of conflict with India. It was also the time when India's profile and presence in Afghanistan was thin. That was an exceptional period because India and Afghanistan acting in concert is more the historical norm.

Starting soon after Independence and Partition, the Pakistani government began complaining to London about India's anti-Pakistan machinations in league with Kabul. Afghanistan's position in 1947 was that because Pakistan's North-west Frontier Province habited by Pashtu-speaking Pathans had been carved out of Afghanistan by Britain after its imperial wars, it should be returned to Kabul's jurisdiction by the departing colonial power. Nehru wanted to make sure that Partition and an independent Pakistan did sever India's historic links with that country. Pakistan–Afghanistan relations have simmered ever since. The British Foreign Minister Harold Macmillan, for instance, noted in his diary of 21 November 1955 that the visiting Pakistani Prime Minister Chaudhary Mohammad Ali whined about Afghan intrigues on the Durand Line 'egged on by Nehru'.[36] Sixty years later, Islamabad continues to squawk, this time about the bigger role the Trump administration has ostensibly assigned India in Afghanistan in its new strategy for the subcontinent.[37]

Governments in Delhi, as part of their approach to Central Asia, have striven to maintain an Indian hand in Afghanistan, making sure that India has a say in the crafting of any final solution for Afghanistan whether on the battlefield or at the negotiating table. With this in mind, Indian intelligence agencies have befriended factions of the Afghan Taliban and, as backup, some groups in the TTP with connections in Taliban quarters across the Durand Line, tempting them with money and/or benefits in kind to pursue dual aims—fight the Americans if they choose to and, on the side, act to undermine Pakistani interests in the country.[38]

The Afghan pot can thus always be kept on the boil or the heat turned down to suit Indian interests even as people-to-people connections are cemented by the normal play of Bollywood films and music and Indian television programmes, and popular goodwill for India strengthened with development projects that visibly remind the Afghan people of India's role in their national life. Managing clandestine Taliban operations targeting Pakistani assets in Afghanistan and supporting the TTP guerilla war in Pakistan are also seen as payback for the ISI's sponsoring of LeT, JeM and Hizbul Mujahideen activity in Indian Kashmir. The Indian approach is a mix of the US and Russian policies. The US believes in strengthening the Ghani government and relying on the National Afghan Army to rid that country of the Taliban. Moscow believes in its low cost, high impact policy of dual support for factions of the Taliban and the Kabul regime to ensure the US effort in Afghanistan is frustrated.[39]

Delhi's priority in nursing a high-trust relationship with the Kabul government has additionally involved periodically replenishing the Afghan army's fighting stock by funding purchases of capital armaments—tanks and helicopters in particular—from eastern Europe, usually Ukraine, and transporting them over Russia's Northern Distribution Network (NDN) into Kabul.[40] It is a multifaceted relationship that now also includes investments in the mining industry, the country being rich in coal and minerals. It was forged with the coalition government, inclusive of India's old Tajik partners in 'the Northern Alliance' during the two-term presidency of the Jawaharlal Nehru University–trained Afghan President Hamid Karzai, and kept in fine fettle since then by the World Bank stalwart Ashraf Ghani, who assumed the presidency in 2014.

As can be seen, while there is some convergence between Indian and US interests, this is entirely coincidental owing to the separate policy interests and thrusts. The programmatic push of Indian policy since 2004 and the ousting of the medievalist Mullah Omar regime, its covert aspects apart, has been mainly constructive, India has built dams and a parliament building in Kabul, constructed roads and the Zaranj–Delaram highway and funded the Afghan government's social welfare projects. The Afghan Taliban are as invested as anyone else in the Zaranj–Delaram link because it is used by them to cart raw opium to refining laboratories on the Iran border for onward transmission to the lucrative European and US markets. The goodwill from this project has spilled over into the Afghan Taliban's acceptance of Indian development programmes.

In a way, this supplements the US emphasis on the military end of the business of fighting the Taliban to an impasse that has prevented it from declaring victory and getting the hell out as Trump once threatened to do.[41] In this context, India's ongoing role in Afghanistan means that Washington has, in a sense, safely outsourced to India 'nation-building' activity, which traditionally was the face-saving rationale of US military interventions abroad and which role Trump has foresworn. As far as Washington is concerned, this division of labour has three benefits. It saves the US money—something Trump is big on; two, it helps Washington refute Islamabad's charge of India's anti-Pakistan actions on Afghan soil by pointing to India's funding and implementing manifestly peaceful and development-oriented programmes. That these fortify the historically close cultural and economic links between the two countries is a bonus. And three, it permits the US to gain from the spillover of goodwill from partnering India to offset the bad vibes generated by US operations, such as encouraging Islamic State to enter Afghanistan via Pakistan, terrorize the Afghan people and wrongly target Afghan villages in Nangarhar province with fuel air explosives (the so-called Massive Ordnance Air Blast, the most powerful non-nuclear weapon in the US inventory).[42] Afghanistan may end up being the graveyard for Trump's policy as it has been for the empires of yore, but India's proximity and connections mean that Delhi will always remain a player in Afghanistan.[43]

Opportunities in South East Asia

Afghanistan is a relative success story, but Pakistan is not and the failure to even try making durable peace with it, says a former foreign secretary, is to miss out on a historic foreign policy opportunity among many such opportunities that the Modi regime, he claims, has missed out on during its first term. Among these is in not using the Philippines's President Duterte's trademark bellicosity against China to speedily arm that country with the Chinese naval ship stopper, the BrahMos missile that

Vietnam, Indonesia and other states are also keen to possess for possible encounters in the South China Sea—an issue that hung undecided for a long time. Included in this list of policy misses is the fact that Australia has still to receive Delhi's nod for participation in the annual trilateral (India, Japan, the US) Malabar naval exercise, which is increasing Canberra's frustration and crimping the chances of the Quadrilateral or even Mod Quad taking off.

There are genuine concerns, though, that Australia is too much the American pony to follow an independent policy line or to detach itself from US policy tilts, a view reinforced by Defence Minister Marisse Payne stating blandly with regard to the 2018 US National Defense Strategy that 'It is for the US to determine what is of concern in relation to its national security, but I would note that Australia shares similar concerns.'[44] Then there is the Modi government's flawed negotiating strategy on RCEP which reflects the unwillingness of the protectionist lobby active in Indian industry and the corporate sector and their enormous diffidence in facing competition. China, he thinks, is only a pretext for the Indian government to go slow because it has the option of negotiating phased, time-bound and sector-wise implementation of the FTA, something the ASEAN states would readily agree to.[45]

The first genuinely geostrategic move that the Modi regime made in its first term was to follow up the summit with the ASEAN states amidst the pomp of the 2018 Republic Day celebrations by holding back Prime Minister Hun Sen of Cambodia for a state visit complete with a colourful guard of honour at the Rashtrapati Bhavan. His formal title in the Khmer language, Lord Prime Minister, Supreme Military Commander, denotes his exalter position as the repository of all political and military power and authority in his country. A comprehensive investment treaty is being negotiated to allow India to consolidate its presence in Cambodia in the pharmaceuticals, information technology, agriculture, horticulture and other sectors. But, more importantly, Hun has agreed to establish close defence ties with India, including the military training of its officers and arms sales.[46]

If India has Hun on its side, Cambodia is lost to China, and why is that important? Cambodia and land-locked Laos in the Chinese bag heretofore allowed Beijing to militarily outflank the pesky Vietnam, which has been a thorn in its soft underbelly in South East Asia. Phnom Penh's separation from China means that the Chinese Navy has no friendly landfall beyond its own South Sea Fleet base at Sanya on Hainan Island, if the synthetic islands in the South China Sea are discounted. Indeed, Hun reiterated his commitment to the cause of freedom of navigation and respect for UNCLOS rules—code words for an anti-China outlook. For Hun, having India on its side allows him greater leeway with China, and an Indo-Cambodian military tie-up would help separate Phnom Penh from Beijing. This could be parlayed into the kind of logistics hook-up the Indian Navy now has with Singapore and Vietnam, with privileges for pre-positioning its stores at the Sihanoukville deep-water port. This will be invaluable, enabling India to increase the frequency of 'innocent passage' missions of its naval ships and/or FoNPs through the contested waters, which is a belated but necessary response to the Chinese Navy's more visible profile in the Indian Ocean.

Further, if Cambodia moves closer to India, will Laos be far behind? And if Laos and Cambodia are both lost to India, China's position in South East Asia becomes shakier still because it will mean a unified ASEAN on the issue of Chinese aggrandizement of disputed maritime territories. A solid mass of alienated countries landward stretching westward to the Indian border will also result in a more coherent maritime scenario of littoral states shrugging off Chinese military pressure by denying the Chinese Navy a friendly port and a green signal to proceed with India's long idling Ganga–Mekong connectivity project. Talking about connectivity, Modi said at the Delhi summit that 'in itself [it] cannot override or undermine the sovereignty of other nations. Only by respecting the sovereignty of countries involved can regional connectivity corridors fulfil their promise and avoid differences and discord'.[47] The ASEAN meet was called to distinguish India as a big good neighbour with whom staying connected entails no cost but only gain, in contrast to the group's experience with the big bad neighbour, China.

Beijing seems aware that the power game could turn against it and sought to pre-empt the success of the Indo-ASEAN summit in Delhi by dispatching Premier Li Keqiang to confer with Hun Sen some ten days prior to the latter's Delhi visit and to bolster the so-called 'Lancang-

Mekong Cooperation' scheme, and hailing its ties with Cambodia as a model for other states in the region.[48] The question is, with so much riding on the Modi government getting things right, will Delhi follow up with substantive actions to realizing this ambitious security design? There's also the worry, considering Delhi's penchant for backing off every time Beijing makes disapproving noises, that Modi will indeed scamper away at the first sign of trouble. And will the BJP government lose strategic interest in Cambodia and Laos if Beijing ramps up its offers of investment, easy credit and concessional terms of trade to Phnom Penh and Vientiane that it cannot match? In that case, affirmative moves will rapidly slide into inaction.

All these moves by India, ASEAN and Japan as the funding source for many of these connectivity projects beg the question: What can they do if the US sits out their crises with China? Merely resolving not to be 'bullied' will not help. Continuing with the frequent sailings of warships by the periphery powers—India, Japan and Australia—even if these are not prosecuted as FoNPs, or surveillance flights by P-3s out of the Clark air force base in the Philippines and the northern Australian coast, will not hugely discomfit the Chinese military as it has become familiar with this kind of activity. What also needs to be proceeded with on a parallel track is to 'reverse China's strategic gains' with its mid-channel islands by counter-narrowing the same waters for China, meaning potentially restricting the freedom of movement of PLA Navy ships and Chinese merchant marines. This can be achieved, as has been adumbrated previously, by empowering ASEAN members with strategic impact armaments.

The Indian government may have finally appreciated the strategic gains from arming Vietnam with the BrahMos cruise missile, agreeing to export it to Hanoi. The Vietnamese BrahMos will likely be deployed on board its Corvettes, affording Vietnam a mobile offensive capability. These supersonic cruise missiles in its coastal batteries would constitute a static seaward defence to deter any 'from the sea' adventures by China. The air-launched and submarine-fired BrahMos variants that may follow will give Vietnam enormous operational flexibility and compel China to alter its plans for the use of force, principally because of the unbearable 'exchange ratio' that Beijing faces.

Pitting a cruise missile costing $10 million against a missile destroyer costing, say, $600 million to $800 million, will inhibit Chinese fleet commanders from casually courting risk and combatant ship captains from undertaking provocative missions. In this scenario, China will discover that the island bases it has created can stockpile only so much fuel and war material and the relatively long distance from the mainland to the disputed area can become a military liability when it comes to sustaining naval or air action in a milieu where the surrounding states can blow its warships out of the water using the BrahMos missile. And that these states with claims in the South China Sea will each be differently motivated to protect their specific interests. It will enormously complicate Beijing's reading of the individual state's intentions and tripwire notions, inducing caution. And the distances advantage the littoral and island states. Consider that the distance between the nearest Philippines islands and the contested Scarborough Shoal is one-fifth the distance from the Shoal to the nearest point on the Chinese coast.

Moreover, Vietnam's success in keeping at bay both the secret Chinese Fourth Fleet meant for the Indian Ocean and the powerful South Sea Fleet co-located at the Sanya naval base on Hainan Island will have a domino effect. In fact, anticipating its deterrence potential, Thailand, the Philippines, Indonesia and Malaysia have also evinced interest in the 'one shot, one kill' BrahMos. Animated by the Delhi summit, the Modi government seems disposed to complying with their requests for this cost-effective weapon to ward off unwanted Chinese attention. If Delhi hesitates, they will procure it directly from Russia.[49]

India's affirmative inaction is one thing, the impatience of the potential South East Asian customers for the BrahMos missile is quite another because it could lead to the US muscling in on the scene. Vietnam is already being actively courted by Washington in terms of defence ties and arms sales, and Hanoi could at any time turn away from India and look to America for such armaments. This will, besides leaving India out in the cold, strain its ties, which Delhi can ill-afford.[50] With the BrahMos and Indian naval presence effectively counter-narrowing the South China Sea and exposing the Chinese Navy and trade traffic to dangers of interdiction, it will make for military equilibrium and durable peace in the region, lengthen the fuse for war of the Mod Quad states and increase their policy options all round.

Standing Firm with Iran

India's historically close relationship with Iran has grown testy in recent years because of the America factor. The Trump administration's annulling the nuclear deal with Tehran has tensed India's ties. Whether India stands up to Washington will be the real test of Modi's fortitude. The Chabahar port—India's entrepot to Afghanistan and Central Asia—is finally functional. The differences over Indian investment in and the pricing of gas from the Farzad-B gas field in eastern Iran are soluble for the reason that Tehran realizes that India has ready recourse in Saudi oil, Qatari gas and American shale oil. It bestows Delhi with many more negotiating cards than it previously possessed. Neither Tehran nor Delhi would wish for a downturn in relations because both are aware that each affords the other leverage in dealing with external forces. Having a friendly Tehran with roaring trade and business ties helps India to limit the show of displeasure for any reason by the Arab states, with Saudi Arabia in the van, and to rein in excessive demands injurious of Indian interests by the United States as well as Israel. And it gives the Indian government the freedom to better calibrate its relations with these countries.

Iran and Afghanistan are tied up with India in a grand strategic infrastructure plan based on Chabahar, whose geostrategic and economic importance cannot be overstated. The proposed rail and road grid fanning out from this port will not only connect this triad of countries but offer a direct land link to them westwards to Russia and Europe, on the one hand, and on the other, link them to Turkmenistan and Kazakhstan via Hajigak, the iron ore and mineral-rich region in the Bamiyan province of Afghanistan where an Indian consortium has mining concessions. India is building the 900 km Chabahar–Hajigak railway and extending the 213 km Delaram–Zaranj highway built by the Border Roads Organization to Milak and Chabahar and northwards to link up with the Russian NDN. Once this entire transportation and communications complex is in place, it will help speed Indian, Iranian and Afghan trade westwards through to St Petersburg and prove a more economical route than through the Suez to reach European markets, and eastwards to the CARs. It will emerge as a competitor to the new 8000 mile Chinese railway connecting Yiwu, outside Shanghai, via Beijing to London.[51] The Trans-Siberian Railway, part of NDN, and this new Chinese 'silk road' incidentally meet in Moscow before diverging to St Petersburg and to the channel ports through Belarus, Poland, Germany and France. The Chabahar port, enlarged and upgraded with Indian investment and technical assistance, is able to annually handle six million tonnes of cargo. This land route, besides sustaining India's ties with its traditional allies in Afghanistan—the Northern Alliance—enables the shipping of Indian grain, freeing Kabul from the fear of Pakistan's tourniquet on the Khyber and Bolan passes. The first consignment of 1,00,000 metric tonnes of wheat was sent in 2011; some 1.1 million tonnes will be shipped in 2017–18.[52]

The leverage Pakistan had of denying Indian trade the use of its Karachi–Peshawar highway to reach points north and north-west won't matter any more. Then there's Chabahar's military importance. Lying just 72 km up the coast from Gwadar in Balochistan, it outflanks any Chinese naval base that will come up there or in nearby Jiwani as part of the ambitious CPEC.[53] It will permit powerful Indian naval flotillas out of that Iranian port, Duqm in Oman, and the French Heron base in Djibouti to bottle up Chinese naval forces ex-Gwadar and Djibouti or lock it in a pincer with the Indian Navy's Western Fleet elements out of Mumbai and Karwar.

The trouble is, none of these benefits that India can derive from a comprehensively developed connectivity out of Chabahar, that will majorly disadvantage China as well, is convincing enough for Washington to relent on pressuring Delhi on its ties with Iran, especially now with NSA John Bolton whispering in Trump's ears.[54] It will require Delhi to be unwavering in communicating to the US that it will under no circumstances or for any reason abandon access to Chabahar and forsake Iran. In the past, Iran was held up as the likely issue to derail the growing Indo-US strategic partnership, with George W. Bush's undersecretary of state, Nicholas Burns, cautioning Delhi's unwillingness to support US-led sanctions as amounting to failure 'to meet its obvious potential to lead globally' and thus, in a spurious sort of way, equating India's ambitions with toeing the American line. It is the sort of conclusion that should have sounded the tocsin about how the US uses India's legitimate ambitions against it. That Iran meets 12 per cent of India's energy needs was brushed off by Burns, who cited Saudi Arabia as an alternative oil source. Except switching over to Saudi oil will require retrofitting existing Indian refineries with new technology and entails considerable expense. Strangely, Burns considered Delhi's willingness to stay linked to Tehran as a sign of uncertainty and unpredictability in India's policy![55] More pressure and balder rhetoric can be expected during the Trump presidency.

Secondly, if India succumbs to pressure and adjusts its policy and presence in Iran accordingly, the vacated strategic space will be immediately filled by China and Delhi will lose out big time. Leaving any space open for China to occupy is, given its Wei Qi mindset, to virtually guarantee India's being elbowed out of Iran altogether. Recall what happened in Myanmar when the Indian government in a foolish attempt to please Washington embraced its human rights campaign: It embittered the ruling military junta so it moved over to China's side and India all but lost Myanmar to China.[56] As it is, China has reached out with its infrastructure investment, trade and military sales tentacles to Iran and West Asia, consolidating its presence there and in Egypt and even Saudi Arabia, a supposedly American bastion.[57] It would be a strategic folly for India to follow the US dictates and lose its advantage in Iran. Tehran continues to be accommodative of Indian economic interests. It has agreed to accept part payment for its oil exports worth $2.5 billion in rupees to fund Indian imports pending a settlement on a more enduring mechanism to bypass US sanctions. In the past, Indian banks, fearful of getting hurt by punitive US policies and hurting their business interests in America, were wary about a role in the otherwise profitable Indo-Iranian trade. Delhi has to roll out measures to facilitate financial transactions and to immunize bilateral relations in the face of Washington's tantrums.[58]

One such mechanism is the PVP instrument established by Moscow and Beijing to protect their trade against punitive Western actions. Delhi and Tehran can negotiate a PVP variant to escape the usual banking processes where the US can intervene and safeguard their economic interests. Owing to the Modi government's pusillanimity, India has already lost in a big way by not reacting quickly enough to the easing of US sanctions, its exports to Iran dipping to $2.4 billion in 2016 from $3.2 billion the previous year. Other than seeking a US waiver on sanction, it may be coming around to installing a payment scheme outside America's purview.[59]

And, finally, there are the religio-cultural reasons for India's close ties to Iran that cannot be victimized by Washington's policy whims. India's Shia population is the second largest in the world after Iran and this makes India a player in the Sunni–Shia tussle which Delhi, if it plays its cards right, can utilize to advance the country's strategic interests. The Indian Shia community and especially the clergy maintains close links with their Iranian counterparts, and are cued into the theological debates and pronouncements emanating from the Iranian religious centre in Qom. It is a live Indo-Iranian link and a direct means by which Iran influences the Indian Shia community, which Tehran has wielded with much discretion and dexterity. A considerable amount of Iranian diplomatic effort is expended in cultivating Indian Shia religious institutions, politicians and intelligentsia, which gets translated into political clout that ruling parties at the centre have always been aware of. It can block any Indian policy hurtful of Iran. This is democracy at work.

There is no such restraint operating on the US or any other Western government, whence very different calculi are at work in their Iran policies. Moreover, unlike Shia Islam that looks to Qom for religious guidance, the Sunni variety in the subcontinent has evolved around the seminaries in Deoband and Bareilly and recognized in the Islamic world as representing serious schools of Islamic thought, discourse and jurisprudence. The Shia–Sunni differences in India have resulted in the smaller Shia community being conciliatory and desirous of joining the mainstream. The attitude of the majority Sunnis (comprising 75 per cent of the Indian Muslim population), on the other hand, is more abrasive.[60] The Shia clergy, for instance, have consistently supported Hindu causes, such as the Ram Temple in Ayodhya.[61] Politically, this has made Shias pals of the ruling BJP dispensation and Hindu organizations. It is a closeness that's mirrored in Delhi's official attitude to Iran. In spring

2016, in response to President Hassan Rouhani's assurances that Iran will be a 'reliable partner' for energy, the visiting External Affairs Minister Sushma Swaraj indicated not just increasing the offtake of Iranian oil from the current level of 3,50,000 barrels a day but revealed that $20 billion had been firmed up as investment in Iran's oil/gas and fertilizer sectors.[62] 'In the West Asia region, India and Iran are two decisive powers,' said Mohammed Haghbin Ghomi, the Iranian consul general in Hyderabad, 'that can cooperate in various fields complementarily.'[63]

If the larger strategic purpose is for a concert of nations to box China into a corner and, at the same time, hold off a too intrusive America in the region, India's strong and growing relations with Iran are an important tool. This may not sit well with Washington or even Israel, but it makes no sense for India to be any part of the problems that the US and Israel separately have with Iran. Even less is Iran's nuclear status of any concern to India and whether the US–Iran nuclear deal survives or not should not occasion other than a passing interest in the MEA. But by threatening to throw out this deal, Trump is in danger of achieving the smaller objective of destabilizing Iran at the expense of the larger, overarching strategic goal of warding off Chinese attempts at putting down roots in the Gulf region. With its diplomacy, Delhi should ensure India's interests are not hurt by Washington's myopia and, under no circumstances, that its military–strategic and economic relations with Iran are damaged. And even more, that India's stake in Chabahar and its connectivity plans are not compromised. There is, however, danger from Modi's over-tilt to the US. Iran represents finely balanced affirmative action which can be upset if Washington's call for isolating Iran is heeded by Delhi. Even drawing back a bit from Iran will signal giving in to America's wishes, which will elicit an adverse reaction from Tehran.

Gross Institutional Deficiencies

China and Pakistan, says Shyam Saran, retired foreign secretary, are the conspicuous policy failures of the Modi government apart from the perennial one of the non-realization of promises and non-implementation of development projects prime ministers have committed India to over the years.[64] These promises are not kept owing to the capability deficit within the MEA, which has frustrated many a friendly country and made still others throw up their hands in despair, leading to loss of faith in India and a rapid slipping of its standing in the region and the developing world at large. This is particularly evident in neighbouring states that have been promised much by Delhi but benefitted little. Saran recalls that as ambassador to Myanmar in 2011–12, he had signed the agreement for the Kaladan project and the construction of numerous border roads ostensibly to connect hinterland Myanmar with the Indian north-east as part of the India–Thailand road corridor in the still bigger Ganga–Mekong connectivity programme. As of 2018, there's little or no progress, he noted, on any of these projects, notwithstanding Modi's trumpeting them as the cutting edge of his Act East policy. It is not surprising, therefore, that the embattled Aung San Suu Kyi government, despite its fears, agreed to China taking charge of the $10 billion Kyauk Pyu economic zone project, inclusive of the $7.3 billion deep-water port, an oil terminal, a 770 km oil pipeline to carry West Asian oil to south-western China that began operating in June 2017 and a $2.3 billion industrial park creating 1,00,000 Myanmarese jobs, the entire project up and running in record time.[65]

Saran recalls that as foreign secretary he established the Development Project Administration (DPA)-I and DPA-II. But he finds that for want of resources they are currently inactive. He proposed, he says, the setting up of a separate cell within the ministry for project implementation to further the country's ambitious foreign aid scheme to be manned by outside experts. That proposal went nowhere.

The nub of the problem, as Saran sees it, are the viscousy and time-wasting procedures on the books that any project proposal has to navigate. Numerous ministries are involved and that leads to interminable delays. Should a project somehow find favour and get on track, resources are never the problem but the minutiae of the implementation process are. For instance, all foreign aid projects are funded, with rules allowing 10 per cent escalation in cost. 'But no financial adviser [FA] worth his name will approve a project at first pass, he will invariably raise questions, which the ambassador in the country will have to send to Delhi for clearance. The responses get inserted into the file and by the time the paper returns to the FA once again for his approval, a lot of time has elapsed, the escalated costs threshold is crossed, and the approval rigmarole begins anew on the now higher-costing project,' explains Saran. 'At the Delhi end, no non-MEA official in government ever moves on approval or does his job expeditiously unless he can attach a face to the phone call, which is when the file comes unstuck from wherever it is stuck at!'

In fact, Saran remembers that as a joint secretary in Narasimha Rao's PMO in 1991–92, he used to follow up on projects the prime minister promised during his foreign trips. There usually was no movement on any of them until the PPS to the prime minister, A.N. Verma, called a meeting of the concerned line ministries—short of which officers invariably postponed, delayed or made excuses for doing nothing.[66]

Phunchok Stobdan, former ambassador to Kyrgyzstan, has other peeves. 'India has been helping the CARs with half-baked skill development and capacity building programmes,' he maintains, rather than exploring 'smart projects' with them or pushing 'direct development processes'. He also complains that 'people-to-people contacts' while talked of never lead to incentivizing air traffic and tourism. The CARs 'undeniably consider India to be a reliable, trustworthy and predictable partner,' he writes, 'but they do not consider it a good performer.' The Indian government's characteristic 'indecisiveness', he continues, 'always influenced the Kazakhstan President Nursultan Nazarbaev against energy deals with India even though they realize the importance of engaging India, [but] they also know well that it is only China that can fit the bill ultimately.'[67]

Another retired foreign secretary explains that the processes are bureaucratically gummed up in the Indian government because each ministry is a fief and any inter-ministry programme or project has inherently low priority and bleak prospects, especially as the IAS officers in line ministries act as if they have no stake whatsoever in foreign aid projects and won't proceed on them short of direct orders from the prime minister or similar extreme pressure, their attention being occupied with working on projects and programmes of interest to their own ministers, members of Parliament and MLAs—which is what they grow up doing in their service careers.[68] Laggardly follow-through is a Government of India hallmark but it is dressed up by diplomats differently.

'[Because] in India no single actor or hierarchy . . . is sufficiently empowered or has the time to ensure that policy is implemented satisfactorily,' writes Shivshankar Menon, 'the corollary to the central role of the prime minister in decision-making is weak institutionalization of foreign policy implementation . . . India has serious capacity issues . . . and lacks the institutional depth to see policy through.'[69] But the cause-and-effect relationship between the prime minister as the locus genesis of foreign policy and why policy is not implemented properly in time, and at the allotted cost that Menon expounds on, is mystifying considering that agencies and bureaucrats manning them deliver on the most arduous tasks when there is accountability. And when there is the political will to drive policies through to full implementation. After all, the 1999 FTA with Sri Lanka was completed—start to finish—inside of a year and India produced and signed in Autumn 2004 the ASEAN Treaty of Amity and Cooperation (TAC), which made India ASEAN's strategic partner, after the Indian ambassador to Thailand alerted the MEA in spring 2003 to the fact that China was preparing to be the first to sign the TAC. In the event, both India and China signed this agreement at the same time.

It is strange, moreover, that Menon does not mention the other factors responsible for the MEA's record of failures, factors like the small cadre strength of the IFS: For every Indian diplomat there are four Brazilian diplomats and seven Chinese diplomats.[70] Nor does he blame the lack of work ethic of Indian diplomats and their 'sense of entitlement'.[71] Or the fact that, because of their generalist liberal arts background, most IFS officers are unfit and incapable of handling the majority of international issues requiring specialist or technical knowledge. And he nowhere refers to the accelerated augmentation of skilled manpower in the IFS by means of lateral entry of experts into its middle ranks, which is resisted by the service itself. Indeed, the lore of dodgy realization of policy by the MEA has spread far and wide, and even friendly countries are aware that the Indian prime minister's words count for little. 'ASEAN has very high expectations of seeing India playing a leading role in bolstering economic growth and regional architecture,' writes Kavi Chongkittavorn, a senior fellow at the Institute of Security and International Studies in

Bangkok, Thailand, 'but the litmus test lies with New Delhi and its bureaucrats'.[72]

This incapacity hints at yet another troubling aspect of Indian diplomacy. The institutional lassitude owing to the structural and regulatory complexities in the Indian government's way of conducting its business to which is added institutional lethargy and dilatory and circuitous procedures, and the already mentioned work ethic of IFS officers. As per the confession of a former ambassador, Vishnu Sahay, the MEA from Nehru's time 'did not get into the habit of reproducing situation reports stating the considerations, analyzing them, and presenting options. There was a marked tendency to wait for the word from the PM.'[73] The MEA still waits for direction from the PMO when not falling back on Nehruvianisms which apparently provide Indian diplomats a 'common frame of reference'.[74] This means two things: The Foreign Office is unable efficiently to prosecute a non-linear, multi-pronged, foreign and military policy, and to pursue on its own the realization of foreign policy aims articulated by the government.

Thus, it seems incapable of simultaneously doing many things at the same time—talking peace and amity with Beijing; negotiating a more equitable trade regime with it, embarking a dance troupe to Beijing; approving a hard-fighting stance on the LAC; drilling for oil in the offshore Vietnamese fields; aggressively deploying Indian combat aircraft and naval ships in the Chinese-designated ADIZ and on FoNPs in the disputed waters of the South China Sea; facilitating the Indian Navy's war exercises with Japanese, Vietnamese, Indonesian, Filipino and Singaporean navies east of Malacca; integrating the Clarke's air force base and the naval base at Subic Bay in the Philippines into the Indian Navy's and IAF's operational grid.

The list of what the MEA doesn't do simultaneously also includes fast-forwarding the Indo-Japanese maritime trade corridor through the Indian Ocean to the East African littoral to compete with the Chinese maritime silk route; arm-twisting the governments of Sri Lanka, the Maldives and Seychelles to minimize the Chinese profile within their territories and compensating these countries for the loss of Chinese infrastructure aid by marshalling Indian technical and manpower capabilities coupled to Japan's aid programmes to build up Indian base and pre-positioning facilities in Singapore, Vietnam and the Philippines in the middle seas and in the Indian ocean region, actively rotating Indian Army, naval and air units out of Duqm, Chabahar, Heron, Seychelles, the Maldives, Mauritius, Ainee in Tajikistan and Na Thrang in Vietnam; having the Indian submarines harass and harry Chinese naval ships and merchant marine units; while all the time belittling China's pretensions as great power, pooh-poohing Chinese protests, issuing combative statements and otherwise getting up China's nose.

It is such a complex, non-linear, 'take no prisoners' approach that India will have to quickly master if it is to have even a glimmer of a chance against a China that has become an expert in it. However, it is precisely this 'in your face' multiple-pronged policies that the MEA, with pronounced antipathy for military diplomacy, seems neither strategically conditioned nor intellectually equipped to handle. Hence, no such policy options get forwarded to the prime minister.[75] It doesn't help that the MEA needs constant prodding and prompting by the prime minister or the PMO to get going. The discursive Look East policy is thirty years old and, strangely, its Act East addendum was a decade in the making and is still in the process of being rolled out. This is the pace that Indian policies keep, unbothered by China's sprawling successes in the extended region. The MEA feels no urgency to counter with competing Indian projects or even to keep India's strategic partners engaged. In 2014, Rizal Sukma, the then foreign policy adviser to Indonesian President Joko Widodo and presently the Indonesian ambassador to Britain, complained during a visit to Delhi that while the two countries had a 'strategic partnership' it hadn't realized 'even half of its potential'.[76] How long it will take for Modi's offer of developing the Indonesian port in Sabang to materialize is anyone's guess.

In March 2013, the director general, shipping, in the Bangladesh government, Captain A.K.M. Shafiqullah, proposed that Sonadia Island in the Bay of Bengal be developed as a deep-water port and main sea access to the seven Indian north-eastern states to rival the Chinese-funded and built Kyaukphyu port in the Western Rakhine province whose development is being financed by India as part of the 2008 Kaladan Multimodal Transit Project. He pointed out that goods from the Indian mainland headed for the Indian north-east have to transit some 800 km—538 km by sea, 225 km by river and 62 km by road—which is an onerous journey for the Indian trade to make compared to Sonadia, only a quarter of this distance away from India's north-eastern states. Even his mentioning of Chinese interest in such a project, he stated, did not motivate the MEA to act.[77] In fact, India's record of delivery on promises is so abysmal and its credibility so low that three years after Modi offered a $1 billion credit line for the ASEAN states to establish digital connectivity, no South East Asian country had availed of the Indian money because of the cumbersome bureaucratic procedures involved in dealing with India's Exim (Export-Import) Bank. (The Exim Bank and the MEA have overlapping responsibility for this programme along with the Ministry of Telecommunications and the Telecom Equipment and Services Promotion Council.) This compelled the MEA to ante up $40 million to 'kick-start' the project among the poorest states in this region: Myanmar, Laos, Cambodia and Vietnam.[78]

It is not that the Indian bureaucracy discriminates against foreign aid programmes; it is an equal opportunity screwer-upper with regard to domestic social welfare schemes that Prime Minister Modi has staked his personal prestige in. Thus, the Swachh Bharat Abhiyan (Clean India Programme), for example, that began with such fanfare has, like other such programmes, petered out. According to the latest report by the Comptroller and Auditor General, no toilets were built since the programme's inception in the National Capital Region, leave alone outlying areas, and in excess of ₹40 crore allocated to the abhiyan lie unused.[79]

The ShinMaywa Tragedy[80]

India and Japan are intent on a concert of like-minded states in the Indo-Pacific to block China. Prime ministers Modi and Shinzo Abe get along well and aspire to mesh Indian manpower with Japanese financial resources to construct a chain of seaports and related infrastructure in island nations and along the East African, Gulf and South Asian and South East Asian littorals to facilitate intra–Indian Ocean Region trade and commerce—the Asia–Africa Growth Corridor—as a rival to China's

BRI. It conceives of economic triangles of cities and manufacturing hubs connecting regions with the promised infusion of $200 billion in this region.[81] And yet the flagship project, other than the Shinkansen high-speed railway linking Mumbai with Ahmedabad, of setting up a production plant in India with transferred technology of the ShinMaywa US-2 amphibious aircraft, a project Tokyo lays much importance by, has not taken off, owing to the obdurate defence ministry bureaucrats in Delhi and, surprisingly, Modi's inaction in pushing this project over the hump.

The Indian bureaucracy is justly famous for being a wrecker of dreams, for gutting the best-laid plans of Indian leaders, but only because the prime ministers have not held the bureaucrats accountable, and otherwise failed ruthlessly and fearlessly to rewrite rules of business and eradicate what a senior diplomat called 'atomised' bureaucratic decision-making in the Indian government. Absent the possibility of being kicked out of service, courtesy Article 311 of the Constitution guaranteeing lifetime job security, the default option of the lowest civil servants on up is to do nothing or as little as possible to get by unless top-driven to produce time-bound results or in crisis situations when non-performance can have costs.[82] Some examples of the MEA's egregious inaction have already been retailed. Even so, a couple more stand out.

In 2013, in the lead-up to the annual India–Russia summit, Manmohan Singh's PMO succeeded in convincing the Russian President Putin, who was pressing the Indian government to buy four Grigorovich-class frigates, that because India was as keen to strengthen its own warship-building industry as Russia was in building and selling its frigates, the two sides could compromise by constructing all these ships in India and sharing equally in equity and effort. Putin was persuaded and agreed to this scheme. That's where the deal still stands with not an inch of movement by the Indian side on this project, because the defence ministry bureaucrats cannot seem to agree on which public sector shipyard to assign the work to and what the role of private-sector shipyards should be. Moscow, meanwhile, has fretted and fumed. Modi hasn't instructed the ministry to get going and, therefore, nothing has happened. A more stunning example of bureaucratic turpitude is the ShinMaywa US-2 programme that Modi and Abe agreed on but, like the Russian frigate proposal, is twisting slowly in the Indian bureaucratic wind with no push from the prime minister, his PMO, the defence minister or the MoD, and thereby hangs a tale that is as much farce as national tragedy.[83]

India's immense maritime domain—1208 islands, most of them bunched in the Andaman Sea, and an EEZ of 2.2 million square miles in the Indian Ocean—cries out for a fleet of amphibious surveillance aircraft to patrol this vast area, a role that the land-based Dornier aircraft with the navy and the Coast Guard can only inadequately perform. In late 2010, a discussion formally began on acquiring an amphibious aircraft and a decision was made that the navy would be the lead agency for procurement purposes because it would operate it, and because seaplanes defined under UNCLOS regulations have to comply with numerous nautical guidelines that the navy is familiar with.

So a request for proposal (RFP) was issued in January 2011, to which seven or eight international companies responded, ranging from the smallest carrying four people to the largest able to carry 200. There were many concerns with range, speed, sea-keeping ability, the amount of cargo that would go through and the kind of specialized roles it would need to perform. A series of discussions within the MoD with the navy, Coast Guard, air force and the Headquarters Integrated Defence Staff followed. After examining all the proposals, it was concluded that there was only one aircraft that met the mission-role—the US-2 aircraft produced by the Japanese ShinMaywa corporation.

This aircraft has several unique features which are not found in any other seaplane. First is its ability to operate in 'sea-state 5', which means 3 metre wave heights which many Indian naval ships find difficult to handle. The second is its short take-off and landing capability—it can take off in 7 seconds inside of 300 metres versus 40 seconds of its nearest competitor. It needs very short runways and can align to whichever direction the wind is blowing and become airborne. The third factor is that it has very low draft—it can go very close to the beach, lower the undercarriage and taxi up the beach as long as it is a hard beach. It also has a glass cockpit and search and rescue (SAR) systems, all very high-technology. No other aircraft in the world has all these features and it is the only military-certified amphibious plane of its kind.

While these discussions were on, India–Japan relations were developing fast with an agreement to ratchet up the 'special relationship' to a higher level. There were also things happening within Japan at the time. The South China Sea issue was on the boil and Tokyo was looking to find allies and partners to hold its own against North Korea and China, and India was its preferred potential partner. There were staff-level talks, 2x2 meetings of defence and foreign ministers, defence and foreign secretary–level talks and a large number of interactions of the Track 1.5 and Track 2 variety between think tanks—the United Service Institution, National Maritime Foundation and the Institute of Defence Studies and Analyses on the Indian side, and the Japan Institute of International Affairs and the National Institute for Defence Studies on the Japanese side. These dialogues tackled maritime issues as that was the easiest thing to do because of the common maritime interests—securing sea lines of communication, accessing markets and resources, maintaining sovereignty at sea and freedom of navigation and of air space.

At this time the Pentagon, particularly the US Navy, was wrestling with China's anti-access, area denial (A2AD) wherewithal and strategy while keeping an eye cocked towards defence budget sequestration, and President Obama's 'Pivot to Asia'. Except the cuts in the US defence spend led to America spending neither on anti-A2AD technology nor on enlarging the contingent of deployable forces. Questions were raised in US circles about whether there was enough funding to field twelve aircraft carriers and how many could be spared for the Indo-Pacific. It was in this context that the issue of Indo-Japanese defence collaboration first came up. It was preceded by Abe's speech in 2007 about the 'confluence of the two seas' and the full-blown emergence of the China threat.

Simultaneously, the Japanese government realized that they couldn't have complete confidence in the US security umbrella because, in a confrontation with China, there were doubts about whether Washington would enter the fray. That's when the Japanese armed forces started reorganizing themselves. For the first time, they created seven theatre commands with the lead service, the navy, looking after it and a CDS system was installed with all the necessary resources assigned. This process of reorganization and change was finished inside of a year—something India has been only debating since 1997—and was imposed on the Japanese military by a political directive, so the services could like it or lump it. Around the same time, the disputed Senkaku/Diaouyu Island dispute started to heat up.

Just then, Beijing came up with its expansive Nine Dash Line claim in the South China Sea, exacerbating Japan's anxiety. It resulted in the Japanese defence forces shifting their focus away from Russia and the Kurile Islands with its naval activity centred on the Hokkaido island base to keep Russian submarines out. This was also the time when the Japanese industry started moving as well on the India front. As a prelude to this development Tokyo had relaxed the rules on arms sales and created a new strategy, with an entirely new division established in the Japanese Ministry of Defence to push military sales, which they had never done before owing to the strictures in the Peace Constitution. Offshore patrol vessels (OPVs) were leased or sold to the Philippines, Indonesia and other countries, and aircraft to Manila. That's when the Indian RFP for the amphibious aircraft was issued and the US-2 shortlisted.

'The US-2 met our requirements fully,' said Commodore Sujeet Samaddar, a consultant with NITI Aayog. 'But India had a defence minister who, afraid of being tainted by corruption, simply stonewalled all procurement proposals, especially those involving single vendors even on a government-to-government basis, and so the bureaucracy too wouldn't touch it.' The reference here is to the defence minister A.K. Antony in the Congress party coalition government, whose antipathy to arms deals was such that he refused in January 2010 to meet with the visiting US Defense Secretary Robert Gates, deliberately absenting himself from Delhi and remaining incommunicado for the duration of Gates's trip.[84] In any case, the US-2 case proceeded without Antony having any role—the interactions being at the level of the NSA and minister of state for defence. The numbers of the aircraft required were debated as between twelve, fifteen and eighteen planes, and finally it was decided that fifteen US-2s would be acquired.

Manmohan Singh's PMO decided that, given its politico-military significance, this was a programme of national importance and should not merely be an MoD project. The concept that was envisioned was that of 'a chariot with two wheels'—one was the US-2 aircraft, the other the commercial aspects of the deal about making India part of the global supply chain of Japanese companies, which produced components for Boeing and Airbus aircraft, some of which work the Japanese hoped to pass on to Indian firms involved in the US-2 work. A joint working group (JWG) was formed to advance this objective with NSA Shivshankar Menon, who saw the potential in this opportunity, leading the initiative.

This is where things began going wrong. The MoD adopted dilatory tactics, claiming the Defence Procurement Policy (DPP) procedures were not followed. A joint secretary in the defence ministry reportedly played a 'bad role'. On the basis of hearsay, she charged that such a deal would hurt relations with China and, more farcically, that the US-2 aircraft was worth nothing because it carried no weapons! The navy responded tartly that a fighter aircraft carries only one passenger—the pilot—and costs in excess of ₹300 crore each and, therefore, was worth nothing either. 'This ignorant and uninformed joint secretary was a complete disaster and really damaged the country,' said a former MoD official.

But now the institutional egos were engaged. The defence secretary, on account of his junior colleague being slighted and because this deal of 'national importance' was handed over by the PMO to Amitabh Kant, then secretary, Department of Industrial Policy and Promotion, to oversee, decided to take his ministry out of the decision-making loop altogether without taking it out of the procurement process. The crafting of the deal for this 'national project' assigned to Kant, presently CEO of NITI Aayog, aimed at building the aerospace business capability and infrastructure in India with a network of micro, small and medium enterprises (MSMEs), with the JWG constituted between the Indian and Japanese governments to explore technical collaboration. Three visits were made by Indian members of the JWG, with the MoD representative instructed to be on a 'listening brief' only, and to say nothing. The rest of the Indians in the group did an independent appraisal and came back very satisfied with what the Japanese were offering.

What Japan was offering—and this was before Make in India—was, firstly, a parts manufacturing project not just for the US-2 but for Boeing and Airbus aircraft. The plan was for this capacity to become the source base for eventually exporting wholly manufactured Indian US-2s to third countries. Secondly, Tokyo offered that ShinMaywa would do the final assembly and integration of the entire aircraft in India after Indian manpower achieved a certain level of expertise and competence. The timeframe for this stage was to be three years. Thirdly, Indian-built US-2s would thereafter be exported to meet the requirement of third countries, with an order of thirty-eight aircraft already in the company's order book. Fourthly, ShinMaywa undertook to create an entire maintenance, repair, overhaul (MRO) facility for this aircraft in India. It was and is a transformational offer. As far as price is concerned the Japanese attitude, according to an industry source, was: 'This is the listed price, but we are prepared to negotiate it.' In addition, the Japanese government and defence ministry said they were willing to look at the additional official development assistance (ODA)–driven offsets in the deal to build up air fields, seaports, navigational aids and other infrastructure around India's peninsular coastline to serve this aircraft, and allotted $200 million of the total offsets commitment of some $750 million to this task. The business model was that the Indian government would incur an expenditure of $2 billion but the revenue the country would earn from worldwide sales would exceed $6 billion.

A bureaucracy scorned can be a dangerous thing. With its institutional bureaucratic ego on the line, the MoD has prevented this programme from going through—even though the fully articulated proposal went to the Defence Acquisition Council (DAC) twice. In both instances, the defence secretary asserted that because the PMO had initiated this project, the decision was for the prime minister to make and that the DAC had no locus standi in the matter. The anomalies in the 'rules of business' are such that the prime minister cannot order the MoD to do anything; he can only send an advisory. Despite the serious interest in obtaining the US-2 by all the end-users and support organizations—the navy, air force, Coast Guard, army and even elements in the defence ministry—it hasn't taken off.

For once, all the armed services were on the same page. The IAF was interested because they knew its flying characteristics, the army because of its utility to the Special Forces, including operations in the north-west against China in the Pangong Lake area, and in the north-east, because the aircraft can land on the Brahmaputra river, as it requires just one and-a-half metres of water depth to operate in. Because of its ability to land on any body of water anywhere, it would be a huge strategic asset. Further, the US-2 can carry 32 fully armed troops, 2 tonnes of cargo and can get the Special Forces troops fast, to wherever they have to be, with a flying speed of 470 km per hour. This aircraft would eliminate the need for paradropping commandos, which is a more onerous job. It can airlift a battalion-sized force with just ten sorties. Besides the maritime dimension, there is island support for operations in Sri Lanka, Lakshadweep, the Maldives, Mauritius and Seychelles. For a perspective on the potential of the US-2, consider the much-lauded evacuation of 4748 Indians and 1962 foreign nationals from Yemen in 2015 (Operation Raahat). It involved two warships, two passenger ships, several Ilyushin-76s of the IAF and a couple of Air India jumbo jets, and took a month. The US-2 on its own could have fetched up at the Sa'ana airport, four-and-a-half-hours flying time from Mumbai, and, in SAR configuration, run like point-to-point buses, packed in the evacuees and completed the entire airlift mission in five days. Ten US-2s, each able to transport 80 people or 3 tonnes sortie, would have brought in 800 people at a time. In military operations, it can lift twenty troops and a full combat load.

'Japanese aircraft are so well constructed and are such workhorses,' says the naval veteran, Commodore Samaddar, 'they do not need switching off, just refuel, and they fly virtually for ever.' Operational range–wise, the US-2 can be in the Red Sea in four and a half hours, and in the same time reach Port Blair in the Andamans and the Maldives in one and a half hours. 'Indeed,' he said, 'one can draw 470 km arcs from anywhere in coastal India as the aircraft's reach.' 'The awful thing is that the joke of a joint secretary, incidentally, a woman, who had originally stiffed the deal returned to the ministry!' said the source. Thus, when the navy put up the proposal again, the MoD reacted with the same objection about the prime minister needing to approve the US-2 deal on his own. Whereupon the navy once again very strongly pitched for this aircraft. This time the MoD put a different spin on the issue. It asked the navy to prioritize between its various needs—US-2s, helicopters, carrier aircraft, etc. 'This is standard stuff from the MoD,' said the source. 'You can't say "will you have dal or roti", you have to have both. You need both and there has to be some balance.'

The navy understands the importance of the US-2, because it combines response and surveillance. Samaddar explained the plane's utility to the navy thus. 'Take an example of apprehending a dhow sailing in from the Gulf with smuggled goods or terrorists. The operation can take over twenty hours and involve a Dornier aircraft to spot it, whence a ship is dispatched to the site by when the whole operation is already compromised—after watching the Dornier circling overhead, the smugglers will simply throw all incriminating goods and papers overboard. A US-2 could land with a Marine commando team next to the dhow and finish that operation inside of an hour and capture the smugglers or terrorists with evidence on them. Just one such demonstration of capability will end all such activity because everybody would come to know that such clandestine forays are not worth the risk. Then there's the problem with floating derelict ships that get beached.' (Like the ship that ran aground on Mumbai's Juhu beach in 2011.[85]) 'The navy looked at all these roles—long-range SAR, fleet deployments, operational defects at sea and their rectification that can be carried out by US-2 transporting equipment, spares to the stricken ship mid-sea, and crew rotation. It will save money and time. It takes three months to ferry naval crews manning facilities for seaward surveillance—land-based radar sweeps and surveillance patrols in the Maldives, Mauritius and Seychelles,' Samaddar said. 'With US-2 the crew rotation can be completed in ten days. Then there are the issues of sovereignty at sea and force projection. A US-2 can put a battalion-sized force in the Maldives in next to no time, obviating the need for paratroops. The flexibility US-2 offers is tremendous.'

The grander aim communicated to the MoD of the intent of both India and Japan to build an aircraft industry on a non-European, non-American foundation is apparently insufficiently appreciated by it. Japan has had sterling successes in adapting American aircraft for their specific use and converting them into entirely new genus of aircraft. Samaddar referred to the 'wonders' the Japanese did on two projects. They undertook the P2 project—the counterpart of the Indian P8I maritime reconnaissance aircraft, but far more advanced because it has fly-by-fibre-optics system, twin propellers controlled by fibre optics so that the weight is reduced, and the C-1 (a development of the C-17 transport plane). Both these Japanese aircraft have composite bodies and Japanese-developed technologies. There's lots of commonality—the same engines are used in both these aircraft. They put two of these engines on the US-2, added two more engines to obtain the C-1. 'In the US-2 deal, moreover, the Japanese,' he said, 'promised the engine technology and hundreds of other technologies.' Apart from what the Japanese were doing, the US-2 had the participation of the Rolls Royce with its turboprop AE 2100 engine which also powers the US-sourced C-130s that are in Indian service. These engines have propellers made by Dowty of the UK and owned by the US company, General Electric. 'Dowty was keen that building on this association with India and the Rolls-Royce on the US-2, they were prepared to set up a propeller-manufacturing unit here, and all this we dumped because of some *** in the MoD!' said a frustrated former MoD official.

After the JWG, the proceedings came to a dead halt in 2013, when the ministry put the US-2 procurement in a twist from which the decision cannot ordinarily be made 'unless some high-up gives the concerned officials a kick where it hurts,' said Samaddar. 'We cannot have the US-2 on just a 'buy' format. When the Japanese offered so much, it was just a matter of the Indian government accepting the offer.' The JWG had made out a whole plan, spelled out the time-frames in which the indigenization would proceed, how India would import primary load-bearing structures, Dowty would bring in its propeller facility into India and Rolls-Royce would have consented to establishing an AE2100 MRO and even a full engine production facility in the country. Because the planned overall demand for engines was sixty engines for US-2, another eighty engines for the C-1/C-17, for a total of some 150 engines, in addition the plant would cater for the engines for the C-130 transporter, which would have required imports from the US as well. 'But all these things can be negotiated once we display the desire and the political will to do so. If you do not have that desire then you keep buying things,' said Samaddar.

Modi can, if he so wishes, bypass the rules of business, give the bureaucrats the required kick in the pants—call in the defence secretary and order him to approve the US-2 deal on pain of instant banishment and transfer to a minor post, say, which demotion no senior civil servant will be able to live with—but this step the prime minister, because he has not so far taken it, seems unwilling to do. Meanwhile, the ShinMaywa contract languishes to India's detriment, as does the Make in India programme.

With this as background, the Japanese were trying to get into the annual Indo-US Malabar naval exercise, but so powerful is the generalist bureaucracy in derailing even official policies that the very same joint secretary in the MoD who had nixed the US-2 proposal with her asinine comments and for fear of hurting Sino-Indian relations proffered the same reason for disapproving Japan's participation in the Malabar exercise, and which decision was reversed by the MoD only after this ridiculously inept officer was posted out of the ministry in 2014. But throughout this period, the Japanese stayed engaged. 'On the soft front there were exercises, training, staff talks, 2x2 talks, etc. And on the hard side,' Samaddar revealed, 'several agreements were signed by them with DRDO for joint development of certain non-lethal technologies, such as radar.'

The Japanese compulsion is that in light of their new orientation they cannot support their military posture on the limited orders of the Japanese armed services, so they have to sell abroad. 'They received and built 32 of the F-35s in Japan, which was very expensive. They wanted to begin a programme to build 22 Soryu-class submarines, which would cost them a pile, and the costing didn't work, so they made overtures to sell the Soryu to Australia as replacement for its Collins-class boats that are being phased out,' Samaddar, who is a former naval attache in the Tokyo embassy, revealed. 'At that time, the Japanese industry did not have the confidence to swing such arms deals, having been reared on definite sales to the Japanese forces. Selling arms abroad was too difficult a business.'

According to Samaddar, the US-2 team briefed the prime minister with a presentation restricted to five slides as advised by the PMO. The slides explained all that the aircraft can do, the diverse missions it can pull, including rescuing carrier aircraft pilots flying the MiG-29K off *Vikramaditya* who ditch at sea, which capability the navy does not currently possess. They showed the aircraft's 'footprint' covering compass points on the Red Sea in the west, the South China Sea in the east and even talked of the aircraft the Chinese displayed at the Zhuhai

Air Show based on the stolen US-2 design but scaled up in size, which will allow the Chinese forces to go anywhere in the Indian Ocean. It was explained to Modi that the underlying aim of the US-2 deal was to create a world-class aircraft industry, rapidly develop skills by setting up a world-class aero-structures design and engineering centre at IIT, Roorkee. This centre was estimated to cost $30 million—with India and ShinMaywa sharing this cost. And the prime minister was told of the setting up of an MRO for the US-2 aircraft, and the programmes for the Dowty propellors and Rolls-Royce engines for capacity building for high technology, technology integration and for the full manufacture in India, as also about the scheme to export the Indian-built US-2s to numerous countries, and how all these various streams would lead to designing and developing a nineteen-seater aircraft in India for the global market that the Japanese would be very keen to help India develop and to sell.

Modi was informed as well, in synoptic form, about the phased manufacturing plan that ShinMaywa had readied for initially taking a contingent of 260 Indian engineers and technicians for training at their factory in Japan where the first three US-2s would be produced. The first aircraft under the joint programme is to be built entirely by Japanese workers with Indians apprenticing with them, the next two are to be built by the now trained Indians under Japanese supervision. Thereafter the production would move completely to India and the next five aircraft constructed by Indians under Japanese supervisory personnel. The ninth US-2 onwards, the manufacture would come under full local supervision and the aircraft would become Indian.

The time-frame for the first Indian-built aircraft is four years with the production reaching the planned rate of one plane every nine months. The total project cost is $3 billion with offsets of $900 million. 'We were saying,' observes Samaddar, 'that the remaining $2 billion could be taken from the $35 billion Japan has promised India as Overseas Development Assistance. This would have defrayed all the costs of the US-2 programme! India, then, would have the design centre and the production capability, and a ready order on the books for thirty-eighth aircraft worth $6 billion in worldwide sales, apart from India's own immediate requirement of fifteen US-2s.' The briefing of Prime

Minister Modi did not, however, lead to any follow-up action, and the joint Indo-Japanese programme has gone into hibernation.

The fallout of the US-2 experience is that it has made the rest of the Japanese industry wary. The Indian Navy wanted the Japanese company Mitsubishi Heavy Industry (MHI) to bid for its Project 75i conventional submarine programme. But MHI did not respond to the RFP. 'They said that they had learned from the ShinMaywa experience where that company had spent close to $30 million on detailed project work, in cultivating potential Indian industrial partnerships, in identifying 117 MSMEs. They spent a lot of money and shareholders got upset because there were no returns on this expenditure and the company's board advised shutting down the India operations,' Samaddar disclosed. ShinMaywa will still be interested, Samaddar speculates, 'if India really wants it, prepares the ground for the project and makes the requisite moves.'

But did Modi try to remove the bureaucratic hurdles stalling the US-2 project in the MoD? 'He has tried,' informs Samaddar and adds, tongue only slightly in cheek, 'but there are six great powers in the world—the P-5 (the US, Russia, China, the UK and France) and the Indian bureaucracy, who don't give a damn for anything in the world. When the prime minister enquires he is shown ten different reports and given the runaround. No politician wants to overrule the MoD and push ahead.' Modi's belief in the bureaucracy is touching even as it brings his government down by its non-performance. But he does not use the whip (instant demotion, postings to the boondocks, imposition of career-ending penalties, etc.) nor does he do anything to put the fear of God into bureaucrats, such as moving to amend Article 311 of the Constitution guaranteeing security of service to everybody on the public payroll. In this respect, he is no more effective as prime minister than his predecessors in office, nor successful in taming the bureaucratized Indian state which remains the stumbling block to realizing policies and plans, big or small.

The obstinate attitude of the bureaucracy is because, a senior civil servant noted, bureaucrats see themselves as 'landlords' who have to look after the assets and permanent interests of the state, and political leaders as 'often unruly tenants who are here today, gone tomorrow' who have by whatever means to be reined in.[86] Juxtaposed against Japanese Prime

Minister Abe's get-go attitude and removal of corporate and procedural obstructions at the Tokyo end, Modi's inability to get the Indian defence ministry to play ball is a sad commentary as much on his limitations as mover and shaker as the dysfunctional Indian bureaucracy. So, the country is stuck with a seemingly unalterable reality: Its leaders are all affirmative and the bureaucracy is all inaction.

[6]

Perennial Security Muddle

'In the midst of chaos, there is also opportunity'—Sun Tzu

THE INDIAN MILITARY in the last seventy-odd years has not been nationalist in desiring and spearheading policies and programmes to attain arms self-sufficiency—the foundation of great national armed forces. Nor has it been creative in strategizing, in tactics and in terms of conceiving new weapons to meet the country's varied security needs. To be fair, this possibly reflects an indisposition of the government and its sometimes competent agencies. What, for instance, stopped the Indian Railways, a technically proficient and hoary organization, from having the foresight to envision high-speed railways and implementing it as China did? China did so by buying trains and technology when and where available from Japan, Germany, France and Canada, reverse engineering them, indigenizing their production—it now boasts of the largest high-speed railway network in the world and is a leading international purveyor of this technology.[1] India, it seems, is happily complacent, content to stay at whatever level imported technologies permit it to be at. It is a situation compounded by the Indian armed services actively discouraging indigenization of the design-to-delivery capability of conventional weapons.

The arms-wise self-sufficient PLA, on the other hand, had a clear forward strategy to make China the military equal of the United States. It wrote the book on modern guerilla warfare—'people's war'—and devised a slew of new tactics to fit the changing mode of war and, in the present day, involving drone weapons and methods to establish cyber dominance in conflict in 'informatized' conditions and conceived and developed unique weapons and weapons platforms to not just blunt the US's military edge but cramp its operational style. Such as the anti-ship ballistic missile system to push the US Navy out of its 'first island chain' comfort zone and, concurrently, to establish China's maritime footprint in the Pacific Ocean, and the so-called 'aircraft carrier barracks ship'—a huge vessel to replenish and sustain distant operations by aircraft carriers and their escort flotillas.[2] (The first island chain in Chinese conceptualization stretches north-east-wards from the Malay Peninsula via Borneo, Taiwan, and the archipelagic Philippines and Japan, to the Kurile Islands.)

The issue that the Indian government and armed services are facing—they apparently haven't realized it yet—is stark: Their preoccupation with replacing dated or obsolescing technologies and military hardware such as combat aircraft, tanks and large ships with newer, imported items of the same type as part of force 'modernization' begs the question whether there's any understanding of the ongoing transformation of the battlefield.[3] The military milieu is changing so fast that an Indian military 'modernized' in this way will face a Chinese PLA that is competing with the US armed forces, and transitioning quickly into the artificial intelligence, cyber robotics and drone technology regimes that will enable Beijing to prosecute its strategy of warfare with dispatch against adversary states such as India that are less tech-savvy.[4] According to a senior military officer who has served in the highest reaches of the Modi government, the Indian capability in cyber warfare is 'Near zero, it is poor quality. It sucks.' The offensive cyber hacker operations have been farmed out to youthful freelancers in the game for the challenges posed in overcoming and breaking through Chinese firewalls, he said, while most Indian government resources are expended on cyber defence carried out by the National Technical Research Organisation (NTRO).[5]

The capacity to think big, act strategic, and create, innovate and apply the latest technologies, with the aim of becoming an unmatchable military power, is enabling China to become one. It showed no scruples, and still doesn't, in the initial stages of its defence industrial growth to pilfer systems and technologies wholesale from Russia and the West and reverse engineer them—an activity facilitated by a massive infrastructure set up for the purpose. Having thus reached a scientific, engineering and industrial threshold, China is channelling huge funds to attain leadership in these and other frontier areas of science and technology, such as unhackable quantum communications, satellites and computers.[6] It is an astonishing achievement for modern China, one vouched for by the US National Science Foundation.[7] China, it may be recalled with some wonder, was economically and technologically on par with India in 1979 and, forty years later, is global technology leader with a GDP four times India's and second only to the US.

India is, frustratingly, an all-round laggard, especially with regard to defence technology, despite a great start. In the main because governments did not build on the foundation laid by Nehru. Under the visionary Homi J. Bhabha, Nehru's 'Janus-faced' nuclear energy programme begot for the country the capability to produce both the Bomb and power plants, and in the aerospace sphere Nehru's policy of commissioning Kurt Tank, the great German designer of Focke-Wulfe fighter bombers for the Nazi Luftwaffe, resulted by 1961 in the indigenously designed and developed Marut HF-24, the first supersonic jet aircraft to be produced outside of North America and Europe. While the nuclear energy, space and missile and nuclear-powered submarine programmes constitute, in self-reliance terms, an oasis in the otherwise DPSU-dominated defence industrial desert, where conventional armaments are concerned, Nehru's imaginative policy to foster a self-sufficient aerospace industry was callously treated by later governments and permitted to atrophy, with the IAF taking the lead in dragging the country into the combat aircraft import regime.

It killed off the successor aircraft to the HF-24, the HF-73 designed by the late Raj Mahindra, a protégé of Tank's, and led to the termination of the fledgling Indian combat aircraft design-to-delivery capability, and to HAL thereafter assembling foreign aircraft under licence.[8] The 'step-by-step approach to develop design know-how,' wrote Mahindra, with exquisite understatement about IAF's role in pressuring the government to end the HF-73 project, 'did not find favour with government machinery as the operational arm of the defence services became more demanding and the ministry decided to rely heavily on licence production.'[9]

Requiring only screwdriver-level skills, licence manufacture has since become the norm for all DPSUs even as India has emerged as the largest arms buyer in the world and, hence, a military dependency that can be jerked around at will for reasons of their national interests by a host of supplier countries, and whose defence industries are enriched and sustained by Indian contracts. Meanwhile, an infant defence industry in the private sector that has invested huge sums in production wherewithal in expectation of large contracts has to make do with job work handed them by the DPSUs with fat order books.[10] The larger outcome is passing strange: India is entirely self-sufficient in strategic armaments (nuclear weapons, missiles, nuclear submarines) but entirely dependent on foreign conventional weaponry. The Indian government does nothing to correct this anomalous situation by simply banning weapons imports to compel the armed services to bank solely on indigenously designed and developed weapon systems as they have had to do with strategic weaponry.

This problem is at the heart of the nation not achieving arms sufficiency, a situation compounded by the inability of senior military officers to differentiate between, say, designing a tank and 'fabricating one' or appreciating that unless economies of scale become possible with very large advance orders, the small numbers of locally designed weapons systems (Arjun MBT and Tejas LCA) will always have imported engines, electronics and components, and become subject to spirit-sapping criticism by a motivated military and an ignorant media, even as armament buys abroad are justified in terms of urgent requirements and 'national security'.

This leads to the army indenting for large numbers of the Russian T-90 tank excelled in every metric by the Arjun MBT, and in the air force prepared to buy the old, fourth-generation American F-16 plane with aluminium body or the Swedish Gripen E still in the development stage while the home-grown, true fly-by-wire 4.5 generation Tejas Mk-1A and Mk2, which are mostly constructed out of composites, are denied consideration and support.[11] Indeed, senior uniformed officers are almost apoplectic with the possibility of India following the successful Chinese model of defence industrial growth founded on 'reverse engineering' foreign technology as a first step in acquiring proficiency in designing and producing advanced weapons systems within the country. 'I hate it,' said the former test pilot and Chief of the Air Staff (CAS) Air Chief Marshal S. Krishnaswamy (retd) about reverse engineering foreign weapons systems. 'Thank God that we didn't do that! We'd have gotten into one hell of a mess had we started copying. Whatever the contractual obligations, we always met them, we paid up and respected IPR (intellectual property rights) constraints, and when we did anything [with the original equipment] it was only when the supplier state okayed it.'

This view conforms to the government's approach of following supplier rules, being a 'responsible state' and observing the proprieties to win the approval of great powers-qua-arms peddlers. Krishnaswamy, however, admitted that whenever some piece of hardware, 'such as sensors, systems, communications, and so on' was reverse-engineered 'it worked well', thus conceding that if implemented on a national scale, these means could have and still can feasibly result in the capacity to produce capital weapons platforms.

By way of decrying such industrial short cuts, however productive they may turn out to be to realize the larger objectives, he pronounced his 'dislike of the Chinese system' because, he claimed, these have resulted in weapons of inferior quality. 'As CAS I visited countries with Chinese armaments, examined them and found them to have serious weaknesses, lacunae,' he declared.[12] It is an assessment of Chinese designed and developed weaponry that seems jaundiced and is belied by Western experts.[13] However, such attitude pleases Western arms companies because it assures them that the Indian military will be no part of any effort to topple their applecart of perennial profit from unending arms sales to India. If China has resorted to underhanded means to become great arms producers, so have other leading arms exporting and selling countries. Israel, for instance, got hold of the Mirage jet engine design from a sympathetic Swiss source, and succeeded in reverse-engineering it to fit the indigenous Kfir combat aircraft.[14]

But this raises the question about why the Indian military leadership has neither bought into the cause to free the nation from the clutches of foreign arms dealers, nor trusted or encouraged the making of home-grown weapons, except rhetorically. It may have everything to do with the colonial antecedents of the Indian armed services. Unlike the American,

French, Russian and Chinese militaries that sprang from revolutionary armies, and the British armed services that grew as a self-sufficient and sovereign enterprise, all of whom per force had to forge their own weapons to fight and were compelled to innovate in-house, the British Indian Army (BIA) was a mercenary force which, like the *condotierri* in the Italy of the fourteenth to the sixteenth centuries, consisted of 'lances for hire' from wherever they could be found. They were by definition, interested only in the tools of war they were supplied with and in honing their 'bread and butter' tactical-level battlefield skills. It was never of any concern to them about where their weapons came from as long as their quality was good.[15] These 'professional' concerns of the BIA were looked after by the British colonial command structure even as the natives were denied exposure to general staff work—strategizing, planning, procurement and weapons R&D. The 'sepoy' made his reputation as a stolid fighter who took well to training, followed orders and held his nerve under fire.

The romanticizing of the BIA by the likes of Philip Mason about this force of disparate South Asian peoples fighting under a foreign flag being motivated by notions of personal honour and pride glosses over the facts of Britain using Indian troops as cannon fodder (in the First and Second World Wars) and expertly crafting the surplus military labour of 'Hindoostan' into a formidable native army that won them the Raj and extended their empire in Asia and Africa.[16] Subsequent accounts papered over the inconvenient truth that this essentially colonial force never really became a national army (or navy or air force) post-1947 in terms of adopting a nationalist strategic mindset and committing to researching and manufacturing weapons at home and promoting a home-grown defence industry for the purpose. Rather, the officer cadre was preoccupied with piffling pipe clay and polish issues and with retaining the British-era traditions and, most damningly, some seven decades after the British departed India, still is. A former vice CAS, Lieutenant General Vijay Oberoi (retd), opposed the changes introduced in the hoary Beating Retreat ceremony to close out the 2018 Republic Day celebrations, for instance, saying, 'Traditions are at the core of the Indian military and flouting them on account of pressures/requests from political and other bosses amounts to letting down the troops.'[17]

The litmus test of an armed force being truly nationalist is its eagerness to develop and rely on home-made weapons. Since 1947, the Indian armed services have been equipped exclusively with imported weaponry—bought off the shelf or licence-produced locally. In historical contrast, consider the armies under Hyder Ali and later his son Tipu Sultan who fought for their king and country against the British. They invented the first practical battlefield rocket system in history and used it to telling effect in the Anglo-Carnatic wars of the late eighteenth century. Indeed, it was a stockpile of these unused 'Mysorean rockets' shipped after the 1799 Battle of Seringapatam to Woolwich Arsenal in Britain that seeded that organization's first R&D project: the reverse-engineered 'Congreve rocket'.[18] This Hyder–Tipu military innovation was, however, an exceptional occurrence. The more normal Indian historical experience resonating with the present conditions is typified by Vasco da Gama's crewmen jumping ship and setting themselves up in business as gunmakers to the Zamorin of Calicut. Inside of a year they had sold 400 canons to the Zamorin. In 1521, the Portuguese reached China and sold guns. By 1524, they discovered Chinese craftsmen making their own artillery pieces. The Chinese pattern was repeated in Japan which the Portuguese reached in 1542. They sold their state-of-the-art muskets to the Japanese only to find local metalworkers making guns as good as any made in Europe by the 1560s.[19]

The Indian government and armed services' record with regard to armaments is more Zamorin than Hyder Ali or Tipu Sultan. When the history of India is compared with that of China and Japan, one can readily see that the ability of the latter to quickly learn and replicate modern arms was one of the reasons why neither of these two Asian countries were ever enslaved and have always been world powers in technology. This raises the issue of culture. War, it has been reasoned, is 'a cultural act . . . How people fight reflects who they are' and 'strategic culture' as 'the sum total of ideas, conditioned emotional responses, patterns of habitual behaviour that members of a national strategic community have acquired through instruction or imitation'.[20] Between these two views and the record since 1947, one can get a fix on the Indian government's attitude to the Indian military as no more than an instrument of a tertiary state activity, namely, protecting Indian territory—in other words, as glorified chowkidars or watchmen. One can also sense the Indian military's attitude to war as something that can be managed wholly by imitation—with imported weapons, tactics and strategy.

Not that history has mattered much to the Indian military other than in terms of regimental glories achieved in colonial times under British direction and of arms they needed to have right away from wherever they could get them. The extension of such thinking is evident in their insistence that home-made weapons be of imported quality which, in practice, has meant that indigenous armament programmes, even when they get off the ground, don't find custom. It also means that with imported weapons are adopted imported military thinking, weapons-use tactics and strategies. And further, with no sign of, or need felt for, innovation and innovative thinking, that the Indian military long ago settled into second-rate status. On the other hand, the Chinese PLA, having to depend on locally produced inferior quality weaponry compensated with fighting spirit combined with innovative battlefield tactics derived from ancient principles of Chinese war-fighting.[21] It is the sort of thing entirely alien to the Indian armed services. The best that Indian officials can come up with is to subtly hint at joining the movement in certain international circles to ban the latest lethal and autonomously operating weapons and robotic warfare spawned by advanced technology. It is a fatalistic view, underscoring the belief that such war-fighting technology is anyway beyond India's ken to develop.[22]

Defence Industry at a Dead End

Arms dependency leads to political dependency and, at a minimum, manipulation by supplier states. Denial of spares on some excuse or the other is a powerful tool to keep a customer state in line, something the country has time and again experienced without learning from it. Modi's Make in India policy was supposed to alleviate this condition but hasn't because of the inherent confusion in the concept and in the guidelines of the Defence Procurement Procedure (DPP) 2016—now in its sixth version, describing a supposedly simplified and streamlined process of acquiring arms and incentivizing indigenous weapons design, development and manufacture. It may well be that as the prime minister first visualized it, it is merely an invitation to international companies of all kinds to make India the workshop of the world, the preferred manufacturing hub over China. 'To my entrepreneur friends from across the globe, I would like to say "Come, Make in India, Invest in India—for India, and for the world",' Modi averred at the Global Investment Entrepreneurship Summit in Hyderabad in November 2017, a line he had repeated previously. 'I invite each one of you to become a partner in India's growth story. And once again assure you of our whole-hearted support.'[23]

So, what's wrong with that? Plenty. The basis for this policy is the belief that owing to the lower comparative cost of skilled manpower, foreign companies will be able to manufacture almost anything at a lower price and higher profit. The prerequisites for attracting international manufacturing industries to India, however, is that firstly they shouldn't face the usual insurmountable difficulties (related to land, water, power and the complicated regulatory maze) in setting up new ventures in India, that all the bureaucratic-procedural impedimenta are removed and the country competes with the best in terms of 'ease of doing business', and that there is surplus trained manpower available for the asking.

None of these pre-conditions exist in India today. Assuming they had existed, Modi's expectation that foreign arms makers would rush to set up factories in India to produce their top-of-the-line goods would still not have been met because their governments would forbid them from doing so. In the present age, cutting-edge military technology is highly prized as the source of 'general purpose technologies' in society, as the spur for sustained economic growth, and as endowing the nation with the decisive edge in war, and is, therefore, highly protected.[24] Which is why despite the assurances by the Indian government and insistent demands for advanced implements of war by the Indian armed services, no foreign company has set up a factory or brought in FDI. In any case, DPP 2016 was not implemented and is apparently superseded by another MoD document, Defence Production Policy (DProP) 2018, which was released to the media on 24 March 2018 and reactions solicited from the public within ten days.[25]

It was met with less enthusiasm than weariness by private sector firms who have gone through such rigmarole earlier to be excited about it. So what chance that DProP 2018 will meet its deadline of 2025 for realization of its hugely ambitious aims of making India one of the 'top five countries in aerospace and defence industries', self-reliant in development and manufacturing' of seventeen leading conventional weapons systems—including fighter aircraft, medium lift and utility helicopters, warships, land combat vehicles, autonomous weapons systems, missile systems, gun systems, small arms, ammunition and explosives, surveillance systems, electronic warfare systems, communications systems, night fighting enablers—reaching an annual turnover level of ₹1,70,000 crore or $26 billion in 'defence goods and services' including, presumably, ₹35,000 crore in arms exports and, as the document says, of 'making India a global leader in cyberspace and AI systems'? The document seems like the Five Year Plans that the erstwhile Planning Commission churned out in the past, which had only passing relevance to reality. Will that be the fate of DProP 2018, another MoD document that means little and achieves even less?

Not, mind you, that these aims cannot be achieved. They can, but not if the Government of India does not (1) first announce a termination of the arms imports option for the armed services, and (2) stop favouring DPSUs and Ordnance Factories Board (OFB) units with, as this document states, are reassured 'infusion of new technologies/ machineries' to 'enable them to take up advanced manufacturing/ development of futuristic weapons and equipment'. It is expected that the OFB/DPSUs will become capital-intensive, high-value, cutting-edge technology centres that private sector companies, big and small, too can readily and without much ado access in order to sharpen their own patented technologies and competence in design, development and production competencies. Except this hope is belied by history and bureaucratic practice which is not unlike the experience of the US. The Trump administration is changing it with the US secretary for the air force Heather Wilson indicating that the current defence decision-making system won't be replaced with another 'where nobody's really accountable, but everybody gets a chance to check off on everything [and] that slows down and adds cost'.[26] The contrast with India is that Modi sees nothing wrong with the bureaucratized system in place that cannot be improved with a little talking to by him.

The suspicion that little will change on the ground and there will be only minimal changes is heightened by the importance accorded OFB/DPSUs. This is most evident in the two things the document is mum about and which reform if promulgated will entirely change the defence production dynamic: Bringing in economies of scale in production alone will enthuse the private sector and prompt huge FDI. There's no hint anywhere in the fifteen-page DProp 2018 document, moreover, that the insidious practice of orders in small tranches will be ended. This is the core reason for the absence of economies of scale. Central to incentivize private sector companies compete for defence contracts is the necessity that they be guaranteed a large production run so as to make their investment in design-development-manufacturing infrastructure financially viable.

This is not possible if orders are given for twenty to thirty units of an item at any given time with no guarantee that the same company will win the production contract for the next procurement tranche of the same item because of the lowest tender (L1) basis. L1 is why no private sector company is interested in setting up modern, robotized assembly lines for armaments, and why the PSUs HAL and Mazagon Dock Shipbuilders Limited (MDL) invariably end up bagging production contracts for aircraft and warships. Working on the basis of cost-plus-profit, they don't care if they are tasked to produce twenty aircraft or 200. For them it makes no difference, but to the private sector it does. This is why DProP 2018, unless radically amended, will make not a whit of difference to the defence procurement system in place and why no great change is expected.

The drafters of DProP 2018 still haven't acknowledged the reason why India is self-sufficient in high-value strategic armaments technology areas of atomic energy, missiles and space, but is an abject dependency in basic conventional weaponry. This is because the former programmes are run in technology mission mode, are outcome/result-oriented and not hung up on the correct process and procedures and are not subject to L1 requirements that end up oxygenating the commercially unviable DPSUs/OFB units. What this document should have done was propose that for all major weapons and weapons platform contracts (aircraft, warships, missiles, tanks) the competition will be for, say, 300 to 500 Tejas LCA, or twenty-plus warships and submarines of a class, rather than twenty to twenty-five Tejas or an order for four warships of this or that class. Then the combat aircraft can be produced in blocks of fifty aircraft, with each block technologically upgraded, so the weapons systems inducted into service will always have a large and tech-wise fresh, in-date, fighting component. There will then be genuine competition with, say, Larsen & Toubro (L&T) going up against MDL to produce conventional Project 75i submarines, etc., and a whole bunch of potential Indian aerospace majors will surface to compete with HAL to produce different, ever more advanced variants of the Tejas, that will phase into the production of the follow-on advanced medium combat aircraft (AMCA). (More on this later.) Short of such reform and contracts for large numbers of equipment for economies of scale, nothing will change. Only the HALs, MDLs and Bharat Dynamics Limited (BDL) for missiles on the Indian scene will end up monopolizing what contracts are on the table, with the private sector companies allotted such minor work as the DPSUs/OFB deign to pass on to them.

The biggest joke is the reference in the document to global leadership in artificial intelligence and autonomous (or robotic) weapons systems. There are already small companies doing stellar work producing ingenious technology in the Cyberabad/Hyderabad–Bangalore belt that could become leaders in these fields, but they will not be given the chance to succeed because DRDO labs and DPSUs/OFB will be assigned the primary development projects in these areas. Moreover, the references to MSMEs in the document notwithstanding, these are unlikely to be encouraged to grow into an Indian version of the German *mittelstand*—as the seedbed of advanced technology in the country.

Such plans will remain on paper, especially because three decades into the IT age, India still does not have many original software packages that Indian IT majors have patented and are international best-sellers, and the country still does not have a 'fab'—a fabrication plant to produce high-end semi-conductor (SC)/integrated circuit (IC) chips. India is hostage to, and its entire communications network compromised by, reliance on Chinese and American SCs/ICs computing hardware and operating systems. And minus a formal end by the government or the MoD of arms imports, foreign arms suppliers will continue using India as the tail-end user of the commercial life and production runs of their best-selling but long in the tooth products to squeeze out the last bit of profit from transferring limited technology to produce dated military weapons systems phased out or being retired from their own militaries (to wit, French Scorpene subs, American F-16/F-18 aircraft, M-777 howitzers). If DProP 2018 means little it may nevertheless be a masking move to retain the same old system of imports-oriented defence procurement. In the event, what happens to the 2025 goals? Will anyone presently in the government at the political and bureaucratic levels still be around then and be held accountable for non-implementation of the policy and non-realization of its stated goals?

Proof that the situation is little changed in the Modi years is available in the Spring 2018 report of the Parliament's Standing Committee on Defence. Acknowledging that something is radically wrong with the scale of foreign dependence that has remained unabated and the inability of the DPSUs to efficiently meet the country's defence requirements, it expressed the need to 'motivate' the private sector with appropriate inducements to get into indigenous arms manufacture. In the period 2015–17, 187 contracts were signed valued at ₹2,40,814 crore, of these 119 contracts worth ₹1,16,523 crore went to mostly DPSU vendors, and sixty-eight contracts for ₹1,24,291 crore to foreign vendors. Except the DPSU contracts still mostly benefitted foreign vendors because of the high foreign content of the military goods they produced. Thus, on average, HAL has 44 to 60 per cent foreign content in the aircraft it assembles, BEL 41 to 49 per cent in its military electronics goods, Hindustan Shipyard Ltd, Kochi, 30 per cent and MDL 54 to 72 per cent in the warships they put together, and the OFB 9 to 15 per cent in the artillery, ammunition and shells it manufactures.[27]

US Paranoia about Its Technology

In the existing order, Russia has been the most forthcoming among supplier states. It has sold India weapons platforms that are top class but with the weapons and electronics-avionics component de-rated 30 per cent quality-wise, and permitted its experts to technically correct design flaws and guide the indigenous development of strategic systems such as missiles and the nuclear submarine.[28] By comparison, the US has been tight-fisted and its offers paltry, with the 2012 Indo-US Defense

Technology and Trade Initiative progressing little beyond the talking stage. Ultra-protective of its technology and seeking to maintain the technological gap with the rest of the world, America has so far cleared for sale and licensed production in India only the technology-wise basic and dated M-777 light howitzer for mountain use by the army and a couple of fifty-year old fighter jets—the Lockheed Martin F-16 Block 70 for the IAF and the Boeing F/A-18IN for Indian aircraft carriers. And even here, the American companies have clarified that the 'transfer of technology' relating to these dated aircraft will not involve the 'know why' element—source codes, operational algorithms of major systems, etc. that could help augment and assist India's combat aircraft designing capability.[29]

Nor are these companies allowed to export 'sensitive' technologies, such as the AESA fire control radar and other avionics fitments other than as 'black boxes' for the duration of the Indian production run of the F-16/18. True, America has offered to sell the advanced non-lethal EMALS for Indian-built carriers but not the advanced arresting gear (AAG) without which the high aircraft launch and recovery rates will not be achieved, nor the nuclear power package for the carriers, which permits EMALS, requiring 3MW of electricity to operate. Further, whether singly or in tandem, these EMALS technologies, according to US military experts, Dan Grazier and the F-16 designer Pierre Sprey, are exorbitantly priced, still 'immature' and, 'at the current failure rate, [with] only a 7 per cent chance that the [carrier] could complete a four-day flight surge without a launch failure'.[30] It is particularly inappropriate for conventionally powered Indian carriers because operating just EMALS, costing nearly a billion dollars per unit to the US Navy and twice as much to the Indian Navy, will be money down the drain because the aircraft carrier platform is frightfully vulnerable to sea-skimming cruise missiles (like the BrahMos) fired from any of a host of platforms ranging from corvettes, warships, aircraft from standoff range, submarines, coastal batteries to even merchant ships. 'Sinking $22.25 billion [Ford-class carrier with its full complement of a fighter wing, early warning planes, and helicopters],' write Grazier and Sprey, 'with $1 million—or even with $20 million—is a good return on investment.'[31] Except, the world is entering the hypersonic anti-ship missile age with attack speeds exceeding seven times the speed of sound. No boat, however well armoured and protected by surface escorts and submarines, will be able to withstand a brace of supersonic BrahMos broadside hits, what to speak of hypersonic missiles. The fact is the aircraft carrier is obsolete, as are technologies related to this platform. The proposed offer of EMALS to India is therefore, motivated, it is reasonable to surmise, owing to the need to reduce its unit cost for the US's own nuclear-powered aircraft carriers.

The Travails of the Tejas LCA

Consider the race to outfit the IAF with a single-engine aircraft (F-16, Gripen) that has now been terminated because the Modi government considered it prudent to back out of another aircraft procurement can of worms in the wake of the Nirav Modi and related scams and the Rafale acquisition fiasco.[32] Deconstructing the single-engine aircraft deal may be instructive about factors impinging on military acquisition decisions generally. The air force requires, it says, a combat aircraft to induct in a hurry to arrest its depleting fighter squadron strength, but the Indian government wants such an aircraft to be produced in India. What's offered by the US is the vintage F-16 with the chosen Indian private sector companies in all probability ending up doing what the DPSU HAL has done for the last six decades: screwdriver the aircraft together from imported semi-knocked down (SKD) and completely knocked down (CKD) kits and equipping them with technology 'black boxes' of highly valued and sensitive technology the US does not want to part with.

Lockheed is covering up for the obsolescence of the F-16 platform by dressing it up with new avionics suites and beyond visual range (BVR) strike wherewithal. But sassing up an old crone does not turn her into a debutante fit for the ball, which is why the IAF is unenthusiastic about the F-16. Moreover, the rationale the US company pitched to the Indian government about the Indian F-16 factory, besides meeting India's needs, producing aircraft and spares for export for the supposedly 2500 F-16s operating worldwide, including in the US Air Force, doesn't hold up. Firstly, all the foreign suppliers lined up for the IAF's single-engine aircraft race, including Lockheed and the Swedish Saab company trying to sell its Gripen E aircraft, are predicating the shifting of the production line to India on the IAF off-taking large numbers of their aircraft.[33] But the Indian government's incentive to produce the F-16 or Gripen in the country is that, beyond the IAF's needs, there is the supposed big market for these aircraft and for spares for the contract to make commercial sense.

But, there's a problem. On Trump's say-so, Lockheed decided that to protect American jobs and the integrity of this item used by the US military, 25 per cent of the F-16 production will be retained in-country to meet the residual need for this aircraft and spares in the US Air Force and the Air National Guard of the various states. The potential order book for the Indian F-16 and spares will thus be cleaved by two-thirds. Further, most of the US allies with F-16s in their inventories are on track to replace them with the F-35, a demand Lockheed is happily gearing up to meet.

So, who and where exactly are the customers—other than the IAF—for the Indian-made F-16s? Is 'Make in India' then to mean that the country produces any old foreign plane without any secondary external market to sell it in, considering Russia has no compunction in selling its most modern fighter bombers like MiG-35/Su-35 that are almost a generation more advanced than the F-16 to any state with the money to pay for it? With Lockheed and the US government having publicly made an economic noose of the F-16 deal, there is no reason why Modi should willingly put India's neck into it. Then again, how is the IAF expected to cope with the consequences of the F-16 in its fleet considering this aircraft has been with the Pakistan Air Force (PAF) for over thirty years, making the Indian F-16s an operational liability from day one? If the BJP government enters into an F-16 deal anyway then the conclusion will be hard to escape that pleasing Washington and enriching the American defence industry coffers take precedence over national security, the IAF's requirement for modern combat aircraft and the imperative to buy more cost-effective combat aircraft.

The supplier companies, however, have learned how to peddle old and inferior defence equipment to India. The modus operandi involves first choosing an Indian strategic partner, as permitted by DPP 2016, usually a big business house, with reach to the prime minister. So, Lockheed has tied up with Tata for the F-16, Dassault with Reliance

Defence for Rafale offsets, and Saab with the Adani Group for the Gripen. Linking up with politically well-placed Indian companies also provides the conduit for meeting the demands of illegal gratification while affording the foreign supplier with plausible deniability. Second, if the procurement proceedings stall for any reason, these foreign companies get their heads of government to gently pressure and sweet-talk Modi into approving the purchase. It worked with the off-the-shelf buy by India of thirty-six Rafale MMRCA whose sale French President Francoise Hollande pitched personally to Modi when he visited Paris in April 2015. It resulted in a $15 billion to $20 billion deal without licence production rights, which compared to the original deal for 126 of this aircraft with transfer of technology for about the same amount of money suggests India ended up paying lots more for a lot less.[34]

'Cost is different from price,' explained a former vice CAS, Air Marshal Satish Inamdar (retd). 'Price depends on how desperately you want it. And regarding Rafale Modi certainly showed desperation,' he said.[35] A similar stratagem of the foreign leader canvassing personally with the Indian prime minister also worked with regard to the $500 million Spike anti-tank guided missile (ATGM). The rescinded contract for this missile was put back on the rails once Israeli Prime Minister Benjamin Netanyahu on a state visit in December 2017 urged Modi to reconsider, even though an indigenous ATGM of spike specifications was tested on the very day Modi was in Tel Aviv earlier in the year.[36] So, the transactions for the F-16 may well happen should Trump intervene to personally pitch this aircraft to Modi. The arms self-reliance angle of all such deals that the Modi government has chosen to ignore is that owing to the paucity of financial resources, fighter aircraft buys from abroad will necessarily be at the expense of the Indian designed and developed 4.5 generation Tejas LCA, which in terms of technology is the same generation as the Rafale and the Gripen, and superior to the F-16.

With the Tejas programme being set up for the kill by slow financial strangulation, the historical analogue springs to mind of how the IAF did away with the HF-73 in the early 1970s, the successor aircraft to the indigenous Marut HF-24. The HF-73 is remembered, forty years later, by former IAF chief Krishnaswamy as a 'beautiful aircraft [that] had overcome 99 per cent of the hurdles [including] safety improvements

... was easy to fly, ergonomically good, great air conditioning and could cruise at 0.9 Mach at altitude [meaning go nearly supersonic or super-cruise without afterburners], something that no aircraft can do today.' Long after the HF-73's killing the IAF feels it safe to praise it! But it was ditched, he explained, because 'it took a long time and the pressure mounted because we needed more aircraft, and such pressure is always there, and we decided to buy [the British Jaguar]; it is simpler to buy'.[37]

This is a remarkable revelation of the IAF tactic of cranking up the pressure on the government to buy foreign aircraft on the basis of urgent need, which procurement is subsequently rationalized in terms of being the 'simpler' option compared to indigenously designing, developing, testing and producing combat aircraft. That episode is being repeated with the IAF's yearning for any foreign aircraft, except Russian, as its choice of single-engine fighter plane, which if it goes through will be at the cost of the Indian LCA, its naval variant, and the follow-on aircraft, the AMCA. The absence of contrary expert advice acceptable to the Modi dispensation means that the IAF will continue importing aircraft even as the development of the Mark-2 and naval versions of the Tejas are throttled in their infancy. If the IAF has its way, F-16s or Gripens or more Rafales may find their way into the country's air fleet. The purchase of additional 90 to 100 Rafales, it is argued, will incentivize the French into helping DRDO iron out the kinks in the indigenous Kaveri jet engine and in the Uttam AESA radar project, and that with these two projects and foreign-assisted capabilities under its belt, India will finally become self-sufficient in combat aircraft.[38] But any weapon with American components is problematic.

The Gripen has an American GE 414 engine and Italian Selex Raven ES-05 AESA fire control radar, and as much as 60 per cent of its technologies are non-Swedish, which will complicate their technology transfer and licensed manufacture because it will necessitate the Indian government negotiating with innumerable companies, each of which will insist on its own terms and conditions. The fact that the engine and other major assemblies are of US origin also leaves open the possibility of Washington exercising leverage in terms of spares denial. If the bilateral Indo-US relations are good, it will be smooth sailing. But if they turn bad as they well might when their non-convergent interests actually diverge, like if Delhi resumes nuclear testing and the US responds with sanctions and if

CAATSA sanctions are imposed to punish India for buying Russian arms, or Delhi sticks to buying Iranian oil and trading with Tehran, contrary to Washington's wishes, the spares supply will be cut off and the Gripen fleet grounded. This happened with the Indian Navy's Sea King anti-submarine helicopter fleet disabled for want of US-sourced components when the Clinton administration sanctioned India in the wake of the 1998 tests.

Stockholm, however, believes that the US and other supplier states will not act to undermine the Gripen deal because it will mean losing India's custom and, in any case, that the US failure to sell its F-16 will be made up to an extent by revenues from the sales of American jet engines and other technologies and components in the Swedish plane.[39] But while the potential loss of the Indian market may deter European firms, it will not deter the US government from disrupting the spares support as it did in the past (also during the 1965 and 1971 India–Pakistan wars). Moreover, the fear of alienating Delhi will not persuade the US government in the least because it will expect the Indian government to make light of it, forget the episode and sue for restoration of the supply relationship as happened post 1965 and 1971 and after the 1974 Indian nuclear test when the US legislature retroactively amended its laws to scupper contractual obligations to supply uranium fuel for the GE light water reactors at the Tarapur atomic power station, only to have India, forty years later, line up to buy Westinghouse AP 1000 reactors!

The main problem an indigenously developed platform such as the Tejas confronts is the insistence by the user armed service that it be delivered in a 'combat ready' state, i.e., it meet 100 per cent of the specifications, including integrated on-board weapons, before the IAF takes delivery of it. Except, this methodology is not followed by any advanced air forces. Thus, the F-35, the newest fighter aircraft with the US Air Force, for example, entered service before it secured initial operational clearance and was improved in stages with feedback from the pilots. The overlapping of development and production phases of this warplane or 'concurrency' is the normal way of producing high-technology combat aircraft.[40] This the IAF rejects, but only selectively, for Indian-made aircraft, because imported planes are showed absolute leniency. Thus, the Mirage 2000 bought from France in the 1990s, for instance, flew with the air force for two years without any weapon whatsoever! The naval LCA was similarly derailed. The Indian Navy rejected the naval variant of Tejas in early 2017 owing to weight constraints. 'It was all completely bullshit!' said Dr V.K. Saraswat, former head of DRDO and currently member of NITI Aayog. 'I went into the reasons—[the] Indian Navy said it is underpowered and they wanted to try out Gripen. But Gripen has the same GE F-414 engine, the same weight category of less than 10 tonnes, where's the question of differences? The dropping of 200 kg even at the design stage can be managed,' he said. 'If the navy had any idea about product development they'd understand that. For instance, when I first produced the Prithvi missile it was 4600 kg, but was delivered at the specified 4000 kg. Weight control is part of the weapon system development process.' Saraswat also decried the 'inconsistency' in armed services' thinking which, he said, is a serious problem. 'Notwithstanding the policies of the armed services and the integrated plan in MoD, every new incoming service chief,' he complained, 'has a different requirement and feels free to change the procurement plans.'[41] While the IAF is on board with the Tejas, the navy's rejection of the navalized variant of the LCA and seeking fifty-seven foreign carrier aircraft is a sore point with the Tejas team, whose perspective needs airing.

Flying into Resistance: Tejas and Navalized LCA[42]

The Tejas LCA programme is the seedbed for the future combat aviation industry in the country and has survived despite every effort to undermine it over the years by the IAF and sections of the MoD with a vested interest in staying with the policy of importing fighter planes programme. IAF chiefs have ridiculed the LCA, one of them calling it 'a cheetah with three legs', and together with an ignorant and illiterate press and electronic media and commentators, have carped incessantly about the ₹8000-odd crore spent on it and the ten-year delay in delivering the aircraft. After years of listening to such uninformed criticism, the DRDO chief Christopher Raj responded. He explained that the decision by the Indian government for the full-scale production of Tejas was taken only in 1998, the real start point of the LCA programme. It had immediately to weather US sanctions in the aftermath of the

Shakti series of nuclear tests, which affected over 200 Indian defence R&D and industrial units. And he blamed the air force for changing aircraft specifications and requirements 'midway through the design and development process'. This delayed the decision on the engine to power the aircraft and, because the plane is designed around the engine, further delayed the development of the Tejas. Learning from the LCA experience, he said the AMCA will roll out faster because the 'critical aspects' of the aircraft have been frozen.[43] The LCA is a remarkable feat considering America's most advanced aircraft, the F-35 Lightning-II, involving a global aerospace giant, Lockheed Martin, has cost over a trillion dollars, taken over twenty-five years to develop and, at the end of which process, is tagged as a lemon![44] In this respect the development of the design-wise more demanding naval variant and the troubles it has encountered is illustrative of the obstacle course indigenous armament programmes have routinely to run.

The navy chief Admiral Sunil Lanba in Spring 2017 explained his service's request for information (RFI) for foreign carrier aircraft as a stop-gap solution to meet immediate needs until the indigenous naval LCA (NLCA) is fully developed, which he reckons will take another decade.[45] What is obvious is the huge gulf between the perceptions of the navy and those responsible for designing and developing the naval Tejas. It may help to have a detailed perspective from the NLCA team.

The cabinet approved the NLCA programme in 2003 when the designers had only vague ideas about what this naval variant should be. There was the air force version to go on but the requirement was for a wing design capable of a 'sink rate'—the vertical rate of descent—of 3 metres per second whereas for a naval version, which goes through a controlled crash on the carrier deck, the sink rate has to be around 7–7.5 metres per second. This means, said Commodore C.D. Balaji (retd), former head of the Aeronautical Development Agency (ADA) and the Tejas LCA project, including its naval version, 'that it is double the velocity and energy-wise it becomes squared. In terms of horizontal energy, a 10 tonne aircraft coming in with a tail hook has to absorb pressure that is four times gravity because it has to land within 90 metres. That means 45 tonnes of load is imposed on the single tail hook. That crashing load is dissipated within the structure of the fuselage frame—that is the sort of concepts that were developed.' The effort required was, however, underestimated by the design team, because it was wrongly assumed that the air force design could be converted easily, with a 15 to 20 per cent design change, which was a wrong assumption. How wrong? The change in the aircraft design was actually as much as 40 per cent to 50 per cent.

The design challenge was that there was only limited volume from the air force version to work with, and it had to fold into it an awkward configuration of the landing gear fitted in the central fuselage structure along the centre line. What was installed initially was not a very efficient landing gear design; it was bulky and overweight. Developing such a plane for the first time led to design conservatism creeping in and incorporation of additional safety features, which caused a big weight penalty. There were problems also with the structural loading, landing gear design, the arrester hook design and their ability to bear the load within the structure. This was despite the fact that the loads on the 14 degree ski jump on the carrier are relatively lesser than on the arrester hook. In terms of the ski jump it was a problem of designing control laws (CLAWS) for an unstable aircraft, which was another challenge for the NLCA team. 'The differences in the CLAWS of the air force and naval variants were in the take-off and landing regimes, not in the up and away envelope, so', Balaji explained, 'the characteristics of the up and away regime had to be blended with the take-off and landing regimes. This required the aircraft to come in at lower speeds for carrier landing and an additional control surface on the leading edge of the aircraft—the leading edge vortex controller [levcon] in the wing root, rather than canards on the plane nose, to reduce the speed of the aircraft by 6-7 knots.' The design went through the certification management techniques, the wind tunnel, etc. Then in April 2012, exactly nine years after the cabinet approval, the NLCA prototype had its first flight. Going from an absolute clean sheet to a flying machine in so short a period of time was a big achievement. Many lessons were learned.

Thereafter, a ski jump and arrested recovery facility had to be built. The option was to look at a US test facility. The carrier suitability of the naval Rafale, for instance, was done by Dassault in the US with four campaigns of testing at an American shore-based catobar (catapult launch arrested recovery) installation. But the US does not have the ski jump facility. So other options were considered. The erstwhile Soviet Union had such a facility in Saki, Ukraine, on the Crimean peninsula now annexed by Russia. It replicated the *Gorshkov* (*Vikramaditya*) deck, but Saki had no aircraft restraining gear. So it was decided to build a facility as a national asset at the Dabolim naval base in Goa, and approval was given in 2007. The arresting gear equipment imported from Russia in 2009 replicated what's on *Gorshkov* and will be installed on the Indian-built carriers. This facility costing ₹500 crore was ready by end-2013, its construction going in parallel with the development of the NLCA. This was fortuitous because by the time *Vikramaditya* was inducted, the MiG-29K pilots couldn't have gone to Saki for training because that facility had by then become defunct. So the carrier pilots had ab initio training in the Goa facility before going to the ship. Moreover, the Goa facility has been configured for a wide spectrum of aircraft. Russian pilots were contracted to test-fly the MiG29K off the Goa ramp and use its arresting gear before they began training Indian Navy pilots. As of early 2017, some ten carrier pilots had been trained there. The navy-headed Goa Shipyard Limited, which maintains the static ski-ramp facility, was part of the entire build-up with the Russians doing some hand-holding.

The Goa ski jump was a major challenge and CLAWS had to be devised for it. So the ski jump was modelled in a wind tunnel and data obtained of the wind currents that would affect take-offs from it. Naval pilots took off in the simulator to generate further data for the CLAWS team. Then a $400,000 consultancy was signed under the Pentagon's Foreign Military Sales Program with the US Navy's test pilot school to audit what was done and to confirm that the NLCA programme was on the right track. The US Navy team validated the NLCA work, saying 95 per cent of the work done was correct and suggested some fine-tuning of the integral controllers to bring it up to 99 per cent. This, Commodore Balaji said, 'was a small-cost, high-value consultancy' with the NLCA team gaining from the unrivalled experience and expertise in carrier aviation of the US Navy. In December 2014, the first ski jump launch went off in textbook fashion. It gave the NLCA team an understanding and the confidence to reduce the design margins. The design improvements were made, especially in the undercarriage of the prototype aircraft such that by the time of the second set of launches from the Goa ski jump the actual flight exactly matched the simulations—proof of a viable aircraft. But the aircraft was 1 to 1.1 tonnes heavier owing to over-designing. These lessons flowed into the NLCA Mk-2 configuration, in which the remnants of the air force variant were jettisoned. The design plan form was the same but the wing was moved outward by 350 mm on either side, freeing up the central fuselage space between the wing and fuselage to fit a simpler, lighter, more elegant landing gear. This also stretched the fuselage by about a metre, increasing the internal fuel volume significantly from 2.4 tonnes in Mk-1 to as much as 3.2 tonnes in Mk-2.

There were significant benefits. Because the aircraft consumes 30 kg of fuel per minute of loiter—the rule of thumb being 3 kg of fuel per kilometre, an additional 700 kg of fuel meant the NLCA can now fly for twenty-four extra minutes, or a radius of action of 250 kms on a typical high-low-high flight profile. Secondly, it had to meet some hard design constraints imposed by the navy, like the wind on deck not exceeding 15 knots and the exit angle of attack (AoA) restricted to 20 degrees pulled by the MiG-29K. (Technically, AoA refers to 'the angle between an aircraft wing's chord line, the imaginary straight line between the wing's leading and trailing edges, and the aircraft's flight path'. What it means in practical terms is that 'Flying at high angles of attack—also known as "high Alpha"—fighter aircraft can gain enhanced nose-pointing capability, allowing pilots to find, fix and target enemy aircraft. Being able to point the nose rapidly is how you outmanoeuvre the enemy, "lock on" to them with your radar and heat-seeking missiles and take the decisive shot'.[46]) These parameters influence the take-off mass for a deck launch and for an unstable aircraft such as the delta-winged Tejas CLAWS were designed to easily handle 24, 25, even 26 degrees of AoA at exit. Every 2 degrees of AoA means the take-off payload increased by 200 to 250 kg. So if the AoA is 22 degrees, the aircraft can take up an additional 200 to 300 kg. If the AoA is 26 degrees the payload increases by an extra tonne.

The NLCA team tried to explain this but the navy was adamant, insisting that the NLCA perform within the specified restrictions. The navy, strangely, seemed unhappy with the NLCA programme exceeding the original performance parameters because, Balaji said, 'They are not used to these kinds of AoAs, even when the flight tests have shown that we can hold the higher Alpha.' In other words, even though the NLCA proved it could handle the wind on deck of 30 knots which means an additional payload capacity of a tonne, it was restricted to 15 knots. The navy, thereby, adopted the IAF procedure of according imported aircraft (Russian MiG-29K) more slack than indigenous aircraft. 'That's what pained me,' said Balaji. 'Because the navy was never that way, this was more the air force thing.' It is revealing of the navy's attitude that no recent chief of naval staff has visited the project. The last one to do so, per Balaji, was Admiral Nirmal Verma in the period 2009–12. Balaji apprised Defence Minister Parrikar with the fact of the Mk-2 emerging as an operationally attractive plane just when Admiral Lanba, on his own, made a formal demand for fifty-seven carrier aircraft from abroad. Going by the timeline, it would appear that the navy's decision to ditch the NLCA Mk-2 was to try and get its demand for foreign aircraft met. Parrikar decided that the navy could import the carrier aircraft but that the development of the Mk-2 would proceed per plans—a ruling in an end-2016 meeting that, Balaji observed, 'the Chief of Naval Staff and Indian Navy brass seemed disappointed by.'

However, the navy's RFP for the fifty-seven aircraft has metrics the NLCA Mk-2 will likely meet before the long and elaborate selection and short-listing process for the imported aircraft is completed. In that case, the government of the day and the navy will be hard put to justify buying the foreign aircraft and spending billions of dollars in hard currency. By end-2018 the NLCA Mk-2 is scheduled to begin doing arrested recovery and that will be the time, said Balaji, 'to begin pitching a near-ready aircraft once again to the navy and government'. The navy, despite its reservations, will be inclined to fly it, which could be the tipping point and, as happened with the IAF, lead to its acceptance. 'The more the navy flies it, the more they will own it, and the more acceptable the NLCA will become,' he averred. For instance, two LCAs were flown by the air force to some bases in South India, and the aircraft put through its paces at the rate of two sorties a day. 'They discovered,' recalled Balaji, 'that the aircraft maintainability is good because the servicing regimes are computerized.' He also revealed that the naval version has a unique 'hot refuelling' feature, which the air force too wants now. This enables a pilot to land, remain in the cockpit and refuel with the engine running. All the pilot and crew have to do is look at the computerized diagnostics visible on the console that the on-board systems are green, meaning that all systems are in good order, and he can take off again. With check-time down to twenty minutes from the earlier forty-five minutes, and speed fuelling taking just six to seven minutes, the lead NLCA test pilot Commodore Jaideep Maolankar once logged three sorties over three hours in a single day. Of course, because ordnance loading will require engine switch-off, the time on the ground would actually be thirty to forty minutes, which can be trimmed with pilot and crew practice to possibly achieve a turnaround time of as low as twenty to twenty-five minutes. The time reduction due to the telescoping of checks, refuelling and ordnance loading was the result of significant feedback from IAF pilots and squadrons that are familiar with the aircraft, in the process helping in fine-tuning the Tejas design.

To return to the navy's RFI, what are the carrier aircraft available internationally that can fit into the first Indian-built aircraft carrier (IAC-1) which is sized about the same as the *Vikramaditya*, around 35,000 tonnes? The size of the lift to carry planes from the hangar to the deck is a limitation. The naval Rafale with 10 metre non-foldable wings cannot be accommodated on *Vikramaditya*'s forward and rear lifts which are only 8.5 meters wide. It will require modification of the lift and of the carrier because there has to be a half-metre space between the wing tips and the lift walls, or the Rafale aircraft would have to undergo a major redesign to have foldable delta wings at the wing root. Neither will happen because the costs involved are too high. A bigger second Indian carrier IAC-2 is an option, except the naval Rafale, oriented to the catapult-based aircraft launch system (Catobar), will have to prove its ski-jump capability. The Boeing F/A-18 with folded wings and a span of 8.6 meters may just fit into the IAC-1 lifts but will have difficulty on the *Vikramaditya*. In fact, a Boeing team that visited this carrier considered the possibility of a system on the lifts to tilt the aircraft just enough for it to be brought up from the hold or taken down to the hangar. The third option is the Gripen (Marine), which is still only a paper plane. 'Saab say they have a design to navalize the air force version into a naval variant,' informed Balaji, 'which will precisely follow the LCA script and face the same conversion problems.' Meanwhile, NLCA Mk-1 with a foldable wing span of 8.2 metres wide is fine but the Mk-2 is 8.9 metres wide and cannot fit into the rear lift of *Vikramaditya*. In the indigenous carrier there will be no problems with this LCA size. With the RFI–RFP–testing-selection process averagely taking five to seven years, the Tejas programme has enough of a time window to produce an NLCA to meet the navy's 2017 specifications for foreign carrier aircraft. This will mean incorporating into the NLCA the more powerful GE F-414 engine requiring, in the main, the stretching of the fuselage by one metre, and the wing outboard. That's why the aircraft is being reconfigured in what Balaji called 'an absolutely new manner'. The thrust of the F-414 engine translates into 16.5 tonnes of take-off mass. 'With the parameters of the RFI and the wind on deck there will be no need for the designers to restrict themselves, because the old wind on deck and AoA constraints on the Tejas are gone,' he claimed. The optimally designed NLCA with the F-414 engine is expected to fly by early 2020. With composites covering 90 per cent of its surface area and constituting 42 per cent by weight (compared to the IAF version with 45 per cent composites), the naval LCA will be light enough while affording more space for fuel and weapons. The NLCA has a slightly lower composites content, because certain structures such as the landing gear that have to take the crash-landing load are built with maraging steel.

Tejas Engine, AESA Radar and Capacity Building

According to Balaji, the 'strength' of the indigenous Tejas LCA is that India owns 100 per cent intelligence of the aircraft. 'We can have aggregates from all over the place. But the intelligence of the flight control software as well as of avionics software is something special,' he declared. 'There are thirty-eight computers on the aircraft and their intelligence is 100 per cent with us. That's our pride both in terms of the software writing and the software quality. That's where the pilot sitting in the simulator and fine-tuning the symbologies and so on finds the aircraft intuitive.' He pointed out that any change in symbology can cost tens of millions of dollars and that's what the country ends up paying for when buying foreign aircraft and the recurring costs of the upgraded software every six months in addition to its lifecycle costs by way of software maintenance in foreign aircraft. 'On the LCA,' he said, 'the costs are minimal, because the intelligence and software is all ours, and we make it the way the Indian pilots want it.' But an indigenous combat aircraft with a foreign jet engine powering it would be anomalous.

The indigenous Kaveri jet engine, designed and under development at the Gas Turbine Research Establishment (GTRE), Bangalore, has achieved 76 kiloNewtons (kN) on a static test bed. This engine was supposed to power the LCA. Balaji identified two or three things about the Kaveri engine that have to be worked on. For higher thrust levels, the air flow scheme and system will have to be redesigned to achieve at least 84 to 85 kNs wet-thrust to reach the GE 404 level; and 97 kNs to attain the F-414 level. ('Wet thrust' is a means of increasing the thrust of a jet engine by injecting methanol in the combustion chamber.) Second, it has a problem; Balaji called it, 'a screech, in the afterburner regime'. The third thing is that the GTRE has to eliminate 'the vibrations in the engine core'. To correct such problems, DRDO 'will likely be using the Rafale offsets and ask the French engine company, Safran, to recover the Kaveri engine,' informed Balaji. 'Engine integration is not a simple task. The aircraft is built around the engine, different mass-flows will require different air intake design. When air intakes are different,' he continued, 'it will mean redesigning the rear fuselage and changing the mounts and, therefore, the central fuselage as well. All this has to be kept in mind, because sometimes there's a tendency to underestimate or underplay the technical difficulties and the effort that is involved. It is not a simple matter of plugging the Kaveri into the Tejas and taking out the F-404.'

A modern combat aircraft is rated, among other things, by the quality of the AESA fire control radar that allows a pilot to instantly switch missions from firing munitions in an air-to-air mode to triggering air-to-ground weapons. The indigenous multi-mode Uttam AESA based on the Israeli Elta 2032 computer is being tested on LCA Mk-1A; its more advanced version based on the Elta 2052 computer may be ready for the Mk-2 Tejas. Uttam can, at any given time, mount surveillance of 100 aircraft, track twenty and target six to seven aircraft and lock on to a 2 square metre target at 170 km. 'As far as Uttam is concerned,' said Balaji, 'I had a separate platform for putting this radar. We have done an enormous amount of interface work. We also tried to keep the space within the Tejas structure to remove the old mechanical radar and replace the transmitter/receiver (T/R) nodule box and plug in the Uttam unit. We had given the interfaces to LRDE [Electronics and Radar Development Establishment, Bangalore] and the exact mountings and so on, to minimize changes, including changing the front plate, and removing the T/R nodule plate.'

The T/R nodules are fabricated in a specialized foundry in Chandigarh. The physical difference between a mechanical radar and the 2052 AESA radar is the requirement for liquid cooling for the latter; the 2032 AESA radar is air-cooled. The AESA was flight-tested by end-2017. Unfortunately, the Uttam AESA radar is being viewed as 'back-up' by HAL, which has compromised it by tendering for a French AESA radar to equip the first lot of eighty-three Tejas Mk-1As, charged Balaji.[47] 'The danger in this is that if we go abroad for eighty-three units, you'll be killing the indigenous Uttam AESA radar,' he asserted. 'My approach would have been—the 2032 is performing well, it meets the Air Staff Requirements [ASRs]. With the quartz radome [supplied by Cobham of UK] markedly reducing transmission losses, the 2032 is giving better performance than what the ASR demanded. We recommended,' he revealed, 'that LCA continue with the 2032, and once the indigenous Uttam AESA is available, it can be easily replaced on the Mk-1A LCA. But without informing the ADA or the LCA project, HAL went ahead and issued the RFP once eighty-three Tejas were sanctioned for IAF.' Balaji wondered how HAL took this decision, considering that even if the MoD's DAC approved this buy, it still had to be authorized by the Cabinet Committee on Security. LRDE should have informed the MoD or the Indian government of this HAL move and conveyed the fact that owing to the indigenous 2032 AESA exceeding the ASRs, there was no need for an imported item. This was not done. Further, in tune with the normal Indian government's stepmotherly treatment of indigenous military technology, the Uttam project has not been sanctioned an Embraer aircraft as a flying test bed that was asked for. A Tejas LCA test bed was likewise denied, forcing the scientists to test it from rooftops in Bangalore!

But how has the LCA programme, starting from zero baseline, become so capable? That's because it did not restrict itself to the government domain and painstakingly nursed an efficient ecosystem, combining the capacities of the ADA, HAL and other PSUs with specialized strengths such as Bharat Heavy Electricals Limited. It resulted in the heat exchangers for the hot-end gas systems, for instance, and in over 400 small and big private sector firms, a good number of them MSMEs, numerous academic institutions and large corporations like L&T participating in the initial phase of software development, getting involved in the LCA project. As a result, several small companies in Chennai are producing the computers and complete hardware for the LCA, a small firm in Bangalore, Turbotech, produces the eleven uplocks that hold the undercarriage system together on each aircraft, and the bellows required for the hot gases in the combustion chamber are manufactured by the Chennai-based Metallic Bellows, a company spawned by the Tejas project. MSMEs contribute between 20 to 25 per cent by value to the programme. And on a consortium basis, the Vikram Sarabhai Space Research Centre, Trivandrum, and Godrej Aerospace, Mumbai, produced the full flight control system actuators. These will replace imports from the US and are of such high quality that they have already found an export market. 'We built up this ecosystem with small investments which have developed technologies and allowed Indian companies to stand out in the world market,' said Balaji. The mission control computers, the flight control computer and the smaller utility computers—there are thirty-eight computers in all in the LCA with software written by the Tejas project for monitoring the hydraulics, pilot health, fuel and so on—are all built from scratch by small private enterprises. These come in as Line Replaceable Units/ modular components that maintenance crews can plug in, plug out.

Among academic institutions, some part of the audit of the control laws was done at Jadavpur University, and the Indian Institute of Science, Bangalore, and the IITs provide the programme close support. The ADA acts as the programme office and nodal body, and has its own avionics unit, which wrote the software and designed the mission control computer hardware for the Tejas and prototyped it before HAL began its work. As elaborated by Balaji, the programme philosophy is that 'If a private company struggled with the programme in its early years, researched and produced the technology, the uplocks, say, why should their manufacturing be handed over to HAL, Lucknow? Our policy is to reward such companies and have these get into the full-scale production of things they struggled to research, design and develop. We funded private firms that helped the programme at the prototype stage to acquire production wherewithal. Large orders for the LCA will mean large repeat orders of spares. It will help the programme amortize the R&D investment.'

Ironically, Balaji says, from a naval person's point of view, the IAF has been more positive about the Tejas. The previous CAS, Arup Raha, flew the two-seater LCA in May 2016. 'I was at the telemetry hearing the conversation in the cockpit. He was very enthusiastic. The script was that after Group Captain Madhav Rangachari takes off, Raha, an experienced MiG-29 pilot, would assume control but because Tejas is such an intuitive aircraft, designed ergonomically, and extremely pilot-friendly,' Balaji recalls, 'Raha took control of the aircraft right away, taking off and doing all the manoeuvres. He was thrilled and kept saying "Beautiful! Beautiful!" as he flew the plane. After he landed he said, yes, this is a good product, we must move ahead, and the first IAF squadron [Number 45 Squadron] with Tejas was formed at Sulur on 1 July that year with whatever number of LCAs were then available (with Rangachari as first commanding officer).' The current strength (in end-March 2018) of the Sulur squadron is some eight Tejas aircraft. The Raha flight, Balaji feels, was 'a turning point for the LCA'. Despite a tradition of not flying single-engine aircraft at the Republic Day parade, the IAF gave the Tejas, staged out of Bikaner, 450 km away, the pride of place in the 2017 fly-past. The current CAS Air Chief Marshal B.S. Dhanoa too seems keen about it, having flown it at the 2017 Bangalore Air Show. 'It led to a perception swing,' says Balaji. 'The navy used to be that way but I found the current dispensation of the air force to be very supportive and keen to move ahead with the Tejas and the AMCA as well.' Raha's positive reaction led the air force to enlarge its order from eighty-three to 123 Tejas Mk-1As.

The galloping confidence of the LCA programme was crowned by Parrikar instructing Balaji to expose the aircraft to a discerning international public, whence the Tejas flew at the 2016 Bahrain Air Show. 'We were given six weeks and it was a huge logistic challenge.'

The LCA flew to Jamnagar on the first leg, to Muscat over the sea in the second leg and then to Bahrain. Persons from *Jane's International Defence Review* timed its manoeuvres in Bahrain and were impressed. Experts offering live commentary on television cameras at the air show followed a manoeuvring Tejas and lauded the LCA's 'excellent handling capabilities'.[48] Interest in the LCA has been shown by several countries.

The chief of the Turkmenistan Air Force in mid-2016 flew the plane and the Bangladesh Air Force chief had a serious interaction with the LCA team. French air chief General Andre Lanata has gone up in a Tejas, as have US Air Force head General David L. Goldfein and Singapore Defence Minister Ng Eng Hen. Ng compared his experience in flying on the LCA to being driven around in a car and praised the IAF pilots for being 'superbly confident, supremely professional and really at the top of the game and I can imagine why my pilots find so much value in training with IAF pilots'.[49] The combination of Tejas and Indian pilots is eliciting a good response and would be a great advertisement for selling the Tejas abroad. Whether this interest translates into worldwide sales will depend on the strength and quality of the after-sale product support system, which requires professional, world-class sales and servicing infrastructure and an export ecosystem and cannot be an extension of HAL's prevailing low-quality product support system that has caused bad blood with the IAF.

In the production aspects, Parrikar pushed a reluctant HAL into becoming the prime integrator of aircraft, divesting it of its manufacturing role. Thus, the major production modules of the LCA have been transferred to the private sector. L&T, Coimbatore, produces Tejas's entire wing assembly, the fuselage is sourced to VEM Technologies, Hyderabad, and the fin and rudder assembly earlier produced at the National Aerospace Laboratories (NAL) is now supplied by Tata Advanced Materials. So from outsourcing parts, the process has transited into outsourcing whole assemblies with HAL as prime integrator and testing done at the Bangalore-based CEMILAC (Centre for Military Airworthiness and Certification). That is how Boeing, Lockheed, Airbus and European Aeronautic Defence and Space work—they get aggregates from various places and integrate them. The NLCA has survived because Parrikar, per Balaji, 'was outstandingly supportive of this programme'.

He physically reviewed the programme eighteen times during his tenure, calling Balaji in for frequent consultations and on the telephone to clear his doubts and otherwise kept abreast of the latest developments to a point, recalls Balaji, wherein at a general body meeting of the ADA (a society chaired by the defence minister), when someone expressed some misgivings about the plane and the project, Parrikar took it on himself to address them. 'He was hands on,' said Balaji, 'and told me, whatever the navy says, the government is 100 per cent behind the NLCA project.'

One reason for the F-16/F-18/Gripen decision being in limbo is because the controversial decision to buy any of these aircraft will have to be made just when the indigenous Tejas is being inducted into service, and its proven technologies provide the basis for upgradation and use in the AMCA programme, which is getting off the ground. And because going in for another foreign aircraft will be seen as both waste of money and refutation of the goal to achieve arms self-sufficiency. Where defence is concerned, is it to assemble/replicate any old technology and weapon system—F-16 or F-18— discarded by the supplier country's military and does it make operational sense to have such aircraft in the IAF? Especially because, as already discussed, there isn't a sufficiently large international market for such dated planes and spares to justify huge expenditures on their production. Clearly there isn't. Dan Gillian, vice president for Boeing's F/A-18 programme, contends that buying and producing a dated American plane 'will lead to the next generation of aeroplane that India will design and build'.[50]

How exactly, considering the next generation of aircraft is Tejas, and that is already being built in the country? If promotion of self-reliance in arms is the overarching objective, setting up a factory in India to produce a technology-wise doddering F-16 plane when there is a budding local industry already putting out the more modern and advanced Tejas aircraft defies logic and good sense. It may be argued that advanced manufacturing processes and skill sets would thus become available to Indian industry. But these can be bought in the international market by Indian companies. So how will India gain? And won't the waste of public funds on the F-16 leave that much less money for the indigenous LCA and the successor AMCA programme, considering Tejas is a ready-to-induct plane that has passed all the technology and production milestones after starting from the ground up (with the complete loss of a generation of aircraft designing and development talent, expertise, skills and capability associated with the HF-24 and HF-73 projects)?

India surely can do without repeating the awful HF-73 tragedy just to generate revenues for an American company, to please Washington and win for India the appellation of 'major strategic partner' from a seller state, which has time and again used coercive means, such as spares cutoff, to compel Delhi to fall in with its foreign policy line. It makes more strategic, technological and economic sense and to turbocharge the Make in India policy if Tata, Reliance, the Adani Group and HAL are all financially incentivized to become stakeholders in the Tejas programme in its entirety, and have the ADA and DRDO transfer to them full technology, including source codes and system algorithms, with HAL already sharing the process/production technology in its possession. This will, on a war-footing, establish a number of competing LCA-seeded combat aircraft design and development bureaus and production facilities, in effect, several combat aircraft complexes. As it is, HAL's bad work culture and low annual aircraft production rate of only sixteen to eighteen Tejas LCA in its two assembly lines only feeds the military's case for buying Western aircraft, and pre-empts the capacity for accelerated production of different variants (Mk-2, naval) of the LCA and the AMCA under development, and the advanced utility and light combat helicopters (LCH) that HAL is on the verge of rolling out to meet the future needs of the three services. The phenomenal savings of hard currency from buying only indigenous military hardware cannot be underestimated in terms of its potential to grow a world-class defence industry and millions of jobs that are presently harvested by foreign countries. Were the Indian government to terminate imports and the private and public sector companies assigned the task to synergize their resources and efforts and granted the permission to export a portion of their Tejas production from the word go, an Indian aerospace industry, driven by the profit motive, would be off and running in next to no time.

The opportunity is there with the F-16/Gripen/Rafale issue running into politically foul weather. Modi's short-circuiting of the MMRCA procurement process with his intervention on behalf of the Rafale aircraft has led to political controversy, handing the opposition a 'corruption' issue to beat the BJP government with. Every time Modi hereon hurls

'Bofors' at the Congress party he may have 'Rafale' thrown back at him.[51] One can see why the release by the government of the Rafale costs has raised a stink. Each aircraft is priced at ₹670 crore, and together with a spares package to ensure 75 per cent serviceability of the aircraft for ten years, the costs zoom to ₹1640 crore per aircraft or ₹59,000 crore for thirty-six Rafales.[52] If the lifetime of a combat aircraft is assumed to be thirty-five years, the serviceability costs growing exponentially for the subsequent two and a half decades will hit stratospheric levels—as much as ₹8212 crore for a single Rafale and ₹2,95,632 crore for the lot of thirty-six planes. In any case, cost escalation of foreign-sourced combat aircraft is inevitable also because of the IAF's stress on 'customization' of the Rafale requiring a wider operating (X Band) bandwidth and a wider 'cone' for the on-board Thales AESA radar to increase the chances of one shot–one kill. Such customization was deemed unnecessary by the French Air Force because it operates as part of NATO air forces involving thousands of planes. In India, the offtake of small numbers of aircraft means the IAF wants each plane to be highly capable. By 2012, the cost had escalated to $25 billion for 126 Rafales. Four years later, the unit cost of a clean aircraft without weapons had gone up yet again to a point where thirty-six of these aircraft cost as much as 126 Rafales did in 2007.[53]

But there's a back story regarding the Rafale which emphasizes why the DPSUs should be denied the lead role in making India independent in armaments, an aim, their sixty-year record shows, is beyond them. The original 2007 Rafale costing for 126 aircraft with 108 to be licence-produced in India was $10.2 billion (₹42,000 crore). The HAL-assembled Rafale was priced at 30 per cent over the Dassault cost of $91 million. After being exposed to the lax DPSU work ethos and quality of work on the shop floor, Dassault backed out of guaranteeing the performance of HAL-made Rafale, whence an impasse ensued which was broken by Modi's decision. The reason for Dassault walking away from HAL is the characteristic attitude of DPSUs summarized by an industry source as 'I will do it my way in my own time, but I'll take no responsibility'.[54]

Finally, consider the economics of indigenous weapons platforms. The IAF has ordered 123 of the LCA Mk-1As worth ₹80,000 crore. This is great returns on the Indian government's investment of less than

₹8000 crore in the Tejas programme. Further, the lifecycle costs are typically 2.5 times the acquisition and induction costs, meaning the initial order will generate ₹2,00,000 crore worth of spares and service support for the Indian defence industry. A fast-maturing LCA with AMCA in train would be an attractive proposition to customers in the global market, particularly in the developing world, who seek effective, economical and modern fighter aircraft and would rather trust India as supplier than some Western countries. Once export orders roll in, the revenues that can be earned will be multiples of the initial IAF order. It is such cascading economic, industrial and politico-military returns which militate towards the Indian government, ordaining an end to imported military hardware. But will Modi do it?

Defence Production Ills

The cost escalation of imported capital military goods can become unbearable. It strengthens the case for Delhi to decree that the military has no alternative other than buying indigenous. This may mean pain in the short term but will assure immeasurable gain for the country in the long term and freedom from external pressure. Such temporary military vulnerability as may be created by the decision to bar all arms imports in the interim period before an indigenous industry gets up to speed can be wiped out by the government articulating a more aggressive first use nuclear weapons policy that will prevent China, say, from taking advantage. (More on this in a later section.) Full indigenization of all weapons and spares production will, moreover, endow the country with the capacity for surge production of spares in times of crisis or war which, in turn, will translate into a capacity to fight long-duration and decisive wars. It is a capacity India and the Indian military has never had, with the duration of the wars it has fought (other than the limited 1999 Kargil border conflict) being determined by the holdings of spares and ammunition. This makes the periodic warnings by the armed services and by the Comptroller and Auditor General about severe shortages in the war wastage reserves (of spares, and POL) and in the war stock of ammunition, artillery shells and other chemical explosives adequate for the army to fight for only ten days at intense levels even more alarming.[55] Serving officers say the actual situation is more dire still, with the war stock for certain kinds of artillery shells and equipment spares enough for just a single day's fighting![56]

The deficient Indian defence industry dominated by PSUs has been as unimaginative as the military services, allowing its shop-floor skills to stagnate at the assembly at the 'build to print' level. Depending on the weapon, it has taken one of three pathways. It has produced items under licence from imported SKD/CKD kits in a screwdriver-assembly regime, meaning the product is put together as per blueprints provided by the original equipment manufacturer (OEM). Sometimes such programmes have gradually transitioned to a production regime where, if the demand is large enough, more and more of the components are sourced from within the country, and included MiG-21s, Jaguar, and Su-30MKIs, armoured and tracked platforms, such as the Vijayanta and T-72 tanks, and the Bofors FH-155 gun. But this route means that for the sensitive 'black box technologies' and certain high-value spares the country remains dependent on the OEM. The second route is for totally indigenous design, development and production, such as those involving strategic systems like SSBN, Agni missiles, nuclear weapons/warheads and satellites that the country has undertaken in 'technology mission mode', where none of the restrictive procurement procedures apply.

The third method encompasses indigenous R&D and development of some sub-systems and 'limited collaboration with an advanced technology collaborator', such as the BrahMos supersonic cruise missile, where the Russian company NPOM (Naochno Proezvodsvyenoye Obyedeenyeneeye Maschinostroyena [Scientific and Production Machine Building Association]) has partnered the Indian government with the latter holding a slight (50.5 per cent) majority equity. This model may well cost less, face fewer technical failures and meet contracted delivery schedules, as A. Sivathanu Pillai, former head of the Indo-Russian joint venture BrahMos Aerospace Limited, claims.[57] But it can be criticized for the fact that other than the guidance software, the high-value front-end of the missile, inclusive of the mono-pulse seeker and ramjet engine, come as 'black boxes' from Russia and constitute 70 per cent of the cost of this missile by value and that the Indian end of the BrahMos venture has not even tried to reverse-engineer either of these technologies. A separate DRDO project is, however, developing a ramjet engine, which is at the testing stage.[58] This is a charge that can be directed as well at the collaborations the DRDO has with Israel to develop MRSAMs and LRSAMs. The funding and work distribution on these projects suggests that India is, in fact, subsidizing the development of weapons and technologies meant primarily for Israel's own use. An Israeli twist to Make in India involves defence industrial interlinks with Indian companies and the establishing by Israeli OEMs of their own constellation of MSMEs in India to supply components and services for their equipment used by the Indian military as part of its 'Make with India' policy.[59]

MSMEs are the foundation of most successful defence high-technology industries. The MSMEs attached to all the defence R&D and industrial programmes and projects in the public and private sectors can be integrated into a production complex and constitute an embryonic Indian mittelstand—a large group of small technology creating and innovating enterprises. In Germany MSMEs provide, *The Economist* says, 'the backbone for the world's fourth largest economy', and which concept President Macron hopes to replicate in France, believing it will generate advanced technologies and millions of jobs.[60] Even though comparatively underdeveloped, the MSME sector in India nevertheless contributes nearly 45 per cent to the manufacturing sector and about 40 per cent to Indian exports. Its contribution to the Indian GDP is 8 per cent with this sector registering a 10.8 per cent growth rate. MSMEs with some 60 million people are the biggest employers in the country, after agriculture, and responsible—and this is a most heartening feature—for 17 per cent (versus 42 per cent for big firms) of 'new to the world' innovations during the course of their business, according to a National Knowledge Commission of India study. The MSMEs would benefit hugely as will the industry as a whole if skilling and vocational training programmes, particularly in smart technologies like artificial intelligence, cyber and robotics were greatly enlarged and more youth persuaded to enrol in them. Some 12.8 million youth enter the job market every year but only 3.5 million avail of the vocational training programmes (versus the capacity of 4.3 million in the country), when the corresponding annual figure for China is 90 million youth undergoing vocational training.[61] The failure of skilling programmes to draw youth and the consequent shortages of trained manpower is a continuing worry.

However, what is seemingly unrectifiable is the bureaucratic attitude to indigenous production. MoD officials explain their own (and by extension the military's) partiality to foreign-sourced weapons systems by saying that encouraging indigenization and growing the local defence industry is no part of their brief and the allotted 'rules of business'. Their task, they assert, is to merely see that the military is adequately armed.[62] The defence production bureaucrats, on the other hand, have the oversight and responsibility for the DPSUs as their remit and are, therefore, committed to ensuring that all major arms licence production contracts are directed to them, that their order books are always overfull and that they are always in good financial health. Incidentally, DPSU facilities have a replacement value of ₹6 lakh crore and are, in a sense, 'unreplicable' with current orders on their books touching ₹7 lakh crore versus a measly contract worth ₹1500 crore for OPVs to the private sector in the period 2014–17. And this small contract accrued only because both L&T and Pipavav shipyard (bought over by Reliance Defence) strongly complained that as regards warship construction, they had invested ₹4000 crore and ₹3000 crore respectively in building up capabilities but that the DPSUs had cornered all the orders valued at ₹2 lakh crore.

So the Parrikar-run MoD opened up the private sector to competitive bidding, to start out, for smaller projects such as for OPVs. The irony is that DPSUs are able to meet their contractual obligations only by outsourcing work to private sector majors like L&T, Tata, Mahindra, et al. The government allows DPSUs to charge 30 per cent over the cost to them from private sector firms. This permits DPSUs to show a healthy bottom line. Except, such DPSU-friendly official milieu is naturally hostile to the private industry and results, as an industry source put it, in MoD/DDP officials 'saying one thing to the industry, and doing the opposite to favour DPSUs, and taking an unconscionably long time—as much as five to six years—to just put a signature to paper'. This last is because of the system of file movement up and down the MoD, defence procurement and defence finance decision-making silos and, because the same people have to sign even a slightly amended paper, it has to make the same journey over and over again.[63]

This is the normal Kafkaesque file-pushing scheme prevailing throughout the government that Prime Minister Modi had promised to eliminate, but has failed to do. It is justified as 'granularities' of the decision-making process in procurement gobbledygook that's hard to make head or tail of.[64] The official mindset has stayed stuck in the socialist-era Deep State principles that perceives private sector defence companies with the gravest suspicion. 'They think of us,' said the head of a new defence manufacturing venture of a major business house, 'as *chors* (thieves)' who need to be given no quarter and who, in fact, ought to be 'squeezed' into conceding more and still more, with a view to limiting their profit margins, the very notion of profitable private sector defence ventures being anathema to them. His company's initiative, for example, of approaching HAL with repeated offers to share its Tejas LCA workload, he said, ran up against just this outlook and was repeatedly rebuffed. This company was confident that after computing the cost of HAL's manufacturing facility and its workforce, it could make a proposal in which it would secure the necessary manufacturing technology and processes on its own and roll out the first LCA inside of two years if allowed to use the existing HAL manpower and facilities—currently utilized to only 30 per cent of its capacity—or, within an additional fifteen to twenty months if the company had to set up its own Tejas production line de novo, and still turn a profit. He did not, he said, hear from HAL again except for a generic reply to forward an RFI.[65]

There is no dearth of such stories illustrating the extraordinary waste of time and resources by DPSUs and their collusion with the MoD and DDP officials. The standard operating procedure of the DPSUs is underscored by the following example retailed by an industry insider. Bharat Electricals Limited (BEL) was tasked to build an electro-optics facility. It was allotted ₹300 crore and 500 acres of land. The first thing it did with the money was lay out an officer's colony complete with a clubhouse and swimming pool and parks, etc. before turning to the government for funds to buy the actual manufacturing paraphernalia. In reality, this source said, a smart electro-optics production unit would cost no more than ₹50 crore and require only about an acre of land. He contrasted the DPSUs' spendthrift ways with a project proposal, he says he had once made to a Tata company to produce the short (25 km) range Akash surface-to-air missiles (SAMs) at the rate of two missiles every three days in a factory on 4 acres of land with an outlay of ₹83 crore, which the company board rejected as a cost-inefficient scheme. In comparison, the premier missile production DPSU, BDL, was budgeted ₹1500 crore and given 500 acres of land, and it produces only six Akash missiles per year. Such appallingly low levels of labour productivity is normal for DPSUs and ordnance factories. A recent NITI Aayog study found that the value produced per worker in OFB units is only ₹6 lakh per year, when the minimum value a worker has to produce is ₹40 lakh to ₹50 lakh annually for an MSME to be economically viable. The total amount spent on R&D and production of the Akash SAM over the years now stands at ₹30,000 crore. Given the differentials in the price and cost of their products and in the lethargic functioning of BDL, why wasn't the production of the Akash missile, powered by a ramjet engine, and the development of its longer range variants, handed over to the private sector? Because, as this person put it pithily: 'There is a *khali sthan* [empty space] between the ears of the MoD and Department of Defence Production (DDP) officials. That the country's resources are wasted this way is not their worry.'[66]

Run Silent, Run Aground: Project 75i

Consider another example with strategic ramifications. India has indigenously built the Arihant-class SSBN—the most potent weapon system in any arsenal, forming at once the most lethal and survivable and the least vulnerable leg of the strategic nuclear triad. It took fifteen years to build the first boat; the second of this type (INS *Arighat*) was launched in twelve years, the third, *Aridhaman*, will take ten years from laying the keel to harbour trials. This compares favourably with the international industry standard of seven years per boat for, say, a US company that has an outstanding order for some fifty to sixty SSBNs and SSNs, and beats the twelve years the first French-origin

Scorpene submarine took to be built at MDL. Compared to this Scorpene sub (INS *Kalvari*) inducted into service with 85 per cent foreign content, which will decrease to 30 per cent in the last of the six Scorpenes at MDL, *Arihant* is 80 per cent indigenous by value, *Arighat* 85 per cent. And production pace-wise, the third Arihant-class vessel, *Aridhaman*, is 75 per cent ready and the fourth boat in this class is 25 per cent ready.

India is completely self-sufficient in nuclear-powered submarines in propulsion systems, control technology and most of the other assemblies in the boat. The nuclear power plants are entirely indigenous in that the improvements in the design in the original power plant in the Arihant (transferred by Russia) have been validated by the Russians. The power plants for the nuclear-powered hunter-killer submarine (SSN) and the larger 260 MW driven next-generation SSBN is already way past the design stage. What will continue to be imported for the foreseeable future until the relevant DRDO projects come good are the diesel engine, the motors, the optronic head of the mast, a communications subsystem, and the torpedoes. The Indian company L&T, the main private sector contractor to build SSBNs, has developed a 3D, fully digitalized submarine design facility able to turn a 'basic' design into engineering design that is as technologically advanced as any in the world and more modern, incidentally, than anything existing in Russia or in the Indian public sector. It would seem reasonable to assume, in these circumstances, that the Indian Navy's Project 75i for a conventional diesel submarine would naturally be handed over to this Indian company with the manufacturing experience, wherewithal and excess capacity to produce it, considering also that a conventional submarine is one-third as complex as a nuclear-powered boat and one-fifth the size, with the complexity factor arising out of three to four redundancies for each major system in the SSBN.

This straightforward decision, like everything else the military undertakes with the MoD, is fouled up, trapped in an endless cycle of delays by indecision. Initiated in the early 2000s, the proposal was approved by the government for a second conventional submarine production line to be built with a foreign partner, Project 75i—the first being for the Scorpene (Project 75)—to flesh out indigenous design capability with the successor Project 76 to be a completely Indian product, with the best mix of design features. The programme cost estimated then was less than half of the ₹70,000 crore that it has ballooned out to when approved in late 2017 by the DAC.[67] L&T as the only firm with experience in building nuclear submarines in the country took the design for SSBN from the submarine design sub-directorate in the warship design directorate at the Naval Headquarters and converted it into an engineering design and constructed the boats on that basis. This process of indigenization of capabilities was helped by Russia transferring the technology for the manufacture of the specialized steel for submarines, and of some other critical items. Until now when this Indian company is entirely capable of building any kind of submarine on its own. Defence Minister Manohar Parrikar, in the meantime, had tweaked the 'strategic partner' concept in DPP 2016 with the extant capability of L&T in mind. He decided that the MoD and L&T would together negotiate with suppliers for just the design and specific technologies and systems the country lacked, as also the best price. The German company ThyssenKrupp—producers of the HDW 209 submarines in service with the Indian Navy whose transfer of technology and full indigenization of production were cut short by the corruption scandal associated with that 1980s procurement decision—was regarded as the most pliable because it desperately wants to sell, having lost the Australian Navy contract to replace its Collins-class vessels. DCNS of France won that race with its Shortfin Barracuda submersible.[68]

This sensible process was undermined by Parrikar deciding in a huff to return to Goa, according to an industry source, because of his frustration with having to have every contract over ₹1000 crore cleared by the finance minister. 'If I can't get anything done on my own,' Parrikar is reported to have told an industry representative, 'there's no point in my staying on.' Once Parrikar left, Arun Jaitley again took concurrent charge as interim defence minister and promptly reverted to the less politically risky lowest tender (L1) process, and terminating in the process the progressive strategic partner scheme the MoD had embarked upon. 'By not protesting and writing a dissenting note,' the source said, 'the naval brass lost the last chance of getting a German submarine they really wanted.'[69] Just the design for the customized German HDW 214 submarine could have been secured for no more than $400 million to $500 million.[70]

L1 means, however, that there will be no scrutiny of the technical capacity and capability of the Indian companies bidding for the contract; it will clear the way for a company with zero experience in building submarines such as, say, Reliance Defence with a turnover of ₹1000 crore to bid for a ₹50,000 crore worth contract of 75i submarines, while L&T with a turnover of ₹1.25 lakh crore may find itself in a position from which it cannot win because its bid will not be the lowest as it has a proper costing scheme on the basis of its Arihant SSBN manufacturing experience. Reliance would then win the Project 75i contract and, because it is bereft of options, will go to a foreign submarine supplier for near 100 per cent foreign-sourced content. The OEM in that case will have the upper hand because it knows this Indian company has zero assets, zero production experience and untested specialized manufacturing capacity. Worse, Jaitley announced publicly that India would be satisfied with even 40 per cent indigenous content possibly by weight and not even value, thereby undercutting what little price negotiating leverage the country had left, as also the leverage to get more advanced technologies while minimizing in percentage terms the foreign content in the 'make and buy Indian' part of the scheme. When a defence minister has no understanding of issues he is to rule on and does not seem to apply his mind—which is the case with most of them—this is the sort of mess that's created for the country. Thus, India, the Indian Navy and the Indian exchequer will all get it in the neck and tens of billions of dollars will be drained from the Indian treasury by the OEM chosen on the L-1 basis, and the existing indigenous capacity and national security will go waste. Pondering the egregiously wasteful practices of the Indian military and the MoD, a West European military attache once wryly commented that 'India is a very rich country; it can afford to do things in a way we can't afford to.'[71]

Aggregating Demand and Choosing a Strategic Partner

More incriminating evidence of how the DPP 2016 is drafted, inadvertently or otherwise, to promote crony capitalism is available in the section on 'strategic partners', a subject on which DProP 2018 is largely silent. According to an industry source, 'In the very first para, it says we are on the lookout for prime integrators with experience of doing large-scale system integration. What's that? Well, it turns out, it means a company that can put up oil refineries and chemical and fertilizer plants! It goes on to say that because there's a lot of difference in manufacturing them, combat aircraft and helicopters should be in different production categories. This would enable a company that has put up a chemical plant or an oil refinery [like say, Reliance tied up with Dassault for Rafale or Adani linked to Saab for Gripen] to bid for making a fighter plane, but would prevent a company making such aircraft from bidding for the production of helicopters! Such is the kind of absurdity found in DPP 2016.'

Defence Minister Parrikar was apprised of such anomalies in the DPP and about the benefits accruing from a strategic partnership for not just a single product but with a company for the full range of products. The armed services, paramilitaries, police and other government agencies want different types of aircraft and helicopters. It makes sense to issue a mega RFP for helicopters with lift capacity ranging from 4 tonnes, 12 tonnes to 25 tonnes, for setting up a factory to produce a whole range of helicopters with the requirement that thereafter all end-users, military included, will have to offtake helicopters only from this source. That is how it is done in advanced countries. All European states have standardized their helicopter requirements to the NH-90 standard.

'We don't have to have a great ectopic like the Sikorsky-60 or whatever. Go to Airbus for the NH-90, it already has an engine deal with Snecma or some other engine manufacturer, build the engine here,' said a former military officer who has also worked in industry. 'With total requirements of two engines per helicopter and a total demand of 1000 helicopters of all kinds, that would be a total of 2000 engines plus another 1000 engines as reserve stock. At 3000 engines every aircraft major—Rolls-Royce, GE, Pratt and Whitney or whoever—will want to set up a plant in India. If you then say, "but your engines don't fit our aircraft", they'll say what's the helicopter you have, and they'll come up with an engine blueprint by the next day. Screw the equity requirements. Look only at the number of jobs that will be created. The

RFP for 1000 helos in the time frame from now to 2025 would be signed on the condition that engines, rotors, and all the avionics will also be made in India. That's all that's needed. Run the business as you wish but deliver the helicopters by this date. We'll give the land, licences, water, power, etc. Sell to us and to the world. The rest is for them to decide and to run their business.' He then held up the automobile manufacturing model. 'The Indian government did not tell Suzuki or Honda or Toyota or Peugeot or General Motors to have this or that level of equity, or Indian managers, or this or that technology, or anything else. These car companies originally brought in all the components, then started out by manufacturing just the tail light, then the bulb, then the cables, and in stages the whole car. I don't know why so commonsensical a route is not comprehensible to the Indian government.'

This same path of global RFP could be taken for small arms— 2 million pieces from 5.56 mm to 12 mm range are required, with the government agencies and the military taking 1,00,000 pieces annually. If the company made an extra 1000 pieces, they would be permitted to export them, with freedom accorded the foreign company to select its Indian partner—whether the OFB or a private sector firm. Such a policy of aggregating the demand and the production has been recommended by NITI Aayog, but the Modi government has paid it no heed, with the result that each new demand is handled as a discrete procurement involving different ministries and the acquisition process remains a boondoggle.[72] However, NITI Aayog is focusing on consolidating military aviation in one place. It has met up with the chief of the integrated defence staff. 'We are clear that for the country to go forward we have to aggregate,' said a NITI Aayog official. 'We can't do this piecemeal—buy two here, three there. Four tomorrow. To make sense, we have to make 50,000! That's the kind of economies of scale we need. If we want some major generic capability, go for the whole thing, not compartmentalize effort and resources.'[73] This initiative was started jointly by the Federation of Indian Chambers of Commerce and Industry, the Aeronautical Society of India, Centre for Air Power Studies, and the MoD and the Ministry of Civil Aviation have signed on.

There are still other problems with DPP 2016. Its limiting foreign equity to 49 per cent is the reason why no foreign company wants to set up a manufacturing base in India. It compelled the South Korean company Kangnam Corporation, for instance, to pull out of the ₹32,640 crore deal to build twelve advanced minesweepers. The 'commercial complications' that Rear Admiral Shekhar Mital (retd), head of the Goa Shipyard, talked about were actually related to this restriction on foreign equity that the Koreans were led to believe would be eased.[74] While the prime minister has talked about allowing 100 per cent equity to foreign entities for select technologies, as far as the DPP is concerned it defines a strategic partner as being permitted only 49 per cent equity, which has been increased to the 76 per cent level in case of certain specialized technologies in DProP 2018. It is also contended that the MoD misinterpreted Modi's 'Come, make in India' as 'Make in India' and the country got trapped, says a source in the debate over indigenous content.

The Tata Avro 748 replacement medium range aircraft for the IAF was supposed to have 40 per cent indigenous content. The amphibious US-2 Japanese plane has 28 per cent Japanese content. So if the Indian government decrees a requirement of 60 per cent indigenous for the C-130J in India, it cannot happen because the original products are put together on the basis of a global supply chain and 'globalized' production. The cost of the engine and propellers alone is 40 per cent of the cost of the aircraft. Of the remaining 60 per cent would the IAF trust an Indian company to make the primary structure? After a few years of production experience under its belt, maybe, but not when Indian companies do not have much to boast about by way of a production record. According to a corporate source, 'We can't make the undercarriage, but avionics we can make—no problems there. We have also learned to make aero-structures, composites and to work the sheet metal—all that can be managed. But that will still fall short of 60 per cent. The problem is there isn't sufficient understanding in the MoD and the Indian government, steeped in statist notions of autarchic development, about the prevailing global supply chains and production networks, he added. Boeing and Lockheed do not make most of their planes. They are all integrators who rely on smart-sourcing—get components from here and there, bring it to a place, assemble it there and that's it. 'The Chinese didn't insist on equity, manning and technology specifications, as does the DPP and, hence, got the Airbus 320 plant, a deal entirely without any preconditions,' he said. 'Apple has only 2 per cent content that is American, but while the name that goes on the instrument is Apple, the small print line says "Made in China". The Indian government is blind to why things succeed in other countries but fail in India.'

Jaitley's Follies

If Jaitley proved himself inept in his short stints as concurrent defence minister, he has been just as maladroit as finance minister. His conception and rollout of the long-awaited Goods and Services Tax (GST) scheme with numerous and confusing rate slabs are growingly being realized as flawed and has impacted the defence sector negatively. 'When I looked at the Japanese ShinMaywa US-2 proposal [discussed in the previous chapter] from the GST angle, one can see the latter is not aligned with the larger objectives of the country of obtaining close military ties with Japan and becoming the sole source for the best amphibious aircraft in the world,' said a former military officer. What should Jaitley ideally have done? He should not have put all capital equipment—production machinery—in the 28 per cent GST bracket. This means, the source said, 'that if I buy machinery—intermediate and capital goods—for ₹100, pay GST of 28 per cent, ₹128 is lost right away. With three years as payback period—which is the average age of the modern machine—where do I get the funds? I can't do Make in India at 28 per cent GST.'

Modi has talked of building infrastructure like roads, highways, etc. 'In that case, shouldn't the excavators, roadrollers and so on have been in the 2 per cent GST bracket instead of 28 per cent as is the case now? The government has its Swachh Bharat Abhiyan, but sanitaryware attracts 18 per cent GST. Insofar as can be made out,' he said, 'the GST slabs are strange at 5 per cent, 12 per cent, 18 per cent and 28 per cent—there is no progression here, not arithmetic, geometric. On what basis did Jaitley decide 5 per cent for this item, 8 per cent for that while deciding the 18 per cent GST slab for services. Why? And who is paying for it? The people to whom it is passed on.' The fundamental flaw in the taxation policy, he averred, is this, 'Assuming these rates were Jaitley's cockeyed notions, what were the generalist civil servants who are *sab jaanta walas* [know-alls] doing? Shouldn't they have used common sense when it came to fitment of the various things into the slabs? Take the Jan Aawas Yojna (for low-cost public housing)—the doors, window frames, etc. that go into a house costing ₹2.5 lakh under this Yojna (Plan) has a GST component of 18 per cent. Won't fewer houses be built for the same fund allocation?'

The GST effect on actual defence production costs is even more skewed. Warships and aircraft are in the 5 per cent slab, but the propulsion system in warships is pegged at 28 per cent, army tanks at 28 per cent, and 3 tonners (trucks most commonly used to move troops) were originally in the 28 per cent category. Moreover, everything connected with the railways attracts 5 per cent GST, anything connected with space is 0 per cent. 'What is this?' asked a bamboozled defence industry person. 'I sent this to a joint secretary in the MoD. He said, "We know all these problems, but tell me what's your interest?" I said as a citizen I don't understand why 28 per cent of the defence budget is thus shaved off as GST. He said the GoI [Government of India] has lots of monies. "If 28 per cent of the defence allocations go in taxes, why should you be concerned? Let it go." I pointed out to him that if the government had not imposed the 28 per cent GST, more would be produced in the country, more people would be employed, the country's wealth would grow faster and India would progress faster. "Do I have to explain all this to you?" I asked him. That's 28 per cent of the budget less spent on military hardware, on job creation, etc. If I make 100 trucks now, without GST I would have made 128 trucks, which would have served as impetus for more steel production, more rubber production for tyres and so on, and faster modernization all round.' Worse still is the working capital requirement. 'The GST rules say that one can claim an input tax credit only when the next guy in the chain pays up,' the industry man said. 'An aircraft is made in three years, so the manufacturer will be waiting for it for three years? How can it work?'

In the matter of defence production, Dr Saraswat opines, 'It is not a problem of resources alone but with the fact that the Indian government has tied itself up into knots, thinking that only DPSUs—HAL, BDL, BEML—can be the production agencies.' A new policy was recommended by the Defence Committee chaired by V.K. Atre, a former science adviser to the defence minister, that recommended offsets to create weapons platform–based clusters in the private sector with one or two big companies heading them. The concept of clusters—'geographic concentrations' of interconnected institutions like businesses, government agencies universities, R&D labs, human resources pool and skilled manpower—is something Israel as the exemplar of a 'start-up nation' has perfected.[75] 'What I have heard is that there was opposition against the cluster idea from within the private sector which felt that they'd be deprived of opportunity to get into the business,' Saraswat said. This would have resulted, for instance, in L&T becoming the sole submarine producer in the country, Bharat Forge and Tata the makers of gun systems, Godrej Aerospace for specialized electronics, etc. This is generally the case abroad except for the US where there are still two companies producing combat aircraft—Boeing and Lockheed—but having multiple producers is not economically sustainable for a country like India. After all, even in the US, the business is getting consolidated with McDonnell-Douglas, for instance, merging into Boeing, etc. But in India, according to Saraswat, Mahindra, L&T and HAL are all producing planes already. 'This can't continue,' he said. 'Look abroad, there's only HDW producing submarines in Germany, Dassault combat aircraft in France, BAE the same in the UK and DCNS ships in France. But we seem not to be able to rationalize the national resources. Can India afford to have six agencies producing subs?'

Atre's cluster idea has not been seriously pursued. There are ten shipyards—four in the private sector—seven of which are working, so each shipyard averages half a ship built a year. Saraswat revealed that he was part of a two-man committee in the PMO during the Manmohan Singh government to examine how best to optimize submarine-building in the country. 'We recommended in end-2012 that private sector companies,' he said, 'should produce submarines, that only L&T can do Project 75i in the private sector, and that this cannot be avoided because MDL's capacity is stretched to the extreme in producing the Scorpene boats. But choosing the production agency was left to the services, in this case the navy. But the government could not enforce the decision because Parrikar took the middle path—that L&T and MDL each make six of the twelve Project 75i subs, and that's where the project is hanging fire ever since; there's been no decision.'

The solution, a retired senior military officer said, is to break the MoD silo. 'We cannot do strategic procurements for the country within the vertical space of the MoD. On Rafale, for instance, we should have said to France, "Set up your reactors, buy 500 of this or that or the other Indian-made products, then we can talk Rafale." The Cabinet Committee on Security has to take this call. Get the procurement business out of the MoD. The MoD's role should be limited to indicating the sort of aircraft that is required, then the process should move to a new central organization established for the purpose, which will carefully examine what India will get in return.'

A proposal along these lines has been forwarded by NITI Aayog to the Modi government, but again the PMO has not responded. A senior official in the Modi regime identifies a brace of more fundamental problems afflicting the defence of the country. One is the MoD bureaucracy, the other is defence production. 'The MoD bureaucracy is the worst in all the Government of India,' he declared. 'Staffed by arts and history BAs and MAs, who are required to pronounce on military issues, there's absolutely no convergence or coordination between the MoD, DDP and DRDO, with each getting in the other's way, and stymieing indigenous projects.' Just how much at odds the three departments are was glimpsed, he said, at the meeting of the intergovernmental committee in Moscow. 'When Parrikar asked a service about a particular weapon system the Russians were ready to sell, the vice chief looked at the director general, acquisitions, MoD, because had he indicated interest the latter would have wondered why the officer had shown interest leading, who knows, to a CBI investigation! Hence, the enormous caution of the military not to get ahead of the bureaucratic overlords.'

He then listed the four factors why arms imports are preferred—the armed services' preference, corruption, vested interests and the influence/inducements offered by the US and France, in particular, among other country suppliers. On the other hand Modi's Make in India in the defence sector is a 'non-starter' in the main because, he said, 'it falls under procurement, rather than industry and, in the event, there are no business plans—the basic foundation for any production project in the private sector—because the cost of capital, technology, infrastructure, etc. has to be accounted for. But these are not considerations uppermost in the mind of the MoD, defence production officials and DRDO. Further, muddying decisions on an economic and commercial basis is that the acquisition is in small tranches, which makes it impossible to plan for economies of scale. Thus, an OEM will make his cost calculations on the demand for six Project 75i submarines. Had the plan been mooted for twenty submarines, it'd be a different, better, more cost-effective sub.'[76]

That the defence procurement system is a disaster is now conceded by the MoD, in a report authored by Subhash Bhamre, minister of state for defence. The report is stunningly honest in saying that weapons acquisition is hobbled by 'multiple and diffused structures with no single-point accountability, multiple decision heads, duplication of processes, delayed comments, delayed execution, no real-time monitoring, no project-based approach and a tendency to fault-find rather than to facilitate' as a result of which Make in India is languishing, it said, 'at the altar of procedural delays and has failed to demonstrate its true potential.' It disclosed that of 144 deals in three financial years (2015–18), only '8 per cent to 10 per cent fructified within the stipulated time period' and that the RFP stage took 2.6 to 15.4 times the allotted time, with RFP clearance taking anything from seventeen weeks to 422 weeks (eight years); that the trials and evaluation stage conducted by the military services takes an average of eighty-nine weeks—three times the allotted time. It is then messed up by issuing 'ambiguous trial directives, leaving scope for varied interpretation' and, by implication, manipulation by foreign vendors. It also concluded that the Technical Oversight Committee is a hindrance, doing no useful work, and that the Cost Negotiation Committee takes ten times its allotted time. If after all this when the proposal reaches the finance ministry it can be shot down, since it is not in the know of the MoD's plans. Bhamre also raises the issue of the finance ministry 'raining . . . numerous queries, a few of them of a basic nature' at every turn, slams the armed services for 'a lack of synergy' between them which 'puts greater strain on the limited defence budget and as a result, we are unable to meet the critical capability requirements' and excoriates the MoD for 'working in independent silos' fuelled by the concerned department's interpretation of policy and procedures.[77]

A pertinent question arises: How come Modi, who was elected on the basis of his 'can do' spirit, has so resisted reforming the existing broken-down system of Indian government? 'Let us assume Modi had asked for changes and for policies to be expedited. The usual thing that happens,' said a former senior military officer, 'is for MoD officials to tell the PMO that the issue is being "reviewed"—which is what it did when Manmohan Singh enquired about the lack of progress on the Japanese US-2 aircraft, but it is a review process without closure.' The constitution of the MoD's DAC doesn't help. For it to be effective, he said, DAC should ideally have only the defence minister, minister of state for defence, defence secretary, the three service chiefs, and chief of the integrated defence staff. In practice, DAC is populated by the defence secretary, secretary, defence production, head of DRDO, financial adviser and director general, acquisitions—all civilians—and the chairman, chiefs of staff committee. 'All these five *goondas* [thugs] gang up against the military man, who knows little about the requirements of the sister services, and so he has no chance, being regularly overwhelmed by technical information, negative attitude, and procedural curveballs thrown at him.'

This does not prevent the defence minister of the day from boasting, as Parrikar did, that he got DAC to approve ₹3 lakh crore worth of acquisition deals. But while such large expenditures are approved, the money is rarely released, other than sparingly. 'The reason,' explained a general who has spent time in the army headquarters and seen how the MoD works, 'is the system of integrated financial advisers (IFAs) overseen by the director general, IFA, MoD, who is ultimately beholden to the finance ministry. The IFA at the formation level usually negatives any procurement proposal that is forwarded without giving any reasons other than financial stringency, paucity of money. The IFAs generally are entirely ignorant of any technical knowledge or even expertise but feel free to overrule acquisition proposals at all higher levels of military organization.'[78] Just how extraordinarily ignorant and strategically blind these IFAs are and just how devastating their impact with regard even to decisive weapons systems can be is exemplified by the case of an additional financial adviser on the board of BrahMos Aerospace. He vetoed the proposal for indigenous manufacture of a light, more compact (at a third of the original length), new generation (NG) BrahMos—that the Russian equity partner had designed and developed—on the basis, as an exasperated missile engineer put it, that the old production line would become defunct, whence he ruled that the company should invest ₹1200 crore in the older, heavier ramjet engines instead! Of course, the fact that a Su-30MKI would be able to carry four of the NGs instead of just one, huge, older BrahMos did not convince him. This decision is of the same ilk as the one earlier mentioned of the joint secretary in the MoD rejecting procurement of the ShinMaywa amphibious US-2 plane because it did not carry weapons or the decision to keep Japan out of the annual Malabar naval exercises because that would upset China! There's nothing in the decision-making system in the entire government of India to reverse, leave alone prevent, such plainly foolish and even farcical decisions by incompetent generalist bureaucrats and IFAs who abound. Significantly, no one strongly objected to this decision because, well, everybody in the BrahMos organization is in his 'comfort zone' where any disturbance is disliked.[79]

The process of getting anything funded, any proposal cleared, is so onerous the military can do little. 'For a procurement proposal to pass requires signatures by 130 entities,' informed a general. 'Approval for Indian military officers to attend courses abroad or to go on a foreign tour involves assent by 137 officials in the government. By way of comparison, on any given issue for every paper generated in the US system, six papers are generated by its Indian counterpart.' Is there any interest in changing this system? Sure there is, but there is 'no political will to make any real big organizational changes or to reform the decision-making process dominated by the civilian bureaucracy and IFAs', he stated. So, why does Modi make promises, announce all sorts of things, but nothing gets done on the ground? 'Because,' he added, 'there's no follow-up. The PM is too busy with other, mostly political things, even with Amit Shah looking after the political end of business, to follow up and ensure implementation of his own decisions, announcements and promises. This is as true of domestic political matters as foreign and military policy issues.'[80]

The lack of progress was so frustrating that the exasperated ShinMaywa has all but pulled out of India, taken a step back, and is waiting for the two governments to forward the US-2 deal. Other Japanese companies, like Mitsubishi Heavy Industry, learning from ShinMaywa's experience, have likewise retreated, unenthusiastic about doing business with the MoD. 'This US-2 project is such a miss for the country,' said a person in the loop. 'They are giving everything in the world—they are so geostrategically keen. They have offered credit at 0.1 per cent interest, a plan to produce a nineteen-seater transport aircraft with Israeli collaboration in India based on the US-2 plan form. Delhi could have insisted that Tokyo offtake twenty to thirty Tejas LCAs as part of the deal—it doesn't matter what, that is the kind of deal the Japanese would agree to just to get the strategic partnership with India going. But the US-2 file is stuck. A fast approval for the production of this amphibious plane could be the biggest technology and industrial game-changer (as already detailed in the previous chapter), it being a straightforward government-to-government deal, involving no negotiation of prices, no *jhatkas* [shocks]. Look at the big picture. Japan is giving India everything—technology, knowledge of how to make parts and put the plane together, maintenance, repair, overhaul facility for the aircraft. So what's the MoD's problem? Too expensive. I can say that a Maruti Alto is too expensive; or if I'm better off that an Audi is too expensive. But you can't say this potato is available for ₹10 per kg and, therefore, why is the Maruti weighing 800 kg not for ₹8000, why are you asking ₹8 lakh for it? What kind of logic is that? That's the stupid logic often used by the MoD.

'Then there's the nonsensical idea of strategic partnership. I said to them, "Don't talk of strategic partnership a priori, it should be post-facto. So I told them,' this person said, 'that there are two kinds of methods to join things together. You can get wedded or you can get welded. When you get wedded the sparks fly after marriage. In the case of welding all the sparks fly before and once you are welded, that's it. Strategic partnership in the MoD is like a wedding—you could go to court, this is wrong, that is the contractual obligation, etc. That's a street to nowhere. Strategic partnership with countries like Japan need to be on the welded basis to be achieved by the highest level of political leadership, with bureaucracies on either side not allowed to intervene. And as far as large orders for hardware are concerned, first have a global tender for 1000 helicopters, say, invite bids, open to all comers. Whoever wins the tender will be the strategic partner. Choosing a strategic partner this way is a welding process because the financial incentive in such large orders will compel the partner to bring in the latest technology and manufacturing and project management practices. Such a simple thing. But DPP 2016 went ahead and broke up this process—how can a helicopter maker produce aircraft? But the winner of aircraft production is apparently the one who has put up a refinery?! This is fantastic logic that can't be beat. Even if the Indian government wants to favour crony capitalists, why make it so obvious? The fact is nobody in government really wants to make anything in India but babus [civil servants] who don't understand the a, b, c of manufacturing give private sector firms gyan [knowledge] on capping equity at this or that level.'[81]

Saraswat summed up the problem this way: 'There's a philosophy of doing things in India. If you continue doing what you have done in the last fifty years the country will continue to face the situation of poor indigenous capability. Certainly this is what's happening in all sectors of our technological growth. Our tendency to only take proven technology has put us in this trouble. Our early leaders thought that to bridge the immediate gap we should have licensed production. But the expectation that our institutions like the IITs and HAL would build their own machines didn't happen because very early licensed production became part of our DNA. By way of analogy, a generation has grown up in India with ready-to-eat foodstuff. Nobody now wants to cook food. And for everything we look abroad and get technology on a turnkey basis—for everything. In this milieu, how do you expect an aeroplane to be manufactured in the country?' Consequently, he said, 'Industry does not support anybody who wants to do anything new. So the gap remains both in terms of R&D and production. Why is it that a Russian company can manufacture 200 missiles per year and BDL only ten? The answer lies in totally revamping the system.'[82] It is the sort of revamp the country urgently needs and Modi promised but his government has not substantively even attempted. The problem of the gangrenous national security system helmed by a malfunctioning bureaucracy has been sought to be addressed by the prime minister with a band-aid solution when what is required is amputation. He has gone in for performance-based 'deep selections'. But when the system itself is so grievously flawed, what are the chances of a few good men turning things around?

The State of the Nuclear Deterrent and Shifting the Focus to China

In the seven decades of India's independent existence, China has had noticeable success in comprehensively outsmarting Delhi in every respect—political, diplomatic, economic and military. In the present day, its wealth and reach is such that it is now the equal of the United States. The Indian tortoise cannot match the Chinese hare, but what the former can do is use its nuclear weapons to regain the initiative on the LAC and elsewhere in Asia. This won't be easy considering the Indian government is not one to depart from the script that I have elsewhere described as 'deterrence by half measures'.[83]

The *Bulletin of Atomic Scientists* has advanced its famous 'Doomsday Clock' to two minutes to midnight, suggesting that nuclear Armageddon is closest to happening since the 1950s.[84] India seems not to have come to terms with this more dangerous world of the 21st century, especially in its nuclear security aspects. The Modi regime seems unperturbed, for instance, by the full-blown emergence of the rogue nuclear triad of China and its risk-taking acolytes, Pakistan and North Korea, which between them have all but dynamited the global nuclear order based on the 1968 Non-Proliferation Treaty (NPT). This is no bad thing to happen. India could have capitalized on the situation had the Modi government shown presence of mind, strategic purpose and nimbleness of policy to use North Korea's successful thermonuclear test in August 2017 and three test-firings of its Hwasong ICBMs in July and November to resume open-ended testing and to obtain proven high-yield fusion weapons that the Indian military can have confidence in. It was a missed opportunity and a strategic blunder the country will pay dearly for. There was sufficient provocation. The North Korean hydrogen bomb test had, after all, upended the comfortable certainties attending on the existing non-proliferation order that Delhi subscribes to. India could have justly explained its resumed underground testing as a reasonable response to unravelling regional and international nuclear security situations.

The Indian government, habitually fearful and fainthearted and eager to respect the strategic sensitivities of the US and China, did nothing. When juxtaposed against Kim Jong-un's airy dismissal of threats by

US President Trump as the ranting of a 'mentally deranged... hard-of-hearing dotard', his unveiling of a plan to nuke Guam, the US military's gigantic mid-Pacific island base and, nearer home, Pakistan Foreign Minister Khwaja Asif's gumption in replying to Trump's demand for Islamabad to 'do more' in Afghanistan with a statement that 'We will not do more', has shown India up as too diffident and weak-willed to matter.[85] North Korea's showing steel and Pakistan cheekiness signal a sea change in the strategic picture of Asia, not that it has even been noticed by Delhi, with Modi intoning such banalities at the 2018 Shangri La Conference in Singapore as 'Asia of rivalry will hold us back. Asia of cooperation will shape this century.'[86]

For one thing, the US nuclear security umbrella counts for a lot less to its Asian treaty allies—Japan, South Korea and the Philippines—because such security guarantees are much less credible now that Pyongyang can take out any city in the continental United States.[87] If Los Angeles is the price to pay for corralling North Korea, Kim Jong-un may be right in calculating that Washington would be unwilling to pay it. The US is unlikely to put itself in danger if Kim Jong-un starts firing his nuclear ordnance. This is at the heart of the problem of the 'extended deterrence' concept, which breaks down when the provider finds itself in the nuclear crosshairs of the very country it is providing security against. It is for these and other reasons that I had argued in 2008 that in the face of China, an unrestrained nuclear proliferator, and pliable nuclear client state, North Korea the chain reaction of Asian states going nuclear is inevitable. And that a nuclear weapons–armed Japan would be quickly followed by a nuclear weaponized South Korea and Taiwan—all countries with highly developed nuclear weapons programmes that were forced to shut down by America. I had also concluded that such a situation would help India because Asian states on the Chinese periphery bristling with nuclear weapons would automatically void China's strivings for hegemony.[88] In the rapidly changing nuclear context, what should India do? What is its best nuclear strategy?

There's always a penalty to be paid for a country getting its conventional military bearings wrong. The costs are infinitely higher in the strategic realm if, cued to a generalized threat and driven by vacuous thinking, the state's nuclear forces end up incapable of dissuading and deterring nuclear-armed adversaries, leave alone coercing or compelling them. It is precisely such concerns about the perceived deficiencies in the Indian nuclear doctrine, capabilities, strategy and posture that are fuelling the growing sentiment in the military and certain policy quarters to rectify them.

The international consensus is that there are two potential nuclear conflict areas—north-east Asia and the Indian subcontinent. The first involves North Korea, China and the US (with its allies South Korea and Japan), the other India, China and Pakistan. Then there's the active 'rogue triad' engaged in clandestine nuclear proliferation—China, Pakistan and North Korea.[89] In the three cases, China is the common factor as enabler and pivot, providing cover for Pakistan's and North Korea's nuclear build-up and relentlessly provocative policies. These two client states, in turn, enhance Beijing's diplomatic leverage as mediator with the US and Japan in the one case, and as security spoiler where India is concerned in the other. It is the capacity strategically to discomfit its main Asian rivals on its two flanks, Japan and India, that China prizes.[90] Without the secret and sustained programme of Chinese transfer of expertise, materials and technologies, Pakistan and North Korea would not be nuclear missile–armed states, or be able to modernize their nuclear arsenals and credibly prosecute their belligerent deterrence strategies premised on the threat of first, and imminent, use of nuclear weapons, while China stands by as cover in case their foolhardy posturing misfires.[91]

There are two ways to deal with these Chinese-centred triads: Try and disrupt the China–Pakistan and China–North Korea nuclear links and/or conceive and implement an aggressive strategy to negate and disturb the Chinese strategy and blunt Beijing's nuclear edge. The option of disruption—by covertly transferring nuclear weapons and missile technologies to Vietnam and any other capable state bordering China that wants them—has not been exercised by India owing to Delhi's traditionally shaky nerves and self-imposed restraint when it would be entirely within its rights to respond in kind and in a tit-for-tat manner.[92] India's inability, moreover, to envision an economic and security architecture in South Asia by co-opting Pakistan and rendering redundant its asymmetric low cost, high returns policy of using terror in Jammu and Kashmir is matched by its losing traction in the Korean peninsula when it thinned out its previous albeit military cooperation arrangement with Pyongyang presumably to please Washington.[93] The more daring policy would have been to solidify relations with a growingly isolated Pyongyang as, say, Russia did at precisely the time that the Xi Jinping regime tilted tactically towards the US at the expense of its North Korean ally, seeking to keep the mutually beneficial Sino-American relationship on an even keel. By strengthening its support for the Kim Jong-un government, Moscow's ability to deal with both Beijing and Washington has become stronger.[94]

India, in contrast, has thought that to be on the right side of the US is more important than the national interest.[95] Despite not being a signatory to the 1968 NPT India has played by its rules at the expense of its national security and gained little. Delhi is apparently unappreciative of the importance of joining the existing international nuclear order on its own terms and of the fact that a country's reputation as an international rule-breaker, spoiler and disruptor fetches bigger diplomatic and political dividends in terms of bargaining outcomes and strengthening nuclear deterrence than lugging the burden of being a 'responsible' state. Not saddled by self-limiting strictures, China, Pakistan and North Korea, which also claim to be responsible nuclear states, have with their keen sense of realpolitik, scrupled to nothing to protect their freedom of sovereign action, enlarge their nuclear arsenals and improve the quality and reach of their weapons and delivery systems while shrugging off Western criticism and pressure to rein in their risky and destabilizing policy of prompt use.[96]

In the last ten years Pakistan has commissioned four Chinese-designed bomb-grade plutonium-producing reactors in Khushab, operationalized a plutonium separation unit and has the fastest-growing nuclear weapons stockpile in the world.[97] In the same time-frame, North Korea conducted six tests and emerged as a thermonuclear military with ICBMs and miniaturized hydrogen warheads.[98] The result is that these two nuclear outlier states have fortified their security, improved their negotiating position and retained their freedom of action. India, meanwhile, has stayed mired in an un-nuanced minimum deterrence stance armed with untested and unproven high-yield fusion weapons, which will be the goad in a serious strategic crisis for China, or even Pakistan, to call Delhi's bluff.

Elsewhere, the Indian government's tendency to keep the Indian deterrent and everything associated with it under wraps is contrasted by Islamabad and Pyongyang injecting credibility into their nuclear postures by either creating conflict situations or using crisis to hint that conventional hostilities could speedily transition to the nuclear level. Regional and international tensions as a consequence get ratcheted upward as do efforts to placate them. These incidents raise temperatures and alarms, but help in legitimating their status as nuclear weapon states. A global NPT-based nuclear order sensitive to instability would sooner concede such status to Pakistan and North Korea and pile them with nuclear deals of the kind India and Iran procured from the US and the NSG than see the extant order breakdown.[99] From the Chinese, Pakistani and North Korean experience, one can surmise that India could resume nuclear testing to obtain for itself a safe and reliable thermonuclear arms inventory without worrying overmuch about the bad consequences as Delhi tends to do. The P-5 states, modernizing their nuclear arsenals and weapons platforms, cannot afford to show ire lest India disavow the NPT system altogether. Moreover, the strategic situation in Asia for most of the rest of the 21st century will likely be such that Washington, the chief objector to India's testing, cannot afford to rub India the wrong way, not if it is serious about having a regional state with the requisite heft on its side to counterbalance China in Asia.

Pakistan's Hollow Threat of 'First Use'

A successful policy to gain political recognition as a nuclear weapon state does not, by itself, transform a state like Pakistan into a meaningful nuclear military power, even less a threat to India. Objectively speaking, Pakistan does not pose a serious danger to the Indian state for the Indian military to overly worry about it. But the Indian armed services have declared that a full-fledged conventional war with Pakistan is unlikely owing to 'the nuclear overhang', in effect, validating the Pakistani view that the threat of 'first use' works.[100] This may embolden Islamabad into taking higher-order military risks.

The threat of first use is stoked by Pakistan's carefully cultivated image as an unpredictable and volatile state. In reality though, the Deep State represented by the Pakistani Army has been remarkably cautious, rational and pragmatic in judging Delhi's tolerance threshold and never crossing it. Consider the 26/11 seaborne strike by the Pakistani Army's ISI-controlled terrorist teams in 2008. I had pointed out at that time that had the Pakistani aim been to cripple the Indian Navy, the strike teams could have easily done that by including frogmen-saboteurs to sink the largely unprotected warships constituting much of India's Western Fleet at anchor in the Mumbai harbour, literally a stone's throw away from where the terrorists landed, and which would have involved only a slight deviation in the team's approach from the sea. Pakistan could have achieved a Pearl Harbor–like spectacular when the Imperial Japanese naval air force sank a large chunk of the US Pacific Fleet in its main base in Hawaii with a surprise attack on 7 December 1941. But, in the no-holds-barred war that would have inevitably followed, Pakistan, facing not the usual inconsequential war of manoeuvre as most India–Pakistan tussles have tended to be, but a war of annihilation, would have been decimated.

In the event, the Pakistani Army was satisfied with the headbutt to the Indian security establishment by the highly motivated jihadis shooting up two Mumbai hotels and a railway terminus and showing up the supposedly multi-tiered Indian maritime security system as weak and leaky. Or, take the 1965 war in which Pakistan agreed to a negotiated peace in Tashkent: Its supplies were down to six days of war (compared to India's ten). The Pakistani Army's propensity to take risks and action is persisted with but only up to a point when India begins to get serious about the war on its hands. Such caution highlights the unique nature of the India–Pakistan conflict dyad marked by restrained wars of manoeuvre and limited counterforce actions owing to the two countries sharing common civilizational and cultural space, and buttressed by the ongoing kith and kinship ties between divided communities.[101]

Countries consider war viable if they stand to gain more from engaging in it than by not doing so. In the modern era of conflict when war can prove fatal to the weaker party instigating it, the 'exchange ratio' (ER) is the metric to decide whether or not to go to war. ER is the ratio of the amount of destruction caused to the adversary to the amount of destruction absorbed by one's own country. If the ER is assessed to be bearable, military action follows, but this ratio will always tilt against Pakistan, the smaller, weaker, state. Despite Islamabad's rapidly enlarging weapons holdings, in any conceivable nuclear war scenario Pakistan will face certain extinction, meaning it will disappear in the Herbert Spencerian sense as a social organism. The destruction of parts of Indian metropolitan areas, say, of Delhi and Mumbai will be horrible but, in the larger scheme of things, these are losses India, with its extensive land mass, can absorb. In exchange the Pakistani state will be terminated. Pakistan's major problem is that it is vulnerable and offers easy target sets. The economic and demographic distribution in that country is such that all its major population centres and wealth-producing areas—Gujranwala, Sialkot, Lahore, Bahawalpur, Rahim Yar Khan and Mirpur Khas—are arrayed in a north-south line not far from the Indian border and within short reach of India's weapons. In fact, in a post-mortem of the 1965 war, General Ayub Khan pointed out to his divisional commanders that this highly vulnerable 'strategic corridor' was Pakistan's fatal weakness.[102]

In this context, how credible is Pakistan's 'first use' philosophy resting on the belief that such threat deters and, in any case, should deterrence breakdown, that the country would somehow survive a nuclear exchange? Given the concentration of exposed high-value Pakistani targets in the 'corridor', this belief doesn't hold. Together with a completely unfavourable ER, it should convince the Special Plans Division (SPD), Chaklala—the Pakistani nuclear secretariat—nuclear forces command and agency with oversight of nuclear arms production all rolled into one, that Pakistan cannot afford a nuclear war no matter what the Indian 'provocation', and why its talk of nuclear first use is, in practical terms, hollow.

Pakistan has a forward defence-in-strength policy nestling within which is the fear of Indian armoured and mechanized forces breaching its defences. The initiation of tactical nuclear weapons against aggressor Indian units inside Pakistani territory is seen by Pakistan as a means of dissuading India from advancing into Pakistan's heartland corridor in the first place by creating uncertainty around the extent of penetration inside its territory that would trigger a tactical nuclear response. Islamabad, perhaps, envisages that between its first tactical nuclear hit and whatever happens next there will be space for concerned big powers (US and/or China, in the main) to step in and even prevent an Indian nuclear retaliation. After all, the US reinforced the bent of the Indian government of Vajpayee after the 2001 attack on Parliament and under Manmohan Singh in 2008 after the seaborne strike on Mumbai not to retaliate.

The possibility of such external intervention can be increased if its initial firing is immediately announced as accidental owing to the confusion and 'fog of war'. In the 'best case' scenario for Pakistan of big powers keeping India from unleashing its full range of nuclear counterstrikes, Pakistan will be able to hold its ground, get away with violating the long-standing nuclear non-use taboo, not really suffer any consequences and, by way of a psychological ploy, slyly send a message to Delhi that it is game for nuclear war-fighting. The 'worst case' would be that as per the 2003 official Indian doctrine, massive retaliation will follow, which Pakistan cannot survive. A 'median' scenario may involve India departing from its doctrinal script and reacting with a proportional nuclear tactical strike—'a flexible response'—on Pakistani armoured units inside Pakistan instead. In the wake of such action-reaction nuclear hits a containable situation could emerge with extraterritorial powers definitely and forcefully intervening to head off further escalation into the uncharted category of uncontrolled nuclear exchange involving densely populated crowded cities.[103] There are three critical assumptions here that (1) the big powers will, in fact, so intervene, (2) India can be so pressured into reacting in the manner Pakistan anticipates, and (3) Pakistan's tactical nuclear first use will have only localized battlefield consequences for it, which last may not be the case, whence the previous two assumptions stand negated.

Consider why such self-serving assumptions are wrong. A single low-yield (1 or 2 kiloton) strike on an aggressor Indian armoured formation inside Pakistan may in fact have strategic ramifications. This is how: The fireball from the mini-nuclear strike will rise, forming an irradiated debris cloud that stabilizes around a 1 to 3 mile altitude where rain-bearing clouds usually form. Further, that radioactive rain would be induced by the seeding effects of the debris downwind of ground zero in a 5 to 10 square km area.[104] In the 'campaign season' of north Indian winters, moreover, the winds blow west to east. Depending on how far inside Pakistan Indian tanks are struck by Pakistani nuclear ordnance, there's every chance of the resulting radioactive clouds drifting over the border with the prevailing winds, and the precipitation occurring on Indian towns well inside India and affecting a large Indian population with radioactivity.[105] Even if not so intended, the Pakistani tactical nuclear use would amount to the targeting of the Indian civilian population. The traditional restraint shown by Delhi, or the possibility Pakistan may be banking on of the retaliatory Indian response being tempered by mediating foreign countries, will not then obtain, and a disproportionate nuclear reply, if not 'massive retaliation', will surely follow.

The initial Pakistani tactical nuclear attack, moreover, may not even succeed in stopping a massed advance by Indian armour. While cities can be destroyed with nuclear devices generating 3 to 5 pound per square inch (PSI) over-pressure, the reason why Pakistan would avoid attacking urban conglomerations for fear of large-scale nuclear bombardment of its own cities by India, a formation of tanks operating in 'hatch-down' mode in an irradiated environment can, however, survive low-kiloton strikes. For instance, a single crewless Centurion tank with the Australian Army, placed 500 yards from Ground Zero of an 8 kiloton air burst in an atomic test on 15 October 1953 (Operation Totem) conducted at the Woomera test range, suffered not at all from radiation and thermal effects. Indeed, that particular tank went on to be used in military operations thereafter. But, a crew inside the tank would have been killed by the shock wave.[106]

Extrapolating from that result, one can surmise that the indigenous 60 tonne Arjun MBT (the equivalent of the US M1A2 Abrams), for instance, with the layered Chobham-type armour, would remain unscathed 500 metres from Ground Zero, with the tactical nuclear weapon exploding at a height of 50 metres and generating 258.6 kiloPascal (or 37.5 PSI) over-pressure.[107] If depleted uranium is made part of Arjun MBT Mk-2's armour material (as is the case with the Abrams tank), it will be even more survivable, because uranium absorbs deadly gamma rays and X-rays emitted by atomic fission. So, the spearhead of a few Arjun tanks (or T-90s/72s) would be stopped because the crews inside them would be killed by the shock wave, and these tanks could end up being deactivated. But the rest of the formation, skirting the radiation zone, can continue advancing to achieve their objective in dispersed mode to minimize the effects of more Pakistani tactical nuclear attacks.[108]

Moreover, Pakistan will need to fire a very large number of tactical nuclear weapons to seriously impede an Indian armoured bull run by independent armoured brigades, leave alone stanch a full-bore armoured attack. But such an attack would only materialize if India goes to war determined on a 'final solution' of dismantling the Pakistani state which, short of sufficient provocation, is inconceivable. Even so, what would the size of the Pakistani tactical nuclear weapons stockpile have to be for such contingency? To destroy 50 per cent of the 500-plus armoured vehicles of all kinds in an armoured division advancing over a 15 km front and deployed to a depth of 25 km will require, by one calculation, expenditure of between 257 and 436 15 kiloton tactical nuclear weapons. With 8 kiloton yield weapons, the number of tactical nuclear weapons to achieve the same result would rise to 391 to 663.[109] Assuming Pakistan has, in fact, miniaturized a 2 kiloton nuclear warhead, say, to fit the 40 mm to 60 mm diameter Nasr battlefield missile which, incidentally, could not have happened without active Chinese help, by linear extrapolation some 2652 of these rockets would have to be fired to have the same effect. Pakistan is nowhere near acquiring such enormous numbers of low-yield atomic weapons. And in any case, the use of even a small fraction of these will herald a war of annihilation of Pakistan. So, Islamabad's huffing and puffing about first use is essentially to play on Delhi's queasiness about such a denouement and should be seen for what it is—a stratagem, a ruse de guerre.

If 'total war' against Pakistan is not the goal and the Indian Army needs a face-saving strategy to justify its capital-draining three armoured, mechanized-unit-heavy strike corps, 'Cold Start' is the wrong one to implement. Incidentally, the Pakistani military believes it was the first to test the concept of space for conventional conflict under the nuclear overhang by surreptitiously capturing the Kargil heights in 1999 and that this operation inspired the Indian Army's 'Cold Start' doctrine.[110] Moving fast, penetrating deep to capture a sizeable amount of real estate as bargaining chip but not deep enough to threaten Pakistan's survival and hasten first use of tactical nuclear weapons, requires the aggregating of eight Independent Battle Groups (IBGs) from the armoured and mechanized units in the three strike corps and pivot formations even as they are on the move to get to the staging areas. This is what the Indian Army trains for and is confident it can pull off in real battle.[111] But such complicated manoeuvres of heavy battle mass is better managed on paper, sand models and even in 'war exercises' (such as the 2009 'Yog Shakti' involving II Corps) than in war, where nothing goes according to plan. And further, because only a 'shallow' penetration is planned for—the capture of some arid acreage around Rahim Yar Khan—such plans make little cost-benefit sense.[112] In fact, Rahim Yar Khan is posited as a likely 'funnel' that the Pakistani Army has deliberately created to draw in Indian IBGs, the easier to destroy them. This is so, says a senior general who has advised the Modi government, because of 'the wrongest decision' by the Vajpayee government in 2001 when having mobilized the military it refrained from going to war. Pakistan learned from that episode and quickly 'plugged all the holes' in terms of sensor placements and surveillance gaps along the rest of the border, leaving the approaches to Rahim Yar Khan invitingly open. Should the Indian Army be tempted to force the issue, it will find Pakistani armour quickly 'closing the trap'. In any case, he believes, the Pakistani Army has so fortified the entire front that the Indian strike forces will make 'little headway' and, in the event, that Cold Start is infructuous.[113]

In 2002, I had detailed a more doable alternative strategy designed to gain valuable assets inside Pakistan as negotiating card while zeroing out the possibility of that country initiating nuclear weapons use. I had dubbed this the 'Sialkot Grab' strategy involving Indian land forces investing cities—such as Sialkot in Pakistan's heartland corridor adjoining the border—in full strength and pressing an advance into them to precipitate hysteria and pandemonium. This advance, I had suggested, was to be maintained in lockstep with the Pakistani civilian population retreating to the hinterland, making defensive actions by the Pakistani army impossible and also rendering infeasible the use of tactical nuclear weapons for fear of vaporizing their own people and urban areas. Pakistani first use, I had argued, would thus be obviated by the civilian population of the city intent on escaping it. This would also make orderly withdrawal for the Pakistani Army units from the besieged city's environs difficult and with the advancing Indian forces there will, in any case, be no space separating the withdrawing Pakistani units from the advancing Indian formations for Pakistan to trigger tactical nuclear weapons in its own urban areas—the first step in the escalatory ladder planned for by the Pakistan Strategic Plans Division (SPD). The idea behind such a border-city-grab strategy is not to offer Pakistan the open terrain in which to exercise its first-use pledge but rather to physically gain a prized city as a card to negotiate a final delineation of the LoC as settled international border, and otherwise to present the Pakistani Army with impossibly difficult choices at every turn, compelling Islamabad to sue for peace.[114] In addition, the Indian Special Forces would be tasked, in this scenario, with destroying the Pakistani nuclear command and control hubs and fighting assets, which IAF chief Air Chief Marshal B.S. Dhanoa has said he can do with aerial strikes.[115] For the strikes to be successful, the Indian armed services, including the Special Forces, would have to be primed by high-order real-time intelligence on targets via a 24/7 'watch and track' regime encompassing seamless intelligence cooperation and coordination between the R&AW, military intelligence, and aerial and satellite-based surveillance and target-tracking information. Leaked news reports about such activity will be a real dampener for nuclear adventurism by Pakistan and be an active psychological means of dissuasion.

Considering how easily the Pakistani threat of first use can thus be thwarted, it is something of a mystery why the Indian government and military continue to give credence to Pakistan as a nuclear threat or support the Cold Start strategy, which is not practicable and which the GHQ considers a nuclear tripwire.[116] And further, it reveals also the institutional habit of mind of the Indian government and armed services of gearing up to tackle the lesser Pakistan threat the old-fashioned way than preparing for the more difficult nuclear war-fighting. This, in turn, indicates that, perhaps, Cold Start is persisted with as justification for a wasteful and outdated force structure featuring armoured and mechanized forces that would have fared well in the Second World War and even the 1965 war with Pakistan. It also reflects the unfamiliarity of Indian policymakers and senior military personnel with the nuclear deterrence dynamic, whence the stock statements emanating from them that nuclear weapons are meant for deterrence, not war-fighting, and their touching belief that the threat of 'massive retaliation' (per the nuclear doctrine) is the answer for all strategic contingencies. The sheer disproportionality of such reaction and its lack of credibility led the 1999 draft nuclear doctrine to talk of 'punitive retaliation with nuclear weapons to inflict damage unacceptable to the aggressor'.[117]

After all, in response to a tactical nuclear strike on an aggressing Indian armoured squadron inside Pakistan, would Delhi really order the nuclear bombing of Karachi or Lahore? The rigidity and predictability of the 'massive retaliation' response that was inserted instead in the doctrine, courtesy the Brajesh Mishra–run PMO, is a liability imposed on the country's nuclear calculus by the 2004 nuclear doctrine. This was pointed out early and has been the grist for such public debate as has taken place on the subject since.[118] As also the fact that should push ever come to nuclear shove, Pakistan is in no position to ensure its own survival. The really skewed 'exchange ratio' is the main motivation, I have argued, for Islamabad doing whatever is necessary to avoid getting into a situation where it has to make good its 'first use' threat.[119] In short, Pakistan has no 'least bad' nuclear option to nurse; its options are all equally bad.

But Pakistan has one huge advantage: It holds its nerves better in crisis. India, on the other hand, is rarely calm and collected. Cases in point: the aftermath of the 2001 attack on Parliament and the 26/11 attack on Mumbai in 2008. Delhi did not, in the first instance, order instantaneous retaliation by air strikes after the terrorist attack on Parliament, but a general mobilization for war and then was unwilling to wage it. In the latter episode, again there was no instant retribution but a whole lot of frenzied helter-skelter. Pakistan has learned not to be intimidated, highlighting in the process that country's success in making much out of what realistically is militarily little and India, in contrast, routinely fluffing it when it comes to exercising hard power even when amply provoked.[120] The only consequential threat India faces is China, but Delhi seems too squeamish to take it on, or even to seriously prepare for it. Would the Deep State in Pakistan not be emboldened by the almost comic Indian response to ISI-managed terrorist incidents to arrange a terrorist strike in an Indian metropolis with a radiation diffusion device or 'dirty bomb'?

And, with respect to the 'modernization' of the 'nuclear' component of Indian strategic forces, how will it be managed without a resumption of nuclear testing to secure a certifiable thermonuclear weapon design? According to K. Santhanam, director of field tests in 1998, the fusion device (S-1) tested in Pokhran was merely 'proof of principle but not maturity of design and technology' and, therefore, 'cannot be' considered 'a one-time execute'. India, he said, 'is jinxed until we have the leadership, the chances of India conducting [more] tests is very, very bleak'.[121] Modi was considered by many to be the man to end this jinx. He has turned out not to be the strong leader he made himself out to be. However, if a strong leader does emerge on the Indian scene, he can nearly instantly carry out nuclear tests because per the DRDO chief Christopher Raj there are L-shaped tunnels available in the Rajasthan desert to do so at 'short notice'.[122]

With the underground testing in abeyance, has the Indian government done the next best thing and provided advanced testing paraphernalia to the weapons-designing unit at the Bhabha Atomic Research Centre (BARC), Trombay to help them finesse the manifestly faulty hydrogen weapon design the best they can? It turns out that the government, in the twenty years after the announcement of the voluntary moratorium on testing, has still not invested in the DARHT (dual axis radiographic hydrodynamic test) facility to generate computer codes for nuclear weapons and to refine the radiation channel and the implosion triggers for them. Worse, the small inertial confinement fusion (ICF) chamber at the Centre for Advanced Technology in Indore used for triggering miniature thermonuclear explosions by concentrating powerful laser beams on nuggets of fissile material to refine to improve and upgrade thermonuclear weapons designs is, according to a senior scientist who worked there, suffering from gross neglect and is in a state of utter disrepair. The air conditioning systems to cryogenically maintain the lasers at extremely low temperatures, for instance, are broken down and have not been repaired for years.[123] When asked about it R. Chidambaram, blamed by many nuclear scientists for deliberately atrophying the Indian nuclear weapons programme, who in early 2018 was finally removed from his post as science adviser to the prime minister, reacted defensively, asking, 'How do you know? Who told you that?'[124]

Meanwhile, China may have gifted the SPD a DARHT system installed at the Special Weapons Facility in Khushab, the site of the four military-dedicated 50 MW weapons-grade plutonium producing reactors built with Chinese help.[125]

Aggressively Blunting the China Threat

If Delhi and the Indian armed services paid as much attention to the long-standing and comprehensive threat posed by China as they do the minimal danger from Pakistan (which can be effectively neutralized with appropriate means such as the use of Special Forces for sustained counter-subconventional warfare, for instance), India would not dissipate its military resources the way it has been doing for the sixty-odd years, the 1962 war having taught the government and military nothing.[126]

In 1979, China and India were at the same economic level, with their militaries too qualitatively on par. Since then, like its economy that has grown five times as large, the Chinese military, fuelled by a hyperactive defence industry, has leapfrogged to become a peer competitor to the US, even conceiving novel armaments to meet specific needs, such as the anti-ship ballistic missile system. There's not a genus of weaponry PLA forces use that China has not designed and developed itself or reverse-engineered from foreign technology that it has bought, stolen or otherwise contrived to lay its hands on.[127] And unlike India, Beijing has been diligent in continually modernizing its strategic arsenal with simulations of thermonuclear tests whose frequency have far exceeded those by the US. Between September 2014 and December 2017, China carried out over 200 nuclear test simulations at its Mianyang facility in south-western Sichuan compared to fifty by the US in the period 2012 to 2017. It has developed a 'multi-stage gas gun' for the purpose. The new more usable thermonuclear weapons being perfected combined with the hypersonic glide weapons—a field China is the leader in—will eventuate in weapons capable of precise destruction with little radioactivity.

This is in the context of $1.2 trillion that President Trump has set aside for modernizing its nuclear weapons inventory, and Russia developing a nuclear torpedo to devastate coastal cities and unveiling new strategic bomber, nuclear-powered submarines, and the 6800 mile range RS-28 Sarmat MIRV missile able to carry fifteen warheads, the RS-26 Rubezh hypersonic missile, and the Kinzhal air-launched cruise missile.[128] To the extent that any Asian country has the potential to take on China, it is India but, sadly, it has shown neither the spirit nor the mettle for such a role. Rather, India has over the decades consistently marginalized itself. It hasn't helped that its armed forces are still mostly industrial age with no institutional capacity for transformative change and totally dependent on imported weaponry and, hence, can be brought to a grinding halt in war by arms-supplying states who, in pursuit of their interests, can close off or tighten to a trickle the spares supply spigot.[129]

Denied the easy option of buying strategic wherewithal from abroad owing to technology sanctions imposed on the country after the 1974 nuclear test, India successfully designed, developed and indigenously met its top strategic needs, including nuclear-powered ballistic missile-firing submarines, advanced and accurate missiles so far limited by government diktat to intermediate range, and nuclear weapons/warheads of proven 20 kiloton yield.[130] For obvious reasons, this is the only military capability that India has whose use cannot be restricted for want of spares and service support. But can this strategic military capability by itself dull the sharp edges of China's comprehensive military prowess? It can and this is how.

China's manifest superiority in the conventional military field and in allied cyber warfare and militarized space systems, driven by a nearly self-sufficient national defence industry, leaves India with no other alternative than to opt for a nuclear 'first use' policy. The revision of the operational doctrine can be done in-house by the Special Programme Staff (SPS) under the NSA in the PMO established during Manmohan Singh's prime ministership with the brief to calibrate strategy and flesh out tactics in a nuclear battlefield, and relay these to the Strategic Forces Command for implementation. It will avoid the very public revision of the nuclear doctrine that the ruling BJP promised in its 2014 election manifesto, which can bring in its train needless external attention and pressure. SPS, styled in the manner of the Pakistani SPD, has, however, failed so far to do even the basic stuff for a nuclear secretariat, such as working out the protocol for mating the warheads to the missiles involving three stakeholders—SFC, BARC and DRDO—and writing qualitative requirements for miniaturized nuclear warheads. This is necessary because SFC won't do it—it's approach to nuclear weapons being that of the armed services to conventional armaments, which a senior rocket scientist summarized as: 'Give us the weapons, tell us what you want done, what to hit, we'll do the rest.'[131]

The Himalayas are not impenetrable, but the high mountain range separating Tibet and the western Chinese provinces from India do constitute a formidable logistics barrier to the PLA undertaking free-flowing military operations across it. It is an obstacle Beijing wants to get around, whence the latest Chinese offer of border settlement of Arunachal Pradesh minus the Tawang division.[132] A Chinese Tawang would be the proverbial foot in the door. Once militarily ensconced on this side of the McMahon Line, the PLA backed by pre-positioned stores continually replenished by the Qinghai-Lhasa railway with its new spur line to Shigatze would expose the Indian mountain defences west of Tawang to attacks from the flank and enable at will concerted Chinese conventional forays to the Brahmaputra. But absent such lodgement in strength in Tawang, the PLA cannot force the issue, not with the three-odd Indian Army divisions emplaced in that sector.

The localized conventional military stalemate in Arunachal Pradesh and generally along the LAC, however, hides a disturbing reality of a strategically outmanoeuvred India. By relentlessly competing with the US for dominance in Asia, China (with its BRI and Asian Infrastructure Investment Bank and its cultivation of naval basing options in the Indian Ocean Region in Kyakpau, Myanmar, Hambantota, Sri Lanka, Gwadar, Pakistan, Mombassa, Kenya, in Djibouti on the Horn of Africa, and possibly the Maldives) has put itself in a geostrategically advantageous position. It joins the US as the other nodal international power, long ago surpassing India in regional, Asian and global power politics. However, none of these ports and potential replenishment stations, other than Gwadar and Djibouti, will be available to China in war, because these other small states cannot afford to have India as an enemy, even though they may get close to China to increase leverage with Delhi.

Further, China's versatile—mainly thermonuclear—fighting arm, the Second Artillery Strategic Forces (SASF), considered a match for the once superior American and Russian nuclear arsenals, can overwhelm the under-strength Indian SFC equipped mainly with the low-yield (20 kiloton) fission weapons and untested, unproven and unreliable higher-yield fusion armaments. Numbers-wise, the block-headed Indian government continues to swear by a small but 'credible' nuclear force that has fewer nuclear warheads and missiles than Pakistan and is half the size of its Chinese counterpart. They seem entirely unmindful of two facts, that its 'massive retaliation' doctrine actually necessitates large nuclear forces and that deterrence has a critical dimension, something the Chinese Second Artillery Strategic Forces and Pakistan's SPD understand well. In the event that use or threat of use of nuclear weapons is, among other things, a function of the numbers in the opponent's weapons inventory as also the yield of these weapons. Meaning that force size matters as does the maximum yield of weapons.[133] A Pakistan with a larger missile force will be psychologically readier to challenge an India it sees as having outmatched, and a China with a far bigger and more advanced and venomous arsenal with high-yield weapons, is like the python moving slowly on a rabbit to consume it, this even as the minders of the puny Indian nuclear force are convinced that what they have is 'credible'.[134]

China struts around menacingly, while a strategically unsure India struggles with managing the ceasefire line in Kashmir with a lowly Pakistan—China's premier client in the region. All Delhi has done so far is talk and then talk some more about security cooperation with littoral countries on the Chinese periphery and Japan, obtaining precious little on the ground to achieve this goal. The bureaucratic hold-ups of decisions that Modi promised, such as regarding the Japanese US-2 amphibious aircraft along with its production technology, to transfer the BrahMos supersonic cruise missiles to Vietnam and other South East Asian nations, to activate a billion-dollar credit line to Mongolia (already dilated on), has strengthened the impression of an India as an indecisive country that cannot be depended on in a crunch.

Worse, Delhi does its reputation no good when it bends over backwards to accommodate Beijing when standing up to it would serve national interests better. Doklam, in that sense, seems a one-off incident. Whatever Delhi's reason for cold-shouldering Canberra, the fact that it disallowed an eager Australian Navy, for example, from participating in the July 2017 annual Malabar naval exercise with the US and Japan in the Bay of Bengal for fear of upsetting China told its own story.[135] Without vision and political will, what has prevented India's strategic deportment from being reduced to nullity is the Agni-5 intermediate range ballistic missile (IRBM) featuring composite rocket motors, guidance on chip and high accuracy at extreme range, and the Arihant-class nuclear submarines. Deemed by China as an ICBM, the Agni-5 has singlehandedly, induced wariness in Beijing.[136] Jitters are also no doubt being induced in Chinese strategic circles by the accelerated schedule of injecting into precise orbits multiple satellites from single space launch vehicles (SLVs), which technology is a MIRV missile capability in situ, enabling a single missile to carry a number of warheads and strike geographically separated targets.[137] It is evidence of the Indian mastery of MIRV technology that will require to be displayed for it to have a multiplier effect. It also showcases the Indian capacity in the making to put up a constellation of indigenous GPS satellites and, in the future, space-based weapons platforms.[138] The Chinese apprehensions about these Indian missile and space capabilities need to be stoked not with words but with deeds as a means of tempering that country's belligerence.

Incorporating Nuclear First Use against China

A China that has risen speedily and spectacularly to prominence is unlikely to be easily diverted from its goal of showing up its notional Asian rival, India, as spineless and as likely to fold at the first hint of trouble. It is something Indian policymakers and war-planners need to focus on, a task that will be helped by clarifying certain basic trends in Chinese strategic thinking relevant in the Sino-Indian context.

Chinese military planners believe, for instance, that coercion and compellance are synonymous with strategic deterrence; that to coerce or compel an adversary state is necessarily to also deter it, albeit pre-emptively. So when the PLA forces staged intrusions or demolished Indian border posts and camera systems and other sensors as happened in the Demchok area of Ladakh in 2014 it was a show of force to warn India that they can at any time do a lot worse. In the Chinese strategic lexicon, moreover, 'challenge' and 'threat' are interchangeable. This is not the case with the Indian foreign and military policy mindset which is imitative of US and Western policy notions. The MEA and MoD view China as challenge and Pakistan as threat and strangely channel more national security attention, resources and effort to dealing with the latter. Also, importantly, China perceives deterrence as the outcome of restraining nuclear weapons use by enemy states, which may be another way of restating the mutually assured destruction principle central to Western and now universal idea of nuclear deterrence. But it takes on a more dynamic meaning when juxtaposed against two other tenets of the new Chinese strategic thought, namely, that 'small wars become big' and because escalation can be deliberate or it can be accidental, that states may be able to control one without being able wholly to control the other.[139] In this respect, senior PLA general staff officers are increasingly vocal about using the DF-21 missile for 'theatre precision strike', campaigning with low-yield weapons and about the utility of missiles with 'special warheads', presumably neutron warheads, to kill the local population without harming the physical structures, and with electromagnetic pulse warheads to knock off communications and power grids.[140]

All these points suggest how China may utilize nuclear weapons. But an understanding about what circumstances would push Beijing into actually using them in an armed conflict may be a better pointer of the Chinese nuclear threshold and indicate how best to shape and leverage a manifestly inferior Indian nuclear weapons position against China. After studying internal debates within PLA and Chinese deterrence literature, Western analysts have concluded that the US is in a position to, if not completely disarm China of its nuclear capability with a conventional counter-force strategy using its superior capabilities, including advanced remote-controlled drones, sensors, and cyber wherewithal, then to hugely damage SASF assets. In this situation, its espousal of 'no first use' notwithstanding, Beijing would risk limited nuclear escalation with low-yield precision weapons.[141]

India is facing a China with a conventional military edge and far superior nuclear forces, backed by proven offensive cyber warfare and unmatchable military infrastructure on its side of the disputed border, the LAC. Hence, in terms of the logistics system, it will be able, if it deploys its full comprehensive might, to conduct decisive conventional military operations. What is India to do? Its present policy of mobile warfare in the mountains to maintain a defensive around a prepared line in the Himalayas has limitations. It can meet hostile Chinese action with localized counter-offensives but, in the prevailing conditions of deficient rail, road and communications systems and border infrastructure, and with inter-valley connectivity in the east missing—gaps that won't be made up until 2025 at the earliest—the Indian presence along the LAC can be overwhelmed by massed PLA actions. Here the value of atomic demolition munitions (ADMs) is self-evident, as I have argued, because these are passive nuclear weapons that could be triggered only after the PLA has advanced in sufficient strength well inside Indian territory. The onus for triggering them will then rest squarely with the aggressor China. Further, ADMs mesh with India's passive-defensive thinking and force alignment on the LAC.[142]

But ADMs bringing down whole mountain sides with minimum venting of radioactivity on deeply intruding PLA units will work best in the east where there are only so many ingress routes for the PLA to consider. The central sector of the LAC features high-altitude mountain passes and are not easy for large military units and elaborate logistics trains to negotiate. The difficult terrain inherently inhibits sustained military activity across it. In the Ladakh–Aksai Chin sector in the west, however, the ground favours easier transgression by the PLA supported by extensive high-quality road and communications networks. Here, ADMs are not a practicable solution but area weapons such as the potentially 1 to 2 kiloton nuclear-tipped, 60 km range, road-mobile Prahar tactical cruise missile can prove an ample deterrent. In a situation where Pakistan and China act in concert—which is probable given an army division's worth of PLA troops already present in Baltistan in POK—the Indian army will be hard put conventionally to resist a determined PLA rush into Ladakh and/or its lunge towards Tawang. Unless the first use of ADMs and the nuclearized Prahar missile is speedily incorporated into nuclear battlefield concepts practised by the SFC coordinating with the Leh-based XIV Corps in the west and the Sukna-based XXXIII Corps in the east.

But such deployment and 'first use' of ADMs and nuclearized Prahar missiles will require prior public hints by the Indian government about the 'red lines' that China better respect lest it find itself in a situation where its actions automatically trigger the use of ADMs and the N-Prahar cruise missiles. Such a position, because it enhances deterrence by shrouding one's own response in uncertainty is, as Thomas Schelling seminally argued, a strategy that 'leave[s] something to chance'.[143] A policy of deliberate escalation to the nuclear level then has to be included in the menu of options available to the Indian strategic forces in-theatre. This innovation would have to be part of the process to rethink deterrence as applicable specifically to India's confrontation with China and, more generally, to ways of beefing up the country's nuclear security. This process has to include the revision of the existing nuclear doctrine stressing the outdated 'massive retaliation' concept.[144]

The possibility of the initiation of tactical nuclear weapon use on the LAC will require as prerequisite a more aggressive conventional military stance on the disputed border. There is a need to show firm resolve especially when dealing with even 'minor' incidents involving PLA or People's Armed Police units as a means of continuously injecting credibility into the first-use threat. The problem here is the reluctance of the Indian government to be clear-headed on nuclear security issues and unambiguous about the nuclear tripwire. But this clarity within the government, the SFC and the military at large has to be complemented by utter opacity about the Indian nuclear posture and its possible nuclear reaction to enemy action other than the certainty of nuclear response should China cross publicly undefined red lines. This is absolutely necessary to befuddle adversaries and keep their war plans unsettled.

The nuclear secretariat of the Special Programmes Staff within the PMO, moreover, will have to work out in great detail the nuclear contingencies, the tripwires, and the precise tactical and strategic nuclear responses. Time and again the country has been blind-sided by China doing what Delhi didn't expect it to do. To revert to the 1962 war, Nehru believed his 'forward policy' of establishing as many posts on the disputed Indo-Tibetan border as possible, never mind the difficulty of adequately supplying them was a masterstroke. By thus pre-emptively and unilaterally demarcating a border on its own, Delhi believed it had in effect solved the border problem by confronting the Chinese with a fait accompli. Far from deterring Beijing, it tripped the PLA into decisive action, which Nehru, advised by the B.N. Mullick–led Intelligence Bureau, had not anticipated.

To believe that China will not at any time in the future press its growing nuclear advantage may be to court precisely the situation Delhi perhaps seeks to avoid—to be pushed into a corner with an all or nothing, use or lose proposition, and generally being unready in terms of neither developing the necessary armaments for specific contingencies, such as a nuclearized Prahar missile, nor a variety of tactical and strategic weapons use options. Tactical nuclear technology was tested in 1998 with the sub-kiloton tests, but there's a need to field small-yield battlefield weapons with different configurations and warheads to fit different missiles. Further, priority needs to be accorded to the canisterization of a goodly portion of the land-based Agni 1s, 2s, 3s, 4s and 5s to support a tactically active nuclear posture, with a launch on warning (LOW) capability. The policy of keeping the canisterized Agni systems de-mated defeats the very purpose of obtaining a LOW capability. But to hold out credible threat of first use, part of the Agni missiles in canisters need to be deployed with their warheads attached and primed for launch, which fact should be 'leaked' to the media. It will signal Beijing that India's tactical-use threat is real and can be easily ratcheted up to the strategic level should it not pay attention to the warning signs of the forward-emplaced Prahars and ADMs. There's also the urgent need for the IAF to be more public about its priority targeting of the Qinghai-Lhasa railway tracks constructed on infirm permafrost that would buckle under the first Indian bombing runs against it at various points to effectively cut Tibet off from the mainland and of the destruction of the gigantic Three Gorges Dam to flood the land all the way downstream to Nanjing, pretty much writing *finis* to China's hard won status as economic super power.[145] This is the sort of targeting plans the SPS has hopefully passed on to the SFC for designated IAF squadrons to practise.

Indian military bosses should talk more pointedly about the China threat and publicly mention these high-value targets as the Indian armed services' focus to induce a healthy respect in Beijing for India's nuclear deterrent and even its conventional strike options with strategic impact. The incorporation of ADMs, nuclear Prahar cruise missiles and other tactical ordnance formally delineating red lines and the Indian nuclear ORBAT will negate, to some extent, the psychological overhang of

China's megaton-yield thermonuclear weaponry. What will help India's nuclear strategy generally is if the Indian government discarded its minimum deterrence thinking. In practical terms, this has resulted in the capping of the country's IRBM strength at thirty to forty Agni-5s and in not prioritizing the Agni-6 (the MIRV-ed version of the Agni-5), which would make up for small numbers of delivery systems with a large number of deliverable warheads. But such decisions have to be taken by Prime Minister Modi, which he hasn't done. In fact, a leading missileer notes, that there have been 'no top-down decisions and direction from the PM, NSA or PMO or anybody else on anything related to the nuclear deterrent and the country's strategic forces. Everything is done by inertia.'[146]

So even with a first-use policy, China will still have the upper hand. But an accelerated Indian nuclear build-up emphasizing useable nuclear weapons and their induction into military service, revision of the nuclear doctrine to make it supple and to stress contingent, tactical and/or strategic first use exclusively with respect to China conceives nuclear deterrence as a changing mix of capabilities, credibility and intent. It will introduce a measure of elasticity and offensive-mindedness that is currently missing in nuclear policy deliberations about just how China can be effectively dissuaded and deterred strategically. Such developments will force Beijing to mull the potentially cascading costs to it of crossing India's tolerance threshold that has to be set deliberately low in order to make Chinese leaders more risk-averse in strategic and nuclear situations and convincing them that once a situation trips the wire they would not be able to control it, and, despite China's distinct military edge, nor guarantee the outcome.

Cyber War with China

There's one aspect of nuclear weapons and strategic deterrence, however, for which there are no easy answers. The PLA has been in the forefront of exploring the use of cyber operations to disarm the enemy and force him into submission without engaging in physical war. What's a credible response, for example, to China's cyber actions to completely disrupt nationwide the power grid and communications and financial networks as a lethal first wave of a strategic offensive that Chinese strategists have hinted may be unleashed by indirect means on an adversary state? Dai Qingmin, director of the PLA communication department of the general staff and in charge of cyber operations, wrote in the early 2000s about using cyber attacks through third-country cyberspace in accordance with traditional Chinese stratagems such as 'kill with a borrowed sword' and 'exhaust the enemy at the gate and attack him at your ease' to pre-empt the enemy and destroy his capacity to wage physical war.[147] It is precisely the sort of action that has baffled US nuclear strategists.

In fact, Pentagon nuclear war planners, drafting the 2018 US Nuclear Posture Review (NPR), after reiterating that nuclear weapon use would only be in 'extreme circumstances', had initially expanded this phrase to include large-scale pre-emptive cyber attacks.[148] The sophistication of the Chinese 'ability to hide the form of its attack will make it difficult', as an analyst noted, 'to recognize a pre-emptive action as it unfolds'.[149] It is this difficulty that likely led to the enunciation of nuclear response to Chinese cyber provocation being dropped in the final version of the NPR. In the section on 'a tailored strategy for China' it merely noted that 'The United States is prepared to respond decisively to Chinese non-nuclear or nuclear aggression.'[150] In the same situation and under pre-emptive cyber attack, how should India react, given that Beijing has made no secret that its particular cyber focus is on four flashpoints: Taiwan, the Korean peninsula, the South China Sea, and its border with India? These are areas where China is confident of marshalling its civilian and military resources to achieve 'information dominance'.[151] China's cyber warfare designs can be thwarted, according to Dean Cheng, a leading expert on China's cyber prowess, by (1) preventing China from collecting information in peacetime, thereby sowing doubts in Beijing about the quality of its capacity to conduct cyber operations, (2) preparing for cyber hostilities by implanting electronic worms, Trojan horses, and other kinds of bugs into Chinese information systems and networks in peacetime, and (3) exacerbating Beijing's fear of loss of internal control, something that the country's communist rulers most dread.[152] But China is the largest seller of Huawei, Xiaomi and Oppo cellphones in India and of the Lenovo family of computers and laptops, all of which have likely embedded malware that can be remotely activated and can transmit to master control information on the communications traffic. With India not fabricating semi-conductors/integrated chips and using imported computer hardware and operating systems, it is as it is immensely vulnerable to Western sources of these machines and software. The Indian government has been extraordinarily lax and complacent about the security threat from these Chinese and Western electronic and computer products, doing next to nothing to reduce the threat.

For all its advanced capability, the PLA still sees itself as 'a half-mechanized, half-informationalized' force.[153] On a comparative scale then, where should India and the Indian military realistically be placed in the cyber domain? A former commander of a leading corps on the China front assessed India's cyber capabilities as 'near zero'.[154] Dr Saraswat, ex-chief of the DRDO and current NITI Aayog member, was of the view that while the 'threat is not new, our vulnerability is very high'. The main reason for this state of affairs, he said, is that the country does not produce its own hardware. 'You may put an app—a four-line code—but the operating system is not yours, even WhatsApp is not yours . . . we say provide end-to-end security, the hardware chap says provide access to your files. We do. We don't care,' he said and, in a soft dig at Prime Minister Modi, added, 'But we are happy with it, we are doing social engineering with it. The point is there's no effort to make things ourselves. We get mired by the fact that we are late entrants in the world of electronics.' Saraswat then made the more significant point: 'In the world's $3 trillion IT industry, India's contribution is not even 1 per cent. So everything manufactured in the country in the electronics sector is assembly, screwdriver level. Value addition is near zero, for a cellphone it may be 5 per cent to 7 per cent, in Apple products even this level of value addition is not there. When there's no value addition, you don't design hardware, what can you control? You are vulnerable.

'India wants to enter this well-established market, except the Indian market is driven by multinational corporations. How will indigenous products find favour? For that we have to have a policy. The Department of Electronics came up with a policy saying that we'll have preferential market access (PMA). What's PMA? All government purchases will be done from indigenous sources. But what is government? Only departments of the central government, not the state governments, not public sector enterprises, not railways, not airlines, not public sector telecommunications units. It's a joke. How many electronic things do Government of India departments purchase? Perhaps one computer per officer or a cellphone for an individual. I have been fighting for changing this policy and I am told, "No no, we can't do that because India has FTAs." I get so frustrated and wonder why I joined NITI Aayog. When a person with indigenization in his blood comes here, when you see what's happening in the civil sector, I think defence was better!' What's remarkable about this statement is that the defence sector, which as previous chapters have shown is abysmal in every respect when it comes to accepting indigenous goods, is rated by Saraswat as ways better than the rest of the government sector!

At the heart of why India does not produce its own electronic hardware, which Saraswat complains about, is that there is no microchip/SC/IC fabrication facility in the country, and acquiring such capability is not a priority for the government. The country's present fab capacity is 180 nanometres, when defence communications, surveillance, satellites, etc. need 29 nanometre capacity. 'The Indian government is ready to invest,' said Saraswat, 'but we can't find foreign investors, because in the present scheme of things, it is after a company invests in a fab that we'll reimburse it.' But for economic viability calculations, the foreign fab has to be first shown the potential market size, and that requires the modification of PMA. In an official report this Indian market is estimated at $400 billion for all electronic products. The percentage of ICs in it is worth $100 billion. 'We have to do two things: Legislate a change in the inverted duties structure to make imports of ICs prohibitive and change PMA to be all-encompassing, meaning every central and state government office, department agency, and all the offtake by the private sector will have to source their ICs from India-based fabs. Thereafter, the government won't have to do a thing—the fabs will come in by themselves.' The reason for the government's inability to do this, Saraswat said, was that India had signed some FTAs listing some 120 commodities in 1995 and couldn't violate these until 2020. Now the economically wealthy countries are pressuring Delhi to sign another FTA under the WTO to keep India dependent on IC and technology. 'And WTO,' Saraswat stated, 'don't allow a country to put conditions on domestic purchases.'[155] In fact Bob van Dijk, the CEO of global internet company Naspers, has warned that if India does not become self-sufficient in electronics hardware or have its own internet infrastructure and driver software, it will become, like Europe, a 'digital colony'.[156] That the Indian government does not have the foresight or the will to oppose such FTAs and, advised by the Ministry of Commerce and the MEA, continues to disregard the leverage that access to the vast Indian market provides Indian negotiators and only accepts defeatist counsel urging patently unfair trade regimes is a problem of the attitude of the man at the top. If Modi or any other strong-minded leader were to say 'No', the WTO and every other country will, per force, come around to accepting India's conditions. After all, that's what the now industrialized states did when building up and maturing their manufacturing base before signing on to FTAs. But Delhi's desire to please, to not be seen as trouble-maker, means big trading powers can use it to manipulate and subdue India. If the Indian government doesn't protect India's interests who will?

Need for a Purposeful, Strategic-minded Military Policy

Great power is a reasonable, even sensible, objective for India to attain. There is a popular consensus about it across political parties and the country. Differences, however, arise over how to achieve it. Many look upon this status as entitlement, Prime Minister Modi included, considering how often and consistently he has talked about the country as a civilizational power and jagat guru, and why the world should so recognize it.[157] This sort of thinking runs smack into the more quotidian metric of might making right, which is what powers international politics.[158] Statesmen of the mid-20th century who founded new nation states had a very realistic view of what it would take to make their countries successful. Even when money was scarce and demands for developmental expenditure serious, Nehru germinated India's dual-use capabilities in the nuclear field and in combat aircraft design and development—the acme of advanced technology. His friend and fellow socialist David Ben-Gurion likewise set up the infrastructure in Israel for it to become a technology leader, saying, 'A high standard of living; a rich culture, spiritual, political and economic independence . . . are not possible without aerial control . . . We need a real aviation industry. We need to be independent.'[159] Some sixty years later, Modi accentuates the spiritual and the cultural without mentioning the military as a great power resource and not merely as a tool to beat up Pakistan with. In a fundamental sense, he seems not to fully comprehend why the armed forces are nation builders, and why meeting the associated need for arms self-reliance with an all-embracing national defence industry is so vital to the country's economic well-being and prospects as great power.

Some military men suspect that apparently Modi has no great love or respect for the Indian armed services and that he perceives the Anglicized officer cadre in the military living in insulated cantonments as purveyors of a tainted and derelict Western culture that is subversive of Hindu norms and values. A former commander of a Gujarat-based army division recalls how during a courtesy call to the state chief minister, Modi asked him if the cantonment in which some of his troops resided could be moved out of the city so that the area could be freed up for popular use. It was explained to him that this being a 'peace station', fighting troops spent three years there with family to recharge their batteries, as it were, and needed the ease and big city comforts to do so. Modi then asked if the general officer was available for further discussion on the subject some evening. But before the officer could answer, Modi piped up, saying, 'After eight, you people are busy' and here he made the gesture with his thumb to his lips, of drinking liquor.[160] Others believe the prime minister soured on the military when politically motivated sections of ex-servicemen continued demonstrating even after his government had conceded the demands on the 'one rank, one pension' issue, and was particularly peeved that none of the then service chiefs stepped up to publicly chastise the demonstrators and publicly set the record straight.[161]

The impressions of the military that a prime minister carries are subjective, but they do matter. If they are positive the armed services have a better chance of being heard and their demands met. But most political leaders are too constituency- and vote-conscious to delve deeply into issues pertaining to national security. In Modi's case, because his exposure to the military in his formative years was superficial—plying troops moving to the front with tea at the railway station, etc.—his views of national security, largely unformed to begin with, have remained in a serious sort of way, uninformed. His NSA and staff in the PMO could have filled the knowledge breach with short, strategically insightful briefs that do not tax Modi's patience on various topics germane to national defence and security. They could have fleshed out policy options and succinctly argued the pros and cons of policy choices to ensure both the best, most effective, use of the scarce defence rupee and of the even scarcer commodity: the prime minister's time. But when the NSA, not known for his intellect and strategic thinking, sees his job as Doval does, and which he described to an official high-up in the Manmohan Singh PMO visiting him as that of 'implementing whatever the Boss wants because the Boss knows what he wants', there's policy trouble.[162] So how does the Boss arrive at his ideas?

As adumbrated in an earlier chapter, these are derived from his own impulses, impressions, bits of information and insights (however he picks them up), from a select sheaf of news stories and opinion pieces his staff puts together for his early morning read, and from short slide presentations made for him by outside experts. To make matters worse, this shallow sourcing of ideas is combined with the fact that Modi brooks no opposition to his own views. In other words, there is no rigorous analyses and process of strategizing on which Modi bases his decisions. A senior diplomat spoke admiringly of the contrasting example of Russian President Putin. Putin, he said, has established an in-house think tank in the Kremlin—the Russian Institute for Strategic Studies headed by a compatriot of the President's from the Federal Secret Service (successor to the Soviet-era KGB)—which has allowed a 'thousand flowers to bloom'. Thus, Putin gets to hear all shades of opinion to cogitate and arrive at a decision. If nothing else, such apparent catholicity provides Putin with cover for his own decisions. This diplomat, with some experience of working with the prime minister, rued that 'Modi's PMO has no bench strength, no in-house source of quality advice, and that the division of labour is that Doval deals with security matters and the foreign secretary with foreign policy; neither interferes in the other's turf, and both proceed along the policy lines and direction laid down by Modi.' So, while the foreign secretary's policy ambit is limited, Doval, he said, 'has too many things to look at, too much on his plate, for him to pay attention to specific policies or to ensure that even priority programmes are pursued and implemented.'[163] It would help if the NSA shared his work load with others in the PMO. This he does not do for fear of diluting his own value to the prime minister and, perhaps, for the same reason, is loath to have domain experts around him.

With the NSA limiting himself to ensuring what the prime minister wants gets done, the reasons for the Modi government's stunted, often half-baked, policies in the external and defence spheres are self-evident. As the head of a private sector defence company supposedly close to the prime minister said, 'Modi's government is a one-man show. He will not delegate decision and policymaking authority.' Thus, despite two reports submitted to the prime minister—one by the MoD and the other by NITI Aayog recommending a permanent committee, council or commission, functionally and institutionally separated from the MoD, specializing only in military acquisitions, staffed with experts in writing defence contracts and steeped in the minutiae of procurement processes, these have not been acted upon because that would mean delegating authority.[164] It does not, therefore, really matter who fills the office of defence minister and the MEA or any other cabinet post, they all act on the prime minister's say-so, failing which, as in the case of the more independent-minded Parrikar in the MoD, is prompted to return home. The main drawback of a top-down system is that Modi has to carry the can for all that his government with a marked parliamentary majority could have done but didn't, and for what his government has done that has not panned out as he had hoped or for all the things that have gone wrong. The consequences of a 'strong man' as prime minister and his working the Westminster system as a presidential form of executive means Modi monopolizes the credit but has to own up to the blame. And there's much that has gone wrong, and is continuing to go wrong, especially with regard to the three armed services. Certain select issues regarding each of them will be very briefly analysed in the following sections.

Pulling the Army out of the Pakistan and Counter-Insurgency Mire

That the Indian military and its support systems are industrial-age is not in doubt.[165] Cyber warfare capabilities that in advanced countries are at the cutting edge of contemporary conventional military and nuclear operations is in the Indian milieu more an aspirational sideshow than manifested in actual wherewithal. So comparing the Indian armed services to the Chinese PLA in terms of integration of the different services and of command, communications and control that allows them to function as a single unit is, in effect, to compare, as the old saw goes, apples and oranges or, more correctly, an old model motor car with one that is a souped-up SUV (while the US and Russian militaries, in this metaphor, are off-road capable Ferraris—if there are such things). In this respect, the Modi government has not helped the cause of the integration of the Indian armed services. Its election campaign promise to install the CDS system has not materialized. Shyam Saran recalls that when as convener of the NSAB he, along with three retired chiefs of service, briefed Modi soon after he took over as the prime minister on the need for a CDS, 'Instead of listening,' said Saran, 'he seemed more interested in negativing the idea.' Saran felt that this was so because Modi did not want to rile the military.[166] True, the old jalopy has advantages—it is sturdy, can keep on going on very little, can be fixed at any roadside workshop and can reliably do its basic tasks well. It is when it is stretched to do more, which it is not equipped for, that its efficiency plummets, and its weaknesses become apparent. It is this deficiency that was the basis for the case made in an earlier section to orientate Indian strategic forces for nuclear first use against China in order to obviate the Indian Army's tangling with the PLA on the LAC.

Counter-insurgency has been the major preoccupation of the army since 1989 when the botched Jammu and Kashmir state elections led to the people's disenchantment with the Indian state and, with Pakistan's assistance, the fanning of the secessionist/separatist fires. Half of the deployed forces on the border with Pakistan and the LoC are on counter-insurgency duty. Similarly, nearly half of the forces under the army's Eastern Command are tasked to maintain peace in the tribal north-east. Over the years, with negotiation and political compromise, most rebels have given up the gun and entered the mainstream, except for the army units in Nagaland and Manipur where Modi has promised early resolution.[167] Pending a settlement, the army and armed rebels have adopted a 'live and let live' attitude and, as long as the armed Naga rebels, representing the oldest rebellion against the Indian Union from the time when Phizo spearheaded it starting in the late 1940s, are not too disruptive; they are even allowed to act out their sovereignty aspirations in areas where they have a presence.[168] In the event, the army in the east and the north-east may soon be free to return to its primary task of securing the border with China and Myanmar. But it is the army's embroilment in Jammu and Kashmir to contain the insurgency that has doubly reduced the Indian army, diverting it from its main job of meeting China's military challenge to tackling not the Pakistani Army which as a secondary foe is bad enough, but a tertiary threat posed by insurgents supported by the Pakistani Army. With so much of the army's effort and manpower resources in the west expended on securing and sanitizing 'the grid' in the insurgency-infected areas of that state, the Indian government has virtually all but handed over the initiative and advantage to the Pakistani Army. But such primary mission for the army became inevitable once the VIF, Doval's old outfit, tasked by the prime minister, produced a paper on threats faced by the country and listed 'Pakistan-sourced terrorism' at the top. It has led to the government devising a two-pronged policy. Priority has been accorded the Special Forces, not the armed services, to hit Pakistan across the LoC with ₹200 crore sanctioned to buy special arms.[169] And offensive counterterrorism operations against Pakistan are enhanced via elements inside that country and using assets cultivated over time within sections of the Afghan Taliban and TTP, which effort explains the influx into the PMO of Doval's professional cronies from the police agencies, Intelligence Bureau and R&AW.[170]

However, what has happened is that at a very small cost to itself—the occasional 'surgical strikes' by Indian Army Special Forces on its forward units and the more routine cross-border artillery and small arms duels, etc. resulting in casualties—the GHQ, has assured itself of two things: (1) the weighted operational focus of the Indian land forces is on the Kashmir insurgency and the LoC, and (2) therefore, it does not have to be too anxious about the Indian Army implementing its 'Cold Start' doctrine (which, as already argued, is not easily implementable anyway). Pakistan has a very good thing going to thus keep the Indian forces busy and distracted and, one can expect that there will be no end to the ISI-supported terrorist activity in J&K, what with its string of safe havens, training facilities and depots of arms and military stores on its side of Kashmir. The mention of Pakistan in the international Financial Action Task Force (FATF) list is likely to result in superficial changes to this arrangement of asymmetric warfare.[171] Islamabad will detach the overt civilian control of J&K terrorist operations managed by Hafiz Saeed and his LeT/Jamaat-ud-Dawa (JuD) group with attendant traceable financial transactions which FATF can track, and return it to ISI, whose secret financial dealings FATF cannot as easily track. Meanwhile, to pacify the US and FATF, LeT/JuD may be disbanded and Saeed returned to house arrest.

The irony is the Modi regime's strongly held view of not talking with Pakistan until it ends the terror campaign plays into this Pakistani strategy.[172] So, the Pakistani Army will continue with its successful *kutayuddha*—covert war in J&K which Chanakya advised as the best means of weakening a more powerful adversary state and its army. The costs for the Indian Army are heavy in terms of troop demoralization and the coarsening of its ethos—after all, hunting down Kashmiri mujahideen may be better than shooting at youthful stone-throwers, but neither is what the army is trained to do, howsoever it may be contrived, to distance the army units from the actual action of subduing a civilian population. In professional terms, because the counter-insurgency operations are the only game in town and can add the extra points in confidential reports for promotion and appointment to high posts, the workload is equally shared as between the combat arms and non-combat arms, with all soldiers pulling time in Kashmir in Rashtriya Rifles dungarees. Time away from their armoured or mechanized artillery or Army Service Corps units means attrition in their specialized combat skills and a general operational degradation of the quality of the strike corps and pivot corps hosting armoured and mechanized formations.

Except, Modi's concern about Pakistan-sponsored Islamic terrorism conflates the RSS's three major bugaboos—Islam, Pakistan and terrorism—to eliminate which the BJP government seems devoted. This is political oxygen for its Hindu support base. Indeed, Modi's initial moves to resolve problems with Pakistan gave way quickly to a more punitive mindset targeting Pakistan on the terror issue at the behest of the RSS to which Modi owes fealty. The RSS, according to a senior military officer, advised the BJP government to make terrorism the priority for both national security policy and foreign policy.[173] This explains just how driven Modi's foreign policy and the MEA have been in getting friendly countries to join Delhi in pillorying Pakistan as the hotbed of terror and source of international turmoil. It has paid off domestically in that with elections somewhere or the other in the country all the time, Modi's anti-Pakistan or anti-terror rhetoric with allusion to the Indian Muslim as the other has kept society divided and vote distribution benefitting the BJP in state elections. The Pakistani Army and the ruling BJP in India, therefore, have a common interest in keeping the Kashmir-qua-Pakistani terror issue alive. But this self-perpetuating situation does not strategically bode well for the Indian Army and the country. Not that Modi or his NSA, Doval, seem much perturbed by the external fallout and the consequences for the army in terms of blunted war-fighting skills and general operational readiness.

The impact of Modi's hard stance on Pakistan is perceived in the adjoining Muslim states that share the subcontinental culture and societal norms as, reflecting anti-Islamic sentiment and the belabouring of a weak neighbouring state. It affects and subconsciously influences their attitude towards India. In the Maldives, it has probably informed President Abdulla Yameen's decision to counter the possibility of Indian interference in its internal politics by forging military bonds with China, even allowing it to establish an 'ocean station' in the Indian Ocean for Chinese submarines.[174] Yameen is risking an adverse Indian reaction but is convinced Modi is all roar and no lion, which has proved so far to be the case.[175] The Sheikh Hasina government in Bangladesh, while professing friendship with India and reassuring Delhi, has justified taking large loans from China because 'we have to take whatever funds come to Bangladesh for the purpose of development', adding pointedly that 'India should also maintain cordial relationship with all its neighbours'.[176] The wariness of India of non-Muslim Nepal and Sri Lanka may be seeping into the thinking of Bhutan as well, with China seen by them as counter-balancing India's presence. This pretty much guts India's larger strategic design—assuming the Modi government has any such plan—of reducing China's footprint in Asia starting out with South Asia.[177]

Bad relations with a Muslim Pakistan also subliminally tenses up what's Modi's otherwise stunning diplomatic coup in courting the states of the Arabian peninsula and the Gulf, topped by the agreement with Oman to use Duqm as a base for the Indian Navy, upgearing India's relations with Israel, reaffirming close ties with Iran by taking operational control of a part of the Chabahar port, presumably to set up a naval/military support facility, even as Tehran sends its pilots to be trained with the Pakistani Air Force and Iran reasserts its strategic autonomy.[178] This entire complex of bilateral ties is delicately balanced on the perception of India in the region as a coming economic and military power, which edifice will fall down if the anti-Pakistan animus begins to be consumed by the Gulf regimes as, in its essence, anti-Islamic. This may transpire if Modi's gambit in the Gulf takes on an overly anti-Pakistan shade.[179]

The BJP regime's synthetic enmity with Pakistan centrally undermine, moreover, the far-reaching strategy of loosening the economic dependence of the CARs on China. The $10 billion Turkmenistan, Afghanistan, Pakistan, India (TAPI) gas pipeline able to pump 90 million standard cubic metres of gas daily is the cornerstone, but how will this project be completed if India and Pakistan are at loggerheads? The Modi government is seriously conflicted on these aspects. It dispatched Minister of State for External Relations M.J. Akbar to Herat for the inauguration of the Afghan start point of TAPI, where he dilated on large investments in the pipeline having to be provided foolproof security but said nothing about what happens when the pipeline, completed section by section, through Afghanistan and Pakistan finally reaches the Indian border.[180] Much is riding on the successful completion of the pipeline for India's relations with Turkmenistan, which sits on the fourth largest gas reserves in the world, and its sister republics in central Asia, where India is a cultural presence but not yet a player with economic or military heft. Any hindrance to TAPI that Ashgabat attributes to Delhi's hand in worsening Indo-Pakistani relations will redound to India's disbenefit.

These are the wider repercussions of militarily concentrating overmuch on Pakistan to the detriment of pacifying the neighbourhood, to achieve which there is no other practical alternative than by an ample show of economic and trade generosity, including absolute freedom and tariff-less entry for their produce and manufactures into the Indian market from all South Asian countries, Pakistan included. This will in turn provide the momentum for countries near and far to begin taking India seriously as a well-meaning economic powerhouse and security provider, and a credible counterweight to China in southern Asia and the Indian Ocean region. Delhi's de-prioritizing Pakistan and instructing its military to concentrate its energies on the China threat and challenge should lead naturally to the restructuring of the Indian Army into a powerful mountain warfare–ready land force (with a total of three offensive mountain corps financed by demobilizing the three strike corps as argued previously in the book). It can then tie down large segments of the PLA—which Beijing can take lightly only at its own peril—with a single composite armoured/mechanized corps and several independent armoured brigades retained for the plains for any unforeseen Pakistan contingency.[181] Such a China-directed force will reassure South East Asian nations as well, particularly Vietnam, because the Indian Army's singular intent to mix it up with the PLA on the Tibetan plateau that will become discernible with the offensive corps in the ORBAT would ease the PLA pressure on their land borders in South East Asia.

In a time of enforced austerity, the government should consider whether the army's extensive use in counter-insurgency warfare within the country is the best use of its military labour and capabilities. From the economic point of view, it costs seventeen times as much to train an army soldier than a paramilitary trooper. Having trained the jawan in war-fighting, he is then deployed to contain and control situations in roles that state police and paramilitaries should be performing. When he redeploys to an army unit, he has to be re-drilled for war situations, which ensures that the army will never be very good at fighting a war, or at taking out insurgents.

Making the IAF Strategic-minded and Imported Aircraft–Free

If Modi has largely achieved his aim of 'Congress-mukt Bharat' there are no signs of his ensuring an air force free of imported aircraft as part of his Make in India policy. Asked what struck him most in his periodic interactions with senior IAF officers, Steve Burgess, a faculty member at the US Air Force Academy, Colorado Springs, replied that it was their seeming unfamiliarity with the basic tenets of professional-level planning required for strategy or for configuring a force.[182] These are institutional deficits. The IAF has still not come to terms with what it wants to be: a strategic air force with aircraft able to deliver ordnance on target at considerable distances from the heartland, or a tactical air force able competently to neutralize aerial threats along the borders with China and Pakistan, threatening destruction in these countries within range of the mostly short-legged aircraft in its inventory.

Strangely, it was Lieutenant General Sir Francis Tuker, commander of the famed Fourth Indian Division active in the Maghreb and the Italian campaigns in the Second World War and the last Briton after 1947 to head India's Eastern Army, who was the first and to date the only military man expansively to envision India's pivotal military role in Australasia as 'the great axis about which the rim of any future war will be revolving'. He emphasized air power as the decisive element for this purpose. The aerial boundaries of Tuker's 'Icarian India' extended from the Australian isthmus to West Asia and into the North African desert in order, he wrote, 'to keep the Indian Ocean air routes well back from a possible enemy' because he thought India 'the natural air transit centre of the East'. 'If India is fit for her destiny,' wrote Tuker with some fervor in August 1945, 'she's one of the coming . . . powers of the world.'[183] True, Partition occurred, dividing the landmass as a unitary military staging area, but his conception is nevertheless relevant to the Indian republic because, geographically, it commands the Indian Ocean and its maritime traffic and the oceanic chokepoints while stretching northwards continentally to be in easy reach of central Asia. Bishkek, the capital of Kyrgyzstan is, after all, nearer to Delhi than Chennai is.

It is revealing that the IAF has never defined its ambit as ambitiously as Tuker did. Given how the Indian armed services have remained limited by their history as colonial forces, the IAF, in a sense, has refused to escape the confines of the tactical role it was assigned during the Second World War for short-range strike and as escort for the Allied medium-range bombers embarked from Kolkata and points east against the Japanese Imperial Army in the China–Burma–India theatre. Indeed, with English officers leading it well after Independence, it, in effect, settled into the restrictive mission as an adjunct to Western strategic forces, and has remained doggedly tactical even when the space for a strategic air force was there for it to fill. The nearest it got to a bomber was the medium-range Canberra, equipping three squadrons, and then it was used in encounters against Pakistan. Indeed, when offered the genuine long-range Tu-22 Backfire bomber by Russia in the summer of 1971, it did not know what to do with it, its notions of its own operational space having by then so shrivelled as to lead to its rejecting this plane, and this despite the commander-in-chief of the Soviet Air Forces, Marshal Pavel Kutukhov, briefing the IAF brass in Delhi on its virtues. What was chosen instead, to Moscow's consternation, was the short-range MiG-23 BN fighter/interceptor.[184]

This selection did several things—it robbed the IAF the opportunity of becoming a strategic bomber force able to hit targets deep within China (at a time when China had no like aircraft), helming the delivery of nuclear fission bombs, a stockpile of which India had begun building after the 1974 underground test and of buttressing its case against the Indian Navy's aircraft carriers for long-range maritime strike. As if to confirm the short-range nature of the IAF, its chief, M.M. Engineer, even said no to the purchase in the mid-1970s of tanker aircraft to extend the range of its fighter fleet that Indira Gandhi, with China in mind, was prepared to fund.[185] And, just a few years back, Air Chief Marshal N.A.K. Browne argued against both the need and the affordability of leasing a squadron of Russian Tu-160 Blackjack strategic bombers.[186] There were unconfirmed reports in late 2017 about the IAF contemplating buying or leasing four of the most advanced Tu-22M3M. Why four? That will mean having just one of these aircraft in the air at any given time, which doesn't make any sense; the better deal would still be to lease a squadron-plus, say, twenty of the refurbished, re-engined, Tu-160s from Russia as the manned bomber leg of the nuclear triad. What a strategic bomber does is lengthen the strategic fuse.

Say, there are reports of serious ingress by the PLA into Indian territory or a major Chinese provocation that has cost military lives; would this be considered a crossing of red lines that will justify firing a canisterized Agni-5? Wouldn't a better option be to send several Tu-160s over the East Sea, affording Delhi the time to confirm what has transpired on the ground with respect to the violation of the Indian red lines, and whether in that situation the Blackjacks cannot be on the way to assigned targets, even as the Agni missiles are activated as fallback or the situation considered a false alarm or at least not meriting a nuclear response, whence the airborne Tu-160s can be called back? It is the recallable aspects of the bomber that is central to its value in nuclear deterrence, which the Indian government, SFC and IAF should ponder, and which capability would be valuable, especially in crisis.

The discussion so far stresses the point that the air force brass—with only fighter-flying experience under their belt—are averse to having a genuine strategic bomber in the fleet which they perhaps believe will dissipate its main mission focus of reducing Pakistan in war, something the IAF, incidentally, has never been able to do, other than over East Pakistan in 1971, and during the Kargil conflict because its aircraft were ordered to operate this side of the LoC. In fact, it has not been able to even keep the Pakistani Air Force aircraft out of Indian skies. And yet it seeks advanced technology combat aircraft to establish air superiority. The problem is this—and it is a dilemma facing other modern air forces—in theory, contemporary fighter planes cost a packet and the country can't afford too many of those, but the technology in it is supposed to compensate for small numbers. This doesn't work in practice because the adversary, say, China, can muster the same if not higher level of technology and lots more aircraft. Constrained financially, the IAF then has to make do with what it can get from wherever the aircraft can be procured for the allotted amount of monies and hope it will be sufficient to at least curtail the operational efficacy of, if not the Chinese air force, at least the Pakistani one. This, in a nutshell and without frills, is what the air force can in fact actually do. Spicing up this dilemma is the fact that the IAF has been resolutely pro-western in its orientation, particularly in sourcing its topline combat aircraft, even though much of its fleet has always comprised Russian fighter planes. So, the air force flies Russian, dreams Western and is sceptical about indigenous fighter planes (leading in an earlier era to the ditching of the HF-24 and HF-73 and, in recent times, initially resisting the Tejas LCA).

It is in this context that the Modi government's decision to scrap altogether the ongoing consideration of a single-engine aircraft for the IAF, a race reduced to just two aircraft—the Lockheed Martin F-16 Block 70 and the Saab JAS 39 Gripen E, one an antique, the other the equal of the Tejas LCA in almost all respects, as the earlier discussion in this chapter showed—was late in coming, even if Modi's controversy-ridden Rafale decision was the prompt.[187] It affords the IAF and the country another opportunity to do something right for a change and the BJP government the chance to make amends and show itself in better light than it has so far managed to do. Other than the unit cost of the plane, Congress party president Rahul Gandhi tweeted two other questions: Whether Modi had secured the approval of the Cabinet Committee on Security before announcing the deal in Paris, and how come the offsets programme related to this transaction was given not to HAL but to a private sector company (Reliance Defence) that has no experience of producing combat aircraft?[188] Turning the knife some more, former defence minister A.K. Antony wondered if the part about doing away with the clauses for the licensed manufacture of 108 Rafales in India and transfer of technology were 'scrapped' before Modi announced his Rafale decision, in which case it was 'gross violation' of the DPP.[189]

Whatever else happens and if past is prologue, when any arms acquisition runs into corruption charges and political controversy, the extended sales of the item in question is usually voided and the foreign company in question goes into eclipse in the Indian market. Recall the fate of the German Howaldtswerke-Deutsche Werft HDW-209 diesel submarine. So the best-laid plans of the IAF to use the purchase of thirty-six Rafale as a wedge to procure its full original requirement for 126 MMRCA likely stands terminated. The race is once again thrown open to all comers and with two-engine aircraft in the fray, single-engine planes—F-16 and Gripen—will be discarded with the Tejas in play. In these circumstances, the question the IAF leadership has to ask itself is this: Should the service forever be the sap, be victimized by aircraft import deals that can at any time turn sour and blunt the fighting edge of the force? No sooner was the Rafale deal confirmed than MBDA, the French-led European missile consortium, put a spoke into the air force's plans by asserting that to avoid compromising them it would not integrate the Scalp subsonic cruise missile and the Meteor air-to-air missile—the main armaments on the Rafale—with the Indian Su-30MKIs and or the Tejas LCA.[190] This unwillingness was not conveyed to the IAF during negotiations when the plans for their retrofitment on the Indian Su-30s and LCAs was made clear to the French companies. This should be reason enough for Modi to cancel the Rafale deal, save the country money and begin the arduous process of changing the Indian military's mindset to economically and indigenously equip the armed services. There's also the danger in buying such Western aircraft and missiles that US-made components in them will provide Washington the handle to render India pliable. Consider in this respect the example of Egypt, a country on friendly terms with the US, which has been denied the Scalp missile for the Rafales it bought from France on America's insistence.[191] Potentially, India could find itself in still bigger trouble because the entire Rafale deal was signed with France without any sovereign guarantees, with the Modi government making do with some kind of a letter from the then President Francoise Hollande, which is worthless. This means that there's no safety net—Dassault can quite literally take the Indian money and run.

This raises the issue of whether it isn't time for the government to say enough's enough and reform the IAF's institutional mindset and close off the import option to the service and the military generally, and order it to become the main stakeholder in the Tejas LCA variants and the AMCA programmes, on pain of not having any aircraft at all? This is the only way to achieve self-sufficiency and permanently insulate the service from the political crosswinds buffeting the country and assure the IAF of the forty-two squadrons it is authorized by the Indian government to have. Opting for a foreign aircraft is perilous because the IAF's future is always one charge of corruption away from blowing up in its face, or a US policy quirk away from having its fighting fleet grounded, something the IAF should by now have realized and accordingly planned for but hasn't.

The IAF's history in this regard is not praiseworthy. Its desire for West European combat aircraft in particular has led to the Air Headquarters time and again resorting to stratagems. In writing the qualitative requirements for the MMRCA, for instance, the IAF was inventive in coming up with the spurious concept of heavy, medium and light aircraft, when no advanced air force anywhere in the world believes in such categories for the good reason that the performance parameters of aircraft of these pheno-types overlap and there's no clear way to distinguish aircraft using the weight metric.[192] The logic of such differentiation for the IAF was, however, simplicity itself—it would at once shove the home-made Tejas to the light category and the Russia-sourced Su-30MKI to the heavy category of aircraft at the two ends of the spectrum, leaving the field free for procurement of a 'medium' European aircraft, the MMRCA of its choice: the Rafale from France, or the EADS Eurofighter from Germany or the Gripen E from Sweden.

The Manmohan Singh–led Congress government's policy of diversifying sources of military supply provided the MMRCA political cover. It is an inherited policy the Modi government endorsed. But diversification makes sense if the supplier has proved to be unreliable and an inconstant friend. While the Soviet Union and its successor state Russia have had hideous problems with supplying spares because of the disrupted Soviet supply chain, with the break-up of that country into many independent republics requiring India to transact with more countries for the same spares, it was not politically unreliable in the sense that the UK, France and Sweden have been in joining the US in imposing sanctions and denying technologies—as has happened frequently in the past. The more telling reason for the West European choices may be that while Russian hardware is good and rugged, repeated trips to, and long stays in, Moscow or Irkutsk to liaise with Russian supply chain officials is not as highly prized by officers in the procurement loop (in the armed services, defence ministry and DRDO) as the more pleasurable trips to Paris, London, Berlin or Stockholm.

But leaving these extraneous factors, once Rafale was in the bag, the IAF was prompted by the Modi government, under pressure from the Obama and Trump administrations to 'buy American', to reconsider the F-16. This aircraft, incidentally, was the first to be dropped in the MMRCA race because it was a dated platform that the Pakistani Air Force has been flying for over three decades—and because the American record of shutting down spares support didn't inspire confidence. The grounding of the navy's UK-sourced Sea King anti-submarine warfare helicopter fleet owing to US sanctions in 1998 because certain components in the aircraft were of American origin was fresh in the IAF's mind.[193] Even so, the IAF, now in a happier frame of mind, came up with new metrics to replace the light-medium-heavy typology that had drawn flak and ridicule with single-engine and two-engine categories.[194] The IAF was never serious about the F-16 but because the evaluation process would take years and get the Modi government off its back, it considered it, with the idea that at the end of the selection process it would ask for the single-engine Gripen, thereby scoring a coup with Rafale as the two-engine plane in the fleet to be joined by the Gripen—a situation many in the IAF had devoutly wished for, especially as licensed production in the country of the Swedish plane would also end up crowding the Tejas out of the funding picture and get it out of its hair for good. Moreover, a force mix of two engine aircraft and single engine aircraft would be more in line with the force structures of advanced air forces. This is how things would have panned out but for the Rafale issue exploding in IAF's face and paying put to this plan.

The IAF will therefore have to go back to the drawing board. Until 2025, the air ORBAT will comprise upgraded fifty-plus or three squadrons of Mirage 2000s, ninety-plus or five squadrons of Jaguars with the indigenous DARIN-III navigation-attack system, and sixty-plus or four squadrons of MiG-29s or roughly twelve squadrons of the residual 4.0 generation combat aircraft. Of the 4.5 generation fighter planes, 123 LCA Mk-1As are already ordered. If the Indian government has the strategic wit, as argued previously, it can get at least two private sector companies to absorb Tejas technology from ADA and join the two HAL assembly lines. With four production lines, the yearly output can easily touch forty to fifty aircraft a year—with the construction of the production lines taking two years. The Tejas Mk-2 is the real item with the more powerful GE 414 engine and the Indian-made Uttam AESA radar, with 30 to 40 per cent commonality between Mk-1A and Mk-2.[195] India will have ready production lines for the Mk-2 and the successor to that aircraft, the AMCA, with two F-414 engines (as Balaji indicated in the section on Tejas), while incorporating some fifth-generation technologies.

With respect to indigenous aircraft, in end-2016 the IAF produced a 'vision paper' according to which the production run was to be forty

Tejas Mk-1s, eighty-three Mk-1As, and eighty to eighty-two Mk-2s. Thereafter, four or five squadrons or sixty-four to eighty AMCAs would be inducted reaching the limit of the Tejas strength in the IAF at some 285 aircraft or seventeen squadrons.[196] This is a large enough number to enable economies of scale and ample incentive for the Indian private sector to enter the Tejas business. In fact, Reliance Defence approached HAL to explore the possibility of co-production of the LCA in January 2018 but, as earlier stated, met with a discouraging bureaucratic non-response. This is an issue Modi can resolve but hasn't. The importance of large numbers of the LCA in the air force cannot be overstated. Tejas is not only the country's aviation standard-bearer and worldwide advertisement and marketing tool but operationally a significantly capable fighter aircraft. Apart from all its other virtues, because it is virtually invisible given its extremely low radar cross-section of 0.3 to 0.5 square metres at 120 km, a closing distance to target that can be counted in just tens of seconds—too little reaction time for the pilot in the enemy aircraft. Its stealth characteristics are furthered by the canopy having a thin indium tin oxide coating of the kind on the US F-22 Raptor.[197] The aircraft is so good to fly it is hugely impressing the air force pilots in major strike bases which Tejas from 45 Squadron have been visiting in order to get the flyers and ground-crews to become acquainted with it.[198] These familiarization visits ought to be extended to hinterland bases as well so that all IAF pilots have a chance to sortie in the LCA and the service begins to generate a stake in the aircraft. The LCA is the natural bulk aircraft for air defence to replace the MiG-21 and the Mirage 2000, and even the Jaguar for low-level strike.

The obvious high-end aircraft will be 270 to 312 of the two-engine Su-30MKI upgraded to 'Super Sukhoi' configuration in a ₹10,900 crore programme, which will include a new 3D vectored AL-31F engine, an advanced new Bars AESA radar and the strengthening of its body to extend its life to 6000 flying hours.[199] And this is where the IAF leadership gets antsy. It is pointed out that as between a Rafale and Su-30, the 'clean cost' (without weapons) is 25 per cent less for Rafale than Su-30, or $75 million versus $100 million, and the 'cost of ownership' (maintenance, servicing for lifetime) is in the ratio 1:1.5 with minimum assured 60 per cent serviceability for Rafale compared to 52 per cent for the Sukhoi. But how does it plan to use such a small fleet of Rafales? The IAF has 'gamed' the situation and concluded that a single Rafale with the Meteor air-to-air missile will take out two Pakistani F-16s. The idea apparently is that because the Pakistani Air Force has only small numbers of F-16s, with Rafales wiping them out with the Meteor, the way will be cleared for the IAF to dominate Pakistani skies. In the same situation, the IAF plans on pitting two Su-30s against a single Pakistani Air Force F-16.[200] Why? To be certain of a kill. This borders on silly because, according to combat aviation experts, Su-30 is superior to the US Super Hornet F-15 which, in turn, is a far superior fighter aircraft to the F-16.[201] Because this is the scenario the IAF came up with, that's how the Rafale will likely be used. Again, the same old issue: So much money deployed to overpower so puny an adversary? But whatever the brouhaha over the plane, the Rafale may stay bought if Delhi does not exercise its prerogative to cancel the deal owing to the French not permitting the integration of the BrahMos missile on Rafale and the Scalp and Meteor missiles on the Su-30s and the LCAs. But, Parrikar made clear soon after Modi's Rafale decision that he foresaw a future IAF as a mix of Rafale, Su-30 and Tejas LCA and its derivatives, with the Rafale here more of an adornment than a fighting asset.[202]

Except, there's the little niggle about the FGFA—the PAK FA or Russian Sukhoi-57—which India has already invested $300 million in as collaborator. The IAF's complaint is that the country had no role in designing the Indian variant of the plane as was originally envisaged. What it doesn't say is that this was because the meagre combat aircraft designing talent available in the country was concentrating on the Tejas LCA programme and, in any case, that such ideas as the IAF came up with in 2011–13 for an Indian Su-57 were either incorporated (such as 360-degree view from cockpit) or subsequently rejected by the air force itself as unwieldy (for instance, the two-seat configuration that would have increased the plane's radar cross-section and decreased its stealth quotient).

The IAF's reluctance to offtake the Su-57 is apparently on the basis that it lacks the US F-35 type performance characteristics.[203] This is curious considering the F-35 aircraft has drawn consistently bad reviews by experts and has been dismissed as a 'trillion-dollar national disaster' with little to commend it other than its data collection and fusion capability. But what good are data and its fusion if the plane can't fly or fight?[204] Maybe the IAF brass should not let their pro-Western bent over-ride reality—something for the MoD to keep in mind when next the Indian military pitches for American or European equipment. In any case, the Modi government has apparently decided to end the collaborative development of the FGFA with Russia because of DRDO's confidence that, learning from the Tejas programme, it has a grip on most of the high-end technologies featured in the FGFA and which the AMCA will have. The unspoken idea being that the $9 billion to $10 billion thus saved on the total transaction can be better invested in the Tejas programme, its variants, and the indigenous AMCA follow-on aircraft.[205] This is no bad direction to move in to minimize aircraft imports and light a fire under the budding aviation sector in the country, which is the reason also—as argued in this book—why the Rafale deal too should be terminated with prejudice. In fact, the Tejas and the Su-30 together would make for a versatile composite battle group.

The IAF is supposed to have evinced interest in the Su-35, which has incorporated into it some FGFA features, such as the 3D thrust vectoring that makes the aircraft highly agile, its manoeuvrability unmatched by any aircraft in the world. But Russia has conceived the Su-35 and the lighter, shorter-range MiG-35 as interim platforms to bridge the 4.5 and 5.0 generation fighter planes in its inventory, before the Su-57 enters its fleet in large numbers. But India is already going in for the 3D-vectored Su-30MKI upgraded to 'Super Sukhoi' standard, so what's the point in also acquiring the Su-35 that's judged to be on par with the Indian Su-30MKI?[206] With four to six squadrons of AMCA at the high end, eighteen to twenty squadrons of the upgraded Su-30s and a like number of LCA Mk-2 squadrons, the country will boast of a modern, terrifically effective, forty-two–squadron air force well into the 2040s without the logistics and operational liability imposed by the diversity of aircraft as is the case at present, and with a thriving Indian combat aviation industry to support it (and to rifle up hundreds of Tejas planes to export for good measure).

The Chinese air threat is at once more and less than it is projected to be. It is more in terms of the extraordinary pace of China's military modernization and the kind of resources it can bring to bear in achieving whatever it wants. It is less in terms of the actual fighting qualities of its air force in that the pilots lack operational savvy and of the quality of aircraft they fly. For instance, the Chinese have always made much of their super-stealthy J-20 that Western experts regard as copy of the F-22.[207] It is, however, fairly easily detected by the radar on the Indian Su-30s deployed on the Tibet border.[208]

The Navy's Sudden Carrier Fixation

Structuring a military force, as Mark Cancian, a stalwart of defence budgeting at the US Office of Management and Budget puts it, is nothing but 'trade-offs, trade-offs, trade-offs'. It means having to deal at the macro level and within the allotted funds with the 'iron triangle of painful tradeoffs' involving 'readiness (the ability of forces to do what they were designed to do), capacity (the size of force) and capability (the ability of forces or equipment to achieve a desired effect)'.[209] The Indian Navy has been more strategic-minded than the other two services in distributing its monies between competing missions owing to its potentially distant operational reach and has impressed the government. Consequently, it has been favoured since the 1990s with 50 per cent of its budget (versus, say around 30 per cent for the air force in the same time-frame) slotted for capital acquisitions. In recent years, however, the trend of strategic good sense has dipped, with the navy not so subtly emphasizing aircraft carriers. This may have to do with more senior officers pulling time at the US Naval War College and being influenced by the US Navy's aircraft carrier ideology. In this milieu, the offer by the US of its cutting-edge EMALS is tipping the scale with the Naval Headquarters now convinced the country should have it. As a result, the third Indian-built carrier (IAC-3) design is being proposed with EMALS in mind. Wisely, Parrikar shot down the EMALS idea, but because no proposal in the MoD and in services' headquarters is ever really terminated, it will be periodically resurrected in the hope that some defence minister and government will approve it.

The flaring of the enthusiasm for large carriers in the navy can be traced to Ashley Tellis's 2015 monograph championing them.[210]

The United Kingdom government jumped in to pre-empt other players and offered to sell India one of its three Queen Elizabeth–class CODOG (combined diesel or gas)–powered carriers the Royal Navy had ordered. This offer was withdrawn because the British Admiralty decided they needed a three-carrier navy after all. But the Royal Navy concluded on the basis of in-depth technical study and analysis that (1) thirty-six was the optimum number of aircraft to have on its Queen Elizabeth–class carriers, (2) a nuclear power plant would double the cost of the carrier, (3) Catobar (catapult assisted take-off and barrier-arrested recovery) was just too expensive and that for a single Catobar system the Royal Navy could get two Stobars (short take-off and barrier-arrested recovery) systems, and (4) the monies saved by these means would be deployed to buy more carrier aircraft: the F-35Cs. The point made by the nuclear submariner, Vice Admiral A.K. Singh (retd), former commander-in-chief of the Eastern Naval Command, is that the spendthrift attitude of the navy in contemplating nuclear propulsion for carriers and even Catobar stands exposed when Britain, with almost the same GDP as India but a population of only 70 million, thinks it too pricey.[211]

If modern large aircraft carriers are built around the power package—whether a nuclear power plant or a bank of combined diesel-gas turbines—the IAC-3, if the Navy has its way, will be unique in being designed around the American aircraft launch system, which is what Tellis advises. The unit cost of EMALS at around a billion dollars is daunting enough for a financially strapped US Navy for it to champion its sale to India so as to reduce its unit cost for its latest Gerald Ford-class nuclear-powered aircraft carriers. Even for the nearly 1,00,000 tonne Ford-class ships carrying an entire air wing (seventy-five to eighty aircraft) and nuclear-powered to boot, EMALS doesn't make economic sense. President Trump in May 2017 blasted it as too costly and 'not good'.[212] So how does it make sense for an Indian 45,000 tonne to 60,000 tonne carrier with no more than twenty-five to thirty aircraft on board?

When the US decided that India would not get the miniaturized carrier nuclear power plant the latter had informally inquired about, that should have ended the Indian Navy's interest in EMALS as well because the massive amount of electricity (3 MW) required to fire up its powerful electromagnets will require enormous hull space to house a very large CODOG/CODAG (combined diesel and gas) power plant and fuel storage tank which space will be obtained at the expense of hangar space for onboard aircraft and ordnance carrying capacity. (This is notwithstanding the 'square-cube law' providing some design relief that Tellis makes much of.[213])

What Tellis does not address, and neither has the Indian Navy, is how it will prevent large carriers from making nonsense of its own plans for sustaining a bigger sea presence in the Indian Ocean or make carriers of any size less vulnerable in supersonic and hypersonic missile regimes. It was for these and other reasons that I have concurred in the view of naval stalwarts such as Rear Admiral K.R. 'Raja' Menon (retd) that if the navy must have carriers they should be the more expendable light carriers of no more than 20,000 tonne size, which will allow more of them to be bought and increase the navy's sea presence.[214] Indeed, a section of the US Navy is coming round to the view that in an age of carrier-killer missiles, small, cheaper carriers may serve better as platforms to launch offensive and defensive aerial and submarine drone operations. This is both clever and in the direction that naval technology is trending, an optimized alternative the Indian Navy must consider rather than plugging the big carrier concept.[215]

But even these drawbacks do not begin to define the real problem for India if it invests in more aircraft carriers—conspicuous and impressive symbols though they might be in peacetime of the country's military might and political and economic power. Consider the conventional military context: The Indian Navy has about thirteen to fourteen submarines, which means that at any given time six or seven of them are in refit or undergoing repairs, and three or four are patrolling on each of the two seaboards. It also has around forty capital surface combatant ships—with roughly a third of them, thirteen warships, unavailable for sea duty. So India's entire naval presence in its ocean is six or seven submarines and twenty-seven frigates and guided missile destroyers. Now pitch the carrier *Vikramaditya* into this picture and one gets an idea of just how lopsided the carrier's prospects are in war and the cost it imposes on sea presence.

According to the US Navy a carrier escort comprises eight warships and two submarines. Even if one halves the US escort numbers accompanying the Indian carrier, *Vikramaditya* will siphon away for its protection four surface combatants and a submarine, leaving the country to make do for its extensive maritime domain with only twenty-three frigates and destroyers and five or six submarines. A second carrier will mean a further diminution of the Indian naval presence on the oceanic highways, unless the frigate/destroyer strength multiplies very fast, which is not on the cards. In the context, moreover, of the Chinese navy expanding furiously, adding more warships and auxiliaries tonnage in the last four years than the total tonnage of the French navy, the large aircraft carrier option sucking up frigates, destroyers, submarines, and fleet tankers just for protection seems foolish.[216] This is reality and a former navy chief pondering these figures threw up his hands and called the navy's hankering for aircraft carriers 'preposterous' given that these can be sunk by supersonic and, in the future, hypersonic missiles fired from shore, from warships, submarines, small seaborne platforms and even launched from long-range strategic bombers and fighter aircraft.[217] The lethality and impact of these missiles will be multiplied, as argued in an earlier chapter, against Chinese naval ships traversing or forcing the two narrow seas that China has created by building the islands as a central verge in the mid–South China Sea, whence my advocacy for speedily arming all the states around the South China Sea with the BrahMos supersonic missile to stifle the Chinese South Sea Fleet and the secret 'Fourth Fleet' ex-Hainan Island tasked for the Indian Ocean. With the local navies thus stymieing the Chinese naval might, there will be lot less steam left in the PLA Navy to create mischief for India in India's maritime backyard. It is time the Indian Navy discarded borrowed notions and stick with what is seen to work. What is good for the US Navy is not necessarily good for India and the Indian Navy.

Unprepared for Future War

The real existential constraint the Indian armed services face are scarce financial resources. India will be a developing country for a long time to come and social welfare and economic development will remain the main national priorities. For the Indian military to expect, in the circumstances, that things will improve and they will have larger budgetary subventions anytime soon is to expect too much. There is no getting away from resource scarcity. Splendid armament platforms such as aircraft carriers and showy armoured forces with a large fleet of tanks in the event may be so much military eye candy that can no longer provide the nation maritime security, assuming they ever did. If the Indian military does not keep pace with the times and is not au fait with advances in technology, it is a sure ticket to military defeat and national humiliation in the near future of robot armies, drone navies and aerial microbot attack swarms.[218] But this is a technology realm the Indian armed services know little about, have showed no real interest and zero investment in and, for whatever reasons, are unprepared to venture into. Between an apparently clueless Indian military and a surprisingly vapid Indian government—and not just under Modi—the country may be setting itself up to be slammed in future armed conflict with China.

Conclusion

AT AN ECONOMIC conclave in February 2018, Narendra Modi talked of a weak and fragile Indian economy turning into a $5 trillion giant, and how his changing the 'work culture' in government had something to do with it.[1] While global corporate bosses talked of India's GDP reaching the $10 trillion level by 2030, the consensus view voiced at the meet was that it cannot be done without the country adopting 'unorthodox measures'.[2] This must have sat uneasily with the prime minister. Anything 'unorthodox' is necessarily outside the ken of the Indian government and, it turns out, Modi's preferred method. But the Indian state's immense limitations are manifest and the prime minister, contrary to the advance advertisements about himself as someone who would take the government out of the 'business of business' and cut down government to provide better 'governance', has proved to be an arch statist believing ardently in the existing bureaucratic system and those running the vast Indian government as the prime agents of change. This despite ample evidence that red tape is in fact the chief barrier to harnessing the resources and the entrepreneurial energies of the people and putting the country on a rocketing growth trajectory, and the bureaucrats are a mostly disinterested lot of time-servers.

The Indian government is no METI (Ministry of Economy, Trade and Industry), which as the Ministry of International Trade and Industry enabled Japan's rapid post-war recovery on the backs of the huge industrial conglomerates, the *zaibatsu* (Mitsubishi, Mitsui, Sumitomo, Suzuki, Furukawa, et al.), to produce the 'Japanese miracle'.[3] Nor is it the far-sighted South Korean state that followed the Japanese model to create its own slate of big companies, the *chaebols*, (Samsung, Hyundai, Daewoo, LG, SsangYong, et al.) and chart as startling a path to economic success.[4] Instead of encouraging and incentivizing and relying on individual enterprise, the profit motive and the private sector to provide the impetus for economic growth, the well-meaning Bloomsbury socialist Jawaharlal Nehru created gigantic public sector enterprises on the Soviet Russian model, which by their very nature not so much competed with as sidelined private companies.

Inevitably, a few of the family-owned firms capitalized on their pre-Independence funding connections to the Congress party to corner production licences to manufacture 1950s-technology cars, scooters, etc. that they did not care to innovate because of a closed and captive market. To consolidate her own power, Indira Gandhi in the 1960s nationalized financial institutions still outside government control—banks and insurance companies—appointing managers beholden to her and not to investors; now, when badly run public sector banks are so habituated to life support they consider periodic capital infusions by the government their right. The BJP regime, instead of privatizing these banks and the rest of the loss-making public sector, announced recapitalization to the tune of ₹2.11 lakh crore with more to follow—monies that are expected 'to go into the drain'.[5] The fact is, almost into the third decade of the 21st century, India is treading water as much economically as in the defence and external realms, all the self-glorifying spiels by Modi about the country and the people never having it so good notwithstanding.[6]

Then again, Modi has proved he is no Shinzo Abe, Vladimir Putin, Recep Tayyip, Erdogan, Donald Trump or even Emmanuel Macron in that he didn't even try radically to reform the system he inherited. Modi failed to follow up his muscular talk of the election campaign with matching action, to advance India's interests in the world or realize any of his slogan-promises for domestic rejuvenation that could only have been done by downsizing and reorganizing the government, restructuring the decision-making processes, bringing in outside experts and fundamentally reforming the decision- and policy-making systems as his 'alpha male' counterparts have done elsewhere. Abe amended Japan's 'peace Constitution', Putin revitalized the military and revived Russia, Erdogan succeeded in ramming a referendum for a strong presidential system in his 'new Turkey', Trump cut the flab and trimmed procedures to end bureaucratic gridlock in Washington, and Macron, the youngest, freshly minted President of France, in his very first year utilized his executive powers to pare the public payroll and tame the powerful, traditionally mollycoddled government sector labour unions by replacing the system of lifetime job security with contractual work.[7]

What Modi has done in comparison is decidedly small bore. He has implemented his Gujarat governance model with indifferent results. It features (1) centralization of decision-making, (2) adoption of IT solutions, (3) improvement in the performance of PSUs, (4) empowerment of senior bureaucrats to make them 'more accountable', and (5) inculcation of pride in civil servants in working for the state.[8] In the event, 'minimum government, maximum governance', explained Rajiv Kumar, vice chairman of NITI Aayog, 'has to be understood as raising the efficiency levels in the delivery of public services, and not the withdrawal of the state'.[9]

Modi's vision for Gujarat, moreover, was by these means to emulate and compete with China.[10] Presumably, it also forms some part of his 'vision' for India. Except, Xi Jinping and his cohort running China, appreciating the limitations of the state, are assigning the private sector a role to even remake the PLA into a slimmer, smarter 'global tier fighting force' by 2050. It is an objective Xi spelled out at the 19th Party Congress in October 2017, for which purpose government research and development organizations expeditiously released to private firms 3000 patents as a first step towards what Xi called 'military-civilian integration'.[11] So, even as Xi—leader of the ultimate Big Brother state—seeks individual drive and private sector initiative to cement China's place as a leading comprehensive power in the world, Modi sees India's deliverance in oiling the creaky colonial-era apparatus of government in the hope of perking up the public sector performance and making the bureaucracy less sclerotic.[12] The pity is that no country in the world has so much talent outside government and so little inside of it.

The BJP government's belated attempt to attract external experts to fill ten joint secretary–level posts in government by lateral entry, while being a recognition that Modi's faith in the entrenched bureaucracy was misplaced, was too late in his term to make a difference. Because as retired IAS officer and now well-regarded columnist Sanjeev Ahluwalia opined, 'Its timing, at the fag end of the government's tenure, loads the dice against persons of outstanding talent applying for this opportunity. Even the best house help is risk averse and abhors untimely disruptions.' And while making the case for the systemic stability that the IAS provides, he contrasted the outcomes from having experts and generalist civil servants running the show. 'Our achievements in space technology, missiles and atomic energy,' overseen by experts, he writes, 'are out of sync with the quality of our roads or public medical care' managed by the IAS.[13] The structure, ethos and attitude of the government system are the maladies afflicting the country that the political class with a vested interest in it doesn't want a cure for.

'India is a story of private success and public failure—its rise is due to its enterprising people rather than the state. Our red tape and bureaucracy breaks the spirit of small and medium enterprises that create the most jobs,' writes Gurcharan Das, corporate guru and public intellectual. 'The World Bank has been pointing this out for fifteen years but every Indian government till now has ignored [its findings], preferring instead to pick holes in its methodology.'[14] The prime minister seems not to sense the contempt the people and the private sector have for politicians, the government and government servants, or to listen to constructive criticism. Modi appears detached from the reality of an India with half its population below the poverty line and having to daily contend with a venal and rapacious, typically Third World administration and government that is responsible for social welfare indices so miserable that the economists Jean Dreze and Amartya Sen felt constrained to point out in 2013 that the country looks 'more and more like islands of California in a sea of sub-Saharan Africa'.[15]

The situation has improved only slightly during Modi's tenure, but not at all in terms of generating employment or skilling programmes to absorb millions of youth annually entering the job market, making it likely that the 'demographic dividend' he foresees will turn into a nightmare. For the prime minister, therefore, to make claims such as 'Digital India has become a way of life' is to mistake aspiration for achievement.[16] A Pakistani financial consultant's take on Modi is sharply relevant. 'Modi is not bad at putting projects together. It is just that they violently lurch from . . . directionless shock-and-awe reforms to those that lack any depth. He has launched dozens of shallow "small-bore government schemes" so far,' avers Saad Khan. 'His social media savvy has served him well in giving each [of these schemes] the sort of digi-buzz that most Instagram influencers would drool over. But they are all symptomatic of a frenzied bureaucrat stuck in the thinking of a small-time glad-hander rather than the leader of a large nation . . . Modi should dial back the number of reforms he releases every month and instead drill down into whether they are short-term band aids or actual solutions. Dense labour laws should be simplified, foreign investment projects should have more follow-through than hollow Make in India campaigns, and small-medium businesses should not have their growth disincentivized by ridiculous retroactive tax measures. Also, less pandering to destructive ideologies would yield better long-term returns than the current display of divisive antics that are so in vogue with contemporary strong men.'[17]

In the Indian society at large, these 'divisive antics' are becoming combustible. Deification of the cow and the stigmatization of, and random violence against, Muslims and Dalits are leading to the unravelling of the complex and delicate sociocultural weave of Indian society, undermining social peace and sowing dissension. Modi's refraining from publicly calling out the Hindu extremist outfits suggests the ruling RSS-inspired BJP is allowing a traditionally tolerant Indian society to turn into an illiberal Hindu state, which has no precedent in India's history.[18] By mixing religion and politics, Modi has seeded a milieu in which censorship of the arts, literature and films, imposition of strictures on couture and cuisine, and the steady assault on the easygoing milieu of the countryside and the cosmopolitanism of the urban areas are obtaining what many fear is a 'Hindu Pakistan'.[19] Thoughtful supporters of Modi in the media see in this trend a dead-ending of the prime minister's agenda.[20] Exacerbating social divisions may lead to grave internal security problems. Thirty-four countries in the new century have fallen apart at the seams or suffered a breakdown owing to sustained domestic disorder. Only four states suffered this fate owing to foreign interventions.[21] Modi's 'Gujarat model' functions in top-down mode with the prime minister as the sole authority and fount of ideas in government, with cabinet ministers and senior bureaucrats alike acting as cogs in the machine to realize his schema of technology-driven growth. Meanwhile, the fervour of the Hindu outliers grows, as do their excesses in terms of straitjacketing the Indian society into RSS-dictated Hindu norms and values resulting—most damagingly for a regime boasting of its business-friendly credentials—in Indian capital and capitalists fleeing the country.[22] His bull-headed nature and strongly held views reinforced by long years in the severely hierarchical Sangh system has conditioned Modi to brook no opposition to his ideas, which he sees as insubordination, and to accept no advice from anyone, whence there's no expert talent around him. He only has his instincts and intuition, his likes and dislikes, his impressions gathered during extensive travels in India and abroad, and nuggets of information and insights he picks up from here and there to guide policy formulation and is surrounded by civil servants waiting to do his bidding.[23]

If the situation inside the country is unsettled by the shenanigans of the looney fringe, India's foreign policy conducted by Modi with a certain showman's flair is facing trouble at its doorstep and in the wider world. His 'neighbourhood first' policy risks going belly-up owing to his government's relentless hostility towards Pakistan that has folded into the anti-Muslim prejudices in society conflated with the anti-terrorism tenor of the times. It has made the lives of Indian Muslims miserable and the abutting Muslim-majority states (Bangladesh, the Maldives) uneasy, Islamic states in the extended region uncomfortable, and friendly states in Central Asia wary putting at risk the TAPI gas pipeline that Ashgabat puts much store by and the IPI gas pipeline that Tehran has assiduously promoted. It also threatens to upend the prime minister's delicate balancing act of cultivating the Sunni Gulf states and Saudi Arabia on the one hand and cooperating with Shia Iran and Israel on the other, and seeds doubts about India's intentions in Sri Lanka, Nepal, and even Bhutan.

But the bellicosity towards Pakistan that the Modi government seems able easily to summon is curious because it seeks single-mindedly to invert the perception of Hinduism as effeminate and passive compared to muscular and robust Islam that American diplomats, for example, used to argue for supporting Pakistan over India in the 1950s.[24]

The manifestations of this hostility geared towards isolating Pakistan have ranged from self-hurting to silly—the postponement, for instance, of the SAARC Summit for reasons of cross-border terrorism, to shifting the 2018 Asia Cup cricket tournament from India to the UAE because of Delhi's prospective denial of visas to the Pakistan team.[25] That the Pakistani tail wags the Indian dog becomes apparent when contrasted with the Modi government's soft-glove and respectful treatment of China: the infinitely more dangerous economic, political and security challenge and threat.[26]

Perhaps the BJP government has realized that it has politically milked 'Pakistan' to the maximum and that it better begin making overtures to Islamabad, particularly the decisive entity in that country, the Pakistani Army, its head, General Javed Bajwa, giving notice of his willingness to talk directly to the Indian government or via his counterpart, the Indian chief of the army staff.[27] Institutionally, this should pose no great problems. After all, if former heads of the R&AW and ISI, Amarjit Singh Dulat and Lieutenant General Assad Durrani respectively, can collaborate in writing a book about the intelligence ventures their agencies have been involved in, there's no reason why the Indian Army and Pakistani Army chiefs cannot sort out problems relating to keeping the disputed border peaceful.[28] It can lead, by way of congealing the dialogue process into a permanent mechanism, to the chiefs negotiating an entente cordiale between the two armies, allowing them to reconnect with each other through the medium of 'divided regiments', renewal of inter-army sports meets and similar social activity—the sort of confidence and security building measures with great potential that have never been mooted but which can be the 'key to peace' in the subcontinent.[29] It is a process that can unfold in step with the composite dialogue at the government level. All it requires is a little strategic imagination and political will. It represents an 'out of the box' type of thinking that Modi has recommended to the country's youth.[30] Apparently, what's good for the youth is not good for the prime minister.

Elsewhere, Modi has sought to strengthen bonds by recommitting to Bhutan and recalibrating India's policy to Nepal. During his third visit in May 2018, he harped on the religio-cultural links and offered a bus service between Janakpur and Ayodhya, and a Kathmandu–Raxaul railway, seeing in such people-pleasing gestures a diplomatic device to overcome ideological tensions (with the Oli-led Leftist coalition government) and the sway of internal Nepali politics revolving around the ethnic divide between the Madhesis and the hill people with Kathmandu suspecting that Delhi favours the former. Except the same old problems about delivering on the prime minister's promises have intruded here as well. Thus, all the many things that Modi promised in his previous trips, among them connecting Lucknow, Pokhara and Nepalgunj by air, establishing the Nepal Police Academy, forming the Pancheshwar Development Authority, creating a Lumbini–Sarnath–Bodh Gaya Buddhist circuit, and actually dispensing the $2 billion in aid to rebuild towns and infrastructure devastated by the 2015 earthquake have remained just 'announcements', the sort of tardiness that former ambassador to Nepal, Rakesh Sood, says 'is no longer tenable' considering that China is 'stepping up its game'.[31] In any case, the small states on India's periphery—Nepal, Maldives, Sri Lanka—have begun to appreciate that the best way to get Delhi's attention is to shake China's hand. This is a new factor that Modi's 'neighbourhood first policy' has not adjusted to.

If India's influence has shrunk in South Asia, it has also lost its international standing as power balancer owing to the Modi policy's over-tilt towards the US and the West. It is a slant supported by a new phenomenon: an ecosystem in Delhi with a distinctly American flavour prominently featuring Indian chapters of Washington think tanks funded by Indian corporate donors that propagate the US line. It flourishes in the context of senior government and military personnel interacting with US counterparts invariably seeking immigrant visas, work permits and other considerations for family members and, in return, easing US-friendly policies through government corridors. This policy tilt is explained by apologists as natural, considering it serves the purpose of having the US on India's side in the looming confrontation with China.[32] Except Washington's agenda seems more ambitious: It is to reduce India into an American dependency, in fact, into another Japan which is advised an 'active denial' military strategy to hold off China and, should matters come to a nuclear crunch, to await US help![33]

The start point for this strategy is for the US to replace Russia as India's prime military supplier, a plan followed by the George W. Bush, Obama and now Trump administrations of getting Delhi to buy high-value non-lethal military goods (C-17 and C-130 transport planes, P-8I maritime surveillance aircraft) and to produce obsolete weapons systems—F-16 aircraft, M-777 howitzers, etc.—which stage is touted as 'a path toward future US–India cooperation on other advanced technologies and mutually beneficial industrial partnerships'.[34] Neither the prime minister nor his advisers seem to understand that Modi's Make in India programme and Trump's 'Make America First' and 'Make America Great Again' policies clash, and that the US is not going to relent. They seem just as unaware of the coercive US strategy and plan for India, to pressure Delhi into buying American arms on the pain of being sanctioned under the 2018 CAATSA.[35]

This plan has been put into action with Washington wanting Delhi to buy its Terminal High Altitude Area Defense System instead of the Russian S-400 India has signed up for.[36] If every major buy of Russian military hardware or instance of military collaboration is 'sanctionable action', as the principal deputy assistant secretary of state Tina Kaidanow has warned, India will always find itself in America's gunsight.[37] There are many deals that are ongoing, already agreed upon or in the pipeline, such as the lease of the second Akula-II SSN, the Indian manufacture of 126-odd Kamov 226 utility helicopters to outfit the army's aviation corps, four Grigorovich-class frigates and the continuing cooperation in sensitive strategic projects, which last the US will not participate in for love, shared democratic values or money. It is a situation not helped by the long and close association in the security sector with Russia, the source of 70 per cent of arms and equipment with the Indian military. The historically intimate ties with Iran, the source of 13 per cent of its oil requirements, and where India has invested heavily in the Chabahar port, in the rail-cum-road grid it is building to Afghanistan and Central Asia, in the Farzad gas field are, likewise, a sore point with Washington and will lead to sanctioning India under CAATSA. A deadline of November 2018 has already been issued for India to end its oil imports from Iran.

CAATSA, it would appear, is a stick to beat Delhi into submission. This much is clear with the threat of sanctions or its waiver being used contingently to obtain the results Washington desires.[38] Like to sink the S-400 deal and/or to persuade the Modi regime, following the LSA to hurry up and sign the other two 'foundational accords', COMCASA and BECA.[39] That getting close to the US entails absolute loss of policy space and military choices dawned late on the government, leading to Modi seeking a mini-summit with Putin on 21 May 2018, where the two leaders countered CAATSA by upgrading their relations, in Russian Foreign Minister Sergei Lavrov's words, to 'a special privileged partnership'—several rungs above the 'strategic partnership' India has with America.[40] This signalled Washington that India will not be easily manipulated or thin out its military relationship with Russia. Whether this also means Delhi getting off the US security bandwagon and getting back to playing its historic role as a 'strategically autonomous' international power balancer remains to be seen, but that seems to be the direction India is headed. This is an overdue and much-needed course correction to regain for India leverage and traction with the US as much as with Russia and China, and can be a solid basis for seeding BRIS and Mod Quad, coalitions derived by cutting the proto-hegemons China and the US out of the BRICS and the original Quadrilateral groupings, which are conceived and detailed in this book, to enhance India's political, economic, diplomatic and military status, standing and leverage.

The slant towards the US makes little sense at a time when Washington has questioned America's leadership role—the latter's alliances are in disarray and their leaders, insulted and alienated by Trump (at the June 2018 G7 summit in Quebec City, for example), are talking of going their separate ways. The Canadian foreign minister Chrystia Freeland said, 'The fact that our friend and ally has come to question the very worth its mantle of leadership puts into sharper focus the need for the rest of us to set our own clear and sovereign course.'[41] If Canada thinks it is difficult to partner the US, will India find it easier? Such a tilt is injurious to India's interests, moreover, also because it discounts what India can do on its own by acting as a strategically autonomous actor and push back against China by undertaking various measures detailed in this book, such as walking back the country's delusional nuclear weapons policy with its moorings in disarmament ideals, resuming testing to obtain proven and credible thermonuclear weapons and incorporating in a revised nuclear doctrine the concept of 'first use' against China.[42] Other actions involve speedily arming countries on the South China Sea littoral and the archipelagic nations with the BrahMos supersonic cruise missile and Agni-1 and Agni-2 short- and medium-range missiles on a priority basis to curtail China's maritime options in the 'narrow seas' created by the synthetic islands it has created mid-channel; activating the Tibet and Uyghur cards and insisting on a strict balancing of trade and reciprocal market access and commercial conditions. The most important measures will be equating Tibet and Taiwan in the Chinese scheme with Kashmir, inclusive of all of POK with Gilgit and Baltistan, and making it clear that if Beijing wants India to accept 'One China' it will only be on the basis of strict reciprocity—'One India' for 'One China'.[43]

But to take on China requires steely resolve and nimble policies—scarce commodities in the Indian milieu. Proactive thinking and articulation of an assertively expansive national vision are desperately needed but missing from the Modi oeuvre. Nor has the prime minister succeeded in shaping Indian foreign policy and diplomacy and the Indian military into agile instruments of state, able to punch and duck out of trouble and be fast on their feet. The Indian state remains what it has always been: a ponderous and incompetent beast.

As Ashley Tellis, the South Asia expert at Carnegie in Washington, said pithily of India, it 'does not have institution in government that can leapfrog, anticipate, deal with surprises, deal with shocks'.[44] Heck, it hasn't even created an investment vehicle for the $76 billion that Qatar generously offered Delhi to fund India's infrastructure build-up. It has dithered in using Japanese capital offered by Shinzo Abe in the Indian Ocean region and the east African littoral to create an Asia–Africa trade corridor to compete with China's maritime silk route and is even hesitating to cement defence-industrial links by agreeing to Tokyo's complete transfer to India on generous terms of the entire production line and manufacturing wherewithal of the one-of-a-kind ShinMaywa US-2 amphibious aircraft to showcase Indo-Japanese security cooperation.[45]

If Delhi keeps looking gift horses in the mouth, they may bolt. Modi's 'Act East' policy spearheaded by 'connectivity' projects that Delhi had conceived as gluing together a combination of 'rimland'

Asian states to counter China have, similarly stalled at the Indian border because railways, roads, pipelines and communications links that Delhi promised proximal countries have not materialized.[46] This is in contrast to the smooth-running Chinese machine that channels billions of dollars in infrastructure credit and magically erects people-pleasing highways, airports, seaports and metro railways, seemingly in a trice and funnels arms to African states to shore up China's near monopoly of minerals and oil extraction industries.[47] Then there is the lumbering India that can't seem to do anything right. It has hurt the country's image, credibility and reputation in southern Asia, the extended region, and Africa where there's still a residual emotional pull because of historical and cultural links and the goodwill from Jawaharlal Nehru's time when India spearheaded campaigns against colonialism and racism in the UN. If there's no delivery on the prime minister's assurances, and timely realization of aid and development programmes is missing because of bureaucratic glitches, ineptitude and absence of coordination at the Indian government end, it is hardly surprising there are so few substantive foreign policy successes that Modi can boast of. Large and imaginative geopolitical/geostrategic economic-cum-security ventures, such as BRIS and Mod Quad are, alas, not even on Modi's radar, even when these would generate enormous political capital for India and serious military clout with the US and China that it cannot otherwise secure.[48] Modi would rather the country pay a higher price for joining existing technology cartels and regional and international conglomerations and clubs than that India constitute new constellations of nations to maximize its own power (as China has done with its BRI, the SCO, and even a China–India–Pakistan trilateral forum proposed by Beijing).[49]

There is little doubt that China has successfully encircled India, and circumscribed it strategically in South Asia and the extended region. That it has done so to a degree where Delhi can't see beyond its borders and without facing any adverse reaction from India suggests something fundamentally wrong with the Indian government's approach even when so besieged and beleaguered. India was an East India Company and then Crown Colony for some 200 years. It is a pity Indians did not imbibe that characteristically British trait of offensive action in difficult circumstances. In 1797, Britain was in desperate straits, hounded and harried by France and its European allies. It had lost the northern European, Baltic and, except for a foothold in Malta, the Mediterranean coasts, and Napoleon was threatening invasion with his 'Army of England'. It was just the time, writes renowned military historian, the late John Keegan, when 'Britain correctly sought to pursue an offensive strategy, directed at checking invasion by forcing France to look to the protection of its own interests, rather than passively waiting to respond to French attacks'. So early in that year, the Royal Navy took on the Spanish Fleet off Cape St Vincent and defeated it, destroyed the Dutch Fleet at Camperdown and its Mediterranean Fleet under Nelson hunted the French Fleet, bringing it to battle at Trafalgar and spoiling Napoleon's designs for the conquest of Egypt and India.[50] Waterloo was still eighteen years away but the erosion of French power had begun. China is approaching its zenith; just the occasion for India, if Delhi musters the iron will to take the fight to Beijing to ensure it never becomes the overlord in Asia. And, as discussed in this book, what it needs least of all to reach this goal is the assistance of a dysfunctional, unreliable and receding America.

The trouble is, Modi, other than with Pakistan, is partial to passivity in the external domain. He truly believes, as he said at the 2018 Shangri La Dialogue in Singapore that 'Asia and the world will have a better future when India and China work together in trust and confidence, sensitive to each other's interests . . .'[51] Delhi has certainly been 'sensitive' to China's concerns, not reacting at all to China's exertions in the near seas to distance the Maldives, Sri Lanka and landward Nepal, Bhutan, Bangladesh and Myanmar from India. Modi has continued, in effect, with the China appeasement policy set in motion in this century by the previous BJP prime minister Atal Bihari Vajpayee, when for the first time India acknowledged Tibet as part of China. India's foreign policy has gone downhill ever since.

Because piecemeal appeasement was seen not to work, Delhi sought intimacy with the US as counter without realizing the costs America would extract or extort for the association. All this time Beijing, far from giving a damn about India's interests, has shafted them. The

Indian government, with the MEA in the lead, has yet to realize two basic tenets of contemporary statecraft: That China's goodwill cannot be bought by plying it with concessions and being nice to it, and that it is less onerous to have America as a friend than 'strategic partner'. In other words, neither China nor the US can be trusted. It is in India's national interest to not take guff from either of these comprehensive powers and to configure coalitions such as BRIS and Mod Quad, unencumbered by their presence, but which can keep them counterweighted and engaged.

At the heart of India's weak foreign and military policies is Modi's imperfect understanding of the international balance of power system. Cleverness alone cannot make up for the lack of the requisite strategic sensibility which is needed to work this system to fully advantage India. In his meetings with President Xi, Modi has stressed 'stability' and with President Putin 'multipolar world order'.[52] These are fairly flexible concepts—stability of what kind, on whose terms, and can a global order be multipolar if major powers tilt towards the dominant powers, other than contingently to restore the balance, for reasons of ideology or ideals? Sure, 'stability' is diplomatic code to suggest the non-tolerance of disruption that China profitably practises, and 'multipolar' denotes a non-G2 order that won't countenance a US–China condominium. But while Modi thinks of these concepts as delimiting and inhibiting a country's options, the cannier practitioner of international diplomacy in Putin thinks it is call to action. 'Stability is important,' declared the Russian president, 'but we can't afford this stability if it holds us back from [what] we need to do.'[53] This statement by Putin goes to the core of Modi's self-limiting policy mindset. Stability serves China's purpose, disrupting and undermining the putative Chinese hegemony in the South China Sea and the East Sea serves India's interest. So what will Modi opt for? His record shows that advised by the China appeasers in government, principally in the MEA, he will choose not to rock the boat.

Modi's one genuine innovation—his personalized diplomacy, replete with the hugging and embracing of foreign leaders, has met with warmth but not, alas, fetched any lasting benefits for the country. Thus, the prime minister talked about 'Mobama' (Modi–Obama) in terms of 'the chemistry [that] has not just brought me and Barack closer but also brought Washington and Delhi and the people of our two countries closer together.' It inverted the view of Joseph S. Nye, Jr, who conceptualized 'soft power', that 'friendship [between leaders] helps, but it is [the] icing on the cake. The cake is national interest.'[54] This last is something Modi has apparently not come to terms with because, the quality of personal relations apart, Obama disregarded the Indian leader's pleas on the H1B visa issue and initiated his 'in-sourcing' policy that penalized US companies for outsourcing back-office operations to India. His successor Donald Trump has further tightened the screws on the Indian IT industry despite enjoying Modi's company in the White House and Delhi's treating his children, Ivanka and Donald Jr, visiting the country as state guests.[55]

Modi has the common 'Indian' failing of believing that just because one gets on well personally with someone that person means well and will act in your interest. Thus the prime minister has not been hard-headed in furthering the national interest, has not forcefully leveraged India's economic clout in terms of using 'denial of access' to the vast Indian market—second largest in the world after China—as a means to get military high-technology from the US and the West, and equitable trade and commercial terms from China and flexibility on resolving the border dispute. On a recent day when NASSCOM reported a dip in India's flagship IT industry growth to single digits, there was a story about Chinese 'next gen tech giants'—Toutiao, Meituan Dianping, Didi Chuxing—gearing up 'to invade India' with plans aggressively to invest $250 million because they espy it as the market of the future.[56] These and the Chinese technology firms already in India (Huawei, Xiaomi, Oppo) have not been required by Delhi to, for instance, transfer technology to Indian partner companies—a condition Beijing has imposed on foreign firms operating in China.[57]

India, moreover, has not received any part of the $20 billion in infrastructure investment that Xi had promised, but Modi seems satisfied with the trifles Xi has doled out. Such as permitting Hindu pilgrims to take the Nathu La route to the Kailash and Mansarovar mountain, visiting which, Modi recalls, proved a spiritually uplifting experience for him.[58] In other words, he has shown that his foreign policy and brand of diplomacy failed to get much out of his opposite numbers who have been intent on securing hard gains for their countries while giving up little. Modi may be India's 'prime marketer' but as to the 'overall success' of Indian foreign policy based on his 'personal chemistry', a supporter of his admits that 'the jury is still out'.[59] Other than state visits, summits and mostly piffling successes that have come India's way—such as votes in the UN General Assembly to extend the term of an Indian judge on the International Court of Justice at the Hague—there are no big gains, unless India's admission into the MTCR and Wassenaar Arrangement (and soon the Nuclear Suppliers Group) that will limit India's freedom of action and strategic latitude are considered accomplishments.[60]

Modi has sought global recognition for India as 'civilizational power' and 'jagat guru' which expansive concepts at one level denote an 'alternative reality' that Modi seems to inhabit. As the fired US Secretary of State Rex Tillerson observed on the basis of his experience with a truth-challenged President Trump, a country's future has to be 'fact-based, not based on wishful thinking, not hoped-for outcomes made in shallow promises, but with a clear-eyed view' of reality, that frees the people 'to seek solutions to ... [the] most daunting challenges'.[61] At a more mundane level, these ideas represent an Indian state with growingly Hindu overtones presided over by Modi that former vice president of India, Hamid Ansari, cagily highlighted. India's composite culture, Ansari stated, is sought to be replaced by a 'mono-culture in the name of new, strident, illiberal, nationalism [that imposes] a form of regressive regimentation'.[62] In any case, a civilizational power is not the same thing as a modern great power, a status that is not an entitlement but has to be earned the old-fashioned way—by gun, grit and gumption, none of which Modi has shown he can summon, especially not when tackling big powers.

This naturally leads to the issue of India's hard power capabilities. Modi's bias against the military's anglicized officer corps is reflected in his disinterest in defence matters generally, except when he has intervened and then only to make wrong decisions (like the Rafale deal and the decision to convert military cantonments roads into public thoroughfares). Other than on 'one rank, one pension', his government has not implemented the other two specific national security–related promises contained in the BJP's 2014 election manifesto, namely, in establishing the CDS system and revising the nuclear doctrine. And just as he did not transform the bureaucracy and the apparatus of government, he left the armed services undisturbed with their trademark deficiencies. Thus, an essentially Second World War–type military is arrayed against the Chinese PLA—a once 'rifle and millet' army that has transmogrified into a 21st century fighting force with advanced cyber, artificial intelligence and robotic systems in its ORBAT that's making America nervous. Against such an overmatched and superior adversary India, as I have argued, will, in a running war, be impelled to resort to nuclear weapons. Preparation for 'total war' will require placing atomic demolition munitions in mountain passes and sub-kiloton nuclear-warhead-armed Prahar cruise missile on the Aksai Chin front, and threatening nuclear first use to take out the Three Gorges Dam with Su-30s and blooding the plains down to Nanjing and targeting China's wealth-producing southeastern and eastern coast by nuclear warheaded-Agni-5 missiles. That will deter China from initiating serious hostilities across the LAC.

Discussion of military options draws attention to India's status as an arms dependency, which mocks its pretensions as even 'a leading power' in the world. The absolute confusion reining in the Modi government in this regard is best exemplified by its muddled procurement policy which whatever rhetorical raiment it comes wrapped in is, in practical terms, a continuation of policy according to which, as a former head of the Headquarters Integrated Command, Vice Admiral Raman Puri, put it, 'India makes armaments when it must, and buys them when it can.'[63] Whence the anomaly of an India entirely self-sufficient in the most demanding and decisive strategic armaments and wherewithal—nuclear weapons, advanced ballistic and cruise missiles, nuclear-powered submarines and satellites—being unable to design, develop and manufacture the far simpler, technologically less complicated conventional weaponry. This situation prevails because the country cannot buy strategic armaments for love or money and has to rely on itself, but it can purchase conventional arms that its military has grown accustomed to and the government procures for them—a habit diligently fostered by foreign arms vendors and governments protecting this lucrative business with a scheme of payoffs involving kickbacks, commissions, foreign trips and immigrant and work visas and other considerations for family members of politicians, bureaucrats and military officers in the procurement loop. So the induction into service is resisted of indigenously produced hardware, such as the Tejas LCA, that has garnered praise as a superb fly-by-wire combat aircraft with quadruplex redundancies, and the Arjun MBT Mk-II that bested the latest Russian T-90 tank in test trials in different terrains, using various procedural and other contrivances, just so there are funds available for imported goods.[64] That in all these years of importing military goods and manufacturing thousands of military use items under licence and of expending by now hundreds of billions of dollars, the Indian government did not think of setting up a massive industrial complex to reverse-engineer every last component of foreign armaments and thus lay the foundation, as China did, for a flourishing defence industry just to observe the proprieties and tells its own sad story.

The obvious solution is, as argued in this book, for a strong-willed prime minister to simply close down the arms import channel and compel the military services to become stakeholders in home-grown conventional weapons design and development projects. Modi has proved he is not that kind of leader. The armed services though complain that they are victimized by the MoD staffed by generalist civil servants steeped in obduracy and ignorance representing a 'business model' that a former naval chief, Admiral D,K. Joshi, described as one in which 'Where there is authority, there is no accountability. And where there is responsibility, there is no authority'.[65] Worse, the nightmarish arms procurement process, based on the lowest tender system while keeping the laggardly defence public sector afloat by providing it licence production deals, was slammed by an internal MoD report as virtually beyond repair.[66] This 'business model' can be junked once the imports option is terminated. Incidentally, this is also essential if the government seeks a manifold increase in the country's arms exports, which the defence attaches in Indian embassies abroad are now being tasked to push.[67] Their sales pitch would be more convincing if the Indian armed services were seen to be using the same indigenous military hardware in large numbers. That this aspect has escaped Modi and his government reveals its jumbled thinking on this, as on other issues.

Modi has also failed to address two of the biggest defence procurement-related issues. The first is the neglect of the solution suggested by experts in NITI Aayog of selecting global companies with a versatile product portfolio and their willingness to manufacture them here for Indian consumption and for export. This will result in one or two companies being chosen to produce, for example, a whole series of small arms and ammunition required by the military, paramilitary and police organizations in the country, which could also lead to economical use of the rupee with a common logistics system for all armed forces of the state. Except the fragmentation of orders, with each service indenting for its own weapons, which is the prevailing scandalous procedure, makes for more deals and, hence, more opportunities for more people—uniformed and civilian—in disparate procurement loops to make more money.[68] The second issue is the government's reversal of the decision by the former defence minister Manohar Parrikar to choose a private sector 'strategic partner' for major projects. Project 75i for the advanced conventional submarine was analysed in detail in the last chapter. Differences over which private sector company to hand the production deal to—L&T with its experience of building the Arihant-class nuclear-powered submarine or Reliance, which bought the Pipavav shipyard but has minimal ship-building and nil submarine construction experience—has been resolved by the MoD going with its default option of contracting the public sector MDL to build it.[69] MDL will rely again on a foreign supplier to not just transmit the design but all the technologies, assemblies, sub-assemblies, components and production wherewithal at great cost to the exchequer, when most of these technologies are available with L&T and, at one stroke, gutting the indigenization thrust of Modi's 'Make in India' programme!

Just how powerful and entrenched the arms import lobby is in the government and military circles that make possible such decisions may be gauged from Defence Minister Nirmala Sitharaman's astonishing statement, ironically at the 2018 Defence Expo in Chennai to promote Indian military manufactures. In a serious abdication of the Indian government's sovereign responsibility to protect and advance the national interest, she asserted that the government will not cross 'the thin line' and compel the armed services to buy Indian.[70] In other words, the military is sovereign and not the Indian government, and as such the armed services are free to source their armament purchases from anywhere. If this is indeed the policy, the Modi government could write *finis* to the still infant Indian defence industry, because without large orders from the Indian armed forces there's no chance whatsoever that the indigenous efforts at achieving self-sufficiency in armaments will take off. Uniquely for a large and potentially great power, India will thus continue enriching foreign defence industries and creating jobs in foreign countries at the expense of its own industry and millions of languishing and unemployed youth guaranteeing, in the process, that the country does not become one.

The impression is thus projected of a country with an addle-brained leadership staggering forward rather than one striding confidently into the future, and of Modi as a big-talking but befuddled prime minister, his government incapable of understanding what the national interest is, leave alone how to protect and advance it. And, more broadly, why he has largely failed to deliver on his promises, a failure that is due to many reasons, chief among them his faith in the decrepit administrative system and careerist civil servants to deliver game-changing results. It may also be that his wildly improbable promises, overblown rhetoric and catchy alliterative slogans have finally caught up with him. Modi was the great hope; he turned out to be so much hype.

At the heart of the failure of India's foreign policy after Jawaharlal Nehru is that a succession of prime ministers, including Modi, have viewed international politics from the vantage point, as Ashley Tellis has written, of 'a subordinate state'.[71] In the present day, the 'subordinate state' notion has melded with Modi's own personal subaltern social status (as a former chaiwala) to inflict a low ceiling on India's ambition. Elected to rule with the boundless support of the Indian people and an impressive majority in Parliament he could have turbo-charged the economy by unshackling it from government control and revolutionized the government by making it over. All Modi has done in his first term is tinker around at the edges and achieved little. Perhaps the expectations attending on Modi were too high or maybe the people were taken in by his take-charge demeanour, mistaking it for Bismarckian will and a desire to truly transform the country and genuinely raise its stock in the world. Narendra Modi, unfortunately, has turned out to be just another Herbert Kitchener, the British minister for war during the First World War and former commander-in-chief, India, of whom Prime Minister Arthur Balfour said that 'he is only great when he has little things to accomplish'.[72]

Notes

Introduction

1. Chidanand Rajghatta, 'Trump Picks Man Who Opposed India's Elevation to UNSC as NSA', *Times of India*, 24 March 2018, https://timesofindia.indiatimes.com/world/us/trump-picks-man-who-opposed-indias-elevation-to-unsc-as-nsa/articleshow/63434685.cms.
2. David E. Sanger and Gardiner Harris, '"America First" Bears a New Threat: Military Force', *New York Times*, 24 March 2018, https://www.nytimes.com/2018/03/24/us/political/trump-nationaal-security-bolton.html.
3. Philip Rucker and Robert Costa, '"Tired of the Wait Game": White House Stabilizers Gone, Trump Calling His Own Shots', *Washington Post*, 31 March 2017, https://www.washingtonpost.com/politics/unhinged-or-unleashed-white-house-stabilizers-gone-trump-calling-his-own-shots/2018/03/31/19447ae2-343b-11e8-8bdd-cdb33a5eef83_story.html.
4. Naresh Mitral, 'India's a Hindu Rashtra, Says RSS Chief Bhagwat', *Times of India*, 18 January 2018, https://timesofindia.indiatimes.com/india/indias-a-hindu-rashtra-says-rss-chief-bhagwat/articleshow/62597063.cms.
5. Bharat Karnad, *Why India Is Not a Great Power (Yet)* (New Delhi: Oxford University Press, 2015).
6. K. Shankar Bajpai, 'At 90, When I Look Back', *Indian Express*, 30 March 2017, http://indianexpress.com/article/opinion/columns/india-growth-challenges-achievements-indian-democracy-government-5116585.
7. 'Modi's India: The Illusion of Reform', *The Economist*, 30 June 2017.
8. James A. Dorn, *China in the New Millennium* (Washington, DC: Cato Institute, 1998); Charles Wolf, Jr., K.C. Yeh, Anil Bamezai, Donald P. Henry and Michael Kennedy, *Long Term Economic and Military*

Trends 1994–2015 (Santa Monica: RAND, National Defense Research Institute, 1995), https://rand.org/content/dam/rand/pubs/monograph_reports/2006/MR627.pdf.

9. Tavleen Singh, 'Good Speech, But Not Enough', *Sunday Express*, 2 July 2017.
10. 'India Takes Its Place in the Sun with Launch of the Solar Alliance', *Times of India*, 12 March 2018, https://timesofindia.indiatimes.com/india/india-takes-its-place-in-the-sun-with-launch-of-solar-alliance/articleshow/63261261.cms.
11. See 'PM Modi Gives a Glimpse of New India at India Today Conclave 2017', *IndiaToday.in*, 18 March 2017, http://indiatoday.intoday.in/story/india-today-conclave-2017-narendra-modi-new-india-bjp-gst-development/1/907382.html; Shadi Hamid, 'How Much Can One Strongman Change a Country?', *Atlantic*, 28 June 2017, https://theatlantic.com/international/archive/2017/06/erdogan-turkey-islamist/531609.
12. Mark Singer, 'Trump Solo', *New Yorker*, 19 May 1997, http://www.newyorker.com/magazine/1997/05/18/trump-solo; P.R. Ramesh, 'Narendra Modi: Still the Unchallenged', *Open*, 18 May 2018, http://www.openthemagazine.com/article/4-years-of-modi/narendra-modi-still-the-unchallenged.
13. Bharat Karnad, 'Message from Modi', *New Indian Express*, 24 September 2011.
14. Rajmohan Gandhi, *Rajaji: A Life* (New Delhi: Penguin Books India, 1997), Chapter 22.
15. Bharat Karnad, 'India First', *Seminar* 519, 2002, http://www.india-seminar.com/2002/519/519%20bharat%20karnad.htm.
16. Bharat Karnad, 'More Disruption Please', *Open*, 17 March 2017, http://www.openthemagazine.com/article/mandate-2017-comment/more-disruption-please.
17. Bharat Karnad, 'Do Not Label Foreign-Made Military Hardware as "Indigenous"', *Hindustan Times*, 24 December 2015.
18. Bharat Karnad, *Why India Is Not a Great Power (Yet)* (New Delhi: Oxford University Press, 2015).

Chapter 1: 'Alpha Male' Leaders and 'Country First' Power Politics

1. Dean Burnett, 'Do Alpha Males Even Exist?', *Guardian*, 16 October 2016, https://www.theguardian.com/science/brain-flapping/2016/oct/10/do-alpha-males-even-exist-donald-trump.

2. Aaron L. Friedberg, *The Weary Titan: Britain and the Experience of Relative Decline, 1895–1905* (Princeton, NJ: Princeton University Press, 2010).
3. Zhang Feng, 'The Tianxia System: World Politics in a Chinese Utopia', *China Heritage Quarterly* 21, March 2010, http://www.chinaheritagequarterly.org/tien-hsia.php?searchterm=021_utopia.inc&issue=021.
4. The central idea in Xi Jinping's predecessor Hu Jintao's foreign policy, for instance, was 'harmonious world'. See Sujian Guo and Jean-Marc Blanchard, eds., *'Harmonious World' and China's New Foreign Policy* (Lanham, MD: Lexington Books, 2008).
5. Brent Griffiths, 'Trump on Alleged Russian Blackmail: I'm a "Germophobe"', *Politico.com*, 11 January 2017, http://www.politico.com/story/2017/01/trump-russia-response-germaphone-233473.
6. Ayesha Perera, 'Modi's Enthusiastic Bear Hug Beats Trump's Handshake', *BBC News*, 27 June 2017, http://www.bbc.com/news/world-asia-india-40414126.
7. 'Japan PM Abe Sends Ritual Offering to Yasukuni Shrine for War Dead', *Reuters*, 16 October 2016, http://www.reuters.com/article/us-japan-yasukuni-idUSKBN12G0ZN.
8. 'Robber Barons Beware', *The Economist*, 24 October 2015, http://www.economist.com/news/china/21676814-crackdown-corruption-has-spread-anxiety-among-chinas-business-elite-robber-barons-beware.
9. 'Xi Jinping's New Titles', *Chinascope*, 10 July 2017, http://chinascope.org/archives/12795.
10. Bill Birtles, 'Xi Jinping Pushes China Back Towards Strongman Era, But Is It Good for the Country?', *ABC News*, 3 August 2017, http://www.abc.net.au/news/2017-08-03/xi-jinping-is-his-power-play-good-for-china/8769284.
11. Caroline Mortimer, 'Emmanuel Macron Says Donald Trump Is like Putin and Erdogan', *Independent*, 29 May 2017, http://www.independent.co.uk/news/world/europe/emmaneul-macron-donall-trump-russia-turkey-diplomacy-public abuse-g7-handshake-recip-tayyp-erdogan-a7761841.html.
12. Susan B. Glasser, 'Madeleine Albright, Michele Flournoy and Wendy Sherman: The Full Transcript', *Politico.com*, 27 February 2017, http://www.politico.com/magazine/story.2017/02/madeleine-albright-michele-flournoy-and-wendy-sherman-the full-transcript-214829.
13. Greg Jaffe, 'For a Trump Adviser, an Odyssey from the Fringes of Washington to the Center of Power', *Washington Post*, 20 February 2017. Internal White House politics led Trump's new chief of staff, retired

General John Kelly firing Gorka in August 2017. See Lauren Gambino, 'Controversial Trump Adviser Sebastian Gorka Out of White House Job', *Guardian*, 26 August 2017, https://www.theguardian.com/us-news/2017/aug/25/donald-trump-sebastian-gorka-out-white-house-breitbart.
14. Glasser, 'Albright, Flournoy, Sherman', op. cit.
15. John Bew, *Realpolitik: A History* (New York: Oxford University Press, 2016), 70–71.
16. Nicholas Vinocur, 'President Marine Le Pen's First 100 Days', Politico.eu, 26 April 2017.
17. Emma Green 'The Specter of Catholic Identity in Secular France', *Atlantic*, 6 May 2017, https://www.theatlantic.com/international/archive/2017/05/christian-identity-france/525558.
18. 'In the current circumstances I see myself as no longer able,' said General Villiers, 'to guarantee the robust defence force I believe is necessary to guarantee the protection of France and the French people, today and tomorrow, and to sustain the aims of our country.' See Lizzie Dearden, 'French Armed Forces Chief Quits after Clash with Emmanuel Macron over Budget Cuts', *Independent*, 20 July 2017, http://www.independent.co.uk/news/world/europe/emmanuel-macron-pierre-de-villiers-head-of-french-armed-forces-quits-france-budget-cuts-army-resigns-a7848186.html.
19. 'How the Dutch Stopped Being Decent and Dull', *Sunday New York Times*, 10 March 2017, https://www.nytimes.com/2-17/03/10/opinion/sunday/how-the-dutch-stopped-being-decent-and-dull.html.
20. 'America First Foreign Policy', White House, https://www.whitehouse.gov/america-first-foreign-policy.
21. Howard Stoffer, 'What Trump's "America First" Policy Could Mean for the World', *Time*, 14 November 2016, http://time.com/4569845/donald-trump-america-first.
22. 'Trade Deals that Work for All Americans', White House, https://www.whitehouse.gov/trade-deals-working-all-americans.
23. Noor Mohammad, 'Commerce Ministry Mulls WTO actions against Trump's Steel Tariffs', *Wire*, 19 March 2018, https://thewire.in/trade/commerce-ministry-mulls-wto-action-against-trump-steel-tariff-barriers.
24. 'China Hits Back on Trump's Tariffs as Europe Off Hook for Now', *Bloomberg*, 22 March 2018, https://www.bloomberg.com/news/articles/2018-03-22/trump-orders-50-billion-hit-on-china-goods-amid-trade-war-fears; Mark Weinraub, Michael Hirtzer, 'China Tariffs on Soy,

Sorghum Spear Fear in US, Farm Country', *Reuters*, 4 April, 2018, https://www.reuters.com/article/us-usa-trade-china-crops/china-tariffs-on-soy-sorghum-spread-fear-in-u-s-farm-country-idUSKCN1HB2R6.

25. 'Making Our Military Strong Again', White House, https://whitehouse.gov/making-our-military-strong-again; Jennifer Epstein, 'Trump Says He Signed Spending Bill, Reversing His Veto Threat', *Bloomberg*, 23 March 2018, https://www.bloomberg.com/news/articles/2018-03-23/trump-says-he-s-signed-spending-bill-reversing-his-veto-threat.
26. 'An America First Energy Plan', White House, https://www.whitehouse.gov/america-first-energy.
27. G. John Ikenberry, 'The Plot against American Foreign Policy: Can the Liberal Order Survive?', *Foreign Affairs* 96.3, May–June 2017.
28. Ibid, 5–6.
29. Sarah Posner, 'Amazing Disgrace', *New Republic*, 27 March 2017, https://newrepublic.com/article/140961/amazing-disgrace-donald-trump-hijacked-religious-right.
30. 'Abe Tells Audience He Favors "Japan First" Policy, but with Global Focus', *Mainichi*, 17 May 2017, https://mainichi.jp/english/articles/20170517/p2a/0na/004000c.
31. 'G-7 Taormina Leaders' Communique', www.consilium.europa.eu/en/meetings/international-summit/2017/05/26-27.
32. See 'Japan and "One Belt, One Road"', *Japan Times*, 24 June 2017, http://www.japantimes.co.jp/opinion/2017/06/24/editorials/japan-one-belt-one-road/#.WXcr_hXyvIU.
33. See 'The Trump Effect on Tokyo', *International Herald Tribune*, 16 November 2016.
34. Cai Hong, '"Japan First" Contradicts Global Ideals', *China Daily*, Asia Weekly, 4 June 2017.
35. Paul Coyer, '(Un)Holy Alliance: Vladimir Putin, the Russian Orthodox Church and Russian Exceptionalism', *Forbes*, 21 May 2015, https://www.forbes.com/sites/paulcoyer/2015/05/21/unholy-alliance-vladimir-putin-and-the-russian-orthodox-church/2/#2387ba192253.
36. The US Congress punished Russia for interfering in the November 2016 US presidential elections with economic sanctions that Trump was advised not to veto, lest his veto be overridden. See Matt Flegenheimer, 'With New Sanctions, Senate Forces Trump's Hand on Russia', *New York Times*, 27 July 2017. https://www.nytimes.com/2017/07/27/us/politics/senate-russia-sanctions-trump.html.

37. John R. Schindler, 'Will Belarus be Putin's Next Victim?', *Observer (London)*, 7 February 2017, http://observer.com/2017/02/belarus-national-security-nato-vladimir-putin.
38. David E. Sanger, Eric Schmitt and Ben Hubbard, 'Trump Ends Covert Aid to Syrian Rebels Trying to Topple Assad', *New York Times*, 19 July 2017, https://www.nytimes.com/2017/07/19/world/middleeast/cia-arming-syrian-rebels.html.
39. 'Trump Seen Hardening Line against Pakistan', *Dawn*, 20 July 2017.
40. Yoko Wakatsuki and Ben Westcott, 'Hot Tub Diplomacy? Putin, Abe Talk Security Ties, Disputed Islands', *CNN*, 16 December 2016, http://edition.cnn.com/2016/12/15/asia/putin-abe-japan-arrival/index.html.
41. Bharat Karnad, 'Why did Turkey's Erdogan Offer to Play Peacemaker on Kashmir?', BloombergQuint.com, 3 May 2017, https://www.bloombergquint.com/opinion/2017/05/03/why-did-turkeys-erdogan-offer-to-play-peacemaker-on-kashmir.
42. Efrat Aviv, 'Erdogan Exploits the Temple Mount Crisis to Foment Anti-Zionism and Anti-Semitism', BESA (Begin-Sadat Center for Strategic Studies) Perspectives Paper 544, 29 July 2017, https://besacenter.org/perspectives-papers/erdogan-temple-mount-crisis.
43. Scott Peterson, 'In Turkey, Erdogan Fans an Islamic Nationalism to Build Ottoman-Style Influence', *Christian Science Monitor*, 22 February 2017, https://www.csmonitor.com/World/Middle-East/2017/0222/In-Turkey-Erdogan-fans-an-Islamic-nationalism-to-build-Ottoman-style-influence.
44. Zia Weise, 'Turkey's New Curriculum: More Erdogan, More Islam', *Politico.com*, 13 February 2017, http://www.politico.eu/article/erdogan-turkey-education-news-coup-analysis-curriculim-history-istanbul.
45. Hikmet Kocamaner, *How New Is Erdogan's 'New Turkey'?*, Middle East Brief 91, Crown Center for Middle East Studies, Brandeis University, Waltham, MA, April 2015, https://www.brandeis.edu/crown/publications/meb/MEB91.pdf.
46. '"India First" at the Core of Government's Foreign Policy: PM Narendra Modi', *Indian Express*, 6 August 2016, http://indianexpress.com/article/india/india-news-india/india-first-mygov-at-the-core-on-governments-foreign-policy-pm-narendramodi-2958398.
47. Bharat Karnad, 'India First', *Seminar* 519, 2002, http://www.india-seminar.com/2002/519/519%20bharat%20karnad.htm.
48. 'PM Narendra Modi Talks of Foreign Policy Goals with Indian Envoys', *Times of India*, 7 May 2017, http://timesofindia.indiatimes.com/india/

pm-narendra-modi-talks-of-foreign-policy-goals-with-indian-envoys/articleshow/58555674.cms.

49. 'Prime Minister Modi Gives a Glimpse of New India at India Today Conclave 2017', *India Today*, 18 March 2017, http://indiatoday.intoday.in/story/india-today-conclave-2017-narendra-modi-new-india-bjp-gst-development/1/907382.html.

50. In his radio show 'Mann Ki Baat' on 25 March 2018, for instance, Modi talked of the 'New India [being] Ambedkar's India, of the Poor and Backward'. See 'Mann Ki Baat: PM focus on farmers, Ambedkar', *Indian Express*, 26 March 2018.

51. John Lloyd, 'It's Time for Liberals to Fight Back', *Reuters*, 28 July 2017, http://www.reuters.com/article/us-lloyd-poland-commentary-idUSKBN1AD27Q.

52. Marlene Laruelle, 'US–Russia relations in Central Asia: Change Within', *Washington Times*, 28 December 2016, http://www.washingtontimes.com/news/2016/oct/28/us-russia-relations-central-asia.

53. M. Naeem Qureshi, *Pan-Islam in British India: The Politics of the Khilafat Movement* (Karachi: Oxford University Press, 2009).

54. Sandipan Sharma, 'BJP–RSS strategy to Make India Forget Nehru by Nixing His Name from Textbooks Won't Fly', *Firstpost*, 9 May 2016, www.firstpost.com/india/bjp-rss-jawaharlal-nehru-prime-minister-history-books-vajpayee-sangh-parivar-2771848.

55. Charles M. Blow, 'Trump's Obama Obsession', *New York Times*, 29 June 2017, https://www.nytimes.com/2017/06/29/opinion/trumps-obama-obsession.html; Paul Waldman, 'Why Trump and the Conservative Media Are Still Obsessed with Hillary Clinton', *Washington Post*, 21 July 2017, 'https://www.washingtonpost.com/blogs/plum-line/wp/2017/07/21/why-trump-and-the-conservative-media-are-still-obsessed-with-hillary-clinton/?utm_term=.0ea568771a40.

56. 'The Republican US Senator Angus King Has Accused President Trump of Conducting "Policy by Twitter"', Anderson Cooper 360, *CNN*, July 2017.

57. 'Modi's Many Tasks', *The Economist*, 23 May 2015, https://www.economist.com/news/special-report/21651329-narendra-modi-has-grand-ambitions-his-country-and-self-confidence-match-he.

58. Daniel Fried, 'Russia's Back-to-the-80s Foreign Policy', *Defense One*, 3 August 2017, http://www.defenseone.com/threats/2017/08/russias-back-80s-foreign-policy/139978.

59. 'Deng Xiaoping's "24-character strategy"', GlobalSecurity.org, http://www.globalsecurity.org/military/world/china/24-character.htm.
60. Graham Allison, 'What Xi Jinping Wants', *Atlantic*, 31 May 2017, https://www.theatlantic.com/international/archive/2017/05/what-china-wants/528561.
61. Bitte Hammergren, 'An Impulsive Actor in the Middle East', *Global Policy*, 28 June 2017, http://www.globalpolicyjournal.com/blog/28/06/2017/impulsive-actor-middle-east.
62. Manoj Joshi, 'Dassault Rafale Deal: New Fighter Is Good but Price Is Worrying', *India Today*, 1 February 2012, http://indiatoday.intoday.in/story/iaf-dassault-rafale-mmrca-deal-aircraft/1/171460.html.
63. 'Will Buy Only 36 Rafales, No Need for 126: Parrikar', *The Hindu*, 31 May 2015.
64. Senior staff member of the foundation.
65. Amelia Stewart, 'The Very Real Impact of India's Demonetization', *Adam Smith Institute*, 6 March 2017, https://www.adamsmith.org/blog/the-very-real-impact-of-indias-demonetization.
66. See 'Samuel Huntington, a Prophet for the Trump Era', *Washington Post*, 18 July 2017, https://www.washingtonpost.com/news/book-party/wp/2017/07/18/samuel-huntington-a-prophet-for-the-trump-era/?utm_term=.cf83a1e72ea2.
67. Mayank Bhardwaj, 'Cattle Trade Ban to Halt Exports, Lead to Job Losses', *Reuters*, 29 May 2017, http://www.reuters.com/article/india-modi-politics-meat-idUSKBN18P129.
68. 'Muslim Women to Thank PM Modi for the Triple Talaq Bill', *ANI*, 31 December 2017, https://www.aninews.in/news/national/general-news/muslim-women-to-thank-pm-modi-for-triple-talaq-bill201712310347580002.
69. Suman Layak, Indulekha Aravind, 'How Fringe Groups Like Hindu Sena and Sanatan Sanstha Are Attempting to Set the Agenda with BJP In Power', *Economic Times*, 8 November 2015, https://economictimes.indiatimes.com/news/politics-and-nation/how-fringe-organisations-like-hindu-sena-and-sanatan-sanstha-are-attempting-to-set-the-agenda-with-bjp-in-power/articleshow/49704443.cms.
70. 'Muslims in India Are Also Hindus: RSS Chief Mohan Bhagwat', *DNA*, 17 December 2017, http://www.dnaindia.com/india/report-muslims-in-india-are-also-hindus-rss-chief-mohan-bhagwat-2568417.

71. Bharat Karnad, 'India's Weak Geopolitics and What to Do about It' in Bharat Karnad, ed., *Future Imperilled: India's Security in the 1990s and Beyond* (New Delhi: Penguin Books India, 1994), 21–22.
72. White House aides said that that Trumpism was an 'impromptu' statement, not a real military threat. See Josh Dawsey and Louis Nelson, 'Trump Aides Downplaying His North Korea Threat As "Impromptu"', Politico.com, 9 August 2017, http://www.politico.com/story/2017/08/09/trump-north-korea-comments-reactions-241434?lo=ap_b1.
73. Patrick Wintour, 'It Is an Honour to Be with You—Trump and Putin Meet at G20 in Hamburg', *Guardian*, 7 July 2017, https://www.theguardian.com/world/2017/jul/07/donald-trump-and-putin-exchange-handshake-at-g20-summit-in-hamburg.
74. John Walcott, 'Trump Ends CIA Arms Support for Anti-Assad Syria Rebels: US Officials', *Reuters*, 19 July 2017, https://www.reuters.com/article/us-mideast-crisis-usa-syria-idUSKBN1A42KC.
75. Shubhajit Roy, 'Accepting PM Modi Invitation, Ivanka Trump Will Head to Hyderabad in November End', *Indian Express*, 8 August 2017.
76. See *Superfast Primetime Ultimate Nation: The Relentless Invention of Modern India* (London: Profile Books, 2017), 289.
77. Aditi Malhotra, 'What Donald Trump Thinks about India', *Wall Street Journal*, 27 January 2016, https://blogs.wsj.com/indiarealtime/2016/01/27/what-donal-trump-thinks-about-india.
78. Dinesh Unnikrishnan, 'Why Modi–Trump Meeting Is a Disappointment for Indian H1B Visa Users, Businesses', *Firstpost*, 27 June 2017, http://www.firstpost.com/world/why-narendra-modi-donald-trump-meeting-is-a-disappointment-for-indian-h-1b-visa-users-businesses-3749643.html.
79. Prabhas K. Dutta, 'Who are Rohingya Muslims and Why the Government Wants to Deport 40,000 of Them?', *India Today*, 10 August 2017, http://indiatoday.intoday.in/story/rohingy-muslim-india-myanmar-deportation/1/1023213.html.
80. Conrad Hackett, 'By 2050, India to Have World's Largest Populations of Hindus and Muslims', *Fact Tank*, Pew Research Center, 21 April 2015, http://www.pewresearch.org/fact-tank/2015/04/21/by-2050-india-to-have-worlds-largest-populations-of-hindus-and-muslims.
81. Barry Sautman, '"Cultural Genocide" and Tibet', *Texas International Law Journal* 38.2, 2003, https://www.tilj.org/content/journal/38/num2/Sautman173.pdf.

82. Lizzie Dearden, 'China Bans Burqas and "Abnormal" Beards in Muslim Province of Xinjiang', *Independent*, 30 March 2017, http://www.independent.co.uk/news/world/asia/china-burqa-abnormal-beards-ban-muslim-province-xinjiang-veils-province-extremism-crackdown-freedom-a7657826.html.
83. For a detailed analysis of the China–Pakistan terrorism nexus, see Andrew Small, *The China-Pakistan Axis: Asia's New Geopolitics* (Gurgaon: Penguin Random House India, 2015), Chapter 3.
84. Ethan Gutmann, *The Slaughter: Mass Killings, Organ Harvesting, and China's Secret Solution to Its Dissident Problem* (Amherst, NY: Prometheus Books, 2014).
85. 'Richard Madsen: China Is Religious Country; 85% Have Some Belief—Part Four', *AsiaNews*, 6 February 2017, http://www.asianews.it/news-en/Richard-Madsen:-China-is-a-religious-country.-85-have-some-belief---Part-Four-39853.html.
86. Hakan Karakurt, 'The Upcoming Civil War in the Islamic World', Geopolitica.ru, 9 March 2017, https://www.geopolitica.ru/en/article/upcoming-civil-war-islamic-world.
87. Nivedita Dash, 'Modi Government Polarizing Society, Destabilizing Institutions: Sonia Gandhi', *IndiaToday.in*, 20 July 2016, http://indiatoday.intoday.in/story/modi-government-polarising-society-destabilising-institutions-sonia-gandhi/1/719169.html.
88. Robert Mickey, Steven Levitsky, and Lucan Ahmad Way, 'Is America Still Safe for Democracy?', *Foreign Affairs*, May–June 2017, https://www.foreignaffairs.com/articles/united-states/2017-04-17/america-still-safe-democracy; Brennan Gilmore, 'What I Saw in Charlottesville Could be Just the Beginning', Politico.com, 14 August 2017, http://www.politico.com/magazine/story/2017/08/14/what-i-saw-in-charlottesville-could-be-just-the-beginning-215487.
89. William Eichler, 'The Making of a Demagogue: How Erdogan Became Turkey's Strongman', *OpenDemocracy*, 18 April 2017, https://www.opendemocracy.net/william-eichler/making-of-demagogue-how-erdo.
90. Joel Wuthnow and Philip C. Saunders, *Chinese Military Reforms in the Age of Xi Jinping: Drivers, Challenges, and Implications*, China Strategic Perspectives No. 10, Center for the Study of Chinese Military Affairs, Institute for National Strategic Studies, National Defense University (Washington, DC: National Defense University Press, March 2017); Chris Buckley, 'China Enshrines "Xi Jinping Thought", Elevating Leader to Mao-like Status',

New York Times, 24 October 2017, https://www.nytimes.com/2017/10/24/world/asia/china-xi-jinping-communist-party.html.
91. William Eichler, 'The Making of a Demagogue', *OpenDemocracy*, 18 April 2017, https://www.opendemocracy.net/william-eichler/making-of-demagogue-how-erdo.
92. Mark Edward Lewis, *China's Cosmopolitan Empire* (Cambridge, MA: Harvard University Press, 2012).
93. Jessica Taylor, 'Trump Thanks Putin for Ordering Expulsion of American Diplomats, Later Says it was Sarcasm', *NPR*, 10 August 2017, http://www.npr.org/2017/08/10/542685154/president-trump-thanks-putin-for-ordering-expulsion-of-u-s-diplomats-from-russia.
94. The Russian TV clip of the interview and this exchange also showed Putin and Modi walking hand-in-hand in a St Petersburg park. See https://www.youtube.com/watch?v=12s_n6F2ZEQ.
95. Bharat Karnad, 'The Doklam Standoff: Hot and Cold at the Creeping Trijunction', BloombergQuint.com, 23 July 2017, https://www.bloombergquint.com/opinion/2017/07/23/the-doklam-india-china-standoff-hot-and-cold-at-the-creeping-trijunction.
96. Hitler's rise in *mitteleuropa* comes to mind. See Edward Hallet Carr, *Twenty Years' Crisis, 1919–1939: An Introduction to the Study of International Relations*, 450th edition (New York: Harper Perennial, 1964).

Chapter 2: Impact of Modi's Persona on Government

1. 'Narendra Modi Anointed BJP's PM Candidate, Advani Disappointed', *PTI*, 13 September 2016, http://timesofindia.indiatimes.com/india/Narendra-Modi-anointed-BJP-PM-candidate-Advani-disappointed/articleshow/22554959.cms.
2. It was the most extensive use of holographic or 3D technology ever that covered 1500 rallies and reached some 5800 locations in the countryside, a large number of these with only spotty supply of electricity. See Andy Marino, *Narendra Modi: A Political Biography* (Noida: HarperCollins India, 2014), 265.
3. K. Balchand, 'Modi Fears a "Pink Revolution"', *The Hindu*, 23 April 2014, http://www.thehindu.com/news/national/other-states/modi-fears-a-pink-revolution/article5864109.ece.
4. Aakar Patel, 'Meeting Disillusionment with Promises', *Business Standard*, 2 February 2018.

5. Erik H. Erikson, *Gandhi's Truth: On the Origins of Militant Nonviolence* (New York: W.W. Norton and Co., 1969).
6. 'Mapping leadership style of Indian leaders', *Economic Times*, 26 April 2009, http://economictimes.indiatimes.com/special-report/mapping-leadership-style-of-indian-leaders/printarticle/4449846.cms.
7. See his *Presidential Character: Predicting Performance in the White House* (Englewood-Cliffs, NJ: Prentice Hall, 1972).
8. Nilanjan Mukhopadhyay, *Narendra Modi: The Man, the Times* (New Delhi: Tranquebar Press, 2013), 72; Marino, *Narendra Modi*, 6.
9. Marino, *Narendra Modi*, 37.
10. Mukhopadhyay, *Narendra Modi*, 305.
11. Ibid, 129.
12. Marino, *Narendra Modi*, 54–60.
13. Ibid, 37, 41.
14. 'Narendra Modi: Leading the race to 7 RCR', *Zee News*, 8 April 2014.
15. Leena Misra, "Watching Shankersinh Vaghela', *Indian Express*, 6 August 2017.
16. Modi has refused to elaborate on his role as chief minister during the 2002 riots. The clearest defence of Modi that has been presented is by Marino with some documentary and other evidence presumably provided by the Gujarat government. See his *Narendra Modi*, Chapter 7.
17. Lance Price, *The Modi Effect: Inside Narendra Modi's Campaign to Transform India* (London: Hodder and Stoughton, 2015), Chapter 13; Marino, *Narendra Modi*, Chapter 9.
18. Marino, *Narendra Modi*, 90.
19. 'Narendra Modi Anointed BJP PM Candidate, Advani Disappointed', *PTI*, 13 September 2013 http://timesofindia.indiatimes.com/india/Narendra-Modi-anointed-BJP-PM-candidate-Advani-disappointed/articleshow/22554959.cms.
20. 'Cracks Appear in BJP over Narendra Modi's PM Candidacy', *PTI*, 12 September 2013, http://www.livemint.com/Politics/tlkSd9JdBKlYZiYlPvDz8N/No-rift-in-party-over-Narendra-Modi-Rajnath-Singh.html.
21. Mukhopadhyay, *Narendra Modi*, 271.
22. Ibid, 28–29; Marino, *Narendra Modi*, 260.
23. Vasudha Venugopal, 'Mohan Bhagwat Backs PM Narendra Modi in Condemning Cow Vigilantes', *Times of India*, 7 September 2017, http://timesofindia.indiatimes.com/india/mohan-bhagwat-backs-pm-narendra-modi-in-condemning-cow-vigilantes/articleshow/60402744.cms.

24. Quotes in Jena McGregor, 'Remembering James MacGregor Burns and His Leadership Wisdom', *Washington Post*, 17 July 2014, https://www.washingtonpost.com/news/on-leadership/wp/2014/07/17/remembering-james-macgregor-burns-and-his-leadership-wisdom.
25. Nilanjana Bhowmick, 'As India's Muslims Are Lynched, Modi Keeps Silent', *Washington Post*, 28 June 2017, https://www.washingtonpost.com/news/global-opinions/wp/2017/06/28/as-indias-muslims-are-killed-modi-keeps-silent.
26. Bhavdeep Kang, 'Ram Rahim Singh's Devotees Are Rampaging: Why Are the Politicians Silent?', *Print*, 25 August 2017, https://theprint.in/2017/08/25/ram-rahim-singhs-devotees-rampaging-politicians-silent.
27. Mona Mishra, 'Ever Noticed that Modi Can't Bring Himself to Say, "Mitron, Muslims Are Equal Citizens"?', *Huffington Post*, 7 July 2017, http://www.huffingtonpost.in/mona-mishra/ever-noticed-that-modi-just-can-t-bring-himself-to-say-mitron_a_23016547.
28. Supriya Nair, 'The Meaning of India's "Beef Lynchings"', *Atlantic*, 24 July 2017, https://www.theatlantic.com/international/archive/2017/07/india-modi-beef-lynching-muslim-partition/533739.
29. See his 'The Harsh Truth about India's "Godmen"', *Japan Times*, 12 September 2017, https://www.japantimes.co.jp/opinion/2017/09/12/commentary/world-commentary/harsh-truth-indias-godmen/#.Wbi1hfOGPIU.
30. For example, Rahul Gandhi, the man ready by his own admission to lead the Congress, reacting to a question about dynastic politics lacked the wit not to say what he did, that the country is run by dynasties in all fields, a statement that sits ill with the predominantly youthful voters, as the 2014 elections proved, and which the BJP is sure to feast on at election time. See 'Rahul Gandhi at UC, Berkeley: Key Takeaways from His Address', *Indian Express*, 12 September 2017, http://indianexpress.com/article/india/rahul-gandhi-at-uc-berkeley-key-takeaways-from-his-address-4839493.
31. 'Modi Government Misusing CBI and Other Agencies: Abhishek Manu Singhvi', *Economic Times*, 6 August 2017, http://economictimes.indiatimes.com/news/politics-and-nation/modi-government-misusing-cbi-and-other-agencies-abhishek-manu-singhvi/articleshow/59943351.cms.
32. Scott London, '*Leadership* by James MacGregor Burns—A Book Review', 2008, http://www.scottlondon.com/reviews/burns.html.
33. In a poll taken in mid-2017, 20 per cent of those polled rated the Modi government's performance as 'Outstanding', 43 per cent as 'Good'. See 'India

Today Mood of the Nation Poll: PM Modi's Invincibility Continues, 10 Big Takeaways', *India Today*, 10 August 2017, http://indiatoday.intoday.in/story/india-today-mood-of-the-nation-poll-10-big-takeaways/1/1028161.html.
34. David Rosen, 'The 6 Political Personality Types', *Campaigns and Elections*, 6 October 2013, https://www.campaignsandelections.com/campaign-insider/the-6-political-personality-types.
35. For Modi's account of his travels that took him from Belur Math in Kolkata to various ashrams in the Himalayas thence back on to the plains before his return to Vadnagar, see Marino, *Narendra Modi*, Chapter 2.
36. Mukhopadhyay, *Narendra Modi*, 280–84.
37. Jyoti Sharma Bawa, 'You Are What You Wear: Modi Changes Clothes Four Times in a Day', *Hindustan Times*, 28 September 2015, http://www.hindustantimes.com/india/you-are-what-you-wear-modi-changes-clothes-four-times-in-a-day/story-NCJ7WBWFXc3Q3p3gSgQ7CN.html.
38. Mukhopadhyay, *Narendra Modi*, 382–84.
39. Interview, February 28, 2017.
40. '"Diwali bomb": L.K. Advani leads BJP revolt against Modi, Shah; Bihar MPs join in as resentment boils over', *Firstpost*, 12 November 2017, http://www.firstpost.com/politics/advani-leads-revolt-by-party-old-guard-says-modi-shah-solely-responsible-for-bihar-defeat-2503028.html.
41. Bobby Azarian, Donald Trump's Narcissistic Personality Makes Him a Dangerous World Leader', *Huffington Post*, 24 March 2016, http://www.huffingtonpost.com/bobby-azarian/donald-trumps-narcissisti_b_9536682.html.
42. Rosen, 'The 6 Political Personality Types'.
43. Marino, *Narendra Modi*, 15.
44. Nilanjan Mukhopadhyay, 'Vakil Sahab's Role in PM Modi's Life Isn't Restricted to Single Sphere', *Economic Times*, 22 September 2017.
45. Ibid, 11. *Economic Times*, 22 September 2017.
46. Mukhopadhyay, *Narendra Modi*, 7.
47. C.J. Polychronion, 'Trump Feels a Kinship with Authoritarian Leaders': Richard Falk on Turmoil in the Middle East', *Global Policy Journal*, 3 July 2017, http://www.globalpolicyjournal.com/blog/03/07/2017/trump-feels-kinship-authoritarian-leaders-richrad-falk-turmoil-middle-east; Philip Rucker, 'Trump Keeps Praising International Strongmen, Alarming Human Rights Advocates', *Washington Post*, 1 May 2017.
48. Rosen, 'The 6 Political Personality Types'.
49. The late American sociologist Seymour Martin Lipset long ago theorized about the causal link between economic development and democratic

politics. See his *Political Man: The Social Bases of Politics* (New York: Doubleday & Co., 1960).
50. Marino, *Narendra Modi*, Chapter 8.
51. In an interview to the *New York Times*, he had this exchange: When asked what he had done for Muslims Modi replied "Nothing.' 'So you admit it?' the reporter queried. Modi then suggested the reporter ask him what he had 'done for Hindus'. 'What have you done for Hindus?' the reporter demanded. 'Nothing', Modi responded. 'Everything I have done has been for Gujaratis.' Ibid, 242.
52. Mukhopadhyay, *Narendra Modi*, 309.
53. Ibid, 270–71.
54. Uday Mahurkar, *Marching with a Billion: Analysing Narendra Modi's Government at Midterm* (Gurgaon: Penguin Random House India, 2017), xliii.
55. Rajeev Deshpande, 'Lack of Muslim Support Has Not Hurt BJP's Poll Prospects', *Times of India*, 29 July 2017.
56. Mukhopadhyay, *Narendra Modi*, 328.
57. Ibid, 34.
58. Ibid.
59. Rosen, 'The 6 Political Personality Types'.
60. Ashish Nandy writes: 'More than a decade ago, when Narendra Modi was a nobody, a small-time RSS *pracharak* trying to make it as a small-time BJP functionary, I had the privilege of interviewing him . . . It was a long, rambling interview, but it left me in no doubt that here was a classic, clinical case of a fascist. I never use the term "fascist" as a term of abuse; to me it is a diagnostic category comprising not only one's ideological posture but also the personality traits and motivational patterns contextualising the ideology. Modi, it gives me no pleasure to tell the readers, met virtually all the criteria that psychiatrists, psycho-analysts and psychologists had set up after years of empirical work on the authoritarian personality. He had the same mix of puritanical rigidity, narrowing of emotional life, massive use of the ego defence of projection, denial and fear of his own passions combined with fantasies of violence—all set within the matrix of clear paranoid and obsessive personality traits. I still remember the cool, measured tone in which he elaborated a theory of cosmic conspiracy against India that painted every Muslim as a suspected traitor and a potential terrorist. I came out of the interview shaken . . . I had met a textbook case of a fascist and a prospective killer, perhaps even a future mass murderer.' See his

'Obituary for a Culture', *Seminar* 513, 2002, http://www.india-seminar. com/2002/513/513%20ashis%20nandy.htm.
61. Mukhopadhyay, *Narendra Modi*, 304, 359.
62. Price, *The Modi Effect*, 86.
63. Pradip Kumar Maitra, 'Now, RSS Begins Drive on What to Eat, Wear and How to Celebrate', *Hindustan Times*, 15 July 2017.
64. 'Personality Predicts Political Preferences', *Science Daily*, 10 June 2010, https://wwwsciencedaily.com/releases/2010/06/100609111312.htm.
65. Ibid, 52, 56–58.
66. Marino, *Narendra Modi*, 176.
67. Personal communication from a senior bureaucrat.
68. This is the view of Amarjit Singh Dulat, head of the R&AW, 1999–2000. See Pankaj Vohra, 'Brajesh Mishra Ran the Vajpayee Government: Dulat', *Sunday Guardian*, 4 July 2015, http://www.sunday-guardian.com/news/brajesh-mishra-ran-vajpayee-government-dulat.
69. Shyam Saran, *How India Sees the World: From Kautilya to the 21st Century* (New Delhi: Juggernaut, 2017), 209–10.
70. The senior functionary; personal communication.
71. Manas Dasgupta, 'Vajpayee's Advice to Modi', *The Hindu*, 5 April 2002. http://www.thehindu.com/2002/04/05/stories/2002040509161100.htm.
72. Price, *The Modi Effect*, Chapter 20, 267.
73. Marino, *Narendra Modi*, 62–63.
74. Mukhopadhyay, *Narendra Modi*, 382; On Indira Gandhi's 'kitchen cabinet' see Raj Thapar, *All the Years: A Memoir* (New Delhi: Penguin Books, 1991).
75. On how centrally Nehru depended on Britishers to craft especially his foreign and national security his policies, see Bharat Karnad, *Nuclear Weapons and Indian Security: The Realist Foundations of Strategy*, second edition (New Delhi: Macmillan India, 2005, 2002), Chapter 2.
76. Price, *The Modi Effect*, Chapter 6, 86.
77. Mukhopadhyay, *Narendra Modi*, 15.
78. Ibid, 359.
79. Ibid, 57, 360.
80. Marino, *Narendra Modi*, 9.
81. Price, *The Modi Effect*, 6.
82. Interview, 28 February 2017.
83. Mishra's curriculum vitae is on the net at http://nset.gov.in/Items/CV%20-%20Dopt%202016%20-%20Dr.%20P.K.%20Mishra.pdf.
84. Mukhopadhyay, *Narendra Modi*, 369–70.

85. See his 'In the New India, Wisdom Is Becoming an Outdated Recipe', *DailyO*, 15 October 2017, https://www.dailyo.in/voices/idea-debate-modi-trump/story/1/20087.html.
86. Welcoming Modi to the White House. President Trump said, 'I'm proud to announce to the media, to the American people, and to the Indian people, that Prime Minister Modi and I are world leaders in social media' which met with much mirth and laughter. See his 'Remarks by President Trump and Prime Minister Modi of India in Joint Press Conference', White House, 26 June 2017, https://www.whitehouse.gov/the=press-office/2017/06/26/remarks-president-trump-and-prime-minister-modi-india-joint-press.
87. Jason Silverstein, 'President Trump Needs Single Page Memos Filled with Charts and His Name for First Foreign Trip', *New York Daily News*, 17 May 2017, http://www.nydailynews.com/news/politics/trump-short-memos-charts-foreign-trip-article-1.3173655.
88. Modi's TV interview with Rajeev Shukla (undated but looks like from when he was Gujarat chief minister), see https://www.youtube.com/watch?v=lTTqEfuD3B8.
89. On Nehru's foreign and defence policy consultations with experts, intellectuals, and fellow politicians see Karnad, *Nuclear Weapons and Indian Security*, Chapter 2; Vinay Sitapati, *Half Lion: How Narasimha Rao Transformed India* (New Delhi: Penguin Random House India, 2016), 313.
90. This was said by Prithviraj Chauhan, Minister of State in Manmohan Singh's PMO, at the Twelfth India Conference at Harvard University, March 2015, https://www.youtube.com/watch?v=9fAmfHILb5s.
91. Deep K. Datta-Ray, *The Making of Indian Diplomacy: A Critique of Eurocentrism* (New Delhi: Oxford University Press, 2015), 74.
92. Mukhopadhyay, *Narendra Modi*, 102–03.
93. Mukhopadhyay, *Narendra Modi*, 360.
94. Ibid, 139.
95. Ibid, 56.
96. Sreeram Chaulia, *Modi Doctrine: The Foreign Policy of India's Prime Minister* (New Delhi: Bloomsbury, 2016), 113.
97. Roberts, *Superfast, Primetime Ultimate Nation*, 50, 52–53. International Chamber of Commerce Open Markets Index 2017, https://iccwbo.org/publication/icc-open-markets-index-2017.
98. This is the impression I had after a meeting with Prime Minister Modi in November 2014, along with an odd assortment of think-tankers and media types—a publisher–editor, reporter or two.

99. Mukhopadhyay, *Narendra Modi*, 57–58.
100. Marino, *Narendra Modi*, 5.
101. Personal communication from a senior VIF member.
102. Mukhopadhyay, *Narendra Modi*, 63–65.
103. Ibid, 76.
104. Margaret G. Hermann, 'Political Psychology' in R.A. Rhodes and Paul 'tHart, eds., *The Oxford Handbook of Political Leadership* (New York: Oxford University Press, 2014), 122
105. Consider the appointment of Rajiv Kumar, a champion of Modi's economic policies, to replace the increasingly disillusioned Columbia University Professor Arvind Panagariya, as vice chairman of NITI Aayog, and the prime minister's decision to revive the Economic Advisory Council filled with economists supportive of the government's policies, such as Surjit Bhalla.
106. Marino, *Narendra Modi*, 54, 61–62.
107. Mihir Sharma, 'The Inside Story of Why BJP's Biggest Policy Champion May Have Jumped Modi's Ship', *Economic Times*, 10 August 2017, http://economictimes.indiatimes.com/news/economy/policy/how-india-lost-another-champion-in-the-form-of-arvind-panagariya/articleshow/59996454.cms.
108. Modi's 'spiritual cronyism', writes Bindu Dalmia, involves 'voter-outsourcing to religious heads [that] comes as a comprehensive package with the lumpen elements and footsoldiers ready to rabble rouse, or riot-on-command in return for state patronage.' See her 'Is Modi Momentum Slowing Down? Crony Spiritualism and a Depressed Economy Could Impede Mission 350', *Times of India*, 31 August 2017.
109. Maseeh Rahman, 'Indian Prime Minister Claims Genetic Science Existed in Ancient Times', *Guardian*, 28 October 2014, https://www.theguardian.com/world/2014/oct/28/indian-prime-minister-genetic-science-existed-ancient-times.
110. 'Science Congress a Circus: Nobel Winner Venkataraman Ramakrishnan', *Times of India*, 6 January 2015, http://timesofindia.indiatimes.com/india/Science-congress-a-circus-Nobel-winner-Venkatraman-Ramakrishnan/articleshow/50460663.cms.
111. Over 250 Indian scientists protested against the obscurantist thrust of funding research into such things as 'panchgavya'—a mix of cow dung, urine, milk, curd and ghee. See 'Scientists Take to Streets against "Obscurantism", Unscientific Ideas', *Hindustan Times*, 10 August 2017.
112. Personal communication from a highly regarded civil servant.
113. See his 'New Wine in Old Bottles', *Times of India*, 21 July 2017.

114. Bharat Karnad, 'India's Foreign Policy: The Foreign Hand', *Open*, 29 April 2016, http://www.openthemagazine.com/article/voices/indias-foreign-policy-the-foreign-hand.
115. Mukhopadhyay, *Narendra Modi*, 221, 384.
116. Ibid, 129, 111–27, 129.
117. Marino, *Narendra Modi*, Chapter 3.
118. Ibid, 260.
119. Ibid, 20.
120. Mukhopadhyay, *Narendra Modi*, 80–97.
121. Ibid, 83.
122. The VMR poll of 30 May 2017 showed 59 per cent of the people polled supported Modi's stance against Pakistan. See https://www.youtube.com/watch?v=wYsTKHxg_yQ.
123. Hermann, 'Political Psychology', 127.
124. Vajpayee's finance minister Yashwant Sinha said the Modi's government ruled by 'fear'. See his interview to Rajdeep Sardesai, *India Today TV*, 27 September 2017. For Congress party Rahul Gandhi's views, see 'PM Narendra Modi Ruling through Fear: Rahul Gandhi', *Economic Times*, 12 January 2017, http://economictimes.indiatimes.com/news/politics-and-nation/pm-narendra-modi-ruling-through-fear-rahul-gandhi/articleshow/56486625.cms.
125. Zoya Hasan and Martha C. Nussbaum, 'India and United States, Spot the Difference', *Indian Express*, 24 July 2017.
126. 'Indira Is India, India Is Indira; JP's Crusade', *Outlook*, 18 August 1997, https://www.outlookindia.com/magazine/story/indira-is-indiaindia-is-indira-jps-crusade/204064.
127. 'Modi Is Now an Accepted World Leader: Shah', *Indian Express*, 28 August 2017.
128. See 'Remarks by President Trump and Prime Minister Modi of India in Joint Press Conference', 26 June 2017, https://www.whitehouse.gov/the-pressoffice/2017/06/26/remarks-president-trump-and-prime-minister-modi--india-joint-press and 'Remarks on "Defining Our Relationship With India for the Next Century"', 18 October 2017, https://www.state.gov/secretary/remarks/2017/10/274913.htm.
129. Mukhopadhyay, *Narendra Modi*, 284.
130. Roberts, *Superfast, Primetime Ultimate Nation*, 212, 249.
131. Mukhopadhyay, *Narendra Modi*, 197.
132. Robert Kagan, 'The Ungreat Washed', *New Republic*, 6 July 2003, https://newrepublic.com/article/90784/fareed-zakaria-democracy.

133. 'BJP Managed to Convince People We Are a Muslim Party: Sonia Gandhi', *Indian Express*, 10 March 2018, http://indianexpress.com/article/india/bjp-managed-to-convince-people-we-are-a-muslim-party-sonia-gandhi-5092572.
134. Amitabh Mattoo and Rory Metcalf, 'How the World Looks from India', *The Hindu*, updated 8 June 2016, http://www.thehindu.com/opinion/op-ed/how-the-world-looks-from-india/article4730431.ece.
135. For insights in this section on 'political capital', see Sabine van 'Credibility As a Source of Political Capital: Exploring political leaders' performance Zuydam, from a credibility perspective', Paper prepared for the 2014 Joint Sessions of the European Consortium of Political Research, https://ecpr.eu/filestore/paperproposal/71691ba3-714b-4f4a-ae59-3d7551645733.pdf.
136. '"Reform, Perform, and Transform": Modi Addresses Indian Diaspora at Mass Tel Aviv Rally', *Times Now TV*, 5 July 2017. http://www.timesnownews.com/india/video/reform-perform-transform-pm-modi-addresses-indian-diaspora-at-mass-tel-aviv-rally/65173.

Chapter 3: Creeper-vine Foreign Policy

1. I gleaned this historical tidbit from a discussion on 15 November 2017 with Professor Andrey Volodin of the Russian Diplomatic Academy, Moscow, who was visiting Delhi.
2. Quote in Pulapre Balakrishnan 'Modi's Unrealistic American Dreams', *The Hindu*, 25 September 2015, http://www.thehindu.com/opinion/lead/lead-article-by-pulapre-balakrishnan-on-prime-minister-narendra-modis-unrealistic-american-dreams/article7678266.ece.
3. Retired US ambassador Teresita Schaffer has talked of a 'family resemblance' between the two concepts. See 'This Is How US Negotiates with India', Stimson Center, Washington, DC, 22 July 2017, https://www.youtube.com/watch?v=qTa6h1M9um0&t=43s.
4. This session with Carafano took place at the Confederation of Indian Industry on 19 January 2018.
5. David Brewster, 'End of Strategic Autonomy', *Indian Express*, 18 November 2014, http://indianexpress.com/article/opinion/columns/end-of-strategic-autonomy. Brewster is a US-schooled researcher at the Australian National University, Canberra.
6. Celeste A. Wallander, 'Global Challenges and Russian Foreign Policy' in Robert Legvold, ed., *Russian Foreign Policy in the Twenty-first Century and the Shadow of the Past* (New York: Columbia University Press, 2007, 446.)

7. Martin Ford, *The Rise of the Robots: Technology and the Threat of Mass Unemployment* (London: One World Publications, 2015).
8. T.X. Hammes, 'The Future of Warfare: Small, Many, Smart Vs. Few & Exquisite?', *War on the Rocks*, 16 July 2014, https://warontherocks.com/2014/07/the-future-of-warfare-small-many-smart-vs-few-exquisite; J. Noel Williams, 'Killing Sanctuary: The Coming Era of Small, Smart, Pervasive Lethality', *War on the Rocks*, 8 September 2017, https://warontherocks.com/2017/09/killing-sanctuary-the-coming-era-of-small-smart-pervasive-lethality.
9. The author has been advocating such arming of the South East Asian countries with the BrahMos cruise missile for over twenty years now. For a recent example, see *Why India Is Not a Great Power (Yet)*, 103–04.
10. The two best books on the old-style gunboat diplomacy are by James Cable. See his *Gunboat Diplomacy: Political Applications of Limited Naval Force* (Westport, CN: Praeger, 1971), and *Gunboat Diplomacy, 1919–1991*, third edition (New York: Palgrave, 1994).
11. That the international system centred on the sovereign state is coming into its own again in the new century is argued in the two recent books by the author, *India's Nuclear Policy* and *Why India Is Not a Great Power (Yet)*.
12. See his 'The End of Globalization? The International Security Implications', *War on the Rocks*, 2 August 2016, https://warontherocks.com/2016/08/the-end-of-globalization-the-international-security-implications.
13. Bharat Karnad, 'Habit of Free-riding' *Seminar* 599, 2009, http://www.india-seminar.com/2009/599/599_bharat_karnad.htm.
14. Mukhopadhyay, *Narendra Modi*, 367.
15. Speech by foreign secretary at Second Raisina Dialogue in New Delhi (18 January 2017), http://mea.gov.in/Speeches-Statements.htm?dtl/27949/Speech_by_Foreign_Secretary_at_Second_Raisina_Dialogue_in_New_Delhi_January_18_2017.
16. 'US–India COMCASA Agreement Crawls, Ash Carter's Farewell Visit to India next month', *Indian Defence News*, 27 November 2016, http://defencenews.in/article/US-India-COMCASA-Agreement-Crawls,-Ash-Carter%E2%80%99s-farewell-visit-to-India-next-month-109306.
17. Pranab Dhal Samanta, 'India, US to Reopen Talks on Comcasa', *Economic Times*, 27 March 2018.
18. Thomas Wright, 'Trump, Xi, Putin, and the Axis of Disorder', Carnegie blog, 8 November 2017, https://www.brookings.edu/blog/order-from-chaos/2017/11/08/trump-xi-putin-and-the-axis-of-disorder.

19. Thomas J. Christensen, *Worse than a Monolith: Alliance Politics and Problems of Coercive Diplomacy in Asia* (Princeton, NJ: Princeton University Press, 2011).
20. For the Srinivasan quote, see Sitapati, *Half Lion*, 273.
21. Strobe Talbott, *Engaging India: Diplomacy, Democracy and the Bomb* (New Delhi: Penguin Books India, 2004).
22. Conveyed to the author in an informal conversation by Jaswant Singh, minister for external affairs in the Vajpayee government in 2002–03.
23. Condoleezza Rice, *No Higher Honour: A Memoir of My Years in Washington* (New York: Simon and Schuster, 2011), 130.
24. On the fizzling of the Indian hydrogen bomb test (S-1) on 11 May 1998, see Karnad, *Nuclear Weapons and Indian Security*, 398–404; Karnad, *India's Nuclear Policy*, 67–71.
25. On the ICBM project just needing Delhi's okay, see Bharat Karnad, *India's Nuclear Policy* (Westport, CN, and London: Praeger, 2008), 77–83.
26. 'Rethinking Deterrence and Assurance', Report, Wilton Park conference, 14–17 June 2017, https://www.wiltonpark.org.uk/wp-content/uploads/WP1545-Report.pdf. The Hwasong-15 ICBM launched by North Korea 29 November 2017, reached an altitude of 4475 km and travelled 950 km before accurately hitting a sea target, per South Korea's military tracking the test-firing. This converts to 13,000 km in standard trajectory or as US scientist David Wright, a physicist who follows Pyongyang's missile and nuclear programmes, has written 'more than enough range to reach Washington, D.C., and in fact any part of the continental United States'. See 'North Korea's Missile Launch Brings Us Closer to War US Isn't Seeking: Nikki Haley', *Hindustan Times*, 30 November 2017, http://www.hindustantimes.com/world-news/north-korea-s-missile-launch-brings-us-closer-to-war-us-isn-t-seeking-nikki-haley/story-kzoxxyCts6MvQBuCWhRknM.html.
27. Bharat Karnad, 'Countering the Rogue Triad of China, Pakistan, North Korea', *Wire*, July 25 2016, https://thewire.in/53338/countering-the-rogue-nuclear-triad-of-china-pakistan-north-korea; Western analysts who until recently did not even acknowledge the rogue triad are finally waking up to the possibility of Pyongyang selling its nuclear goods to third countries without, however, identifying China as the source of both the Pakistani and North Korean nuclear weapons and missiles. See Dominic Tierney, 'North Korea Wants to End Up Like Pakistan, Not Libya', *Defense One*, 29 May

2018, https://www.defenseone.com/ideas/ 2018/05/north-korea-wants-end-pakistan-not-libya/148549; Bharat Karnad, 'India Must Revise Its Nuclear Policy and Keep Its Strategy Opaque', *Hindustan Times*, 11 May 2018, https://www.hindustantimes.com/opinion/india-mus t- revise-its-nuclear-policy-and-keep-its-strategy-opaque/story-MRwcgzYXypIHf1j0V5iUoI.html.
28. Karnad, *Nuclear Weapons and Indian Security*, 299–300.
29. Most of these anti-nuclear deal articles complied in in P.K. Iyengar, A.N. Prasad, A. Gopalakrishnan, Bharat Karnad, *Strategic Sell-out: Indian–US Nuclear Deal* (New Delhi: Pentagon Press, 2009).
30. Talbott, *Engaging India*, 230.
31. 'This Is How US Negotiates with India', op.cit.
32. Personal communication, unattributable, senior Indian diplomat.
33. For the US Secretary of State Condoleezza Rice's reading of the emerging international situation in Asia, see Shivshankar Menon, *Choices: Inside the Making of India's Foreign Policy* (Gurgaon: Penguin Random House India, 2016), 54–55.
34. For India's border dispute resolution strategy, see Ibid, Ch. 1.
35. Quote in Ibid, 55.
36. Ibid, 69–70.
37. Karnad, *Why India Is Not a Great Power (Yet)*, Ch. 3, 16.
38. Quoted in Condoleezza Rice, *No Higher Honour: A Memoir of My Years in Washington* (New York: Simon and Schuster, 2011).
39. C. Raja Mohan, *Modi's World: Expanding India's Sphere of Influence* (Noida: HarperCollins India, 2015), 11.
40. Datta-Ray, *The Making of Indian Diplomacy*, 71, 56, 58.
41. Frederic Gare, *India Turns East: International Engagement and US–China Rivalry* (New York: Oxford University Press, 2017), 72–88.
42. William A. Callahan, Elena Barabantseva, eds., *China Orders the World: Soft Power and Foreign Policy* (Baltimore, MD: Johns Hopkins University Press, 2012).
43. Jennifer Rubin, 'Trump Is Xi's Lapdog', *Washington Post*, 10 November 2017, https://www.washingtonpost.com/blogs/right-turn/wp/2017/11/10/trump-is-xis-lapdog.
44. Adam Roberts, *Superfast Primetime Ultimate Nation*, 212–14.
45. Ibid, 214–16. Ram Madhav, a foreign affairs adviser to Modi said: 'We are changing the contours of diplomacy and looking at new ways of strengthening India's interests abroad. [The NRIs] can be India's voice even while being loyal citizens in those countries.' This quote in Sreeram

Chaulia, *Modi Doctrine: The Foreign Policy of India's Prime Minister* (New Delhi: Bloomsbury, 2016), 76.

46. 'India Needs to Cherish and Nurture its Muslims: Obama', *Pioneer*, 2 December 2017, http://www.dailypioneer.com/top-stories/india-needs-to-cherish-and-nurture-its-muslims-obama.html.
47. Michael Maccoby, *Narcissistic Leaders: Who Succeeds and Who Fails* (Cambridge, MA: Harvard University Press, 2007).
48. A biographer of his observed that Modi is not open-minded and uses 'power to demand—and secure—subservience from those around him'. See Mukhopadhyay, *Narendra Modi*, 57.
49. Personal communication; unattributable.
50. *The Economist* in a lead story depicted him as a 'one man band', See its 23 May 2015 edition, https://www.economist.com/printedition/2015-05-23.
51. 'Remarks on India and the United States: Vision for the 21st Century', 20 July 2011, https://2009-2017.state.gov/secretary/20092013clinton/rm/2011/07/168840.htm.
52. Quote in Lisa Curtis, 'Steady Progress on India–US Security Ties under Modi Government' in Ganguly, Chauthaiwale, Sinha, *The Modi Doctrine*, 39–40.
53. 'Remarks on India and the United States: Vision for the 21st Century'.
54. 'Joint Statement during the visit of Prime Minister to USA', Ministry of External Affairs, 30 September 2014, http://www.mea.gov.in/bilateral-documents.htm?dtl/24051/Joint+Statement+during+the+visit+of+Prime+Minister+to+USA.
55. See Jaishankar's 20 July 2015, IISS Fullerton Lecture where he talks of India as 'leading power not a balancing power', http://mea.gov.in/Speeches-Statements.htm?dtl/25493/IISS_Fullerton_by_Foreign_Secretary_in_Singapore; Ram Madhav, 'Emerging Challenges in the Indo-Pacific Region', *India Foundation Journal*, March-April 2017, http://www.indiafoundation.in/wp-content/uploads/2017/03/India-Foundation-JOURNAL-Mar-Apr-2017-colour.pdf.
56. Mahurkar, *Marching with a Billion*, xxx.
57. Quote in Pravin Sawhney and Ghazala Wahab, *Dragon at the Doorstep: Managing China Through Military Power* (New Delhi: Aleph, 2017), 153.
58. Personal communication.
59. Pavan K. Varma, *The Great Indian Middle Class*, revised edition, (New Delhi: Penguin Books India, 2007), 161–62.
60. Karnad, *Nuclear Weapons and Indian Security*, Chapter 3.

61. M.K. Rasgotra, *A Life in Diplomacy* (New Delhi: Penguin Random House India, 2016), 165.
62. Karnad, *Nuclear Weapons and Indian Security*, 199–211.
63. Ibid, 278–331.
64. McGeorge Bundy, *Danger and Survival: Choices about the Bomb in the First Fifty Years* (New Delhi: East-West Press, 1989), 503, 585.
65. Karnad, *Why India Is Not a Great Power (Yet)*, Ch. 1.
66. 'India in Another Non-proliferation Regime, Slap on China for NSG', *Times of India*, 9 December 2017.
67. Indrani Bagchi, 'Nuclear Deal in Place, India and Japan Now Eye Investments, JVs', *Times of India*, 9 December 2017.
68. Karnad, *Nuclear Weapons and Indian Security*, 20–22.
69. See his speech, ironically, at the function in Mumbai formally to induct INS *Kalvari*, the first of the Scorpene-class submarines into the Indian Navy on 14 December 2017, https://www.youtube.com/watch?v=r1IizJIu67c.
70. Modi said this in one of his weekly 'Maan Ki Baat' radio addresses. See 'India Spreading Message of Peace Across World: PM', *Times of India*, 30 October 2017.
71. Manmohan Bahadur, 'The Power Play in Peacekeeping', *The Hindu*, 12 December 2017, http://www.thehindu.com/opinion/op-ed/the-power-play-in-peacekeeping/article21420388.ece?homepage=true.
72. John Bew, *Realpolitik: A History* (New York: Oxford University Press, 2016), 3, 15.
73. Raj Chengappa, "Modi's Global Rush', *India Today*, 30 September 2015.
74. Anirban Ganguly, 'Modi and India's Civilizational Quest' in Ganguly, Chauthaiwale, Sinha, *The Modi Doctrine*, 183.
75. Bew, *Realpolitik*, 106.
76. Karnad, *Why India Is Not a Great Power (Yet)*, 187–219.
77. Quote in Datta Ray, *The Making of Indian Diplomacy*, 82.
78. Quote, Ibid, 84.
79. Ramanna's quote in Karnad, *Nuclear Weapons and Indian Security*, 312.
80. Ibid, 313.
81. Karnad, *India's Nuclear Policy*, 54.
82. Karnad, *Nuclear Weapons and Indian Security*, 313, 339.
83. Ibid, 340–44.
84. Ibid, 397.
85. Menon, *Choices*, 92–94.
86. Rice, *No Higher Honour*, 720–21.

87. Menon, *Choices*, 98–99.
88. 'India a Responsible Nuclear State; Pakistan an Unstable One', *Times of India*, 29 September 2016, https://timesofindia.indiatimes.com/india/India-a-responsible-nuclear-state-Pakistan-an-unstable-one-US/articleshow/54573880.cms.
89. Alyssa Ayres, 'US Secretary of State Rex Tillerson Thinks India Is More Responsible Than China', *Forbes*, 18 October 2017, https://www.forbes.com/sotes.alyssaayres/2017/10/18/u-s-secretary-of-state-rex-tillerosn-thinks-india-is-more-responsible-than-china/#2b4005d82d64.
90. Rasgotra, *Life in Diplomacy*, 243, 246.
91. Jaishankar's quote in Datta-Ray, *The Making of Indian Diplomacy*, 71.
92. Karnad, *Nuclear Weapons and Indian Security*, 261–63.
93. Quote in Datta-Ray, *The Making of Indian Diplomacy*, 46.
94. Personal communication, 10 November 2017.
95. Personal communication.
96. Personal communication.
97. Congressional Budget Justification: Foreign Operations, Appendix 3, US Department of State, Fiscal Year 2017, 293, https://www.state.gov/documents/organization/252734.pdf.
98. Ibid, 1, 258, 289.
99. See his 'Patronage As a US Force Multiplier', *The Hindu*, 14 December 2010, http://www.thehindu.com/todays-paper/tp-opinion/Patronage-as-a-U.S.-force-multiplier/article15592583.ece.
100. Personal communication, 10 November 2017.
101. Personal communication.
102. Correspondence, 22 November 2017.
103. 'Enhancing Defense and Security Cooperation with India', Fiscal Year July 2017, Joint Report to the Congress, US Department of State and US Department of Defense, 4, 2, https://www.defense.gov/Portals/1/Documents/pubs/NDAA-India-Joint-Report-FY-July-2017.pdf.
104. Bharat Karnad, 'India's Foreign Policy: The Foreign Hand', *Open*, 29 April 2016, http://www.openthemagazine.com/article/voices/indias-foreign-policy-the-foreign-hand. For the case that for rich Indians charity begins abroad, see Alya Mishra, 'India: Charity not beginning at home for universities', *University World News* 157, 6 February 2011, http://www.universityworldnews.com/article.php?story=20110204222722977.
105. Eric Lipton and Brooke Williams, 'How Think Tanks Amplify Corporate America's Influence', *New York Times*, 7 August 2016, https://www.

nytimes.com/2016/08/08/us/politics/think-tanks-research-and-corporate-lobbying.html.
106. http://www.anantaaspencentre.in.
107. The Delhi Carnegie head, C. Raja Mohan, for instance, is also a foreign affairs editorial consultant with the *Indian Express*.
108. S. Jaishankar, 'Navigating an Uncertain World', K. Subrahmanyam Memorial Lecture 2017, 4 August 2017, National Institute of Advanced Studies, Bengaluru, http://www.nias.res.in/event/k-subrahmanyam-memorial-lecture-navigating-uncertain-world-dr-s-jaishankar-foreign-secretary
109. Indrani Bagchi, 'China Specialist Gokhale Takes Over As Foreign Secy', *Times of India*, 30 January 2018.
110. A prominent such tandem operating for a while was that of Foreign Secretary Jaishankar and C. Raja Mohan, director of Brookings India and a newspaper columnist. This is what the former said of the latter: 'Raj and I have known each other for more than four decades; I am possibly his oldest acquaintance in this room. We have studied and debated together and represent the JNU generation that first impacted on this city. Some of you may not know that we even initially wrote together. Our shared journey moved comfortably from our university days into our professional lives. Though our paths diverged, we inhabit connected worlds and for many years, have been each other's sounding boards. Therefore, I do follow Raja Mohan's endeavours and achievements with special attention—and might I say—even a sense of pride.' See 'Remarks by Foreign Secretary at the Release of C. Raja Mohan's book *Modi's World: Expanding India's Sphere of Influence*' Ministry of External Affairs, 18 July 2015, http://mea.gov.in/Speeches-Statements.htm?dtl/25491/Remarks_by_Foreign_Secretary_at_the_release_of_DrC_Raja_Mohans_book_Modis_WorldExpanding_Indias_Sphere_of_InfuencequotJuly_17_2015.
111. Rahul Bedi, 'Patronage As a US force Multiplier'.
112. *A Resource Guide to the US Foreign Corrupt Practices Act*, US Department of Justice, US Government, 14 November 2012, https://www.sec.gov/spotlight/fcpa/fcpa-resource-guide.pdf
113. Two Indian intelligence officers; personal communication.
114. Shyam Saran, *How India Sees the World: Kautilya to the 21st Century* (New Delhi: Juggernaut, 2017), 211–12.
115. See his piece 'The Americans Are Back: F-16 for IAF, F/A-18 for the Indian Navy', Carnegie, 2 August 2017, http://carnegieendowment.org/2017/08/02/americans-are-back-f-16-for-iaf-and-f-18-for-indian-navy-pub-72706.

116. Ashley J. Tellis, Sean Mirski, 'Crux of Asia: China, India, and the Emerging Global Order', 13 January 2013, http://carnegieendowment.org/2013/01/10/crux-of-asia-china-india-and-emerging-global-order-pub-50551.
117. Tellis, Mirski, 'Crux of Asia'.
118. Robert Kagan, 'The Ungreat Washed', *New Republic*, 6 July 2003, https://newrepublic.com/article/90784/fareed-zakaria-democracy.
119. Quote in Chaulia, *Modi Doctrine*, 84.
120. US Vice President Michael Pence has repeated this many times. See Jonathan Chait, 'Mike Pence Strongly Believes Donald Trump's Shoulder-width Guarantees His Foreign Policy Acumen', *New York Magazine*, 22 August 2017, http://nymag.com/daily/intelligencer/2017/08/12-times-mike-pence-praised-donald-trumps-shoulders.html.
121. 'India Can Supply Manpower for Running Industries Globally: PM Modi', *Times of India*, 19 January 2016, https://timesofindia.indiatimes.com/india/India-can-supply-manpower-for-running-industries-globally-PM-MOdi/articleshow/50641918.cms.
122. Ayan Pramanik, 'Wage Hike for H1B Visa Holders in US Push Indian IT for Local Hiring', *Business Standard*, 6 January 2017, http://www.business-standard.com/article/economy-policy/wage-hike-for-h1b-visa-holders-in-us-push-indian-it-for-local-hiring-117010601065_1.html.
123. Sachin Parashar, 'Safe Havens for Terror Groups in Pak Won't be Tolerated: Tillerson', *Times of India*, 26 October 2017; 'Trump Talks of New Plan to Punish Cos that Outsource', *Times of India*, 11 October 2017; 'US Makes it Tougher to Renew L1, H1B Visas', *Times of India*, 26 October 2017.
124. Guillermina Jasso, Mark R. Rosenzweig, 'How Donald Trump's New Immigration Plan Could Harm the American Workforce', *Time*, 18 August 2017, http://time.com/4887558/legal-family-immigration-skilled-workforce.
125. 'If Donald Trump Goes for Merit-based Immigration in US, Here's What Happens', *Economic Times*, 2 November 2017, https://economictimes.indiatimes.com/nri/visa-and-immigration/if-donald-trump-goes-for-merit-based-immigration-in-us-heres-what-happens/articleshow/61450965.cms.
126. Jennifer Epstein, 'Trump Says He'll End US Visa Lottery and Chain Migration', *Bloomberg*, 12 December 2017, https://www.bloomberg.com/news/articles/2017-12-12/trump-says-he-ll-end-u-s-visa-lottery-and-chain-migration.
127. Yashwant Raj and Gireesh Chandra Prasad, 'Indians with H-1B visas Highly Skilled, Legal: Jaitley in US', *Hindustan Times*, 16 October 2017.

128. Interview with Rentala Chandrashekhar, *Times of India*, 1 January 2018.
129. Fact sheet of IT and BPM industry, http://meity.gov.in/content/fact-sheet-it-bpm-industry
130. Nilesh Christopher, 'NASSCOM Pegs BPM Income to $55 billion by 2025', *Economic Times*, 13 October 2017, https://economictimes.indiatimes.com/tech/ites/nasscom-sees-big-scope-for-indias-bpm-sector/articleshow/61053731.cms. For the annual growth figures see the Ministry of Electronics and Information Technology statistics in http://meity.gov.in/content/performance-contribution-towards-exports-it-ites-industry.
131. 'President Obama Issues Call to Action to Invest in America at White House Insourcing American Jobs Forum', 11 January 2012, https://obamawhitehouse.archives.gov/the-press-office/2012/01/11/president-obama-issues-call-action-invest-america-white-house-insourcing.
132. 'H1B Visa: Jaitley Discusses India's Concerns with US Commerce Secretary', *Hindustan Times*, 21 April 2017, http://www.hindustantimes.com/business-news/arun-jaitley-discusses-india-s-concerns-over-h-1b-visa-issue-with-us-commerce-secretary/story-8MgaO5xzNOCMO4uMouq0zJ.html.
133. Yashwant Raj, 'H1B Visa Rules: Trump Admin Considers Tweak That May Send Indian Techies Home', *Hindustan Times*, 3 January 2018, http://www.hindustantimes.com/business-news/arun-jaitley-discusses-india-s-concerns-over-h-1b-visa-issue-with-us-commerce-secretary/story-8MgaO5xzNOCMO4uMouq0zJ.html; Chidanand Rajghatta, 'Trump Administration Considers Proposal that May Send Back More than 500,000 Indian Tech Workers', *Times of India*, 3 January 2018, https://timesofindia.indiatimes.com/business/india-business/trump-admin-considers-proposal-that-may-send-back-more-than-500000-indian-tech-workers/articleshow/62341416.cms.
134. Ishani Duttagupta, 'Will Ya Rob Our Jobs?', *Economic Times* magazine, January 2018.
135. 'Relief for H1B Visa Holders! Trump Administration Rejects Deportation Plan Reports', *Business Today*, 9 January 2018, http://www.businesstoday.in/current/world/h1b-visa-donald-trump-green-card-united-states-india-jobs-nasscom-us-work-visa/story/267583.html.
136. 'Says US Industry Body: 'Ending Extension of H1B Visas Bad Policy', *Sunday Express*, 7 January 2018.
137. Prachi Verma, 'IT Cos Push for Hiring in US to Deal with New H1B Visa Rules, Say Experts', *Economic Times*, 5 January 2018.

138. 'Saeed's Name Is Not on US List: Pakistan', *Indian Express*, 26 October 2017.
139. 'If Pakistan Doesn't Act against Terror Groups, We Will Find "a Different way"', *Express Tribune*, 27 October 2017, https://tribune.com.pk/story/ 1542898/1-pakistan-doesnt-act-terror-groups-well-find-different-way-us.
140. Anwar Iqbal, 'US Bill Delinks LeT from Haqqani Network', *Dawn*, 14 November 2017, https://www.dawn.com/news/1370332/u-bill-delinks-let-from-haqqani-network
141. 'President Trump has put Pakistan on notice,' said Pence. 'As the president said, so I say now: Pakistan has much to gain from partnering with the United States, and Pakistan has much to lose by continuing to harbour criminals and terrorists.' See Mariana Baaber, 'War of Words: Pence, Pakistan Trade Verbal Volleys', *News*, 23 December 2017, https://www.thenews.com.pk/print/259544-war-of-words-pence-pakistan-trade-verbal-volleys.
142. Pamela Constable, 'US Wants to Build "Tsunami of Air Power" in Afghanistan, but Impact Is Years Away', *Washington Post*, 12 November 2017, https://www.washingtonpost.cm/world/asia_pacific/us-wants-to-build- tsunami-of-air-power-in-afghanistan-but-impact-is years-away/2017/1 1/10/91c453ae-c3e1-11e7-9922-4151f5ca6168_story.html; Umair Jama l, 'If China Does Build a Naval Base in Pakistan, What Are the Risks for Islamabad?', *Diplomat*, 24 June 2017, https://thediplomat.com/2017/06/if-china-does-build-a-naval-base-in-pakistan-what-are-the-r isks-for-islamabad.
143. Zamir Akram, 'Dangerous Delusions', *Express Tribune*, 31 October 2017, https://tribune.com.pk/story/1545460/6-dangerous-delusion/. Akram is a retired Pakistani ambassador.
144. '"Our Stand Vindicated," Says India After Trump Rips into Pak on Terrorism', Agencies, *NDTV*, 2 January 2018, https://ndtv.com/india-news/our-stand-vidicated-says-india-afet-us-president-donald-trump-rips-into-pakistan-on-terrorism-1794603?pfrom=home-topscroll.
145. Roshan Kishore, 'US Aid Pull May Not Dent Pak's Fortunes', *Hindustan Times*, 8 January 2018.
146. Lt Col (Res) Mordechai Kedar, 'The US Betrayal of Kurdistan Is a Warning Sign for Israel', Perspectives Paper No. 651, Begin-Sadat Center, Bar Ilan

University, 22 November 2017, https://besacenter.org/perspectives-papers/us-betraya-kurdistan-warning-israel.
147. Tom Hals, Emily Fitter, 'How Two Cutting Edge US Nuclear Projects Bankrupted Westinghouse', *Reuters*, 1 May 2017, https://www.reuters.com/article/us-toshiba-accounting-westinghouse-nucle/how-two-cutting-edge-u-s-nuclear-projects-bankrupted-westinghouse-idUSKBN17YOCQ.
148. 'India Interested in Acquiring V-22 Osprey for Special Operation [sic]', *Defence Update*, 31 August 2017, https://defenceupdate.in/india-interested-acquiring-v-22-osprey-special-operation.
149. Tillerson, 'Remarks on "Defining Our Relationship With India for the Next Century"'.
150. Kirtika Suneja, 'Prabhu Reaches Out to China and S Africa to Put Up United Front', *Economic Times*, 12 December 2017; Kirtika Suneja, 'India's Food Security Intact', *Economic Times*, 15 December 2017.
151. See the interview of Harsha Vardhana Singh, deputy director general, WTO, *Times of India*, 25 November 2017; Anirudh Bhattacharya and Yashwant Raj, 'Trump Lashes Out at India Before Leaving G-7 Summit', *Hindustan Times*, 11 June 2018; Michael D. Shear, 'Trump Threatens to End Trade with G-6, Says US No Longer a "Piggy Bank"', *NYT News Service*, *Times of India*, 10 June 2018.
152. Steven Mufson, 'Trump-appointed Regulators Reject Plan to Rescue Coal and Nuclear Plants', *Washington Post*, 8 January 2018.
153. 'Areva's Finland Reactor to Start in 2019, After Another Delay', *Reuters*, 9 October 2017, https://www.reuters.com/article/us-finland-nuclear-olkiluoto/arevas-finland-reactor-to-start-in-2019-after-another-delay-idUSKBN1CE1ND.
154. *National Security Strategy of the United States of America*, White House, December 2017, https://www.whitehouse.gov/wp-content/uploads/2017/12/NSS-Final-12-18-2017-0905.pdf.
155. Jeffrey A. Bader and Ryan Hass, 'Order from Chaos: Was Pre-Trump Policy towards China Based on "False" Premises?', *Brookings*, 22 December 2017, https://www.brookings.com/edu/blog/order-from-chaos/2017/12/22/was-pre-trump-u-s-policy-towards-china-based-on-false-premises.
156. Kevin Breuninger and Kayla Tausche, 'Trump Slaps China with Tariffs on Up to $60 billion on Imports: "This Is the First of Many"', *CNBC*, 22 March 2018, https://www.cnbc.com/2018/03/22/trump-moves-to-slap-china-with-50-billion-in-tariffs-over-intellectual-property-theft.html.

157. 'Global Stocks Decline on Report China May Slow US Bond Buy', *Hindustan Times*, 11 January 2018.
158. Emily Fitter, 'What Is Plan B if China Dumps its US Debt?', *Reuters*, https://www.reuters.com/article/us-usa-treasuries-china/analysis-what-is-plan-b-if-china-dumps-its-u-s-debt-idUSTRE70H5NX20110118.
159. *National Security Strategy of the United States of America*, 45–50.
160. Ibid.
161. Menon, *Choices*, 55.
162. On the Indo-US trust deficit and the US offer of arms and technology as influence multipliers, see Karnad, *Why India Is Not a Great Power (Yet)*, 187–219.
163. 'US, China and Thucydides' Trap', videographed discussion between Henry Kissinger and Graham Allison, Harvard University, 2 August 2017, www.youtube.com/watrch?v=IKI6M2UiCGk.
164. Linda J. Bilmes, 'The $5 trillion Wars', *Boston Globe*, 17 October 2016, https://www.bostonglobe.com/opinion/2016/10/17/the-trillion-wars/uPVfSuDutnTZI5fiQ7YIIK/story.html.
165. 'This Is How US Negotiates with India'.
166. See C. Raja Mohan, 'How India Can Negotiate Trump's World', *Indian Express*, 25 December 2017. Raja Mohan heads Carnegie India.
167. Rasgotra, *A Life in Diplomacy*, 243.
168. For the Subrahmanyam quote, see Karnad, 'The Foreign Hand'. For Tellis' F-16 advocacy, see his 'The Americans Are Back: F-16s for the IAF, F-18s for the Indian Navy', Carnegie Endowment, 2 August 2017, http://carnegieendowment.org/2017/08/02/americans-are-back-f-16-for-iaf-and-f-18-for-indian-navy-pub-72706.
169. Karnad, 'India's Foreign Policy: The Foreign Hand'.
170. Testimony of the vice chairman of the US joint chiefs of staff, General Paul Selva, before the US Senate Armed Services Committee, 18 July 2017, https://www.armed-services.senate.gov/hearings/17-07-18-nomination_--selva; Peter Drombowski, 'Can America Compete with China's Great Military Leap Forward?', *War on the Rocks*, 15 September 2015, https://warontherocks.com/2015/09/is-america-ready-for-chinas-great-leap-forward; Albert R. Hunt, 'China Has Upper Hand, while the US Is Hobbled by Trump', *Bloomberg*, 5 November 2017, https://www.bloomberg.com/view/articles/2017-11-05/china-has-upper-hand-while-u-s-is-hobbled-by-trump.
171. Karnad, *Why India Is Not a Great Power (Yet)*, 187–219.

172. This was said by Verma in the interaction period after the formal release at the Centre for Policy Research, New Delhi, on 16 January 2018 of the Center for American Progress Task Force Report on US–India Relations titled 'The United States and India: Forging an Indispensable Democratic Partnership' (Washington, DC: 2018).
173. Datta-Ray, *The Making of Indian Diplomacy*, 46, 48.
174. Iyengar, et al., *Strategic Sell-out*.
175. Small, *China–Pakistan Axis*, 35.
176. Karnad, *India's Nuclear Policy*, 29–33.
177. Ashley J. Tellis, 'New Delhi, Washington, Who Gets What', *Times of India*, 30 January 2010.
178. Summary of the 2018 National Defense Strategy of the United States of America: Sharpening the American Military's Competitive Edge, https://www.defense.gov/Portals/1/Documents/pubs/2018-National-Defense-Strategy-Summary.pdf.
179. See his 'India As a Leading Power', Carnegie Endowment for International Peace, 4 April 2016, http://carnegieendowment.org/2016/04/04/india-as-leading-power-pub-63185.
180. Athanassios Platias, Constantinos Koliopoulus, *Thucydides on Strategy: Grand Strategies in the Peloponnesian Wars and Their Relevance Today* (New York: Oxford University Press, 2017).
181. Lance Pritchett, 'Is India a Flailing State? Detours on the Four Lane Highway to Modernization', John F. Kennedy School, Harvard University, 2009, https://dash.harvard.edu/handle/1/4449106.
182. Mayank Jain, 'What Can be Done to Revive India's Sluggish Economic Growth? Here's What Five Economists Prescribe', Scroll.in, 21 September 2017, https://scroll.in/article/851337/what-can-be-done-to-revive-indias-sluggish-economic-growth-heres-what-five-economists-prescribe; Amy Kazmin, 'India's Faltering Economy Poses Questions for Mr. Modi', *Financial Times*, 18 September 2017, https://www.ft.com/content/9dd3bff4-9871-11e7-a652-cde3f882dd7b.

Chapter 4: Adversarial Geopolitics: BRIS and Mod Quad

1. Sushant Sareen of VIF in the panel discussion programme 'The Big Picture', Rajya Sabha TV, 11 November 2017.
2. See his 'Remarks on "Defining Our Relationship with India for the Next Century"', Center for Strategic and International Studies,

Washington, DC, 18 October 2017, https://www.state.gov/secretary/remarks/2017/10/274913.htm.
3. Dinakar Peri, 'China's Rise a Big Disruption, Says Jaishankar', *The Hindu*, 19 January 2018, http://www.thehindu.com/news/national/chinas-rise-a-big-disruption-says-jaishankar/article22466659.ece.
4. Ibid.
5. Ganguly, Chauthaiwala and Sinha, *The Modi Doctrine*, 191.
6. True this naysayer aspect is formally touted with respect to India's posture at the WTO and multilateral economic forums. See Indrani Bagchi, 'India Looks to Change Global "Naysayer" Image', *Times of India*, 19 March 2018. But surely it applies to India's neighbourhood policy even more, as the record shows.
7. Personal communication from a senior naval person.
8. 'Maldives' Security, Stability in India's Interest: PM Modi', *Indian Express*, 12 April 2016, http://indianexpress.com/article/india/india-news-india/narendra-modi-meets-maldives-president-abdullah-yameen-in-delhi.
9. The India-friendly Nasheed's statement that 'I believe it is India's Ocean and therefore it is right that India has a stake in what goes on here. She has a right to protect her interests' and his further elaboration that in case Yameen remains obstreperous 'I hope that India will impose further robust measures' was an open invitation for Delhi to assert its 'strategic imperative'. He pointed out that under Yameen's rule China had 'grabbed large tracts of land, several islands in the Maldives, without firing a shot'. See Jyoti Malhotra and Shubhajit Roy, 'Maldives Back on Boil after Apex Court Frees Mohammad Nasheed, Opp Leaders', *Indian Express*, 2 February 2018.
10. 'Amid Political Crisis, Yameen Sends Out Envoys to "Friendly" Countries, India Excluded', *Deccan Chronicle*, 8 February 2018, https://www.deccanchronicle.com/world/asia/080218/amid-political-crisis-maldives-sends-envoys-to-friendly-nations-in.html; Saibal Dasgupta, 'China says it is against external intervention in the Maldives', *Times of India*, 8 February 2018, https://timesofindia.indiatimes.com/world/china/china-says-it-is-against-external-intervention-in-maldives/articleshow/62825671.cms.
11. 'PM Narendra Modi, Donald Trump Discuss Maldives Crisis over Phone Call: White House', *Indian Express*, 9 February 2018, http://indianexpress.com/article/world/donald-trump-narendra-modi-discuss-maldives-crisis-over-phone-call-white-house-5056893.

12. 'Chinese Warships Enter Eastern Indian Ocean Amid Maldives Tension', *Reuters*, 20 February 2018, https://www.reuters.com/article/us-maldives-politics-china/chinese-warships-enter-east-indian-ocean-amid-maldives-tensions-idUSKCN1G40V9.
13. Quotes in Jyoti Malhotra, 'Stepping Back from Maldives: India to China', *Indian Express*, 28 March 2018.
14. 'Why haven't we gone into the Kashmir issue . . . and asked to be [an] intermediary? Because they are internal matters . . . India should stay away from our issue. We are independent and capable of dealing with the situation. If we need help, we will let India know,' said Yameen's Fisheries Minister, Mohammad Shainee. See Arun Ram, 'Yameen Cites Kashmir, Tells India to Back Off', *Times of India*, 14 March 2018.
15. Shubhajit Roy, 'Eye on China, India and France Focus on Defence, Maritime Ties', *Sunday Express*, 11 March 2018.
16. Abantika Ghosh, 'Govt Sends Out Note: Very Sensitive Time for Ties with China, So Skip Dalai Lama Events', *Indian Express*, 2 March 2018.
17. Jayanth Jacob, 'Govt Looks to Reset China Ties with Modi–Xi Summit', *Hindustan Times*, 17 March 2018.
18. Zeeshan Shaikh, 'China responds: Dragon and Elephant Must Not Fight, but Dance Together', *Indian Express*, 9 March 2018.
19. See 'Iran Offers Pak, China Role in Chabahar', *Times of India*, 14 March 2018; the Rajpaksa interview in *Indian Express*, 24 March 2018; and Indrani Bagchi, 'Seychelles Oppn Blocks Military Deal with India', *Times of India*, 28 March 2018.
20. 'Middle Powers in the Twenty-first Century World Order with Ambassador Richard Verma', Georgetown University, Washington, DC, 28 February 2017, https://india.georgetown.edu/features/middle-powers-in-the-twenty-first-century-world-order-with-ambassador-rich-verma.
21. Richard A. Bitzinger,'Does North Korean Missile Parade Augur a New Asian Super Power?', *Asia Times*, 17 April 2017, http://www.atimes.com/make-way-north-korea-asias-new-superpower.
22. David E. Sanger, David D. Kirkpatrick and Nicole Perlroth, 'The World Once Laughed at North Korean Cyberpower. No more', *New York Times*, 15 October 2017, https://nytimes.com/2017/10/15/world/asia/north-korea-hacking-cyber-sony.html.
23. Uzi Rubin, 'What Parades in Pyongyang Ends Up in Tehran', *Perspectives Paper No. 598*, 28 September 2017, Begin-Sadat Center, Bar Ilan

University, Israel, https://besacenter.org/perspectives-papers/parades-pyongyang-ends-up-tehran.
24. Karnad, 'Countering the Rogue Nuclear Triad of China, Pakistan, and North Korea'.
25. Karnad, *Why India Is Not a Great Power (Yet)*, 50–51.
26. India has 'soaked up' $4.3 billion credit from the China-funded Asian Infrastructure Investment Bank for infrastructure projects. See Kiran Stacey, Simon Mundy, Emily Feng, 'India Soaks Up Funds from Chinese-led Bank Despite Tension', *Financial Times*, 20 March 2018.
27. Quote in Ganguly, Chauthaiwala and Sinha, *The Modi Doctrine*, 189.
28. Shaikh, 'China Responds: Dragon and Elephant Must Not Fight, but Dance Together'.
29. See her 'America's Pacific Century', *Foreign Policy*, October 2011, http://www.foreignpolicy.com/2011/10/11/Americas-pacific-century.
30. Quote in Joseph Joffe, 'Of Allies and Adversaries: Trump's "Principled Realism"', in Joseph Joffe, Robert G. Kaufman, Angelo M. Codevilla, Bruce Thornton, *The Practice of 'Principled Realism'*, Strategika: *Conflicts of the Past as Lessons for the Present*, 45.2, September 2017, https://www.hoover.org/sites/default/files/issues/resources/strategika_45_web.pdf.
31. Maggie Haberman, '"Relaxed" Trump Says What He Really Feels', *New York Times*, 20 March 2018.
32. Andrew Bacevich, 'Trump's Strategy Prepares for a "Long War" without End', *Boston Globe*, 21 December 2017, https://www.bostonglobe.com/opinion/2017/12/21/trump-security-strategy-prepares-for-long-war-without-end/vIMOGrg5LljWiFrmePLcpN/story.html; Quinn Mecham, 'Will Trump's "Principled Realism" Leave Autocrats Off the Hook?', *Washington Post*, 24 May 2017, https://www.washingtonpost.com/news/monkey-cage/wp/2017/05/24/trump-outlined-his-idea-of-principled-realism-in-riyadh-heres-how-it-lets-autocrats-off-the-hook/?utm_term=.e3b4997cf72e.
33. Angelo M. Codevilla, 'What Can We Expect from Trump's Foreign Policy of "Principled Realism"?', in Joffe, Kaufman, Codevilla, Thornton, *The Practice of 'Principled Realism'*, 8.
34. Joseph Joffe, 'Of Allies and Adversaries: Donald Trump's "Principled Realism"', Ibid, 3.
35. See his *War: What Is It Good for? The Role of Conflict in Civilization from Primates to Robots* (London: Profile Books, 2014), 357.
36. Ibid, 363.

37. Henry Kissinger, *Diplomacy* (New York: Simon and Schuster, 1994), 835.
38. Ibid, 108.
39. See his 'Get Smart: Combining Hard and Soft Power', *Foreign Affairs* 88.4, July–August 2008.
40. Quote in Kissinger, *Diplomacy*, 45.
41. See his *The Big Stick: The Limits of Soft Power and the Necessity of Military Force* (New York: Basic Books, 2016), 116.
42. Robert G. Kaufmann, 'Two First Quarter Cheers for Trump's Principled Realism', ibid, 6.
43. See his *How India Sees the World: Kautilya to the 21st Century* (New Delhi: Juggernaut, 2017), 147–48.
44. Menon, *Choices*, 168–69.
45. See https://www.youtube.com/watch?v=M9-w8kMdKsI&t=287s.
46. Derek Grossman, 'Vietnam's Remarkable Month of Balancing against China in the South China Sea', *RAND Blog*, 26 March 2018, https://www.rand.org/blog/2018/03/vietnams-remarkable-month-of-balancing-against-china.html.
47. Rajya Sabha Debate on Foreign Policy, *Rajya Sabha TV*, 4 August 2017.
48. Keith Johnson, 'What Kind of Game Is China Playing?', *Wall Street Journal*, 11 June 2011, https://www.wsj.com/articles/SB10001424052702304259304576374013537436924; For a comparison of Wei Qi and Indian chess (shatranj), see Karnad, *Why India Is Not a Great Power (Yet)*, 167–69.
49. John Schaus, 'The Limits of Good Strategy: The United States in the Asia Pacific of 2018', *Defense Outlook 2018*, Center for Strategic and International Studies, February 2018, www.defense360.csis.org/wp-content/uploads/2018/02/Schaus_Limits-of-Good-Strategy_D360.pdf.
50. Richard Haass, 'America and the Great Abdication', *Atlantic*, 28 December 2017, https://www.theatlantic.com/international/archive/2017/12/America-abdication-trump-foreign-policy/549296.
51. Bharat Karnad, 'Why Donald Trump Is Good for India', *Open* magazine, 29 July 2016, http://www.openthemagazine.com/article/politics/why-donald-trump-is-good-for-india; Bharat Karnad, 'Trust in Trump', *Open*, 11 November 2016, http://www.openthemagazine.com/article/the-american-dream-2016/trust-in-trump; Bharat Karnad, 'Habit of Free-riding', *Seminar* 599, 2009, http://www.india-seminar.com/2009/599/599_bharat_karnad.htm.

52. Export-Import Bank of India, 'Intra-BRICS Trade: An Indian Perspective,' Working Paper No. 56, 27–28 October 2016, https://www.eximbankindia.in/Assets/Dynamic/PDF/Publication-Resources/ReasearchPapers/80file.pdf.
53. Ibid, 45, 47–49.
54. Ibid, 57–59.
55. 'Total Trade', *Department of Commerce, 2015–16.*
56. Alissa Wang, Brittaney Warren, Irina Popova, Andey Shelepov and Andrei Sakharov, '2016 BRICS Goa Summit Final Compliance Report, 17 October 2016–14 August 2017,' 29 August 2017, www.ranepa.ru/images/News/2017-08/29-08-2016-goa-final-report.pdf.
57. 'Russia's Trade with China Up 22%', *Moscow Times*, 17 October 2017, https://themoscowtimes.com/articles/russias-trade-with-china-up-22-to59285.
58. Joseph V. Micallef, 'Are the US and Russia on a Collision Course?', Military.com, 9 August 2017, https://www.military.com/daily-news/2017/08/09/are-us-russia-collision-course.html; 'A Defiant Russia Build Barriers to US Sanction', *Stratfor*, 29 May 2018, https://worldview.stratfor.com/article/defiant-russia-builds-barriers-us-sanctions; Text of Prime Minister's keynote address at Shangri La Dialogue, 1 June 2018, http://pib.nic.in/newsite/PrintRelease.aspx?relid=179711.
59. Modi raised the terrorism issue and why eradicating it was essential to development and economic progress. See 'PM's Opening Remarks at the SCO Summit in Astana, Kazakhstan', 9 June 2017, https://www.narendramodi.in/pm-s-opening-remarks-at-the-sco-summit-in-astana-kazakhstan-535799; 'Joint Communique' issued at the end of the 16th Meeting of Heads of Government Council attended by the Indian External Affairs Minister Sushma Swaraj, Shanghai Cooperation Council, 1 December 2017, http://eng.sectsco.org/news/20171201/361743.html.
60. Salvatore Babones, 'Why Is Democratic India Joining Russia and China's "Anti-Western" Club, the SCO?', *Forbes*, 29 November 2017, https://www.forbes.com/sites/salvatorebaboes/2017/11/29/why-is-democratic-india-joining-russia-and-china-anti-western-club-the-sco/#345cOff4cac7.
61. See his 'Main Results of 2017: Energetic Russia and the Greater Eurasia Community', Valdai Club, 28 December 2017, Valdai Club, http://valdaiclub.com/a/highlights/main-results-of-2017-energetic-russia.
62. Ibid.
63. 'Large Section of the Russian Gas Pipeline to China Completed', *RT News*, 18 October 2017, https://www.rt.com/business/407063-gazprom-power-of-siberia.

64. 'Russia Tightens Grip with Second Oil Pipeline', *Bloomberg*, 1 January 2018, https://www.bloomberg.com/news/articles/2018-01-01/second-chinese-crude-oil-pipeline-linked-to-russia-s-espo-opens.
65. This happened in 2009 with the brewing Ukraine crisis as backdrop. See Robert Lea, 'Europe Plunged into Energy Crisis as Russia Cuts Off Gas Supply via Ukraine', *Daily Mail*, 7 January 2009, http://www.dailymail.co.uk/news/article-1106382/Europe-plunged-energy-crisis-Russia-cuts-gas-supply-Ukraine.html.
66. Danny Vinik, 'Why Germany Doesn't Want to Sanction Russia, in Two Charts', *New Republic*, 3 March 2014, https://newrepublic.com/article/116836/why-germany-doesnt-want-sanction-russia-invading-ukraine.
67. https://www.youtube.com/watch?v=mshLcvjB3AY.
68. 'India–Russia Cooperation Not about Arms Trade, but about Trust: Narendra Modi', 2 June 2017, https://www.youtube.com/watch?v=qj_UooFvaj8&t=605s
69. Personal communication, 16 April 2016.
70. Aniket Chakraborty, 'Spare Parts for Russian Weapons May be Made in India', *Russia Beyond*, 14 March 2017, https://www.rbth.com/defence/2017/03/14/spare-parts-for-russian-weapons-may-be-made-in-india_719206.
71. Konstantin Bogdanov, Ilya Kramnik, 'What Will the Indian Navy's New Carrier Look Like?', *Russia Beyond*, 12 March 2016, https://www.rbth.com/economics/defence/2016/03/11/what-will-the-indian-navys-new-carrier-look-like_574805.
72. Personal communication.
73. For the contrasting modes of Indo-Russian and Indo-US military technology cooperation, see Karnad, *Why India Is Not a Great Power (Yet)*, 178–80, 187–219.
74. Quote in Admiral Vishnu Bhagwat (retd), 'Friend in Need', *Force*, February 2018, 13.
75. Bharat Karnad, 'India's Weak Geopolitics and What to Do About It', in Bharat Karnad, ed., *Future Imperilled: India's Security in the 1990s and Beyond* (New Delhi: Viking, 1994), 34–41.
76. Dmitriy Frolovskiy, 'The Coming India–Russia Split', *Diplomat*, 9 January 2018, https://thediplomat.com/2018/01/the-coming-india-russia-split.
77. Matthew Bodner, 'In Arms Trade, China Is Taking Advantage of Russia's Desperation', *Moscow Times*, 1 November 2016, https://themoscowtimes.

com/articles/in-arms-trade-china-is-taking-advantage-of-russian-desperation-55965.
78. Personal communication from a Russian-trained very senior Indian naval officer.
79. Personal communication.
80. See the interview of Andrew Korybko published in Geopolitica.ru, 14 September 2017, https://www.geopolitica.ru/en/article/russia-and-pakistan; Stephen Blank, 'What Drives Russo-Pakistan Relations and Where Are They Going?', *Central Asia-Caucasus Analyst*, 29 August 2017, https://www.cacianalyst.org/publications/analytical-articles/item/13463-what-drives-russo-pakistan-relations-and-where-are-they-going?.html.
81. See his 'New South Asia Geography', *Dawn*, 26 March 2018, https://www.dawn.com/news/1397602/new-south-asia-geography.
82. Personal communication, Russian foreign policy expert.
83. Quote in Sitapati, *Half Lion*, 275–76.
84. Bharat Karnad, *Nuclear Weapons and Indian Security: The Realist Foundations of Strategy*, second edition (New Delhi: Macmillan India, 2005), 185–86.
85. For the full text of the Juster speech at Carnegie India, see *Firstpost*, 12 January 2018, http://www.firstpost.com/world/full-text-of-kenneth-justers-remarks-on-us-india-relations-us-envoy-outlines-ambitious-agenda-for-bilateral-ties-4299325.html; for the Q&A session that followed this speech, see Shubhajit Roy, 'US Sends Clear Signal: At Some Point, Let Us Post Officers at Each Other's Combatant Commands', *Indian Express*, 12 January 2018.
86. Shishir Gupta, 'Soon, India Defence Attache at US Navy Bahrain Command', *Hindustan Times*, 22 March 2018.
87. Kenneth I. Juster, C. Raja Mohan, 'India–US Relations: Building a Durable Relationship for the 21st Century', *Carnegie India*, 11 January 2018, http://carnegieindia.org/2018/01/11/india-u.s.-relations-building-durable-partnership-for-21st-century-event-5789; 'US Gives India "Us or Russia" Choice', *Times of India*, 29 May 2018; Chidanand Rajghatta, 'New US Law Attacks India's Russia Defence Ties', *Times of India*, 21 May 2018; 'US, China Drop Tariffs, Put Trade War "On Hold"', *Times of India*, 21 May 2018.
88. Charles Bybelezer, 'Washington's Back and Forth with Egypt', *Jerusalem Post*, 7 September 2017, http://www.jpost.com/Middle-East/Courting-Egypt-Washingtons-options-in-a-changed-Middle-East-504516.

89. David D. Kirkpatrick, 'In Snub to US, Russia and Egypt Move toward Deal on Air Bases', *New York Times*, 30 November 2017, https://www.nytimes.com/2017/11/30/world/middleeast/russia-egypt-air-bases.html.
90. Steve Holland, Roberta Rampton, Jeff Mason, 'Exclusive: Trump Accuses Russia of Helping North Korea Evade Sanctions, Says US Needs More Missile Defence', *Reuters*, 17 January 2018, https://www.reuters.com/article/us-usa-trump-exclusive/exclusive-trump-accuses-russia-of-helping-north-korea-evade-sanctions-says-u-s-needs-more-missile-defense-idUSKBN1F62KO.
91. 'US Army in Asia-Pacific: Ensuring Stability and Security', Department of the Army, Washington, November 2013, http://www.arcic.army.mil/app_Documents/US-Army-In-Asia-Pacific-Ensuring-Stability-And-Security_Nov2013.pdf.
92. Franz Stephan-Gady, '3 Carrier Strike Groups Enter Asia-Pacific Ahead of Trump's Visit', *Diplomat*, 25 October 2017, https://thediplomat.com/2017/10/3-us-carrier-strike-groups-enter-asia-pacific-ahead-of-trumps-visit; 'PacAf units', Pacific Air Forces, http://www.pacaf.af.mil/Info/PACAF-Units.
93. 'A Shift in the International Security Environment: Potential Implications for Defense: Issues for Congress, Congressional Research Service, US Congress', Washington, 7 June 2017, https://www.everycrsreport.com/files/20170607_R43838_39b7e5f7b661a1ec055b5d750fc642a3973ee9f8.pdf.
94. Sydney J. Freedberg Jr., 'HASC EW expert Bacon: US Not Prepared for Electronic Warfare versus Russia, China', Breaking Defense, 8 January 2018, https://breakingdefense.com/2018/01/hasc-ew-expert-bacon-us-not-prepared-for-electronic-warfare-vs-russia-china.
95. Lucy Pasha Robinson, 'EU Leaders Defiant over US Pressure to Increase Nato Defence Budgets', *Independent*, 18 February 2017, http://www.independent.co.uk/news/world/europe/eu-leaders-angela-merkel-jean-claude-juncker-donald-trump-us-president-nato-defence-budgets-a7587461.html; Tim Street, 'Taking Back Control? UK, Europe and NATO', *Oxford Research Group*, 30 September 2016, http://www.oxfordresearchgroup.org.uk/publications/briefing_papers_and_reports/taking_back_control_uk_europe_and_nato.
96. Alex Lockie, 'For the First Time Since WWII, No US Aircraft Carriers Are Deployed—but Russia's and China's Are', *Business Insider*, 6 January 2017, https://www.businessinsider.in/For-the-first-time-since-WWII-no-US-aircraft-carriers-are-deployed-but-Russias-and-Chinas-are/articleshow/56380624.cms.

97. See his 'The US Navy's Indo-Pacific Challenge', *Journal of Indian Ocean Region* 9.1, 2013, 100, http://www.eisa-net.org/be-bruga/eisa/files/events/warsaw2013/Yoshihara_USNavyIndoPacificChallenge.pdf.
98. Kimberley Amadeo, 'US Military Budget: Components, Challenges, Growth', *Balance*, 15 February 2018, https://www.thebalance.com/u-s-military-budget-components-challenges-growth-3306320.
99. Vaqas Asghar, 'No Aid Till You Act, US Tells Pakistan', *Express Tribune*, 5 January 2018, https://tribune.com.pk/story/1601075/1-no-aid-till-act-us-tells-pakistan.
100. Qadeer Tanoli, 'US Is Trumpeting India's "lies and deceit": Khwaja Asif', *Express Tribune*, 4 January 2018, https://tribune.com.pk/story/1600568/1-us-trumpeting-indias-lies-deceit-khawaja-asif.
101. 'Pakistan Is Impregnable', *News*, 4 January 2018, https://www.thenews.com.pk/print/264151-pakista-is-impregnable-says-coas.
102. Iain Marlow and Ismail Dilawar, 'With Chinese Support, Pakistan Can Ignore Trump on Afghanistan', *Bloomberg*, 23 August 2017, https://www.bloomberg.com/news/articles/2017-08-23/with-chinese-support-pakistan-can-ignore-trump-on-afghanistan.
103. Talat Masood, 'The Insatiable Demands of US', *Express Tribune*, 3 January 2018, https://tribune.com.pk/story/1599053/6-insatiable-demands-us.
104. See their *An Uncertain Glory: India and Its Contradictions* (New Delhi: Allen Lane, 2013).
105. See his *The Geography of the Peace* (New York: Harcourt, Brace & Company, 1944). The use of Spyman's rimland concept to bolster an Indian security architecture first articulated in Karnad 'India's Weak Geopolitics and What To Do About It'; Sam Parker and Gabrielle Chefitz, 'Debtbook diplomacy', Belfer Center for Science and International Affairs, Harvard University, Boston, 24 May 2018, https://www.belfercenter.org/index.php/publication/debtbook-diplomacy.
106. Personal communication.
107. Commodore Sujeet Samaddar (retd), former Indian Naval Attache in Tokyo; currently a consultant with NITI Aayog.
108. Demetri Sevastopulo, 'North Korea "Months Away" from Ability to Strike US, Says CIA Head', *Financial Times*, 19 October 2017, https://www.ft.com/content/834279f8-b51f-11e7-aa26-bb002965bce8.
109. Rachael Revesz, 'US and South Korea Fly Advanced Bombers over Korean Peninsula Amid Growing Tensions with Pyongyang', *Independent*, 18 September 2017, http://www.independent.co.uk/news/world/asia/us-

south-korea-north-pyongyang-bombers-peninsula-air-force-fly-nuclear-weapons-missile-tests-japan-a7953931.html; Franz-Stefan Gady, 'Russia Flies Nuclear Capable Near North Korea', *Diplomat*, 29 August 2017, https://thediplomat.com/2017/08/russia-flies-nuclear-capable-bombers-near-north-korea; Lucas Mikelionis, 'US fighter jets intercept Russian nuclear bombers near North Korea', *Fox News*, 1 November 2017, http://www.foxnews.com/world/2017/11/02/us-fighter-jets-intercept-russian-nuclear-bombers-near-north-korea.html.

110. Jesse Johnson, 'Trump Warns China It Could Face Big Problems with "Warrior Nation" Japan over North Korea', *Japan Times*, 4 November 2017, https://www.japantimes.co.jp/news/2017/11/04/national/politics-diplomacy/trump-warns-china-face-big-problem-warrior-nation-japan-north-korea/#.Wf2Rk49SzIU.

111. Mark Landler and Julie Hirschfeld Davis, 'Trump: Japan Can Protect Itself by Buying US Arms', *New York Times*, 7 November 2017.

112. Alex Ward, 'South Korea Wants the US to Station Nuclear Weapons in the Country. That's Bad News', *Vox*, 5 September 2017, https://www.vox.com/world/2017/9/5/16254988/south-korea-nuclear-weapons-north-korea-trump.

113. For the text of the Australian 2017 Foreign Policy White Paper, 'Foreign Policy in Action', https://www.fpwhitepaper.gov.au.

114. Quote in Jason Scott, 'Australia Fears Asia Power Shift to China if US Withdraws', *Bloomberg*, 22 November 2017, https://www.bloomberg.com/news/articles/2017-11-22/australian-policy-paper-warns-of-china-s-rise-in-asia-afr-says.

115. *2016 Defence White Paper*, Australian Government, Department of Defence, http://www.defence.gov.au/WhitePaper/Docs/2016-Defence-White-Paper.pdf.

116. David C. Gompert and Philip C. Saunders, *The Paradox of Power: Sino-American Strategic Restraint in an Age of Vulnerability* (Washington, DC: National Defense University, NDU Press, 2011).

117. Akhilesh Pillalamarri, 'Project Mausam: India's Answer to China's "Maritime Silk Road"', *Diplomat*, 18 September 2014, https://thediplomat.com/2014/09/project-mausam-indias-answer-to-chinas-maritime-silk-road.

118. Dipanjan Roy Chaudhury, 'Pushing Back against China's One Belt, One Road, India, Japan Build Strategic "Great Wall"', *Economic Times*, 16 May 2017, https://economictimes.indiatimes.com/news/economy/

infrastructure/pushing-back-against-chinas-one-belt-one-road-india-japan-build-strategic-great-wall/articleshow/58689033.cms.
119. Personal communication: Commodore Sujeet Samaddar.
120. For an interesting, but slightly dated, discussion on this subject, see David W. Lovell, 'The Challenge for Australian Foreign-Policy professionals', undated (but probably 1990s), http://press-files.anu.edu.au/downloads/press/p239321/pdf/ch027.pdf.
121. 'Speech by Dr S. Jaishankar, Foreign Secretary to Mark 25 years of India–Singapore Partnership at Shangri La Hotel, Singapore, 11 July 2017, http://mea.gov.in/Speeches-Statements.htm?dtl/28609/Speech_by_Dr_S_Jaishankar_Foreign_Secretary_to_mark_25_years_of_IndiaSingapore_Partnership_at_Shangri_La_Hotel_Singapore_July_11_2017.
122. Tina Nguyen, 'An "Idiot" and a "Dope": McMaster Unloads on Trump During a Private Dinner', *Vanity Fair*, 20 November 2017, https://www.vanityfair.com/news/2017/11/hr-mcmaster-calls-trump-idiot-dope.
123. Timofei Bordachev, 'Security of Macro-regions?', *Valdai Discussion Club*, 1 August 2017, http://vadaiclub.com/a/highlights/security-ofmacro-regions.
124. Mark Landler, 'Trump, the Insurgent, Breaks with 70 years of American Foreign Policy', *New York Times*, 28 December 2017, https://www.nytimes.com/2017/12/28/us/politics/trump-world-diplomacy.html.
125. See 'Henry Kissinger and Graham Allison on the US, China, and the Thucydides Trap', 2 August 2017, www.youtube.com/watch?v=IKI6M2UiCGk.
126. See Table 19, ASEAN Statistics ASEAN trade by selected partner country or region, 2015 (as of November 2016), http://asean.org/storage/2016/11/Table19_as-of-6-dec-2016.pdf.
127. 'Japan Posts Trade Deficit with China in 2016', *Standard*, 25 January 2017, http://www.thestandard.com.hk/breaking-news.php?id=84089; Gregory O'Brien, 'Australia's trade in figures', Parliament of Australia, https://www.aph.gov.au/About_Parliament/Parliamentary_Departments/Parliamentary_Library/pubs/BriefingBook45p/AustraliaTrade.
128. Surojit Gupta, 'Indo-ASEAN Trade Rises 10% to $72bn in FY17, but Is Long Way Off Potential', *Times of India*, 26 January 2018.
129. Sachin Parashar, 'ASEAN Leaders Push Delhi to Conclude RCEP Talks by This Yr', *Times of India*, January 26, 2018; Amanda Hodge, 'Modi Takes a Dig at Chinese Expansionism' *Weekend Australian*, 27–28 January 2018.
130. Jayanth Joseph Jacob, 'Modi Pitches for a "Balanced" Trade Pact', *Hindustan Times*, 26 January 2018.

131. Sachin Parashar, 'Terror, Maritime Cooperation Top Agenda at ASEAN Summit', *Times of India*, 26 January 2018; Amy Kazin, John Reed, 'India woos ASEAN bloc to foil China', *Financial Times*, 25 January 2018.
132. 'Increase in Chinese Investment, but Barriers Still Remain', *Quint*, 4 September 2017, https://www.thequint.com/news/india/china-investment-india-polical-economic-barriers.
133. Ajay Banerjee, 'Indian Navy Gets Logistics Base East of Malacca in Singapore', *Tribune*, 29 November 2017, http://www.tribuneindia.com/news/nation/indian-navy-gets-logistics-base-east-of-malacca-in-singapore/505455.html.
134. 'India–Indonesia Exercise CORPAT concludes', Indian Navy (undated, but likely October 2014), https://www.indiannavy.nic.in/content/india-indonesia-exercise-corpat-concludes; 'Indonesia, India Plan to Develop Strategic Indian Ocean Port', *Reuters*, 30 May 2018, https://af.reuters.com/article/worldNews/idAFKCN1iVOSB.
135. 2016 Defence White Paper, Australian Government, 134–35.
136. Cheng Feng and Larry M. Wortzel, 'PLA Operational Principles and Limited War: The Sino-Indian War of 1962' in Mark A. Ryan, David M. Finkelstein and Michael A. McDevitt, eds., *Chinese Warfighting: The PLA Experience Since 1949* (Armonk, NY, London: ME Sharpe, 2003), 187–88.
137. The Radhakrishnan quote in Bew, *Realpolitik: A History*, 102.
138. The Machiavelli quote, Ibid, 192.
139. Saran, *How India Sees the World*, 142, 145–46.
140. 'China Defends Pakistan against Criticism by India, US on Terrorism', *Hindustan Times*, 26 October 2017, http://www.hindustantimes.com/world-news/china-defends-pakistan-against-criticism-by-india-us-on-terrorism/story-tZrQRS7dBQLol9eOlForgK.html.
141. China Objects to Vietnam's Call for Indian Investment in the South China Sea', *Times of India*, 11 January 2018, https://timesofindia.indiatimes.com/business/india-business/china-objects-to-vietnams-call-for-indian-investment-in-south-china-sea/articleshow/62457912.cms.
142. The concerned provision in the 1963 Treaty is Article 6. For the text of this agreement, see https://en.wikipedia.org/wiki/Sino-Pakistan_Agreement.
143. Karnad, *Why India Is Not a Great Power (Yet)*, 254–65.
144. Shubhajit Roy, 'Big Investment in Island Nations, with Eye on Maritime Diplomacy', *Indian Express*, 2 February 2018.
145. Regarding China's strong and evolving surface fleet, see Peter A. Dutton and Ryan D. Martinson, eds., *China's Evolving Surface Fleet* (Newport, RI: US Naval War College, China Maritime Studies, 2017).

146. Shyam Saran, personal communication, 10 November 2017.
147. Sutirtho Patranobis, 'China Welcomes India's "Rejection" of Australian Request to Join Malabar Exercise', *Hindustan Times*, 31 May 2017, http://www.hindustantimes.com/world-news/china-welcomes-indias-rejection-of-australian-request-to-join-malabar-exercise/story-N5ujAItgrEShsnGyLh3faL.html.
148. Indrani Bagchi, 'India, Australia Kick Off Joint Exercise Down Under', *Times of India*, 15 June 2017, https://timesofindia.indiatimes.com/india/india-australia-kick-off-joint-exercise-down-under/articleshow/59152044.cms.
149. The following exposition on the South China Sea issue is adapted from Bharat Karnad, 'China Narrows the South China Sea', *Policy Forum*, Asia and the Pacific Policy Society, Australian National University, 26 August 2017, http://www.policyforum.net/china-narrows-south-china-sea.
150. Milan N. Vego, *Naval Strategy and Operations in Narrow Seas*, second revised edition (London, Portland, OR: Frank Cass, 2003).
151. Minnie Chan, 'South China Sea: "Provocative US Action" Could Prompt Faster Chinese Military Build-up', *South China Morning Post*, 13 July 2016, http://www.scmp.com/news/china/diplomacy-defence/article/1989125/south-china-sea-provocative-us-action-could-prompt.
152. 'Remarks by Secretary Mattis at Shangri-La Dialogue', US Department of Defense, 3 June 2017, https://www.defense.gov/News/Transcripy-View/Article/1201780/remarks-by-secrtary=mattis-at-shangri-la-dialogue; Ben Westcott and Barbara Starr, 'US Warship Challenges China's Claims with First Operation under Trump', *CNN*, 25 May 2017, http://edition.cnn.com/2017/05/24/politics/south-china-sea-us-mischief-reef/index.html.
153. Sydney J. Freedberg, Jr., 'UN Ruling Won't End South China Sea Dispute: Navy Studies Next Clash', *Breaking Defense*, 20 June 2016, https://breakingdefense.com/2016/06/un-ruling-wont-end-south-china-sea-dispute-navy-studies-next-clash.
154. Joe Cirincione, 'Trump's Nuclear Insanity', *Politico*, 30 March 2016, https://www.politico.com/magazine/story/2016/03/trumps-nuclear-insanity-213781.
155. 'Trump: N Korea Will be Met with "Fire and Fury"', *Associated Press*, 8 August 2017, https://www.youtube.com/watch?v=8p1JIgTuKQk.
156. Justin Sink, Jennifer Jacobs and Nick Wadhams, 'Trump Chases US Arms Deals in Asia to Help Him Win Re-election', *Bloomberg*, 14 November 2017, https://www.bloomberg.com/news/articles/2017-11-14/trump-in-asia-kept-one-eye-on-re-election-with-push-for-deals.

157. 'Full Text of President Donald Trump's Speech at APEC CEO Summit', *Da Nang Today*, 10 November 2017, http://www.baodanang.vn/english/politics/201711/full-text-of=president-donald-trumps-speech-at-apec-ceo-summit-2577482.
158. Ian Talley, 'Trumps's Vow to Target China's Currency Could be First Step to Trade War', *Wall Street Journal*, 15 November 2016, https://www.wsj.com/articles/donald-trumps-pledge-to-get-tough-on-china-raises-threat-of-trade-war-1478804077.
159. Sink, et al, 'Trump Chases US Arms Deals'; Justin McCurry, 'What Have Trump and Kim Signed? We Read between the Lines', *Guardian*, 12 June 2018, https://www.theguardian.com/world/ng-interactive/2018/jun/12/trump-and-kim-document-analysis-singapore-agreement-denuclearisation.
160. David E. Sanger, Choe Sang-Hun and Motoko Rich, 'North Korea Rouses Neighbors to Reconsider Nuclear Weapons', *New York Times*, 28 October 2017, https://wwwnytimes.com/2017/10/28/world/asia/north-korea-nuclear-weapons-japan-south-korea.html.
161. With a sharp sense for the dramatic, Duterte, who had called US President Obama 'son of a bitch', rather grandly announced at the Great Hall of the People in Beijing 'a separation from the United States', adding that 'Both in military, not maybe social, but economics also. America has lost.' Buoyed by deals worth $13.5 billion signed with Beijing he added for good measure that he had 'realigned' Philippines with China and Russia, and that it was now 'three of us against the world—China, Philippines and Russia. It's the only way'. The expression of bafflement by Washington led to ministers in Manila clarifying, 'We will maintain relations with the West but we desire stronger integration with our neighbors [as] we share the culture and a better understanding with our region.' See Ben Blanchard, 'Duterte Aligns Philippines with China, Says US Has Lost', *Reuters*, 19 October 2016, https://www.reuters.com/article/us-china-philippines/duterte-aligns-philippines-with-china-says-u-s-has-lost-idUSKCN12K0AS.
162. President Xi declared, 'Our national sovereignty and our maritime rights and interests in the South China Sea will not be affected in any way by the ruling and case brought about by the Philippines.' His Foreign Minister Wang Yi sounded more truculent. Calling it a 'political farce made under the pretext of law', he warned that it 'has put the dispute into dangerous territory of worsening tensions and confrontation'. See Kor Kian Beng, 'China President Xi Dismisses Hague Arbitration on South China Sea but

Says "Committed to Peace"', *Straits Times*, 12 July 2016, http://www.straitstimes.com/asia/east-asia/china-dismisses-hague-ruling-maintains-sovereignty-over-south-china-sea.

163. 'Courting Trouble', *The Economist*, 16 July 2016, https://www.economist.com/news/china/21702069-region-and-america-will-now-anxiously-await-chinas-response-un-appointed-tribunal.
164. David Ignatius, 'Trump Shouldn't Take Jordan for Granted', *Washington Post*, 6 February 2018, https://www.washingtonpost.com/opinions/trump-shouldnt-take-jordan-for-granted/2018/02/06/2520556e-0b75-11e8-95a5-c396801049ef_story.html?utm_term=.50c09208ecb3.
165. 'Australia–China Ties in a Difficult Phase', *Indian Express*, 2 March 2018.
166. Kirtika Suneja, 'US-China Tariff War May be Boon for India, Say Experts', *Economic Times*, 5 April 2018.
167. Mark the words of US official Alex Wong speaking at the Ananta Aspen Centre in Delhi about what the Trump Administration expects of the Indian government in the Indo-Pacific: 'It is our policy to *ensure* that India *does* play' a 'weighty role' (my italics). See 'Trump's Indo-Pacific Policy Expects India to Play a More "weighty role"', *Times of India*, 4 April 2018.
168. 'Turkey and NATO Are Growing Apart', *The Economist*, 1 February 2018, https://www.economist.com/news/europe/21736190-they-will-probably-have-stick-together-turkey-and-nato-are-growing-apart; Steven Erlanger, 'EU Moves Closer to a Joint Military Force', *New York Times*, 13 November 2017, https://www.nytimes.com/2017/11/13/world/europe/eu-military-force.html.
169. See the insightful discussion on this topic on Pakistan TV, https://www.youtube.com/watch?v=OUhuHGF25hA.
170. Quote in Kevin Mitchell, 'Jake LaMotta Was Not a Great Champion but One of the Toughest, a Boxing Beast', *Guardian*, 21 September 2017, https://www.theguardian.com/sport/blog/2017/sep/21/jake-lamotta-not-great-champion-but-one-of-toughest-boxing-beast.

Chapter 5: Affirmative Inaction

1. See his 'Best Foot Forward', *Indian Express*, 14 February 2018, http://indianexpress.com/article/opinion/columns/best-foot-forward-pm-modi-foreign-visit-bjp-5062848.
2. Anil Sasi, 'On Govt Drawing Board: Tool to Hardsell Soft Power in Diplomacy', *Indian Express*, 14 February 2018.

3. Pramit Pal Chaudhuri, 'Think West to Go West: Origins and Implications of West Asia Policy Under Modi (Part I)', Middle East Institute, 26 September 2017, http://www.mei.edu/content/map/india-s-west-asia-policy-under-modi-part-one; Tina Edwin, 'With Love from Gulf', *Hindu BusinessLine*, 29 April 2018, https://www.thehindubusinessline.com/opinion/columns/from-the-viewsroom/with-love-from-gulf/article23720968.ece.
4. Quote in Datta-Ray, *The Making of Indian Diplomacy*, 208.
5. Sugata Bose, *A Hundred Horizons: The Indian Ocean in the Age of Global Empire* (Cambridge, MA: Harvard University Press, 2006); Scott C. Levi, *India and Central Asia: Culture and Commerce 1500–1800* (New York: Oxford University Press, 2007).
6. Syed Munir Khusru, 'Narendra Modi Charmed with His Words, It Is Now High Time for Action', *South China Morning Post*, 24 May 2017, http://www.scmp.com/comment/insight-opinion/article/2095514/indias-narendra-modi-charmed-his-words-it-now-high-time; Happymon Jacob, 'Losing the Neighbourhood', *The Hindu*, updated 18 October 2016, http://www.thehindu.com/opinion/lead/Losing-the-neighbourhood/article14324718.ece.
7. Small, *The China–Pakistan Axis*.
8. For Nehru's visioning of India as the indispensable power, see Karnad, *Nuclear Weapons and Indian Security*, 175–76.
9. Karnad, *India's Nuclear Policy*, 115–17. For another analysis along these lines, see Walter C. Ladwig III, 'Indian Military Modernization and Conventional Deterrence in South Asia', *Journal of Strategic Studies*, published online 11 May 2015.
10. Bharat Karnad, *Nuclear Weapons and Indian Security*, Chapter 5; Bharat Karnad, 'Sialkot Grab' and 'Capturing the "Corridor": Objectives and Tactics in a Nuclear Battlefield', *War College Journal* 34.2, Army War College, Autumn 2005.
11. Sune Engel Rassmussen, 'Isis in Afghanistan: "Their Peak Is Over, but They Are Not Finished"', *Guardian*, 18 November 2016, https://www.theguardian.com/world/2016/nov/18/isis-in-afghanistan-their-peak-is-over-but-they-are-not-finished; 'US Supplying Weapons to ISIS in Afghanistan', *Pakistan Today*, 8 October 2017, https://www.pakistantoday.com.pk/2017/10/08/us-supplying-weapons-to-isis-in-afghanistan; 'British Research Showed a Large Number of ISIS Weapons Originated in China', *Duowei*, 3 January 2018, *Chinascope*, http://chinascope.org/archives/14079.
12. The earlier attacks and the early 2017 Pathankot raid did not result in corrective measures. This was evident in the 12 February 2018 suicidal

terrorist assault on the Sanjuwan military area in Jammu, which elicited the same old empty threats. See 'Pak Will Have to Pay for J&K Misadventure: Def Minister', *Times of India*, 13 February 2018.

13. Husain Haqqani, *India vs Pakistan: Why Can't We Just Be Friends?* (New Delhi: Juggernaut, 2016).
14. Bharat Karnad, 'Scaring-up Scenarios: An Introduction' in Gurmeet Kanwal and Monika Chansoria, eds., *Pakistan's Tactical Nuclear Weapons: Conflict Redux* (New Delhi: Centre for Land Warfare Studies and Knowledge World, 2014).
15. Bharat Karnad, 'No More Hand-holding, Please', *Hindustan Times*, 30 January 2009, https://www.hindustantimes.com/india/no-more-handholding-please/story-aol3o7ZCMyiup1JhQtEsHM.html.
16. Steve Coll, *Directorate S: The CIA and America's Secret Wars in Afghanistan and Pakistan* (New York: Penguin, 2018).
17. Shubhajit Roy, Anand Mishra, 'Narendra Modi's Independence Day Speech: PM Throws Down Balochistan Gauntlet', *Indian Express*, 16 August 2016, http://indianexpress.com/article/india/india-news-india/pm-narendra-modi-balochistan-independence-day-congress-pakistan-salman-khurshid-2977554.
18. Bharat Karnad, 'Uses of Ambush Diplomacy', *Open*, 30 May 2014, http://www.openthemagazine.com/article/voices/uses-of-ambush-diplomacy.
19. Nilanjan Mukhopadhyay, 'How Will Modi Deal with Pakistan?', *Friday Times* (Lahore), 4 March 2014, http://www.thefridaytimes.com/tft/how-will-modi-deal-with-pakistan.
20. Indrani Bagchi, 'PM Modi Sets Terms for Pakistan, Woos China for Trade', *Times of India*, 18 January 2018, https://timesofindia.indiatimes.com/india/pakistan-must-walk-away-from-terror-if-it-wants-dialogue-with-india-pm-modi/articleshow/56630523.cms.
21. Mukhopadhyay, *Modi*, 73–74.
22. Marino, *Narendra Modi*, 20.
23. Michael Kugelman and Robert M. Hathaway, eds., *Pakistan-India Trade: What Needs to be Done? What Does It Matter?* (Washington, DC: Woodrow Wilson Center, 2013), 27, https://www.wilsoncenter.org/sites/default/files/ASIA_121219_Pakistn%20India%20Trade%20rptFINAL.pdf.
24. 'Threat of Nuclear and Chemical Weapons Becoming a Reality, Says Army Chief Bipin Rawat', *Indian Express*, 12 January 2018, http://indianexpress.com/article/india/general-bipin-rawat-asserts-china-as-powerful-nation-says-india-not-weak-either-5021785.

25. Roberta Lampton, Jonathan Landay, 'Trump Rejects Peace Talks with Taliban in Departure from Afghan Strategy', *Reuters*, 29 January 2018, https://in.reuters.com/article/afghanistan-blast-trump/trump-rejects-peace-talks-with-taliban-in-departure-from-afghan-strategy-idINKBN1FI2B6.
26. Karnad, *Nuclear Weapons and Indian Security*, Karnad, *India's Nuclear Policy, 2.*
27. Nirupama Subramaniam, 'Internal Threat More Immediate Than External: Kayani', *The Hindu*, 4 July 2009, http://www.thehindu.com/todays-paper/tp-international/Internal-threat-more-immediate-than-external-Kayani/article16547021.ece; Devirupa Mitra, '"Threat from Militants, Not from India", Pakistan's New Army Chief Once Said', *Wire*, 27 November 2016, https://thewire.in/82911/threat-from-militants-not-from-india-pakistans-new-army-chief-once-said.
28. The said book is *Army and Nation: The Military and Indian Democracy Since Independence* by Steven Wilkinson. See Rezaul. H. Laskar, 'Pakistan Army Chief Asks Officers to Read Book on Success of Indian Democracy', *Hindustan Times*, 15 February 2017, https://www.hindustantimes.com/world-news/pakistan-army-chief-asks-officers-to-read-book-on-success-of-indian-democracy/story-wa7Ii1EiHEkBYmmiHVZTmK.html.
29. Sushant Singh, 'Pak Considers Proposal for DGMO-level Meet: Report', *Indian Express*, 17 January 2018.
30. For instance, see Salman Rafi, 'CPEC Could be an Expensive Albatross around Pakistani Necks', *Asia Times*, 31 July 2017, http://www.atimes.com/article/cpec-expensive-albatross-around-pakistani-necks.
31. Karnad, *Why India Is Not a Great Power (Yet)*, 173.
32. Ibid.
33. https://nation.com.pk/18-Mar-2018/thank-you-modi.
34. Satish Chandra, 'India's China and Pakistan Policies Must be Based on Realism not Hope', 14 January 2018, http://www.vifindia.org/article/2018/january/14/india-s-pakistan-and-china-policies-must-be-based-on-realism-not-hope.
35. Personal communication.
36. Peter Caterall, ed., *The Macmillan Diaries: The Cabinet Years 1950–1957* (London: Pan Books, 2003), 509.
37. 'Pakistan PM Complains to US about Greater Role for India in Afghanistan', *Economic Times*, 20 September 2017, https://economictimes.indiatimes.com/news/politics-and-nation/pakistan-pm-complains-to-us-about-greater-role-for-india-in-afghanistan/articleshow/60768837.cms.

38. Bharat Karnad, 'Afghanistan, Pakistan and the F-16: Mattis Has to Hardsell These Issues on His Visit to India', *Hindustan Times*, 21 September 2017, http://www.hindustantimes.com/analysis/afghanistan-pakistan-and-the-f-16-mattis-has-to-hardsell-these-issues-on-his-visit-to-india/story-qvL9NS6wgl17sy756hE2WN.html.
39. Praveen Swami, 'How Significant Is Jaish-e-Muhammad in Kashmir Today', *Indian Express*, 10 November 2017; David Lewis, 'Why Russia is back in Afghanistan', *The Conversation*, 15 November 2017, http://theconversation.com/why-russia-is-back-in-afghanistan-86663
40. Sanjeev Miglani, 'Afghans Push India for More Arms, Despite Pakistan's Wary Eye', *Reuters*, 22 August 2016, https://www.reuters.com/article/us-afghanistan-india-defence/afghans-push-india-for-more-arms-despite-pakistans-wary-eye-idUSKCN10X29W.
41. 'Remarks by President Trump on the Strategy in Afghanistan and South Asia', 21 August 2017, https://www.whitehouse.gov/the-press-office/2017/08/21/remarks-president-trump-strategy-afghanistan-and-south-asia.
42. Interview with Hamid Karzai, *The Hindu*, 3 May 2017, http://www.thehindu.com/opinion/interview/hamid-karzai-on-uss-stand-on-af-pak-and-why-india-must-stay-invested-in-afghanistan/article18358469.ece.
43. Seth G. Jones, *In the Graveyard of Empires: America's War in Afghanistan* (New York: W.W. Norton & Co., 2010).
44. Paul Maley, 'Our Strategy: All the Way with USA', *Weekend Australian*, 27–28 January 2018.
45. Personal communication.
46. 'India, Cambodia Sign 4 Pacts, Agree to Enhance Defence, Cultural ties', *Hindustan Times*, 27 January 2018, https://www.hindustantimes.com/india-news/india-cambodia-sign-4-pacts-agree-to-enhance-bilateral-defence-ties/story-taD4EUlr6ldga1JgPGcT8I.html; 'India, Cambodia to Expand Ties in IT, Infrastructure Sectors', *LiveMint*, 27 January 2018, http://www.livemint.com/Politics/9JywUlgANvAdB2oUTnuYFI/India-Cambodia-to-expand-ties-in-IT-infrastructure-sectors.html.
47. https://www.youtube.com/watch?v=DZ_79xJFmKc.
48. Zhang Yue, 'China to Strengthen LMC Ties' and Pan Mengqi, 'Cambodia Relationship Hailed as Good Model' in *China Daily*, 15–21 January 2018.
49. 'Indonesian Navy Successfully Tests Russian Anti-ship Missile', *Sputnik News*, 21 April 2011, https://sputniknews.com/military/20110421163634028.

50. 'Vietnam, US, Talk Political, Security, Defence Matters', *Voice of Vietnam*, 31 January 2018, http://english.vov.vn/diplomacy/vietnam-us-talk-political-security-defence-matters-367802.vov.
51. Jonathan Webb, 'The New Silk Road: China Launches Beijing-London Freight Train Route', *Forbes*, 3 January 2017, https://www.forbes.com/sites/jwebb/2017/01/03/the-new-silk-road-china-launches-beijing-london-freight-train-route/#7d5ed4b41f13.
52. 'India Formally Start Exports to Afghanistan via Chabahar with 1.1.M Tons of Wheat', *Defence News India*, 29 October 2017, https://www.defencenewsindia.com/india-formally-start-exports-to-afghanistan-via-chabahar-with-1-1m-tons-of-wheat.
53. 'China Denies Plans to Set Up Military Base at Jiwani In Pakistan's Balochistan', PTI, *LiveMint*, 9 January 2018, http://www.livemint.com/Politics/stB8WVXUBhca96JR3YtvKP/China-denies-plans-to-set-up-military-base-at-Jiwani-in-Paki.html.
54. Colin Kahl and Jon Wolfstahl, 'John Bolton Is a National Security Threat', *Foreign Policy*, 23 March 2018, http://foreignpolicy.com/2018/03/23/john-bolton-is-a-national-security-threat/
55. Bharat Karnad, 'US Wrong on India's Iran Policy', *Diplomat*, 19 March 2012, https://thediplomat.com/2012/03/u-s-wrong-on-indias-iran-policy.
56. For a comparative analysis of the classical Indian and Chinese games of shatranj (chess) and Wei Qi emphasizing seizing spaces so as to limit the adversary's room for manoeuvre, which provide the policy templates to India and China respectively, see Karnad, *Why India Is Not a Great Power (Yet)*, 167–69.
57. Lily Hindy, 'A Rising China Eyes the Middle East', Century Foundation, 6 April 2017, https://tcf.org/content/rising-china-eyes-middle-east.
58. Payam Mohseni and Sahar Nowrouzzadeh, 'Trump's Dangerous Shift on Iran', *Foreign Affairs*, 15 October 2017, https://www.foreignaffairs.com/articles/iran/2017-10-15/trumps-dangerous-shift-iran.
59. Nidhi Verma & Manoj Kumar 'India Tries to Fix Iran Trade Payments as Donald Trump Hardens Line', *Reuters*, 22 March 2017, https://www.reuters.com/article/us-india-iran-trade/india-tries-to-fix-iran-trade-payments-as-trump-hardens-line-idUSKBN16T0PE; Sanjeev Choudhary, 'India may seek exemptions from US buy Iranian oil', *Economic Times*, 15 June 2018.

60. On the differences in the outlook and attitude of Shias and Sunnis in India, see the interview with the Qom-trained Iranian cleric Seyed Mohammad Asgari in *Religioscope*, 12 January 2011, https://english. religion.info/2011/01/12/islam-reviewing-shiite-sunni-relations-in-india-an-interview-with-seyed-mohammad-asgari.
61. 'With Shia Waqf Board Coming In Support, Will Ram Temple be a Reality Now?', IndiaToday.in, 17 October 2017, http://indiatoday.intoday.in/programme/shia-waqf-board-support-ram-temple-ayodhya-yogi-adityanath/1/1070741.html.
62. 'Iran Is India's Reliable Partner, Says Rouhani', *The Hindu*, 18 April 2016, http://www.thehindu.com/news/Iran-is-India%E2%80%99s-reliable-partner-says-Rouhani/article14242401.ece.
63. 'Iranian President Rouhani Keen to Visit India, Says Envoy', *India Today*, 20 December 2018, https://www.indiatoday.in/pti-feed/story/iranian-president-rouhani-keen-to-visit-india-says-envoy-1113662-2017-12-20.
64. Centre for Policy Research, 27 July 2017.
65. Yimou Lee, Wa Lone, 'China's $10 Billion Strategic Project in Myanmar Sparks Local Ire', *Reuters*, June 8, 2017, https://www.reuters.com/article/us-china-silkroad-myanmar-sez/chinas-10-billion-strategic-project-in-myanmar-sparks-local-ire-idUSKBN18Z327.
66. Personal communication, 9 January 2018.
67. See his 'Modi in Central Asia: Widening the Strategic Perimeter' in Ganguly, Chauthaiwala, Sinha, eds., *The Modi Doctrine*, 119–20.
68. Personal communication, 29 January 2018.
69. Menon, *Choices*, 191–92.
70. Datta-Ray, *The Making of Indian Diplomacy*, 71.
71. Ibid, 71–73.
72. See his 'China's Effect on Asean–India Ties', *Straits Times*, 27 January 2018.
73. Datta-Ray, *The Making of Indian Diplomacy*, 72, 216.
74. Ibid, 76.
75. For the MEA's antipathy to military diplomacy, see Karnad, *Why India Is Not a Great Power (Yet)*, 267–70.
76. Personal communication from retired ambassador Girish Dhume.
77. See his 'Deep Sea Port in Sonadia: A Unique Opportunity for Bangladesh', *Daily Star* (Dhaka), 30 March 2013, http://archive.thedailystar.net/beta2/news/deep-sea-port-in-sonadia-a-unique-opportunity-for-bangladesh.

78. Sushant Singh, '3 Yrs, No Takers for India's $1-bn Credit Line for Asean Digital Links', *Indian Express*, 4 April 2018.
79. 'Not One Toilet Built under Swachh Bharat', *Hindustan Times*, 4 April 2018.
80. Most of the content in this section was pieced together on the basis of a discussion with certain unattributable sources in the MoD and with Commodore Sujeet Samaddar (retd), former Indian Naval Attache in the Tokyo Embassy and sometime head of the ShinMaywa Office in India.
81. Wade Shepard, 'India and Japan Join Forces to Counter China and Build Their Own New Silk Road', *Forbes*, 31 July 2017, https://www.forbes.com/sites/wadeshepard/2017/07/31/india-and-japan-join-forces-to-counter-china-and-build-their-own-new-silk-road/#4932da704982.
82. Personal communication; Bharat Karnad, 'The 311 Problem', *Open*, 2 December 2016, http://www.openthemagazine.com/article/comment/the-311-problem
83. Personal communication from a former foreign secretary.
84. This revealed by K.P. Nayar, of the *Telegraph* (Kolkata) in a television panel discussion. See Rajya Sabha TV programme, 'The Big Picture', 16 August 2017, https://www.youtube.com/watch?v=OhtHUIDn054.
85. 'Another Ship Grounded at Mumbai's Juhu Beach', *The Hindu*, 1 August 2011, http://www.thehindu.com/news/national/other-states/another-ship-grounded-at-mumbais-juhu-beach/article2311514.ece.
86. This take on the IAS's role in government conveyed to Commodore Samaddar by an IAS friend of his.

Chapter 6: Perennial Security Muddle

1. Gerald Chan, 'From Laggard to Super Power: Explaining China's High Speed Railway "miracle"', *International Affairs*, Japan Institute of International Affairs, Number 661, May 2017, http://www2.jiia.or.jp/en/pdf/kokusaimondai/kokusaimondai661_Dr_Gerald_Chan.pdf.
2. 'The Second Chinese Naval Carrier Barracks Ship Will Be in Service Soon', *Sina*, 2 January 2018, *Chinascope*, http://chinascope.org/archives/14077.
3. Karnad, *Why India is Not a Great Power (Yet)*, Chapter 5.
4. For an outline of the Chinese strategy of warfare against systems, Jeffrey Engstrom, 'China Has Big Plans to Win the Next War It Fights', *National Interest*, 9 February 2018, http://nationalinterest.org/prit/blog/the-buzz/china-has-big-plans-win-the-next-war-it-fights-24449?page=show; for

China's development of drone ships for its navy and trade, see Kristin Huang, 'China Starts Work on World's Biggest Test Site for Drone Ships at Gateway to South China Sea', *South China Morning Post*, 12 February 2018, http://www.scmp.com/news/china/diplomacy-defence/article/2133076/china-starts-work-worlds-biggest-test-site-drone-ships; Elsa B. Kania, 'Chinese Sub Commanders May Get AI help for Decision-making', *Defense One*, 12 February 2018, http://www.defenseone.com/ideas/2018/02/chinese-sub-commanders-may-get-ai-help-decision-making/145906/?oref=defenseone_today_nl. Regarding the US army already field-testing elements of a robotic land and air forces, see Jen Judson, 'US Army Tackles Teaming Robots and Ground Forces on the Battlefield', *Defense News*, 25 August 2018, https://www.defensenews.com/land/2017/08/25/us-army-tackles-teaming-robots-and-ground-forces-on-battlefield; Patrick Tucker, 'Pentagon Requesting $66M for Laser Drones to Shoot Down North Korean Missiles', *Defense One*, 12 February 2018, http://www.defenseone.com/technology/2018/02/pentagon-requesting-66-million-laser-drones-shoot-down-north-korean-missiles/145939/?oref=defenseone_today_nl.
5. Personal communication.
6. Patrick Tucker, 'China Has a Breakthrough in Spy-proof Quantum Communications', *Defense One*, 9 November 2017, http://www.defenseone.com/technology/2017/11/china-has-breakthrough-spy-proof-quantum-communications/142415.
7. 'Overview of the State of the US S&E Enterprise in a Global Context', Science and Engineering Indicators 2018, National Science Foundation, National Science Board, Washington, DC, January 2018, https://www.nsf.gov/statistics/2018/nsb20181/report/sections/overview/introduction.
8. On Nehru's nursing the dual-use nuclear energy programme, and the HF-24 project, see Karnad, *Nuclear Weapons and Indian Security*, Chapter 2 and 186 respectively; for more details on Tank and the HF-24/HF-73 project, refer Karnad, *Why India is Not a Great Power (Yet)*, 12, 62, 422–24.
9. See Mahindra's obituary of his senior colleague, V.M. Ghatge, 'Aircraft Industry Pioneer', *Current Science*, Vol. 62, No. 9, 10 May 1992, www.repository.ias.ac.in/84720/1/84720.pdf.
10. 'India is World's Largest Arms Importer: SIPRI', *Hindustan Times*, 20 February 2018, https://www.hindustantimes.com/india-news/india-is-world-s-largest-arms-importer-sipri/story-Ahi6LhqR7WcZStOyDuIRKL.html.

11. Refer the views of Air Marshal Vinod Patney (retd), former vice chief of the air staff and currently head of the Centre for Air Power Studies, and Major General Chakraborty in a Lok Sabha TV panel discussion programme, 18 November 2017, https://www.youtube.com/watch?v=epdJRXA23o8.
12. Interview, 25 March 2017.
13. Kyle Mizokami, '5 Chinese Weapons of War America Wishes It Had', *National Interest*, August 2016, http://nationalinterest.org/blog/the-buzz/5-chinese-weapons-war-america-wishes-it-had-17264.
14. Senor and Singer, *Start-up Nation*, 180.
15. Pauline Montagna, 'The Scourge of Italy: Condotierri and Their Mercenary Armies', *History Buff*, 6 August 2016, https://medium.com/the-history-buff/the-scourge-of-italy-the-condottieri-and-their-mercenary-armies-7fca2cc626a8.
16. See his *A Matter of Honour: An Account of the Indian Army, Its Officers and Men* (London: Jonathan Cape, 1974).
17. Ajai Shukla, 'Beating Retreat Ceremony with Nationalised Flavor Disappoints Many', *Business Standard*, 4 February 2018, http://www.business-standard.com/article/current-affairs/beating-retreat-ceremony-with-nationalised-flavour-disappoint-many-118020301059_1.html.
18. See the chapter on 'Mysorean rockets' in Estefania Wenger, *Tipu Sultan: A Biography* (New Delhi: Vij Books, Alpha editions, 2017); Sanchari Pal, 'The Story of Tipu Sultan and His Mysorean Rockets, the World's First War Rockets', *Better India*, 26 October 2017, https://www.thebetterindia.com/119316/tipu-sultan-mysore-rockets-hyder-ali-first-war-rocket.
19. Ian Morris, *War, What Is It Good For: The Role of Conflict in Civilisation from Primates to Robots* (London: Profile Books, 2014), 182.
20. Patrick Porter, *Military Orientalism: Eastern War through Western Eyes* (New York: Columbia University Press, 2009), 1, 95, 207.
21. Alison Kaufman and Peter Mackenzie, *The Culture of The Chinese People's Liberation Army* (Quantico, VA: US Marine Corps Intelligence Activity, 2009), https://info.publicintelligence.net/MCIA-ChinaPLA.pdf.
22. See former deputy NSA and ex-diplomat Arvind Gupta's piece, 'India Should Take Up Challenge of Lethal Autonomous Weapons Systems', *Economic Times*, 15 February 2018.
23. 'Come, Make in India, for India and the World: Modi at GES', *Rediff*, 28 November 2017, http://www.rediff.com/money/report/ges-2017-narendra-modi-address-make-in-india-ivanka-trump/20171128.htm.

24. Vernon W. Ruttan, *Is War Necessary for Economic Growth?: Military Procurement and Technology Development* (New York: Oxford University Press, 2006).
25. Makeinindiadefence.gov.in/Defence%20Production%202018.pdf. This draft policy document was taken off the site after ten days.
26. Marcus Weinbgerber, 'Here's how the USAF is using its new purchasing power', *Defense One*, 25 May 2018, https://www.defenceone.com/business/2018/05/air-force-secretarys-plan-run-acquisition-business/148506.
27. Amrita Nair-Ghaswalla, 'House Panel Suggests Sops to Motivate Indigenous Defence Manufacturers', *Hindu BusinessLine*, 28 March 2018.
28. Personal communication by a retired vice admiral.
29. Ajai Shukla, 'Lockheed Martin Says F-16 Orders Flowing in', *Business Standard*, 16 December 2017, http://www.business-standard.com/article/companies/lockheed-martin-says-f-16-orders-flowing-in-117121600953_1.html.
30. See their 'How Not to Build a Ship: USS Ford', *San Diego Union-Tribune*, 7 June 2017, http://www.sandiegouniontribune.com/military/guest-voices/sd-me-grazier-ussford-20170606-story.html.
31. Ibid.
32. Rajat Pandit, 'Govt Scraps Single-engine Fighter Plane', *Times of India*, 23 February 2018.
33. Anurag Kotoki and N.C. Bipindra, 'Boeing, Saab Hanker for Scale to Meet Modi's Make in India Plea', *Bloomberg*, 15 February 2017, https://www.bloomberg.com/news/articles/2017-02-15/boeing-saab-hanker-for-scale-to-meet-modi-s-make-in-india-plea.
34. John Irish, Elizabeth Pineau, 'India Orders 36 French-made Rafale Jets: PM Modi', *Reuters*, 15 April 2015, https://www.reuters.com/article/us-india-france-rafale/india-orders-36-french-made-rafale-fighter-jets-pm-modi-idUSKBN0N10R020150410.
35. Personal communication, 13 April 2015.
36. Herb Kienon, 'Israel–India Spike Deal Back On, Says Netanyahu', *Jerusalem Post*, 17 January 2018, http://www.jpost.com/Israel-News/Israel-India-spike-missile-deal-back-on-says-Netanyahu-537003.
37. Interview.
38. Sumit Walia, 'MiG-35, F-16, Gripen or Better Choice?', *Indian Defence Review*, 14 August 2017, http://www.indiandefencereview.com/news/mig-35-f-16-gripen-or-better-choice.

39. Communication from senior Swedish government officials visiting Delhi.
40. Loren Thompson, 'How Concurrency in Building F-35 Fighter Has Proven to be a Big Plus', *Forbes*, 29 September 2017, https://www.forbes.com/sites/lorenthompson/2017/09/29/how-concurrency-in-building-the-f-35-fighter-has-proven-to-be-a-big-plus/#14f472a57147.
41. Interview, 20 March 2017.
42. This section was put together in a long discussion on 8 April 2017 in Bangalore with Commodore C.D. Balaji (retd), head of the ADA and the Tejas Light Combat Aircraft Programme, including the naval LCA project, 2015–17.
43. Sudhi Ranjan Sen, 'As Tejas Inches Towards Final Clearance, DRDO Chairman Explains Why the Fighter Jet Programme Was Delayed', *Mail Today*, 29 April 2018, https://www.indiatoday.in/india/story/as-tejas-inches-towards-final-clearance-drdo-chairman-explains-why-the-fighter-programme-was-delayed-1222844-2018-04-29.
44. A 2012 expert assessment of the aircraft said this: 'At $395.7 billion, the F-35 is now the most expensive weapons system in U.S. history, and the costs are still rising. It has constant problems with its engine, "unexplained" hot spots on the fuselage, and software that doesn't function properly . . . Canadians had some sticker shock when it turned out that the price tag for buying and operating the F-35 would be $45.8 billion . . . Lockheed Martin was counting on US allies to buy at least 700 F-35s as a way to lower per-unit costs. The US is scheduled to purchase 2,457 F-35s at $107 million apiece (not counting weapons). The plane cost $35,200 per hour to fly.' See Conn Hallinan, 'Conn Hallinan's 'Are You Serious' Awards', Foreign Policy in Focus, 31 December 2012, https://fpif.org/conn_hallinans_2012_are_you_serious-Awards.
45. See his interview to *The Hindu*, 25 March 2017, http://www.thehindu.com/news/national/we-will-be-able-to-liquidate-the-shortage-of-women-officers-in-five-to-six-years-navy-chief/article17664481.ece.
46. 'The F-35's High Angle of Attack Explained', *F-35 Lightning II*, Lockheed Martin, 12 July 2016, https://www.f35.com/in-depth/detail/the-f-35s-high-angle-of-attack-explained.
47. Anil Urs, 'Thales Develops Active Array Radar for HAL', *Hindu BusinessLine*, 16 October 2017, https://www.thehindubusinessline.com/companies/thales-develops-active-array-radar-for-hal/article9908310.ece.
48. 'Outstanding Performance of TEJAS Fighter at Bahrain Air Show 2016', https://www.youtube.com/watch?v=Hrs044wMqhc.

49. Nirmala Ganapathy, 'Defence Minister Ng Flies in India's Tejas Combat Aircraft, Says Bilateral Relation "Very Strong"', *Straits Times*, 28 November 2017, http://www.straitstimes.com/asia/se-asia/defence-minister-ng-flies-in-indias-tejas-combat-aircraft-says-bilateral-ties-very.
50. 'Boeing Offers to Set Up Production Facility for F/A-18 Fighter Jets in India', *Indian Express*, 28 August 2017, http://indianexpress.com/article/india/boeing-offers-to-set-up-production-facility-for-fa18-in-india-4817696.
51. Calling it 'the great Rafale mystery', Rahul Gandhi, president of the Congress Party, accused Modi of involvement in a 'scam'. 'Modiji had personally gone to Paris,' he said. 'Personally the deal was changed . . . What does this mean? This only means there is some scam'. He added that this deal promoted the financial interests of the prime minister's 'crony capitalist friends'. See 'Rahul Target PM on Rafale Deal', *Times of India*, 7 February 2018.
52. Rajat Pandit, 'Centre Divulged Rafale Cost in '16 but Is Mum Now', *Times of India*, 8 February 2018.
53. Personal communication.
54. Ibid.
55. The 2017 CAG Report noted that of the 152 types of ammunition and artillery shells the army uses, it had sufficient stocks of only thirty types. See Sudhi Ranjan Sen, 'Indian Army Ammunition Stock Will Exhaust After 10 Days of War: CAG Report', *India Today*, 21 July 2017, https://www.indiatoday.in/india/story/indian-army-ammunition-war-supply-shortfall-cag-report-1025676-2017-07-21.
56. Personal communications from numerous flag rank officers.
57. See his *The Path Unexplored: Success Mantra of Brahmos* (New Delhi: Pentagon Press, 2014), 204.
58. Personal communication from a senior missile scientist; DRDO's solid fuel ducted ramjet engine had partial success in its first test-firing. See Manu Pubby, 'India Tastes Only Partial Success in Ramjet Test, *Economic Times*, 3 June 2018.
59. Tamir Eshel, 'Indo-Israeli Relations: Make with India', *Indian Defence Review* 32.3, July–September 2017, http://www.indiandefencereview.com/news/indo-israel-relations-make-with-india/2.
60. 'German Lessons', *The Economist*, 12 July 2014, https://www.economist.com/news/business/21606834-many-countries-want-mittelstand-germanys-it-not-so-easy-copy-german-lessons; Tim Wallace, 'We Want to Create a French Mittelstand, Says Macron's Right Hand Man', *Telegraph* (London), 13 September 2017, http://www.telegraph.co.uk/

business/2017/09/13/want-create-french-mittelstand-says-macrons-right-hand-man.
61. This is slightly old data but still illustrative of the MSME potential and shortfalls. Refer *Innovation: Changing the MSME Landscape*, PriceWaterhouseCoopers India, 2011, 2, 5, 7, 9, https://www.pwc.in/assets/pdfs/publications-2011/innovation-msme-2011.pdf.
62. A senior military officer.
63. Industry source.
64. For an instance of this procurement gobbledygook, see the explanation of the Rafale deal by a former financial adviser (acquisitions), MoD, Amit Cowshish. See his 'Decoding the Deal', *Indian Express*, 12 February 2018.
65. Not for attribution.
66. Personal communication.
67. 'Four Contenders Vying for the Indian Navy's Project 75i: Here Are the Project Details', *Money Control*, 20 October 2017, http://www.moneycontrol.com/news/india/four-contenders-vying-for-indian-navys-project-75-i-here-are-the-project-details-2416737.html.
68. Victoria Craw, 'Australia's 12 New Shortfin Barracuda Submarines Described As "Most Lethal Weapon" the nation has', News.com.au, 15 December 2016, http://www.news.com.au/technology/innovation/design/australias-12-new-shortfin-barracuda-submarines-described-as-most-lethal-weapon-the-nation-has/news-story/a1f423bd9b30aef5259da42ba87cf503.
69. Industry source.
70. Another industry source.
71. Personal communication.
72. 'After Sunjuwan, Guns Worth Rs 16,000 cr Okayed for Infantry', *Times of India*, 14 February 2018.
73. Personal communication.
74. Rahul Singh, 'Navy's Minesweeper Deal Falls through After South Korea Talks Fail', *Hindustan Times*, 9 January 2018, https://www.hindustantimes.com/india-news/navy-s-minesweeper-deal-falls-through-after-south-korea-talks-fail/story-Fo9J1XaYlNEFgBSEGBNcRN.html.
75. Senor and Singer, *Start-up Nation*, 196.
76. Personal communication.
77. Vishnu Som, 'Defence Ministry Report: India's Weapons-buying Process in a Shambles', *NDTV*, 26 February 2018, https://www.ndtv.com/india-news/defence-ministry-report-weapons-procurement-process-in-tatters-1817153.

78. Personal communication.
79. Ibid.
80. Personal communication.
81. Personal communication.
82. Interview.
83. Karnad, *Nuclear Weapons and Indian Security*, 452–703.
84. The minute hand on the famous 'Doomsday Clock' has been advanced by 30 seconds to 2 minutes to midnight by the *Bulletin of Atomic Scientists*, the nearest to nuclear Armageddon since the 1950s. 'It is Two Minutes to Midnight', *Bulletin of Atomic Scientists*, 26 January 2018, https://thebulletin.org/press-release/it-now-2-minutes-midnight11464.
85. Peter Baker and Choe Sang-Hun, 'Trump Threatens "Fire and Fury" against North Korea if It Endangers US', *New York Times*, 8 August 2017, https://www.nytimes.com/2017/08/08/world/asia/north-korea-un-sanctions-nuclear-missile-united-nations.html; Krishnadev Calamur, 'Why Would North Korea Want to Drop a Hydrogen Bomb in the Ocean?', *Atlantic*, 22 September 2017, https://www.theatlantic.com/international/archive/2017/09/trump-north-korea/540783;
86. Saba Aziz, 'US–Pakistan War of Words over Donald Trump's Tweet', *Aljazeera.com*, 8 January 2018, http://www.aljazeera.com/news/2018/01/pakistan-war-words-donald-trump-tweet-180102055709366.html; Choe Sang-hun, 'North Korean Threat to Guam Tests Credibility of Kim and Trump', *New York Times*, 10 August 2017, https://www.nytimes.com/2017/08/10/world/asia/north-korea-guam-missiles-kim-trump.html.
87. Text of prime minister's keynote address at Shangri La Dialogue, 1 June 2018 (Press Information Bureau, Government of India, PMO), http://pib.nic.in/newsite/PrintRelease.aspx?reid=179711.
88. This according to CIA chief Mike Pompeo and General Paul Selva, vice chief, US joint chiefs of staff, 'North Korea May Perfect ICBM within Months, US General Says', *Japan Times*, 31 January 2018, https://www.japantimes.co.jp/news/2018/01/31/asia-pacific/not-yet-north-korea-soon-perfect-icbm-knows-spy-satellites-pass-u-s-general/#.WovK6rynHIU.
89. Bharat Karnad, *India's Nuclear Policy* (Westport, RI, and London: Praeger International, 2008), Chapter 1.
90. Bharat Karnad, 'Countering the Rogue Nuclear Triad of China, Pakistan and North Korea', *Wire*, 25 July 2016, https://thewire.in/53338/countering-the-rogue-nuclear-triad-of-china-pakistan-north-korea.

91. Bharat Karnad, *Why India Is Not a Great Power (Yet)* (New Delhi: Oxford Global, Oxford University Press, 2015), 98–102.
92. Ibid.
93. Karnad, *Nuclear Weapons and Indian Security*, 540–42; Karnad, *India's Nuclear Policy*, 30, 36–37.
94. Kadayam Subramanian, 'Modi Is to Blame for India's Failure on Pakistan Policy', *Asia Times*, 13 October 2016, http://www.atimes.com/modi-blame-indias-failure-pakistan-policy; Nilanjana Bhowmick, 'India's Embarrassing North Korean Connection', *Al Jazeera*, 26 June 2016,
95. http://www.aljazeera.com/indepth/features/2016/06/india-embarrassing-north-korean-connection-160620195559208.html; Manu Pubby and Dipanjan Roy Chaudhury, 'No Indian Language Training for North Korean Soldiers', *Economic Times*, 1 May 2017, http://timesofindia.indiatimes.com/world/rest-of-world/no-indian-language-training-for-north-korean-soldiers/articleshow/58453668.cms.
96. 'Russia Seizes an Opportunity in North Korea', *Stratfor*, Worldview, 5 May 2017, https://worldview.stratfor.com/article/russia-seizes-opportunity-north-korea.
97. Bharat Karnad, *Nuclear Weapons and Indian Security: The Realist Foundations of Strategy*, second edition (New Delhi: Macmillan India, 2005, 2002), 391–430.
98. Michael Krepon and Toby Dalton, 'Nuclear Mainstream', *Dawn*, 20 May 2016, https://www.dawn.com/news/1203017/nuclear-mainstream; 'Kim Jong-un: North Korea Is a Responsible Nuclear State', *Al Jazeera*, 3 May 2016,
99. http://www.aljazeera.com/news/2016/05/north-korea-nuclear-weapons-160508040813994.html.
100. David Albright and Serena Kelleher-Vergantini, 'Pakistan's Chashma Plutonium Separation Plant: Possibly Operational', Institute for Science and International Security, Imagery Brief, 20 February 2015, http://isis-online.org/uploads/isis-reports/documents/Chashma_February_20_2015_Final.pdf; 'North Korea's Nuclear Programme: How Advanced Is It?', *BBC News*, 6 January 2017, http://www.bbc.com/news/world-asia-pacific-11813699.
101. 'North Korea's Nuclear Programme: How Advanced Is It?', *BBC News*, 6 January 2017, http://www.bbc.com/news/world-asia-pacific-11813699.
102. Michael Krepon, 'Treaty and Pakistan's Nuke Arsenal', *Korea Herald*, 17 February 2012, http://www.koreaherald.com/view.php?ud=20120217000973; Robert S. Litwak, 'An Iran-Style Nuclear Deal with North Korea Is

the Best America Can Hope for', *Atlantic*, 4 May 2017, https://www.theatlantic.com/international/archive/2017/05/iran-deal-north-korea-jcpoa/525372/?mkt_tok=eyJpIjoiTkRZMllXTTBaalUyT1Rkay-IsInQiOiJBajZ3dWQyMzh6WnpORTBvOUBV1FEd-WRDR3VZb21sNVFaVUJQRlBTcVpHR1lDQnVTb3pWUW05K3h5UVFKQ25qeFNRZFZkcERrbWFSNys2Zk8xaTM1OWJKSX-JSeGNNcFBrTkJpYkw2WVFwQ3hyQm5WdVk5cE5tOWlSaVFxV3p-mZCJ9.

103. See *Joint Doctrine Indian Armed Forces*, Headquarters Integrated Defence Staff, Ministry of Defence, 18 April 2017, 50, http://bharatshakti.in/wp-content/uploads/2015/09/Joint_Doctrine_Indian_Armed_Forces.pdf.
104. Karnad, *Why India Is Not a Great Power (Yet)*, 165–67.
105. Karnad, *Nuclear Weapons and Indian Security*, 677–78.
106. This composite view of the three scenarios put together by the author from informal soundings of a number of Pakistani Flag–rank officers over the past twenty years.
107. Theodore A. Postol, 'Targeting' in Ashton B. Carter, John D. Steinbruner, Charles A. Zracket, eds., *Managing Nuclear Operations* (Washington, DC: Brookings Institution, 1987), Figure 11.9, 386, 403.
108. Ibid.
109. See www.io9.gizmodo.com/the-atomic-tank-survived-a-nuclear-test-then-went-to-w-1542451635.
110. Refer https://worldbuilding.stackexchange.com/questions/12323/could-a-tank-survive-a-nuclear-blast.
111. For an analysis of how armoured operations will proceed after the first tactical nuclear weapon attack on the forward units, see Karnad, *Nuclear Weapons and Indian Security*, Chapter 5.
112. Ibid, 681.
113. Pakistani Air Force Air Vice Marshal (retd) Shehzad Chaudhury in a 2013 Pakistani TV panel discussion, see https://www.youtube.com/watch?v=1nLRMb4CyBM.
114. National Seminar on 'Conduct of Operations in Nuclear Environment', Centre for Land Warfare Studies, Ministry of Defence, South Block, New Delhi, 13 February 2018.
115. Personal communication.
116. Ibid; Bharat Karnad, '"Sialkot Grab" and Capturing the "Corridor": Objectives and Tactics in a Nuclear Battlefield', *War College Journal*, Army War College, Autumn 2005, 1–12.

117. Rajat Pandit, 'India Can Handle Pakistan, China in Two-front War, says IAF chief', *Times of India*, 6 October 2017.
118. Ajai Shukla, 'Army Chief Says Militancy Must Prepare for Cold Start', *Business Standard*, 14 January 2017, http://www.business-standard.com/article/current-affairs/army-chief-says-military-must-prepare-for-cold-start-117011301174_1.html; Pandit, 'India Can Handle Pakistan, China in Two-front War, says IAF chief', *Times of India*, 6 October 2017.
119. See the section on 'Objectives' in the text of the 1999 draft doctrine. Available at http://mea.gov.in/in-focus-article.htm?18916/Draft+Report+of+National+Security+Advisory+Board+on+Indian+Nuclear+Doctrine.
120. Karnad, *Nuclear Weapons and Indian Security*, 504–13. For an analysis of the public debate on the salience of massive retaliation versus flexible response between ex-foreign secretary and then convener of the NSAB, Shyam Saran, and former foreign secretary and NSA, Shivshankar Menon, on one side and the author on the other, see Karnad, *Why India Is Not a Great Power (Yet)*, 482–84.
121. Bharat Karnad, *Nuclear Weapons and Indian Security*, 557–611.
122. Bharat Karnad, 'Shaping the Indian Special Forces into a Strategic Asset' in Lieutenant General Vijay Oberoi, ed., *Special Forces: Doctrine, Structures and Employment Across the Spectrum of Conflict in the Indian Context* (New Delhi: Centre for Land Warfare Studies and Knowledge World, 2006), 235–48.
123. Panel discussion on 'Two Decades of the Pokhran Tests: India and the Global Nuclear Order', Institute of Defence Studies and Analyses, New Delhi, 11 May 2018.
124. Pallava Bagla, 'India Capable of Nuclear Test at Short Notice: Defence Research Chief', *NDTV*, 28 May 2018, https://www.ndtv.com/india-news/india-capable-of-nuclear-test-at short-notice-defence-research-chief-1858949.
125. Personal communication from a former CAT scientist.
126. On the sidelines of a 'closed' seminar involving senior army officers.
127. Personal communication from an Indian engineer working in China on cutting-edge quantum communications. As regards the plutonium reactors, see 'Pakistan's Fourth Nuclear Reactor at Khushab Now Appears Operational', *Times of India*, 17 January 2015, https://timesofindia.indiatimes.com/world/pakistan/Pakistans-fourth-nuclear-reactor-at-Khushab-now-appears-operational/articleshow/45919653.cms.

128. Karnad, *Nuclear Weapons and Indian Security*, 499–517
129. 'Beg, Borrow or Steal: How Trump Says China Takes Technology', 24 March 2018, https://www.youtube.com/watch?v=x01fvNyLdqM.
130. Stephen Chen, 'China Steps Up Pace in New Nuclear Arms Race with US and Russia As Experts Warn of Risking Conflict', *South China Morning Post*, 28 May 2018, http://www.scmp.com/news/china/society/article/2147304/china-steps-pace-new-nuclear-arms-race-us-and-russia-experts-warn; For US and Russian nuclear modernization and build-up, refer 'US Nuclear Arsenal to Cost $1.2 trillion over Next 30 Years', *Reuters*, 31 October 2017, https://in.reuters.com/article/usa-nuclear-arsenal/u-s-nuclear-arsenal-to-cost-1-2-trillion-over-next-30-years-cbo-idINKBN1D033E; Kingston Reif, 'New Russian Weapons Raise Arms Race Fears', *Arms Control Today*, April 2018, https://www.armscontrol.org/act/2018-04/news/new-russian-weapons-raise-arms-race-fears.
131. Karnad, *Why India Is Not a Great Power (Yet)*, Chapter 5.
132. Ibid, 375–78; Karnad, *India's Nuclear Policy*, 77–83.
133. Personal communication.
134. 'Concession on Tawang Can Resolve India–China Border Dispute, Says Former Diplomat', *Hindustan Times*, 3 March 2017, http://www.hindustantimes.com/world-news/concession-on-tawang-can-resolve-india-china-border-dispute-says-former-diplomat/story-g8BRaViOpTvjKbMcA46g5I.html.
135. Karnad, *Why India Is Not a Great Power (Yet)*, 366–393; Karnad, *Nuclear Weapons and Indian Security*, 561–646.
136. Rajat Pandit, 'Pakistan Remains Ahead in Nuclear Warheads but India Confident of its Deterrent Capability', *Times of India*, 19 June 2018, https://timesofindia.indiatimes.com/india/pakistan-has-more-nuclear-warheads-india-credible-deterrence/articleshow/64641056.cms.
137. Andrew Greene, 'India to Block Australia from Naval Exercise amid Concerns It Could Inflame Diplomatic Tensions with China, *ABC Net*, 20 April 2017, http://www.abc.net.au/news/2017-04-21/india-tipped-to-block-australia-from-naval-exercise-china/8459896.
138. 'India's successful test of nuclear-capable Agni 5 leaves China worried', *Deccan Chronicle*, 28 December 2016, http://www.deccanchronicle.com/nation/current-affairs/281216/indias-successful-test-of-nuclear-capable-agni-5-leaves-china-worried.html.
139. Vishaka Saxena, 'From 3 Satellites in One Launch to 104: All You Need to Know about ISRO's PSLV Rocket', IndiaToday.in, 15 February 2017,

http://indiatoday.intoday.in/story/pslv-104-satellite/1/883213.html; A. Raghu Raman, 'Isro's 4-decade Journey: From 40 kg to 4000 kg', *Deccan Chronicle*, 6 June 2017, http://www.deccanchronicle.com/science/science/060617/isros-4-decade-journey-from-40-kg-to-4000-kg.html.

140. Bharat Karnad, *India's Nuclear Policy* (Westport, CN, and London: Praeger Security International, 2008), 69, 80–82, 142.

141. These Chinese nuclear weapons and deterrence-related views extracted from Li Bin and Tong Zhao, eds., *Understanding Chinese Nuclear Thinking* (Washington DC: Carnegie Endowment for International Peace, 2016).

142. Brandon Thomas-Noone, *Tactical Nuclear Weapons in the Modern Nuclear Era* (Lowy Institute for International Policy, 2016), 13.

143. Caitlin Talmadge, 'Would China Go Nuclear?', *International Security* 41.4 (Spring 2017), 50–92; Noone, *Tactical Nuclear Weapons*, 16.

144. Karnad, *Why India Is Not a Great Power (Yet)*, 388–93.

145. Thomas C. Schelling, *Arms and Influence* (New Haven, CN: Yale University Press, 1966).

146. Karnad, *Nuclear Weapons and Indian Security*, 512–612.

147. The targeting of the Qinghai-Lhasa Railway and the Three Gorges Dam and the economic effects of such strikes on China analysed in Karnad, *Why India Is Not a Great Power (Yet)*, 330–33.

148. Personal communication.

149. Timothy L. Thomas, 'Nation-state Cyber Strategies: Examples from China and Russia', March 2014, http://ctnsp.dodlive.mil/files/2014/03/Cyberpower-I-Chap-20.pdf.

150. David E. Sanger William J. Broad, 'Pentagon Suggests Countering Devastating Cyberattacks with Nuclear Arms', *New York Times*, 16 January 2018, https://www.nytimes.com/2018/01/16/us/politics/pentagon-nuclear-review-cyberattack-trump.html.

151. Thomas, 'Nation State Cyber Strategies'.

152. *Nuclear Posture Review 2018*, Office of the Secretary of Defense, February 2018, https://media.defense.gov/2018/Feb/02/2001872886/-1/-1/1/2018-NUCLEAR-POSTURE-REVIEW-FINAL-REPORT.PDF, 32.

153. Dean Cheng, *Cyber Dragon: Inside China's Information Warfare and Cyber Operations* (Santa Barbara, CA: Praeger Security International, 2017), 175.

154. Ibid, 218–219.

155. Ibid, 143.

156. Personal communication.

157. Interview.
158. See his interview, *Economic Times*, 26 February 2018.
159. Rajiv Kumar, *Modi and His Challenges*, 167.
160. For a book analysing the competing notions of great power and why hard power is the decisive factor in making a nation great, ibid.
161. Quotes in Senor and Singer, *Start-up Nation*, 143.
162. Personal communication. The former Northern Army commander Lieutenant General H.S. Panag (retd) writes of a similar incident thus: 'A recent "Langar gupp"—generally a simplistic version of real facts—in the armed forces with respect to the state of the politico-military relationship tells the tale. A very senior politician is alleged to have made a casual remark with respect to interaction with the military: "We do not call the military top brass for meetings because our meetings are held at odd times and after 8 p.m. their [top brass] 'happy hour' starts." Implying that the military brass gets down to their drinking after 8 p.m. If this is the impression the political masters have about the work ethics of their military hierarchy, what can one say?' Perhaps the 'senior politician' Panag is referring to is Modi. See his 'Generals Must Speak but on What Issues?', 'General Analyses', *Newslaundry*, 20 December 2017, https://www.newslaundry.com/2017/12/20/army-generals-india-government-military-strategy.
163. A retired vice admiral who keeps close tabs on 'the political'; personal communication.
164. Personal communication.
165. Ibid.
166. Ibid.
167. Karnad, *Why India Is Not a Great Power (Yet)*, Chapter 5.
168. Personal communication.
169. Dipankar Ghose, 'PM Narendra Modi: Naga Political Issue May be Solved in a Few Months', *Indian Express*, 23 February 2018, http://indianexpress.com/article/north-east-india/nagaland/pm-modi-naga-issue-may-be-solved-in-a-few-months-5074710.
170. See the interview with Phungting Shingrang, commander of the rebel Naga army, *Week*, 23 April 2017, http://www.theweek.in/theweek/cover/interview-phungting-shimrang.html.
171. Senior retired military officer. Also see Colonel R. Hariharan, 'Defence Forces: A Low Priority?' *India Legal*, 24 February 2018, http://www.indialegallive.com/viewpoint/defence-forces-a-low-priority-44273.

172. Rajesh Ahuja and Jayanth Jacob, 'India's Revamped Security Set-up Gets IPS, Intel Influx', *Hindustan Times*, 5 January 2018.
173. 'Act Now or Face Action in 90 Days: FATF', *News*, 24 February 2018, https://www.thenews.com.pk/print/284927-terror-financing-act-now-or-face-action-in-90-days-fatf.
174. 'No Talks until Pakistan Ends "Export of Terrorism" to India: Rajnath in Telengana', *Deccan Chronicle*, 17 September 2017, https://www.deccanchronicle.com/nation/current-affairs/170917/talks-meaningless-until-pak-stops-aiding-cross-border-terrorism-rajnath.html.
175. Personal communication.
176. Sachin Parashar, 'China's Proposed "Ocean Stn" in Maldives Worries India', *Times of India*, 26 February 2018.
177. Sachin Parashar and Rajat Pandit, 'Male Snubs Delhi again, Returns Gift', *Times of India*, 4 April 2018.
178. Madhuparna Das, 'India Need Not Worry about B'desh–China ties: Hasina', *Economic Times*, 23 February 2018.
179. Prashant Jha, 'Up North: In 10 Yrs, a New Nepal with a New Neighbor', and Saubhadra Chatterji and Rahul Singh, 'What if China, Bhutan Strike Deal: Rahul to House Panel', *Hindustan Times*, 23 February 2018; Shakthi de Silva, 'Will Sri Lanka be Able to Balance between China and India?', *Daily Mirror* (Colombo), 25 January 2018, http://www.dailymirror.lk/article/Will-Sri-Lanka-be-able-to-balance-between-China-and-India—144571.html.
180. Pakistan TV panel discussion, https://www.youtube.com/watch?v=BSiK0CmdL7Y.
181. Jawed Naqvi, 'Modi Steps into Pakistan–UAE Breach', *Dawn*, 18 August 2015, https://www.dawn.com/news/1201143.
182. 'TAPI Is a People's Pipeline; Safety, Assured Supply of Gas Is Vital, Says Akbar', *Indian Express*, 24 February 2018.
183. Such restructuring detailed in Karnad, *Why India Is Not a Great Power (Yet)*, 351–59.
184. Discussion with Burgess.
185. Karnad, *Nuclear Weapons and Indian Security*, 174–75.
186. This entire episode with the Air Marshal Shiv Deo Singh mission to Moscow, its test-flying the Backfire and rejecting it in favour of the MiG-23 detailed in Ibid, 663–68.
187. Ibid.
188. Bharat Karnad, *Why India Is Not a Great Power (Yet)*, 335–36.

189. Rajat Pandit, 'Govt Scraps Single-engine Fighter Plane', *Times of India*, 23 February 2018.
190. 'Rahul Gandhi Poses Three Questions to Nirmala Sitharaman on Rafale Deal', *News18*, 18 November 2017, http://www.news18.com/news/india/rahul-gandhi-poses-three-questions-to-nirmala-sitharaman-on-rafale-deal-1581027.html.
191. See his interview, *Economic Times*, 27 February 2018.
192. Ajit Kumar Dubey, 'Setback for IAF's Plans to Arm Fighter Jets with Meteor Missiles', *Mail Today*, 4 June 2018, https://www.indiatoday.in/mail-today/story/iaf-s-meteor-miisle plans-likely to-take-a-hit-1249650-2018-6-4.
193. Bob Stevenson, 'Scalp Missile Sale Reportedly being Blocked', *Jane's 360*, 20 February 2018, http://www.janes.com/article/scalp-missile-sale-reportedly-being-blocked.
194. Karnad, *Why India Is Not a Great Power (Yet)*, 427–28.
195. Ibid, 194.
196. Ibid, 427–28.
197. Saurav Jha, 'Single Engine Fighter Cancellation Provides an Opening for Tejas MK-2', *Delhi Defence Review*, 26 February 2018, http://www.delhidefencereview.com/2018/2/26/single-engine-fighter-cancellation-provides-an-opening-for-tejas-mk-2.
198. Discussion with Commodore C.D. Balaji, former head of the LCA programme.
199. Information from a source.
200. IAF sources.
201. 'After Super Sukhoi-30 Upgrade India's Sukhoi-30MKI Will Be Better than China's Su-35', *Defence Update*, 15 August 2017, https://defenceupdate.in/after-super-sukhoi-30-upgrade-indias-su-30-mki-will-be-superior-to-chinese-sukhoi-35.
202. Discussion with senior IAF officers.
203. Refer the leading combat aviation analysts Dr Carlo Kopp's 'F/A-18 E/F Super Hornet versus Sukhoi Flanker', *Air Power Australia*, April–May 2007, http://www.ausairpower.net/DT-SuperBug-vs-Flanker.html; Dario Leone, 'F-15 Eagle Vs CF-18 Hornet Vs F-16 Fighting Falcon: A Pilot's Perspective', *Aviationist*, 18 September 2014, https://theaviationist.com/2014/09/18/f-15vsf-16vs-cf18.
204. Ajay Banerjee, 'Rules Changed? Rafale Not the Only Choice', *Tribune* (Chandigarh), 13 April 2015.

205. Vivek Raghuvanshi, 'Indian Air Force Wants out of Fighter Program with Russia', *Defense News*, 20 October 2017, https://www.defensenews.com/air/2017/10/20/indian-air-force-wants-out-of-fighter-program-with-russia.
206. Dan Grazier, 'The F-35 Is a $1.4 trillion National Disaster', *National Interest*, 1 April 2017, http://nationalinterest.org/blog/the-buzz/the-f-35-14-trillion-dollar-national-disaster-19985.
207. Manu Pubby, 'DRDO's Tech Claim Fells $9b Indo-Russian aircraft', *Economic Times*, 13 June 2018.
208. Pinaki Bhattacharya, 'Indian Sukhoi-30MI and Russian Su-35 Nearly on Par: Indian Aviation Expert', *Defence World*, 23 November 2015, http://www.defenseworld.net/news/14672/Indian_Sukhoi_Su_30MKI_And_Russian_Su_35_nearly_on_par__Indian_Aviation_Expert#.WscjHtTwbIU.
209. Ryan O'Hare, 'China Proudly Debuts its New Stealth Jet it Built "By Hacking into US Computers and Stealing Plans"', *Daily Mail*, 1 November 2016, http://www.dailymail.co.uk/sciencetech/article-3893126/Chinese-J-20-stealth-jet-based-military-plans-stolen-hackers-makes-public-debut.html.
210. 'Indian Air Force Claims China's J-20 Stealth Fighters are not Undetectable', *Sputnik News*, 23 March 2018, https://sputniknews.com/asia/201803231062835269-chinese-j20-not-undetectable-iaf.
211. See his 'Military Structure: Trade-offs, Trade-offs, Trade-offs', *Breaking Defense*, 27 February 2018, https://breakingdefense.com/2018/02/military-force-structure-trade-offs-trade-offs-trade-offs.
212. See his *Making Waves: Aiding India's Next-Generation Aircraft Carrier* (Washington, DC: Carnegie Endowment for International Peace, April 2015), http://carnegieendowment.org/files/making_waves.pdf.
213. Vice Admiral A.K. Singh (retd), former FOC-in-C, Eastern Naval Command; personal communication.
214. See Trump's interview, *Time*, 11 May 2017, http://time.com/4775040/donald-trump-time-interview-being-president.
215. Karnad, *Why India Is Not a Great Power (Yet)*, 350–51.
216. Tellis, *Making Waves*, 9.
217. Karnad, *Why India is Not a Great Power (Yet)*, 350–51.
218. Sydney K. Freedbarg, Jr, 'F-35C and Ford Carriers: A Wrong Turn for Navy: CNAS', Breaking Defense, 19 October 2015, http://breakingdefense.com/2015/10/f-35c-a-wrong-turn-for-navy-cns.

Conclusion

1. 'A Journey from Fragile 5 to a $5-trillion Economy', *Economic Times*, 24 February 2018.
2. 'India Poised to be a $10tn Eco by 2030, Say Biz Leaders', *Times of India*, 24 February 2018.
3. Chalmers Johnson, *MITI and the Japanese Miracle: The Growth of Industrial Policy, 1925–1975* (Stanford, CA: Stanford University Press, 1982).
4. Daniel Kim, 'The Institutional Rise of the Chaebols throughout South Korea's Transitional Vulnerabilities', Dudley Knox Library, Naval Post-Graduate School, Monterrey, CA, March 2014, https://calhoun.nps.edu/bitstream/handle/10945/41403/14Mar_Kim_Daniel.pdf?sequence=1.
5. Anand Adhikari, 'Modi Govt Comes to the Rescue of Public Sector Banks with Recapitalization, at What Cost?' *Business Today*, 26 October 2017, https://www.businesstoday.in/current/economy-politics/modi-govt-psb-recapitalisation-public-sector-banks-recapitalisation-arun-jaitley-fiscal-stimulus/story/262527.html.
6. Paul Staniland, 'America Has High Expectations for India. Can New Delhi Deliver?' *War on the Rocks*, 22 February 2018, https://warontherocks.com/2018/02/america-has-high-expectations-for-india-can-new-delhi-deliver.
7. Angelique Chrisafis, 'Tens of Thousands of Public Sector Workers Strike across France', *Guardian*, 22 March 2018, https://www.theguardian.com/world/2018/mar/22/thousands-of-public-sector-workers-go-on-strike-across-france.
8. Rajiv Kumar, *Modi and his Challenges* (New Delhi: Bloomsbury, 2016), 49–83.
9. Ibid, 31.
10. Ibid, 48.
11. Meia Nouwens and Lucie Beraud-Sudreau, 'Xi Looks to China's Private Sector as He Pursues a Slimmer, Smarter PLA', *War on the Rocks*, 23 February 2018, https://warontherocks.com/2018/02/xi-looks-chinas-private-sector-pursues-slimmer-smarter-pla.
12. Indian officials confess that procedures have not changed from the 1910s. See Wilson, *India Conquered*, 4.
13. See his 'India's Elite Bureaucrats: Unshakably Resilient', *Asian Age*, 18 June 2018, http://www.asianage.com/opinion/oped/180618/govts-lateral-hiring-great-idea-bad-timing.html.

14. Gurcharan Das, 'Here's Tangible Proof of Minimum Govt, Maximum Governance', *Sunday Times of India*, 19 November 2017.
15. Quote in Alex von Tunzelmann, 'An Uncertain Glory: India and its Contradictions', *Telegraph* (London), 3 August 2013, http://www.telegraph.co.uk/culture/books/10211435/An-Uncertain-Glory-India-and-itsContradictions-by-Jean-Dreze-and-Amartya-Sen-review.html.
16. 'PM Modi at World Congress: Digital India Has Become a Way of Life', *Economic Times*, 19 February 2018, https://economictimes.indiatimes.com/news/politics-and-nation/pm-modi-at-world-congress-digital-india-has-become-a-way-of-life/articleshow/62979194.cms.
17. Saad Khan, 'OzyModi', *Express Tribune*, 15 November 2017, https://tribune.com.pk/story/1558396/6-ozymodi.
18. At a large convention called by the RSS, its chief Mohan Bhagwat declared that there's no alternative to all Indians becoming members of the Sangh even if that requires coercion. *News 24* panel discussion, 26 February 2018.
19. Zafar Agha, 'By Mixing Religion with Politics, India is Going Down Pakistan's Road', *Wire*, 20 April 2017, https://thewire.in/126070/by-mixing-religion-with-politics-india-is-going-down-pakistan-road; Nirupama Subramanian, 'Is India Becoming a Hindu Pakistan?', *Indian Express*, 28 June 2017, http://indianexpress.com/article/opinion/india-is-becoming-a-hindu-pakistan-kashmir-police-ballabhgarh-lynching-beef-muslim-dadri-4722104/; Sadanand Dhume, 'Towards a Hindu Pakistan?', *Times of India*, 18 November 2017.
20. 'The result of [the] absence of revolutionary "parivartan" [change] is that India continues to remain in the rut created over 70 yrs of Congress-style dynastic democracy,' writes Tavleen Singh. 'Could it be because the zeal that we have seen for love jihad and beef has made everyone in the BJP forget that it was the promise of parivartan and vikas [progress] that made Modi win a full majority?' See her 'Broken Promises', *Sunday Express*, 4 February 2018.
21. This statistic provided by Vijaya Kumar, IPS, joint director, Intelligence Bureau, during a panel discussion titled 'Internal Security Scenario', Phase III Mid-Career Training Programme, National Police Academy, Hyderabad, 15 June 2018.
22. Sanjay Pugalia, 'Why Are Rich Indians Moving out of the Country?' *Quint*, 9 February 2018, https://www.thequint.com/news/india/why-are-rich-indians-moving-out-of-the-country.

23. This is a point made as well by Ashley J. Tellis, see his 'The Long Road from Delhi: To Define the Indian Grand Strategy', Hudson Institute, 6 January 2015, https://uaclips.com/video/nvs7jC-LRz0/the-long-road-from-delhi-to-define-the-indian-grand-strateg.html.
24. Patrick Porter, *Military Orientalism: Eastern War through Western Eyes* (New York: Columbia University Press, 2009), 3.
25. 'India: Not Possible to Go Ahead with Saarc Summit under Current Condition', *Times of India*, 8 April 2018; 'Presence of Pakistan Prompts Asia Cup Shift from India to UAE', *Free Press Journal*, 11 April 2018, http://www.freepressjournal.in/cricket/presence-of-pakistan-prompts-asia-cup-shift-from-india-to-uae/1254819.
26. Shubhajit Roy, 'Delhi Works on Beijing to Drop Objections on N-club Entry', *Indian Express*, 11 April 2018.
27. Amit Baruah, 'Pakistan Army Ready to Join Dialogue Process with India', *The Hindu*, 17 May 2018, http://www.thehindu.com/news/national/ready-to-join-dialogue-with-india-pak-army/article23905872.ece.
28. 'Dialogue between Ex-spy Chiefs of India, Pakistan forms basis of new book', *Times of India*, 20 May 2018, https://timesofindia.indiatimes.com/india/dialogue-between-ex-spy-chiefs-of-india-pakistan-forms-basis-of-new-book/articleshow/64244908.cms.
29. Bharat Karnad, 'Key to Peace in South Asia: Fostering "Social" Links between the Armies of India and Pakistan', *The Round Table: The Commonwealth Journal of International Affairs* 338, April 1996.
30. Gyan Varma, 'Narendra Modi Tells Youth to Gain New Experiences, Think Out of the Box', *LiveMint*, 1 May 2017, https://www.livemint.com/Politics/BRNgzODigGQgJmFF6eRsoO/PM-Modi-on-Mann-Ki-baat-Ban-on-red-beacons-aimed-at-ending.html.
31. Rakesh Sood, 'A "Pilgrimage" to Nepal', *The Hindu*, 17 May 2018, http://www.thehindu.com/opinion/lead/a-pilgrimage-to-nepal/article23906250.ece.
32. Ashley J. Tellis, 'India–US Bonding: It's Not about Give and Take', *Hindustan Times*, 22 January 2015, https://hindustantimes.com/ht-view/india-us-bonding-it-s-not-about-give-and-take/story-aesTlo7vCnc3bLcwFiQ3BN.html.
33. Eric Heginbotham and Richard J. Samuels, 'Active Denial: Redesigning Japan's Response to China's Military Challenge', *International Security* 42.4, Spring 2018.

34. See the interview of Vivek Lall, vice president, Lockheed Martin Aeronautics, to the Atlantic Council, http://www.atlanticcouncil.org/blogs/new-atlanticist/the-us-india-defense-partnership-trending-upward.
35. Marcus Weingerber, 'US to India: Buy American, Not Russian', *Defense One*, 8 June 2018, https://www.defenseone.com/politics/2018/06/us-india-buy-american-not-russian/148853.
36. Pranab Dhal Samanta, 'US May Offer Air Defence System to Block S-400 Deal with Russia', *Economic Times*, 27 June 2018, https://economictimes.indiatimes.com/news/defence/us-may-offer-air-defence-system-to-block-s-400-deal-with-russia/articleshow/64753870.cms.
37. For Kaidanow's statements after her India visit in May 2018, see note 34.
38. Chidanand Rajghatta, 'New US Law Attacks India's Russia Defence Ties', *Times of India*, 21 May 2018; Sandeep Unnithan, 'The Sanctions Shadow', *India Today*, 16 June 2018, https://www.indiatoday.in/magazine/defence/story/20180618-the-sanctions-shadow-s400-india-russia-nirmala-sitharaman-1252730-2018-06-16.
39. Official Indian sources.
40. 'PM–Putin Meet Elevates Ties to "Spl Privileged Strategic Partnership"', *Times of India*, 22 May 2018.
41. Tonda MacCharles, 'Trump Takes Trade Shots at G-7 and Trudeau but Plays Nice in Person', *Toronto Star*, 8 June 2018, https://www.thestar.com/news/canada/2018/06/08/trump-throws-shade-on-g7-calls-for-russia-to-be-readmitted-to-group.html. The Freeland quote in Eliot A. Cohen, 'How Trump Is Ending the American Era', *Atlantic*, October 2017, https://www.theatlantic.com/magazine/archive/2017/10/is-trump-ending-the-american-era/537888.
42. Bharat Karnad, 'Walking Back Delusional Nuclear Policies', *Strategic Analysis, Special Issue: Two Decades of the Pokhran Tests: India and the Global Nuclear Order* 42.3, 2018, https://doi.org/10.1080/09700161.2018.1463955.
43. 'India in Talks with Friendly Nations to Export Missiles', *Times of India*, 10 April 2018.
44. See his 'The Long Road from Delhi: To Define the Indian Grand Strategy', Hudson Institute, 6 January 2015, https://uaclips.com/video/nvs7jC-LRz0/the-long-road-from-delhi-to-define-the-indian-grand-strateg.html.
45. 'India, Qatar Sign 7 Agreements', *Zee Business*, 5 June 2016, http://www.zeebiz.com/world/news-india-qatar-sign-7-agreements-1976.

46. Shyam Saran, 'Marginalised in Our Own Backyard', *Hindustan Times*, 12 April 2018.
47. Marcel Plichta, 'China Is Filling the Africa-sized Gap in US Strategy', *Defense One*, 28 March 2018, https://www.defenseone.com/ideas/2018/03/china-filling-africa-sized-gap-us-strategy/146985; Abdi Latif Dahir, 'Beijing Announces Inaugural China–Africa Defense Forum', *Defense One*, 5 June 2018, https://www.defenseone.com/threats/2016/06/china-announces-inaugural-china-africa-defense-forum/148753.
48. A US–China deal of mutual compromise will likely be followed by an entente where both sides agree not to push the military confrontation envelope. Thus, despite Trump's initial tough talk on trade, once Xi's China threatened to retaliate strongly, his ardour cooled appreciably and he was even offered 'the loss of jobs in China' as a reason for lifting the technology ban on the Chinese communications giant, ZTE, and putting the trade war on hold. Refer Ana Swanson, Mark Landler and Keith Bradsher, 'Trump Shifts from Trade War Threats to Concessions in Rebuff to Hard-Liners', *New York Times*, 14 May 2018, https://www.nytimes.com/2018/05/14/business/china-trump-zte.html; 'US, China Drop Tariffs, Put Trade War on Hold', *Times of India*, 21 May 2018.
49. 'Chinese Envoy Pitches for India–China–Pakistan Trilateral Meet', IANS, *Business Standard*, 18 June 2018, https://www.business-standard.com/article/news-ians/chinese-envoy-pitches-for-india-china-pakistan-trilateral-meet-118061800601_1.html.
50. John Keegan, *Intelligence in War: Knowledge of the Enemy from Napoleon to Al-Qaeda* (London: Pimlico, 2004), 36–37.
51. 'Text of Prime Minister's Keynote Address at Shangri La Dialogue, 1 June 2018' (New Delhi: Press Information Bureau, Government of India, PMO), http://pib.nic.in/newsite/PrintRelease.aspx?relid=179711.
52. Devirupa Mitra, 'Modi and Xi Seek to Project the Image of Stability in an Uncertain World', *Wire*, 9 June 2017, https://thewire.in/diplomacy/despite-uncertainty-over-chinas-belt-road-forum-modi-and-xi-bond-over-dangal; Dipanjan Roy Chaudhury, 'Narendra Modi, Vladimir Putin Agree on Building Multipolar World Order', *Economic Times*, 22 May 2018, https://economictimes.indiatimes.com/news/politics-and-nation/narendra-modi-vladimir-putin-agree-on-building-multipolar-world-order/articleshow/64266272.cms.

53. Kathrin Hille and Henry Foy, 'Russia to Deploy "Unstoppable" Nuclear Weapons, Says Putin', *Financial Times*, 1 March 2018, https://www.ft.com/content/57710046-1d4e-11e8-aaca-4574d7dabfb6.
54. Modi's and Nye's quotes in Chaulia, *The Modi Doctrine*, 35.
55. 'Indian Tech Cos May Stumble over Tighter H1B Visa Rules', *Economic Times*, 24 February 2018.
56. Ayan Pramanik, 'Nasscom Sees Single Digit Growth', and Supraja Srinivasan, 'Next-gen Tech Giants from China Gear Up to Invade India', *Economic Times*, 21 February 2018.
57. Jethro Mullen, 'How China Squeezes Tech Secrets from US Companies", *CNN Money*, 14 August 2017, http://money.cnn.com/2017/08/14/news/economy/trump-china-trade-intellectual-property/index.html.
58. https://www.youtube.com/watch?v=604NshhAtps.
59. Manoj Ladwa, 'Modi's Economic Diplomacy: Turning Conventions on Their Head', in Ganguly, Chautahiwale, Sinha, eds., *The Modi Doctrine*.
60. The amount of column space allotted by Indian newspapers to this story and the ballyhooing by the Modi government of its success in seating Justice Dalveer Bhandari on the Hague bench as a tremendous victory for Indian diplomacy was ridiculous. Shubhajit Roy, 'How Focused Diplomacy Won India the International Court of Justice Battle', *Indian Express*, 22 November 2017, http://indianexpress.com/article/india/how-focussed-diplomacy-won-india-the-icj-battle-dalveer-bhandari-4948701. For a warning by an ex-diplomat not to make too much of this 'success', see K.C. Singh, 'India's ICJ win: Don't Overdo the Rejoicing', *Asian Age*, 23 November 2017.
61. Quote in Sara Boboltz, 'Rex Tillerson Warns Grads of Living in "Alternative Realities"', *Hufffington Post*, 17 May 2018, https://www.huffingtonpost.in/entry/rex-tillerosn-fact-truth-vmi-commencement-speech_us_5afc7303e4b0779345d548f5.
62. Third Annual Lecture of the Centre for Policy Analysis (transcribed text), 22 February 2018, New Delhi.
63. Personal communication.
64. Thus, after first agreeing to buy the Tejas Mk-1A under Defence Minister Parrikar's pressure, the IAF has stalled its entry into squadron service by insisting that the aircraft incorporate into its design 'smart multi-function displays' for the cockpit, a 'combined interrogator and transponder' to differentiate friendly and enemy aircraft, a digital map generator and an improved radio altimeter. This will delay induction by four or five years.

See Ajai Shukla, 'Tejas Mark 1A Faces Delay As Air Force Adds on Demands', *Business Standard*, 19 May 2018, http://ajaishukla.blogspot.in/2018/05/tejas-mark-1a-faces- delay-as-air-force.html.

65. Quote in P.R. Ramesh, 'Something Is Rotten in the Indian Navy', *Open*, 27 February 2015, http://www.openthemagazine.com/article/india/something-is-rotten-in-the-indian-navy.
66. Vishnu Som, 'India's Weapons-buying Process in a Shambles: Defence Ministry Report', *NDTV.com*, 26 February 2018,' https://www.ndtv.com/india-news/defence-ministry-report-weapons-procurement-process-in-tatters-1817153?pfrom=home-topstories.
67. Indrani Bagchi, 'To Push Exports, Govt Calls All 44 Defence Attaches', *Times of India*, 8 April 2018.
68. Bharat Karnad, 'India Needs to Find a Solution to Its Arms and Ammo Shortages', *Hindustan Times*, 14 June 2018, https://www.hindustantimes.com/opinion/india-needs-to-find-a-solution-to-its-arms-and-ammo-shortages/story-ihvvuEu2aZ3THVP7ZDhsxK.html.
69. Manu Pubby, 'L&T Opposes Plan to Give Sub Project to Mazagon Dock', *Economic Times*, 20 June 2018.
70. 'Can't Force "Made in India" Arms on Military: Nirmala', *Times of India*, 12 April 2018.
71. Tellis, 'India–US bonding'.
72. Quote in Robert K. Massie, *Dreadnought: Britain, Germany, and the Coming of the Great War* (NY: Ballantine Books, 1991), 663.